WITHDRAWN

lonely planet

New England

Maine
p367

Vermont
p277

New
Hampshire
p324

Central
Massachusetts Around Boston p88
& the Berkshires Boston p34
p175

Connecticut Rhode
p241 Island
p208

Cape Cod,
Nantucket &
Martha's Vineyard
p124

D0068383

THIS EDITION WRITTEN AND RESEARCHED BY

Mara Vorhees,

Gregor Clark, Ned Friary, Paula Hardy, Caroline Sieg

Contents

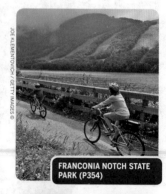

FRANCONIA NOTCH STATE PARK (P354)

BEACON HILL (P38)

Contents

Welcome to New England

Come to New England to mount spectacular summits and to feel the ocean breeze. Come to tantalize your taste buds with succulent seafood and sweet maple syrup. Come for history and high culture.

History

The history of New England is the history of America. It's the Pilgrims who came ashore at Plymouth Rock and the minutemen who fought for American independence. It's the ponderings of Ralph Waldo Emerson and the protests of Harriet Beecher Stowe. It's hundreds of years of poets and philosophers, of progressive thinkers who dared to dream and dared to do. It is generations of immigrants who have shaped New England into the dynamic region that it is today.

Outdoor Adventure

New England is big on outdoor adventure. The region undulates with the rolling hills and rocky peaks of the ancient Appalachian Mountains, from the beautiful birch-covered Berkshires in Western Massachusetts, to the lush Green Mountains in Vermont and the towering White Mountains that stretch across New Hampshire and Maine.

Nearly 5000 miles of coastline means that New Englanders are into water sports: opportunities for fishing, swimming, surfing, sailing and sunbathing are unlimited. So pack your sunglasses and your sunblock and settle in for some quality time on the open ocean.

Culture

New England is at the cutting edge of culture. The region is home to two exciting, experimental contemporary art museums, as well as traditional art museums. Indie bands rock out in Boston, Portland and Burlington. The world-renowned Boston Symphony Orchestra takes its show on the road in summer, delighting audiences in the Berkshires. Meanwhile, there are blues jams in Maine, folk festivals in Newport and Lowell and classical music in Rockport. Concert series, film festivals and theater productions mean the cultural calendar is jam-packed.

Food

New England is delicious. Just check out the calendar of events celebrating local delicacies, such as Maine lobsters, Wellfleet oysters and Vermont beer. Blessed with a burgeoning locavore movement and a wealth of international culinary influences, New England cuisine fuses the best of both worlds. A pile of pancakes drenched in maple syrup; fresh farm produce and sharp cheddar cheese; fish and shellfish straight from the sea; exotic dishes with influences of Portugal, Italy or Asia: this is just a sampling of the epicurean delights that travelers will find in New England.

Why I Love New England

By Mara Vorhees, Author

For a place that is steeped in history, New England is ever moving forward. I am proud of the region's 18th-century revolutionary roots, but I'm even prouder that all six states have embraced marriage equality in the 21st century. Trinity Church is glorious, but even more so when reflected in the facade of the Hancock Tower. Emerson and Thoreau are inspiring, but it's Geraldine Brooks, Jhumpa Lahiri and Elizabeth Strout that keep me up reading late into the night. New England's history is rich, to be sure, but the here-and-now is downright exhilarating.

For more about our authors, see p456

Above: Kent Falls State Park (p275)

New England

100 miles
120 km

CANADA

ONTARIO

NEW BRUNSWICK

MAINE

VERMONT

45°N

St Lawrence River

St John River

Allagash River

Kennebec River

Montmagny

Québec City

Montréal

Malone

Massena

Saranac Lake

Lake Champlain

Lake Placid

Drummondville

Victoriaville

Sherbrooke

Berlin

St Albans

Burlington

Montpelier

Mt Mansfield (4393ft)

Stowe

Franconia Notch State Park

North

Edmundston

Gand Falls

Fort Kent

Van Buren

Caribou

Presque Isle

Florenceville

Woodstock

Fredericton

St Stephen

Eastport

Grand Manan Island

Houlton

Lincoln

Bangor

Ellsworth

Bar Harbor

Acadia National Park

Penobscot Bay

Belfast

Camden

Rockland

Pittsfield

Waterville

Augusta

Millinocket

Mt Katahdin (5267ft)

Chamberlain Lake

Moosehead Lake

Flagstaff Lake

West Grand Lake

Mt Katahdin
Northern terminus of the Appalachian Trail (p408)

Acadia National Park
Where the mountains meet the sea (p403)

White Mountains
Outdoor adventure and inspiring landscape (p349)

ROAD DISTANCES (miles)
Note: Distances are approximate

	Boston, MA	Burlington, VT	Hartford, CT	Portsmouth, NH	Providence, RI
Burlington, VT	215				
Hartford, CT	100	235			
Portsmouth, NH	60	210	150		
Providence, RI	50	265	90	110	
Provincetown, MA	115	330	205	175	120
Bar Harbor, ME	285	335	375	230	335	400

Portland
Lit up by America's oldest lighthouse (p377)

Boston
History and eye-catching architecture (p34)

Provincetown
Whale-watching cruises to Stellwagen Bank (p151)

Martha's Vineyard
Sun-drenched cliffs and refreshing surf (p166)

Newport
Fabulous mansions along Cliff Walk (p222)

Lenox
Open-air classical music at Tanglewood (p201)

Litchfield Hills
Rolling hills blanketed with forests (p272)

ELEVATION

1500m
1200m
900m
600m
300m
0

ATLANTIC OCEAN

Portland
Harbor
Kennebunk
Kennebunkport
Portsmouth
Cape Ann
Gloucester
Marblehead
Salem
Boston
Cambridge
Provincetown
Cape Cod National Seashore
Plymouth
Cape Cod
Hyannis
Falmouth
Woods Hole
Edgartown
Martha's Vineyard
Nantucket
Nantucket Island

Harbor
Hanover
Lakes Region
Lake Winnipesaukee
Concord
Manchester
NEW HAMPSHIRE
Quabbin Reservoir
Worcester
Northampton
Brattleboro

Rutland
Green Mountain National Forest
Williamstown
Connecticut River
Springfield
MASSACHUSETTS
Providence
RHODE ISLAND
Newport
Narragansett
Block Island

Manchester
Bennington
Pittsfield
Lenox
Hartford
CONNECTICUT
Norwich
New London
Mystic

Albany
Woodstock
New Haven
Waterbury
Danbury
Bridgeport
Stamford
New Canaan
NEW YORK
Newburgh

Long Island
New York
NEW JERSEY
Belmar
Point Pleasant

43°N
42°N
41°N
40°N
67°W
68°W
69°W
70°W
71°W
72°W
73°W

New England's
Top 15

1

Appalachian Trail

1 The Appalachian Trail (p429) runs more than 2100 miles from Georgia to Maine, passing through 14 states along the way. If anyone is counting, 730 of those miles and five of those states are in New England. This means ample opportunities for hikers to hop on and tackle a piece of the trail. Western Massachusetts offers easy access to the rolling hills of the Berkshires, while Vermont promises the pastoral splendor of the Green Mountains. In New Hampshire and Maine, the trail traverses the alpine peaks of the White Mountains, with its northern terminus at Mt Katahdin. Mt Katahdin, Baxter State Park (p408)

College Town, USA

2 From the Five Colleges to the Seven Sisters (well, four of them), New England is crowded with colleges and overrun with universities, making for a dynamic, diverse student scene (p424). Hundreds of institutions of higher education are located in Boston and across the river in Cambridge, Massachusetts. But Boston is only the beginning of this college tour. Providence, Rhode Island, and New Haven, Connecticut, are home to their own Ivy League institutions, while smaller towns around the region are dominated by lively leafy campuses of their own. Yale University (p262)

GEORGE LEPP / GETTY IMAGES ©

Freedom Trail

3 The best introduction to revolutionary Boston is the Freedom Trail (p37). This red-brick path winds its way past 16 sites that earned the town its status as the cradle of liberty. The 2.5-mile trail follows the course of the conflict, from the Old State House – where British regulars killed five men in the Boston Massacre – to the Old North Church, where the sexton hung two lanterns to warn that the British troops would come by sea. Follow the road through American revolutionary history. Old State House (p247)

Acadia National Park

4 Acadia National Park (p403) is where the mountains meet the sea. Miles of rocky coastline and even more miles of hiking and cycling trails make this wonderland Maine's most popular destination, and deservedly so. The high point (literally) is Cadillac Mountain, the 1530ft peak that can be accessed by foot, bike or vehicle. Early risers can catch the country's first sunrise from this celebrated summit. Later in the day, cool off with a dip in Echo Lake or take tea and popovers at the teahouse overlooking Jordan Pond.

White Mountains

5 The White Mountains (p349) are New England's ultimate destination for outdoor adventure and inspiring landscape, with 1200 miles of hiking trails and 48 peaks over 4000ft. Franconia Notch is a perfect place to start, with trailheads for dozens of different hiking routes, an aerial tramway that whisks passengers to the top of Cannon Mountain, and the spectacular rush of water through Flume Gorge. It's a destination for all seasons, with opportunities for hiking and cycling, skiing and snowboarding, sitting fireside and sitting lakeside.

5

Lobster Trap

6 Nowhere is more closely associated with this crustacean (p19) than Maine. The mighty lobster was once so plentiful it was fed to prisoners and used for fertilizer. Now the state symbol is deservedly esteemed as a delicacy. Crack the shell of a freshly steamed lobster with drawn butter at one of Maine's many summertime lobster pounds. Or catch (and eat) your own on board a do-it-yourself lobster boat. Either way, don't forget to tie on a plastic bib – Maine's most endearing and enduring fashion statement.

6

BRUCE MCINTOSH / GETTY IMAGES ©

Sailing Penobscot Bay

7 Explore the rugged coast of Maine the old-fashioned way – on board one of the grand, multimasted windjammers that fill the harbors of Rockland and Camden (p396). These majestic sailing ships offer cruises around the islands and coves of Penobscot Bay, all under the power of the wind. Feel the breeze through your hair and the spray on your face as you sail the high seas, stop for a spot of souvenir shopping and a lobster roll for lunch, venture a quick dip in the afternoon, and dine as the sun sets over the rocky Maine coastline.

Mansions of Newport

8 Eleven fabulous mansions are vestiges of the 19th-century capitalist boom when bankers and businesspeople built their summer homes overlooking the Atlantic. Managed by the Preservation Society of Newport County, the mansions offer a glimpse into a world of unabashed wealth, and include grand homes modeled after an Italian Renaissance palace, an English manor and a Parisian chateau. See them all from the Cliff Walk (p226), a narrow footpath along the ocean's edge, offering stunning views all around. Kingscote (p225)

Litchfield Hills

9 With scenery to match the Green Mountains, pre-colonial villages worthy of any movie set, and the finest food, culture and music in Connecticut, Litchfield Hills (p272) attracts a sophisticated crowd of weekending Manhattanites and celebrities escaping the limelight. No wonder it's often described as 'the Hamptons for people who like privacy'. Give yourself some time here and you'll be rewarded with classical concerts in Norfolk, colonial farmhouse breakfasts in Kent, vintage car races at the Lime Rock Race Track and fly-fishing worthy of Brad Pitt's performance in *A River Runs Through It*.

Beachy Keen

10 Summer in New England is humid, so it's no surprise that the region's entire population flocks to the coast for cool ocean breezes. Fortunately, it's a long coastline. In Massachusetts, the island of Martha's Vineyard is ringed with beaches, which means plenty of sea and sand for everyone. At Aquinnah Public Beach, the cliffs of Gay Head radiate incredible colors in the late afternoon light, attracting serious sun worshippers and photographers. Alternately, Katama Beach is best for good old-fashioned sand and surf.
Gay Head Cliffs (p174)

Architecture

11 From Charles Bulfinch to Henry Hobson Richardson to IM Pei, the world's most renowned architects and designers have left their mark on Boston (p34). See the city's signature buildings clustered around Copley Square, including the Renaissance Revival Boston Public Library, the Richardsonian Romanesque Trinity Church and the modernist John Hancock Tower. Of course urban design is much more than just buildings. Some of Boston's most striking features are its green spaces, including the city's newest innovation in urban design, the Rose Kennedy Greenway.
Trinity Church (p48)

Whale Watching

12 Nothing matches the thrill of spotting a breaching humpback or watching a pod of dolphins play in the boat's wake (p151). Off the coast of Massachusetts, Stellwagen Bank is an area of 842 sq miles of open ocean rich in marine life. The National Marine Sanctuary was designated to conserve the area's biological diversity and facilitate research and other activity. Informative whale-watching cruises are offered from Boston, Plymouth, Barnstable, Provincetown and Gloucester, Massachusetts.

Farm Fresh

13 New England cuisine is a treat, thanks in part to the abundance of fruits, vegetables and dairy products that come from local farms. Depending on the season, visitors can pick their own apples, cherries, berries and pumpkins, relishing the flavor of the produce. In winter, farmers tap the local trees for the incomparable flavor of maple syrup. Vermont is leading the regional movement toward artisanal cheeses, with a 'Cheese Trail' mapping the route between dozens of local producers.

Tanglewood

14 Come summer, culture beckons in the Berkshires. At this renowned music festival in Lenox, you can spread a blanket on the lawn and uncork a bottle of wine as one of the finest symphony orchestras in the USA takes the stage. Not only does the Boston Symphony Orchestra summer in these cool hills, but guest musicians of every stripe, from James Taylor to jazz greats, make it onto the schedule. The setting of meadows and lawns, once part of a Gilded Age estate, is as sweetly refined as the music.

Shine the Light

15 Lighthouses have long served to communicate across dangerous waters, guiding ships through dark nights and darker storms. The image of the lonely beacon is borne out by hundreds of lighthouses up and down the New England coast. Nowadays, you can take a tour of a lighthouse, spend the night in a lighthouse, share a romantic dinner in a lighthouse, or even become a lighthouse keeper. Or you can just keep your camera handy and admire the stoic beauty of these iconic New England buildings. Portland Head Light (p379)

Need to Know

For more information, see Survival Guide (p431)

Currency
US Dollars ($)

Language
English

Visas
Citizens of many countries are eligible for the Visa Waiver Program, which requires prior approval via Electronic System for Travel Authorization (ESTA).

Money
ATMs are widely available, except in the smallest towns and most remote wilderness. Credit cards are accepted at most hotels and restaurants.

Cell Phones
Check with your service provider. For US travelers, Verizon, Cingular and Sprint have coverage throughout New England (except in rural and mountainous areas).

Time
Eastern Standard Time (GMT/UTC minus four hours)

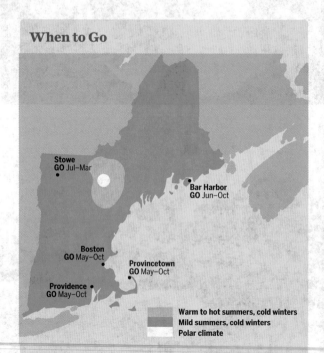

When to Go

Stowe
GO Jul–Mar

Bar Harbor
GO Jun–Oct

Boston
GO May–Oct

Provincetown
GO May–Oct

Providence
GO May–Oct

Warm to hot summers, cold winters
Mild summers, cold winters
Polar climate

High Season
(May–Oct)

➡ Accommodation prices increase by 50% to 100%; book in advance.

➡ Temperate spring weather and blooming fruit trees. July/August are hot and humid, except in mountain areas.

➡ Becomes cooler in September and October.

Shoulder
(Mar–Apr)

➡ Weather remains wintry throughout March; April sees some sunshine and spring buds.

➡ Less demand for accommodations; negotiate lower prices (also applies to beach areas in May/early June).

Low Season
(Nov–Feb)

➡ Significantly lower prices for accommodations.

➡ Some sights in seasonal destinations close.

➡ With snow comes ski season (December to March), meaning higher prices in ski resorts.

Useful Websites

Visit New England (www.visitnewengland.com) Listings for events, sights, restaurants and hotels in all six states.

New England Guide (www.boston.com/travel/newengland) Travel tips and itineraries from the Boston Globe.

Lonely Planet (www.lonelyplanet.com/usa/new-england) What better place to start?

National Parks Service (www.nps.gov/parks) Facts about national parks, recreation areas and historic sites.

New England Lighthouses (www.lighthouse.cc) A list of lighthouses by state.

Important Numbers

Emergency	☑ 911
Local Directory	☑ 411
Country Code	☑ +1
International Dialing Code	☑ 011 + country code
National Park Service Visitor Center	☑ 617-242-5642

Exchange Rates

Australia	A$1	$0.91
Canada	C$1	$0.96
Euro zone	€1	$1.30
Japan	¥100	$1.00
New Zealand	NZ$1	$0.78
UK	UK£1	$1.51

For current exchange rates see www.xe.com

Daily Costs
Budget:
Less than $100

➡ Camping or dorm bed: $30–$60 per night

➡ Public transportation

➡ Self-catering

➡ Taking advantage of free admissions and walking tours

Midrange:
$100–$200

➡ Double room in midrange hotel: $100–$200 per night

➡ Car rental for a portion of the trip

➡ Admission to museums, parks and other activities

Top End:
Over $200

➡ Double room in high-end hotel: from $200 per night

➡ Eat at the region's finest restaurants

➡ Enjoy concerts, events and other activities

Opening Hours

Restaurants, bars and shops may have shorter hours (or may be closed completely) during low or shoulder seasons.

Banks and Offices From 9am or 10am to 5pm or 6pm Monday to Friday

Restaurants Breakfast from 7am to 10am; lunch 11:30am to 2:30pm; dinner 5pm to 10pm Monday to Sunday

Bars and Pubs From 5pm to midnight, some until 2am

Shops From 10am to 5pm Monday to Saturday, some open noon to 5pm Sunday, or until evening in tourist areas

Arriving in New England

Logan International Airport (p438), **Boston** The subway (T) and the bus (silver line) connect the airport to city center from 5:30am to 12:30am; take a taxi for $15 to $25, which takes about 15 minutes.

Bradley International Airport (p438), **Hartford, Connecticut** A bus runs to the city center from 4:30am to midnight; a taxi is $45 and takes about 20 minutes to the center.

Getting Around

Car The most convenient option for seeing rural New England, exploring small towns and partaking of outdoor adventure. Driving and parking can be a challenge in Boston.

Train Amtrak travels up and down the Northeast Corridor, connecting Boston to coastal towns like Portland, Salem, Providence and New Haven.

Bus Regional bus lines connect bigger towns throughout the region.

For much more on **getting around**, see p439

PLAN YOUR TRIP NEED TO KNOW

If You Like...

Outdoor Activities

Sailing Take to the waters in an America's Cup yacht for thrilling sunset tours. (p228)

Cycling Pedal the region's many rail trails, including the Cape Cod Rail Trail, the Ashuwillticook Rail Trail in the Berkshires or the cycling River Bikeway in Rhode Island. (p139) (p203) (p177)

Hiking Make your way over the rocky precipices of Cadillac Mountain (p403) or through the narrow pass of the Flume Gorge. (p356)

Kayaking Paddle your kayak around Nauset Marsh in the Cape Cod National Seashore. (p146)

Skiing Hit the slopes above Stowe, Vermont's coziest ski village. (p313)

Beaches

Cape Ann, Massachusetts Come to Wingaersheek Beach at low tide to investigate the tide pools. (p109)

Cape Cod, Massachusetts Race Point Beach in Provincetown and Nauset Beach in Orleans are wildly spectacular beaches backed by sand dunes. (p153) (p144)

Block Island, Rhode Island Stroll north from Old Harbor to sink your feet into the sand at Benson Town Beach. (p237)

Vermont Even land-locked Vermont has some great lakeside beaches at Branbury State Park, Lake Willoughby and Burton Island. (p299) (p323) (p317)

Ogunquit, Maine Frolic on the family-friendly 3-mile stretch of sand at Ogunquit Beach. (p372)

Shopping

Newbury St Boston's most famous shopping destination is lined with boutiques, galleries and high-fashion outlets. (p81)

Brimfield Antique Show The largest outdoor antiques fair in North America sprouts on farmers' fields in rural Brimfield. (p179)

Galleries Art aficionados will find plenty to catch their eye at galleries in Wellfleet and Provincetown. (p147) (p151)

Artist Colony Find handcrafted jewelry, Shaker rugs and ceramics at the rural artists' colony in Tiverton. (p220)

Street Markets In Burlington, the pedestrianized Church Street Marketplace offers easygoing shopping, Vermont-style. (p303)

LL Bean Head to the flagship store in Freeport, Maine for an amazing selection of outdoor gear and wear. (p386)

Scenic Byways

MA 127 Drive around the edge of Cape Ann for views of salt marshes and windswept beaches, oases of art and antiques, and more clam shacks than you can shake a shucker at.

MA 6A The Old King's Highway on Cape Cod is as antique as the shops along it.

Mohawk Trail Massachusetts' top fall foliage route.

CT 169 Tool around the Quiet Corner, between orchards and 200-year-old villages.

VT 100 This iconic road runs right along the base of the Green Mountains, showcasing

---

IF YOU LIKE... NATIVE AMERICAN CULTURE

The exhibit at the Peabody Essex Museum in Salem shouldn't be missed. (p101)

the state's idyllic farmland, fiery foliage and renowned ski areas.

Kancamangus Hwy The river hugs the road on this cruise through leafy mountain panoramas.

Park Loop Rd This 27-mile loop circumnavigates the northeastern section of Mt Desert Island.

Historic Towns

Nantucket, Massachusetts Cobblestone streets and sea captains' mansions to whisk you back to the island's whaling heyday. (p158)

Deerfield, Massachusetts This historic village is a museum of colonial living. (p191)

Newport, Rhode Island The 18th-century downtown was thankfully preserved by Doris Duke's millions. (p222)

Portsmouth, New Hampshire A bustling port city with a fine collection of historic houses from the 17th and 18th centuries. (p326)

Woodstock, Vermont A perfectly preserved slice of old New England, with 18th- and 19th-century architecture surrounding a village green. (p293)

Seafood

You might be tempted to go on a self-directed lobster tour of US 1 in Maine, stopping at every lobster pound for fresh-steamed crustaceans dripping with clarified butter. But there's more to life than lobster: there's also scallops, crabs, clams, oysters and fresh flaky fish.

Lobster Tie on a bib at Ford's Lobster in Noank, Connecticut or any one of Maine's Best Lobster Pounds. (p260)

(Above) Cobblestone street, Nantucket (p158)
(Below) Kayaking, Cape Cod (p126)

IF YOU LIKE... GRAVEYARDS

Ralph Waldo Emerson and others are buried on Authors' Ridge at Sleepy Hollow Cemetery. (p94)

Lobster rolls Pull up one of the picnic tables at Sesuit Harbor Café in Dennis, Massachusetts. (p138)

Lobster bisque The perfect beginning to any meal at Brewster Fish House in Brewster, Massachusetts. (p140)

Fried clams Go to Woodman's and order Chubby's Original to see how the fried clam thing started. (p114)

Oysters on the half shell Slurp some down at Matunuck Oyster Bar in Matunuck, Rhode Island, or Neptune Oyster in Boston. (p232) (p65)

Beer

Northampton Brewery Hoist a microbrew at New England's oldest operating brewpub. (p188)

Long Trail Brewing Company Sip Vermont's number-one amber. (p297)

Shipyard Brewing Company Partake of tours and tastings in Portland, Maine. (p383)

Mohegan Cafe & Brewery Sample the jalapeño pilsner at the Block Island brewery. (p239)

Cisco Brewers Imbibe island brew at this friendly, laid-back Nantucket spot. (p166)

Vermont Brewers Festival Sample dozens of local craft brews at this annual event in Burlington. (p307)

Lighthouses

Boston Light This historic lighthouse can be visited on special tours of the Boston Harbor Islands. (p44)

Portland Head Light Maine's oldest lighthouse was built by order of George Washington in 1791. (p379)

Gay Head Lighthouse Perched on the colorful cliffs of Martha's Vineyard. (p174)

Cape Cod lighthouses Climb to the top of Chatham Light in Chatham, Nauset Lighthouse in Eastham or Cape Cod Highland Light in Truro for vast ocean views. (p142) (p146) (p150)

Beavertail Lighthouse Built in 1898, this Jamestown lighthouse is still signaling ships into Narragansett Bay. (p232)

Literature

In the mid-19th century – sometimes called the American Renaissance – New England was the epicenter of American literature.

Robert Frost Pay a visit the poet's former homes in Bennington and Franconia. (p287) (p356)

Louisa May Alcott Visit Orchard House, where the author wrote *Little Women*. (p95)

Henry David Thoreau Follow the philosopher to his hideaway at Walden Pond. (p97)

Mark Twain Discover the irascible writer's penchant for opulence in his Gothic Revival mansion in Hartford. (p245)

Month by Month

February

The deepest, darkest part of winter, with snow and cold temperatures. Many New Englanders retreat to warmer climes, making this an ideal time for museums, restaurants, theaters and other indoor attractions.

🏃 Ski Season

Though the ski season extends from mid-December until the end of March, its peak is President's Day weekend (third weekend in February). Book your accommodations well in advance if you plan to hit the slopes during this time.

March

New England is officially sick of winter. In Vermont and New Hampshire, ski season continues through to the end of the month.

🍴 Maple Syrup Tasting

Vermont's maple sugar producers open the doors for two days in late March during the Vermont Maple Open House Weekend. Maine maple syrup producers do the same on the last Sunday in March (www.mainemapleproducers.com).

April

Spring arrives, signaled by the emerging crocuses and the blooming forsythia. Baseball fans await Opening Day at Fenway Park. Temperatures range from 40°F to 55°F, although the occasional snowstorm also occurs.

🏃 Boston Marathon

At the country's 'longest-running' marathon, tens of thousands of spectators watch runners cross the finish line at Copley Sq in Boston on the third Monday in April.

🎉 Patriots' Day

Also on the third Monday in April, companies of minutemen and regulars don Colonial dress for Pa-triots' Day and reenact the historic battles of April 19, 1775 on the greens in Lexington (p91) and Concord, Massachusetts (p92). Arrive just after dawn.

🍴 Boothbay Fisherman's Festival

Activities at this long-standing Maine event in Boothbay Harbor on the last weekend in April include a cod relay race, an old-fashioned fish fry and the Miss Shrimp Pageant.

May

The sun comes out on a semipermanent basis and the lilac and magnolia trees bloom all around the region. Memorial Day, the last Monday in May, officially kicks off the beach season (though few would go in the water this early).

🎓 College Graduations

As the academic year ends, students around the region celebrate their accomplishments. Boston, Cambridge, the Pioneer Valley and other university towns get overrun with students and their proud parents during graduation ceremonies, which might take place anytime in May or early June.

June

Temperatures range from 55°F to 70°F, with lots of rain. After graduation, students leave town, causing a noticeable decline in traffic and noise.

⊙ Fields of Lupine Festival

This little-known floral festival (p358) in early June in Franconia, New Hampshire, celebrates the annual bloom of lovely lupine with garden tours, art exhibits and concerts.

☆ International Festival of Arts & Ideas

New Haven dedicates three weeks in June to dance, music, film and art. Besides the ticketed concerts and performances, there are free events and special programming for kids and families.

July

July is the region's hottest month and public beaches are invariably crowded. Temperatures usually range from 70°F to 85°F, but there's always a week or two when the mercury shoots above 90°F.

🎊 Harborfest

This week-long festival is an extension of the Fourth of July weekend in Boston, Massachusetts. Kids' activities, chowder tasting and other events culminate in

the annual fireworks and Pops concert on the Esplanade. (p58)

🎊 Mashpee Wampanoag Pow Wow

On the weekend nearest July 4, Native Americans from around the country join the Mashpee Wampanoag for a big three-day heritage celebration (p132) in Mashpee, Massachusetts, that includes Native American dancing, crafts, competitions and after-dark fireball.

🎊 American Independence Festival

Exeter, New Hampshire, celebrates Independence Day a little late (p331), on the second Sunday after July 4, with reenactments, Colonial cooking, road races and free concerts.

☆ North Atlantic Blues Festival

If you're feeling blue, go to Rockland, Maine in mid-July for the region's biggest blues festival. Nationally known performers and local-brewed beers guarantee a good time.

🍺 Vermont Brewers Festival

The third weekend in July is dedicated to discussing beer, brewing beer and of course drinking beer, featuring Vermont's finest craft brews.

☆ Newport Folk Festival

One of the region's most exciting music events, this folk festival at Newport, Rhode Island, in late July attracts national stars as

well as new names to perform all weekend long.

August

Summer continues unabated, with beaches packed to the gills. Only at the end of August do we begin to feel fall coming on.

✕ Maine Lobster Festival

If you love lobster like Maine loves lobster, why not come along for the week-long Lobster Festival held in the first week in August in Rockland? King Neptune and the Sea Goddess oversee a week full of events and – of course – as much lobster as you can eat.

☆ Rhode Island International Film Festival

The region's largest public film festival, held in the second week of August in Providence, Rhode Island, attracts interesting, independent films and sophisticated film-savvy audiences.

🎊 Provincetown Carnival

Carnival in P-town, held in the third week in August, is a week of crazy dance parties and streets filled with beautiful boys in colorful costumes (even more than usual). (p155)

✕ Machias Wild Blueberry Festival

In its 38th year, this festival includes pie-eating contests, cook-offs and hundreds of artisans hawking everything from blueberry jam to blueberry-themed artwork (www.machiasb-lueberry.com). Held on the third weekend in August.

September

The humidity disappears, leaving slightly cooler temperatures and a crispness in the air. Students return and city streets are filled with U-Hauls during the first week. The first Monday in September is Labor Day, the official end of summer.

Big E

Officially known as the Eastern States Exposition, this fair in West Spring-field, Massachusetts, in the second half of September features animal shows, car-nival rides, cheesy perform-ances and more. (p183)

October

New England's best month. The academic year is rolling; the weather is crisp and cool; and the trees take on shades of red, gold and amber.

Fryeburg Fair

This old-fashioned agri-cultural fair in Maine has something for everyone, from live animals to live music, fun rides and fire-works. First week in Octo-ber. (p360)

Foliage Season

Witness Mother Nature at her most ostentatious. The colors all around the region are dazzling, but especially as they blanket the moun-tainsides in the Berkshires in Western Massachusetts, the Green Mountains in Vermont and the White Mountains in New Hamp-shire and Maine.

Wellfleet OysterFest

Who can be surprised that a food festival in Wellfleet celebrates oysters? Come to this huge event the week-end after Columbus Day for plenty of eating, drinking and slurping. (p149)

Haunted Happenings

The 'Witch City' of Salem celebrates Halloween all month long, with special exhibits, parades, con-certs, pumpkin carvings and trick-or-treating. Pub crawls and costume parties keep the carousing going late into the evenings, all month long.

Head of the Charles

This, the world's largest rowing event, takes place in Boston on the River Charles on the third weekend in October, attracting thou-sands of rowers and thou-sands more spectators.

Keene Pumpkin Festival

Help Keene win back its title by building a tower of jack-o'-lanterns as high as the sky. The size of the town triples for this annual festival (p340), held on the third weekend in October.

November

Winter is coming and you can feel it in the air. You may even see snow flurries. Thanksgiving Day – the third Thursday in November – kicks off the holiday season.

America's Hometown Thanksgiving Celebration

Plymouth, Massachu-setts, is the birthplace of Thanksgiving, so it's ap-propriate that the town celebrates this heritage with a parade, concerts, crafts and – of course – food. Held the weekend before Thanksgiving.

December

Winter sets in, with at least one big snow storm in December to prove it. Christmas lights and holiday fairs make the region festive.

Boston Tea Party Reenactment

New Englanders take their reenactments seriously. In the case of the Tea Party, they dress up like Mohawk warriors and dump tea into the Boston Harbor, just like their forebears in 1773. It's held on the Sunday before December 16.

First Night

It actually starts on the 'last night', New Year's Eve, and continues into the wee hours of the New Year. Activities, performances and other events are held at venues all around Boston and Burlington. Buy a but-ton and attend as many as you can.

Plan Your Trip
Itineraries

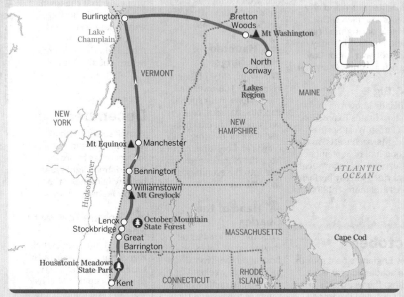

RON AND PATTY THOMAS PHOTOGRAPHY / GETTY IMAGES ©

10 DAYS Fall Foliage

The brilliance of fall in New England is legendary. Scarlet and sugar maples, ash, birch, beech, dogwood, tulip tree, oak and sassafras all contribute to the carnival of autumn color.

Start in Connecticut's **Kent**. Hike up Cobble Mountain in Macedonia Brook State Park for sweeping views of the forested hills against a backdrop of the Taconic and Catskill mountain ranges. Heading north on Rte 7, stop at **Housatonic Meadows State Park** to snap a photo of the Cornwall Bridge, then continue into Massachusetts.

Blanketing the westernmost part of the state, the rounded mountains of the Berkshires turn crimson and gold as early as mid-September. Set up camp in **Great Barrington**, a formerly industrial town now populated with art galleries and upscale restaurants. It's a good base for exploring **October Mountain State Forest**, a multicolored tapestry of hemlocks, birches and oaks. This reserve's name – attributed to Herman Melville – gives a good indication of when this park is at its loveliest.

Cruising north from Great Barrington, you pass through the Berkshires' most charming towns: **Stockbridge**, **Lenox**

Maple trees, Vermont

and **Williamstown**. Stop for a few hours or days for fine dining, shopping and cultural offerings. Dedicate at least one day to **Mt Greylock State Reservation**: the summit offers a panorama stretching up to 100 miles across more than five states.

Cross into Vermont and continue north through the historic villages of **Bennington** and **Manchester**. For fall foliage views head to the top of **Mt Equinox**, where the 360-degree panorama includes the Adirondacks and the lush Battenkill Valley. Continue north to **Burlington**, your base for frolicking on Lake Champlain, and sail away on a schooner for offshore foliage views.

Head southeast through Montpelier and continue into New Hampshire. Your destination is **Bretton Woods**, where you can admire the foliage from the porch of the historic hotel or from a hanging sky bridge. Then make your way to the summit of **Mt Washington**, whether by car, by train or on foot.

When you're ready to come down from the clouds, descend into **North Conway**. Many of the town's restaurants and inns offer expansive views of the nearby mountains, making it an ideal place to wrap up a fall foliage tour.

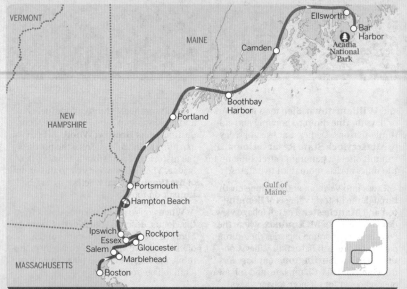

VERMONT

MAINE

Ellsworth

Bar
Harbor

Acadia
National
Park

Camden

Boothbay
Harbor

NEW
HAMPSHIRE

Portland

Portsmouth

Gulf of
Maine

Hampton Beach

Ipswich
Essex

Rockport

Gloucester

Salem

Marblehead

MASSACHUSETTS

Boston

Coastal New England

New England is intrinsically tied to the sea – historically, commercially and emotionally. To see this connection firsthand, just follow the coastline.

Start in **Boston**; follow the HarborWalk along the water's edge from Christopher Columbus Park, stopping at the New England Aquarium and the Institute for Contemporary Art. The next day, board a ferry out to the Harbor Islands.

Head north to **Marblehead** and **Salem**, both rich in maritime history. Don't miss the Peabody Essex Museum and its wonderful maritime exhibit. To glimpse New England's fishing industry at work (and sample its culinary treats) journey to **Gloucester**. This is your jumping-off point for a whale-watching cruise to Stellwagen Bank.

Circle around Cape Ann to discover the charms of the **Rockport** and the mysteries of Dogtown. Then continue up the coast to frolic in the waves at Crane Beach in **Ipswich** and feast on fried clams in **Essex**.

The New Hampshire seacoast is scant, but not without merit: walk the boardwalk at **Hampton Beach** and admire the old houses in historic **Portsmouth**.

In Maine, spend a day or two exploring **Portland**. Eat, drink and shop the Old Port District and check out the collection at the Portland Museum of Art. Don't leave town without snapping a photo of the Portland Head Light on Cape Elizabeth. Continuing north, stroll around lovely (but crowded) **Boothbay Harbor**, perhaps stopping for a seafood lunch on the harbor.

Don't miss a stop in pretty **Camden**, where you can take a windjammer cruise up the rocky coast. When you return to dry land, clamber to the top of Mt Battie in Camden Hills State Park, for sweeping views of Penobscot Bay.

End your trip in beautiful **Bar Harbor** and **Acadia National Park**, which are highlights of the New England coast. You'll have no problem occupying yourself for a weekend or a week, exploring Mt Desert Island's beautiful scenery while hiking, biking, kayaking, camping and more. For a fun and delicious detour, head to the Trenton Bridge Lobster Pound in **Ellsworth**. This is your last chance to get your fill of fresh Maine lobster, so tie on your bib and enjoy.

Top: Acadia National Park (p403)
Bottom: Boothbay Harbor (p392)

1 WEEK Mountain Meander

If you long to breathe pure mountain air and gaze over mountain majesty, follow this route through the region's most glorious peaks.

Start your Mountain Meander at **Franconia Notch State Park**, where you can hike down the Flume, ride a tramway up Cannon Mountain and see what little remains of the Old Man of the Mountain. Spend a few nights at one of many welcoming inns in **Franconia** or **Bethlehem** and don't miss dinner at the creative Cold Mountain Cafe.

The next day, head east on Rte 302, relishing the spectacular views of the White Mountains. Stop at the historic Mount Washington Hotel at **Bretton Woods**. This is the base for a ride on the Cog Railway to the top of **Mt Washington**, New England's highest peak. Or, if you prefer to make the climb on your own two feet, continue on Rte 302 to **Crawford Notch State Park**, the access point for countless hikes in the area.

To give your legs a break, drive west across the **White Mountain National Forest** on the scenic Kancamagus Hwy. This route offers countless opportunities for hiking, camping and other outdoor adventuring. Otherwise, just enjoy the scenery and motor through to I-93, continuing southwest into Vermont.

Expansive vistas unfold with abandon as you approach the Green Mountains on US 4. Continue on to **Killington**, for a day of wintertime skiing or summertime mountain biking.

Continue north on VT 100, often called 'the spine of the state.' Snaking north through the mountains, this classic route feels like a backcountry road, littered with cow-strewn meadows and white-steepled churches. Spend a few hours or a few days exploring, turning off on the gap roads and stopping in any number of tiny towns along the way. Don't miss **Warren** and **Waitsfield**, excellent for browsing art galleries and antique shops, while the nearby ski resorts offer mountain biking and horseback riding.

Sidle up to **Stowe**, where looming **Mt Mansfield** is the outdoor capital of northern Vermont. After exerting yourself sledding or skiing, cycling or hiking, indulge in some Ben & Jerry's ice cream from the factory in **Waterbury**. After climbing many peaks, skiing many slopes and snapping many photos, you've earned it.

Top: Railway in Crawford Notch State Park (p363)
Bottom: Waterway off the Kancamagus Hwy (p353),
White Mountain National Forest

MICHAEL P. GADOMSKI / GETTY IMAGES ©

FOTOSEARCH / GETTY IMAGES ©

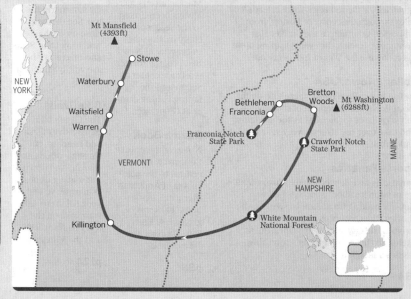

Regions at a Glance

Boston

History
Academia
Sports

Freedom Trail

For a sampler of Boston's Revolutionary sights, follow the red-brick road. It leads 2.4 miles through the center of Boston, from the Boston Common to the Bunker Hill Monument, tracing the events leading up to and following the War of Independence.

College Town, USA

Boston is a college town; there's no doubt about it. No other element of the population is quite as influential as the students, who take over the streets every year in September.

Sports Fanatics

'Fanatic' is no idle word here. Boston fans are passionate about sports, whether they are waking up at 5am to scull on the Charles River, running countless miles through the city streets or yelling at the pitcher to throw something – anything – besides a fast ball.

p34

Around Boston

History
Seafaring
Literature

Pilgrims & Presidents

From the Pilgrims' landing at Plymouth to witch hysteria in Salem, and from the first Revolutionary battle at Lexington to the presidents who were born and buried in Quincy, this region has shaped history.

Ocean Economy

The fate of eastern Massachusetts has always been linked to the sea, especially in the whaling capital at New Bedford, the former sea-trade center at Salem and the fading fishing center at Gloucester.

Read a Book

Nineteenth-century Concord was central to the golden age of American literature, being home to literary greats like Emerson, Thoreau and Hawthorne.

p88

Cape Cod, Nantucket & Martha's Vineyard

Beaches
Wildlife
Cycling

Seashore

Surrounded by sea, it's hard to imagine a place with more world-class beaches: from tidal flats to gnarly open-ocean surf, and from soft sandy dunes to aeons-old clay cliffs.

Creature Features

Humpback whales find the region ideal for summering, too. See them up close on a whale-watching tour. Seals and migratory birds are wildly abundant as well.

Bike Trails

The Cape's bike paths skirt marshes and beaches, cut through woods and soar up and down undulating dunes. When you've had your fill there, take your bike on the ferry to Nantucket and the Vineyard.

p124

Central Mass & the Berkshires

Culture
Food
Hiking

Summer Performances

Each summer a major symphony orchestra, top-notch dance troupes and renowned theater performers land in the hills of the Berkshires.

Locavore Heaven

Apple orchards and farm fields are more than just scenery here. Their harvest is yours for the picking: menus are ripe with farm-to-table dishes, from organic veggies and cheeses to grass-fed meats.

Trails Galore

From the river valleys to the mountaintops, you're never far from a trailhead. Parks, forests and nature preserves offer everything from good birding to sweaty outings along the Appalachian Trail.

p175

Rhode Island

Nightlife
History
Beaches

Pumping Providence

From punk dives and hip art bars to loungy neighborhood joints with an art nouveau aesthetic, there's something for everyone in Providence.

History Writ Small

From Providence's drawing-room radicals and Bristol's slave trading profiteers to the Colonial clapboards of Little Compton and the mansions of Newport's capitalist kings, the East Bay tells the American story in microcosm.

Ocean State

From South County's multi-mile stretches of white sand to the bluff-backed shores of Block Island, the 'Ocean State' has some of the most beautiful beaches in the northeast, perfect for swimming, surfing or building sand castles.

p208

Connecticut

Art
Hiking
Wine

Artistic Gems

Connecticut's reputation as a culturally barren NYC suburb is belied by its wonderful galleries and museums. See avant-garde installations at the Aldrich, American masterpieces in New Britain and esteemed collections in Hartford and New Haven.

Ponds & Peaks

With rolling hills and picturesque ponds, Connecticut is wonderful walking country. Hike to Caleb's Peak, amble along Squantz Pond or wander the trails of the Quiet Corner for the perfect antidote to big city life.

Wine Tasting

Connecticut's gently rolling hills may not be the most famous wine country, but among the state's two dozen or so wineries, there are some real gems, including Hopkins Vineyard in New Preston.

p241

Vermont

Outdoors
Food & Drink
Villages

Four-Season Outdoor Fun

Kayak Jamaica State Park's raging springtime rapids, mountain bike Kingdom Trails' 200-plus miles of cycling paths, survey Mt Mansfield's colors on a fall hike or ski the best slopes in the east.

Dairies & Breweries

Vermont's patchwork of small farms is home to organic producers, sugar shacks, cheesemakers and microbreweries; products appear on menus and at farmers markets statewide.

Vintage Villages

Vermont values small towns: billboards are prohibited and big stores heavily restricted, allowing historic villages to show off their timeless charms. Among the most picturesque are Newfane, Grafton and Woodstock.

p277

New Hampshire

Lakes
Leaf Peeping
Culture

Lake Life

On Golden Pond didn't do it justice. Something about paddling in a kayak, cruising on a boat, taking a sunset dip or gazing out at the bobbing loons from a deck makes time stand still in the Lakes Region.

Scenic Drives

Enjoy Kancamagus Hwy's winding turns through state parks and past gushing gorges, or village-hop along state roads in the Monadnock region. During the fall foliage season, almost every road qualifies as a scenic byway.

Urban Living in Miniature

One walk around pretty little Portsmouth yields sophisticated restaurants, hopping nightlife and historic attractions galore.

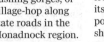

p324

Maine

Boating
Lobster
Antiquing

Take to the Sea

From the multi-masted windjammers of Camden and Rockport, to whale-watching cruises of Bar Harbor and kayak trips amid the islands of Penobscot Bay, Maine is paradise for those who feel at home on the water.

Lobster by the Pound

Maine's famous crustaceans come hot and fresh from the ocean at its many lobster pounds and seafood shacks. Tie on a bib, grab a metal cracker, and go to town on these succulent beasties.

Antique Road Show

Trolling the antiques stores of Maine's pretty fishing villages and mountain towns is a summer visitors' tradition.

p367

On the Road

Maine
p367

Vermont
p277

New
Hampshire
p324

Central
Massachusetts
& the Berkshires
p175

Around Boston p88

Boston p34

Connecticut
p241

Rhode
Island
p208

Cape Cod,
Nantucket &
Martha's Vineyard
p124

Boston

☎ 617 / POP 636,000

Includes ➡

Best Places to Eat

➡ Paramount (p63)

➡ Courtyard (p68)

➡ El Pelon (p69)

➡ Neptune Oyster (p65)

➡ Gourmet Dumpling House (p67)

Best Places to Stay

➡ Liberty Hotel (p59)

➡ Newbury Guest House (p61)

➡ Inn @ St Botolph (p61)

➡ Oasis Guest House (p62)

➡ Kendall Hotel (p62)

Why Go?

The winding streets and stately architecture recall a history of revolution and renewal; and still today, Boston is among the country's most forward-looking and barrier-breaking cities.

For all intents and purposes, Boston is the oldest city in America. And you can hardly walk a step over its cobblestone streets without running into some historic site. But Boston has not been relegated to the past.

A history of cultural patronage means that the city's art and music scenes continue to charm and challenge contemporary audiences. Cutting-edge urban planning projects are reshaping the city even now, as neighborhoods are revived and rediscovered. Historic universities and colleges still attract scientists, philosophers and writers, who shape the city's evolving culture.

When to Go

Boston

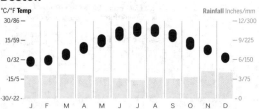

April On Patriots' Day, hordes of sports fans attend the world's oldest marathon.

Summer Hot and humid; many locals make for the beach.

Fall The city comes alive in fall, when students fill the streets.

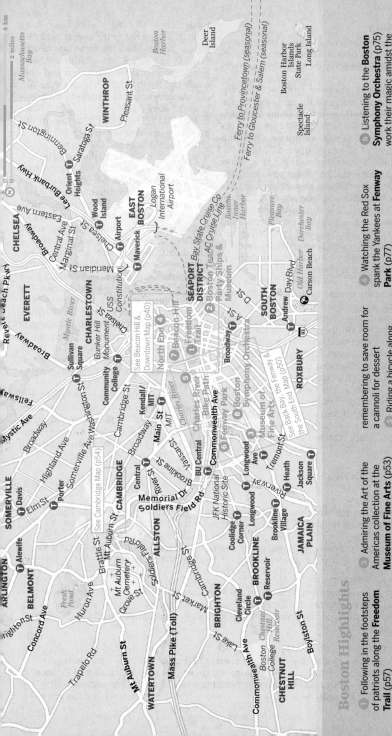

Boston Highlights

1 Following in the footsteps of patriots along the **Freedom Trail** (p57)

2 Fomenting revolution at the **Boston Tea Party Ships & Museum** (p46)

3 Admiring the Art of the Americas collection at the **Museum of Fine Arts** (p53)

4 Feasting on a plate of pasta and a bottle of wine in the **North End** (p65), but remembering to save room for a cannoli for dessert

5 Riding a bicycle along the **Charles River Bike Path** (p48)

6 Watching the Red Sox spank the Yankees at **Fenway Park** (p77)

7 Strolling the brick sidewalks and admiring the architecture on **Beacon Hill** (p38)

8 Listening to the **Boston Symphony Orchestra** (p75) work their magic amidst the grandeur of Symphony Hall

History

Boston is rich in history, made by successive generations of political and social nonconformists inspired by the idea of a better way to live.

In 1630 a thousand Puritans made the treacherous transatlantic crossing to the New World. Upon arrival, John Winthrop gazed upon the Shawmut Peninsula and declared, 'we shall be as a city upon a hill, with the eyes of all people upon us.' Massachusetts Bay Colony was founded as a 'model Christian community,' where personal virtue and industry replaced aristocratic England's class hierarchy and indulgence. A spiritual elite governed in a Puritan theocracy. They established America's first public school and library. Harvard College was founded to supply the colony with homegrown ministers.

When Britain became entangled in expensive wars, it coveted Boston's merchant wealth. The Crown imposed trade restrictions and tariffs. Bostonians protested; Britain dispatched troops. In 1770 a mob provoked British regulars with slurs and snowballs until they fired into the crowd, killing five in the Boston Massacre. In 1773 the Tea Act incited further resentment. Local radicals disguised as Mohawks dumped 90,000 pounds of tea into the harbor in an event known as the Boston Tea Party. The King took it personally: the port was blockaded and city placed under military rule.

Defiant colonists organized a militia. British troops marched to Concord to seize hidden arms. The Old North Church hung two signal lanterns in the steeple, and Paul Revere galloped into the night, and history. Next morning, redcoats skirmished with minutemen on Lexington Green and Concord's Old North Bridge, beginning the War of Independence. Boston figured prominently in the early phase of the American Revolution. Finally, in March 1776, the British evacuated and Boston was liberated.

By the middle of the 19th century, industrial wealth transformed Boston. The hilltops were used as landfill, forming the Back Bay. The city acquired lush public parks and great cultural institutions. Boston was a center of Enlightenment, creating America's first homegrown intellectual movement, transcendentalism. Bostonians were at the forefront of progressive social movements, like abolitionism and suffrage. The city was a vibrant center for arts and science, earning the reputation as the Athens of America.

With industry came social change. The city was inundated with immigrants: Boston Brahmans were forced to mix with Irish, Italians and Portuguese. Anti-immigrant and anti-Catholic sentiments were shrill. Brahman dominance subsided. The Democratic Party represented the new ethnic working poor and featured flamboyant populist politicians.

A decline in manufacturing caused economic recession in the mid-20th century. But as a center of intellectual capital, the region rebounded, led by high technology and medicine. More recently, Boston was again

BOSTON IN...

Two Days

Spend one day reliving revolutionary history by following the Freedom Trail. Take time to lounge on the Boston Common, peek in the Old State House and visit the Paul Revere House. Afterwards, stroll back into the North End for an Italian dinner. On your second day, rent a bike and ride along the Charles River Route. Go as far as Harvard Square to cruise the campus and browse the bookstores.

Four Days

On your third day, peruse the impressive American collection at the Museum of Fine Arts. Spend your last day discovering Back Bay. Window-shop and gallery-hop on Newbury St, go to the top of the Prudential Center and browse the Boston Public Library.

One Week

If you have a week to spare, you also have time to escape the city for a day. Head out to the Harbor Islands to visit Fort Warren and go berry-picking on Grape Island. On your remaining days, explore the quaint streets of Beacon Hill or the edgy urbane South End. Visit the newly renovated New England Aquarium and catch a Red Sox game.

Walking Tour
Freedom Trail

START BOSTON COMMON
FINISH BUNKER HILL MONUMENT
LENGTH 2.4 MILES; 3 HOURS

Start at ➊ **Boston Common** (p38), America's oldest public park. On the northern side, you can't miss gold-domed ➋ **Massachusetts State House** (p38) sitting atop Beacon Hill. Walk north on Tremont St, passing the soaring steeple of ➌ **Park Street Church** (p38) and the Egyptian revival gates of the ➍ **Granary Burying Ground** (p38).

At School St, the columned ➎ **King's Chapel** (p39) overlooks the adjacent burying ground. Turn east on School St, and take note of the plaque commemorating this spot as the ➏ **site of the first public school** (p42).

Continue down School St past the ➐ **Old Corner Bookstore**. Diagonally opposite, the ➑ **Old South Meeting House** (p42) saw the beginnings of the Boston Tea Party.

Further north on Washington St, the ➒ **Old State House** (p42) was the scene of the city's first public reading of the Declaration of Independence. Outside the Old State House a ring of cobblestones marks the ➓ **Boston Massacre site**, yet another uprising that fueled the revolution. Across the intersection, historic ⓫ **Faneuil Hall** (p43) has served as a public meeting place and marketplace for over 250 years.

From Faneuil Hall, follow Hanover St across the Rose Kennedy Greenway. One block east, charming North Sq is the site of ⓬ **Paul Revere House** (p45). Back on Hanover St, the Paul Revere Mall offers a lovely vantage point to view the ⓭ **Old North Church** (p45). From the church, head west on Hull St to ⓮ **Copp's Hill Burying Ground** (p45), with grand views across the river to Charlestown.

Across the Charlestown Bridge, Constitution Rd brings you to the Charlestown Navy Yard, home of the world's oldest commissioned warship, the ⓯ **USS Constitution** (p46). Finally, wind your way through the historic streets of Charlestown center to the ⓰ **Bunker Hill Monument** (p46), site of the devastating American Revolution battle.

a battle site for social reform, this time for gay rights. In 2004 the country's first legal gay marriage occurred in Cambridge. Meanwhile, Massachusetts elected its first (the nation's second) African-American governor.

⊙ Sights

◎ Beacon Hill & Boston Common

When the local news reports the day's events 'on Beacon Hill' it's usually referring to goings-on in the Massachusetts State House, the focal point of politics in the commonwealth, the building famously dubbed 'the hub of the solar system.' Beacon Hill is also famed as the home of centuries of great thinkers. In the 19th century it was the site of literary salons and publishing houses, as well as the center of the abolitionist movement.

But neither politics nor history is what makes this neighborhood the most prestigious in Boston. The appeal of Beacon Hill is its utter loveliness: the narrow cobblestone streets lit with gas lanterns; the distinguished brick town houses decked with purple windowpanes and blooming flower boxes; and grand streets such as stately Louisburg Square.

★ **Boston Common**   PARK
(Map p40; btwn Tremont, Charles, Beacon & Park Sts; ⏰6am-midnight; ⊞; ⓣPark St) The Boston Common has served many purposes over the years, including as a campground for British troops during the Revolutionary War and as green grass for cattle grazing until 1830. Although there is still a grazing ordinance on the books, the Common today serves picnickers, sunbathers and people-watchers.

In the winter, the Frog Pond attracts iceskaters, while summer draws theater lovers for Shakespeare on the Common. This is also the starting point for the Freedom Trail. The on-site information kiosk is a great source of information, maps and tour guides.

ⓘ FREEDOM TRAIL TICKET

The Freedom Trail ticket (adult/child $13/2) includes entry to the Paul Revere House, the Old State House and the Old South Meeting House (a savings of $5 if you visit all three).

The Common is the country's oldest public park. If you have any doubt, refer to the plaque emblazoned with the words of the treaty between Governor Winthrop and William Blaxton, who sold the land for £30 in 1634.

★ **Massachusetts State House**   NOTABLE BUILDING
(Map p40; www.sec.state.ma.us; cnr Beacon & Bowdoin Sts; ⏰9am-5pm, tours 10am-4pm Mon-Fri; ⓣPark St) **FREE** High atop Beacon Hill, Massachusetts' leaders and legislators attempt to turn their ideas into concrete policies and practices within the State House. Charles Bulfinch designed the commanding state capitol, but it was Oliver Wendell Holmes who called it 'the hub of the solar system' (thus earning Boston the nickname 'the Hub').

A free 40-minute tour of the State House covers its history, artwork, architecture and political personalities. Knowledgeable 'Doric Docents' provide details about the many statues, flags and murals that decorate the various halls. Tours also visit the legislative chambers: the House of Representatives, also house of the famous 'Sacred Cod;' and the Senate Chamber, where Angelina Grimké spoke out against slavery in 1838.

On the front lawn, statues honor important Massachusetts figures, among them orator Daniel Webster, religious martyrs Anne Hutchinson and Mary Dyer and President John F Kennedy. Unfortunately, these lovely grounds are closed to the public, so you'll have to peek through the iron fence to catch a glimpse.

Park Street Church   CHURCH
(Map p40; www.parkstreet.org; 1 Park St; ⏰9am-4pm Tue-Sat mid-Jun–Aug; ⓣPark St) Shortly after the construction of Park St Church, powder for the War of 1812 was stored in the basement, earning this location the moniker 'Brimstone Corner.' But that was hardly the most inflammatory event that took place here. Noted for its graceful, 217ft steeple, this Boston landmark has been hosting historic lectures and musical performances since its founding.

Granary Burying Ground   CEMETERY
(Map p40; Tremont St; ⏰9am-5pm; ⓣPark St) Dating to 1660, this atmospheric atoll is crammed with historic headstones, many with evocative (and creepy) carvings. This is the final resting place of all your favorite

revolutionary heroes including Paul Revere, Samuel Adams, John Hancock and James Otis. Benjamin Franklin is buried in Philadelphia, but the Franklin family plot contains his parents.

The five victims of the Boston Massacre share a common grave. Other noteworthy permanent residents include Peter Faneuil, of Faneuil Hall fame, and Judge Sewall, the only magistrate to denounce the hanging of the so-called Salem witches.

Museum of Afro-American History MUSEUM (Map p40; www.afroammuseum.org; 46 Joy St; adult/senior/child $5/3/free; ⊗10am-4pm Mon-Sat; ⊤Park St or Bowdoin) The Museum of Afro-American History occupies two adjacent historic buildings: the African Meeting House, the country's oldest black church and meeting house; and Abiel Smith School, the country's first school for blacks.

Today the Museum of Afro-American History offers rotating exhibits about these historic events. The museum is also a source of information about – and the final destination of – the Black Heritage Trail (p57).

⊙ Downtown & Waterfront

It's hard to tell that downtown Boston was once the domain of cows. The well-trodden paths eventually gave rise to the maze of streets occupied by today's high-rises. Although vestiges of 17th-century Boston are not uncommon in this part of town, the atmosphere of these streets is hardly historic. Downtown is a bustling commercial center, its streets lined with department stores and smaller shops.

Along the waterfront, sailing ships once brought exotic spices, tea and coffee into these docks. Again, some remnants of this maritime trade are still visible in the architecture, especially on Long Wharf, but the waterfront is now a center for a new industry: tourism. Tourists and residents stroll the HarborWalk; ferries shuttle visitors between historic sights; and alfresco diners enjoy the breeze off the harbor.

★ **New England Aquarium** AQUARIUM (Map p40; www.neaq.org; Central Wharf; adult/ child/senior $23/16/21; ⊗9am-5pm Mon-Fri, to 6pm Sat & Sun, 1hr later Jul & Aug; ⓟ♿; ⊤Aquarium) ⬛ Teeming with sea creatures of all sizes, shapes and colors, this giant fishbowl is the centerpiece of Boston's waterfront. Harbor seals and sea otters frolic in a large

observation tank at the entrance. Rays and sharks cruise around a touch-tank. But the main attraction is the newly renovated, three-story cylindrical saltwater tank, swirling with more than 600 creatures great and small, including turtles, sharks and eels.

At the base of the tank the penguin pool is home to three species of fun-loving penguins. Countless side exhibits explore the lives and habitats of other underwater oddities, including exhibits on ethereal jellyfish and playful marine mammals. Daily programs include tank dives, penguin presentations and harbor seal training exhibits. The Simons IMAX Theatre (Map p40; www. neaq.org; Central Wharf; adult/senior & child $10/8; ⊗10am-10pm; ♿; ⊤Aquarium) features films with aquatic themes. The aquarium also organizes whale-watching cruises. Combination tickets are available.

King's Chapel & Burying Ground CHURCH, CEMETERY (Map p40; www.kings-chapel.org; 58 Tremont St; self-guided tour $2 donation, Bells & Bones tours $5-8; ⊗10am-4pm Mon-Sat & 1:30-4pm Sun Jun-Aug, Sat & Sun only Sep-May; ⊤Park St) Bostonians were not pleased when the original Anglican church was erected on this site in 1688. (Remember, it was the Anglicans – the Church of England – whom the Puritans were fleeing.) The granite chapel standing today was built in 1754, while the adjacent burying ground is the oldest in the city. Request a brochure to take a self-guided tour of the church's architectural and historical highlights.

The church was built on a corner of the city cemetery because the Puritans refused

Beacon Hill & Downtown

BOSTON

500 m
0.25 miles

Boston Inner Harbor

Boston Harbor

Constitution Wharf

Callahan Tunnel (toll)
Sumner Tunnel (toll)

Union Wharf
Battery Wharf
Sargents Wharf
Lewis Wharf
Commercial Wharf

US Coast Guard Piers

Atlantic Ave

Christopher Columbus Park

Salem Ferry

Boston Harbor Cruises
25
29
4

WATERFRONT

Aquarium
114

Commercial St

North St
Clark St
Fleet St

54
80
49
71
21
23
62
53
86
87
124

North End Playground

Charter St
Hull St
Tileston St
N Bennet St
Salem St
Prince St

17
8

NORTH END

Fulton St
Commercial St

30

Boston Harbor Islands Pavilion
27
37
State St
Commercial St

118 113
50
72
117

9
79

NPS
Visitors
Center

121
125
64
59
78
58
111
22
70
14

N Margin St
Thatcher St
Endicott St

Hanover St

Congress St

N Washington St

Charlestown Bridge

Lovejoy Wharf
Beverly St

North Station

Haverhill St
Canal St
Friend St
Merrimac St

36
99
144

N Charter St
Causeway St

15

Haymarket

John F Kennedy Federal Building

City Hall Plaza

Boston City Hall

31
Court St

New Sudbury St

Government Center
Center Plaza
Somerset St
Cambridge St

Bowdoin

Bowdoin St

56
Temple St
Hancock St
Joy St

12

Derne St
Myrtle St
S Russell St
Irving St
Garden St
Anderson St

WEST END

Lomasney Way
Stanfords St
Martha Rd
Nashua St

Zakim Bridge

John F Fitzgerald Expwy

Science Park

Charles St

Massachusetts General Hospital

Blossom St
Grove St
Fruit St
Parkman St
Phillips St
Revere St

Liberty Hotel

Charles/MGH

84
41
110
105
40
119
115

Storrow Dr

The Esplanade

Charles River

Charles Rose Canoe & Kayak Center (0.5mi)

Science Park

13
100

Figs (0.25mi); Warren Tavern (0.5mi);
Zumes Coffee House (0.5mi);
Bunker Hill Monument (0.45mi);
USS Constitution Museum (0.5mi);
USS Constitution (0.5mi);
Navy Yard Bistro & Wine Bar (0.6mi);
ConstitutionInn (0.7mi)

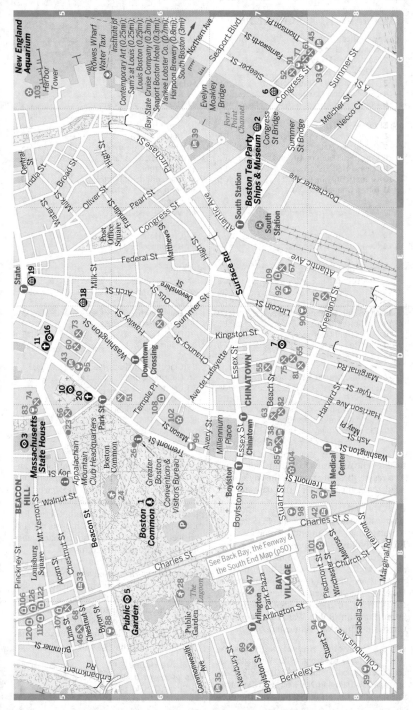

Beacon Hill & Downtown

to allow the Anglicans to use any other land. As a result, these are some of the city's oldest headstones, including one that dates to 1623.

Old City Hall
HISTORIC SITE

(Map p40; www.oldcityhall.com; 45 School St; Ⓣ State) This monumental French Second Empire building occupies a historic spot. Out front, a plaque commemorates the site of the first public school, Boston Latin, founded in 1635 and still operational in Fenway. The hopscotch sidewalk mosaic, *City Carpet,* marks the spot where Benjamin Franklin, Ralph Waldo Emerson and Charles Bulfinch were educated.

Old South Meeting House
HISTORIC BUILDING

(Map p40; www.osmh.org; 310 Washington St; adult/child/senior & student $6/1/5; ⊙9:30am-5pm Apr-Oct, 10am-4pm Nov-Mar; ☖; Ⓣ Downtown Crossing) 'No tax on tea!' That was the deci-

sion on December 16, 1773, when 5000 angry colonists gathered here to protest British taxes, leading to the Boston Tea Party. The graceful meeting house is still a gathering place for discussion, although there's less rabble-rousing now. Instead, it hosts concert and lecture series, as well as reenactments and other historical programs.

This brick meeting house, with its soaring steeple, was also used as a church house back in the day. When you visit today, you can check out an exhibit about the history of the building and listen to an audio of the historic pre–Tea Party meeting. Kids will be engaged by activity kits and scavenger hunts designed for their age groups.

Old State House
HISTORIC BUILDING

(Map p40; www.bostonhistory.org; 206 Washington St; adult/child $8.50/free; ⊙9am-5pm; ☖;

T State) Dating to 1713, the Old State House is Boston's oldest surviving public building, where the Massachusetts Assembly used to debate the issues of the day before the revolution. The building is best known for its balcony, where the Declaration of Independence was first read to Bostonians in 1776.

It occupies a once prominent spot at the top of State St (then known as King St), which was Boston's main thoroughfare. Inside, the Old State House contains a small museum of revolutionary memorabilia, with videos and multimedia presentations about the Boston Massacre.

Faneuil Hall   HISTORIC BUILDING
(Map p40; www.faneuilhall.com; Congress St; ⊙9am-5pm; T Haymarket or Aquarium) FREE 'Those who cannot bear free speech had best go home,' said Wendell Phillips. 'Faneuil Hall is no place for slavish hearts.' Indeed, this public meeting place was the site of so much rabble-rousing that it earned the nickname the 'Cradle of Liberty.'

The brick colonial building – topped with the beloved grasshopper weather vane – was constructed in 1740 at the urging of Boston benefactor and merchant Peter Faneuil. In 1805 Charles Bulfinch enlarged the building, enclosing the 1st-floor market and designing the 2nd-floor meeting space, where public ceremonies are still held today. It's normally open to the public, who can hear about the building's history from National Park Service (NPS) rangers.

New England Holocaust Memorial   MEMORIAL
(Map p40; www.nehm.org; btwn Union & Congress Sts; T Haymarket) Constructed in 1995, the six luminescent glass columns of the New England Holocaust Memorial are engraved with

DON'T MISS

PUBLIC GARDEN

The Public Garden (Map p40; www.friendsofthepublicgarden.org; btwn Charles, Beacon, Boylston & Arlington Sts; ⊙ 6am-midnight; ⊕; T Arlington) is a 24-acre botanical oasis of Victorian flowerbeds, verdant grass and weeping willow trees shading a tranquil lagoon. Until it was filled in the early 19th century, it was (like Back Bay) a tidal salt marsh. Now, at any time of year, it is an island of loveliness, awash in seasonal blooms, gold-toned leaves or untrammeled snow.

The garden's centerpiece is a tranquil lagoon with old-fashioned pedal-powered Swan Boats (Map p40; www.swanboats.com; Public Garden; adult/child/senior $2.75/1.50/2; ⊙ 10am-4pm, to 5pm mid-Jun–Aug; T Arlington). Also a favorite among tiny tots, *Make Way for Ducklings* is a bronze sculpture depicting the Mallard family from Robert McCloskey's beloved book.

six million numbers, representing those killed in the Holocaust. Each tower – with smoldering coals sending plumes of steam up through the glass corridors – represents a different Nazi death camp. The memorial sits along the Freedom Trail, a sobering reminder of its larger meaning.

Rose Kennedy Greenway PARK
(Map p40; www.rosekennedygreenway.org; ⊕; T Aquarium or Haymarket) The completion of the infamous Central Artery Project, aka the Big Dig, has had major implications for the city above ground, reclaiming 27 acres of industrial wasteland for parks and civic plazas and reconnecting Boston to its waterfront.

Ever evolving, the Greenway now hosts a weekly open market for Saturday shoppers and a slew of food trucks for weekday lunchers. The light-enhanced Ring Fountain is a cool place for visitors to rest and recover. There's also a custom-designed Boston-themed carousel, created by a local artist with help from local school children.

◎ Boston Harbor Islands

Boston Harbor is sprinkled with 34 islands, many of which are open for bird-watching, trail walking, fishing and swimming. Now designated as a national park, the Boston Harbor Islands (www.bostonharborislands.org; admission free; ⊙ 9am-dusk, mid-Apr–mid-Oct; ⊛ Boston's Best Cruises from Long Wharf) offer a range of ecosystems – sandy beaches, rocky cliffs, freshwater and saltwater marsh and forested trails – only 45 minutes from downtown Boston. Learn everything you need to know at the Boston Harbor Islands Pavilion (Map p40; www.bostonharborislands.org; Rose Kennedy Greenway; ⊙ 9am-5pm May-Oct; T Aquarium) on the Greenway.

Georges Island is the site of Fort Warren, a 19th-century fort and Civil War prison. NPS rangers give guided tours of the fort, which is largely abandoned, with many dark tunnels, creepy corners and magnificent lookouts to discover. On weekends, Georges Island offers plenty of family fun, with live music, theater, participatory sports and other special events.

The revamped Spectacle Island has a marina, visitor center, restaurant and supervised beaches. Rangers lead half-hour introductory kayak tours for newbies. Five miles of walking trails provide access to a 157ft peak overlooking the harbor.

Islands with walking trails, campgrounds and beach access include Bumpkin, Grape and Lovells. Open for camping from Memorial Day to Columbus Day, each island has 10 to 12 individual sites and one large group site. If you are camping here, make sure to bring your own water and supplies; hang your food high in the trees out of reach of animals; and expect rather primitive sites and composting toilets. Make reservations (☏ 877-422-6762; www.reserveamerica.com; reservation fee $8.65, campsite per person $6-8) in advance.

To get to most of the islands, Harbor Express (www.bostonbestcruises.com; 1 Long Wharf; roundtrip adult/senior/child $15/9/11, inter-island $3; ⊙ service 9am-5pm May-early Oct) offers a seasonal ferry service from Long Wharf. Purchase a round-trip ticket to Georges Island or Spectacle Island, where you catch the inter-island shuttle to the smaller islands.

◎ North End & West End

One of Boston's oldest neighborhoods, the North End has a history that is rich with diversity and drama. These days, the North

End's Italian flavor is the strongest. Old-timers still carry on passionate discussions in Italian and shop at specialty stores selling handmade pasta and fresh-baked bread.

The West End is sometimes called the 'Old West End' because there's not much left of this formerly vibrant neighborhood. What few vestiges remain are found in the little byways between Merrimac and Causeway Sts. The massive institutions that now dominate this neighborhood include Boston City Hall and Mass General Hospital. Of more interest to travelers is North Station and the TD Banknorth Garden.

Paul Revere House   HISTORIC HOUSE
(Map p40; ☎ 617-523-2338; www.paulreverehouse. org; 19 North Sq; adult/child/senior & student $3.50/1/3; ☉ 9:30am-5:15pm, shorter hours Nov-Apr; ☻; ☏ Haymarket) When silversmith Paul Revere rode to warn patriots of the British march to Lexington and Concord, he set out from his home on North Sq. This small clapboard house was built in 1680, making it the oldest house in Boston. A self-guided tour through the house and courtyard gives a glimpse of what life was like for the Revere family (which included 16 children!).

Old North Church   CHURCH
(Map p40; www.oldnorth.com; 193 Salem St; donation $1, tour adult/child $5/4; ☉ 9am-5pm Mar-Oct, 10am-4pm Tue-Sun Nov-Feb; ☏ Haymarket or North Station) 'One if by land, and two if by sea...' Everyone knows the line from Longfellow's poem, *Paul Revere's Ride*. It was here, on the night of April 18, 1775, that the sexton hung two lanterns from the steeple, a signal that the British would march on Lexington and Concord via the sea route.

Also called Christ Church, this 1723 place of worship is Boston's oldest church. This remains an active church; the grand organ is played at the 11am Sunday service. All visitors are invited to enjoy a 10-minute presentation about the history of the Old North Church. For more detailed information, the Behind the Scenes tour takes visitors up into the belfry and down into the crypt.

Copp's Hill Burying Ground   CEMETERY
(Map p40; Hull St; ☉ dawn-dusk; ☏ North Station) The city's second-oldest cemetery – dating to 1660 – is the final resting place for an estimated 10,000 souls. It is named for William Copp, who originally owned this land. While the oldest graves belong to Copp's children, there are several other noteworthy residents.

Near the Charter St gate you'll find the graves of the Mather family – Increase, Cotton and Samuel – all of whom were politically powerful religious leaders in the colonial community. Front and center is the grave of Daniel Malcolm, whose headstone commemorates his rebel activism. British soldiers apparently took offense at this claim and used the headstone for target practice.

New England Sports Museum   MUSEUM
(Map p40; www.sportsmuseum.org; TD Banknorth Garden; adult/child $10/5; ☉ 10am-4pm except event days; ☏ North Station) For a nostalgic look at Boston sports history, spend an afternoon at this museum, housed in the concourse area at the Garden.

The highlight is the penalty box from the old Boston Garden – gifted to Bruin Terry O'Reilly because he spent so much time there. Also on display are Larry Bird's locker, Adam Vinatieri's shoes and Tony Conigliaro's baseball (yes, the one that damaged his left eye and derailed his career). The museum sometimes closes for special events at the Garden; closing days are posted on the website.

Museum of Science   MUSEUM
(Map p40; www.mos.org; Charles River Dam; adult/child/senior $22/19/20, theater & planetarium $10/8/9; ☉ 9am-5pm Sat-Thu Sep-Jun, to 7pm Jul & Aug, to 9pm Fri year-round; ☻☻; ☏ Science Park) ☻ This educational playground has more than 600 interactive exhibits. Favorites include the world's largest lightning-bolt generator, a full-scale space capsule, a world population meter and a virtual fish tank. The museum also houses the **Charles Hayden Planetarium & Mugar Omni Theater** (Map p40).

The amazing array of exhibits and presentations explores computers, technology, complex systems, algae, maps, models, dinosaurs and birds. Many others focus on the natural world, including exploration of issues such as organic waste as an alternative fuel source, pathogens on produce and the impact of the changing environment on various species. The Discovery Center offers other hands-on fun that's cool for the youngest set (ages 3 to 8).

☉ Charlestown

The Charlestown Navy Yard was a thriving shipbuilding center throughout the 19th century. Although the navy yard was closed in 1974, the surrounding neighborhood has been making a comeback ever since. The impressive granite buildings have been transformed into shops, condos and offices, which enjoy a panoramic view of Boston. To find these places, walk across the Charlestown Bridge from the North End or take the ferry from Long Wharf.

USS Constitution   HISTORIC SITE
(www.oldironsides.com; Charlestown Navy Yard; ⊙10am-6pm Tue-Sun Apr-Oct, to 4pm Thu-Sun Nov-Mar; ⛴; ☐93 from Haymarket, ⛴F4 from Long Wharf) **FREE** 'Her sides are made of iron!' So cried a crewman as he watched a shot bounce off the thick oak hull of the USS *Constitution* during the War of 1812. This bit of irony earned the legendary ship her nickname. Indeed, she won no less than three battles during that war, and she never went down in a battle. The USS Constitution is the oldest commissioned US Navy ship, dating to 1797.

She has been moored here since 1897, when Congressman John F 'Honey Fitz' Fitzgerald introduced a bill to make Massachusetts her permanent residence. Navy personnel give 30-minute guided tours of the top deck, gun deck and cramped quarters (last tour 4:30pm in summer, 3:30pm in winter). You can also wander around the top deck by yourself, but access is limited. Plus, you won't learn all the USS *Constitution* fun facts, like how the captain's son died on her maiden voyage (an inauspicious start).

USS Constitution Museum   MUSEUM
(www.ussconstitutionmuseum.org; First Ave, Charlestown Navy Yard; adult/senior/child $5/3/2; ⊙9am-6pm Apr-Oct, 10am-5pm Nov-Mar; ⛴; ☐93 from Haymarket, ⛴F4 from Long Wharf) For a play-by-play of the USS *Constitution*'s various battles, as well as her current role as the flagship of the US Navy, head indoors to the museum. More interesting is the exhibit on the Barbary War, which explains the birth of the US Navy during this relatively unknown conflict – America's first war at sea. Upstairs, kids can experience what it was like to be a sailor on the USS *Constitution* in 1812.

Bunker Hill Monument   MONUMENT
(www.nps.gov/bost; Monument Sq; ⊙9am-5pm Sep-Jun, to 6pm Jul & Aug; ☐93 from Haymarket, ⛈Community College) **FREE** 'Don't fire until you see the whites of their eyes!' came the order from Colonel Prescott to revolutionary troops on June 17, 1775. Considering the ill-preparedness of the revolutionary soldiers, the bloody Battle of Bunker Hill resulted in a surprising number of British casualties. Ultimately, however, the Redcoats prevailed. Today, the 220ft granite obelisk monument is visible from all around the city.

Walk through Charlestown's winding cobblestone streets up to the monument's hilltop perch and climb 294 steps to the top of the monument to enjoy the panorama of the city, the harbor and the North Shore. By the way, the name 'Battle of Bunker Hill' is misleading, as most of the fighting took place on Breed's Hill, where the Bunker Hill Monument stands today.

Bunker Hill Museum   MUSEUM
(43 Monument Sq; ⊙9am-5pm; ☐93 from Haymarket, ⛈Community College) **FREE** Opposite the Bunker Hill Monument, this red-brick museum contains two floors of exhibits, including historical dioramas, a few artifacts and an impressive 360-degree mural depicting the battle. If you can find where the artist signed his masterpiece, you win a prize. NPS rangers give summer talks and musket-firing demonstrations.

◉ Seaport District

Separated from Boston proper by the jellyfish-laden Fort Point Channel, this area has always afforded spectacular views of downtown Boston. But until recently it had been neglected by city officials and ignored by developers. Such prime waterside real estate can only go unexploited for so long, however, and the Seaport is now the target of an ambitious development project, as evidenced by the huge convention center, several luxury hotels and the ICA on the water's edge. The goal is to turn this neighborhood into an **Innovation District** (www.innovationdistrict. org), with business incubators, research labs and affordable housing to attract Boston's best and brightest young thinkers. Following the **HarborWalk**, it's a pleasant stroll across the Northern Ave Bridge to the Seaport District.

★ Boston Tea Party
Ships & Museum   MUSEUM
(Map p40; www.bostonteapartyship.com; Congress St Bridge; ⛴; ⛈South Station) After years of anticipation and restoration, the Tea Party Ships are moored at the reconstructed Griffin's Wharf, alongside a shiny new museum dedicated to the revolution's most catalytic event. Interactive exhibits allows visitors to

meet re-enactors in period costume, explore the ships, learn about contemporary popular perceptions through multimedia presentations and even participate in the protest.

At the time of opening in 2012, visitors can board the fully-rigged *Eleanor* and the whaler *Beaver* to experience life aboard an 18th-century vessel. (The *Dartmouth* is expected to be built later.) Would-be rebels can throw crates of tea into the harbor, in solidarity with their fiery forebears.

Institute of Contemporary Art   MUSEUM

(ICA; www.icaboston.org; 100 Northern Ave; adult/child/student/senior $15/free/10/13; ☉10am-5pm Tue, Wed, Sat & Sun, to 9pm Thu & Fri; P ♿; ☐ SL1 or SL2, T South Station) A work of art in itself, the ICA is housed in a glass structure cantilevered over a waterside plaza. The vast light-filled interior allows for groundbreaking exhibits, multimedia presentations and performance art, in addition to the ICA's growing collection of cutting-edge contemporary art.

The museum's primary strategy has been to acquire pieces by artists featured in its past exhibits, so the permanent collection is a sort of history of the museum itself. It showcases both national and international artists, including the likes of graffiti artist Shepard Fairey; video artist Christian Jankowski; photographer Boris Mikhailov; local boy Josiah McElheny; and sculptors Tara Donovan, Mona Hatoum and Cornelia Parker.

Boston Children's Museum   MUSEUM

(Map p40; www.bostonchildrensmuseum.org; 300 Congress St; admission $14, Fri evening $1; ☉10am-5pm Sat-Thu, 10am-9pm Fri; ♿; T South Station) 🖋 The interactive, educational exhibits at the delightful Children's Museum keep kids entertained for hours. Highlights include a bubble exhibit, rock-climbing walls, a hands-on construction site and intercultural immersion experiences, not to mention the amazing three-story climbing structure in the atrium. In nice weather kids can enjoy outdoor eating and playing in the waterside park. Look for the iconic Hood milk bottle on Fort Point Channel.

👁 Chinatown & Theater District

These neighborhoods are home to Boston's lively theater scene, its most hip-hop-happening nightclubs and its best international dining. Ethnically and economically diverse, they border Boston's downtown districts, but they are edgier and artier.

Although tiny by New York standards, Boston's Theater District has long served as a pre-Broadway staging area. In the 1940s Boston had over 50 theaters. Many landmark theaters have recently received long-needed face-lifts, and their colorful marquees and posh patrons have revived the aura of 'bright lights, big city.'

Chinatown is overflowing with ethnic restaurants, live poultry and fresh produce markets, teahouses and textile shops. In addition to the Chinese, who began arriving in the late 1870s, this tight-knit community also includes Cambodians, Vietnamese and Laotians. The official entrance is China-town Gate (Map p40; cnr Beach St & Surface Rd; T Chinatown), a gift from the city of Taipei. Surrounding the gate and anchoring the southern end of the Rose Kennedy Greenway is the new Chinatown Park. Incorporating elements of feng shui, the park design is inspired by the many generations of Asian immigrants that have passed through this gate.

👁 South End

What the Castro is to San Francisco and Dupont Circle is to Washington, DC, so the South End is to Boston: a once-rough neighborhood that was claimed and cleaned up by the gay community, and now everyone wants to live there.

And why not? The South End boasts the country's largest concentration of Victorian row houses, many of which have been painstakingly restored. The most enticing corners of the South End are those with exquisite London-style row houses, with steep stoops and tiny ornamental gardens. Several sweet streets run between Tremont St and Shawmut Ave, particularly the lovely elliptical Union Park and intimate Rutland Square.

The South End offers Boston's most innovative and exciting options for dining out, especially along trendy Tremont Street. And now, the area south of Washington St has earned the moniker SoWa for the artistic community that is converting the old warehouses into studio and gallery space. On the first Friday of every month, check out the open studios event at the SoWa Artists Guild (Map p50; www.sowaartistsguild.com; 450 Harrison Ave; ☉5-9pm first Fri; ☐ SL4 or SL5, T Tufts Medical Center).

Back Bay

Up until the 1850s Back Bay was an uninhabitable tidal flat. Boston was experiencing a population and building boom, so urban planners embarked on an ambitious 40-year project: filling in the marsh, laying out an orderly grid of streets, erecting magnificent Victorian brownstones and designing high-minded civic plazas. So Back Bay was born.

The grandest of Back Bay's grand boulevards is **Commonwealth Avenue** (more 'commonly' Comm Ave). Boston's Champs Élysées, the dual carriageway connects the Public Garden to the Back Bay Fens, a green link in Olmsted's Emerald Necklace.

North of here is lovely **Marlborough Street**, its brick sidewalks lit with gas lamps and shaded by blooming magnolias. South is swanky **Newbury Street**, destination for the serious shopper or gallery hopper. And **Copley Square** represents the best of Back Bay architecture, as it gracefully blends disparate elements from all eras.

★**Charles River Esplanade** PARK
(Map p50; www.esplanadeassociation.org; ⊞; ⓣCharles/MGH or Kenmore) The southern bank of the Charles River Basin is an enticing urban escape, with grassy knolls and cooling waterways, all designed by Frederick Law Olmsted. The park is dotted with public art, including an oversized bust of Arthur Fiedler, long-time conductor of the Boston Pops. Paths along the river are ideal for bicycling, jogging or walking.

The Esplanade stretches almost 3 miles along the Boston shore of the Charles River, from the Museum of Science to BU Bridge. Further west, the **Charles River Bike Path** runs along both sides of the Charles River all the way to Watertown Center, making a 17-mile loop.

★**Boston Public Library** LIBRARY
(Map p50; www.bpl.org; 700 Boylston St; ⊙9am-9pm Mon-Thu, 9am-5pm Fri & Sat year-round, 1-5pm Sun Oct-May; ⓣCopley) FREE Dating from 1852, the esteemed Boston Public Library lends credence to Boston's reputation as the 'Athens of America.' The old McKim building is notable for its magnificent facade and exquisite interior art. Pick up a free brochure and take a self-guided tour; alternatively, free guided tours (times vary) depart from the entrance hall.

This original BPL building, inspired by Italian Renaissance palazzi, features Daniel Chester French's enormous bronze doorways, flanked by iron gates and lanterns. From there a marble staircase leads past Pierre Puvis de Chavannes' inspirational murals depicting poetry, philosophy, history and science, which he considered 'the four great expressions of the human mind.'

The staircase terminates at the splendid **Bates Hall Reading Room**, where even the most mundane musings are elevated by the barrel-vaulted, 50ft coffered ceilings. Nearby, the **Abbey Room** is named for the author of the 1895 murals recounting Sir Galahad's quest for the Holy Grail. The 3rd floor features John Singer Sargent's unfinished **Judaic and Christian murals**, which were criticized for anti-Semitic messages.

Besides this amazing artistry, the library holds untold treasures in its special collections, including John Adams' personal library. Frequent exhibits showcase some of the highlights – check the BPL website for details. The enchanting **Italianate courtyard** is a peaceful place to read.

★**Trinity Church** CHURCH
(Map p50; www.trinitychurchboston.org; 206 Clarendon St; adult/child/senior & student $7/free/5; ⊙10am-3:30pm Mon-Fri, 9am-4pm Sat, 1-5pm Sun; ⓣCopley) A masterpiece of American architecture, Trinity Church is the country's ultimate example of Richardsonian Romanesque. The interior is an awe-striking array of vibrant murals and stained glass, most by artist John LaFarge, who cooperated closely with architect Henry Hobson Richardson to create an integrated composition of shapes, colors and textures. Free architectural tours are offered on Sunday at 12:15pm.

The walls of the great central tower are covered by two tiers of murals, soaring more than 100ft. These thousands of square feet of exquisite, jewel-toned encaustic paintings established John LaFarge as the father of the American mural movement. Inside, his stained glass windows are the jewels of the church, distinctive for their use of layered opalescent glass. *Christ in Majesty*, the spectacular three-panel clerestory window at the west end, is now considered one of America's finest examples of stained-glass art.

New Old South Church CHURCH
(Map p50; www.oldsouth.org; 645 Boylston St; ⊙8am-7pm Mon-Fri, 10am-4pm Sat & Sun; ⓣCopley) This magnificent puddingstone Venetian Gothic church on Copley Sq is

called the 'new' Old South because up until 1875, the congregation worshiped in the Old South Church on Milk St (now the Old South Meeting House). The Congregational church has an impressive collection of stained-glass windows, all shipped from London, and an organ that was rescued from a Minneapolis church just before demolition.

Prudential Center Skywalk Observatory
LOOKOUT

(Map p50; www.prudentialcenter.com; 800 Boylston St; adult/child/senior & student $15/10/13; ☉10am-10pm Mar-Oct, to 8pm Nov-Feb; P⏹; T Prudential) Get a bird's-eye view of Boston from the 50th floor of the Prudential Center. Completely enclosed by glass, the Skywalk Observatory offers spectacular 360-degree views of Boston and Cambridge, accompanied by an entertaining audio tour (with a special version catering to kids). Alternatively, get the same view from the Top of the Hub (Map p50; ☑617-536-1775; www.topofthehub. net; 800 Boylston St; ☉11:30am-1am; ☏; T Prudential) for the price of a drink.

Christian Science Church
CHURCH

(Map p50; www.christianscience.com; 175 Huntington Ave; ☉noon-4pm Tue, 1-4pm Wed, noon-5pm Thu-Sat, 11am-3pm Sun, service 10am Sun; T Symphony) Known to adherents as the 'Mother Church,' this is the international home base for the Church of Christ, Scientist (Christian Science), founded by Mary Baker Eddy in 1866. Tour the grand classical revival basilica, which can seat 3000 worshippers, listen to the 14,000-pipe organ, and linger on the expansive plaza with its 670ft-long reflecting pool.

Mary Baker Eddy Library & Mapparium
LIBRARY

(Map p50; www.marybakereddylibrary.org; 200 Massachusetts Ave; adult/child/senior & student $6/free/4; ☉10am-4pm Tue-Sun; ⏹; T Symphony) The Mary Baker Eddy Library houses one of Boston's hidden treasures, the intriguing Mapparium. The Mapparium is a room-size, stained-glass globe that visitors walk through on a glass bridge. It was created in 1935, which is reflected in the globe's geopolitical boundaries. The acoustics, which surprised even the designer, allow everyone in the room to hear even the tiniest whisper.

Besides the Mapparium, the library has an odd amalgam of exhibits related to its full name, the MBE Library for the Betterment of Humanity. Second-floor galleries deal with the 'search for the meaning of life,' both on a personal and global level.

BOSTON FOR CHILDREN

Boston is a giant living history museum, the setting for many educational and lively field trips. A handy reference book is *Kidding Around Boston* by Helen Byers.

You'll have no trouble taking your kid's stroller on the T. The city's crowded old streets and sidewalks may present more of a challenge.

Sights

Don't forget to think outside the box: many adult-oriented museums and historic sites have special programs geared toward kids. Check out their websites in advance.

Children's Museum (p47) Hours of fun climbing, constructing and creating. Especially good for kids aged three to eight years.

Museum of Science (p45) More opportunities to combine fun and learning than anywhere in the city. Exhibits will entertain kids aged four and up.

New England Aquarium (p39) Explore the most exotic of natural environments: under the sea. For ages three and up.

Activities

Freedom Trail (p57) Download a scavenger hunt or a reading list from Freedom Trail Foundation for your child before setting out. Also consider Boston for Little Feet (p57).

Urban Adventours (p57) Bike tour company offering baby seats, trailers and child-size bicycles so kids can get in on the cycling action.

Boston Duck Tours (p56) Kids of all ages are invited to drive the duck on the raging waters of the Charles River. Bonus: quacking loudly is encouraged.

Back Bay, the Fenway & the South End

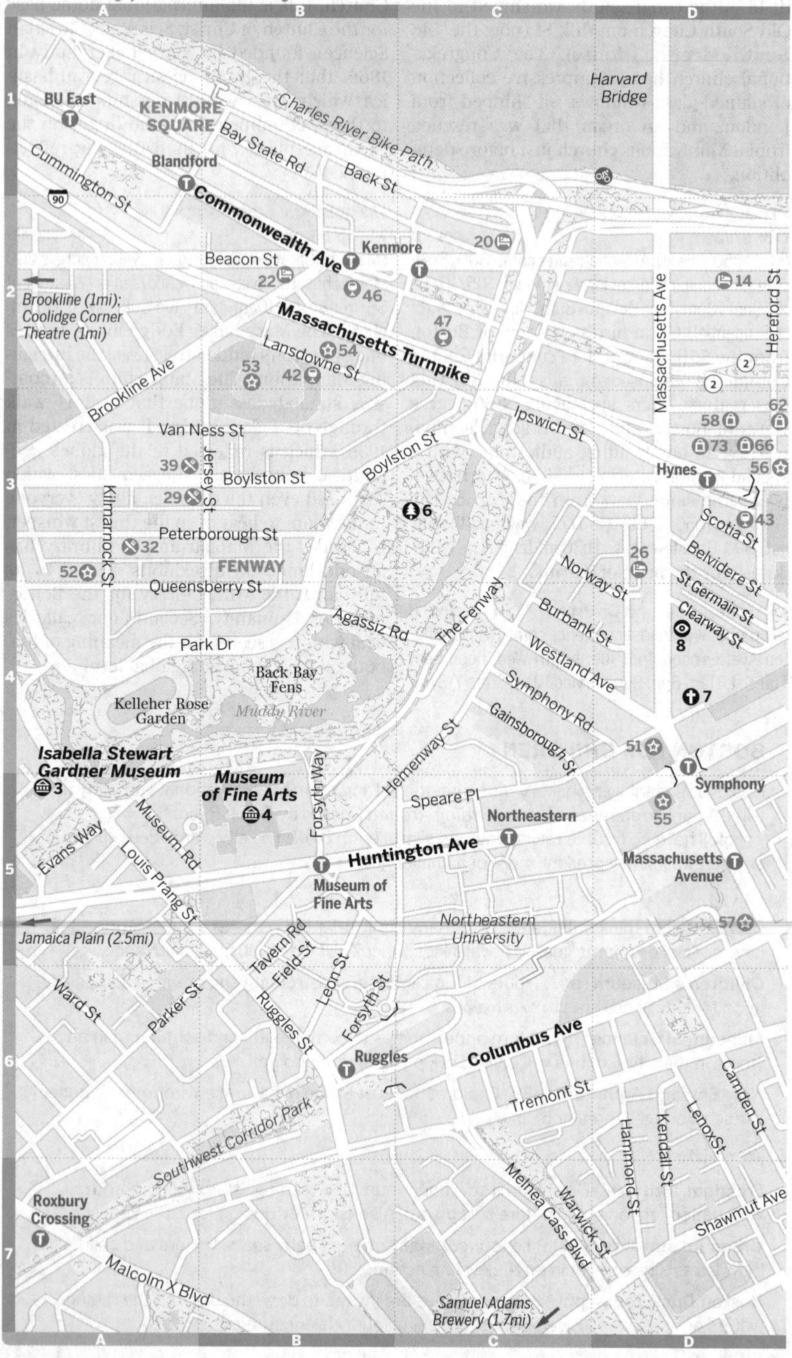
A
B
C
D
1
2
3
4
5
6
7
BU East
KENMORE SQUARE
Charles River Bike Path
Bay State Rd
Back St
Harvard Bridge
Blandford
Cummington St
90
Commonwealth Ave
Kenmore
Beacon St
20
22
46
14
Massachusetts Ave
Hereford St
Brookline (1mi); Coolidge Corner Theatre (1mi)
Massachusetts Turnpike
47
54
Lansdowne St
53
42
Brookline Ave
62
58
Ipswich St
Van Ness St
73
66
Boylston St
56
Hynes
39
Jersey St
Boylston St
29
6
Kilmarnock St
Scotia St
43
Peterborough St
32
26
Belvidere St
52
FENWAY
Norway St
St Germain St
Queensberry St
Clearway St
8
Agassiz Rd
The Fenway
Burbank St
Park Dr
Westland Ave
Back Bay Fens
7
Symphony Rd
Kelleher Rose Garden
Muddy River
Gainsborough St
Isabella Stewart Gardner Museum
3
51
Museum of Fine Arts
4
Hemenway St
Forsyth Way
Symphony
Speare Pl
55
Museum Rd
Northeastern
Evans Way
Huntington Ave
Massachusetts Avenue
Louis Prang St
Museum of Fine Arts
Northeastern University
57
Jamaica Plain (2.5mi)
Tavern Rd
Field St
Leon St
Ward St
Forsyth St
Parker St
Ruggles St
Columbus Ave
Ruggles
Camden St
Tremont St
Lenox St
Kendall St
Hammond St
Southwest Corridor Park
Roxbury Crossing
Melnea Cass Blvd
Warwick St
Shawmut Ave
Malcolm X Blvd
Samuel Adams Brewery (1.7mi)

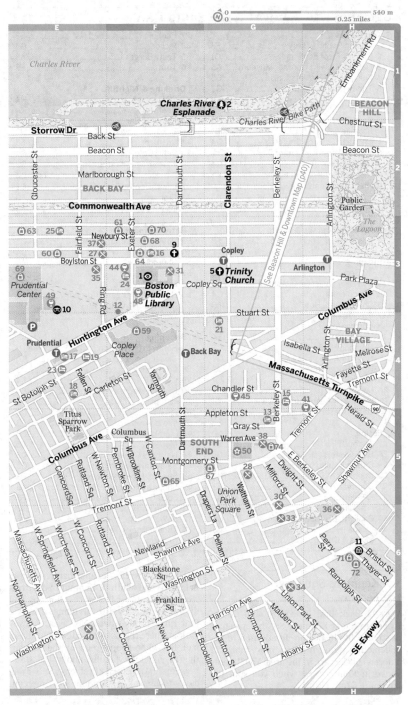

BOSTON SIGHTS

Back Bay, the Fenway & the South End

⊙ Kenmore Square & the Fenway

West of Back Bay, Beacon St and Comm Ave converge at Kenmore Sq, the epicenter of student life in Boston. In addition to the behemoth Boston University, more than half a dozen colleges are in the area. You'll know you're in Kenmore Sq when you spot the landmark Citgo sign.

The Fenway refers to an urban residential neighborhood south of Kenmore Sq, attractive to students for its low-cost housing and dining. Fenway is also the name of a road that runs through here. Not least, Fenway Park is where the Boston Red Sox play baseball. But when people refer to 'the Fenway,' they're generally talking about the Back Bay Fens (Map p50; Park Dr at Jersey St; ⊙ dawn-dusk; Ⓣ Museum), a tranquil and interconnected park system that's an integral link in the Emerald Necklace.

⭐ **Museum of Fine Arts** MUSEUM
(MFA; Map p50; www.mfa.org; 465 Huntington Ave; adult/child/senior & student $22/10/20; ⊙10am-5pm Sat-Tue, to 10pm Wed-Fri; 🚻; Ⓣ Museum of Fine Arts or Ruggles) The Museum of Fine Arts holdings encompass all eras, from the ancient world to contemporary times, and all areas of the globe, making it truly encyclopedic in scope. The museum's latest additions are new wings dedicated to the Art of the Americas and to contemporary art, which has significantly increased its exhibition space and broadened its focus, contributing to Boston's emergence as an art center in the 21st century.

The Art of the Americas wing is the undisputed highlight of the MFA, featuring myriad portraits by John Singleton Copley and Gilbert Stuart (including the dollar-bill portrait), as well as paintings by Winslow Homer, John Singer Sargent and Mary Cassatt. Edward Hopper and the Hudson River School are well represented. The decorative arts are also on display, including Paul Revere's famous Liberty Bowl.

In addition to American art, the museum has one of the world's most comprehensive collections of Japanese art and a significant collection of Nubian art. In 1905, the museum joined forces with Harvard for a 1905 archaeological expedition at the Great Pyramids at Giza, hauling back a world-famous collection of mummies and funerary objects. The collection of European paintings is outstanding, especially the huge stash of French impressionist paintings, featuring many masterpieces by Claude Monet and Edgar Degas.

⭐ **Isabella Stewart Gardner Museum** MUSEUM
(Map p50; www.gardnermuseum.org; 280 The Fenway; adult/child/student/senior $15/free/5/12; ⊙11am-5pm Wed-Mon, to 9pm Thu; 🚻; Ⓣ Museum of Fine Arts) The Gardner is filled with almost 2000 priceless objects, primarily European, including outstanding tapestries and Italian Renaissance and 17th-century Dutch paintings. The four-story greenhouse courtyard is a masterpiece and a tranquil oasis that alone is worth the price of admission.

This Venetian-style palazzo was home to 'Mrs Jack' Gardner herself until her death in 1924. Now with a brand new wing (designed by Renzo Piano), the museum hosts a vibrant artist-in-residence program, as well as performing arts events. It remains a monument to one woman's taste for exquisite art.

👁 **Cambridge**

Boston's neighbor to the north was home to the country's first college and first printing press. Thus Cambridge established early on its reputation as fertile ground for intellectual and political thought – a reputation that

---

WORTH A TRIP

JFK SITES

The legacy of JFK is ubiquitous in Boston, but the official memorial to the 35th president is the John F Kennedy Presidential Library & Museum (www.jfklibrary.org; Columbia Point; adult/child/senior & student $12/9/10; ⊙9am-5pm; Ⓟ; Ⓣ JFK/UMass), a striking, modern, marble building designed by IM Pei. The architectural centerpiece is the glass pavilion, with soaring 115ft ceilings and floor-to-ceiling windows overlooking Boston Harbor. The museum is a fitting tribute to JFK's life and legacy. The effective use of video recreates history for visitors who may or may not remember the early 1960s. A highlight is the museum's treatment of the Cuban Missile Crisis: a short film explores the dilemmas and decisions that the president faced, while an archival exhibit displays actual documents and correspondence from these gripping 13 days.

In the streetcar suburb of Brookline, the John F Kennedy National Historic Site (www.nps.gov/jofi; 83 Beals St; ⊙9:30am-5pm Wed-Sun May-Oct; Ⓣ Coolidge Corner) FREE occupies the modest three-story house that was JFK's birthplace and boyhood home. Matriarch Rose Kennedy oversaw its restoration and furnishing in the late 1960s; today her narrative sheds light on the Kennedys' family life. Guided tours allow visitors to see furnishings, photographs and mementos that have been preserved from the time the family lived here. Take the Green Line (C branch) to Coolidge Corner and walk north on Harvard St.

BOSTON

Cambridge

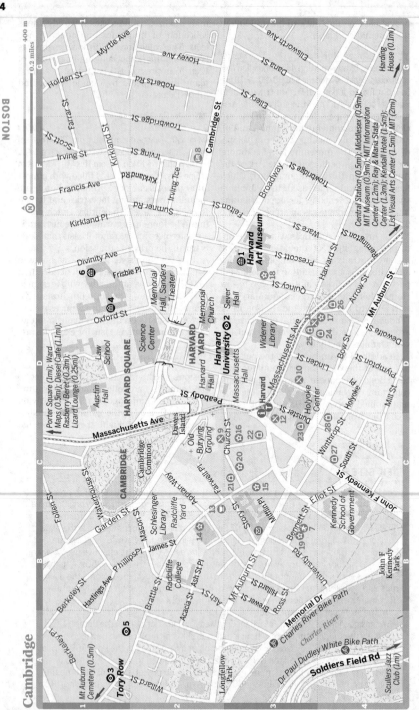

Myrtle Ave
Holden St
Hovey Ave
Ellsworth Ave
Dana St
Farrar St
Scott St
Roberts Rd
Cambridge St
Ellery St
Irving St
Kirkland St
Trowbridge St
Irving St
Francis Ave
Kirkland Rd
Irving Tce
Broadway
Trowbridge St
Kirkland Pl
Sumner Rd
Felton St

Central Station (0.5mi); Middlesex (0.9mi);
MIT Museum (0.9mi); MIT Information
Center (1.2mi); Ray & Maria Stata
Center (1.3mi); Kendall Hotel (1.5mi);
List Visual Arts Center (1.5mi); MIT (2mi)

Harding
House (0.1mi)

Divinity Ave
6 🏛
Frisbie Pl
Harvard
Art Museum
1 🏛
4 🏛
Oxford St
Memorial
Hall, Sanders
Theater
Ware St
Prescott St
Harvard St
18
Quincy St

Porter Square (1mi); Ward
Maps (0.5mi); Diesel Cafe (1.1mi);
Rasberry Beret (0.3mi);
Lizard Lounge (0.25mi)

HARVARD
SQUARE
Science
Center
HARVARD
YARD
Memorial
Church
Sever
Hall
Harvard
University ⊙2
Arrow St
26
Mt Auburn St
Law
School
Austin
Hall
Harvard
Hall
Massachusetts
Hall
Widener
Library
Linden St
10 ✕
25
24
17
Bow St

Massachusetts Ave

Dawes
Island

Peabody St

Harvard ✕
Holyoke
Center
Dunster St
12
Plympton St
Dewolfe St

CAMBRIDGE
Cambridge
Common
Old
Burying
Ground
9 ✕
16
22
Church St
20
28
23
Holyoke
Pl
Mill St

Farwell Pl
21
15 ✪
27
Winthrop St
South St
John F Kennedy St

Watercourse St
Garden St
Appian Way
Mifflin Pl
Story St
13
Bennett St
Eliot St
Kennedy
School of
Government

Follen St
Phillips Pl
Mason St
Schlesinger
Library
Radcliffe
Yard
14 ✪
James St
7
19
University Rd

John F
Kennedy
Park

Berkeley St
Hastings Ave
Brattle St
Radcliffe
College
Ash St Pl
Acacia St
Ash St
Mt Auburn St
Hilliard St
Brewer St
Ross St

Memorial Dr
Charles River Bike Path

Berkeley Pl
5 ⊙
Longfellow
Park
Willard St

Mt Auburn Cemetery (0.5mi)
3 ⊙
Tory Row

Charles River
Dr Paul Dudley White Bike Path
Soldiers Field Rd
Scullers Jazz
Club (1mi)

Cambridge

has been upheld over 350 years (and counting). Harvard Sq is overflowing with cafes, bookstores, restaurants and street musicians, while gritty Central Sq is the stomping ground of MIT students.

Cambridge is fondly called the 'People's Republic' for its progressive politics. In this vein, Cambridge City Hall was the first to issue marriage licenses to gay and lesbian couples, when same-sex marriages became legal in Massachusetts in 2004.

★ **Harvard University**   UNIVERSITY
(Map p54; www.harvard.edu; Massachusetts Ave; tours free; ☉ tours 10am, noon & 2pm Mon-Fri, 2pm Sat; ⊤ Harvard) Founded in 1636 to educate men for the ministry, Harvard is America's oldest college. The original Ivy League school has eight graduates who went on to be US presidents, not to mention dozens of Nobel laureates and Pulitzer Prize winners. Learn more fun facts about Harvard on the free campus tour that departs from Holyoke Center.

The geographic heart of Harvard University – where red-brick buildings and leaf-covered paths exude academia – is **Harvard Yard** (through Anderson Gates from Mass Ave). The focal point of the yard is the John Harvard statue, where every Harvard hopeful has a photo taken (and touches the statue's shiny shoe for good luck).

Outside the Yard, the university hosts several excellent museums. The two-in-one science museums include the myriad stuffed animals and famous glass flowers at the **Harvard Museum of Natural History** (Map p54; www.hmnh.harvard.edu; 26 Oxford St; adult/child/senior & student $12/8/10; ☉ 9am-5pm; ⊕; ⬚ 86, ⊤ Harvard), as well as impressive exhibits on indigenous cultures at the **Peabody Museum of Archaeology & Ethnology** (Map p54; www.peabody.harvard.edu; 11 Divinity Ave; adult/child/senior & student $12/8/10; ☉ 9am-5pm; ⊕; ⬚ 86, ⊤ Harvard). The **Harvard Art Museum** (Map p54; www.harvardartmuseum.org; 32 Quincy St; ⊤ Harvard) is expected to reopen in 2014 with an all-new state-of-the-art facility to show off its extensive holdings.

★ **Tory Row**   STREET
(Map p54; Brattle St; ⊤ Harvard) Heading west out of Harvard Square, Brattle St is the epitome of colonial posh. Lined with mansions that were once home to royal sympathizers, the street earned the nickname Tory Row. About 100 years later, Brattle St's most famous resident was the poet Henry Wadsworth Longfellow, whose stately manor is now the **Longfellow National Historic Site** (Map p54; www.nps.gov/long; 105 Brattle St; ☉ tours 9:30am-4pm Wed-Sun Jun-Oct, grounds dawn-dusk year-round; ⬚ 71 or 73, ⊤ Harvard) **FREE**.

Mt Auburn Cemetery CEMETERY
(www.mountauburn.org; 580 Mt Auburn St; admission free, guided tour $5; ⊘8am-5pm Oct-Apr, to 7pm May-Sep; P; ☑71 or 73, THarvard) On a sunny day, this delightful spot at the end of Brattle St is worth the 30-minute walk west from Harvard Sq. Developed in 1831, it was the first 'garden cemetery' in the US. Maps pinpoint the rare botanical specimens and notable burial plots.

Famous long-term residents include Mary Baker Eddy (founder of the Christian Science Church), Isabella Stewart Gardner (socialite and art collector), Winslow Homer (19th-century American painter), Oliver Wendell Holmes (US Supreme Court Justice) and Henry W Longfellow (19th-century writer).

🏃 Activities

Cycling

More than 50 miles of bicycle trails originate in the Boston area, including the Charles River Bike Path (see Charles River Esplanade, p48) and the **Minuteman Bikeway** (www.minutemanbikeway.org; TAlewife or Davis) from Cambridge to Bedford. You can take your bike on any of the MBTA subway lines except the Green and Silver Lines, but you must avoid rush hours (7am to 10am and 4pm to 7pm weekdays) and always ride on the last train car. For bike rental:

➜ **Urban AdvenTours** (p57)

➜ **Cambridge Bicycle** (www.cambridge bicycle.com; 259 Massachusetts Ave; per day/week $30/$150; ⊘10am-7pm Mon-Sat, noon-6pm Sun; TCentral)

Kayaking & Canoeing

Besides canoe and kayak rental, **Charles River Canoe & Kayak** (www.ski-paddle.com; 500 Broad Canal St; per hr canoe $17, kayak $15-19, kids' kayak $8; ⊘noon-8pm Mon-Fri, 9am-8pm Sat-Sun, longer hours in summer; ⓘ; TKendall/MIT) offers classes and organized outings. Experienced kayakers can venture out to the harbor, but the river and basin are lovely for skyline views and fall foliage. There is another outlet in Allston (near Harvard Sq), which allows for an excellent one-way five-mile trip between the two rental centers.

Skating

The cycling routes listed are also suitable for in-line skating. Check out the **Inline Club of Boston** (ICB; www.sk8net.com) for more information. In winter, there are several outdoor skating rinks:

➜ **Boston Common Frog Pond** (Map p40; www.bostonfrogpond.com; Boston Common; adult/child admission $5/free, rental $9/5; ⊘10am-4pm Mon, to 9pm Tue-Thu & Sun, to 10pm Fri & Sat mid-Nov–mid-Mar; ⓘ; TPark St)

➜ **Rink at the Charles** (Map p54; www .charleshotel.com; 1 Bennett St; adult/child $5/3, skate rental $5/3; ⊘4-8pm Mon-Fri, 10am-6pm Sat & Sun Dec-Mar; ⓘ; THarvard)

☞ Tours

Boat Tours

Boston Duck Tours BOAT TOUR
(Map p50; ☎617-267-3825; www.bostonducktours. com; adult/child/senior $34/23/28; ⓘ; TAquarium, Science Park or Prudential) These ridiculously popular tours use WWII amphibious

---

DON'T MISS

MASSACHUSETTS INSTITUTE OF TECHNOLOGY

The MIT campus near Central Sq offers a completely novel perspective on Cambridge academia: proudly nerdy, but not quite so tweedy as Harvard. The **MIT Information Center** (www.mit.edu; 77 Massachusetts Ave; ⊘tours 11am & 3pm Mon-Fri; TCentral) offers excellent guided campus tours, where you can learn all about MIT's amazing contributions to the sciences.

Alternatively, get an up-close look at robots, holograms, strobe photography, kinetic sculptures and other scientific wonders at the **MIT Museum** (http://museum.mit.edu; 265 Massachusetts Ave; adult/child $8.50/4; ⊘10am-5pm; P; TCentral)

A stroll around campus is proof that MIT supports artistic as well as technological innovation. The **List Visual Arts Center** (http://listart.mit.edu; 20 Ames St, Weisner Bldg; donation $5; ⊘noon-6pm Tue-Sun, to 8pm Thu; P; TKendall/MIT) mounts sophisticated shows of contemporary art across all media. You can also pick up (or download) a map of the public art that bejewels the East Campus (east of Massachusetts Ave). Don't miss the funky **Ray & Maria Strata Center** (CSAIL; http://csail.mit.edu; 32 Vassar St; TKendall/MIT), an avant-garde building designed by architectural legend Frank Gehry.

LOCAL KNOWLEDGE

THE STATUE OF THREE LIES

In Harvard Yard, the sculpture by Daniel Chester French is inscribed with 'John Harvard, Founder of Harvard College, 1638.' Hardly living up to the university's motto, *Veritas* (truth), this Harvard symbol is known as the statue of three lies:

➡ It does not actually depict Harvard (since no image of him exists), but a student chosen at random.

➡ John Harvard was not the founder of the college, but its first benefactor in 1638.

➡ The college was actually founded two years earlier, in 1636.

vehicles that cruise the downtown streets before splashing into the Charles River. Tours depart from the Aquarium, the Museum of Science or the Prudential Center. Reserve in advance.

Boston Harbor Cruises CRUISE
(Map p40; www.bostonharborcruises.com; 1 Long Wharf; 👤; 🚇 Aquarium) Boston Harbor Cruises offers a slew of options for those who want to get out on the water, from a Historic Sightseeing Tour around the Inner Harbor to an all-day Lighthouse Tour that goes out to Boston Light. Kids love the high-speed thrill-ride on Codzilla, where passengers are guaranteed to get wet.

Cycling Tours

⭐**Urban AdvenTours** BICYCLE TOUR
(Map p40; 📞 617-670-0637; www.urbanadventours. com; 103 Atlantic Ave; tours $50; 👤; 🚇 Aquarium) 🔰 Founded by avid cyclists who believe the best views of Boston are from a bicycle. The City View Ride provides a great overview of how to get around by bike, but there are other specialty tours such as Bikes at Night and Bike & Brew Tour.

Trolley Tours

Trolley tours offer great flexibility because you can hop off at sites along the route and hop on the next trolley that comes along. The trolley tickets also include a harbor cruise and/or admission to a few museums.

Beantown Trolley TROLLEY TOUR
(📞 781-986-6100, 800-343-1328; www.brush hilltours.com; adult/child/senior $35/15/33; ⏰ 9:30am-4:30pm) Includes a short harbor cruise or admission to the Mapparium.

Upper Deck Trolley Tours TROLLEY TOUR
(Map p40; www.bostonsupertours.com; adult/ child/senior $33/22/30; 👤; 🚇 Aquarium) A two-day pass that includes a harbor cruise and admission to one of five museums.

Old Town Trolley Tours TROLLEY TOUR
(Map p40; www.historictours.com; Long Wharf; adult/child/senior $36/17/33; 👤; 🚇 Aquarium) A two-day pass that includes a harbor cruise or admission to the Boston Tea Party Ships.

Walking Tours

⭐**Freedom Trail** WALKING TOUR
Follow the red-brick path for 2.4 miles, past the city's most prominent historic sites. The NPS covers parts of the Freedom Trail on its free guided tours (www.nps.gov/bost; ⏰ 1-3pm Mon-Fri, 10am-3pm Sat & Sun Apr-Oct) **FREE**, departing from Faneuil Hall. The Freedom Trail Foundation (Map p40; www.thefreedom trail.org; 👤) is also a popular option, departing from the Boston Common. If you prefer to go it alone, follow the Freedom Trail walking tour (p37).

Black Heritage Trail WALKING TOUR
(Map p40; www.nps.gov/boaf; ⏰ tours 2pm Mon-Sat, more frequently in summer; 🚇 Park St) **FREE** This free 1.6-mile walking tour explores the history of the abolitionist movement and African American settlement on Beacon Hill. The NPS conducts guided tours, but maps and descriptions for self-guided tours are available at the Museum of Afro-American History. Departs from the Robert Gould Shaw memorial.

Boston by Foot WALKING TOUR
(www.bostonbyfoot.com; adult/child $12/8; 👤) This fantastic nonprofit offers 90-minute walking tours, with specialty theme tours like Literary Landmarks, the Dark Side of Boston and Boston for Little Feet – a kid-friendly version of the Freedom Trail.

Harvard Tour WALKING TOUR
(Trademark Tours; www.harvardtour.com; $10; 🚇 Harvard) This company was founded by a couple of Harvard students who share the inside scoop on history and student life at The University. Tours depart from the Cam-

bridge Visitor Information Kiosk in Harvard Sq; see the website for schedule details.

Photo Walks WALKING TOUR
(✆800-979-3370; www.photowalks.com; adult/youth $30/15; ⊕) A walking tour combined with a photography lesson. Different routes cover Boston's most photogenic neighborhoods.

✹ Festivals & Events

★ **Boston Marathon** SPORTING EVENT
(www.baa.org; ⊙ 3rd Mon Apr) One of the country's most prestigious marathons takes runners on a 26.2-mile course ending at Copley Sq on Patriots' Day, a Massachusetts holiday on the third Monday in April.

Independent Film Festival of Boston FILM
(www.iffboston.org) During the last week in April, venues around the city host screenings of independent films, including shorts, documentaries and drama produced locally and nationally.

Harborfest PATRIOTIC FESTIVAL
(www.bostonharborfest.com) The week-long Independence Day (July 4) festival starts on the last weekend in June. One of the days is Children's Day, with face painting, balloons and children's entertainment at venues around the city. The tastiest part of the festival is Chowderfest, where you sample dozens of fish and clam chowders prepared by Boston's top chefs.

Independence Day PATRIOTIC FESTIVAL
(www.july4th.org; ⊙ Jul 4) Boston hosts a line-up of free performances that culminates with the Boston Pops playing Tchaikovsky's 1812 Overture, complete with brass cannon and synchronized fireworks. Half a million people descend on Boston to watch it live. The event traditionally takes place on the Esplanade.

Head of the Charles Regatta SPORTING EVENT
(www.hocr.org) Spectators line the banks of the Charles River on a weekend in mid-October to watch the world's largest rowing event.

Boston Tea Party Reenactment HISTORIC REENACTMENT
(www.oldsouthmeetinghouse.org) On the Sunday prior to December 16, costumed actors march from Old South Meeting House to the waterfront and toss crates of tea into the harbor. Nowadays, the event takes place on the newly rebuilt Griffin's Wharf, where the Tea Party Ships are docked.

First Night NEW YEAR'S
(www.firstnight.org; ⊙ Dec 31) New Year celebrations begin early and continue past midnight, culminating in fireworks over the harbor. Purchase a special button that permits entrance into events citywide.

Boston Pride Festival GLBT
(www.bostonpride.org) During the first full week in June, Boston does its part for this now-national celebration, kicking off with the raising of a rainbow flag on City Hall Plaza and culminating in the colorful Pride Parade on the following weekend.

🛏 Sleeping

From poor student backpackers to high-class business travelers, Boston's tourist industry caters to all types of visitors. That means the city offers a complete range of accommodations, from backpacker-style dorms and hostels, to inviting guesthouses in historic quarters, to swanky hotels with all the amenities you would expect.

A few agencies maintain databases of B&Bs in the area:

B&B Agency of Boston ACCOMMODATION SERVICES
(Map p40; ✆617-720-3540, 800-248-9262, free from the UK 0800-89-5128; www.boston-bnbagency.com; r $120-200, 2-bed $200-350, 3-bed $300-400) Lists more than 100 different properties, including B&Bs and furnished apartments. Properties are in Beacon Hill, Back Bay, North End and South End.

Bed & Breakfast Associates Bay Colony ACCOMMODATION SERVICES
(✆781-449-5302, 888-486-6018, from UK 08-234-7113; www.bnbboston.com) A huge database of furnished rooms and apartments in Boston, Brookline, Cambridge and the suburbs. Most are unhosted.

🛏 Beacon Hill

John Jeffries House HOTEL **$$**
(Map p40; ✆617-367-1866; www.johnjeffrieshouse.com; 14 David Mugar Way; r $125-160, ste $175-195; P❄🕱⊕; T Charles/MGH) Reproduction furnishings, original molding, hardwood floors and mahogany accents warmly recall the era when Dr John Jeffries founded what is now the world-renowned Massachusetts Eye & Ear Infirmary. Many patients reside here

when they come to town for treatment, as do travelers.

While the parlor is a lovely spot to enjoy your complimentary breakfast, you can also whip up your own meal in your in-room kitchenette (available in most rooms).

Beacon Hill Hotel & Bistro BOUTIQUE HOTEL **$$$**
(Map p40; ☎ 617-723-7575; www.beaconhillhotel. com; 25 Charles St; r $245-345, ste $365-425; P ✳ ☎; T Charles/MGH) Upscale European-style inn that blends into its namesake neighborhood without flash or fanfare. Carved out of former residential buildings typical of Beacon Hill, the hotel has 12 small but stylish rooms, individually decorated with black-and-white photographs, plantation shutters and a designer's soothing palette of paint choices. Added perks include the exclusive roof deck and complimentary breakfast at the urbane, on-site bistro.

Downtown & Waterfront

★**Harborside Inn** BOUTIQUE HOTEL **$$**
(Map p40; ☎ 617-723-7500; www.harborsideinn boston.com; 185 State St; r from $169; P ✳ @ ☎; T Aquarium) Ensconced in a respectfully renovated 19th-century warehouse, this waterfront hostelry strikes just the right balance between historic digs and modern conveniences. Nautical-themed guest rooms feature classy, custom-designed teak furniture and plenty of multimedia entertainment options. Add $20 for a city view.

Nine Zero BOUTIQUE HOTEL **$$$**
(Map p40; ☎617-772-5810; www.ninezero.com; 90 Tremont St; r from $299; P ✳ ☎ ✻; T Park St) ✿ This chic boutique hotel appeals to a broad audience, offering amenities from ergonomic workspace to in-room yoga mats. Marvelous views of the State House and the Granary Burying Ground from the upper floors.

Intercontinental Hotel HOTEL **$$$**
(Map p40; ☎ 617-747-1000; www.intercontinental boston.com; 510 Atlantic Ave; r from $280; P ✳ ☎ ✻; T South Station) ✿ The fancy marble bathrooms alone are worth the price of staying in this first-class hotel. The bathtub is enormous, perfect for soaking, with sliding windows yielding a view of the flat-screen TV in the bedroom, not to mention the separate shower, fragrant soaps and plush luxurious towels.

The rooms are sumptuous and sophisticated, while the location – perched on the edge of the Seaport District – is ideal.

Ames Hotel BOUTIQUE HOTEL **$$$**
(Map p40; ☎ 617-979-8100; www.ameshotel.com; 1 Court St; r from $299; P ✳ ☎; T State) It's easy to miss this understated hotel, tucked behind the granite facade of the historic Ames Building (Boston's first skyscraper). Starting in the lobby and extending to the guest rooms, the style is elegant but eclectic, artfully blending modern minimalism and old-fashioned ornamental details. The upper floors yield wonderful views over the city.

West End

Friend Street Hostel HOSTEL **$**
(Map p40; ☎ 617-934-2413; www.friendstreethostel. com; 234 Friend St; dm $48-54; @ ☎; T North Station) We believe them when they say it's the friendliest hostel in Boston. But there are other reasons to love this affable hostelry, such as the spic-and-span kitchen and the comfy common area with the huge flat-screen TV. Sleeping six to 10 people each, dorm rooms have painted brick walls, wide-plank wood floors and bunkbeds and lockers for everyone.

Also: breakfast, bikes and lots of free activities. What's not to love? Street noise.

★**Liberty Hotel** HOTEL **$$$**
(Map p40; ☎ 617-224-4000; www.libertyhotel.com; 225 Charles St; r from $375; P ✳ ☎; T Charles/MGH) It is with intended irony that the notorious Charles Street Jail has been converted into the luxurious Liberty Hotel. Today, the spectacular lobby soars under a 90ft ceiling. Guest rooms boast floor-to-ceiling windows with amazing views of the Charles River and Beacon Hill, not to mention luxurious linens and high-tech amenities such as LCD TVs and iPod docking stations.

Onyx Hotel BOUTIQUE HOTEL **$$$**
(Map p40; ☎ 617-557-9955; www.onyxhotel.com; 155 Portland St; d $229-289; P ✳ ☎ ✻; T North Station) ✿ Done up in jewel tones and contemporary furniture, the Onyx exudes warmth and style – two elements that do not always go hand in hand. Attractive features of the hotel (a member of the Kimpton Hotel Group) include morning car service, passes to a local gym and an evening wine reception. 'Pet-friendly' goes to a whole new level with gourmet doggy biscuits and a dog-sitting service.

Boxer Hotel BOUTIQUE HOTEL **$$$**
(Map p40; ☎ 617-624-0202; www.theboxerboston. com; 107 Merrimac St; r from $269; P ✳ @ ☎ ✻;

T North Station) Exemplifying the up-and-coming character of this once-downtrodden district, this new boutique hotel occupies a fully restored flatiron building. The lobby hearkens back to the 19th century, its ceiling plastered with a map of Boston from that era. The guest-room decor is industrial chic, with tufted bed frames and metallic fixtures and furnishings, all in a soothing palette of slate blues and greys.

Charlestown

Constitution Inn   HOTEL **$$**
(📋 617-241-8400; www.constitutioninn.org; 150 Third Ave; d $199-209; P ❄ 🛜 🏊 🎿; 🚇 93 from Haymarket, 🚢 F4 from Long Wharf) Housed in a granite building in the historic Charlestown Navy Yard, this excellent, affordable hotel accommodates active and retired military personnel. But you don't have to have a crew cut to stay here. The rooms are clean, crisp and comfortable, with plain cherry furniture and kitchenettes. Guests gain free access to the Olympic-class fitness center.

Seaport District

Seaport Boston Hotel   HOTEL **$$$**
(📋 617-385-4000; www.seaportboston.com; 1 Seaport Lane; r $239-319; P ❄ 🛜 🏊 🎿 🐾; 🚇 SL1 or SL2, T South Station) 🏊 With glorious views of the Boston Harbor, this business hotel is up-to-snuff when it comes to high-tech amenities (eg automatic motion-sensitive lights so you never have to enter a dark room, and privacy/service lights instead of the old-fashioned 'Do not disturb' signs). Soothing tones, plush linens and robes, and a unique no-tipping policy guarantee a relaxing retreat.

Now the Seaport is reaching out to families, offering Nintendo, baby gear and treats for your pet.

Residence Inn Marriott   BOUTIQUE HOTEL **$$$**
(Map p40; 📋 617-478-0840; www.residenceinn.com/bosfp; 370 Congress St; r $349-399; P ❄ 🛜; 🚇 SL1 or SL2, T South Station) This is not your typical Marriott. Housed in a historic, brick warehouse, this boutique hotel now features an old-style atrium and glass elevators leading up to spectacular, spacious suites. Twelve-foot ceilings and enormous windows are in every room, as is a floor-to-ceiling cityscape mural. King-size beds, fully-equipped kitchens and up-to-date gadgetry ensure guests' optimal comfort and convenience.

Chinatown & Theater District

HI Boston   HOSTEL **$**
(Map p40; 📋 617-536-9455; www.bostonhostel.org; 19 Stuart St; dm $50-60, d $179; ❄ @ 🛜 🎿; T Chinatown or Boylston) 🏊 HI Boston has a brand-new facility! The historic Dill Building has been revamped to allow for expanded capacity and community space, handicap access and state-of-the-art green amenities. A tad impersonal for a hostel, but facilities are up to standard and the institution still offers an excellent line-up of fun activities for guests.

Milner Hotel   HOTEL **$$**
(Map p40; 📋 617-453-1731, 617-426-6220; www.milner-hotels.com; 78 Charles St S; s/d from $159/189; P 🛜 🎿; T Boylston) Mr Milner said it himself back in 1918: 'A bed and a bath for a buck and a half.' Prices have gone up since then, but the Milner Hotel still offers excellent value for this central location. Itinerant actors and international travelers frequent this affordable Theater District hotel, which offers cramped but comfortable rooms and free continental breakfast.

South End

40 Berkeley   HOSTEL **$$**
(Map p50; 📋 617-375-2524; www.40berkeley.com; 40 Berkeley St; s/d/tr/q from $108/130/144/169; 🛜 🎿; T Back Bay) Straddling the South End and Back Bay, this safe, friendly hostelry rents over 200 small rooms (some overlooking the garden) to guests on a nightly and long-term basis. Bathrooms are shared, as are other useful facilities such as the telephone, library, TV room and laundry. All rates include a generous and delicious breakfast. Weekly rates also available.

Chandler Inn   HOTEL **$$**
(Map p50; 📋 617-482-3450, 800-842-3450; www.chandlerinn.com; 26 Chandler St; r from $170; ❄ 🛜 🎿; T Back Bay) The Chandler Inn is looking fine, after a complete overhaul. Small but sleek rooms have benefited from a designer's touch, giving them a sophisticated, urban glow. Modern travelers will appreciate the plasma TVs and iPod docks, all of which come at surprisingly affordable prices. As a bonus, congenial staff provide super service. On site is the South End drinking institution, Fritz.

Hotel 140   HOTEL **$$**
(Map p50; 📋 617-585-5440; www.hotel140.com; 140 Clarendon St; r from $179; P ❄ @ 🛜; T Co-

pley or Back Bay) Once the headquarters of the YWCA, this classic brick building is now one of Boston's hidden hotel bargains. The smallish rooms are stylish and contemporary, with large windows and lots of sunlight. Steps from Back Bay shopping and South End dining, this is a popular spot among theater people, thanks to weekly and monthly rates.

🛏 Back Bay

463 Beacon Street
Guest House   GUESTHOUSE $$
(Map p50; ☑617-536-1302; www.463beacon.com; 463 Beacon St; d without/with bath from $99/149; P ✳ 🛜; T Hynes) What's more 'Boston' than a handsome, historic brownstone in Back Bay? This guesthouse lets you live the blueblood fantasy – and save your cash for the boutiques and bars on Newbury St. This c 1880 building retains plenty of highfalutin' architectural frolics, like a spiral staircase, wrought-iron filigrees and impossibly high ceilings. Alas, there is no elevator.

Rooms vary in size and decor, but they all have the basics (except daily maid service, which is not offered). Bathrooms are cramped, but hopefully you won't be spending too much time in there.

Charlesmark Hotel   BOUTIQUE HOTEL $$
(Map p50; ☑617-247-1212; www.thecharlesmark. com; 655 Boylston St; r $159-219; P ✳ 🛜; T Copley) The Charlesmark's small but sleek rooms are at the crossroads of European style and functionality. The design is classic modernism; and the effect is upscale, urbane and surprisingly affordable. This hip hotel is backed by a small group of warmly efficient staff that see to every detail. The downstairs lounge spills out onto the sidewalk where the people-watching is tops. Complimentary continental breakfast.

Copley Inn   GUESTHOUSE $$
(Map p50; ☑617-236-0300, 617-232-0306; www. copleyinn.com; 19 Garrison St; r $211; T Prudential) This sweet old brownstone is tucked into the residential streets behind Copley Place: it's about as close as you can get to Newbury St while preserving the sense that you're nesting in a slightly quieter neighborhood. Equipped with kitchens, rooms in this four-story walkup are relatively roomy, if a bit plain.

Copley House   APARTMENTS $$
(Map p50; ☑800-331-1318, 617-236-8300; www.cop leyhouse.com; 239 W Newton St; studio $145-212;

✳; T Prudential) Copley House occupies four different buildings, straddling Back Bay and the South End. The simple, plain studios each have a kitchenette and dining area. A judicious use of antique wood and big windows beaming with light make this Queen Anne–style inn a place of respite, while the location makes it a handy base of operations for exploring Boston. Weekly rates are available.

⭐ Newbury Guest House   GUESTHOUSE $$$
(Map p50; ☑617-437-7666, 617-437-7668; www. newburyguesthouse.com; 261 Newbury St; r $219-249; P ✳ 🛜; T Hynes or Copley) Dating to 1882, these three interconnected brick and brownstone buildings offer a prime location in the heart of Newbury St. A recent renovation has preserved the charming features, such as ceiling medallions and in-room fireplaces, but now the rooms also feature clean lines, luxurious linens and modern amenities. Each morning, a complimentary continental breakfast is laid out next to the marble fireplace in the salon.

Inn @ St Botolph   BOUTIQUE HOTEL $$$
(Map p50; ☑617-236-8099; www.innatstbotolph. com; 99 St Botolph St; ste $259-329; P ✳ 🛜; T Prudential) Whimsical but wonderful, this delightful brownstone boutique emphasizes affordable luxury. Spacious, light-filled rooms feature bold patterns and contemporary decor, fully equipped kitchens, and all the high-tech bells and whistles. Foreshadowing a coming trend, the hotel keeps prices down by offering 'edited service,' with virtual check-in, keyless entry and 'touch-up' housekeeping, minimizing the need for costly staff. Complimentary continental breakfast.

College Club   GUESTHOUSE $$$
(Map p40; ☑617-536-9510; www.thecollegeclubof boston.com; 44 Commonwealth Ave; s without bathroom from $129, d with bathroom $249-289; ✳ 🛜; T Arlington) Originally a private club for female college graduates, the College Club has 11 spacious rooms with high ceilings, now open to both sexes. Period details – typical of the area's Victorian brownstones – include claw-tooth tubs, ornamental fireplaces and bay windows. Local designers have lent their skills to decorate the various rooms, with delightful results. Prices include a continental breakfast.

Colonnade   HOTEL $$$
(Map p50; ☑617-424-7000; www.colonnadehotel. com; 120 Huntington Ave; r from $259; P ✳ 🛜 ✳ ✳ ✳; T Prudential) 🌿 There are many

reasons to stay at the Colonnade, such as its handsome guest rooms, which are well equipped with both high-tech gadgetry and simple pleasures (like a rubber duck in your bathtub). There's the VIPets program, complete with fluffy beds and walking services. And of course there's the excellent dining and the fabulous location.

But the real reason to stay at the Colonnade is the rooftop pool, or RTP, as it's known. A glamorous place to see and be seen in your bikini, it's also optimal for al fresco dining, sunbathing and yes, even swimming. Open to nonguests weekdays only.

Lenox Hotel   HISTORIC HOTEL **$$$**
(Map p50; ☑ 617-536-5300, 617-225-7676; www.lenoxhotel.com; 61 Exeter St; r $265-305; P ✳ ☎; T Copley) ✔ For three generations, the Saunders family has run this gem in Back Bay. And while the atmosphere is a tad old-world, you don't have to forgo modern conveniences to live with that ethos. Guest rooms are comfortably elegant (with chandeliers and crown molding), without being stuffy. If your pockets are deep enough, it's worth splurging for a junior suite, as they boast the best views.

Kenmore Square & the Fenway

★Oasis Guest House   GUESTHOUSE **$$**
(Map p50; ☑ 617-230-0105, 617-267-2262; www.oasisgh.com; 22 Edgerly Rd; r $136-228, without bath $114-148; P ✳ ☎; T Hynes or Symphony) True to its name, this homey guesthouse is a peaceful, pleasant oasis in the midst of Boston's chaotic city streets. Thirty-odd guest rooms occupy four attractive, brick, bow-front town houses on this tree-lined lane. The modest, light-filled rooms are tastefully and traditionally decorated, most with queen beds, floral quilts and nondescript prints.

The common living room does not exactly encourage lingering, but outdoor decks and kitchen facilities are nice touches. Complimentary continental breakfast.

Hotel Buckminster   HOTEL **$$**
(Map p50; ☑ 617-727-2825; www.bostonhotelbuckminster.com; 645 Beacon St; r $149-209, ste from $219; P ✳ ☎ ✱; T Kenmore) Designed by the architect of the Boston Public Library, the Buckminster is a convergence of Old Boston charm and affordable elegance. It offers nearly 100 rooms of varying shapes and sizes: European-style rooms are small and

stuffy, with elegantly worn furniture (but still a great bargain); by contrast, the suites are quite roomy, with all the tools and toys of comfort and convenience.

Each floor has its own laundry and kitchen facilities.

★Gryphon House   B&B **$$$**
(Map p50; ☑ 617-375-9003; www.innboston.com; 9 Bay State Rd; r $225-275; P ✳ ☎; T Kenmore) A premier example of Richardson Romanesque, this beautiful five-story brownstone is a paradigm of artistry and luxury overlooking the picturesque Charles River. Eight spacious suites have different styles, including Victorian, Gothic, and Arts and Crafts, but they all have 19th-century period details. And they all have home-away-from-home perks such as entertainment centers, wet bars and gas fireplaces.

Inquire about discounts for Red Sox fans (seriously!). Prices include a continental breakfast.

Cambridge

★Kendall Hotel   BOUTIQUE HOTEL **$$**
(☑ 617-566-1300; www.kendallhotel.com; 350 Main St; r from $189; P ✳ ☎; T Kendall/MIT) Once the Engine 7 Firehouse, this city landmark is now a cool and classy all-American hotel. The 65 guest rooms retain a firefighter riff, without a whiff of 'cutesy.' There's no scrimping at the breakfast table, either, with a full buffet included.

The on-site Black Sheep restaurant, filled with memorabilia from the old days of fightin' fires, features organic, locally grown produce pleasing to omnivores and vegetarians alike.

★Harding House   INN **$$**
(☑ 617-489-2888, 617-876-2888; www.hardinghouse.com; 288 Harvard St; r $175-265; P ✳ @ ☎; T Central) This treasure brilliantly blends refinement and comfort, artistry and efficiency. Old wooden floors toss back a warm glow and sport throw rugs. Antique furnishings complete the inviting atmosphere. Other perks: all-day munchies, a thoughtfully designed continental breakfast and complimentary museum passes.

Irving House   GUESTHOUSE **$$**
(Map p54; ☑ 617-547-4600; www.irvinghouse.com; 24 Irving St; r $165-270; s with shared bath $135-160, d with shared bath $165-205; P ✳ @ ☎ ✱; T Harvard) ✔ Call it a big inn or a homey ho-

LATE-NIGHT GRUB

Boston might be called 'the city that goes to bed early' for all its late-night eating options. If you have a case of the midnight munchies, you have to know where to look for your cure:

➡ Franklin Café (p68), the South End's most beloved place for meeting and eating, is even more beloved after midnight.

➡ New Jumbo Seafood (p67) is one of many Chinatown joints that stay open late for the post-clubbing crowd.

➡ South Street Diner (p67) serves breakfast around the clock. Amen.

➡ Tasty Burger (p69) serves burgers and beers into the wee smalls.

➡ Clover Food Lab (p70) is the place to get your chickpea fritter before the clock strikes 12.

tel, this property welcomes the most world-weary travelers. The 44 rooms range in size, but every bed is covered with a quilt and big windows let in plenty of light. There is a bistro-style atmosphere in the brick-lined basement, where you can browse the books on hand, plan your travels or munch on free continental breakfast.

Perks include museum passes and laundry facilities.

✖ Eating

In the last decade Boston has developed a multifaceted local cuisine, drawing on its unique regional traditions and its rich international influences. Boston presents some fine opportunities to feast on Italian and Chinese fare, but other more exotic ethnic cuisines are also well represented, especially Korean, Thai, Portuguese and Indian. Seafood still reigns supreme, and you are advised to take advantage of every opportunity to eat it.

Eating cheaply does not mean eating badly. But, if you want to splurge, you will find some of the country's most highly regarded chefs in Boston. Expect to pay less than $15 per person for a meal at a budget eatery, and from $15 to $30 per person at midrange establishments (not including drinks). Top-end restaurants will set you back at least $30 per person.

✖ Beacon Hill

★ Paramount   CAFETERIA $$
(Map p40; www.paramountboston.com; 44 Charles St; breakfast & lunch $8-12, dinner $15-30; ⊘ 7am-10pm Mon-Thu, from 8am Sat-Sun, to 11pm Fri-Sat; ☑ ⑪; ⓣ Charles/MGH) This old-fashioned cafeteria is a neighborhood favorite. Basic din-

er fare includes pancakes, steak and eggs, burgers and sandwiches, and big, hearty salads. The dinner menu is enhanced by homemade pastas, a selection of meat and fish dishes and an impressive roster of daily specials. Add table service and candlelight, and the place goes upscale without losing its down-home charm.

75 Chestnut   AMERICAN $$
(Map p40; www.75chestnut.com; 75 Chestnut St; mains $15-25; ⊘ brunch Sat & Sun, dinner daily; ⑪; ⓣ Charles/MGH) You might not think to take a peek around the corner, away from the well-trod sidewalks of Charles St. But locals know that Chestnut St is the place to go for tried-and-true steaks and seafood and a genuine warm welcome. It's a perfect place to stop for a drink, but you'll probably end up staying for dinner because the place is that comfy-cozy.

And once you catch a glimpse of the signature desserts, you'll certainly want to stay for hazelnut ganache or molten chocolate cake.

Scollay Square   AMERICAN $$
(Map p40; www.scollaysquare.com; 21 Beacon St; lunch mains $10-16, dinner mains $17-23; ⊘ lunch Mon-Fri, brunch Sun, dinner daily; ⓣ Park St) Down the road from the former Scollay Sq, this retro restaurant hearkens back to the glory days of its namesake. Old photos and memorabilia adorn the walls, while suits sip martinis to big-band music. The classic American fare is reliably good, with the lobster mac and cheese the perennial favorite.

Grotto   ITALIAN $$
(Map p40; ☑ 617-227-3434; www.grottorestaurant. com; 37 Bowdoin St; mains $21, 3-course prix fixe $38; ⊘ 11:30am-3pm Mon-Fri, 11am-3pm Sun,

5-11pm daily; T Bowdoin) Tucked into a basement on the back side of Beacon Hill, this cozy, cavelike place lives up to its name. The funky decor – exposed brick walls decked with rotating art exhibits – reflects the innovative menu (which also changes frequently).

No 9 Park
EUROPEAN $$$

(Map p40; 617-742-9991; www.no9park.com; 9 Park St; mains $39, 3-course prix fixe $69; dinner; T Park St) Set in a 19th-century mansion opposite the State House, this swanky place tops many fine-dining lists. Chef-owner Barbara Lynch has been lauded by food and wine magazines for her delectable French and Italian culinary masterpieces and her first-rate wine list. She has now cast her celebrity-chef spell all around town, but this is the place that made her famous. Reservations recommended.

Downtown & Waterfront

Quincy Market
FOOD COURT $

(Map p40; Congress St; 10am-9pm Mon-Sat, noon-6pm Sun; T Haymarket) At the center of the tourist action, this food hall is packed with about 20 restaurants and 40 food stalls. Choose from chowder, bagels, Indian, Greek, baked goods and ice cream, and take a seat at one of the tables in the central rotunda.

Chacarero
SANDWICHES $

(Map p40; www.chacarero.com; 101 Arch St; meals $5-10; 8am-6pm Mon-Fri; T Downtown Crossing) A *chacarero* is a traditional Chilean sandwich made with grilled chicken or beef, Muenster cheese, fresh tomatoes, guacamole and the surprise ingredient: steamed green beans. Stuffed into homemade bread, these sandwiches are the hands-down favorite for lunch around Downtown Crossing.

Falafel King
MIDDLE EASTERN $

(Map p40; 48 Winter St; mains $5-7; 11am-8pm Mon-Fri, 11am-4pm Sat; T Downtown Crossing) Two words: free falafels. That's right, everyone gets a little free sample before they order. There's no disputing that this sketchy-looking carry-out spot is indeed the falafel king of Boston. The sandwiches are fast, delicious and cheap. Besides the namesake falafel, the King sells *shawarma* and shish kebab made from the meat of your choice, as well as many vegetarian delights.

Sam La Grassa's
DELI $

(Map p40; www.samlagrassas.com; 44 Province St; sandwiches $11; lunch Mon-Fri; T Downtown Crossing) Step up to the counter and place your order for one of Sam La Grassa's signature sandwiches, then find a spot at the crowded communal table. You won't be disappointed by the famous Romanian pastrami or the 'fresh from the pot' corned beef. All of the sandwiches are so well stuffed that they can be tricky to eat, but this is part of the fun.

Durgin Park
AMERICAN $$

(Map p40; www.durgin-park.com; North Market, Faneuil Hall; lunch mains $9-15, dinner $15-30; 11:30am-9pm; T Haymarket) Known for no-nonsense service and sawdust on the floorboards, Durgin Park hasn't changed much since the restaurant opened in 1827. Nor has the menu, which features New England standards such as prime rib, fish chowder, chicken pot pie and Boston baked beans, with strawberry shortcake and Indian pudding for dessert. Be prepared to make friends with the other parties seated at your table.

Marliave
AMERICAN, FRENCH $$

(Map p40; www.marliave.com; 10 Bosworth St; sandwiches $14-16, mains $18-32; 11am-10pm; T Park St) A French immigrant, Henry Marliave first opened this restaurant way back in 1885. After a recent rehab, the Marliave has reopened with all of its vintage architectural quirks still intact, from the mosaic floor to the tin ceilings. The black-and-white photos on the wall add to the old-Boston ambience, as do the cleverly named drinks (Molasses Flood, anyone?).

Note that the downstairs area feels more historically authentic, but the glass-enclosed upstairs has a unique view of the surrounding neighborhood.

Union Oyster House
SEAFOOD $$

(Map p40; www.unionoysterhouse.com; 41 Union St; mains $15-25; 11am-9:30pm; T Haymarket) The oldest restaurant in Boston, ye olde Union Oyster House has been serving seafood in this historic red-brick building since 1826. Countless history-makers have propped themselves up at this bar, including Daniel Webster and John F Kennedy. Apparently JFK used to order the lobster bisque, but the raw bar is the real draw here. Order a dozen on the half-shell and watch the shucker work his magic.

North End

Volle Nolle
SANDWICHES **$**

(Map p40; 351 Hanover St; sandwiches $8-12; ⊙11am-11pm; ✎🖥; Ⓣ Haymarket) Apparently, *volle nolle* is Latin for 'willy-nilly,' but there is nothing haphazard about this much-beloved North End sandwich shop. Black-slate tables and pressed-tin walls adorn the simple, small space. The chalkboard menu features fresh salads, delicious flatbread sandwiches, dark rich coffee and – bonus – beer and wine.

Galleria Umberto
PIZZERIA **$**

(Map p40; 289 Hanover St; mains $2-6; ⊙lunch Mon-Sat; ✎🖥; Ⓣ Haymarket) Paper plates, cans of soda, Sicilian pizza: can't beat it. This lunchtime legend closes as soon as the slices are gone. And considering their thick and chewy goodness, that's often before the official 2:30pm closing time. Loyal patrons line up early so they are sure to get theirs.

Pizzeria Regina
PIZZERIA **$**

(Map p40; www.pizzeriaregina.; 11½ Thatcher St; pizzas $14-20; ⊙lunch & dinner; ✎; Ⓣ Haymarket) The queen of North End pizzerias is the legendary Pizzeria Regina, famous for brusque but endearing waitresses and crispy, thin-crust pizza. Thanks to the slightly spicy sauce (flavored with aged romano) Regina repeatedly wins accolades for her pies. Reservations are not accepted, so be prepared to wait.

★ Giacomo's Ristorante
ITALIAN **$$**

(Map p40; www.giacomosblog-boston.blogspot.com; 355 Hanover St; mains $14-19; ⊙4:30-10pm Mon-Sat, 4-9:30pm Sun; ✎; Ⓣ Haymarket) Customers line up before the doors open so they can guarantee themselves a spot in the first round of seating at this North End favorite. Enthusiastic and entertaining waiters, plus cramped quarters, ensure that you get to know your neighbors. The cuisine is no-frills southern Italian fare, served in unbelievable portions.

The specialty of the house is *zuppa di pesce* ($55 for two), chock-full of shrimp, scallops, calamari, mussels and lobster. Cash only.

Daily Catch
SEAFOOD **$$**

(Map p40; www.dailycatch.com; 323 Hanover St; mains $18-26; ⊙lunch & dinner; Ⓣ Haymarket) Although owner Paul Freddura long ago added a few tables and an open kitchen, this shoe-box fish joint still retains the atmosphere of a retail fish market (complete with wine served in plastic cups). Fortunately, it also retains the freshness of the fish. The specialty is calamari, fried to tender perfection. Cash only.

★ Pomodoro
ITALIAN **$$**

(Map p40; ☎617-367-4348; 319 Hanover St; brunch mains $12, dinner mains $23-24; ⊙dinner daily, brunch Sat-Sun; Ⓣ Haymarket) This hole-in-the-wall place on Hanover is one of the North End's most romantic settings for delectable Italian. The food is simply but perfectly prepared: fresh pasta, spicy tomato sauce, grilled fish and meats, and wine by the glass. Credit cards are not accepted and the bathroom is smaller than your closet, but that's all part of the charm.

★ Neptune Oyster
SEAFOOD **$$$**

(Map p40; ☎617-742-3474; www.neptuneoyster.com; 63 Salem St; mains $25-35; ⊙11:30am-10pm, till 11pm Fri-Sat; Ⓣ Haymarket) Neptune's menu hints at Italian, but you'll also find elements

---

SWEET NORTH END

It wouldn't be a night in the North End if you didn't end it with a cannoli or some other sweet thang. Here's where to get yours:

Maria's Pastry (Map p40; www.mariaspastry.com; 46 Cross St; ⊙7am-7pm; ✎; Ⓣ Haymarket) Three generations of Merola women are now working to bring you Boston's most authentic Italian pastries, especially *sfogliatelle* (layered, shell-shaped pastry filled with ricotta).

Modern Pastry Shop (Map p40; www.modernpastry.com; 257 Hanover St; snacks $2-4; ⊙breakfast, lunch & dinner; Ⓣ Haymarket) While crowds of tourists and suburbanites are queuing out the door at Mike's Pastry across the street, pop into the Modern Pastry for divine cookies and cannolis.

Lulu's Sweet Shoppe (Map p40; www.lulussweetshoppeboston.com; 57 Salem St; ⊙11am-7pm; Ⓣ Haymarket) If you prefer cupcakes over cannolis. Red velvet? Boston cream cupcake? Don't take too long to decide or you will annoy the counter girl.

of Mexican, French and old-fashioned New England. The daily seafood specials and impressive raw bar (featuring several kinds of oysters, plus littlenecks, cherrystones, crabs and mussels) confirm that this is not your traditional North End eatery.

The retro interior offers a convivial – if crowded – setting, with an excellent option for solo diners at the marble bar.

Taranta FUSION $$
(Map p40; ☑ 617-720-0052; www.tarantarist.com; 210 Hanover St; mains $25-35; ☺ dinner; ⓣ Haymarket) ✐ Europe meets South America at this Italian restaurant with a Peruvian twist. So, for example, gnocchi is made from yucca and served with a spicy lamb ragout; salmon filet is encrusted with macadamia nuts, and filet mignon with crushed espresso beans. There's an incredible selection of Italian, Chilean and Argentinean wines, all of which are organic or biodynamic. Taranta is a Certified Green Restaurant.

✕ Charlestown

Figs ITALIAN $$
(www.toddenglish.com; 67 Main St; mains $15-20; ☺ lunch & dinner; ☑ ⓐ; ⓣ Community College) This creative pizzeria – which also has an outlet in Beacon Hill – is the brainchild of celebrity chef Todd English, who tops whisper-thin crusts with interesting, exotic toppings. Case in point: the namesake fig and prosciutto with gorgonzola cheese. The menu also includes sandwiches and fresh pasta.

Navy Yard Bistro & Wine Bar FRENCH $$
(www.navyyardbistro.com; cnr Second Ave & Sixth St; mains $15-25; ☺ dinner; ⓐ 93 from Haymarket, ⓕ F4 from Long Wharf) Dark and romantic, this hideaway is tucked into an unlikely spot behind the Tedeschi convenience store. It does not sound like an ideal location, but it faces a pedestrian walkway, allowing for comfortable outdoor seating in summer months. Inside, the cozy, carved-wood interior is an ideal date destination – perfect for tuna tartare or grilled hanger steak.

The menu always features seasonal vegetables and an excellent wine list, from which the owner will be pleased to help you make a selection.

✕ Seaport District

Flour BAKERY, CAFE $
(Map p40; www.flourbakery.com; 12 Farnsworth St; snacks $2-3, salads & sandwiches $7-9; ☺ 7am-8pm Mon-Fri, 8am-6pm Sat, 9am-5pm Sun; ☑ ⓐ; ⓐ SL1 or SL2, ⓣ South Station) ✐ Flour implores patrons to 'make life sweeter...eat dessert first!' It's hard to resist at this pastry-lover's paradise. If you can't decide – and it can be a challenge – go for the melt-in-your-mouth sticky buns. But dessert is not all: delicious sandwiches, soups, salads and pizzas are also available.

Yankee Lobster Co SEAFOOD $
(www.yankeelobstercompany.com; 300 Northern Ave; mains $10-18; ☺ 10am-9pm Mon-Sat, 11am-6pm Sun; ⓐ SL1 or SL2, ⓣ South Station) The Zanti family has been fishing for three generations, so they definitely know their stuff. A relatively recent addition is this retail fish market, scattered with a few tables in case you want to dine in. And you do. Order something simple like clam chowder or a lobster roll, accompany it with a cold beer, and you will not be disappointed.

Sportello ITALIAN $$
(Map p40; ☑ 617-737-1234; www.sportelloboston. com; 348 Congress St; mains $12-25; ☺ 11:30am-2:30pm Mon-Fri, 4:30-10pm daily, till 11pm Fri-Sat; ⓣ South Station) Modern and minimalist, this brainchild of Barbara Lynch fits right into this up-and-coming urban 'hood. At the *sportello*, or lunch counter, suited yuppies indulge in sophisticated soups and salads and decadent polenta and pasta dishes. It's a popular spot, which means it's usually a tight squeeze, but the attentive waitstaff ensure that everybody is comfortable and contented.

Sam's at Louis MODERN AMERICAN $$$
(☑ 617-295-0191; www.samsatlouis.com; 60 Northern Ave, Louis Boston; sandwiches $13-16, mains $25-30; ☺ 11:30am-10pm Mon-Thu, 11:30am-11pm Fri-Sat, 11am-9pm Sun; ⓟ ⓢ ☑; ⓐ SL1 or SL2, ⓣ South Station) Unarguably, the highlight of Sam's is the three walls of windows, yielding a 180-degree view of city and sea. Chrome and leather, post-industrial decor complements this spectacular view. It's a delightfully casual-chic place, with an interesting, innovative menu to match. Live music on Friday nights.

Menton FRENCH, ITALIAN $$$
(Map p40; ☑ 617-737-0099; www.mentonboston. com; 354 Congress St; 4-course prix-fixe $95; ☺ dinner; ⓐ; ⓣ South Station) Boston's favorite celebrity chef, Barbara Lynch has outdone herself at this high-class conglomeration of classic European cuisine and modern Amer-

ican innovations. She has set her latest venture in a revamped warehouse in the edgy, eclectic Seaport District. The setting and the cooking are sophisticated, stylish and wholly satisfying – sure ingredients for a memorable night out.

✕ Chinatown & Theater District

Wrapmi
ASIAN $

(Map p40; 66 Kneeland St; mains $3-5; ⊙11am-9pm Mon-Sat; ✍; ☂Chinatown) The specialty of Wrapmi is best described as an Asian burrito. The 'wrap' is a thin crepe and a sheet of nori; and the filling is a scrumptious combination of Asian flavors, such as shrimp, avocado and cucumber or duck and red peppers. It's cheap, fast and delicious – a great option for lunch on the go (especially since this place has hardly any seating).

South Street Diner
DINER $

(Map p40; www.southstreetdiner.com; 178 Kneeland St; mains $6-12; ⊙24hr; ☂South Station) A divey diner that does what a diner is supposed to do – that is, serve bacon and eggs and burgers and fries, at any time of the day or night. Plonk yourself into a vinyl-upholstered booth and let the sass-talking waitstaff satisfy your midnight munchies.

Considering the location, this place is bound to attract some sketchy characters. But again, that's what a diner is supposed to do.

Xinh Xinh
VIETNAMESE $

(Map p40; www.xinhxinhboston.com; 7 Beach St; mains $8-12; ⊙lunch & dinner; ✍; ☂Chinatown) Wins the award for Boston's favorite *pho* (pronounced 'fuh'), the sometimes exotic, always fragrant and flavorful Vietnamese noodle soup. These hot, hearty meals come in big bowls and warm you from the inside out. The lemongrass tofu is especially recommended, as are the roll-it-yourself spring rolls (work for your food!).

My Thai Vegan Café
THAI $

(Map p40; 3 Beach St; mains $8-12; ⊙lunch & dinner; ✍; ☂Chinatown) Formerly Buddha's Delight, this welcoming cafe is tucked into a sunlit second-story space. It's still an animal-free zone – but good enough that meat-eaters will enjoy eating here too. The menu has a Thai twist, offering noodle soups, dumplings and pad thai. The bubble tea gets raves. Service can be slow, so bring a book.

★ Gourmet Dumpling House
CHINESE, TAIWANESE $

(Map p40; www.gourmetdumpling.com; 52 Beach St; lunch $8, dinner mains $10-15; ⊙11am-1am; ✍; ☂Chinatown) *Xiao long bao*. That's all the Chinese you need to know to take advantage of the specialty at the Gourmet Dumpling House (or GDH, as it is fondly called). They are Shanghai soup dumplings, of course, and they are fresh, doughy and delicious. The menu offers plenty of other options, including scrumptious crispy scallion pancakes. Come early or be prepared to wait.

Shōjō
ASIAN FUSION $$

(Map p40; www.shojoboston.com; 9A Tyler St; mains $18-26; ⊙lunch Mon-Fri, dinner Mon-Sat; ☂Chinatown) Clean, contemporary and super cool, Shōjō is unique in Chinatown for its upscale atmosphere. The menu picks and chooses from all over Asia (and beyond), effortlessly blending disparate elements into original, enticing fare. If you're not afraid for your arteries, the duck fat fries are highly recommended.

Jacob Wirth
GERMAN $$

(Map p40; ✆617-338-8586; www.jacobwirth.com; 31-37 Stuart St; sandwiches $8-12, mains $16-22; ⊙lunch & dinner; ♿; ☂Boylston) Boston's second-oldest eatery is this atmospheric Bavarian beer hall. The menu features Wiener schnitzel, sauerbraten, potato pancakes and pork chops, but the highlight is the beer – almost 30 different drafts, including Jake's House Lager and Jake's Special Dark. On Friday night (open until 1am), Jake hosts a sing-along that rouses the *haus*.

New Jumbo Seafood
CHINESE, SEAFOOD $$

(Map p40; www.newjumboseafoodrestaurant.com; 5 Hudson St; lunch $6-10, dinner mains $12-22; ⊙11am-2am; ✍; ☂Chinatown) You know the seafood is fresh when you see the huge tanks of lobster, crabs and fish that constitute the decor at this Chinatown classic. But it's not only seafood on the menu, which represents the best of Hong Kong cuisine. Other specialties include braised duck with mushrooms and Szechuan-style shrimp. Lunch specials are a bargain.

O Ya
SUSHI $$$

(Map p40; ✆617-654-9900; www.oyarestaurant boston.com; 9 East St; nigiri & sashimi pieces $12-24; ⊙dinner Tue-Sat; ✍; ☂South Station) Who knew that raw fish could be so exciting? Each piece of nigiri or sashimi is dripped with something unexpected but exquisite, ranging from honey truffle sauce to banana pepper mousse. Shrimp tempura is topped with a bacon truffle emulsion. Homemade soba noodles are chilled and served with sea urchin, nori and scallions. The service is impeccable, with knowledgeable waiters ready to offer advice and explanations.

✗ South End

Picco   PIZZERIA $$

(Map p50; www.piccorestaurant.com; 513 Tremont St; mains $9-15; ☺ lunch & dinner; 🛜 🖉 ♿; Ⓣ Back Bay) The crust of a Picco pizza undergoes a two-day process of cold fermentation before it goes into the oven and then into your mouth. The result is a thin crust with substantial texture and rich flavor. You can add toppings to create your own pie, or try the specialty Alsatian (sautéed onions, shallots, garlic, sour cream, bacon and Gruyère cheese).

The menu also features sandwiches, salads and delectable homemade ice cream. The breezy decor and free wi-fi access lure those who might like to linger.

Toro   TAPAS $$

(Map p50; ✒ 617-536-4300; www.toro-restaurant. com; 1704 Washington St; tapas $6-15; ☺ lunch & dinner; 🖉; 🚊 SL4 or SL5, Ⓣ Massachusetts Ave) 🖋 True to its Spanish spirit, this place is bursting with energy, from the open kitchen to the lively bar to the communal butcher-block tables. The menu features simple but sublime tapas – grilled chilies with sea salt, corn on the cob dripping with lemon and butter, and delectable, garlicky shrimp.

For accompaniment, take your pick from rioja, sangria or any number of spiced-up mojitos and margaritas.

Franklin Café   AMERICAN $$

(Map p50; www.franklincafe.com; 278 Shawmut Ave; mains $15-20; ☺ 5:30pm-1:30am; 🖉; 🚊 SL4 or SL5, Ⓣ Back Bay) The Franklin is probably the South End's longest-standing favorite neighborhood joint – and that's saying something in this restaurant-rich neighborhood. It's still friendly and hip – a fantastic spot for people-watching (especially the beautiful boys in the 'hood).

The menu is New American comfort food prepared by a gourmet chef: duck pot pie with root vegetables and cranberry jam or oyster-mushroom ravioli in sage brown butter.

Gaslight, Brasserie du Coin   FRENCH $$

(Map p50; ✒ 617-422-0224; www.gaslight560.com; 560 Harrison Ave; mains $17-27; ☺ brunch Sat & Sun, dinner daily; Ⓟ 🖉; 🚊 SL4 or SL5, Ⓣ Back Bay) Gaslight is the friendly and affordable 'brasserie on the corner' that we all wish we had in our own neighborhood. Mosaic tiles, wood-beam ceilings and comfy cozy booths set up the comfortable, convivial atmosphere, which is enhanced by classic French fare and an excellent selection of wines by the glass.

Coppa   ITALIAN $$

(Map p50; ✒ 617-391-0902; www.coppaboston. com; 253 Shawmut Ave; dishes $10-22; ☺ lunch Mon-Fri, brunch Sun, dinner daily; 🚊 SL4 or SL5, Ⓣ Back Bay) This South End *enoteca* (wine bar) serves up *salumi* (cured meats), antipasti, pasta and other delicious Italian small plates. Wash down with an Aperol spritz and you might be tricked into thinking you're in Venice. The setting is delightfully informal and small.

B&G Oysters   SEAFOOD $$

(Map p50; ✒ 617-423-0550; www.bandgoysters. com; 550 Tremont St; oysters $3 each, mains $25-30; ☺ lunch & dinner; 🛜; Ⓣ Back Bay) Patrons flock to this casually cool oyster bar to get in on the raw delicacies offered by chef Barbara Lynch. Sit inside at the marble bar or outside on the peaceful terrace, and indulge in the freshest oysters from local waters. An extensive list of wines and a modest menu of mains and appetizers (mostly seafood) are ample accompaniment for the oysters.

Myers & Chang   ASIAN $$$

(Map p50; ✒ 617-542-5200; www.myersandchang. com; 1145 Washington St; small plates $10-18; ☺ 11:30am-11pm Fri & Sat, to 10pm Sun-Thu; 🖉; 🚊 SL4 or SL5, Ⓣ Tufts Medical Center) This hip Asian spot blends Thai, Chinese and Vietnamese cuisines, which means delicious dumplings, spicy stir-fries and oodles of noodles. The kitchen staff does amazing things with a wok, and the menu of small plates allows you to sample a wide selection of dishes. The vibe is casual but cool, international and independent.

✗ Back Bay

★ Courtyard   MODERN AMERICAN $$

(Map p50; www.thecateredaffair.com; 700 Boylston St; mains $12-17; ☺ lunch Mon-Fri; 🖉; Ⓣ Copley) The perfect destination for an elegant luncheon with artfully prepared food is – believe it or not – the Boston Public Library. Overlooking the beautiful Italianate courtyard, this grown-up restaurant serves seasonal, innovative and exotic dishes (along with a few standards). The only downside is the lack of alcohol, but we understand the concern about drinking and reading.

Parish Café
SANDWICHES **$$**

(Map p40; www.parishcafe.com; 361 Boylston St; sandwiches $12-15; ⊙noon-2am; ⚑; ⊤Arlington) Sample the creations of Boston's most famous chefs without exhausting your expense account. The menu at Parish features a rotating roster of salads and sandwiches, each designed by a local celebrity chef, including Lydia Shire, Ken Oringer and Barbara Lynch.

Despite the creative fare, this place feels more 'pub' than 'cafe.' The long bar – backed by big TVs and mirrors – attracts a lively after-work crowd.

Bistro du Midi
FRENCH **$$$**

(Map p40; ☎617-426-7878; www.bistrodumidi. com; 272 Boylston St; mains $12-24; ⊙lunch & dinner; ⊤Arlington) The upstairs dining room is exquisite, but the downstairs cafe exudes warmth and camaraderie, inviting casual callers to linger over wine and snacks. In either setting, the Provençal fare is artfully presented and simply delicious. Reservations are required for dinner upstairs, but drop-ins are welcome at the cafe all day.

Piattini
ITALIAN **$$**

(Map p50; www.piattini.com; 226 Newbury St; lunch $8-15, dinner $18-24; ⊙lunch Mon-Fri, dinner daily; ⚑; ⊤Copley) If you have trouble deciding what to order, Piattini can help. The name means 'small plates,' so you don't have to choose just one. The list of wines by the glass is extensive, each accompanied by tasting notes and fun facts. This intimate *enoteca* (wine bar) is a delightful setting to sample the flavors of Italy, and you might just learn something while you're there.

Atlantic Fish Co
SEAFOOD **$$**

(Map p50; www.atlanticfishco.com; 761 Boylston St; lunch $12-22, dinner $24-32; ⊙lunch & dinner; ⊤Copley) New England clam chowder in a bread bowl. For a perfect lunch at Atlantic Fish Co, that's all you need to know. For the nonbelievers, we will add Maine lobster pot pie, lobster ravioli and jumbo lump crabcakes. There's more, of course, and the menu is printed daily to showcase the freshest ingredients. Enjoy it in the seafaring dining room or the flower-filled sidewalk patio.

L'Espalier
FRENCH **$$$**

(Map p50; ☎617-262-3023; www.lespalier.com; 774 Boylston St; lunch mains $25, dinner prix fixe $90-110; ⊙lunch & dinner Mon-Sat; ⊤Prudential) This tried-and-true favorite remains the crème de la crème of Boston's culinary scene, thanks to impeccable service and a variety of prix-fixe and tasting menus. The menus change daily, but usually include a degustation of caviar, a degustation of seasonal vegetables and recommended wine pairings.

Kenmore Square & the Fenway

★El Pelon
TAQUERIA **$**

(Map p50; www.elpelon.com; 92 Peterborough St; tacos $3-6; ⊙11am-11pm; ⚑⚑; ⊤Museum) If your budget is tight, don't miss this chance to fill up on Boston's best burritos, tacos and tortas, made with the freshest ingredients. The *tacos de la casa* are highly recommended, especially the *pescado*, made with Icelandic cod and topped with chili mayo. Plates are paper and cutlery is plastic.

Tasty Burger
BURGERS **$**

(Map p50; www.tastyburger.com; 1301 Boylston St; burgers $4-6; ⊙11am-2am; ⚑; ⊤Fenway) Once a Mobile station, it's now a retro burger joint, with picnic tables outside and a pool table inside. The name of the place is a nod to *Pulp Fiction*, as is the poster of Samuel L Jackson on the wall. You won't find a half-pound of Kobe beef on your bun, but you will have to agree 'That's a tasty burger.'

Aside from the burgers, this is a fun place to drink cheap beer and watch sports on TV.

Citizen Public House
MODERN AMERICAN **$$**

(Map p50; ☎617-450-9000; www.citizenpub.com; 1310 Boylston St; oysters $2-3, mains $15-23; ⊙dinner daily, brunch Sun; ⊤Fenway) Long overdue on this side of Fenway Park, this is a modern, urban gastropub with food and drinks for a sophisticated palette. There is an eye-catching and daily-changing raw bar, while the selective list of main dishes focuses on roasts and grills. The food is top-notch and it's all complemented by an extensive bar menu, featuring 75 varieties of whisky.

Sample the award-winning Ideal Manhattan, if you dare.

Eastern Standard
COCKTAIL BAR

(Map p50; www.easternstandardboston.com; 528 Commonwealth Ave; mains $15-25; ⊙lunch Mon-Fri, brunch Sat & Sun, dinner daily; ⊤Kenmore) Whether you choose to sit in the sophisticated, brassy interior or on the heated patio (open year-round), you're sure to enjoy the upscale atmosphere at this Kenmore Sq favorite. French bistro fare, with a hint of New American panache, caters to a pre-game crowd that prefers wine and cheese to peanuts and crackerjacks. Great people-watching on game nights.

Cambridge

★ Clover Food Lab   VEGETARIAN $
(Map p54; www.cloverfoodlab.com; 7 Holyoke St; mains $6-7; ⊙7am-midnight; 🖉🖐; ⊤Harvard) 🖉 Clover is on the cutting edge. It's all high-tech with its 'live' menu updates and electronic ordering system. But it's really about the food – local, seasonal, vegetarian food – which is cheap, delicious and fast. How fast? Check the menu. Interesting tidbit: Clover started as a food truck (and still has a few trucks making the rounds).

Veggie Planet   VEGETARIAN $
(Map p54; www.veggieplanet.net; 47 Palmer St; mains $8-12; ⊙lunch & dinner; 🖉🖐; ⊤Harvard) 🖉 Vegetarians and vegans can go nuts on creative interpretations of pizza (literally nuts: try the peanut curry pizza with tofu and broccoli). Stirfries and oddly shaped pies call on all the ethnic cuisines – but none of the animals – for their tantalizing tastes. By night, these basement digs double as the famous folk music venue, Club Passim (p75).

Mr Bartley's Burger Cottage   BURGERS $
(Map p54; www.mrbartley.com; 1246 Massachusetts Ave; burgers $10-15; ⊙11am-9pm Mon-Sat; 🖐; ⊤Harvard) Packed with small tables and hungry college students, this burger joint has been a Harvard Sq institution for more than 50 years. Bartley's offers at least 40 different burgers; if none of those suit your fancy, create your own 7oz juicy masterpiece with the toppings of your choice. Sweet potato fries, onion rings, thick frappes and raspberry-lime rickeys complete the classic American meal.

Cambridge, 1   PIZZERIA $$
(Map p54; www.cambridge1.us; 27 Church St; pizzas $17-22; ⊙11:30am-midnight; 🖉; ⊤Harvard) Set in the old fire station, this pizzeria's name comes from the sign chiseled into the stonework out front. The interior is sleek, sparse and industrial, with big windows overlooking the Old Burying Ground in the back. The menu is equally simple: pizza, soup, salad, dessert. These oddly-shaped pizzas are delectable, with crispy crusts and creative topping combos.

Russell House Tavern   MODERN AMERICAN $$
(Map p54; www.russellhousecambridge.com; 14 John F Kennedy St; sandwiches & pizza $12-13, mains $19-24; ⊙lunch & dinner; ⊤Harvard) Smack dab in the middle of Harvard Sq, this attractive gastropub has a classy, classic atmosphere, enhanced by good-looking, effervescent patrons. The menu – with hints of Southern goodness – includes a raw bar and a list of intriguing but irresistible small plates, not to mention a well-selected all-American wine list and killer cocktails.

🍷 Drinking & Nightlife

Boston is a beer-drinking city, thanks to the presence of the country's largest brewer, a host of microbreweries and a huge Irish population. But drink connoisseurs will find a venue accommodating every palate: brewpubs, swanky martini lounges and stylish wine bars...it just depends what your poison is. Keep in mind that the T stops running at 12:30am, while the bars are open until 1am or 2am.

The thriving club scene is fueled by the constant infusion of thousands of American and international students. Cover charges vary widely, from free (if you arrive early) to $20, but the average is usually $10 to $15 on weekends. Most clubs are open 10pm to 2am and require proper dress.

🍺 Beacon Hill

21st Amendment   PUB
(Map p40; www.21stboston.com; 150 Bowdoin St; ⊙11:30am-10pm Sun-Thur, to 11pm Fri & Sat; ⊤Park St) Named for one of the most important amendments to the US Constitution, this quintessential tavern has been an ever-popular haunt for overeducated and underpaid statehouse workers to whinge about the wheels of government. The place feels especially cozy in the winter, when you'll feel pretty good about yourself as you drink a stout near the copper-hooded fireplace.

Cheers   PUB
(Map p40; www.cheersboston.com; 84 Beacon St; ⊙11am-1am; ⊤Arlington) We understand that this is a mandatory pilgrimage place for fans of the TV show. But be aware that the bar doesn't look like its famous TV alter ego, nor is it charming or local or 'Boston' in any way. In short, nobody knows your name. The fact

BREW HA HA

A few national brews originate right here in Boston. Visit the facilities to see how your favorite beer is made and to partake of free samples.

Samuel Adams (www.samueladamsbrewery.com; 30 Germania St; donation $2; ☺10am-3pm Mon-Sat, to 5:30pm Fri; Ⓣ Stony Brook) **FREE** One-hour tours depart every 45 minutes. Learn about the history of Sam Adams the brewer and Sam Adams the beer.

Harpoon Brewery (www.harpoonbrewery.com; 306 Northern Ave; ☺tastings 2pm & 4pm Mon-Fri, tours 10:30am-5pm Sat & 11:30am-3pm Sun; 🚌 SL1 or SL2, Ⓣ South Station) **FREE** Very popular weekend tours of the brewery include a free souvenir beer mug. Alternatively, come during the week for free samples in the tasting room, which offers a view into the brewery at work.

that there is another outlet in Quincy Market proves our point.

🍷 Downtown & Waterfront

Thinking Cup CAFE
(Map p40; www.thinkingcup.com; 165 Tremont St; ☺7am-10pm Mon-Wed, to 11pm Thu-Sun; Ⓣ Boylston) There are a few things that make the Thinking Cup special. One is the French hot chocolate – ooh la la. Another is the Stumptown Coffee, the Portland brew that has earned accolades from coffee-drinkers around the country. But the best thing? It's across from the Boston Common, making it a perfect pitstop for a post–Frog Pond warm-up.

Silvertone PUB
(Map p40; www.silvertonedowntown.com; 69 Bromfield St; ☺11:30-2am Mon-Fri, 5pm-2am Sat; Ⓣ Park St) Black-and-white photos and retro advertising posters create a nostalgic atmosphere at this still-trendy pub and grill. The old-fashioned comfort food is always satisfying (the mac and cheese comes highly recommended), as is the cold beer drawn from the tap. The only downside is that the service suffers when the place gets crowded – and it does get crowded.

🍷 West End

Alibi COCKTAIL BAR
(Map p40; www.alibiboston.com; 215 Charles St, Liberty Hotel; ☺5pm-2am; Ⓣ Charles/MGH) There are actually two hot-to-trot drinking venues in the Liberty Hotel, both architecturally impressive and socially oh-so-trendy. Downstairs, Alibi is set in the former 'drunk tank' of the Charles St Jail. The prison theme is played up, with mugshots hanging on the brick walls and iron bars on the doors and

windows. Upstairs, Clink is the opposite, set under the soaring ceiling of the hotel's lobby. Both places are absurdly popular, so you'd best come early if you care to sit down.

West End Johnnies SPORTS BAR
(Map p40; www.westendjohnnies.com; 138 Portland St; ☺5pm-2am Tue-Sat, 11am-4pm Sun brunch; Ⓣ North Station) Despite the black leather furniture and big picture windows, this West End venue cannot escape the fact that it's a sports bar, with flatscreen TVs and sports paraphernalia adorning the walls. But it's a sports bar for grown-ups, with a good wine list and cocktail selection and tasty food.

Attention brunchies: JC's corned-beef hash and eggs and live reggae music make for an excellent way to recover from your Saturday night.

🍷 North End

Caffé Vittoria CAFE
(Map p40; www.vittoriacaffe.com; 290-96 Hanover St; ☺7am-midnight; Ⓣ Haymarket) A delightful destination for dessert or aperitifs. The frilly parlor displays antique espresso machines and black-and-white photos, with a pressed-tin ceiling reminiscent of the era. Grab a marble-topped table, order a cappuccino and live it up in Victorian pleasure. Cash only, just like the olden days.

Caffé Dello Sport SPORTS BAR, CAFE
(Map p40; www.caffedellosport.us; 308 Hanover St; ☺6am-midnight; Ⓣ Haymarket) An informal crowd of thick-accented guys from the 'hood sit at glass-topped tables and drink coffee and Campari. The espresso drinks are surprisingly excellent. This is a great place to watch a football game (and yes, we mean soccer), and watching the other patrons is equally entertaining. Cash only.

Charlestown

Warren Tavern
HISTORIC PUB

(www.warrentavern.com; 2 Pleasant St; ⊙11am-1am; ⊤Community College) One of the oldest pubs in Boston, the Warren Tavern has been pouring pints for its customers since George Washington and Paul Revere drank here. It is named for General Joseph Warren, a fallen hero of the Battle of Bunker Hill (shortly after which – in 1780 – this pub was opened).

Zumes Coffee House
CAFE

(www.zumescoffeehouse.com; 223 Main St; ⊙6am-6pm Mon-Fri, 7am-6pm Sat & Sun; 🛜📶; ⊤Community College) This is slightly off the beaten path (aka the Freedom Trail), but locals love it for the comfy leather chairs, big cups of coffee and decadent doughnuts. Also on the menu: soup, sandwiches and lunchy items. Paintings and photographs by local artists adorn the walls; books and games keep the kiddies busy.

Seaport District

★ Drink
COCKTAIL BAR

(Map p40; www.drinkfortpoint.com; 348 Congress St S; ⊙4pm-1am; 🚃SL1 or SL2, ⊤South Station) There is no cocktail menu at Drink. Instead you have a little chat with the bartender, and he or she will whip something up according to your specifications. The bar takes seriously the art of drink mixology – and you will too, after you sample one of its concoctions. The subterranean space creates a dark, sexy atmosphere, which makes for a great date destination.

Lucky's Lounge
DIVE COCKTAIL BAR

(Map p40; www.luckyslounge.com; 355 Congress St S; ⊙11am-2am Sun-Fri, 6pm-2am Sat; 🚃SL1 or SL2, ⊤South Station) One of Boston's top-notch bars, Lucky's earns street cred by having no sign. Step inside and you'll return to a delightfully gritty lounge that looks like it's straight from 1959. Enjoy well-priced drinks, excellent martinis and Motown-inspired bands playing tunes to which people actually dance (Thursday to Sunday). Sinatra Sunday remains a perpetual favorite, and the after-work scene is one of the liveliest around.

Chinatown & Theater District

Les Zygomates
WINE BAR

(Map p40; www.winebar.com; 129 South St; ⊙11:30am-10pm Mon-Thu, 11:30-11pm Fri, 5:30-11pm Sat; ⊤South Station) This Parisian bistro serves up live jazz music alongside classic but contemporary French cuisine. Tuesday-night wine tastings ($45; 7pm) attract a clientele that is sophisticated but not stuffy. Dinner is pricey, but the tempting selection of starters and cocktails make it a perfect pre- or post-theater spot.

DANCE!

There's really only one neighborhood in Boston where the dancing goes down in earnest: the Theater District. Boylston St is the main drag for over-the-top megaclubs, but there are other venues all over this groovy 'hood. Go online to get on the guest list. And don't forget to dress sharp.

Bijou (Map p40; www.bijouboston.com; 51 Stuart St; ⊤Boylston) Named after the old Bijou Theater, which was the first electrically lit playhouse back in 1882 (wired by Thomas Edison himself).

District (Map p40; www.districtboston.com; 180 Lincoln St; ⊙10pm-2am Wed & Fri-Sat; ⊤South Station) Eclectic is an understatement, and that goes for the decor as well as the clientele.

RISE (Map p40; www.riseclub.us; 306 Stuart St; cover $20, students $10; ⊙1-6am Fri & Sat; ⊤Arlington) The clubs are closing and you still want more – that's when you head to RISE.

Underbar (Map p40; www.underbaronline.com; 275 Tremont St; cover $10-20; ⊙10pm-2am Fri-Sun; ⊤Tufts Medical Center) A basement club with a tiny dance floor and a hard-working sound system.

Venu & Rumor (Map p40; www.venuboston.com; 100 Warrenton St; cover $15-20; ⊙11pm-2am Tue-Wed & Fri-Sat; ⊤Boylston) Two side-by-side clubs with an impeccably dressed, international guest list.

GAY & LESBIAN BOSTON

Out and active gay communities are visible all around Boston, especially in the South End and Jamaica Plain. **Calamus Bookstore** (Map p40; www.calamusbooks.com; 92 South St; ⏰9am-7pm Mon-Sat, noon-6pm Sun; ⓣSouth Station) is also an excellent source of information about community events and organizations.

There is no shortage of entertainment options catering to LGBTs. From drag shows to dyke nights, this sexually diverse community has something for everybody.

Diesel Cafe (www.diesel-cafe.com; 257 Elm St; ⏰6am-11pm Mon-Sat, 7am-11am Sun; ⓣDavis Sq) Shoot stick, drink coffee and swill beer in this industrial cafe popular with students and queers.

Fritz (Map p50; www.fritzboston.com; 26 Chandler St; ⏰noon-2am; ⓣBack Bay) Watch the boys playing sports on TV or watch the boys watching the boys playing sports on TV.

Club Café (Map p40; www.clubcafe.com; 209 Columbus Ave; ⏰11am-2am; ⓣBack Bay) Always hopping, it's a cool cafe by day and a crazy club by night. Aimed at men, open to all.

Jacques Cabaret (Map p40; www.jacques-cabaret.com; 79 Broadway; admission $6-10; ⏰11am-midnight, showtimes vary; ⓣArlington) Life is a cabaret, old friend. Come to the cabaret.

South End

★**Delux Café**   DIVE BAR
(Map p50; ☎617-338-5258; 100 Chandler St; ⏰5pm-1am Mon-Sat; ⓣBack Bay) If Boston has a laid-back hipster bar, this is it. The small room on the 1st floor of a brownstone comes covered in knotty pine paneling, artwork from old LPs and Christmas lights. A small TV in the corner plays silent cartoons (not sports), and a noteworthy kitchen serves incredible grilled-cheese sandwiches and inspired comfort food. Cash only.

★**Beehive**   JAZZ, COCKTAIL BAR
(Map p50; ☎617-423-0069; www.beehiveboston.com; 541 Tremont St; ⏰5pm-1am Mon-Wed, 5pm-2am Thu-Fri, 10am-2am Sat-Sun; ⓣBack Bay) The Beehive has transformed the basement of the Boston Center for the Arts into a 1920s Paris jazz club. This place is more about the scene than the music, which is often provided by students from Berklee College of Music. But the food is good and the vibe is definitely hip. Reservations required if you want a table.

28 Degrees   COCKTAIL BAR
(Map p50; www.28degrees-boston.com; 1 Appleton St; ⏰5pm-midnight; ⓣBack Bay or Arlington) Twenty-eight degrees is the optimum temperature for a martini. Now, perhaps you're getting an idea about what to order at this this super-slick bar on the edge of the South End. The blue basil and cucumber martini is just an example from a long list of perfectly chilled treats, which change seasonally.

The uber-chic interior makes this a sweet spot to impress a date. Don't leave without checking out the loo.

Back Bay

Bukowski Tavern   DIVE BAR
(Map p50; www.bukowskitavern.net; 50 Dalton St; ⏰11am-2am; ⓣHynes) This sweet bar lies inside a parking garage next to the canyon of the Mass Pike. Expect sticky wooden tables, loud rock, lots of black hoodies, a dozen different burgers and dogs and more than 100 kinds of beer. In God we trust; all others pay cash.

City Bar   COCKTAIL BAR
(Map p50; www.citybarboston.com; 710 Boylston St; ⏰4:30pm-2am; ⓣCopley) For an intimate atmosphere and impressive selection of cocktails, you can't go wrong at this swish bar in the Lenox Hotel. It's not exactly a destination in and of itself, but it's ideal for after-work or early-evening drinks. Sink into the leather couch or sidle up to the polished bar for a fancy martini, and amuse yourself by observing the clientele giving each other the eye.

Storyville   NIGHTCLUB
(Map p50; www.storyvilleboston.com; 90 Exeter St; ⏰8pm-2am Wed-Thu, 7pm-2am Fri-Sat; ⓣCopley) The legendary Storyville jazz club occupied this same spot in the 1940s, when it hosted

the likes of Dave Brubeck and Billie Holiday (who even recorded an album here). The contemporary nightclub recalls that era with its loungey atmosphere and sexy New Orleans–inspired vibe. One room is reserved for dancing, with live music on Wednesday nights.

Along with potent drinks, the place serves excellent modern New England fare well into the night.

Kenmore Square & the Fenway

★ Bleacher Bar   SPORTS BAR

(Map p50; www.bleacherbarboston.com; 82a Lansdowne St; T Kenmore) Tucked under the bleachers at Fenway Park, this classy bar offers a view onto center field (go Jacoby baby!). It's not the best place to watch the game, as the place gets packed, but it's an awesome way to experience America's oldest ballpark, even when the Sox are not playing.

If you want a seat in front of the window, get your name on the waiting list an hour or two before game time; once seated, diners have 45 minutes in the hot seat.

Lower Depths Tap Room   BEER BAR

(Map p50; www.thelowerdepths.com; 476 Commonwealth Ave; T Kenmore) This subterranean space is a beer-lovers' paradise. It has all the atmosphere (and beer knowledge) of its sister establishment, Bukowski Tavern, but the Lower Depths classes it up. Besides the impressive beer selection, the kitchen turns out excellent comfort food, including one-dollar Fenway Franks with exotic one-dollar toppings. Cash only, friends.

Cambridge

La Burdick   CAFE

(Map p54; www.burdickchocolate.com; 52D Brattle St; ⊙8am-9pm Sun-Thu, 8am-10pm Fri-Sat; T Harvard) This boutique chocolatier doubles as a cafe, usually packed full of happy patrons drinking hot cocoa. Whether you choose dark or milk, it's sure to be some of the best chocolate that you'll drink in your lifetime. There are only a handful of tables, so it's hard to score a seat when temperatures are chilly.

Middlesex   NIGHTCLUB

(www.middlesexlounge.us; 315 Massachusetts Ave; cover $5-10 Fri & Sat; ⊙5pm-1am Mon-Wed,

5pm-2am Thu-Sat; T Central) Sleek and sophisticated, Middlesex brings the fashionable crowd to the Cambridge side of town. Black modular furniture sits on heavy casters, allowing the cubes to be rolled aside when the place transforms from lounge to club, making space for the beautiful people to become entranced with DJs experimenting with hip hop and electronica.

☆ Entertainment

From high culture to low-down blues, Boston's entertainment scene has something for everyone. The vibrant university culture enhances the breadth and depth of cultural offerings on both sides of the river.

Live Rock & Indie

From legends like Aerosmith and the Cars to modern rockers like the Mighty Mighty Bosstones and the Dropkick Murphys, plenty of nationally known bands trace their roots back to Boston clubs. To help you figure out who's playing where, check out the listings in the *Boston Phoenix* or the *Weekly Dig*.

★ Lizard Lounge   LIVE MUSIC

(www.lizardloungeclub.com; 1667 Massachusetts Ave, Cambridge; cover $5-10; ⊙7:30pm-1am, to 2am Fri-Sat; T Harvard) The underground Lizard Lounge doubles as a jazz and rock venue. The big drawcard is the Sunday night poetry slam, featuring music by the jazzy Jeff Robinson Trio. Also popular are the Monday open-mic challenge and regular appearances by local band Session Americana. The bar stocks an excellent list of New England beers, which are complemented by the sweet-potato fries.

Located a quarter-mile north of Cambridge Common (the park), below Cambridge Common (the restaurant).

★ Red Room @ Café 939   LIVE MUSIC

(Map p50; www.cafe939.com; 939 Boylston St; T Hynes) Run by Berklee students, the Red Room @ Café 939 is emerging as one of Boston's best music venues. The place has an excellent sound system and a baby grand piano; most importantly, it books interesting, eclectic up-and-coming musicians. This is where you'll see that band that's about to make it big. Buy tickets in advance at the Berklee Performance Center.

Sinclair   LIVE MUSIC

(Map p54; www.sinclaircambridge.com; 52 Church St; tickets $15-18; ⊙11am-1am Tue-Sun, 5pm-1am

Mon; T Harvard) Music lovers are raving about this new, small live-music venue. The acoustics are excellent and the mezzanine level allows you to escape the crowds on the floor. The club attracts a good range of local and regional bands and DJs. Bonus: under the direction of Michael Schlow, the attached kitchen puts out some delicious and downright classy food (though service seems to be a little spotty).

Great Scott
NIGHTCLUB

(www.greatscottboston.com; 1222 Commonwealth Ave; cover $5-12; T Harvard Ave) A great place to hear rock and indie. Get up close and personal with the bands, hang out with them after the set, buy them some beers. The place rarely gets uncomfortably crowded, and the stage is well raised.

On Friday nights, the club turns into a comedy club known as the Gas (7:30pm), after which it turns into an awesome indie dance club, aka the Pill (10pm). Both guarantee a rockin' good time.

Church
LIVE MUSIC

(Map p50; www.churchofboston.com; 69 Kilmarnock St; cover $10-12; ⊘5pm-2am; T Museum or Kenmore) Say a prayer of thanks for this neighborhood music venue. It books cool bands nightly, which is the most important thing. But it's also stylish, with pool tables, a pretty slick restaurant and attractive people. And plasma TVs, of course. Music starts most nights at 9pm.

Paradise Rock Club
LIVE MUSIC

(www.crossroadspresents.com; 967 Commonwealth Ave; cover $20-40; T Pleasant St) Top bands rock at this landmark club – like U2, whose first gig in the USA was on this stage. Nowadays, you're more likely to hear the likes of the Del Fuegos, Los Compesiños, Trombone Shorty, and plenty of Boston bands that made good but still come home to play the Dise.

House of Blues
LIVE MUSIC

(Map p50; www.hob.com/boston; 15 Lansdowne St; T Kenmore) The HOB is bigger and better than ever. Well, it's bigger. Nevermind the ridiculously tight security measures, this is where national acts play if they want something more intimate than the Garden (eg, the reunited J Geils Band, Lady Gaga, Dropkick Murphys, etc). The balcony seating offers an excellent view of the stage, while fighting the crowds on the mezzanine can be brutal.

Live Folk, Blues & Jazz

★ Wally's Café
BLUES, JAZZ

(Map p50; http://wallyscafe.com; 427 Massachusetts Ave; ⊘2pm-2am; T Massachusetts Ave) When Wally's opened in 1947, Barbadian immigrant Joseph Walcott became the first African American to own a nightclub in New England. Old-school, gritty and small, it still attracts a racially diverse crowd to hear jammin' jazz since 365 days a year. Berklee students love this place, especially the weekend jam sessions (6pm to 8pm Saturday and Sunday).

★ Club Passim
FOLK MUSIC

(Map p54; ✆617-492-7679; www.clubpassim.org; 47 Palmer St; tickets $15-30; T Harvard) Folk music in Boston seems to be endangered outside of Irish bars, but the legendary Club Passim does such a great job booking top-notch acts that it practically fills the vacuum by itself. The colorful, intimate room is hidden off a side street in Harvard Sq, and those attending shows are welcome to order filling dinners from Veggie Planet (p70).

Scullers Jazz Club
JAZZ

(✆617-642-4111; www.scullersjazz.com; 400 Soldiers Field Rd; tickets $20-45; ☐47 or 70, T Central) A more mature music experience, this club books big names (Dave Brubeck, Dr John, Michael Franks) in a small room. Though it enjoys impressive views over the Charles, the room itself lacks the grit you might hanker for in a jazz club. It feels like it's inside a Doubletree Hotel (which it is). Book in advance.

Regattabar
JAZZ

(Map p54; ✆617-395-7757; www.regattabarjazz.com; 1 Bennett St; tickets $15-35; T Harvard) Why does Boston have such clean jazz clubs? Regattabar looks just like a conference room in a hotel – in this case the Charles Hotel. They get big enough names (Virginia Rodrigues, Keb Mo) to transcend the mediocre space, though. As it only has 225 seats, you're guaranteed a good view and the sound system is excellent.

Classical Music

★ Boston Symphony Orchestra
CLASSICAL MUSIC

(BSO; Map p50; ✆617-266-1200; www.bso.org; Symphony Hall, 301 Massachusetts Ave; tickets $30-115; T Symphony) The world-renowned Boston Symphony Orchestra has welcomed a new Musical Director, the dynamic young Andris Nelsons. From September to April, the BSO performs in the beauteous Symphony Hall, featuring an ornamental high-relief ceiling and attracting a fancy-dress crowd. The building was designed in 1861 with the help of a Harvard physicist who pledged to make the building acoustically perfect (he succeeded).

In summer months, the Boston Pops take over Symphony Hall. Led by the dashing Keith Lockhart and sometimes fronted by real live 'pop' stars, the Pops play crowd-pleasers like holiday fare and movie scores.

Theater

Though it lives in the shadow of New York, Boston's theater culture is impressively strong for a city of its size. Multiple big-ticket venues consistently book top shows, produce premieres and serve as testing grounds for many plays that eventually become hits on Broadway.

Tickets are available online or at individual theater box offices. **BosTix** (www.bostix.org; ◷10am-6pm Tue-Sat, 11am-4pm Sun) has discounted tickets to productions citywide. Discounts of up to 50% are available for same-day purchase: check the website, but purchases must be made in person in cash at the **Faneuil Hall outlet** or the **Copley Square outlet**.

The big venues in the Theater District are lavish affairs, all restored to their early-20th-century glory. Other venues include:

➔ **American Repertory Theater** (ART; Map p54; ✆617-547-8300; www.amrep.org; 64 Brattle St; tickets $40-75; Ⓣ Harvard) A prestigious Cambridge-based company famous for its innovation.

 CLASSIC ON THE CHEAP

The BSO often offers various discounted ticket schemes, which might allow you to hear classical music on the cheap:

➔ Same-day 'rush' tickets ($9) are available for Tuesday and Thursday evening performances (on sale from 5pm), as well as Friday afternoon performances (on sale from 10am).

➔ Check the schedule for open rehearsals, which usually take place in the afternoon midweek. Tickets are $18 to $30.

➔ Occasionally, discounted tickets are offered for certain segments of the population (eg $20 for under 40s).

➔ **Boston Center for the Arts** (Map p50; www.bcaonline.org; 539 Tremont St; Ⓣ Back Bay) A nexus for small theater in Boston, this venue hosts dozens of companies.

➔ **Huntington Theatre** (Boston University Theatre; Map p50; www.huntingtontheatre.org; 264 Huntington Ave; Ⓣ Symphony) An award-winning company that has premiered the works of many fine playwrights.

Dance

Boston Ballet DANCE
(✆617-695-6950; www.bostonballet.org; tickets $15-100) Boston's skillful ballet troupe performs both modern and classic works at the **Opera House** (Map p40; www.bostonoperahouse.com; 539 Washington St; Ⓣ Downtown Crossing). During the Christmas season, they put on a wildly popular performance of the *Nutcracker*. Student and child 'rush' tickets are available for $20 two hours before the performance; seniors get the same deal, but only for Saturday and Sunday matinees.

Comedy Clubs

Wilbur Theatre COMEDY
(Map p40; www.thewilburtheatre.com; 246 Tremont St; tickets $20-50; Ⓣ Boylston) The colonial Wilbur Theatre dates to 1914, and over the years has hosted many prominent theatrical productions. These days it is Boston's premier comedy club. Once known as the Comedy Connection (and located in Quincy Market), this long-running operation has hosted the likes of Chris Rock and other nationally known cut-ups.

★ **Comedy Studio** COMEDY
(Map p54; www.thecomedystudio.com; 1238 Massachusetts Ave; admission $10-12; ◷show 8pm Tue-Sun; Ⓣ Harvard) The 3rd floor of the Hong Kong noodle house contains a low-budget comedy house with a reputation for hosting cutting-edge acts. This is where talented future stars (eg Brian Kiley, who became a writer for Conan O'Brien) refine their racy material. Each night has a different theme, eg on Tuesday you can usually see a weird magician show.

Sports

Boston loves its sports teams. And why not, with its professional teams bringing home the 'Grand Slam of American Sports' by winning all four championships in recent years. In addition to professional sports, many local college teams earn devotion from spir-

LET'S GO OUT TO THE MOVIES

Catch a flick at one of Boston's historic theaters or academic institutions.

Brattle Theatre (Map p54; www.brattlefilm.org; 40 Brattle St; T Harvard) This film lover's *cinema paradiso* features repertory series showcasing particular directors or series.

Coolidge Corner Theatre (www.coolidge.org; 290 Harvard St; T Coolidge Corner) An art-deco neighborhood palace, this old theater blazes with exterior neon and a line-up of indie fare.

Harvard Film Archive Cinematheque (Carpenter Center for the Arts; Map p54; http://hcl.harvard.edu/hfa; 24 Quincy St; ☺ Fri-Mon; T Harvard) Housed in the esteemed Carpenter Center (designed by Le Corbusier), the Cinematheque presents thoughtful film events, often featuring the filmmakers themselves.

ited students and alums. The local rivalries come out in full force during the **Beanpot** (www.beanpothockey.com), an annual hockey tournament which occurs the first two weeks in February.

Boston Red Sox SPORTS
(www.redsox.com) The intensity of baseball fans has only grown since the Boston Red Sox broke their agonizing 86-year losing streak and won the 2004 World Series (and repeated the feat in 2007). The Red Sox play at **Fenway Park** (Map p50; www.redsox.com; 4 Yawkey Way; tickets $25-125; T Kenmore), the nation's oldest and most storied ballpark, built in 1912. Unfortunately, it is also the most expensive – not that this stops the Fenway faithful from scooping up all the tickets.

Boston Celtics SPORTS
(www.nba.com/celtics) The Boston Celtics have won more basketball championships than any other NBA team, most recently in 2008. From October to April, the Celtics play at **TD Garden** (www.tdgarden.com; 100 Legends Way; T North Station).

New England Patriots SPORTS
(www.patriots.com) Super Bowl champions in 2002, 2004 and 2005 – that's a 'three-peat' for football fans – the New England Patriots are considered a football dynasty. They play in the state-of-the-art Gillette Stadium, 32 miles south of Boston in Foxborough. The season runs from late August to late December.

Boston Bruins SPORTS
(www.bostonbruins.com) Stanley Cup winners in 2011, the Boston Bruins play ice hockey at the TD Garden (p77) from mid-October to mid-April.

 Shopping

Boston may not be very alluring for bargain hunters, but it does boast its fair share of Bohemian boutiques, distinctive galleries and offbeat shops. Boston's classic shopping destinations are **Charles St** on Beacon Hill or **Newbury St** in the Back Bay.

Nowadays, there are chic boutiques and artsy galleries sitting side by side with the irresistible restaurants in both the **South End** and the **North End**. Across the river in Cambridge, **Harvard Square** has spirited street life with plenty of musicians and performance artists to entertain. Unfortunately, most of the independent stores have been replaced by national chains due to rising rents.

Beacon Hill

⭐ **Artifaktori Vintage** CLOTHING
(Map p40; www.artifaktori.com; 121 Charles St; ☺ Tue-Sun; T Charles/MGH) Vintage meets Beacon Hill. Stop by this sweet spot for a choice selection of oldies-but-goodies, as well as fantastic retro-inspired designs that are brand new. The eye-popping colors and bold patterns cater to dapper men and women who are passionate about fashion from any era.

But here's a modern concept: Artifaktori combines style-conscious with eco-conscious, featuring ethically produced clothing (fairly traded or locally made with all-natural materials).

NOA JEWELRY, HANDICRAFTS
(Map p40; www.noagifts.com; 88 Charles St; T Charles/MGH) Candles, glasswork, jewelry, furniture, handbags, mobiles, mosaics, photography, pottery, soaps, stationery,

woodwork and more. And all of it – *all* of it – made by local artists.

Beacon Hill Chocolates FOOD & DRINK

(Map p40; www.beaconhillchocolates.com; 91 Charles St; T Charles/MGH) This artisanal chocolatier puts equal effort into selecting fine chocolates from around the world and designing beautiful keepsake boxes to contain them. Using decoupage to affix old postcards, photos and illustrations, the boxes are works of art even before they are filled with truffles. Pick out an image of historic Boston as a souvenir for the sweet tooth in your life.

Blackstone's of Beacon Hill GIFTS, ACCESSORIES

(Map p40; www.blackstonesbeaconhill.com; 46 Charles St; T Charles/MGH) Here's a guarantee: you will find the perfect gift for that certain someone at Blackstone's. This little place is crammed with classy, clever and otherwise unusual items. Highlights include the custom-designed stationery, locally made handicrafts and quirky Boston-themed souvenirs like clocks and coasters. If none of that fits your fancy, there's always a Vera Bradley handbag.

Crush Boutique CLOTHING

(Map p40; www.shopcrushboutique.com; 131 Charles St; T Charles/MGH) Fashion mavens rave about this cute, cozy basement boutique on Charles St, which features both well-loved designers and up-and-coming talents. The selection of clothing is excellent, but it's the expert advice that makes this place so popular. Co-owners (and childhood BFFs) Rebecca and Laura would love to help you find something that makes you look fabulous.

Helen's Leather SHOES, ACCESSORIES

(Map p40; www.helensleather.com; 110 Charles St; ☉ Wed-Mon; T Charles/MGH) You probably didn't realize that you would need your cowboy boots in Boston. Never fear, you can pick up a slick pair right here on Beacon Hill. (In-deed, this is the number-one distributor of cowboy boots in New England.) Helen also carries stylish dress boots and work boots, as well as gorgeous jackets, classy handbags and sharp wallets and belts.

Red Wagon & Pixie Stix CHILDREN'S CLOTHING

(Map p40; www.theredwagon.com; 69 Charles St; T Charles/MGH) At street level, the Red Wagon carries adorable outfits for little tykes (up to age 8), while upstairs, Pixie Stix caters to their older sisters (to 13). The shop treats each age with cuteness and coolness, if that's possible. The fun fashions at Pixie Stix will appeal to parent and child with bright colors, bold patterns and funky styles.

🏠 Downtown & Waterfront

Greenway Open Market ART MARKET

(Map p40; www.greenwayopenmarket.com; Surface Ave; ☉ 11am-5pm Sat Jun-Oct; T Aquarium) One of the newest features on the Greenway, the Saturday-only Open Market brings dozens of vendors to display their wares in the open air. Look for unique, handmade gifts, jewelry, bags, paintings, ceramics and other arts and crafts – many of which are locally and ethically made.

Brattle Book Shop BOOKS

(Map p40; www.brattlebookshop.com; 9 West St; ☉ 9am-5:30pm Mon-Sat; T Park St) Since 1825, the Brattle Book Shop has catered to Boston's literati: it's a treasure trove crammed with out-of-print, rare and first-edition books. Ken Gloss – whose family has owned this gem since 1949 – is an expert on antiquarian books, moonlighting as a consultant and appraiser (see him on *Antiques Roadshow*!). Don't miss the bargains on the outside lot.

Lucy's League CLOTHING

(Map p40; www.thecolorstores.com; North Bldg, Faneuil Hall; T Government Center) We're not

NEW BALANCE FACTORY STORE

Runners rejoice over New Balance shoes, but regular people wear them too. The **New Balance Factory Store** (40 Life St, Brighton; ☉ 9am-7pm Mon-Sat, 11am-6pm Sun; 🚌 64) sells these comfortable, supportive running shoes at discounted prices. This warehouse of a place also carries factory seconds and overruns of fleece jackets and synthetic clothing. You may have to search for your size, but you can easily save 50% or more off any given item. This place is not so easy to get to: take bus 64 from Central Sq (about 20 minutes).

advocating those pink Red Sox caps. But sometimes a girl wants to look good while she's supporting the team. At Lucy's League, fashionable sports fans will find shirts, jackets and other gear sporting the local teams' logos – but in super-cute styles designed to flatter the female figure.

Funusual   GIFTS, GAMES
(Map p40; www.funusual.com; 8 North Building, Faneuil Hall; ⊤ Government Center) It's hard to describe this silly gift shop without using the obvious adjectives. It's filled with quirky, clever and crazy toys, games and knick-knacks. Shop here and you too can serve drinks in Matchbox-car shotglasses at your next party. Popular 'Life is Crap' T-shirts give 'Life is Good' a run for their money, and there are plenty of other funny T-shirts that are more optimistic.

Local Charm   JEWELLERY
(Map p40; 2 South Market; ⊤ State) These days, Quincy Market is packed with chain stores that you can find anywhere in America. Wouldn't it be nice to experience a little local charm? This tiny jewelry boutique delivers, offering up exquisite things with sterling silver and gemstones. The jewelry is tasteful yet artful, interesting yet unique. Best of all, it's handmade by local artisans.

🛍 North End

Every visitor goes to the North End to savor the flavors of Italian cooking. But as a local points out, 'Where do you think the chefs get their food from?'

Polcari's Coffee   FOOD & DRINK
(Map p40; polcariscoffee.com; 105 Salem St; ⊗ 9:30am-6pm Mon-Sat; ⊤ Haymarket) Since 1932, this corner shop is where North-Enders stock up on their beans. Look for 27 kinds of imported coffee, over 150 spices and an impressive selection of legumes, grains, flours and loose teas. Don't bypass the chance to indulge in a fresh Italian ice.

Salumeria Italiana   FOOD & DRINK
(Map p40; www.salumeriaitaliana.com; 151 Richmond St; ⊗ 7am-6pm Mon-Thu, to 7pm Fri & Sat; ⊤ Haymarket) Shelves stocked with extra virgin olive oil and aged balsamic vinegar; cases crammed with cured meats, hard cheeses and olives of all shapes and sizes; boxes of pasta; jars of sauce: this little store is the archetype of North End specialty shops.

DePasquale's Homemade Pasta Shoppe   FOOD & DRINK
(Map p40; www.homemade-pasta.com; 66a Cross St; ⊗ 10am-8pm Sun-Thu, 10am-10pm Fri & Sat; ⊤ Haymarket) Peek into this little storefront and catch a glimpse of the pasta maker working her magic, crafting pasta in various shapes, sizes and flavors. The store carries more than 50 fresh varieties, including specialty ravioli and tortellini with mouth-watering fillings. If you can't decide, browse the recipe cards for some ideas.

In-Jean-ius   CLOTHING
(Map p40; www.injeanius.com; 441 Hanover St; ⊤ Haymarket) You know what you're getting when you waltz into this denim haven. Offerings from over 30 designers include tried-and-true favorites and little-known gems, and staff are on hand to help you find the pair that fits you perfectly. Warning: the Surgeon General has determined that it is not healthy to try on jeans after a gigantic plate of pasta; come here before dinner.

Sedurre   CLOTHING
(Map p40; www.sedurreboston.com; 281/2 Prince St; ⊗ noon-8pm Mon-Sat, noon-6pm Sun; ⊤ Haymarket) If you speak Italian, you'll know that Sedurre's thing is sexy and stylish. (It means 'seduce.') The shop started with fine lingerie – beautiful lacy nightgowns and underthings for special occasions. Sisters Robyn and Daria were so good at that they created an additional space next door for dresses and evening wear (for other kinds of special occasions).

Shake the Tree   CLOTHING, ACCESSORIES,
(Map p40; www.shakethetreeboston.com; 67 Salem St; ⊗ 11am-7pm; ⊤ Haymarket) You can't know what you will find at this sweet boutique, but it's bound to be good. The little shop carries a wonderful, eclectic assortment of jewelry by local artisans, interesting stationery, designer handbags and clothing and unique housewares.

Seaport District

Louis Boston CLOTHING & ACCESSORIES
(www.louisboston.com; 60 Northern Ave; 🚇 SL1 or
SL2, 🚈 South Station) It was big news when
this high-class fashion institution moved
shop from its fancy Back Bay quarters to
the gritty, industrial Seaport District. But
the influential design icon is clearly at the
forefront of something. Now in slick modern digs with wall-to-ceiling windows, Louis
inhabits a space that matches its trendy, on-
point designs.

By the way, this being Boston, Louis is
not pronounced the way you expect: it's *Loo-
eeez* with a zed. Louis Boston.

South End

★ Bobby From Boston CLOTHING, VINTAGE
(Map p50; 19 Thayer St; ⊗ noon-6pm Mon-Sat;
🚇 SL4 or SL5, 🚈 Tufts Medical Center) Bobby is
one of Boston's coolest cats. Men from all
over the greater Boston area come to the
South End to peruse Bobby's amazing selection of classic clothing from another era.
This is stuff that your grandfather wore – if
he was a very stylish man. Smoking jackets,
bow ties, bomber jackets and more.

The women's section is smaller, but there
is enough here to make sure the lady looks
as good as her date.

South End Open Market HANDICRAFTS, MARKET
(Map p50; www.sowaopenmarket.com; 540 Harrison Ave; ⊗ 10am-4pm Sun May-Oct; 🚇 SL4 or
SL5, 🚈 Tufts Medical Center) Part flea market
and part artists' market, this weekly outdoor
event is a fabulous opportunity for strolling,
shopping and people-watching. More than
100 vendors set up shop under white tents.
It's never the same two weeks in a row, but
there's always plenty of arts and crafts, as
well as edgier art, vintage clothing, jewelry,
local farm produce and homemade sweets.

SoWa Vintage Market MARKET, VINTAGE
(Map p50; www.sowavintagemarket.com; 460 Harrison Ave; ⊗ 10am-4pm Sun, 5-9pm first Fri; 🚇 SL4
or SL5, 🚈 Tufts Medical Center) Where the Open
Market is for cool handmade stuff, the Vintage Market is for cool old stuff. It's like an
indoor flea market, with dozens of vendors
selling clothes, furniture, posters, housewares and loads of other trash and treasures.

Sault New England CLOTHING, GIFTS
(Map p50; www.saultne.com; 577 Tremont St;
⊗ 11am-7pm Tue-Sun; 🚈 Back Bay) Blending
prepster and hipster, rustic and chic, this
little basement boutique packs in a lot of intriguing stuff. The eclectic mix of merchandise runs the gamut from new and vintage
clothing to coffee-table books and homemade terrariums. A New England theme
runs through the store, with nods to the
Kennedys, *Jaws*, and LL Bean.

Motley CLOTHING, GIFTS
(Map p50; www.shopmotley.com; 623 Tremont St;
🚈 Back Bay) This little shoebox of a store lives
up to its name, offering a 'motley' array of
hip clothing, funny books and novelty gift
items. The ever-changing product line includes supercomfy, clever T-shirts and true-
blue vintage Boston sports-fan gear. You
absolutely do not need anything that is on
offer at Motley, but you will absolutely find
something that you *have* to own.

Uniform CLOTHING
(Map p50; www.uniformboston.com; 511 Tremont St;
⊗ Tue-Sun; 🚈 Back Bay) With its cool collection
of men's casual wear, Uniform caters to all
the metrosexuals in this hipster 'hood. Guys

ANTIQUING ON BEACON HILL

There was a time when Charles St was lined with antique shops and nothing else: some
historians claim the country's antique trade began right here on Beacon Hill. Many vestiges remain from those days of old. A few of our favorites:

Eugene Galleries (Map p40; www.eugenegalleries.com; 76 Charles St; ⊗ 11am-6pm Mon-
Sat, noon-6pm Sun; 🚈 Charles/MGH) A tiny shop with a remarkable selection of antique
prints and maps, especially focusing on old Boston.

Marika's Antique Shop (Map p40; 130 Charles St; 🚈 Charles/MGH) A treasure trove of
jewelry, silver and porcelain.

Twentieth Century Ltd (Map p40; www.boston-vintagejewelry.com; 73 Charles St;
🚈 Charles/MGH) Not just jewelry, but vintage costume jewelry made by the great designers of yesteryear.

leave this place decked out in designers like Ben Sherman and Penguin, with Freitag bag slung over shoulder. Hot men looking good in hot fashions: it's very South End.

Bromfield Art Gallery GALLERY
(Map p50; www.bromfieldgallery.com; 450 Harrison Ave; ⊙noon-5pm Wed-Sat; TTufts Medical Center) The city's oldest cooperative, this South End gallery hosts solo shows by its members, as well as occasional visiting artists. The work runs the gamut in terms of media, but you can always expect something challenging or entertaining.

Back Bay

If you prefer to go shopping in a climate-controlled setting, there are two vast, light-filled shopping malls replete with pricey shops:

➡ **Shops at Prudential Center** (Map p50; www.prudentialcenter.com; 800 Boylston St; ⊙10am-9pm; ☎; TPrudential)

➡ **Copley Place** (Map p50; www.simon.com; 100 Huntington Ave; ⊙10am-8pm Mon-Sat, noon-6pm Sun; TBack Bay)

Life is Good CLOTHING, GIFTS
(Map p50; www.lifeisgood.com; 285 Newbury St; THynes) Life *is* good for this locally designed brand of T-shirts, backpacks and other gear. Styles depict the fun-loving stick figure Jake engaged in guitar playing, dog walking, coffee drinking, mountain climbing and just about every other good-vibe diversion you might enjoy. Jake's activity may vary, but his theme is constant.

Converse SHOES, CLOTHING
(Map p50; www.converse.com; 348 Newbury St; THynes) Converse started making shoes right up the road in Malden, Massachusetts way back in 1908. Chuck Taylor joined the 'team' in the 1920s and the rest is history. This retail store (one of three in the country) has an incredible selection of sneakers, denim and other gear.

The iconic shoes come in all colors and patterns; you can even design your own at the in-store customization area.

Newbury Comics MUSIC
(Map p50; www.newburycomics.com; 332 Newbury St; THynes) Any outlet of this local chain is usually jam-packed with teenagers clad in black and sporting multiple piercings. Apparently these kids know where to find cheap CDs and DVDs. The newest alt-rock

and the latest movies are on sale here, along with comic books, rock posters and other silly gags. No wonder everyone is having such a wicked good time.

Trident Booksellers & Café BOOKS
(Map p50; www.tridentbookscafe.com; 338 Newbury St; ⊙9am-midnight; ☎; THynes) Pick out a pile of books and retreat to a quiet corner of the cafe to decide which ones you really want to buy. You'll come away enriched, as Trident's stock tends toward New Age titles. But there's a little bit of everything here, as the 'hippie turned back-to-the-lander, turned Buddhist, turned entrepreneur' owners know how to keep their customers happy.

Ibex CLOTHING
(Map p50; www.retail.ibex.com/boston; 303 Newbury St; THynes) Based in snowy, cold Vermont, Ibex makes outdoor clothing from soft, warm, breathable merino wool. It's not the itchy stuff you remember – this wool is plush and pleasurable, thanks to the fineness of the fiber. Categorized as base layer, midlayer or outerlayer, the clothing is guaranteed to keep you cozy, even through the coldest, snowiest Vermont winter. Bonus: it looks good too.

Hempest CLOTHING, HOMEWARES
(Map p50; www.hempest.com; 207 Newbury St; ⊙11am-8pm Mon-Sat, noon-6pm Sun; TCopley) All of the products at the Hempest are made from cannabis hemp, the botanical cousin of marijuana. It's all on the up and up: men's and women's clothing, organic soaps and lotions, and fun home-furnishing items.

These folks argue that hemp is a rapidly renewable and versatile resource that is economically and environmentally beneficial... if only it were legal to grow it in the United States.

Marathon Sports SPORTS
(Map p50; www.marathonsports.com; 671 Boylston St; TCopley) Specializing in running gear, this place could not have a better location: it overlooks the finish line of the Boston Marathon. It's known for attentive customer service, as staff work hard to make sure you are getting a shoe that fits. Besides the latest styles and technologies, Marathon also carries a line of retro running shoes.

Society of Arts & Crafts HANDICRAFTS
(Map p50; www.societyofcrafts.org; 175 Newbury St; ⊙10am-6pm Mon-Sat; TCopley) This prestigious

nonprofit gallery was founded in 1897. With retail space downstairs and exhibit space upstairs, the society promotes emerging and established artists and encourages innovative handicrafts. The collection changes constantly, but you'll find weaving, leather, ceramics, glassware, furniture and other hand-crafted items.

Eastern Mountain Sports
SPORTS, OUTDOOR EQUIPMENT

(Map p50; www.ems.com; 855 Boylston St; T Hynes) EMS is all over the east coast, but it began right here in Boston, when a couple of rock climbers started selling equipment they couldn't buy elsewhere. Now this tree-hugger retailer sells not only rock-climbing equipment, but also camping gear, kayaks, snowboards and all the special apparel you need to engage in the aforementioned activities.

Cambridge

★ Ward Maps
MAPS, SOUVENIRS

(www.wardmaps.com; 1735 Massachusetts Ave; T Porter) If you're into maps, you'll be into Ward Maps. They have an incredible collection of original antique and reproduction maps. What's more, they print the maps on coffee mugs, mouse pads, journals and greeting cards, creating unique and personal gifts. Some stuff is ready-made, or you can custom order. Located midway between Harvard and Porter.

Cardullo's Gourmet Shop
FOOD & DRINK

(Map p54; www.cardullos.com; 6 Brattle St; ⏰ 9am-9pm Mon-Sat, 10am-7pm Sun; T Harvard) We've never seen so many goodies packed into such a small space. You'll find every sort of imported edible your heart desires, from caviar to chocolate. The excellent selection of New England products is a good source of souvenirs.

Cambridge Artists' Cooperative
HANDICRAFTS

(Map p54; www.cambridgeartistscoop.com; 59a Church St; T Harvard) Owned and operated by Cambridge artists, this three-floor gallery displays an ever-changing exhibit of their work. The pieces are crafty – handmade jewelry, woven scarves, leather products and pottery. The craftspeople double as sales staff, so you may get to meet the creative force behind your souvenir.

Garage
MALL

(Map p54; 36 John F Kennedy St; ⏰ 10am-9pm; T Harvard) This gritty mini-mall in the midst of Harvard Sq houses an eclectic collection of shops. Highlights include an outlet of Newbury Comics, as well as the crazy costume store Hootenanny, and an edgy urban boutique and skate shop, Proletariat. Also, for hungry people, a sort of upscale food court.

ℹ Information

EMERGENCY
Ambulance, Police & Fire (✆ 911)
City of Boston Police Headquarters (✆ 617-343-4200; cnr Ruggles & Tremont Sts; T Ruggles)
Road & Traffic Conditions (✆ 511, 617-986-5511)

INTERNET ACCESS
If you are traveling without a computer, you can log on at the following locations:
Boston Public Library (www.bpl.org; 700 Boylston St; ⏰ 9am-9pm Mon-Thu, to 5pm Fri & Sat

---

SECOND-HAND ROSE

The best clothes are not always new clothes. If you appreciate high-quality duds, you can give them a second chance by shopping at one of Boston's excellent consignment shops.

Closet, Inc (Map p50; www.closetboston.com; 175 Newbury St; T Copley) Feels like a fashion maven's overstuffed closet.

Raspberry Beret (www.raspberryberet.us; 1704 Massachusetts Ave, Cambridge; T Porter) Contemporary consignment and awesome vintage pieces.

Oona's Experienced Clothing (Map p54; www.oonasboston.com; 1210 Massachusetts Ave; ⏰ 11am-8pm; T Harvard) Kitschy clothes from all eras.

Second Time Around (Map p50; www.secondtimearound.net; 176 Newbury St; T Copley) A gold mine of barely worn designer clothing (including lots of denim). Outlets all around Boston and Cambridge.

BOOKSTORES OF HARVARD SQUARE

Harvard Sq has long been famous for its used and independent bookstores. There are not as many as there used to be, but there are still enough to fill up your afternoon with browsing. Some of the more unusual bookstores:

Grolier Poetry Bookshop (Map p54; www.grolierpoetrybookshop.org; 6 Plympton St; ☺11am-7pm Tue & Wed, to 6pm Thu-Sat; Ⓣ Harvard) Founded in 1927, Grolier is the oldest – and perhaps the most famous – poetry bookstore in the USA.

Harvard Bookstore (Map p54; www.harvard.com; 1256 Massachusetts Ave; ☺9am-11pm Mon-Sat, 10am-10pm Sun; Ⓣ Harvard) The university community's favorite place to come to browse (though not officially affiliated with the university).

Raven Used Books (Map p54; www.ravencambridge.com; 52 John F Kennedy St; ☺10am-9pm Mon-Sat, 11am-8pm Sun; Ⓣ Harvard) Its 16,000 books focus on scholarly titles, especially in the liberal arts.

Schoenhof's Foreign Books (Map p54; www.schoenhofs.com; 76A Mt Auburn St; ☺10am-8pm Mon-Sat, to 6pm Sun; Ⓣ Harvard) Since 1856, Schoenhof's has been providing Boston's foreign-language-speaking literati with reading material in some 700 languages.

BOSTON INFORMATION

year-round, 1-5pm Sun Oct-May; 🛜; Ⓣ Copley) Internet access free for 15-minute intervals. Or get a visitor courtesy card at the circulation desk and sign up for one hour of free terminal time. Arrive first thing in the morning to avoid long waits.

Wired Puppy (www.wiredpuppy.com; 250 Newbury St; ☺6:30am-7:30pm; 🛜; Ⓣ Hynes) Free wireless access and free computer use in case you don't have your own. This is also a comfortable, cozy place to just come and drink coffee.

MEDIA

Bay Windows (www.baywindows.com) Serves the gay and lesbian community.

Boston Globe (www.boston.com) One of two major daily newspapers, the *Globe* publishes an extensive Calendar section every Thursday and the daily Sidekick, both of which include entertainment options.

Boston Herald (www.bostonherald.com) The more right-wing daily, competing with the *Globe*; has its own Scene section published every Friday.

Open Media Boston (www.openmediaboston.org) An alternative voice for local news and events.

Boston Magazine (www.bostonmagazine.com) The city's monthly glossy magazine.

Improper Bostonian (www.improper.com) A sassy biweekly distributed free from sidewalk dispenser boxes.

MEDICAL SERVICES

CVS Pharmacy (www.cvs.com) Cambridge (1426 Massachusetts Ave; ☺24hr; Ⓣ Harvard); Back Bay (587 Boylston St; ☺24hr; Ⓣ Copley)

Massachusetts General Hospital (☎617-726-2000; www.massgeneral.org; 55 Fruit St; ☺24hr; Ⓣ Charles/MGH) Arguably the city's biggest and best hospital. It can often refer you to smaller clinics and crisis hotlines.

POST

Main Post Office (www.usps.com; 25 Dorchester Ave; ☺6am-midnight; Ⓣ South Station)

Post Office (Map p54; 125 Mt Auburn St, Cambridge; ☺7:30am-6:30pm Mon-Fri, 7:30am-3:30pm Sat; Ⓣ Harvard)

TOURIST INFORMATION

Appalachian Mountain Club Headquarters (AMC; Map p40; www.outdoors.org; 5 Joy St; ☺8:30am-5pm Mon-Fri; Ⓣ Park St) *The* resource for outdoor activities in Boston and throughout New England.

Cambridge Visitor Information Kiosk (Map p54; www.cambridge-usa.org; Harvard Sq; ☺9am-5pm Mon-Fri, 1-5pm Sat & Sun; Ⓣ Harvard) Detailed information on current Cambridge happenings and self-guided walking tours.

Greater Boston Convention & Visitors Bureau (GBCVB; www.bostonusa.com) Boston Common (Map p40; ☎617-426-3115; 148 Tremont St; ☺8:30am-5pm Mon-Fri, 9am-5pm Sat & Sun; Ⓣ Park St); Prudential Center (GBCVB; ☎888-5515, 536-4100; www.bostonusa.com; suite 105, 2 Copley Pl; Ⓣ Back Bay or South End)

National Park Service Visitor Center (NPS; www.nps.gov/bost; State ST) Downtown (Map p40; Faneuil Hall; ☺9am-5pm; Ⓣ Haymarket); Charlestown (Bldg 5, Charlestown Navy Yard; ☺9am-5pm; 🚌 93 from Haymarket, ⛴ F4 from Long Wharf)

WI-FI ACCESS

Wireless access is free at most hotels and many cafes. Look for the 🛜 icon in the listings. The city of Boston provides free wi-fi in the area around City Hall Plaza and Faneuil Hall, as well as the Rose Kennedy Greenway parks. For a long list of free wi-fi locations around the city, see www.openwifispots.com.

WEBSITES

www.bostoncentral.com A fantastic resource for families, with listings for activities, outings, shopping and restaurants that are good for kids.

www.boston-online.com An offbeat source of local news and information; includes such important resources as a glossary of 'Bostonese' and a guide to public restrooms in the city.

www.cityofboston.gov Official website for the city government.

www.designmuseumboston.org See what this pop-up museum is planning for public space around town.

www.sonsofsamhorn.net Dedicated to discussion of all things Red Sox.

www.universalhub.com Bostonians talk to each other about whatever is on their mind (sometimes nothing).

Getting There & Away

AIR

In East Boston, Logan International Airport (p438) has five separate terminals that are connected by a frequent shuttle bus (11). Public information booths are located in the baggage claim areas of terminals A, B, C and E.

BOAT

Boats operate from mid-May to mid-October:

Bay State Cruise Company (www.boston-ptown.com; Commonwealth Pier, Seaport Blvd; round trip adult/child $85/62; 🚊 SL1 or SL2, 🚆 South Station) Bay State Cruise Co operate ferries between Boston and Provincetown. The 90-minute trip runs three or four times a day.

Boston Harbor Cruises (Map p40; www.bostonharborcruises.com; 1 Long Wharf; round trip adult/child/senior $85/62/73; 🚆 Aquarium) Boston Harbor Cruises operate ferries between Boston and Provincetown. The 90-minute trip runs once, twice or three times a day.

Salem Ferry (Map p40; www.salemferry.com; Central Wharf; round trip adult/child $27/22; 🚆 Aquarium) A commuter service between Boston Central Wharf and Salem. The boat docks in Salem, leaving early enough so commuters are in Boston before 8am on weekdays. Boats run four to six times daily; check the time of the last return to Boston.

BUS

For intercity travel, Boston has a modern, indoor, user-friendly **bus station** (700 Atlantic Ave) at Summer St, conveniently adjacent to the South Station.

Greyhound (www.greyhound.com) buses travel across the country. A seven-day advance purchase on one-way tickets often beats all other quoted fares.

All of these regional lines operate out of the South Station bus station:

C&J Trailways (www.ridecj.com; 🛜) Provides daily service to Newburyport, Massachusetts, as well as Portsmouth, Dover and Durham, New Hampshire. Kids free when accompanied by a full-paying adult.

Concord Coach Lines (www.concordcoachlines.com; 🛜) Plies routes from Boston to New Hampshire (Concord, Manchester, and as far up as Conway and Berlin) and Maine (Portland, Bangor and Augusta, as well as coastal Maine).

Megabus (www.megabus.com; 🛜) Goes up and down the East Coast, south to Washington, DC and north to Portland, Maine and Burlington, Vermont. One-dollar tickets are very limited, but with minimal foresight you can get your fare for $10 or less.

Peter Pan Bus Lines (www.peterpanbus.com) Serves 52 destinations in the northeast, as far north as Concord, New Hampshire, and as far south as Washington, DC, as well as Western Massachusetts. Check online for $1 deals to New York City.

Plymouth & Brockton Street Railway Co (📞508-746-0378; www.p-b.com) Provides frequent service to the South Shore and to most towns on Cape Cod, including Hyannis and Provincetown.

CAR & MOTORCYCLE

Two major highways cut through Boston: the Massachusetts Turnpike (I-90) heading east and west; and the Central Artery (I-93) heading north and south.

The Mass Pike, as I-90 is lovingly called, is a toll road that terminates in East Boston at Logan Airport. In downtown Boston, the highway runs through the Ted Williams Tunnel, where it intersects with the Central Artery somewhere below Chinatown. Then the Pike reemerges above ground, continuing west through the Back Bay, and exiting Boston and heading to Western Massachusetts.

The Central Artery starts south of the city in Neponset (where it intersects with I-95). It traverses Boston via the Tip O'Neill Tunnel (which spans downtown) and the Zakim Bunker

Hill Bridge (which spans the Charles River). There are five exits in downtown Boston, including the intersection with I-90, then the artery continues to the North Shore of Massachusetts and on to New Hampshire.

A few sample distances from Boston to various points around New England:

DESTINATION	DISTANCE (MILES)	DURATION (HR)
Burlington, VT	220	4½
New York City, NY	227	4½
Portland, ME	108	2¼
Portsmouth, NH	57	1
Providence, RI	45	1

TRAIN

Amtrak (✆ 800-872-7245; www.amtrak.com; South Station) trains leave from South Station, located on the corner of Atlantic Ave and Summer St, but also stop at Back Bay station on Dartmouth St. Service to New York City's Penn Station takes four to 4½ hours, while the high-speed *Acela Express* train (3½ hours) is a lot more expensive; reservations are required. Amtrak's online 'Rail Sale' program offers substantial discounts on many reserved tickets.

MBTA commuter rail (✆ 800-392-6100, 617-222-3200; www.mbta.com) trains heading west and north of the city, including to Concord, leave from bustling North Station on Causeway St. Catch the 'beach trains' to Salem, Gloucester and Rockport here. Trains heading south, including to Plymouth, leave from South Station.

ℹ Getting Around

TO/FROM THE AIRPORT

Downtown Boston is just a few miles from Logan International Airport and is accessible by bus, subway, taxi and water shuttle.

Bus The Silver Line is the 'bus rapid transit service' operated by the **MBTA** (www.mbta. com; per ride $1.50-2; ⏱5:30am-12:30am). It travels between Logan International Airport and South Station (which is the railway station, as well as a Red Line T station), with stops in the Seaport District. Silver Line buses pick up directly at the airport terminals. This is the most convenient way to get into the city if you are staying in the Seaport District, Theater District or South End, or anywhere along the Red Line.

If you're heading straight out of town, the regional bus lines (Concord Coach Lines, Peter Pan and P&B) operate **Logan Direct** (✆ 800-235-6426; adult/child $10/5), which provides direct bus service between Logan airport and the bus station.

Subway The MBTA subway (p86), known as 'the T', is another fast and cheap way to reach the city from the airport. From any terminal, take a free, well-marked shuttle bus (22 or 33) to the Blue Line T station called Airport and you'll be downtown within 30 minutes.

Taxi Taxis are plentiful but pricey; traffic snarls can translate into a $25 fare to downtown.

Water Shuttle Several water shuttles operate between Logan and the waterfront district in Boston, including City Water Taxi (p86; adult/child $10/free) and Rowes Wharf Water Taxi (p86; one way/round trip $10/17).

BICYCLE

In recent years, Boston has made vast improvements in its infrastructure for cyclists, including painting miles of bicycle lanes, upgrading bike facilities on and around public transportation and implementing a cutting-edge bike-share program.

Hubway (www.thehubway.com; 30min free, 60/90/120min $2/6/14; ⏱24hr) Boston's brand new bike-share program (sponsored by New Balance, as you will be repeatedly reminded) is the Hubway. There are now 60 Hubway stations around town (as well as in Brookline, Cambridge and Somerville), stocked with 600 bikes that are available for short-term loan. Purchase a temporary membership at any bicycle kiosk, then pay by the half-hour for

---

ℹ GETTING TO NYC

The infamous 'Chinatown Buses' originated as an inexpensive way for Chinese workers to travel to and from jobs. They offered super-cheap tickets between Boston and New York, traveling from Chinatown to Chinatown. Young, savvy travelers caught wind of the bargain transportation, and the phenomenon began to spread. It was crowded and confusing and probably not that safe, but it sure was cheap.

Some years down the line, the feds have finally shut down most of the Chinatown services between Boston and New York, due to safety violations. But the competition has spurred a few other companies to offer better service and safety records on the four-hour journey, while prices remain blissfully low.

➡ Yo! Bus (p438) is a Greyhound subsidiary offering six daily buses, with wi-fi.

➡ Go Buses (p438) has six daily bus departures to Manhattan from Cambridge.

the use of the bikes (free under 30 minutes). Return the bike to any station in the vicinity of your destination. Check the website for a map of Hubway stations.

The Hubway pricing is designed so a bike ride can substitute for a cab ride (eg to make a one-way trip or run an errand), not for leisurely riding or long trips (in which case you should rent a bike; see p56).

BOAT

In addition to these water taxi services, Boston Harbor Cruises (p84) operates a commuter service to Charlestown Navy Yard.

City Water Taxi (www.citywatertaxi.com; ⊙8am-10pm Mon-Sat, 10am-8pm Sun) Makes on-demand taxi stops at about 15 waterfront points, including the airport, the Barking Crab, the Seaport District, Long Wharf, Sargents Wharf in the North End and the Charlestown Navy Yard. Call to order a pick-up.

Rowes Wharf Water Taxi (Map p40; ☑617-406-8584; www.roweswharfwatertaxi.com; Rowes Wharf; ⊙7am-10pm Mon-Sat, to 8pm Sun Apr-Nov, 7am-7pm daily Dec-Mar) Serves Rowes Wharf near the Boston Harbor Hotel, the Moakley Federal Courthouse on the Fort Point Channel and the World Trade Center in the Seaport District. Taxis also go to the North End and Charlestown for a higher fare.

CAR & MOTORCYCLE

With any luck you won't have to drive in or around Boston. Not only are the streets a maze of confusion, choked with construction and legendary traffic jams, but Boston drivers use their own set of rules.

Two highways skirt the Charles River: Storrow Dr runs along the Boston side and Memorial Dr (more scenic) parallels it on the Cambridge side. There are exits off Storrow Dr for Kenmore Square, Back Bay and Government Center. Both Storrow Dr and Memorial Dr are accessible from the Mass Pike and the I-93.

Car Rental All major car rental agencies are represented at the airport; free shuttle vans will take you to their nearby pick-up counters. When returning rental cars, you'll find gas stations on US 1, north of the airport.

Parking A pair of Back Bay parking spaces recently sold for more than half a million dollars. The explanation is simple economics: supply and demand. Since on-street parking is limited, you could end up paying $25 to $35 daily to park in a lot. Rates are generally more affordable after 4pm or 5pm, when you can usually park for about $10 and leave your car until morning.

Most Boston hotels offer parking for $15 to $30 a day. Some museums, restaurants and venues offer discounted rates at local parking facilities. That said, it may be easier (and cheaper) to get around town using public transportation and taxis. See **BestParking.com** (www.boston. bestparking.com) to compare rates at locations around the city.

PUBLIC TRANSPORTATION
Bus

The **MBTA** (☑617-222-5215; www.mbta.com; per ride $1.50-2) operates bus routes within the city. These can be difficult to figure out for the short-term visitor, but schedules are posted on the website and at some bus stops along the routes. The fare for a regular bus is $2 if you pay in cash and $1.50 if you pay with a Charlie Card. The Silver Line bus fare to Logan airport is $2-$2.50 depending on the kind of ticket.

Subway

The **MBTA** (☑800-392-6100, 617-222-3200; www.mbta.com; per ride $2-2.50; ⊙5:30am-

---

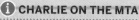

ⓘ CHARLIE ON THE MTA

Did he ever return?
No, he never returned
And his fate is still unlearned
He may ride forever
'Neath the streets of Boston
He's the man who never returned.

Immortalized by the Kingston Trio, Charlie's sad story was that he could not get off the Boston T because he did not have the exit fare.

Charlie has been immortalized – yet again – by the MBTA's fare system: the Charlie Card. The plastic cards are available from attendants at any T station. Once you have a card, you can add money at the automated fare machines; at the turnstile you will be charged $2 per ride.

The system is designed to favor commuters and cardholders. If you do not request a Charlie Card, you can purchase a paper fare card from the machine, but the turnstile will charge you $2.50 per ride. Similarly, those with a Charlie Card pay $1.50 to ride the bus, while with cash you pay $2.

BRING YOUR BIKE ON THE T

You can bring bikes on the T, the bus and the commuter rail for no additional fare. Bikes are not allowed on Green Line trains or Silver Line buses, nor are they allowed on any trains during rush hour (7am to 10am and 4pm to 7pm, Monday to Friday). Bikes are not permitted inside buses, but most MBTA buses have bicycle racks on the outside.

12:30am) operates the USA's oldest subway, which was built in 1897. It's known locally as 'the T' and has four lines – Red, Blue, Green and Orange – that radiate out from the principal downtown stations. These are Park St (which has an information booth), Downtown Crossing, Government Center and State. When traveling away from any of these stations, you are heading outbound.

The T operates from approximately 5:30am to 12:30am. The last Red Line train rolls through Park St around 12:30am, but check the postings at individual stations for exact times.

Subway fares:
➡ Buy a paper fare card ($2.50 per ride) or a Charlie Card ($2 per ride) at any station.

➡ Kids under 11 ride for free.

➡ Tourist passes with unlimited travel (on subway, bus or water shuttle) are available for periods of one week ($18) and one day ($11).

➡ For longer stays, you can buy a monthly pass allowing unlimited use of the subway and local bus ($70).

➡ Passes may be purchased at the following T stations: Park St, Government Center, Back Bay, Alewife, Copley, Quincy Adams, Harvard, North Station, South Station, Hynes and Airport.

TAXI

Cabs are plentiful (although you may have to walk to a major hotel to find one) but expensive. Rates are determined by the meter, which calculates miles. Expect to pay about $10 to $20 between most tourist points within the city limits, without much traffic. You may have trouble hailing a cab during bad weather and between 3:30pm and 6:30pm weekdays. Again, head to major hotels.

Recommended taxi companies:

Chill Out First Class Cab (✆ 617-212-3763; www.chilloutfirstclasscab.com)

Planet Tran (✆ 617-756-8876; www.planettran. com)

Top Cab & City Cab (✆ 617-536-5100, 617-266-4800; www.topcab.us)

Around Boston

781, 978, 508 / POP 4.6 MILLION

Best Places to Eat

➡ Concord Cheese Shop (p96)

➡ Life Alive (p99)

➡ Plum Island Grille (p116)

➡ Roy Moore Lobster Co (p111)

➡ JT Farnham's (p114)

➡ Carmen's Cafe Nicole (p121)

Best Places to Stay

➡ Inn at Castle Hill (p113)

➡ Morning Glory (p104)

➡ Accommodations of Rocky Neck (p108)

➡ Blue (p116)

Why Go?

Boston may be the state capital, but it's not the only town in Massachusetts with traveler appeal. Destinations with rich histories, vibrant cultural scenes and unique events merit a visit. Easily accessible from Boston, most of these are ideal day-trip destinations.

From the moment the Pilgrims stepped ashore at Plymouth Rock, this area was on the map. The towns that surround Boston represent every aspect of New England history – colonial, revolutionary, maritime, literary and industrial.

Inspired by intriguing events of the past and spectacular seascapes in the present, writers, artists and filmmakers continue to enrich the region's cultural life. Miles of pristine coastline draw beachcombers and sunbathers. Hikers and cyclists, canoeists and kayakers, bird-watchers and whale-watchers have myriad opportunities to engage with the local active lifestyle.

When to Go
Boston

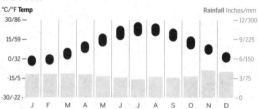

Apr Lexington and Concord recreate the battles that launched the American War of Independence.

Summer North Shore beaches are irresistible in July and August, with hot sun and cold sea.

Fall Halloween is a hoot in Salem in October; while Plymouth hosts Thanksgiving in November.

1 Cycling the **Minuteman Commuter Bikeway** (p92) from Cambridge to Lexington

2 Continuing on to Concord for a cooling dip in **Walden Pond** (p97)

3 Traversing **Minute Man National Historic Park** (p91) and recalling the beginnings of American independence

4 Admiring the collection of treasures from around the world at the **Peabody Essex Museum** (p101) in Salem

5 Frolicking in the waves at **Crane Beach** (p113) in Ipswich

6 Experiencing the realities of Pilgrim life at **Plimoth Plantation** (p119)

7 Enjoying the cultural diversity at the **Lowell Folk Festival** (p99)

History

The original inhabitants of Massachusetts belonged to several different Algonquian tribes, including the Wampanoag and the Pennacook. After running aground off the coast of Cape Cod, the Pilgrims established their permanent settlement at Plymouth Colony in 1620. The Puritans followed them in 1628, establishing the Massachusetts Bay Colony on the sites of present-day Boston and Salem. In the following years, daring souls in search of religious freedom or economic opportunity would settle right along the coast of Massachusetts. When these colonies finally broke free from Mother England, the War of Independence started with the Battles of Lexington and Concord.

Eastern Massachusetts played a crucial role in the country's economic development. In the early 19th century, during the age of sails and whales, towns such as Salem, Newburyport and New Bedford amassed great wealth from maritime trade, shipbuilding and whaling. At the same time, Lowell was an exemplary textile town, instigating the industrial revolution. Villages on Cape Ann – especially Gloucester – were leaders in the fishing industry.

With the decline of these sectors in the 20th century, the area has turned to tourism to pick up the economic slack, with varying degrees of success. In an attempt to revitalize their aging city centers, Salem, Lowell and New Bedford have created National Historic Sites, turning old industrial buildings into museums and opening restaurants and cafes to cater to tourists. Gloucester, too, touts its working waterfront as a heritage center, where visitors can book a whale-watching tour or learn about marine life.

National & State Parks

The region around Boston includes several diverse sites, significant to the region's revolutionary, mercantile and industrial past, that have been designated as National Historical Parks by the National Park Service (NPS). The Minute Man National Historical Park incorporates Battle Rd between Lexington and Concord, where the first skirmishes of the American Revolution developed into full-blown fighting. This area remains much as it was 200 years ago. Other National Historical Parks are less pristine, but still capture a significant piece of the nation's history. They include the Lowell National Historical Park, Salem Maritime National Historic Site and the New Bedford Whaling National Historical Park.

State, county and private efforts have made great strides toward limiting intrusive development and preserving ecosystems, especially on the North Shore: much of Cape Ann is protected, as are vast swaths of land further north. Sandy Point is a lovely state park, while Halibut Point Reservation, the Crane Wildlife Refuge and Parker River Wildlife Refuge are managed by the ever-attentive Trustees of Reservations. Walden Pond is an inspirational, wonderful natural resource, also managed by the Commonwealth of Massachusetts, while the acres of undisturbed woods around it are protected by the efforts of private institutions. Just a few miles south of Boston, the Blue Hills Reservation is the little-known but much-appreciated result of the Massachusetts Department of Conservation and Recreation.

❶ Getting There & Away

Many sights around Boston are accessible by the **Massachusetts Bay Transportation Authority commuter rail** (MBTA; www.mbta.com). Trains depart from Boston's North Station to destinations on the North Shore, including a line to Gloucester and Rockport, and another line to Newburyport. Salem is served by both these train lines. North Station is also the departure point for trains heading west to Concord and Lowell. Plymouth is served by trains departing from South Station in Boston. Other destinations are reached by bus, but it's preferable to use a private vehicle to get the most from a trip out of the city.

WEST OF BOSTON

Some places might boast about starting a revolution, but Boston's western suburbs can actually make the claim that two revolutions were launched here. Most famously, the American Revolution – the celebrated War of Independence that spawned a nation – started with encounters on the town greens at Lexington and Concord. And the industrial revolution – the economic transformation that would turn this new nation from agriculture to manufacturing – began in the textile mills of Lowell.

Lexington

POP 31,400

This upscale suburb, about 18 miles from Boston's center, is a bustling village of white churches and historic taverns, with tour buses surrounding the village green. Here, the skirmish between patriots and British troops jump-started the War of Independence. Each year on April 19, historians and patriots don their 18th-century costumes and grab their rifles for an elaborate reenactment of the events of 1775.

While this history is celebrated and preserved, it is in stark contrast to the peaceful, even staid, community that is Lexington today. If you stray more than a few blocks from the green, you could be in Anywhere, USA, with few reminders that this is where it all started. Nonetheless, it is a pleasant enough Anywhere, USA, with restaurants and shops lining the main drag, and impressive Georgian architecture anchoring either end.

⊙ Sights

Massachusetts Ave cuts through the center of Lexington. The Battle Green is at the northwestern end of the business district, at the corner of Mass Ave and Waltham St.

Battle Green   HISTORIC SITE
(Massachusetts Ave) The historic Battle Green is where the skirmish between patriots and British troops jumpstarted the War of Independence. The Lexington Minuteman Statue (crafted by Henry Hudson Kitson in 1900) stands guard at the southeast end of Battle Green, honoring the bravery of the 77 minutemen who met the British here in 1775, and the eight who died.

The Parker Boulder, named for their commander, marks the spot where the minutemen faced a force almost 10 times their strength. It is inscribed with Parker's instructions to his troops: 'Stand your ground. Don't fire unless fired upon. But if

they mean to have a war, let it begin here.' Across the street, history buffs have preserved the Old Belfry that sounded the alarm signaling the start of the revolution.

**Lexington Historic
Society Houses**   HISTORIC SITES
(www.lexingtonhistory.org; 1 bldg adult/child $7/5; 3 bldgs $12/8) Facing the green next to the visitor center, Buckman Tavern (www.lexingtonhistory.org; 1 Bedford Rd; adult/child $7/5; ⊗10am-4pm Apr-Oct), built in 1709, was the headquarters of the minutemen. The tense hours between the midnight call to arms and the dawn arrival of the Redcoats were spent here. The tavern and inn also served as a field hospital where the wounded were treated after the fight. Today it is a museum of Colonial life, with instructive tours given every half-hour.

The Lexington Historical Society also maintains two historic houses. Munroe Tavern (www.lexingtonhistory.com; 1332 Massachusetts Ave, Lexington; adult/child 1 house $7/5, all houses $12/8 ; ⊗noon-4pm Jun-Oct), built in 1695, was used by the British as a command post and field infirmary. It's about seven blocks southeast of the green. The Hancock-Clarke House (www.lexingtonhistory.org; 36 Hancock St, Lexington; adult/child 1 house $7/5, all houses $12/8; ⊗10am-4pm Sat-Sun Apr-May, daily Jun-Oct), built in 1698, was the parsonage of the Reverend Jonas Clarke and the destination of Paul Revere on April 19, 1775.

Minute Man National Historic Park   PARK
(www.nps.gov/mima; 250 North Great Rd, Lincoln; ⊗9am-5pm Apr-Oct, 9am-4pm Nov; 🐾) **FREE** Two miles west of Lexington center, the route that British troops followed to Concord has been designated the Minute Man

AROUND BOSTON LEXINGTON

PATRIOTS' DAY

The Patriots' Day celebration in Lexington starts early – really early. On the third Monday in April, as dawn breaks, local history buffs are assembled on the village green, some decked out in 'redcoats' while others sport the scruffy attire of minutemen, firearms in hand, ready to reenact the fateful battle that kicked off the American War of Independence.

Later in the day, the conflict at the Old North Bridge in Concord is reenacted, as are skirmishes at Meriam's Corner and Hartwell Tavern in Minute Man National Historic Park. Spectators can witness the arrival of Paul Revere in Lexington, as well as his capture along Battle Rd.

Massachusetts is one of only two states in the USA that recognize Patriots' Day as a public holiday. This is where the action went down on April 19, 1775. And this is where it goes down every year on the third weekend of April. For a complete schedule of events, visit Battle Road (www.battleroad.org).

National Historic Park. The visitors center at the eastern end of the park shows an informative multimedia presentation depicting Paul Revere's ride and the ensuing battles.

Within the park, Battle Rd is a five-mile wooded trail that connects the historic sites related to the battles – from Meriam's Corner, where gunfire erupted while British soldiers were retreating, to the Paul Revere capture site. Minute Man National Historical Park is about 2 miles west of Lexington center on Rte 2A.

🏃 Activities

★ Minuteman
Commuter Bikeway   CYCLING
The Minuteman Commuter Bikeway follows an old railroad right-of-way from near the Alewife Red Line subway terminus in Cambridge, through Arlington to Lexington and Bedford, a total distance of about 14 miles. From Lexington center, you can also ride along Massachusetts Ave to Rte 2A, which parallels the Battle Rd trail, and eventually leads into Concord center.

👉 Tours

Liberty Ride   BUS TOUR
(www.libertyride.us; adult/child $25/10; ⊙ 10am-4pm Sat-Sun Apr-May, daily Jun-Oct) The 90-minute bus route covers the major minuteman sites in Lexington and Concord, as well as some of Concord's places of literary importance. Your ticket includes parking as well as admission to the three historical houses. Departs from the Lexington Visitors Center.

🍴 Eating & Drinking

More than a dozen eateries lie within a five-minute walk of Battle Green.

Via Lago Café   CAFE $
(www.vialagocatering.com; 1845 Massachusetts Ave; mains $5-8; ⊙ breakfast, lunch & dinner Mon-Sat; 🖼) This cafe has high ceilings, intimate tables, a scent of fresh-roasted coffee and a great deli case. You'll often see cyclists in here kicking back with the daily paper, a cup of exotic java or tea, and a sandwich of roasted turkey, Swiss and sprouts.

Rancatore's Ice Cream   ICE CREAM $
(www.rancs.com; 1752 Massachusetts Ave; ⊙ 10am-11pm; 🖼) Cool off with a scoop of homemade ice cream or sorbet from this family-run

place. Some of Ranc's flavors inspire worshipful devotion, such as bourbon butter pecan and classic coconut. The hot fudge sundaes are also legendary.

Nourish   MODERN AMERICAN $$
(www.nourishlexington.com; 1727 Massachusetts Ave; lunch $10-18, dinner $15-23; ⊙ lunch & dinner; 🖼) 🌱 The goal is to satisfy all comers – vegans, vegetarians, meat-eaters – and to do so using locally sourced and organically produced ingredients whenever possible. The result is a diverse and delicious menu, with items ranging from quinoa salad to sirloin steak tips. There's a burger here to suit every taste, plus local beers and wines.

Ride Studio Cafe   CAFE
(www.ridestudiocafe.com; 1720 Massachusetts Ave; ⊙ 7am-6pm Mon-Fri, 8am-5pm Sat & Sun) Part bike store, part cafe, this is a novel concept in retail and coffee. Come hang out with other cyclists, browse the gear and drink invigorating coffee. A perfect stop pre-, post- or mid-ride.

ℹ Information

Lexington Visitors Center (Lexington Chamber of Commerce; www.lexingtonchamber.org; 1875 Massachusetts Ave; ⊙ 9am-5pm Apr-Nov, 10am-4pm Dec-Mar) Opposite Battle Green, next to Buckman Tavern.

ℹ Getting There & Away

Bicycle The most enjoyable way to get to Lexington – no contest – is to come by bicycle via the Minuteman Commuter Bikeway.

Bus MBTA (www.mbta.com) buses 62 (Bedford VA Hospital) and 76 (Hanscom Field) run from the Red Line Alewife subway terminus through Lexington center at least hourly on weekdays, and less frequently on Saturday; no buses on Sunday.

Car Take MA 2 west from Boston or Cambridge to exit 54 (Waltham St) or exit 53 (Spring St). From I-95 (MA 128), take exit 30 or 31.

Concord
POP 17,700

Tall, white church steeples rise above ancient oaks, elms and maples in colonial Concord, giving the town a stateliness that belies the American Revolution drama that occurred centuries ago. Indeed, it is easy to see how writers such as Ralph Waldo Emerson, Nathaniel Hawthorne, Henry David Thoreau and Louisa May Alcott found their inspiration here. Concord was also the home of famed sculptor Daniel Chester French (who went on to create the Lincoln Memorial in Washington, DC).

These days travelers can relive history in Concord. Indeed, every year on Patriots' Day history buffs reenact the minutemen's march to Concord, commemorating the battle with a ceremony at the Old North Bridge and a parade later in the day. Literary mavens might still experience Thoreau's Garden of Eden at Walden Pond; and French's legacy lives on at the DeCordova Sculpture Park. The homes of literary figures such as Ralph Waldo Emerson, Nathaniel Hawthorne and Louisa May Alcott are also open for visitors. For the less culturally inclined, the placid Concord River and the country roads are excellent for canoeing and cycling.

◉ Sights

The center of this sprawling, woodsy town is Monument Sq, marked by its war memorial obelisk. Main St runs westward from Monument Sq through the business district to MA 2. Walden and Thoreau Sts run southeast from Main St and out to Walden Pond some 3 miles away. The MBTA commuter rail station, Concord ('the Depot'), is on Thoreau St at Sudbury Rd, a mile west of Monument Sq.

★ Concord Museum   MUSEUM
(www.concordmuseum.org; 200 Lexington Rd; adult/child/senior & student $10/5/8; ⊙9am-5pm Mon-Sat & noon-5pm Sun Apr-Dec, 11am-4pm Mon-Fri & 1-4pm Sun Jan-Mar; ⊞) Southeast of Monument Sq, Concord Museum brings the town's diverse history under one roof. The museum's prized possession is one of the 'two if by sea' lanterns that hung in the steeple of the Old North Church in Boston as a signal to Paul Revere.

It also has the world's largest collection of Henry David Thoreau artifacts, including his writing desk from Walden Pond. Scavenger hunts and other activities make this little museum a great destination for kids.

★ Old North Bridge   HISTORIC SITE
(www.nps.gov/mima; Minute Man National Historic Park, Monument St; ⊙dawn-dusk) A half-mile north of Memorial Sq in Concord center, the wooden span of Old North Bridge is the site of the 'shot heard around the world' (as Emerson wrote in his poem *Concord Hymn*). This is where enraged minutemen fired on British troops, forcing them to retreat to Boston. Daniel Chester French's first statue, *Minute Man*, presides over the park from the opposite side of the bridge.

On the far side of the bridge, the Buttrick mansion contains the visitor center (p97), where you can see a video about the battle and admire the Revolutionary War brass cannon, the Hancock. On your way up to Old North Bridge, look for the yellow Bullet Hole House (262 Monument St), at which British troops purportedly fired as they retreated from North Bridge.

WORTH A TRIP

FRUITLANDS MUSEUMS

In the early 19th century, Concordian thinkers were at the forefront of Transcendentalism, a philosophical movement that espoused that God 'transcends' all people and things. Bronson Alcott (1799–1888), educational reformer and father of Louisa May Alcott, was a leader amongst this group pursuing Transcendental ideals. Toward this end, he founded Fruitlands, an experimental vegetarian community (read: commune) in Harvard, Massachusetts.

The site of this experiment now houses the Fruitlands Museums (www.fruitlands. org; 102 Prospect Hill Rd, Harvard; adult/child $12/5, grounds only $6/3; ⊙11am-4pm Mon & Wed-Fri, 10am-5pm Sat & Sun Apr-Oct), a beautifully landscaped 210-acre property. The original hillside farmhouse was actually used by Alcott and his utopian 'Con-Sociate' (communal) family. Other museums have since been moved to the 200-acre estate, including the 1794 Shaker House, a Native American museum and a gallery featuring paintings by 19th-century itinerant artists and Hudson River School landscape painters.

Fruitlands hosts all kinds of special events, including a summer concert series. There is a cafe on site. Fruitlands is in Harvard, about 30 miles west of Boston. Take Rte 2 to exit 38A, Rte 111, then take the first right onto Old Shirley Rd.

Concord

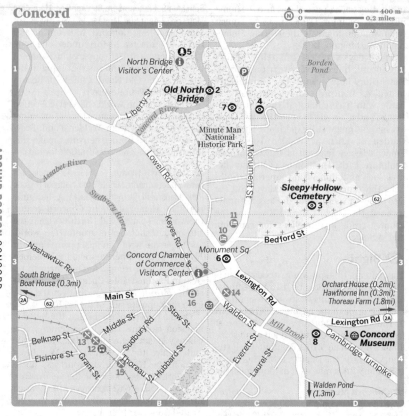

★ **Sleepy Hollow Cemetery** CEMETERY
(www.friendsofsleepyhollow.org; Bedford St;
☉ dawn-dusk) This is the final resting place
for the most famous Concordians. Though
the entrance is only a block east of Monument Sq, the most interesting part, **Authors' Ridge**, is a 15-minute walk along
Bedford St. Henry David Thoreau and his
family are buried here, as are the Alcotts
and the Hawthornes. Ralph Waldo Emerson's tombstone is a large uncarved rose
quartz boulder, an appropriate Transcendentalist symbol.

Nearby is the **Melvin Memorial**, a much
photographed monument to the memory of
three Concord brothers who died in the Civil
War. It's the work of Daniel French, who is
also buried in Sleepy Hollow.

Monument Square SQUARE
The grassy center of Monument Sq is a favorite resting and picnicking spot for cyclists touring Concord's scenic roads. At the
southeastern end of the square is **Wright
Tavern**, one of the first places the British
troops searched in their hunt for arms on
April 19, 1775. It became their headquarters
for the operation.

Old Hill Burying Ground, with graves
dating from colonial times, is on the hillside
at the southeastern end of Monument Sq.

Old Manse HISTORIC HOUSE
(www.thetrustees.org; 269 Monument St; adult/
child/senior & student $8/5/7; ☉ noon-5pm
Tue-Sun May-Oct, Sat & Sun only Mar-Apr & Nov-
Dec) Right next to Old North Bridge, the
Old Manse was built in 1769 by Ralph
Waldo's grandfather, the Reverend William Emerson. Today it's filled with mementos, including those of Nathaniel and
Sophia Hawthorne, who lived here for a
few years. The highlight of Old Manse is
the gorgeously maintained grounds – the
fabulous organic garden was planted by

Concord

Henry Thoreau as a wedding gift to the Hawthornes.

Ralph Waldo Emerson
Memorial House   HISTORIC HOUSE
(www.rwe.org; 28 Cambridge Turnpike; adult/child/senior & student $7/free/5; ⊙ 10am-4:30pm Thu-Sat, 1-4:30pm Sun mid-Apr–Oct) The Ralph Waldo Emerson Memorial House is where the philosopher lived for almost 50 years (1835–82). Emerson was the paterfamilias of literary Concord, one of the great literary figures of his age and the founding thinker of the Transcendentalist movement. The house often hosted his renowned circle of friends and still contains many original furnishings.

Orchard House   HISTORIC HOUSE
(www.louisamayalcott.org; 399 Lexington Rd; adult/child/senior & student $10/5/8; ⊙ 10am-4:30pm Mon-Sat, 1-4:30pm Sun Apr-Oct, 11am-3pm Mon-Fri, 10am-4:30pm Sat, 1-4:30pm Sun Nov-Mar) Louisa May Alcott (1832–88) was a junior member of Concord's august literary crowd, but her work proved to be durable: *Little Women* is among the most popular young-adult books ever written. The mostly autobiographical novel is set in Concord. Take a tour of Alcott's childhood home, Orchard House, to see how the Alcotts lived and where the novel was actually written.

Thoreau Farm   HISTORIC HOUSE
(www.thoreaufarm.org; 341 Virginia Rd; adult/child $6/free; ⊙ tour 11am, 1pm & 3pm Sat-Sun) Fans of Thoreau can travel off the beaten path to the house where he was born, which is about 4 miles east of Concord center. Henry David lived in his grandmother's farmhouse for only a few months after his birth; but the rural retreat would prove influential and inspirational throughout his life. The grounds are still an inviting place for exploration and reflection.

Guided tours show off the restored farmhouse. Midway between Lexington center and Concord center, turn north on Old Bedford Rd.

🏃 Activities

South Bridge Boat House   CANOEING
(☑ 978-369-9438; 502 Main St; canoes per hr $14-16, kayaks per hr $16-20; ⊙ 10am-dusk Mon-Fri & 9am-dusk Sat & Sun Apr-Oct) A mile west of Monument Sq, you can rent canoes for cruising the Concord and Assabet Rivers. The favorite route is downstream to the Old North Bridge, and back past the many fine riverside houses and the campus of prestigious Concord Academy – a paddle of about two hours.

👉 Tours

Concord Bike Tours   BICYCLE TOUR
(☑ 978-501-7097; www.concordbiketours.com; adult/child $50/35) Highly recommended bicycle tours explore different themes of Concord's history, such as revolutionary sites, Concord authors or the Underground Railroad. Guides are knowledgeable and entertaining, the scenery is marvelous and the riding is not too rigorous for novice cyclists.

Concord Walking Tours   WALKING TOUR
(☑ 978-369-3120; www.concordchamberofcommerce.org; adult/child $20/5; ⊙ 1pm Fri, 11am & 1pm Sat, noon Sun Apr-Oct) The chamber of commerce offers tours of both revolutionary and literary Concord. Tours depart from the chamber of commerce visitors center.

🛏 Sleeping

While there is a paucity of hotels and motels in Concord, travelers will find dozens of B&Bs in the area. Get a complete list from the Concord Chamber of Commerce.

LONGFELLOW'S WAYSIDE INN

This **inn** (☑978-443-1776; www.wayside.org; 76 Wayside Inn Rd, Sudbury; d incl breakfast $140-175; ❋🛜) was made famous by Longfellow's poems *Tales from a Wayside Inn*, and now offers nine period rooms and lovely landscaped grounds. Also on-site is an extensive archive of the history of the inn, which has been operating since 1707, making it the oldest functioning inn in the country. The inn is 13 miles south of Concord on US 20.

Colonial Inn
INN **$$**

(☑978-369-9200; www.concordscolonialinn.com; 48 Monument Sq; d $111-185, ste from $250; P❋) Dating from 1716, the Colonial Inn boasts a role in the Revolution, when it was used as a storehouse for Colonial arms and provisions. Original architectural details like wide plank floors and post beam ceilings make the 15 rooms in the oldest section of the building the most atmospheric (and the most expensive).

North Bridge Inn
INN **$$$**

(☑888-530-0007; www.northbridgeinn.com; 21 Monument St; ste $200-235; P❋🛜🍴) Six suites are decked out with down comforters, plush pillows, tiled bathrooms and kitchenettes. A hearty breakfast is served in the sunfilled morning room. All guests are warmly welcomed by Posey, the resident corgi.

Hawthorne Inn
B&B **$$$**

(☑978-369-5610; www.concordmass.com; 462 Lexington Rd; r $299-349; P❋🛜) The artist owners here have put their passion and skill into turning their home into a creative sanctuary, with gardens filled with flowers and figures, china cabinets packed with kitschy collectibles and rooms adorned in luxury. Homemade gourmet breakfasts served on hand-painted pottery are a highlight.

🍴 Eating

Concord Cheese Shop
DELI **$**

(www.concordcheeseshop.com; 29 Walden St; sandwiches $6-10; ⊙10am-5:30pm Tue-Sat;) This is a cheese shop, as it claims, with an excellent selection of imported and local cheese, as well as wine and other specialty food items. But the folks behind the counter can whip those ingredients into an amazing sandwich (or soup or salad) – perfect for a picnic on Memorial Sq. Or find a spot at the cozy (but comfortable) seating area.

Bedford Farms
ICE CREAM **$**

(www.bedfordfarmsicecream.com; 68 Thoreau St; ⊙11-9:30pm Mar-Nov; 🍴) Dating to the 19th century, this local dairy specializes in delectable ice cream, and frozen yogurt that tastes like delectable ice cream. If prices seem a tad high, it's because the scoops are gigantic. Their trademark flavor is Moosetracks (vanilla ice cream, chocolate swirl, peanut-butter cups). Conveniently located next to the train depot.

Country Kitchen
SANDWICHES **$**

(181 Sudbury Ave; sandwiches $5-10; ⊙breakfast & lunch Mon-Fri; 🍴) At lunchtime, this little yellow house often has a line out the door, which is testament to its tiny size, as well as its amazing sandwiches. The Thanksgiving sandwich is the hands-down favorite, with roasted turkey carved straight off the bird. They don't accept credit cards and there's no seating, save the picnic table out front.

80 Thoreau
MODERN AMERICAN **$$$**

(☑978-318-0008; www.80thoreau.com; 80 Thoreau St; mains $21-31; ⊙dinner Mon-Sat) Understated and elegant, this modern restaurant is an anomaly in historic Concord – but that's a good thing. The menu – short but sweet – features deliciously unexpected combinations of flavors, mostly using seasonal, local ingredients. There's also a busy bar area, which offers a short selection of classic cocktails and long list of wines by the glass.

🔒 Shopping

Concord Bookshop
BOOKSTORE

(www.concordbookshop.com; 65 Main St; ⊙9:30am-6pm Mon-Sat, noon-5pm Sun) An independent bookstore packed with good reads, especially featuring local authors.

ℹ Information

Concord Chamber of Commerce & Visitors Center (www.concordchamberofcommerce.org; 58 Main St; ⊙9:30am-4:30pm Apr-Oct) Concord Chamber of Commerce has full details on sites, including opening hours for the homes, which vary with the season.

Concord Magazine (www.concordma.com) This community website is replete with information about Concord history, sights and current events.

North Bridge Visitor's Center (www.nps.gov/mima; Liberty St; ⊙9am-5pm Apr-Oct, 9am-4pm Nov-Mar)

❶ Getting There & Away

CAR

Driving west on MA 2 from Boston or Cambridge, it's some 20 miles to Concord. Coming from Lexington, follow signs from Lexington Green to Concord and Battle Rd, the route taken by the British troops on April 19, 1775.

TRAIN

MBTA commuter rail (☑617-222-3200, 800-392-6100; www.mbta.com; Concord Depot, 90 Thoreau St) trains run between Boston's North Station and Concord Depot ($8, 40 minutes, 12 daily) in either direction on the Fitchburg/South Acton line.

Around Concord

DeCordova Museum

The magical **DeCordova Sculpture Park** (www.decordova.org; 51 Sandy Pond Rd; adult/senior, student & child $14/10; ⊙10am-5pm) encompasses 35 acres of green hills, providing a spectacular natural environment for a constantly changing exhibit of outdoor artwork. As many as 75 pieces are on display at any given time. The entry fee includes admission to the on-site **museum** (⊙10am-5pm Tue-Sun), which hosts rotating exhibits

of contemporary sculpture, painting, photography and mixed media. From Concord center, drive east on Rte 2 and turn right on Bedford Rd.

Discovery Museums

The **Discovery Museums** (www.discoverymuseums.org; 177 Main St, Acton; admission $11) consist of two unique side-by-side museums, both great for children. Occupying an old Victorian house, the **Children's Museum** (⊙9am-4:30pm Tue-Sun) invites kids to play make-believe, cooking up some eats in a bite-size diner, hunting for wildlife on safari, conducting a toy train and more. The **Science Museum** (⊙1:30-4:30pm Tue-Fri, 10am-4:30pm Sat & Sun) is for slightly older kids, but it's equally playful, with hands-on exhibits such as earth science and an inventor's workshop. The museums are reserved for school groups on weekday mornings during the school year.

Lowell

POP 107,600

In the early 19th century, textile mills in Lowell churned out cloth by the mile, driven by the abundant waterpower of Pawtucket Falls. Today, the city at the confluence of the Concord and Merrimack Rivers does not have such a robust economy, but its historic center recalls the industrial revolution glory days – a working textile mill, canal boat tours and trolley rides evoke the birth of America as an industrial giant.

DON'T MISS

WALDEN POND

'I went to the woods because I wished to live deliberately, to front only the essential facts of life, and see if I could not learn what it had to teach, and not, when I came to die, discover that I had not lived.' So wrote Henry David Thoreau about his time at **Walden Pond** (www.mass.gov/dcr/parks/walden; 915 Walden St; ⊙dawn-dusk) **FREE**. Thoreau took the naturalist beliefs of Transcendentalism out of the realm of theory and into practice when he left the comforts of the town and built himself a rustic cabin on the shores of the pond. His famous memoir of his time spent there, *Walden; or, Life in the Woods* (1854), was full of praise for nature and disapproval of the stresses of civilized life – sentiments that have found an eager audience ever since.

The glacial pond is now a state park, surrounded by acres of forest preserved by the Walden Woods project, a nonprofit organization. It lies about 3 miles south of Monument Sq, along Walden St (MA 126) south of MA 2. There's a swimming beach and facilities on the southern side, and a footpath that circles the large pond (about a 1.5 mile stroll). The **site of Thoreau's cabin** is on the northeast side, marked by a cairn and signs. The park gets packed when the weather is warm; the number of visitors is restricted, so arrive early in summer. Parking costs $5.

In modern Lowell, 25 miles north of Boston, an influx of Southeast Asian immigrants has diversified the culture (and cuisine) of this classic New England mill town. A short walk away from the historic center into the ethnic neighborhood known as the Acre reveals that Lowell has definitely changed from the city it was 150 years ago.

Besides being the birthplace of the textile industry, Lowell was also the birthplace of two American cultural icons, painter James Abbott McNeill Whistler and writer Jack Kerouac.

◉ Sights & Activities

Merrimack St is the main commercial thoroughfare, holding the Downtown Transit Center, the chamber of commerce office and several restaurants. The historic multiethnic neighborhood known as the Acre lies west of the Merrimack Canal.

Lowell is arguably undergoing a transformation to an urban artistic center, thanks to its gritty, post-industrial setting and its diverse cultural influences. Evidence lies within the growing artistic communities. Visit the Brush Art Gallery & Studios (www.thebrush.org; 256 Market St; ⊙11am-4pm Tue-Sat & noon-4pm Sun), housed in a restored mill building next to the NPS visitor center.

Lowell National Historical Park   HISTORIC SITE
(⊞) The historic buildings in the city center – connected by the trolley and canal boats – constitute the national park, which gives a fascinating peek at the workings of a 19th-century industrial town. Stop first at the Market Mills Visitors Center (p100) to pick up a map and check out the general exhibits. An introductory multimedia video on historic Lowell is shown every half-hour.

Five blocks northeast along the river, the fascinating Boott Cotton Mills Museum (www.nps.gov/lowe; 115 John St; adult/child/student $6/3/4; ⊙9:30am-5pm) has exhibits that chronicle the rise and fall of the industrial revolution in Lowell, including technological changes, labor movements and immigration. The highlight is a working weave room, with 88 power looms. A special exhibit on Mill Girls & Immigrants (☑info 978 970 5000; 40 French St; ⊙1:30-5pm) FREE examines the lives of working people.

American Textile History Museum   MUSEUM
(www.athm.org; 491 Dutton St; adult/child $8/6; ⊙10am-5pm Wed-Sun; ⊞) On the southern edge of the historic district, this Smithsonian outpost is an excellent, interactive and comprehensive look at textiles and their role in American history. The permanent exhibit is *Textile Revolution,* which highlights the advances made by textiles and technology. Appropriate for a textile museum, the exhibit is very hands-on, encouraging visitors to touch fabrics, work looms and even design clothes.

The museum is two long blocks south of Market St.

Jack Kerouac Sites   LITERARY SITES
Dedicated in 1988, the Jack Kerouac Commemorative (Bridge St) features a landscaped path where excerpts of the writer's work are posted, including opening passages from his five novels set in Lowell. They are thoughtfully displayed with Catholic and Buddhist symbols, representing the belief systems that influenced him. The memorial is northeast of the visitors center along the Eastern Canal.

Two miles south of Lowell center, Kerouac is buried in the Sampas family plot at Edson Cemetery (cnr Gorham & Saratoga Sts). His grave site remains a pilgrimage site for devotees who were inspired by his free spirit. Stop by the front desk for directions to the Sampas plot. For more insight into Kerouac's life in Lowell, catch a screening of *Lowell Blues,* a film at the Market Mills Visitors Center shown daily at 4pm.

Whistler House Museum of Art   MUSEUM
(www.whistlerhouse.org; 243 Worthen St; adult/senior, student & child $5/4; ⊙11am-4pm Wed-Sun) James McNeill Whistler's birthplace, built in 1823, is the home of the Lowell Art Association. It houses a small collection of work by New England artists, including some etchings by Whistler himself. Outside, an 8ft bronze statue of the artist by sculptor Mico Kaufman is the centerpiece of the Whistler Park and Gardens.

Whistler House is on the west side of the Merrimack Canal, two blocks west of the Market Mills Visitors Center.

New England Quilt Museum   MUSEUM
(www.nequiltmuseum.org; 18 Shattuck St; adult/senior & student $7/5; ⊙10am-4pm Tue-Sat year-round, noon-4pm Sun May-Oct) This little museum has found its niche. The friendly, knowledgeable staff show off a collection of over 150 antique and contemporary quilts from around New England. Rotating exhib-

LOCAL KNOWLEDGE

GO CAMBODIA

Adventurous eaters can delve into Lowell's interior to discover authentic, delicious Khmer cuisine.

Red Rose Restaurant (716 Middlesex St; mains $8-15; ⊘ breakfast, lunch & dinner) In a word: authentic. As in Khmer-speaking waitstaff and delicious adventurous food straight from Phnom Penh. If you don't know what to order, try the *loc lac*: cubes of beef marinated in soy sauce, grilled or fried, and served with a lime dipping sauce. The Red Rose is about three blocks west of the train station.

Simply Khmer (www.simplykhmerrestaurant.com; 26 Lincoln St; $10-18; ⊘ breakfast, lunch & dinner) When TV personality Andrew Zimmern wanted to sample some *Bizarre Foods* from Cambodia, this is where he came. The place was popular before that though, thanks to its clean interior and approachable menu. The restaurant is southwest of the train station, off Chelmsford St.

its highlight thematic work such as modern quilting, regional traditions and the Red Sox (of course). Great gift shop.

Tours

NPS Tours BOAT TOUR
(☏ 978-970-5000; www.nps.gov/lowe; canal tours adult/child $8/6, walking tours free; ⊘ 10am-3pm Jun-Aug) Canal tours are offered throughout summer, with themes such as Engineering Innovations and Working the Water. The schedule varies according to season and water levels. Park rangers also lead free walking tours of Lowell Cemetery, the Acre and the Riverwalk.

✿✿ Festivals & Events

Lowell Folk Festival MUSIC
(www.lowellfolkfestival.org) Three days of food, music (on six stages!), parades and other festivities honoring the diverse multicultural community that Lowell has become. It takes place every year at the end of July.

Lowell Celebrates Kerouac LITERATURE
(LCK; www.lowellcelebrateskerouac.org) Every October, this local nonprofit organization hosts four days of events dedicated to Beat writer Jack Kerouac, featuring tours of many places in his novels, as well as panel discussions, readings, music and poetry. Literature buffs travel from around the world for this unique event.

🛏 Sleeping

There are not many places to stay in Lowell, nor reasons to stay here. However, if you must spend the night, a few options meet standard needs.

UMass Lowell Inn & Conference Center HOTEL $
(☏ 877-886-5422; www.acc-umlinnandconference center.com; 50 Warren St; r from $89; ❋ 🛜 ♿ 🐾) Located in the heart of downtown Lowell overlooking the canals. Some rooms have scenic views of the Merrimack, and all rooms are modern with standard amenities.

Courtyard Lowell HOTEL $$
(☏ 978-458-7575; http://marriott.com; 30 Industrial Ave E; r from $139; P ❋ 🛜 ♿ 🐾) Although it's a Marriott Hotel, the Courtyard Lowell manages to maintain a bit of New England charm with its Colonial-style building.

🍴 Eating & Drinking

Arthur's Paradise Diner DINER $
(112 Bridge St; meals $6-10; ⊘ breakfast & lunch; 🐾) The epitome of 'old school,' this place is open only for breakfast and lunch and specializes in something called the Boot Mill sandwich (egg, bacon, cheese and home fries on a grilled roll). Housed in an authentic Worcester Diner Car #727.

Viet-Thai Restaurant VIETNAMESE, THAI $$
(www.vietthailowell.com; 368 Merrimack St; mains $8-15; ⊘ 9:30am-9:30pm) In a town that's known for its southeast Asian food, this restaurant is one of the best, serving hearty portions of pad thai and delicious pho. Regulars rave about the *mekathung*, spicy sauteed flat noodles. Go for the lunchtime buffet and you won't leave hungry.

★ Life Alive VEGETARIAN $$
(www.lifealive.com; 194 Middle St; meals $10-15; ⊘ lunch & dinner; 🍴) 🍃 Scrumptious salads, fresh fantastic food and jubilant juices fill out the menu at this funky cafe. The choices

MARVELOUS MARBLEHEAD

First settled in 1629, Marblehead is a maritime village with winding streets, brightly painted Colonial and Federal houses, and 1000 sailing yachts bobbing at moorings in the harbor. As indicated by the number of boats, this is the Boston area's premier yachting port and one of New England's most prestigious addresses.

While wandering the streets, stop by **Abbott Hall** (☑781-631-0000; Washington Sq, Washington St; ⊙9am-4pm) **FREE**, the seat of Marblehead's town government to see *The Spirit of '76*, the famous patriotic painting (c 1876) by Archibald M Willard. Two blocks up the street, a few of the historic mansions are open to the public as museum and art exhibition space.

From Salem, MA 114 – locally called Pleasant St – passes through modern commercial Marblehead en route to the Marblehead Historic District (Old Town). The **Marblehead Chamber of Commerce information booth** (☑639 8469; www.marblehead chamber.org; cnr Pleasant, Essex & Spring Sts; ⊙noon-5pm Mon-Fri, 10am-5pm Sat & Sun) has information about local B&Bs, restaurants and art galleries.

can be overwhelming, but you can't go wrong with the signature dish known as 'The Goddess': veggies and tofu served over rice with a zinger ginger nama shoyu sauce. The food is healthy and veg-friendly; the setting is arty and appealing.

Worthen House PUB
(141 Worthen St; meals $12-20; ⊙lunch & dinner) This old brick tavern is famed for its amazing, pulley-driven fan system (which is still operational). The pressed-tin ceiling and wooden bar remain from the early days, giving this place an old-fashioned neighborhood feel. Stop by for a pint of Guinness and a burger.

☆ Entertainment

Lowell Spinners SPECTATOR SPORT
(www.lowellspinners.com; tickets $10; 🅱) This Class A baseball organization is a Red Sox feeder-team. Locally, it plays at LeLacheur Park, which is north of the center on the Merrimack River. If your kid's not into baseball, check out the Swampland Kids Area in the left-field corner of the ball park, featuring a giant slide, a bouncy house and lots more fun and games.

ℹ Information

Market Mills Visitors Center (www.nps.gov/lowe; 246 Market St, Market Mills; ⊙9am-5pm) Starting place for the Lowell National Historical Park.

ℹ Getting There & Around

BUS
The **Lowell Regional Transit Authority** (www.lrta.com) runs a shuttle bus that departs every 15 minutes from the Downtown Transit Center, stopping near the museums and visitors center.

CAR
From I-495, follow the Lowell Connector to its end at exit 5-C to reach the city center.

TRAIN
MBTA commuter rail (www.mbta.com) trains depart Boston's North Station for Lowell ($8.75). Trains go in either direction 10 times a day during the week, four times on weekends. Trains from Boston terminate at the Gallagher Transportation Terminal on Thorndike St, a 15-minute walk southwest of the city center (or take the shuttle).

NORTH SHORE

The entire coast of Massachusetts claims a rich history, but no part offers more recreational, cultural and dining diversions than the North Shore of Boston. Salem was among America's wealthiest ports during the 19th century; Gloucester is the nation's most famous fishing port; and Marblehead remains one of the premier yachting ports. Trade and fishing have brought wealthy residents, sumptuous houses, and great collections of art and artifacts to the area. Explore the region's rich maritime history and spectacular coastal scenery, and don't miss the opportunity for a seafood feast.

Salem

POP 41,700
This town's very name conjures up images of diabolical witchcraft and women being

burned at the stake. The famous Salem witch trials of 1692 are engrained in the national memory. Indeed, Salem goes all out at Halloween, when the whole town dresses up for parades and parties, and shops sell all manner of wiccan accessories.

These incidents obscure Salem's true claim to fame: its glory days as a center for clipper-ship trade with the Far East. The responsible party, Elias Hasket Derby, benefited enormously from his enterprise, eventually becoming America's first millionaire. Derby built half-mile-long Derby Wharf, which is now the center of the Salem Maritime National Historic Site.

Many Salem vessels followed Derby's ship *Grand Turk* around the Cape of Good Hope, and soon the owners founded the East India Marine Society to provide warehousing services for their ships' logs and charts. The new company's charter required the establishment of 'a museum in which to house the natural and artificial curiosities' brought back by members' ships. The collection was the basis for what is now the world-class Peabody Essex Museum.

Today Salem is a middle-class commuter suburb of Boston with an enviable location on the sea. And its rich history and culture, from witches to ships to art, continue to cast a spell of enchantment on all those who visit.

◉ Sights

Commercial Salem centers around Essex St, a pedestrian mall running east to west from Washington St to the historic Salem Common. To the southeast, Derby Wharf stretches out into Salem Harbor. The train station is a short walk north of Essex St.

The 1.7 mile Heritage Trail is a route connecting Salem's major historic sites. Follow the red line painted on the sidewalk.

★ **Salem Maritime**
National Historic Site   HISTORIC SITE
(www.nps.gov/sama; 193 Derby St; ⊘9am-5pm)
FREE This National Historic Site comprises the Custom House, the wharves and the other buildings along Derby St that are remnants of the shipping industry that once thrived along this stretch of Salem. Of the 50 wharves that once lined Salem Harbor, only three remain, the longest of which is Derby Wharf.

Visitors can stroll out to the end and peek inside the 1871 lighthouse or climb aboard the tall ship Friendship. The most prominent building along Derby St is the Custom House, where permits and certificates were issued and, of course, taxes paid. Other buildings at the site include warehouses, the scale house and Elias Hasket Derby's home. Stop by at the West India Goods Store, a working store with spices and other items similar to those sold two centuries ago.

★ **Peabody Essex Museum**   MUSEUM
(www.pem.org; 161 Essex St; adult/child $15/free; ⊘10am-5pm Tue-Sun; ♿) All of the art, artifacts and curiosities that Salem merchants brought back from the Far East were the foundation for this museum. Founded in 1799, it is the country's oldest museum in continuous operation. The building itself is impressive, with a light-filled atrium, and is a wonderful setting for the vast collections, which focus on New England decorative arts and maritime history.

AROUND BOSTON SALEM

DON'T MISS

WITCH CITY

The city of Salem embraces its witchy past with a healthy dose of whimsy. But the history offers a valuable lesson about what can happen when fear and frenzy are allowed to trump common sense and compassion.

By the time the witch hysteria of 1692 had finally died down, a total of 156 people had been accused, 55 people had pleaded guilty and implicated others to save their own lives, and 14 women and six men who would not confess had been executed. Stop by at the Witch Trials Memorial (Charter St), a simple but dramatic monument that honors the innocent victims.

Now for the whimsy. After remembering this very real tragedy, you can head over to the TV Land statue (cnr Washington & Essex Sts) to have your picture taken with Samantha Stephens, the spell-casting, nose-twitching beauty from the classic show *Bewitched*.

Salem

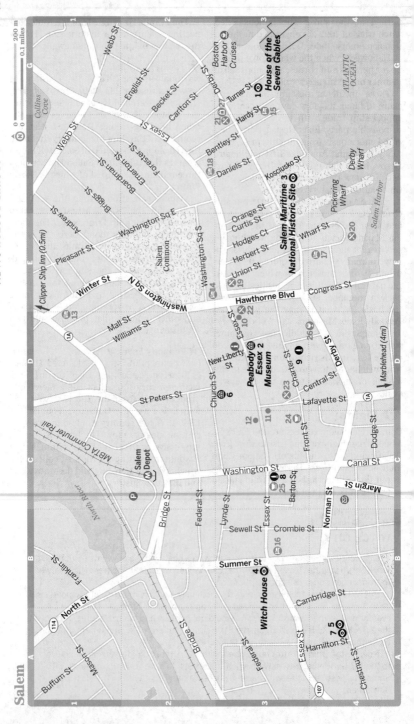

0 200 m
0 0.1 miles

House of the Seven Gables 1

Boston Harbor Cruises

ATLANTIC OCEAN

Salem Maritime 3 National Historic Site

Derby Wharf

Pickering Wharf

Salem Harbor

Salem Common

Clipper Ship Inn (0.5mi)

Hawthorne Blvd

Peabody Essex 2 Museum

Salem Depot

MBTA Commuter Rail

North River

Witch House 4

Marblehead (4mi)

Webb St
English St
Becket St
Carlton St
Derby St
Turner St
Hardy St
Essex St
Bentley St
Daniels St
Orange St
Curtis St
Hodges Ct
Herbert St
Union St
Kosciusko St
Wharf St
Congress St
Webb St
Forester St
Emerton St
Boardman St
Briggs St
Andrew St
Washington Sq E
Washington Sq S
Pleasant St
Winter St
Washington Sq N
Mall St
Williams St
New Liberty St
Church St
St Peters St
Essex St
Charter St
Central St
Lafayette St
Front St
Derby St
Dodge St
Canal St
Washington St
Barton Sq
Norman St
Margin St
Federal St
Lynde St
Sewell St
Crombie St
Summer St
Bridge St
Federal St
Bridge St
Franklin St
North St
Cambridge St
Hamilton St
Essex St
Chestnut St
Buffum St
Mason St

Collins Cove

114

1A

107

Salem

Predictably, the Peabody Essex is particularly strong on Asian art, including pieces from China, Japan, Polynesia, Micronesia and Melanesia. The collection from preindustrial Japan is rated as the best in the world. **Yin Yu Tang** (adult/child $5/free) is a Chinese house that was shipped to the museum from China's southeastern Huizhou region.

The interactive **Art & Nature Center** has games and exhibits specifically designed for children, while age-specific 'Gallery Discovery Kits' make the other exhibits intriguing for the little ones.

★**House of the
Seven Gables**   HISTORIC HOUSE
(www.7gables.org; 54 Turner St; adult/child/senior $12.50/7.50/11.50; ⊙10am-5pm Nov-Jun, 10am-7pm Jul-Oct) 'Halfway down a by-street of one of our New England towns stands a rusty wooden house, with seven acutely peaked gables facing towards various points of the compass, and a huge clustered chimney in their midst.' So wrote Nathaniel Hawthorne in his 1851 novel about Salem's most famous house, the *House of Seven Gables*.

The novel brings to life the gloomy Puritan atmosphere of early New England and its effects on the people's psyches; the house does the same. Look for wonderful seaside gardens, many original furnishings and a mysterious secret staircase.

★**Witch House**   HISTORIC HOUSE
(Jonathan Corwin House; www.salemweb.com/witchhouse; 310 Essex St; adult/child/senior $8.25/4.25/6.25, tour add $2; ⊙10am-5pm May-Nov) The most authentic of more than a score of witchy sites, this house was once the home of Jonathan Corwin, a local magistrate who was called on to investigate witchcraft claims. He examined several accused witches, possibly in the 1st-floor rooms of this house. Open longer hours in October.

Chestnut Street   HISTORIC STREET
Lovers of old houses should venture to Chestnut St, which is among the most architecturally lovely streets in the country. (Alternatively, follow the McIntire Historic District Walking Trail). One of these stately homes is the **Stephen Phillips Memorial Trust House** (www.phillipsmuseum.org; 34 Chestnut St; adult/child/senior & student $5/2.50/4; ⊙10am-5pm Tue-Sun Jun-Oct, Sat & Sun Nov-May), which displays the family furnishings of Salem sea captains, including a collection of antique carriages and cars.

Salem Toy Museum   MUSEUM
(Museum Place Mall, 1 E India Sq; admission $6; ⊙10:30am-5:30pm Tue-Sun, shorter hours in winter; ⊕) This small museum is packed with fun for anyone who was ever young, but especially if you were young in the 1960s, '70s and '80s. Discover (or rediscover) all the toys that have entertained previous generations

of kids. The owner Frank is a wealth of fun facts about all the vintage toys in his collection.

☞ Tours

Due to Salem's witch history, there is an unusual interest in the paranormal, as evidenced by the many spooky tours on offer.

Hocus Pocus Tours
HISTORY TOUR
(www.hocuspocustours.com; adult/child $16/8) It's called Hocus Pocus, but it's not hokey (or pokey). This is an informative, historically accurate overview of Salem's sordid past, given by an enthusiastic and entertaining couple.

Spellbound Tours
SPOOKY TOUR
(www.spellboundtours.com; adult/child/senior & student $13/7/10; ⊗8pm mid-Apr–Oct) Created by a parapsychologist and licensed ghost hunter, this 75-minute nighttime tour promises you will see real ghosts. Tours depart nightly from the bell outside the NPS visitors center.

Salem Night Tours
SPOOKY TOUR
(www.salemghosttours.com; 127 Essex St; adult/child $13/7) Lantern-led tours start at 8pm, offering insights into Salem's scariest ghost stories. Guides are 'specially trained paranormal investigators.'

Salem Trolley
TROLLEY TOUR
(www.salemtrolley.com; adult/child/senior $15/5/14; ⊗10am-5pm Apr-Oct) This one-hour tour starts at the NPS visitor center and covers most of the town's places of interest. Catch the courtesy shuttle from the MBTA commuter rail station.

✯ Festivals & Events

★ Haunted Happenings Halloween
FESTIVAL
(www.hauntedhappenings.org) Everyone in Salem celebrates Halloween, not just the witches. And they celebrate for much of the month of October with special exhibits, parades, concerts, pumpkin carvings, costume parties and trick-or-treating. It all culminates on October 31, with the crowning of the King and Queen of Halloween. Book your lodging way in advance and expect to pay more.

🛏 Sleeping

Many of Salem's historic houses have been converted into B&Bs and guesthouses –

some of which claim a resident ghost. Prices increase during the Haunted Happenings Halloween festival in October. Breakfast is included unless otherwise stated.

Morning Glory
B&B $$
(☎978-741-1703; www.morningglorybb.com; 22 Hardy St; d $160-175, ste $210; P✷@♠) 𝄐 Tucked in behind the House of Seven Gables, this glorious B&B is hard to beat. To make his guests feel welcome, innkeeper and Salem native Bob Shea pulls out all the stops, not the least of which are the delectable homemade pastries prepared by his mother. Three frilly rooms and one sweet suite are named for Salem celebrities – that is, the witch victims of 1692.

Stephen Daniels House
B&B $$
(☎978-744-5709; www.thedanielshouse.com; 1 Daniels St; r $115-135; P♠) Two blocks north of the waterfront, this must be Salem's oldest lodging, with parts dating from 1667 – before the witch trials. Two walk-in fireplaces grace the common area, and the rooms are filled with period antiques. It is appropriate in this spooky town that such an old house be haunted: rumor has it that a ghost cat roams the ancient halls and has even been known to jump in bed with guests.

Amelia Payson Guest House
B&B $$
(☎978-744-8304; www.ameliapaysonhouse.com; 16 Winter St; d $135-175; ⊗Apr-mid-Nov; P✷@♠) Ada and Don Roberts have been in the innkeeping business for more than 50 years, so they know what they're doing. Just steps from Salem Common, their Greek Revival home is decorated with floral wallpaper, Oriental rugs, rich drapes and ornamental fireplaces. Breakfast is fresh fruit and homemade pastries, served in the lovely parlor around the grand piano.

Salem Waterfront Hotel & Suites
HOTEL $$
(☎978-740-8788; www.salemwaterfronthotel.com; 225 Derby St; r $179-199, ste from $219; P✷@♠✷☇) This modern property has a prime location overlooking Pickering Wharf and Salem Harbor. Eighty-six spacious rooms and suites have graceful decor and all the expected amenities, but breakfast is not included.

Salem Inn
INN $$
(☎978-741-0680; www.saleminnma.com; 7 Summer St; d $169-219, ste $219-289; P✷♠☇✷) Forty rooms are located in three different historic houses including the Captain West

House, a large brick sea captain's home from 1834. The rooms vary greatly, but they are all individually decorated with antiques, period detail and other charms, while still providing modern amenities. Suites are equipped with kitchenettes, making them ideal for families.

Hawthorne Hotel   HOTEL $$
(☎978-744-4080; www.hawthornehotel.com; 18 Washington Sq W; r $140-210; P❋@🤍📶🛏🐾) This historic Federalist-style hotel is at the very heart of Salem's center. For years it was the only full-service hotel, with 84 double rooms, a fancy (if staid) restaurant and a cozy pub. Rooms are decked out with reproduction 18th-century furnishings, so you can feel like a wealthy merchant from Salem's glory days. It also operates the Fidelia Bridges House, a small B&B in an 1807 federal house.

Clipper Ship Inn   MOTEL $$
(☎978-745-8022; www.clippershipinn.com; 40 Bridge St; r $95-145; P❋📶🛏) Crisp, clean rooms and efficient service make this red-brick motel a comfortable place to lay your head, even if it's not in a historic home. Breakfast not included.

✖ Eating

Pickering Wharf has a nice selection of cafes and restaurants overlooking the Salem waterfront.

Red's Sandwich Shop   DINER $
(www.redssandwichshop.com; 15 Central St; mains $5-8; ◷breakfast & lunch) This Salem institution has been serving eggs and sandwiches to faithful customers for over 50 years. The food is hearty and basic, but the real attraction is Red's old-school decor, complete with counter service and friendly faces. It's housed in the old London Coffee House building (around since 1698).

In a Pig's Eye   PUB $$
(www.inapigseye.com; 148 Derby St; mains $8-13; ◷lunch & dinner) This dark, friendly pub boasts an eclectic menu of burgers and beef stroganoff, homemade soups and tasty salads, and 'Pig's Eye Favorites' like steak tips or pork chops. Despite the small space, it has live music (usually acoustic) six nights a week. The Friday afternoon Blues Jam is legendary.

Old Spot   PUB $$
(www.theoldspot.com; 121 Essex St; sandwiches $8-10, mains $15-18; ◷lunch Fri-Sun, dinner daily) It's pub food, to be sure, but so perfectly prepared that it becomes a dining experience – a meat pie with beef and lamb in a Guinness stew; a slow-roasted pork sammie where the pork melts in your mouth; irresistible sweet potato fries. Dim lighting and plush pillows make the place extra comfortable and cozy.

Bella Verona   ITALIAN $$
(www.bellaverona.com; 107 Essex St; mains $12-20; ◷dinner; 🅿) The striped awning and overflowing flower boxes are the perfect gateway into this romantic trattoria in the heart of Salem. Owner Giogio Manzana has brought the flavors from his home region (Verona, of course) and the results are delightful. Aside from the impeccable food and service, this place is cozy, ie crowded.

AMERICA'S OLDEST CANDY COMPANY

For more than 200 years Ye Olde Pepper Companie (www.yeoldepeppercompanie.com; 122 Derby St, Salem; ◷10am-6pm) has been making sweets – you gotta believe that they know what they are doing.

In 1806, an English woman named Mrs Spencer survived a shipwreck, and she arrived in Salem with hardly a penny to her name. Her new neighbors were kind enough to lend her some cash to purchase a barrel of sugar. Mrs Spencer used the sugar to create 'Salem Gibraltar,' a candy that sated the sweet tooth of sea captains and sailing merchants. She hawked the candy from the front steps of the local church, eventually earning enough to purchase a horse and wagon and sell her products in neighboring towns. In 1830, Mrs Spencer sold her by-then-successful company to John William Pepper, hence the current name.

The Burkenshaw family has owned the candy company for four generations, but they continue to use Mrs Spencer's and Mr Pepper's original recipes for old-fashioned delights like Black Jacks (flavored with blackstrap molasses) and Gibraltars (lemon and peppermint treats). Sweet!

Finz SEAFOOD $$$
(www.hipfinz.com; 76 Wharf St; sandwiches $8-12, mains $18-28; ⊘lunch & dinner) The highlight here is the gracious, spacious dining room with three walls of windows and a sweet patio overlooking Salem Harbor. The kitchen keeps customers sated, with a seductive raw bar and other fresh-out-of-the-water local seafood. The carefully chosen wine list is an added perk.

🍷 Drinking

★ **Gulu-Gulu Café** CAFE
(www.gulu-gulu.com; 247 Essex St; mains $6-8; ⊘8am-11pm Sun-Tue, to 1am Wed-Sat; ⏰) Gulu-gulu means 'gulp, gulp' in French and it's named after a now-defunct cafe in Prague. That is an indication of how eclectic this place is, featuring (in no particular order) delicious coffee, art-adorned walls, sinful crêpes, live music, a great wine list and board games. Come for a snack but you might be tempted to stay all day.

Salem Beer Works MICROBREWERY
(www.beerworks.net; 178 Derby St; ⊘11:30am-midnight) Part of the Boston Beer Works family, this microbrewery serves 15 different brews on tap, as well as a full menu of pub grub, sandwiches and more. The specialty seems to be things fried, which undoubtedly encourages more beer-drinking. There are pool tables and outdoor seating.

Front Street Coffeehouse CAFE
(www.frontstreetcoffeehouse.com; 20 Front St; ⊘7am-8pm; ⏰💿) A cool place to sip a caffe latte or munch on a giant sandwich. This is where multipierced urban youths, well-groomed soccer moms and out-of-town visitors all find common ground.

ℹ️ Information

Hawthorne in Salem (www.hawthorneinsalem.org) An extensive site with loads of articles about Nathaniel Hawthorne, his life in Salem and his writings about the town.

NPS Regional Visitor Center (www.nps.gov/sama; 2 New Liberty St; ⊘9am-5pm) Free screening of *Where Past is Present*, a short film about Salem history. Pick up a map and description for one of several self-guided walking tours.

Official Guide (www.salem.org) A useful information site with links to local businesses, up-to-date events calendar and an ongoing blog.

ℹ️ Getting There & Around

BOAT
Boston Harbor Cruises operates the **Salem ferry** (Salem Ferry; www.bostonharborcruises.com; 10 Blaney St; round-trip adult/child $27/22; ⊘May-Oct) (round-trip adult/child $27/12, one hour, five daily), which makes the scenic trip between Salem Ferry Center and Long Wharf in Boston.

CAR
Salem lies 20 miles northeast of Boston. From MA 128, take MA 114 east into Salem center.

TRAIN
The Rockport/Newburyport line of the **MBTA commuter rail** (www.mbta.com) runs from Boston's North Station to Salem Depot ($6.75, 30 minutes). Trains run every 30 minutes during the morning and evening rush hours, hourly during the rest of day, and less frequently on weekends.

Gloucester

Founded in 1623 by English fisherfolk, Gloucester is one of New England's oldest towns. This port, on Cape Ann, has made its living from fishing for almost 400 years, and it has inspired books and films like Rudyard Kipling's *Captains Courageous* and Sebastian Junger's *The Perfect Storm*. And despite some recent economic diversification, this town still smells of fish. You can't miss the fishing boats, festooned with nets, dredges and winches, tied to the wharves or motoring along into the harbor, with clouds of hungry seagulls hovering expectantly above.

◉ Sights

Washington St runs from Grant Circle (a rotary out on MA 128) into the center of Gloucester at St Peter's Sq, an irregular brick plaza overlooking the sea. Rogers St, the waterfront road, runs east– west from the plaza; Main St, the business and shopping thoroughfare, is one block inland. East Gloucester, with the Rocky Neck artists' colony, is on the southeastern side of Gloucester Harbor.

St Peter's Square SQUARE
Don't leave Gloucester without paying your respects at St Peter's Sq, where Leonard Craske's famous statue, *Gloucester Fisherman* is dedicated to 'They That Go Down to the Sea in Ships, 1623–1923.'

Gloucester Maritime Heritage Center

MUSEUM

(www.gloucestermaritimecenter.org; 23 Harbor Loop; adult/child $6/4; ⊙10am-6pm Jun-Oct; ❀) Visit Gloucester's working waterfront and see the ongoing restoration of wooden boats, watch the operation of a marine railway that hauls ships out of the water, and compare the different kinds of fishing boats that were used over the years. From the Grant Circle rotary, take Washington St to its terminus then turn left on Rogers St to Harbor Loop.

The interactive exhibit Fitting Out focuses on the many different businesses that grew up around Gloucester's fishing industry. Doesn't sound so interesting, until you chart your course through the local waters or try your hand at rope making. **Sea Pocket Lab** is a hands-on outdoor aquarium with exhibits on local marine habitats. It is a great chance for kids to get down and dirty with sea stars, sea urchins, snails, crabs and seaweed. The Stellwagen Bank Marine Sanctuary Exhibit is an excellent introduction for whale watchers heading out on an excursion.

Cape Ann Historical Museum

MUSEUM

(www.capeannhistoricalmuseum.org; 27 Pleasant St; adult/children $10/free; ⊙10am-5pm Tue-Sat, 1-4pm Sun Mar-Jan) This tiny museum is a gem, particularly for its paintings by Gloucester native Fitz Hugh Lane. Exhibits also showcase the region's granite quarrying industry and – of course – its maritime history. The museum is in the heart of downtown Gloucester, just north of Main St.

Rocky Neck Art Colony

ART COLONY

(www.rockyneckartcolony.org) The artistic legacy of Gloucester native Fitz Hugh Lane endures, as Gloucester still boasts a vibrant artists community at Rocky Neck Art Colony. This association operates the cooperative **Rocky Neck Gallery** (53 Rocky Neck Ave; ⊙mid-May—mid-Oct) in a beautiful space overlooking Smith Cove. Follow Main St east and south around the northeastern end of Gloucester Harbor to East Gloucester.

Visit on the first Thursday of the month, from June to October, for **Nights on the Neck,** when many galleries host receptions with refreshments, live performances and other entertainment.

Beauport

HISTORIC HOUSE

(www.historicnewengland.org; 75 Eastern Point Blvd, Eastern Point; adult/student $15/8; ⊙10am-5pm Tue-Sat Jun–mid-Oct) The lavish home of interior designer Henry Davis Sleeper is known as Beauport, or the Sleeper-McCann mansion. Sleeper scoured New England for houses that were about to be demolished and scavenged wood paneling, architectural elements and furniture. In place of unity, he created a wildly eclectic but artistically surprising – and satisfying – place to live.

Now in the care of Historic New England, Beauport is open to visitors, and holds afternoon teas, evening concerts and other events.

🏃 Activities

Gloucester is perfectly situated to launch your whale-watching expedition, thanks to the proximity of **Stellwagen Bank** (www.stellwagen.noaa.gov), 842 sq miles of open ocean rich in marine life. The area was declared a National Marine Sanctuary in 1992 to conserve the area's biological diversity and to facilitate research and other beneficial activity. Today it's a destination for whale watching, diving and managed fishing.

Whale-watching cruises usually depart several times a day in summer, but only once a day or only on weekends in April, May, September and October. Reservations are recommended. Whale sightings are practically guaranteed.

Schooner Thomas E Lannon

SAILING

(☑978-281-6634; www.schooner.org; Rogers St; adult/child $40/27.50; ❀) This 65ft ship is the spitting image of the Gloucester fishing schooners. It leaves on two-hour sails from the Seven Seas wharf. A daily sunset cruise features live music and – on Saturday – lobster! Bonus for families: on Saturday mornings one kid sails for free with the purchase of one adult fare.

Cape Ann Whale Watch

WHALE WATCHING

(☑978-283-5110; www.seethewhales.com; Rose's Wharf, 415 Main St; adult/child $48/33; ❀) Cruises depart from Rose's Wharf, east of Gloucester center (on the way to East Gloucester).

Capt Bill & Sons Whale Watch

WHALE WATCHING

(☑978-283-6995; www.captainbillandsons.com; 24 Harbor Loop; adult/child $48/32; ❀) The boat leaves from behind Captain Carlo's Seafood Market & Restaurant.

Seven Seas Whale Watch

WHALE WATCHING

(☑888-283-1776, 978-283-1776; www.7seaswhalewatch.com; 63 Rogers St; adult/child $48/32; ❀) Seven Seas Whale Watch vessels depart from Rogers St in the center of Gloucester, between St Peter's Sq and the Gloucester House Restaurant.

🎆 Festivals & Events

St Peter's Festival
RELIGIOUS FESTIVAL

(www.stpetersfiesta.org) Honoring the patron saint of fisherfolk, this carnival at St Peter's Sq takes place over five days in late June. Besides rides and music, the main event is the procession through the streets of a statue of St Peter. Customarily, the cardinal of the Catholic Archdiocese of Boston attends to bless the fishing fleet.

🛏 Sleeping

Contact the chamber of commerce for local B&Bs.

Crow's Nest Inn
INN $

(☑ 978-281-2965; www.crowsnestgloucester.com; 334 Main St; r $75) If you want to wake to the sound of fisherfolk's cries and the smell of salt air, and you don't mind the most basic of bunks, stay at the Crow's Nest, upstairs from the pub made famous by *The Perfect Storm*.

★ Accommodations of Rocky Neck
STUDIO APARTMENTS $$

(☑ 978-381-9848; www.rockyneckaccommodations.com; 43 Rocky Neck Ave; r $135-155, ste $265-285; ᴾ🛜) You don't have to be an artiste to live the bohemian life in Gloucester. The colony association offers light-filled efficiencies – all equipped with kitchenettes – at the Rocky Neck Artist Colony. The rooms are sweet and simple, most with beautiful views of Smith Cove. Weekly rates also available.

Sea Lion Motel & Cottages
MOTEL $$

(www.sealionmotel.com; 138 Eastern Ave; r $138-169, ste $169-199; 🛁🛜🅿️🐾) Less than a mile from Good Harbor Beach, this welcoming woodsy spot offers excellent value. The accommodations are simple and spotless, whether you opt for a basic double or a more fitted-out suite. All suites and cottages have kitchenettes – ideal for families.

Julietta House
GUESTHOUSE $$

(☑ 978-281-2300; www.juliettahouse.com; 84 Prospect St; r $140-185; ᴾ🛁🛜) Steps from Gloucester Harbor, this grand Georgian house has eight spacious and elegant rooms with period furnishings and private bathrooms. This place promises privacy and comfort, without the overwrought frills and

friendliness of some guesthouses. Breakfast is not included.

Atlantis Oceanfront Inn
MOTEL $$$

(☑ 978-283-0014; www.atlantisoceanfrontinn.com; 125 Atlantic Rd; d $195-235; ᴾ🛁🛜🐾🐾) The institutional rooms at this large motel-style facility are spruced up by ocean views and private terraces. This place takes full advantage of its oceanfront setting, with its lovely rocky waterside walkway and a light-filled breakfast cafe. From the terminus of MA 128, take Bass Ave east to Atlantic Rd.

🍴 Eating

Virgilio's Italian Bakery
DELI $

(29 Main St; sandwiches $5-8; ⊙9am-5pm) Primarily a takeout joint, Virgilio's has excellent sandwiches and other Italian treats. Try the famous St Joseph sandwich – like an Italian sub on a fresh-baked roll. Pick one up and head down to the waterfront for a picnic.

Two Sisters Coffee Shop
DINER $

(27 Washington St; mains $5-8; ⊙breakfast & lunch; 🐾) This local place is where the fisherfolk go for breakfast when they come in from their catch. They are early risers, so you may have to wait for a table. Corned beef hash, eggs in a hole and pancakes all get rave reviews. Service is a little salty.

Franklin Cape Ann
AMERICAN $$

(www.franklincafe.com; 118 Main St; mains $15-20; ⊙dinner daily, til midnight Fri & Sat; 🐾) The North Shore branch of a South End favorite in Boston, this cool place has an urban atmosphere and an excellent, modern New American menu. More often than not, daily specials feature fresh seafood and seasonal vegetables, always accompanied by an appropriate wine. Regulars rave about the cocktails too.

The Causeway Restaurant
SEAFOOD $$

(78 Essex St; mains $12-18; ⊙lunch & dinner) Gloucester's favorite seafood shack is about a mile west of town, on the mainland. It's a convivial, crowded place serving irresistible clam chowder, heaping portions of fried clams and twin lobster specials. Expect to wait for a table and don't forget to BYOB.

Duckworth's Bistrot
AMERICAN $$$

(☑ 978-282-4426; www.duckworthsbistrot.com; 197 E Main St; mains $22-28; ⊙dinner Tue-Sat; 🐾) Half-portions and wines by the glass (or carafe) mean that Duckworth's won't break

LIFE'S A BEACH ON CAPE ANN

Cape Ann has several excellent beaches that draw thousands of Boston-area sun-and-sea worshippers on any hot day in July or August.

Wingaersheek Beach (Atlantic Rd; parking weekdays/weekends $20/25) A wide swath of sand surrounded by Ipswich Bay, the Annisquam River and lots of sand dunes. At low tide a long sandbar stretches for more than half a mile out into the bay. Take Rte 128 to Exit 13.

Good Harbor Beach (Thatcher Rd, Rte 127A; parking weekdays/weekends $25/20) A spacious, sandy beach midway between Gloucester and Rockport. The parking lot fills up before the beach does, so if you get here early enough, you will enjoy the minimal crowds all day long.

Stage Fort Park (978-281-9785; parking Mon-Fri $10, Sat & Sun $15) Includes two lovely small beaches: the picturesque Half-Moon Beach and the more remote Cressy's Beach. It's off MA127, just south of the cut.

your bank. But the menu of fresh seafood and local produce means you will dine like a gourmand. Specialties include the oysters of the day – served with two special sauces – and the to-die-for lobster risotto, which features ever-changing seasonal vegetables. Reservations recommended.

Drinking & Entertainment

Crow's Nest PUB
(www.crowsnestgloucester.com; 334 Main St; ⊘11am-1am) The down-and-dirty fisherfolk bar made famous in *The Perfect Storm*. But this is the real deal, not the set the movie folks threw up for a few weeks during filming. Come early if you want to drink with the fish crews in summer.

Rhumb Line LIVE MUSIC
(www.therhumbline.com; 40 Railroad Ave; ⊘11:30am-1am) This club across from the train station is the best place on Cape Ann to hear live music, with performances six nights a week. Acts range from mellow acoustic and blues to high-energy rock, with the occasional open-mike night.

Gloucester Stage Company THEATER
(www.gloucesterstage.com; 267 E Main St) This company stages excellent small-theater productions of classics and modern works. Excellent summer theater.

Shopping

Bookstore of Gloucester BOOKSTORE
(www.gloucesterbooks.com; 61 Main St; ⊘9am-6pm Mon-Sat, till 8pm Thu, noon-5pm Sun) This

Main St bookstore features local authors and themes.

ℹ Information

Cape Ann Chamber of Commerce (www.capeannvacations.com; 33 Commercial St; ⊘8am-5:30pm Mon-Fri, 10am-6pm Sat, 10am-4pm Sun) South of St Peter's Sq.

ℹ Getting There & Away

CAR
You can reach Cape Ann quickly from Boston or North Shore towns via four-lane Rte 128, but the scenic route on MA 127 follows the coastline through the prim villages of Prides Crossing, Manchester-by-the-Sea and Magnolia.

TRAIN
Take the Rockport line of the **MBTA commuter rail** (www.mbta.com) from Boston's North Station to Gloucester ($9.25, one hour).

Rockport

At the northern tip of Cape Ann, Rockport is a quaint contrast to gritty Gloucester. Rockport takes its name from its 19th-century role as a shipping center for granite cut from the local quarries. The stone is still ubiquitous: monuments, building foundations, pavements and piers remain as a testament to Rockport's past.

That's about all that remains of this industrial history, however. A century ago, Winslow Homer, Childe Hassam, Fitz Hugh Lane and other acclaimed artists came to Rockport's rugged shores, inspired by the hearty fisherfolk who wrested a hard but satisfying living from the sea. Today Rockport makes its living from tourists who come to look at the artists. The artists have long since given up looking for hearty fishermen because the descendants of the fishers are all running boutiques and B&Bs.

⊙ Sights & Activities

The center of town is Dock Sq, at the beginning of Bearskin Neck. Parking in Rockport is difficult on summer weekends. Unless you arrive very early, you'd do well to park at one of the lots on MA 127 from Gloucester and take the shuttle bus to Rockport's center.

Dock Square   SQUARE
Dock Sq is the hub of Rockport. Visible from here, the red fishing shack decorated with colorful buoys is known as Motif No 1, since it has been captured by so many artists for so many years. (Actually, it should be called Motif No 1-B, as the original shack vanished during a great storm in 1978 and a brand-new replica was erected in its place.)

Bearskin Neck   STREET
(www.bearskinneck.net) Bearskin Neck is the peninsula that juts into the harbor, lined with galleries, lobster shacks and souvenir shops.

The name Bearskin Neck apparently comes from a historic account of a young boy who was attacked by a bear. In an attempt to save the boy, his uncle, Ebenezer Babson, went after the bear with the only weapon he had available at the time – his fish knife. Babson managed to kill the bear and save the child, and then he skinned the bear and laid the pelt on the rocks to dry. The legend lives on in rhyme: 'Babson, Babson, killed a bear, with his knife, I do declare.'

Paper House   NOTABLE BUILDING
(www.paperhouserockport.com; 52 Pigeon Hill St; adult/child $2/1; ⊙10am-5pm Apr-Oct) In 1922, long before there was any municipal recycling program, Elis F Stenman decided that something useful should be done with all those daily newspapers lying about. He and his family set to work folding, rolling and pasting the papers into suitable shapes as building materials. Twenty years and 100,000 newspapers later, they had built the Paper House.

The walls are 215 layers thick, and the furnishings – table, chairs, lamps, sofa, even a grandfather clock and a piano – are all made of newspaper. Some pieces even specialize: one desk is made from *Christian Science Monitor* reports of Charles Lindbergh's flight, and the fireplace mantel is made from rotogravures drawn from the *Boston Sunday Herald* and the *New York Herald Tribune*. The text is still legible on all of the newspapers so there is built-in reading material (literally).

The Paper House is inland from Pigeon Cove. From MA 27, take Curtiss St to Pigeon Hill Rd.

North Shore Kayak
Outdoor Center   OUTDOORS
(☑978-546-5050; www.northshorekayak.com; 9 Tuna Wharf; kayaks per day $35-50, bikes per day $25) Rockport is a perfect base for sea kayaking – a great way to explore the rocky coast of Cape Ann. Besides renting kayaks, this outfit offers kayak tours, starting at $40/25 adult/child for a two-hour tour.

✪ Festivals & Events

★ Rockport Chamber
Music Festival   MUSIC
(☑978-546-7391; www.rcmf.org; 37 Main St) In June and July, this festival hosts concerts by internationally acclaimed performers. Concerts take place at the Shalin Liu Performance Center, a gorgeous hall overlooking the ocean. Most concerts sell out, so it's advisable to order tickets in advance.

🛏 Sleeping

Every year B&Bs open around Cape Ann: search out this emerging market at www.capeannvacations.com or www.innsofrockport.com. Breakfast is included unless otherwise indicated.

★ Tuck Inn   B&B $$
(☑978-546-7260; www.tuckinn.com; 17 High St; r $145-165, ste $185; P❄@🛜♨👯) Despite the unfortunate name, this inn offers excellent value. The renovated 1790s Colonial home has nine rooms and a four-person suite. Elegant communal rooms feature period decor. Local artwork and homemade quilts are some of the little touches that make the rooms special. The breakfast buffet – complete with fresh, seasonal fruit salads, and fresh-baked muffins and pastries – will be a highlight of your stay.

Lantana House   B&B $$
(☑978-546-3535; www.thelantanahouse.com; 22 Broadway; r $120-140, ste $160-235; P❄🛜) Conveniently located, Lantana House features

spacious rooms with floral bedspreads and lace curtains. The wide, airy porch and sundeck are wonderful places to have breakfast in the morning or a rest in the afternoon.

Addison Choate Inn   B&B $$
(✆978-546-7543; www.addisonchoateinn.com; 49 Broadway; r $155-179, ste $195; P❄🛜) This Greek Revival residence stands out among Rockport's historic inns. The traditional decor includes canopy beds, wide-plank hardwood floors and period wallpaper. The third-floor suite overlooks Rockport harbor.

Captain's Bounty on the Beach   MOTEL $$
(✆978-546-9557; www.captainsbountymotorinn.com; 1 Beach St; r from $180, ste $220; P❄🛜🖥) The draw here is the prime location, right on Front Beach and a short stroll from Dock Sq. The 24 rooms are simple, but they all have lovely views of the beach, where the local lobsterfolk check their traps at dawn. Breakfast is not included, but you can make your own, as all of the rooms have refrigerators and microwaves, while some are equipped with full kitchens.

Sally Webster Inn   B&B $$
(✆978-546-9251, 877-546-9251; www.sallywebster.com; 34 Mt Pleasant St; r $130-160; P❄@🛜) This handsome brick Colonial place, built in 1832, offers eight rooms with early American decor. Many have working fireplaces, and all have authentic architectural details and period furniture. Well-groomed flower beds and cool ocean breezes make the terrace a wonderful respite.

Inn on Cove Hill   B&B $$
(✆978-546-2701; www.innoncovehill.com; 37 Mt Pleasant St; r $150-165, ste $250; P) This is a Federal-style house built in 1791 with, so they say, pirates' gold that was discovered nearby. It has been lovingly restored down to the tiniest detail. Doubles have wide-plank hardwood floors, ornate moldings and canopy beds. The location, a block from Dock Sq, is hard to beat.

Bearskin Neck Motor Lodge   MOTEL $$
(✆978-546-6677; www.bearskinneckmotorlodge.com; 64 Bear Skin Neck; d $189-209; P🛜) The only lodging on Bearskin Neck is this motel-style lodge near the end of the strip. Needless to say, every room has a great view and a balcony from where you can enjoy it. Otherwise, the rooms are pretty plain and probably overpriced. Breakfast not provided.

✗ Eating & Drinking

Dock Sq has several cafes, while Bearskin Neck is crowded with ice-cream stores, cafes and cozy restaurants – and plenty of seafood. Many places reduce hours or close completely for the winter. Rockport is a dry town, meaning that alcohol is not sold in stores and rarely in restaurants, and there are no bars. However, most restaurants allow you to bring your own drinks (though they may charge a corkage fee).

You can buy liquor outside Rockport at **Lanesville Package Store** (1080 Washington St/MA 127, Lanesville; ⊘8am-9pm Mon-Sat, noon-6pm Sun) or **Liquor Locker** (www.liquorlocker gloucester.com; 287 Main St, Gloucester; ⊘8am-10pm Mon-Sat, noon-6pm Sun).

Top Dog   HOTDOGS, SEAFOOD $
(www.topdogrockport.com; 2 Doyle's Cove Rd; dogs $5-8; ⊘11am-4pm Mon-Thu, 11am-7pm Fri & Sat Apr-Oct; 🖥) More than a dozen kinds of dogs, from a German Shepherd (with fresh sauerkraut) to a Chihuahua (with jalapenos, salsa and cheese). Located on the Neck.

Helmut's Strudel   BAKERY $
(69 Bearskin Neck; desserts $5-8; ⊘breakfast & lunch; 🖉🖥) For dessert, try this bakery, almost near the outer end, serving various strudels, filled croissants, pastries, cider and coffee. Four shaded tables overlook the yacht-filled harbor.

★Roy Moore Lobster Company   SEAFOOD $$
(39 Bearskin Neck; mains $5-20; ⊘8am-6pm) This takeout kitchen has the cheapest lobster-in-the-rough on the Neck. Your beast comes on a tray with melted butter, a fork and a wet wipe for cleanup. Find a seat at a picnic table on the back patio. Don't forget to bring your own beer or wine.

Flav's Red Skiff   SEAFOOD $$
(15 Mount Pleasant St; mains $8-15; ⊘breakfast & lunch; 🖥) Be prepared to wait for a table at this old-fashioned seafood shack, in the heart of Rockport, close to the T Wharf. Come for pancakes and eggs for breakfast, or clam chowder and lobster rolls for lunch. It doesn't look like much, but the service is friendly and the fish is fresh.

Ellen's Harborside   DINER $$
(www.ellensharborside.com; 1 Wharf Rd; mains $10-22; ⊘breakfast, lunch & dinner Apr-Oct; 🖥) By the T-wharf in the center of town, Ellen's has grown famous serving a simple menu

LOCAL KNOWLEDGE

DOGTOWN

Much of the interior of Cape Ann is wild and undeveloped, partially protected by reservations, but mostly left to the whims of nature and history. This vast territory is known as Dogtown.

Those who venture into Dogtown might discover the mysterious glacial **rock formations** that inspired artist Marsden Hartley; the ruins of an ancient, **abandoned Colonial settlement**; or strange, stern **rock inscriptions** that date to the Great Depression. It's a beautiful but foreboding place, which has seen more than its fair share of mystery and tragedy, as detailed in Elyssa East's award-winning book *Dogtown: Death and Enchantment in a New England Ghost Town*.

Dogtown contains miles and miles of trails, but they are poorly maintained and mostly unmarked. Simply put, it's not easy to navigate. Let a local expert show you the way, with **Walk the Words** (www.walkthewords.com; adult/child $15/7; ⊙9am daily), a two-hour hike to Dogtown's most intriguing spots. If you want to go it alone, pick up a map from the Bookstore of Gloucester (p109). You can access Dogtown between Gloucester and Annisquam. From MA 127, take Reynaud St to Cherry St.

of American breakfasts, chicken, ribs and lobster since 1954. You get decent portions, fresh food and low prices. Consider the award-winning clam chowder.

Brothers Brew Coffee Shop   CAFE
(27 Main St; ⊙7am-4pm Mon-Sat, 7am-noon Sun) Two words: coffee and doughnuts. There are other (perhaps healthier) options for breakfast, but go for the doughnuts. You won't regret it.

ⓘ Information

Rockport Chamber of Commerce (www.rockportusa.com; Upper Main St; ⊙9am-5pm Mon-Sat Apr-Oct, 11am-2pm Mon, Wed & Fri Nov-Mar) Located about 1 mile out of town on Rte 127.

See Cape Ann (www.seecapeann.com) Cape Ann's online information booth.

ⓘ Getting There & Around

BUS

The **Cape Ann Transportation Authority** (www.canntran.com) operates bus routes between the towns of Cape Ann.

CAR

MA 127/127A loops around Cape Ann, connecting Magnolia and Gloucester to Rockport. Driving the entire loop is worth it for the seaside scenery in East Gloucester, Lanesville and Annisquam.

Street parking in Rockport is in short supply in summer, but you can park for free in the **Blue Gate Parking Lot** (Upper Main St; ⊙11am-7pm Jun-Oct), then take the trolley (or walk) the three quarters of a mile to Dock Sq.

TRAIN

Take the **MBTA commuter rail** (www.mbta.com) from Boston's North Station to Rockport ($10, one hour).

Around Cape Ann

Hammond Castle Museum

Dr John Hays Hammond, Jr (1888–1965) was an electrical engineer and inventor who amassed a fortune fulfilling defense contracts. With this wealth, Hammond pursued his passion for collecting European art and architecture. His eccentric home is a **medieval castle** (www.hammondcastle.org; 80 Hesperus Ave, Magnolia; adult/child $10/8; ⊙10am-4pm Sat & Sun Apr-Jun, Tue-Sat Jul & Aug), which he built to house all his treasures, dating from the Romanesque, medieval, Gothic and Renaissance periods. Furnishings are eclectic and interesting, including a magnificent 8200-pipe organ in the Romanesque Great Hall.

Hammond Castle overlooks several spectacular natural features. Painted by Fitz Hugh Lane and many other artists over the years, **Rafe's Chasm** is a cleft in the rocky shoreline that is characterized by turgid and thrashing water. Near it is **Norman's Woe**, the reef on which the ship broke up in Longfellow's poem *The Wreck of the Hesperus*.

Halibut Point Reservation

Only a few miles north of Dock Sq along MA 127 is **Halibut Point Reservation** (www.thetrustees.org; ⊙dawn-dusk; [P]) **FREE**. A 10-minute walk through the forest brings you to yawning, abandoned granite quarries, huge hills of broken granite rubble, and a granite foreshore of tumbled, smoothed rock, perfect for picnicking, sunbathing, reading or painting. The surf can be strong here, making swimming unwise, but natural pools are good for wading or cooling your feet. A map is available at the entrance. Parking costs $2.

Ipswich & Essex

POP IPSWICH 13,200, ESSEX 3500

Heading up the North Shore from Cape Ann, Ipswich and Essex are pretty New England towns surrounded by rocky coast and sandy beaches, extensive marshlands, forested hills and rural farmland.

Ipswich is one of those New England towns that is pretty today because it was poor in the past. Because it had no harbor, and no source of waterpower for factories, commercial and industrial development went elsewhere in the 18th and 19th centuries. As a result, Ipswich's 17th-century houses were not torn down to build grander residences. Today the town is famous for its ample antique shops and succulent clams. Formerly the home of novelist John Updike, it is also the setting for some of his novels and short stories like *A&P*, which is based on the local market.

◎ Sights & Activities

Crane Beach   BEACH
(www.thetrustees.org; Argilla Rd, Ipswich; admission $2; ⊙8am-dusk; ⬦) One of the longest, widest, sandiest beaches in the region is Crane Beach, with 4 miles of fine-sand barrier beach on Ipswich Bay. It is set in the midst of the Crane Wildlife Refuge, so the entire surrounding area is pristinely beautiful. Five miles of trails traverse the dunes. The only downside is the pesky greenhead flies that buzz around (and bite) in late July and early August. Parking costs $25/15 on weekends/weekdays.

Crane Estate   HISTORIC HOUSE
(www.thetrustees.org; Argilla Rd, Ipswich; per car/bike $10/2; ⊙8am-dusk; [P]) Above Crane Beach, on Castle Hill sits the 1920s estate of Chicago plumbing-fixture magnate Richard T Crane. The 59-room Stuart-style **Great House** (290 Argilla Rd, Ipswich; adult/child $12/7;

⊙10am-4pm Wed-Thu, 10am-1pm Fri-Sat Jun-Oct) is the site of summer concerts and special events. It's open for tours in summer, but only a few days a week. The lovely landscaped grounds, which are open daily, contain several miles of walking trails.

Appleton Farms   FARM
(www.thetrustees.org; 219 County Rd, Ipswich; ⊙8am-dusk; ⬦) **FREE** Four miles of trails wind along old carriageways, past ancient stonewall property markers and through acres of beautiful grasslands. The store sells fresh, organically grown produce, not to mention tantalizing jams, spreads and sauces made with said produce. From MA 128 take MA 1A north. Turn left on Cutler Rd and drive 2 miles to the intersection with Highland Rd.

Essex Shipbuilding Museum   MUSEUM
(www.essexshipbuildingmuseum.org; 66 Main St, Essex; guided tour adult/child $10/5, self-guided $7; ⊙10am-5pm Wed-Sun Jun-Oct, Sat & Sun Nov-May; ⬦) This unique museum was established in 1976 as a local repository for all of the shipbuilding artifacts of the local residents. Most of the collections of photos, tools and ship models came from local basements and attics, allowing Essex to truly preserve its local history. Most of the collections are housed in the town's 1835 schoolhouse (check out the Old Burying Ground behind it).

The historical society also operates the Waterline Center in the museum shipyard, a section of waterfront property where shipbuilding activities have taken place for hundreds of years. The historic Essex-built schooner, *Evelina M Goulart*, is moored here.

Essex River Basin Adventures   KAYAKING
(☏978-768-3722; www.erba.com; 1 Main St, Essex; tours $45-75; ⊙10am-5pm Mon-Sat, noon-5pm Sun) Explore the tidal estuaries of the Essex River. Tours include basic kayak instruction, as well as plenty of opportunities for birdwatching. Romantics will have a hard time choosing between a sunset paddle around the Essex River Basin and a moonlight paddle to Crane's Beach.

🛏 Sleeping & Eating

Inn at Castle Hill   INN $$$
(☏978-412-2555; innatcastlehill.thetrustees.org; 280 Argilla Rd, Ipswich; r woodland-view $195-240, ocean-view $250-425; [P]✳🛜) 🍴 On the grounds of the Crane Estate, this inn is an example of understated luxury. In the midst

of acres of beautiful grounds, the inn boasts 10 rooms, each uniquely decorated with subtle elegance. Turndown service, plush robes and afternoon tea are some of the very civilized perks. Instead of televisions (of which there are none), guests enjoy a wraparound verandah and its magnificent views of the surrounding sand dunes and salt marshes.

★ **JT Farnham's**　　SEAFOOD $$$
(88 Eastern Ave, Essex; mains $15-25; ☺ lunch & dinner; 🖶) When the Food Network came to Essex to weigh in on the fried-clam debate for the show *Food Feud*, the winner was JT Farnham, thanks to the crispiness of his clams. Pull up a picnic table and enjoy the amazing estuary view.

Clam Box　　SEAFOOD $$$
(www.ipswichma.com/clambox; 246 High St/MA 133, Ipswich; mains $15-25; ☺ lunch & dinner) You can't miss this classic clam shack, just north of Ipswich center. Built in 1938, it actually looks like a clam box, spruced up with striped awnings. Folks line up out the door for crispy fried clams and onion rings – arguably the best in the land.

Woodman's　　SEAFOOD $$$
(www.woodmans.com; 121 Main St/MA 133, Essex; mains $7-25; ☺ lunch & dinner; 🖶) This roadhouse is the most famous spot in the area to come for clams, any way you like them. The specialty is Chubby's original fried clams and crispy onion rings. But this place serves everything from boiled lobsters to homemade clam cakes to a seasonal raw bar.

❶ Getting There & Away

CAR
From Gloucester, MA 133 heads north to Essex and on to Ipswich. If you're coming from Boston, get off I-95 at Topsfield Rd, which takes you into Ipswich.

TRAIN
Ipswich is on the Newburyport line of the **MBTA commuter rail** (www.mbta.com). Trains leave Boston's North Station for Ipswich ($8.75, 50 minutes) about 12 times each weekday and five times on Saturday (no trains Sunday).

Newburyport

POP 17,600
At the mouth of the Merrimack River, Newburyport prospered as a shipping port and silversmith center during the late 18th century. Not too much has changed in the last 200 years, as Newburyport's brick buildings and graceful churches still show off the Federal style that was popular back in those days. Today the center of this town is a model of historic preservation and gentrification. Newburyport is also the gateway to the barrier Plum Island, a national wildlife refuge with some of the best bird-watching in New England.

◉ Sights & Activities

All major roads (MA 113, US 1 and US 1A) lead to the center of the town's commercial and historic district, around the junction of Water and State Sts.

Custom House Maritime Museum　　MUSEUM
(www.customhousemaritimemuseum.org; 25 Water St; adult/senior & child $7/5; ☺ 10am-4pm Tue-Sat & noon-4pm Sun May-Dec, Sat-Sun only Jan-Apr) The 1835 granite Custom House is an excellent example of Classic Revival architecture, built by Robert Mills (of Washington Monument fame). It now houses the Maritime Museum, which exhibits artifacts from Newburyport's maritime history as a major shipbuilding center and seaport. Seafaring folk will have a field day in the Moseley Gallery with its collection of model clipper ships.

Cushing House Museum & Garden　　HISTORIC HOUSE
(www.newburyhist.com; 98 High St; adult/child & student $8/2; ☺ 10am-4pm Tue-Fri, noon-4pm Sat & Sun Jun-Oct) This 21-room Federal home is decked out with fine furnishings and decorative pieces from the region. Collections of portraits, silver, needlework, toys and clocks are all on display, not to mention the impressive Asian collection from Newburyport's early Chinese trade. The museum offers guided tours, exhibits, special events and lectures.

Newburyport Whale Watch　　WILDLIFE WATCHING
(☎ 800-848-1111; www.newburyportwhalewatch. com; 54 Merrimac St; adult/child $48/33; 🖶) Offers bird- and whale-watching tours, as well as occasional cruises to the Isle of Shoals.

⎚ Sleeping

Like many historic North Shore towns, Newburyport has become full of B&Bs. Several motels and hotels are in nearby towns. For a complete list of places to stay and website links, check out www.newburyportchamber. org. Breakfast is included unless otherwise indicated.

Essex Street Inn BOUTIQUE HOTEL **$$**
(☎978-465-3148; www.essexstreetinn.com; 7 Essex St; r $135-165, ste $215-275; P ❄ 🕏 🛗) This Victorian inn was built as a lodging house in 1880. Today it's an elegant place to stay, albeit less intimate than some of the other options in Newburyport. The 37 rooms are nicely decorated with elegant 19th-century furnishings and details (some with fireplaces), while some of the more expensive rooms feature whirlpools and kitchenettes.

Clark Currier Inn GUESTHOUSE **$$**
(☎978-465-8363; www.clarkcurrierinn.com; 45 Green St; r $155-190, ste $205-215; P ❄ @ 🕏) Travelers in search of a genteel experience can luxuriate in this 1803 Federal mansion, with its stately parlor and welcoming library. A fish pond and gazebo adorn the gardens, which are gorgeous in season. Details such as fireplaces and canopy beds make the seven guest rooms extra charming.

Garrison Inn BOUTIQUE HOTEL **$$$**
(☎978-499-8500; www.garrisoninn.com; 11 Brown Sq; d $190-270, ste from $290; P ❄ 🕏 🛏 🛗) Once a private mansion, this gracious, red-brick building is named for William Lloyd Garrison, the abolitionist who was born in Newburyport. After a recent overhaul, its 24 luxurious 'boudoirs' are done up in an elegant, eclectic mix of contemporary and classic. Original architectural features such as exposed-brick walls, cathedral ceilings and spiral staircases are highlighted.

The restaurant on-site, David's Tavern, is acclaimed for its menu of eclectic American haute cuisine (not to mention child care while you dine!).

🍴 Eating & Drinking

Revitalive Cafe & Juice Bar VEGAN **$**
(www.revitalive.com; 50 Water St, The Tannery Mall; mains $8-10; ☺9am-6pm Mon-Thu, 9am-5pm Fri-Sun; 🍴) Vegan, gluten-free, raw – whatever your dietary restriction, this sweet little cafe has got you covered. Even if you're an omnivore, you'll drool over the fresh salads, fresh-made soups and fresh-squeezed juices. Or feast on a deliciously healthy 'bowl,' built on quinoa or rice. Also: smoothies.

Loretta AMERICAN **$$**
(www.lorettarestaurant.com; 27 State St; sandwiches $8-10, dinner $13-23; ☺lunch & dinner) With memorabilia on the walls and barbecue and burgers on the menu, Loretta specializes in all-American goodness. While local, seasonal ingredients are in full play, the menu features many regional dishes from around the country, such as crawfish étouffé and St Louis smoked barbecue ribs. Giant portions, small space.

Glenn's Restaurant &
Cool Bar INTERNATIONAL, SEAFOOD **$$$**
(www.glennsrestaurant.com; 44 Merrimac St; mains $20-30; ☺dinner Tue-Sun) Glenn is out to spice up your life. He's got the seafood you are looking for, but he's serving it in ways you never imagined. Oysters might come baked with chili pesto. Spiced lobster gets stuffed in a spring roll with Szechuan sauce. The menu changes frequently, but it's always exciting.

Aside from the creative cooking, there's an excellent wine list and live jazz on Sunday afternoons. The only downside is that service is unreliable – if you come on a bad night, stay cool!

ℹ Information

Greater Newburyport Chamber of Commerce
(www.newburyportchamber.org; 38 Merrimac St; ☺9am-5pm Mon-Fri, 10am-4pm Sat, noon-4pm Sun) Seasonal information booth in Market Sq from June to October.

ℹ Getting There & Away

BUS
C&J Trailways (www.ridecj.com; Storey Ave) runs hourly buses from Logan International Airport (one way/round-trip $22/40) and Boston's South Station (one way/round-trip $16/27). Kids under 18 ride free with a full-fare adult.

CAR
From I-95 north, take exit 57 and follow signs to downtown Newburyport. There are free parking lots on Green and Merrimack Sts.

TRAIN
MBTA commuter rail (www.mbta.com) runs a line from North Station to Newburyport ($10, one hour). There are more than 10 trains daily on weekdays, and there's six on weekends.

Plum Island

A barrier island off the coast of Massachusetts, Plum Island is named for the smallish plum shrubs that grow wild along the coast. The long, skinny island has 9 miles of wide, sandy beaches surrounded by acres of wildlife sanctuary. These are among the nicest beaches on the North Shore, especially if you head to the furthest points on the island.

Unfortunately, the beaches in the Parker River Wildlife Refuge are generally closed April to June because of nesting piping plovers, but you can go to the public beaches at the north end of the island, where there is a community of vacation homes. In 2013, this area was battered by storms, resulting in eight houses washing into the ocean and many others remaining in danger.

Plum Island is 5 miles east of downtown Newburyport, along the Plum Island Turnpike.

◉ Sights & Activities

Parker River National Wildlife Refuge
WILDLIFE REFUGE
(www.fws.gov/refuge/parker_river; Plum Island; per car/bike or pedestrian $5/2; ☉ dawn-dusk) The 4662-acre sanctuary occupies the southern three-quarters of Plum Island. More than 800 species of birds, plants and animals reside in its many ecological habitats, including beaches, sand dunes, salt pans, salt marshes, freshwater impoundments and maritime forests.

There are several observation areas that are excellent for spotting shorebirds and waterfowl, including herons and egrets. Large portions of the refuge are closed because they provide an important habitat for the endangered piping plover. Inland, there are freshwater impoundments, as well as an extensive swamp and forest. During spring and fall, you can observe migrating songbirds, including magnificent wood-warblers in the woods. In winter the refuge is a good place to see waterfowl, the rough-legged hawk and snowy owl.

Foot trails allow access to much of the area. Observation towers and platforms dot the trails at prime bird-watching spots.

Sandy Point State Reservation
BEACH
(www.mass.gov/dcr; ☉ dawn-8pm; ♿) At the southern tip of Plum Island, Sandy Point is a 77-acre state park that is popular for swimming, sunning and tidepooling. Walking trails and an observation tower also make for good bird-watching. Access Sandy Point through the Parker River National Wildlife Refuge.

Plum Island Kayak
KAYAKING
(☑ 978-462-5510; www.plumislandkayak.com; 38 Merrimac St, Newburyport; single/tandem kayaks per day $60/80; ☉ 9am-5pm Mon-Wed, 9am-8pm Thu-Sun Apr-Oct) Rent a kayak and explore Plum Island on your own, or join one of several tours during the day (or night) exploring the islands, mud bars, salt marshes and shorelines. Expect to see lots of birds, or for a truly unique experience, paddle among the resident seals.

🛏 Sleeping & Eating

★ Blue
INN $$$
(☑ 978-465-7171; www.blueinn.com; 20 Fordham Way; d from $385; 🅿 ❋ 🛜) In a drop-dead gorgeous location on a beautiful beach, this sophisticated inn is quite a surprise on unassuming Plum Island. Room decor features high ceilings, contemporary decor, fresh white linens and streaming sunlight. Private decks and in-room fireplaces are a few of the perks you will find, not to mention a bottle of wine chilling for your arrival.

Plum Island Grille
SEAFOOD $$$
(☑ 978-463-2290; www.plumislandgrille.com; Sunset Blvd, Plum Island; lunch mains $14-22, dinner mains $26-34; ☉ lunch Sat-Sun, dinner nightly) Cross the bridge to Plum Island and come across this sophisticated seafood grill, serving up grilled fish and a specialty oyster menu. The food is good but the setting is spectacular. Watch the sun set over the salt marsh and feast on the fruits of the sea. Reservations are recommended in season.

ⓘ Information

Parker River Visitors Center (www.fws.gov/ refuge/parker_river; 6 Plum Island Turnpike; ☉ 11am-4pm) On the mainland, just east of the causeway. Stop by for maps, exhibits and other information about the refuge.

SOUTH SHORE

As with much of the Massachusetts coast, the South Shore is blessed with historic sites and natural beauty. Seeing firsthand the challenges faced by the Pilgrims who first landed at Plymouth Rock is a vivid reminder of the value of religious tolerance and stubborn endurance – both at the core of the nation's foundation. Generations later, these values were lived out by founding father John Adams and his son John Quincy Adams.

Quincy

POP 92,900

Like all good New England towns, Quincy, about 10 miles south of Boston, is not pronounced the obvious way: say '*Quin*-zee' if you want to talk like the locals.

Quincy was first settled in 1625 by a handful of raucous colonists who could not stand the strict and stoic ways in Plymouth. History has it that this group went so far as to drink beer, dance around a maypole and engage in other festive Old English customs, which enraged the Puritans down the road. Nathaniel Hawthorne immortalized this history in his fictional account, *The Maypole of Merrimount*. Eventually, Myles Standish arrived from Plymouth to restore order to the wayward colony.

Quincy was officially incorporated as its own entity in 1792, named after Colonel John Quincy, a respected local leader and ancestor of revolutionary Josiah Quincy and First Lady Abigail Adams.

What makes Quincy notable – and earns this town the nickname 'The City of Presidents' – is that it is the birthplace of the second and sixth presidents of the United States: John Adams and John Quincy Adams. The collection of houses where the Adams family lived now makes up the Adams National Historic Park.

In more recent history, Quincy is the birthplace of the Dropkick Murphys and Dunkin' Donuts.

⊙ Sights & Activities

Adams National
Historic Park   HISTORIC HOUSES
(www.nps.gov/adam; 1250 Hancock St; adult/child $5/free; ⊙ 9am-5pm mid-Apr–mid-Nov; Ⓣ Quincy Center) The Adams family sights are accessible by guided tours departing from the Adams National Historic Park Visitor Center. Every half-hour (until 3:15pm), trolleys travel to the **John Adams and John Quincy Adams Birthplaces**, the oldest presidential birthplaces in the United States. These two 17th-century saltbox houses stand side by side along the old Coast Rd, which connected Plymouth to Boston.

The houses are furnished as they would have been in the 18th century, so visitors can see where John Adams started his law career, started his family and wrote the Massachusetts Constitution (which was later used as the basis for the US Constitution).

From here, the trolley continues to the **Old House**, also called Peacefields, which was the residence of four generations of the Adams family from 1788 to 1927. The house contains original furnishings and decora-tions from the Adams family, including the chair in which John Adams died on July 4, 1826, the 50th anniversary of the Declaration of Independence (and, spookily, the same day that Thomas Jefferson died on his estate in Virginia). On the grounds, the spectacular two-story library and the lovely formal gardens are highlights.

United First Parish Church   CHURCH
(www.ufpc.org; 1306 Hancock St; adult/child/senior & student $4/free/3; ⊙ 11am-4pm Mon-Fri & noon-4pm Sat-Sun mid-Apr–mid-Nov; Ⓣ Quincy Center) John and Abigail Adams and John Quincy and Louisa Catherine Adams are all interred in the basement of this handsome granite church in Quincy Center. The crypt is open by guided tour.

Reverend John Hancock (father to the famous patriot) had been the preacher at the old wooden meeting house that previously stood on this spot. In 1822, John Adams established a fund to replace the wooden church with the fine granite structure that stands today. The church was built in 1828 by Alexander Parris, who was also responsible for designing Quincy Market in Boston.

Hancock Cemetery   CEMETERY
(1307 Hancock St; Ⓣ Quincy Center) Opposite the church, Hancock Cemetery is the final resting place of many notable Quincy residents, including most of the Quincy and Adams families. The Adams family vault, near the street, was the original site of the graves of the presidents and their wives, before they were interred in the Presidential Crypt. A map to Hancock Cemetery is available at the United First Parish Church.

✕ Eating & Drinking

For eating in Quincy center, there is no shortage of ethnic restaurants, including Chinese, Japanese, Mongolian and Filipino. For drinking, take your pick from many Irish pubs.

Craig's Cafe   CAFE $
(1354 Hancock St; mains $8-10; ⊙ 7am-5pm Mon-Fri, 7am-1pm Sat; Ⓣ Quincy Center) Perfect for a light lunch or a packed picnic, this simple cafe serves soups, salads and sandwiches with a smile. Folks behind the counter seem to know most of the patrons by name.

Fat Cat   AMERICAN $$
(www.fatcatrestaurant.com; 24 Chestnut St; sandwiches $6-10, mains $13-18; ⊙ 11am-1am; Ⓣ Quincy Center) Quincy native Neil Kiley transformed

the city's old market place into a cool contemporary restaurant and bar, complete with exposed-brick walls and painted pipes, lending a hip post-industrial vibe. The menu has been created to match, featuring traditional pub fare with a twist. The specialty is the Fat Cat Wings, served with a dipping sauce of your choice.

Paddy Barry's   IRISH PUB
(www.paddybarrys.com; 1574 Hancock St; ⊙from 1pm Mon-Thu, from noon Fri-Sun; T Quincy Center) No food, just friendly folks, inviting atmosphere and perfectly poured Guinness. You might catch some live music, but the good craic is guaranteed.

ℹ Information

Adams National Historic Park Visitor Center (www.nps.gov/adam; 1250 Hancock St; ⊙9am-5pm mid-Apr–mid-Nov; T Quincy Center) Directly opposite the T-station. Tours of the national park start here, and plenty of information about the surrounding area is also available.

ℹ Getting There & Away

BOAT

The **MBTA F2 Ferry** (www.bostonharborcruises.com) travels between Long Wharf in Boston and Fore River Shipyard in Quincy (adult/child $8/free, 30 minutes, hourly).

CAR

If you are traveling by car, drive south from Boston on I-93 to exit 12 and follow the signs over the Neponset Bridge. Take Hancock St into Quincy Center.

METRO

The easiest way to reach the Adams National Historic Park from Boston is to take the Red Line to Quincy Center (Braintree line).

Plymouth

POP 56,500

Plymouth calls itself 'America's Home Town.' It was here that the Pilgrims first settled in the winter of 1620, seeking a place where they could practice their religion as they wished, without interference from government. An innocuous, weathered ball of granite – the famous Plymouth Rock – marks the spot where they supposedly first stepped ashore in this foreign land, and many museums and historic houses in the surrounding streets recall their struggles, sacrifices and triumphs.

◉ Sights

'The rock' is on Water St at the center of Plymouth, within walking distance of most museums and restaurants. Main St, the main commercial street, is a block inland. Some lodgings are within walking distance, but most require a car.

As New England's oldest European community, Plymouth has its share of fine old houses, some very old indeed.

★**Plymouth Rock**   MONUMENT
(Water St) Thousands of visitors come here each year to look at this weathered granite ball and to consider what it was like for the Pilgrims, who stepped ashore on this strange land in the autumn of 1620. We don't really know that the Pilgrims landed on Plymouth Rock, as it's not mentioned in any early written accounts. But the story gained popularity during Colonial times.

In 1774, 20 yoke of oxen were harnessed to the rock to move it – splitting the rock in the process. Half of the cloven boulder went on display in Pilgrim Hall from 1834 to 1867. The sea and wind lashed at the other half, and innumerable small pieces were chipped off and carried away by souvenir hunters over the centuries. By the 20th century the rock was an endangered artifact, and steps were taken to protect it. In 1921 the reunited halves were sheltered in the present granite enclosure. In 1989 the rock was repaired and strengthened to withstand weathering. And so it stands today, relatively small, broken and mended, an enduring symbol of the quest for religious freedom.

★**Mayflower II**   HISTORIC SITE
(www.plimoth.org; State Pier, Water St; adult/child $10/7; ⊙9am-5pm Apr-Nov; ♿) If Plymouth Rock tells us little about the Pilgrims, *Mayflower II* speaks volumes. It is a replica of the small ship in which they made the fateful voyage. Actors in period costume are often on board, recounting harrowing tales from the journey.

As you climb aboard, you have to wonder how 102 people – with all the household effects, tools, provisions, animals and seed to establish a colony – could have lived together on this tiny vessel for 66 days, subsisting on hard, moldy biscuits, rancid butter and brackish water as the ship passed through the stormy north Atlantic waters. But they did, landing on this wild, forested shore in the frigid months of December 1620 – testimony to their courageous spirit and the strength of their religious beliefs.

★Pilgrim Hall Museum   MUSEUM

(www.pilgrimhall.org; 75 Court St; adult/child/senior $8/5/7; ☉9:30am–4:30pm Feb-Dec; 🖐) Claiming to be the oldest continually operating public museum in the country, Pilgrim Hall Museum was founded in 1824. Its exhibits are not reproductions, but real objects that the Pilgrims and their Wampanoag neighbors used in their daily lives – from Governor Bradford's chair to Constance Hopkins' beaver hat.

The exhibits are dedicated to correcting the misrepresentations about the Pilgrims that have been passed down through history.

★Plimoth Plantation   MUSEUM

(www.plimoth.org; MA 3A; adult/child $26/15; ☉9am–5pm Apr-Nov; 🖐) Three miles south of Plymouth center, Plimoth Plantation authentically recreates the Pilgrims' settlement, in its primary exhibit entitled **1627 English Village**. Everything in the village – costumes, implements, vocabulary, artistry, recipes and crops – has been painstakingly researched and remade. Costumed interpreters, acting in character, explain the details of daily life and answer your questions as you watch them work and play.

During the winter of 1620–21, half of the Pilgrims died of disease, privation and exposure to the elements. But new arrivals joined the survivors the following year; by 1627 – just before an additional influx of Pilgrims founded the colony of Massachusetts Bay – Plymouth Colony was on the road to prosperity. Plimoth Plantation provides excellent educational and entertaining insight into what was happening in Plymouth during that period.

In the **crafts center**, you can help artisans as they weave baskets and cloth, throw pottery and build fine furniture using the techniques and tools of the early 17th century. Exhibits explain how these manufactured goods were shipped across the Atlantic in exchange for Colonial necessities.

The **Wampanoag Homesite** replicates the life of a Native American community in the same area during that time. Homesite huts are made of wattle and daub (a framework of woven rods and twigs covered and plastered with clay); inhabitants engage in traditional crafts while wearing traditional garb. Unlike the actors at the English Village, these individuals are not acting as historic characters, but are indigenous people speaking from a modern perspective.

Plimoth Grist Mill   MUSEUM

(www.plimoth.org/mill; 6 Spring Lane; adult/child $6/4.50; ☉9am–5pm Apr-Nov; 🖐) In 1636, local leaders constructed a gristmill on Town Brook, so the growing community could grind corn and produce corn meal. Today, the replica mill is on the site of the original, still grinding corn the old-fashioned way.

Visit on Wednesday or Saturday afternoon to see the waterwheel at work, hear the crackling of corn and smell the cornmeal as it is produced. On other days, tours demonstrate the process of grinding whole corn into cornmeal and discuss the ecology of the area.

Myles Standish State Forest   PARK

(www.friendsofmssf.com; Cranberry Rd, South Carver; 🖐) About six miles south of Plymouth, this 16,000-acre park is the largest public recreation area in southeastern Massachusetts. It contains 15 miles of biking and hiking trails and 16 ponds – two with beaches. It's a wonderful wilderness for picnicking, fishing, swimming and camping. From MA 3, take exit 5 to Long Pond Rd.

1667 Jabez Howland House   HISTORIC HOUSE

(www.pilgrimjohnhowlandsociety.org; 33 Sandwich St; adult/child/senior & student $4/2/3; ☉10am–4:30pm late May–mid-Oct) The only house in Plymouth that was home to a known *Mayflower* passenger. John Howland lived here with his wife Elizabeth Tilley and their son Jabez and his family. The house has been restored to its original appearance, complete with period furnishings and many artifacts and documents from the family.

Plymouth Antiquarian
Society   HISTORIC HOUSE

(www.plymouthantiquariansociety.org) Maintains three historic houses from three different centuries. The oldest is the **1677 Harlow Old Fort House** (119 Sandwich St; ☉2-6pm Thu Jun-Aug), one of the few remaining 'First Period' structures in Plymouth. Newly renovated, the **1749 Spooner House** (27 North St; ☉2-6pm Thu-Sat Jun-Aug) showcases 200 years of domestic life, complete with original furniture and housewares. Finally, the **1809 Hedge House** (126 Water St; ☉2-6pm Wed-Sun Jun-Aug) is a grand, Federal edifice overlooking Plymouth Harbor.

The society also oversees **Sacrifice Rock** (394 Old Sandwich Rd), the oldest of its historic

Plymouth

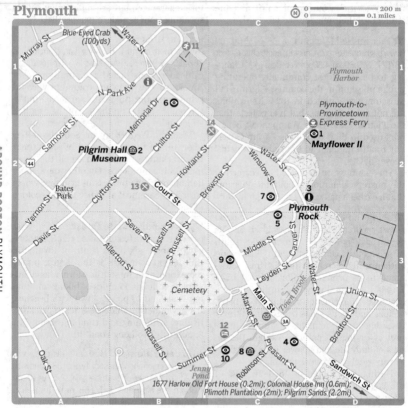

sites. 'The other rock' is an ancient landmark, where Wampanoag travelers would place branches and stones, as an offering in exchange for safe travels. It's about 6 miles south of Plymouth center.

Mayflower Society Museum   HISTORIC HOUSE
(www.themayflowersociety.com; 4 Winslow St; ⊙11am-4pm daily Jul-Sep, Sat & Sun Jun & Oct) The offices of the General Society of Mayflower Descendants is housed in the magnificent 1754 house of Edward Winslow, the great-grandson of Plymouth Colony's third governor. Guided tours show off antique furniture, family portraiture and stunning architectural details.

Richard Sparrow House   HISTORIC HOUSE
(www.sparrowhouse.com; 42 Summer St; adult/child $2/1; ⊙10am-5pm) Plymouth's oldest house, built by one of the original Pilgrim settlers in 1640. Today the house contains a small art gallery.

🏃 Activities

Capt John Boats   BOAT TOUR
(☑508-746-2643; www.captjohn.com; Town Wharf; adult/child $47/29; ⊙tours Apr-Oct; ⓐ) Offers loads of options to get you out on the water, including whale-watching cruises and fishing trips.

👉 Tours

Pilgrim Path   AUDIO TOUR
(www.pilgrimpathtours.com) The Plymouth Area Chamber of Commerce offers this free audio tour. Pick up an audio headset at the Destination Plymouth visitors center or download the audio clips from the website to your MP3 player before you arrive. The tour includes all the major historic sites, as well as other sites that were significant during Pilgrim times and some statues of 17th-century personalities that are scattered around town.

Plymouth

Plymouth Trolley Tours   TROLLEY TOUR
(www.p-b.com; 1 ride adult/child $10/5, all-day pass $15/7.50; ◷10am-5pm late Jun-Aug) This traditional trolley tour covers the history of Plymouth, from the Pilgrims to the fisherfolk. It includes all of the major sites – the all-day pass allows you to hop off to check them out, then hop back on the next trolley.

✷✷ Festivals & Events

**America's Hometown
Thanksgiving Celebration**   THANKSGIVING
(www.usathanksgiving.com) On the weekend before Thanksgiving, historic Plymouth comes to life as pilgrims, pioneers and patriots parade the streets of 'America's Hometown.' The weekend event features a food festival, a concert series, a craft show and the ongoing festivities at the 'historic village.' Have some fun, then stop by Plimoth Plantation to see how the Pilgrims really celebrated (or rather, didn't celebrate) Thanksgiving.

⊨ Sleeping

Continental breakfast is included unless otherwise indicated.

Pilgrim Sands   HOTEL **$$**
(☑508-747-0900; www.pilgrimsands.com; 150 Warren Ave; d $159-199, apt $309; ℗❄@☒♿) This mini resort is a good option for families as it's right on a private beach and directly opposite Plimoth Plantation. Rooms with an

ocean view are pricier, but the other rooms look out over Plimoth Plantation, which has its own charm. Rates decrease outside of summer months.

Colonial House Inn   B&B **$$**
(☑508-747-4274; www.thecolonialhouseinn.com; 207 Sandwich St; d $120-160; ℗❄☇♿) About a mile south of Plymouth center, this pleasant house has five guest rooms and one loft apartment, all of which are spacious and comfortable with a hint of elegance. The setting is pleasant for its views of the inner harbor and its location across from the salt marshes. Guests have access to a neighboring resort's private beach and swimming pool.

John Carver Inn   HOTEL **$$$**
(☑508-746-7100; www.johncarverinn.com; 25 Summer St; d $169-229, ste $309; ℗❄☇☒♿) This 80-room inn is a boon for families: special packages allow kids to stay for free and include entry to local sights. Best of all, the indoor Pilgrim-theme swimming pool (complete with a *Mayflower* replica!) will keep your little ones entertained for hours. All rooms feature traditional colonial decor, while the fancier ones boast four-poster beds and fireplaces.

✗ Eating

Fast-food shops line Water St opposite the *Mayflower II*. For better food at lower prices, walk a block inland to Main St, the attractive thoroughfare of Plymouth's business district, where restaurants are open year-round.

All-American Diner   DINER **$$**
(60 Court St; mains $6-12; ◷breakfast & lunch; ♿) Here in America's Hometown, what better place to eat than the All-American Diner? It's a classic red-white-and-blue place, with a breakfast menu that reads like a novel. From corn-beef hash to eggs Benedict and amazing omelets, all of the breakfast items get rave reviews (especially the home fries). If you prefer lunch, try the Thanksgiving sandwich.

Carmen's Café Nicole   MEXICAN, SEAFOOD **$$**
(www.carmenscafenicole.com; 114 Water St; mains $10-20; ◷breakfast & lunch) Boasting a wonderful view of Plymouth Harbor and outdoor seating, this eclectic cafe pulls off a wide variety of delicious dishes, from decadent breakfasts (featuring the signature bananas foster French toast) to traditional seafood to

surprisingly satisfying Mexican combos (eg tacos del mar). The 'famous' Pilgrim wrap with turkey, stuffing and cranberry sauce is famous for a good reason.

Blue-Eyed Crab SEAFOOD $$$
(www.blue-eyedcrab.com; 170 Water St; sandwiches $10-13, dinner mains $20-30; ⊙lunch & dinner) There are a few tried-and-true seafood restaurants clustered around Town Wharf. But if you like a little innovation with your fish (and perhaps a cocktail or a glass of wine), head a bit further east to this fun and funky joint, with sea-blue walls and fish floating from the ceiling.

You can still get clam chowder and lobster rolls, but you can also try shrimp croquettes, pan-seared scallop salad or a crispy crab burger.

❶ Information

Destination Plymouth (www.seeplymouth. com; 130 Water St; ⊙9am-5pm Apr-Nov, until 8pm Jun-Aug) Located at the rotary across from Plymouth Harbor; provides loads of information about local attractions, as well as assistance with B&B reservations.

Plymouth Guide Online (www.plymouthguide. com) Lots of information about tourist attractions and local events.

❶ Getting There & Away

BOAT
The **Plymouth-to-Provincetown Express Ferry** (☑508-747-2400; www.p-townferry. com; State Pier, 77 Water St; adult/child/senior $43/33/38) deposits you on the tip of Cape Cod faster than a car would. From late June to early September, the 90-minute journey departs Plymouth at 10am and leaves Provincetown at 4:30pm.

---

❶ HERITAGE PASS

If you intend to visit all of Plymouth's most significant history sites, consider purchasing the **Heritage Pass** (adult/child $35/21), which includes admission to all the exhibits at Plimoth Plantation (two days), as well as the Mayflower II and Plimoth Grist Mill (one day each). Alternatively, the **Combination Ticket** (adult/child $30/19) includes Plimoth Plantation and one of the other sites. Both passes are good for one year after the date of purchase.

BUS
Buses operated by **Plymouth & Brockton** (www.p-b.com) travel hourly to South Station ($14, one hour) or Logan International Airport ($20) in Boston. The Plymouth P&B terminal is at the commuter parking lot, exit 5 off MA 3. Hop on a PAL bus into Plymouth center.

CAR
Plymouth is 41 miles south of Boston via MA 3; it takes an hour with some traffic. From Providence, it's the same distance and time, but you'll want to head west on US 44.

TRAIN
You can reach Plymouth from Boston by **MBTA commuter rail** (☑617-222-3200, 800-392-6100; www.mbta.com) trains, which depart from South Station three or four times a day ($10, 90 minutes). From the station at Cordage Park, PAL buses connect to Plymouth center.

❶ Getting Around

The **Plymouth Area Link** (PAL; www.gatra.org; adult/child $1/0.50) links the P&B bus terminal, Plymouth station at Cordage Park and Plymouth center. Passengers can flag down a bus from anywhere on the route.

New Bedford

POP 95,200

During its heyday as a whaling port (1765–1860), New Bedford commanded as many as 400 whaling ships. This vast fleet brought home hundreds of thousands of barrels of whale oil for lighting America's lamps. Novelist Herman Melville worked on one of these ships for four years, and thus set his celebrated novel, *Moby-Dick; or, The Whale,* in New Bedford. Nowadays, the city center constitutes the New Bedford Whaling National Historic Park (www.nps.gpv/ nebe; 33 Williams St; ⊙9am-5pm), with maps and other information available at the visitor center.

The centerpiece is the excellent, hands-on Whaling Museum (www.whalingmuseum.org; 18 Johnny Cake Hill; adult/child/senior & student $14/6/12/9; ⊙9am-5pm daily Jun-Dec, 9am-4pm Tue-Sun Jan-May), occupying seven buildings situated between William and Union Sts. A 66ft skeleton of a blue whale and a smaller skeleton of a sperm whale welcome you at the entrance. To learn what whaling was all about, you need only tramp the decks of the *Lagoda,* a fully rigged, half-size replica of an actual whaling bark.

LIZZIE BORDEN

Lizzie Borden took an axe
And gave her mother forty whacks.
And when she saw what she had done
She gave her father forty-one.

This children's rhyme is just one of many inconsistencies in the account of what happened in Fall River one night in 1892. Actually, Abby Borden was assaulted with 18 blows to the head with a hatchet, while Andrew Borden received 11. Ouch.

Although Lizzie Borden was acquitted of this crime, her story was rife with contradictions. That nobody else was ever accused was enough indication for Lizzie Borden to go down in popular history as America's most famous murderess.

Today, the Greek Revival Borden House in Fall River is the **Lizzie Borden Bed & Breakfast** (508-675-7333; www.lizzie-borden.com; 92 Second St; r $219-274). Decked out with period furnishings and decor, the eight rooms are named for the family members that actually stayed there. It's artfully and accurately remodeled, which makes it all the creepier. If you don't care to spend the night in the room where Abby Borden was found murdered, you can just come for a **tour** (adult/child $15/8; 11am-3pm).

Across the street from the museum, **Seamen's Bethel** (15 Johnny Cake Hill; admission by donation; 10am-5pm Mon-Fri late May–mid-Oct) **FREE** is the chapel that was immortalized in *Moby Dick*. This is where the marathon, nonstop reading of the novel takes place every year on January 3, the anniversary of Melville's embarkation from New Bedford harbor.

Getting There & Away

BOAT

Martha's Vineyard Express Ferry (www.mvexpressferry.com) runs from New Bedford to Vineyard Haven and Oak Bluffs on Martha's Vineyard (one-way adult/bike/child $38/7/22, one hour, at least four daily from mid-May to mid-October).

BUS

Peter Pan Bus (www.peterpanbus.com) offers bus services to/from Providence ($16, one hour, six daily) from the New Bedford ferry dock. **Dattco** (www.dattco.com) runs buses to Boston South Station (adult/child $13/9, 1½ hours, 12 daily), departing from the Southeastern Regional Transit Authority (SRTA) station at the corner of Elm and Pleasant Sts.

CAR

From I-195 take MA 18 south to exit 18S.

Fall River

'You sank my battleship!' This cry was ne'er heard aboard the mighty USS *Massachusetts*, a hulk of a craft that survived 35 battles in WWII, gunning down almost 40 aircraft and never losing a man in combat. Today, this heroic ship sits in a quiet corner of Mt Hope Bay known as **Battleship Cove** (www.battleshipcove.com; 5 Water St; adult/child $17/10.50; 9am-5pm). This beaut – longer than two football fields and taller than a nine-storey building – is only one of eight historic ships that visitors can explore at Battleship Cove.

The USS *Joseph P Kennedy Jr*, named for President John F Kennedy's older brother, did battle in the Korean and Vietnam Wars and is now a museum. The USS *Lionfish* is a WWII submarine still in full working condition. The Soviet-built *Hiddensee* is a fast attack craft that was obtained from Germany after the communist collapse. There are also two Patrol Torpedo (PT) boats, a landing craft, a Japanese attack boat and other craft.

To further experience life on board one of these fine ships, spring for **Nautical Nights** (per person $50 to $55), which allows you to sleep on one of the battleships. The price includes three meals as well as a host of movies and activities while on board.

Getting There & Away

BUS

Peter Pan Bus Lines (p84) runs six buses a day to Providence ($12, 30 minutes) and the same number to Boston ($19, one hour).

CAR

Fall River is about 50 miles south of Boston. Take I-93 south to Route 24, then merge onto Route 79. Otherwise it's 17 miles southeast of Providence on I-195.

Cape Cod, Nantucket & Martha's Vineyard

Best Places to Eat

➡ Chatham Fish Pier Market (p143)

➡ Company of the Cauldron (p164)

➡ Mews Restaurant & Cafe (p156)

➡ Bistrot de Soleil (p135)

➡ BlackFish (p151)

Best Places to Stay

➡ Carpe Diem (p155)

➡ Centerboard Inn (p161)

➡ Outermost Inn (p174)

➡ Wequassett Inn (p141)

➡ Anchor-In (p134)

Why Go?

When summer comes around, New England's top seashore destination gets packed to the gills. Cars stream over the two bridges that connect Cape Cod to the mainland, ferries shuttle visitors to and from the islands and coconut-oiled bodies plop down on towels all along the shore.

This trio of destinations offers a beach for every mood. You can surf a wild Atlantic wave or dip a paddle into a quiet cove. Or just chill out and watch the kids build sand castles.

But there's much more than sun, sand and surf. You'll find lighthouses to climb, clam shacks to frequent, and beach parties to revel in. The Cape and Islands have scenic cycling paths and hiking trails, intriguing art galleries and summer theater – and any one of them alone would be reason enough to come here.

When to Go
Barnstable

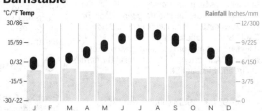

Jun–Aug In summer the ocean's warmest, the partying's hardest and the festivities are maxed.

Sep The beaches still dazzle, but the crowds thin, hotel rates drop and traffic jams disappear.

Oct–Nov Fall is ideal for cycling, hiking, kayaking – and even a little swimming.

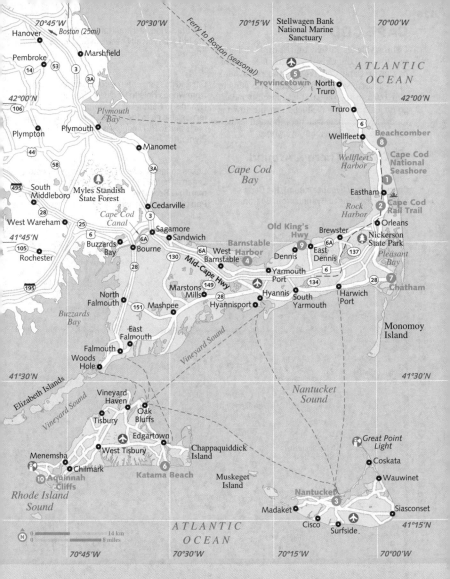

Cape Cod, Nantucket & Martha's Vineyard Highlights

1 Climbing dunes at **Cape Cod National Seashore** (p152)

2 Enjoying your own swimming hole on the **Cape Cod Rail Trail** (p139)

3 Wandering the cobbled *Moby Dick*–era streets of **Nantucket** (p158)

4 Ogling humpbacks from a **whale-watching** boat (p132)

5 Reveling in the carnival street scene in **Provincetown** (p151)

6 Riding a wave at **Katama Beach** (p171)

7 Eating fresh-off-the-boat seafood at **Chatham Fish Pier Market** (p143)

8 Joining the party scene at the **Beachcomber** (p150)

9 Antiquing your way along the **Old King's Highway** (p134)

10 Drinking up the sunset at the **Aquinnah Cliffs** (p174)

CAPE COD

Fishing villages, kitschy tourist traps and gen-teel towns – the Cape has many faces. Families favor Cape Cod Bay on the peninsula's quieter north side. College students looking to play hard in the day and let loose after dark go for Falmouth or Wellfleet. Provincetown is for art lovers, whale watchers, gay and lesbian travelers…well, just about everyone.

ⓘ Getting There & Around

AIR

Cape Air (www.flycapeair.com), the Cape's main carrier, flies to Hyannis from Boston,

Martha's Vineyard and Nantucket. Fares fluctuate but are typically between $50 and $100 one-way.

BOAT

Car and passenger ferries operate year-round from Woods Hole to Martha's Vineyard and from Hyannis to Nantucket. Seasonal passenger-only ferries also go to the islands from several Cape ports and to Provincetown from Boston and Plymouth.

BUS

Buses connect several Cape towns with Boston's Logan airport. Find schedules and fares at **Plymouth & Brockton** (www.p-b.com) and **Peter Pan** (www.peterpanbus.com).

Cape Cod

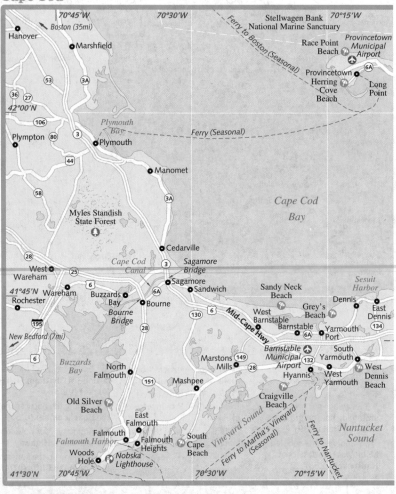

CAR

Two bridges, one in Bourne and the other in Sagamore, connect the Cape with the mainland. In summer they can back up for hours coming on Cape on Saturdays and going off Cape on Sundays, so avoid getting caught in the weekend snarl.

The Cape is fairly easy to navigate. MA 28 runs through the heart of Falmouth and most southside towns. MA 6A connects the northside towns. Most beaches and sights are on or near these roads.

Sandwich

POP 20,675

The Cape's oldest town (founded in 1637) makes a perfect first impression as you cross

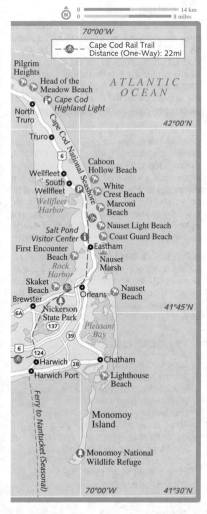

over the canal from the mainland. Head straight to the village center, where white-steepled churches, period homes and a grist mill surround a swan pond.

⊙ Sights & Activities

Cape Cod Canal CANAL
(www.capecodcanal.us; 🚹 🚲) **FREE** Cape Cod isn't connected by land to the mainland, but it's not exactly an island, or at least wasn't until the Cape Cod Canal was dug in 1914. The 7-mile-long canal saves ships from having to sail an extra 135 miles around the treacherous tip of the Cape.

The canal is also a great recreational resource bordered on both sides by bike paths that attract not only cyclists but also in-line skaters, power walkers and kids with fishing poles. On a sunny day it looks like a scene from a Norman Rockwell painting.

For the scoop on the how, what and why of the canal, stop by the **Cape Cod Canal Visitor Center** (📞 508-833-9678; www.capecodcanal.us; 60 Ed Moffitt Dr; ⊙10am-5pm) **FREE**, near the Sandwich Marina, where interactive exhibits capture the interest of kids. Follow your visit with a 10-minute walk along the canal to the beach. Unlike at other beaches, parking here is free. The center offers free programs throughout the summer, including guided hikes and bike rides, beach walks and talks; call for the current schedule.

Heritage Museums & Gardens MUSEUM
(📞 508-888-3300; www.heritagemuseumsandgardens.org; 67 Grove St; adult/child $15/7; ⊙10am-5pm; 🚹) Fun for kids and adults alike, the 76-acre Heritage Museums & Gardens sports a superb vintage automobile collection in a Shaker-style round barn, an authentic 1912 carousel (rides free with admission) and unusual folk art collections. The grounds also contain one of the finest rhododendron gardens in America; from mid-May to mid-June thousands of 'rhodies' blaze with color.

Sandwich Glass Museum MUSEUM
(📞 508-888-0251; www.sandwichglassmuseum.org; 129 Main St; adult/child $6/1.25; ⊙9:30am-5pm) Sandwich glass, now prized by collectors, had its heyday in the 19th century, and this heritage is artfully displayed here. But don't think it's just a period glass collection – there are also glass-blowing demonstrations given hourly throughout the day and a cool contemporary gallery.

ℹ CAPE-WIDE INFO

For Cape-wide tourist information, stop at the Cape Cod Chamber of Commerce (☑ 508-362-3225; www. capecodchamber.org; MA 132 at US 6, Hyannis; ⊙ 9am-5pm Mon-Sat, 10am-2pm Sun). The Cape Cod Times (www. capecodonline.com) also has oodles of visitor info online.

Dexter Grist Mill　　HISTORIC SITE
(☑ 508-888-5144; 2 Water St; adult/child $3/2; ⊙ 10am-5pm Mon-Sat, 1-5pm Sun) This restored mill on the edge of Shawme Pond dates to 1654 and has centuries-old gears that still grind cornmeal. Bring a camera; with its spinning waterwheel and paddling swans, it's one of the most photographed scenes on the Cape.

Thornton W Burgess Museum　　MUSEUM
(☑ 508-888-4668; www.thorntonburgess.org; 4 Water St; adult/child $3/1; ⊙ 10am-4pm Mon-Fri, 10am-1pm Sat; ⊕) A treat for young kids is the tiny Thornton W Burgess Museum, named for the Sandwich native who wrote the *Peter Cottontail* series. Storytime on the lawn, overlooking the pond featured in Burgess' works, can be particularly evocative – call for times.

Hoxie House　　HISTORIC BUILDING
(☑ 508-888-1173; 18 Water St; adult/child $3/2; ⊙ 11am-4:30pm Mon-Sat, 1-4:30pm Sun) Get a feel for what life was like for early settlers by touring Hoxie House, the oldest house on Cape Cod (c 1640). The saltbox-style house has been faithfully restored to the colonial period, complete with antiques, brick-fire hearth and the like.

🛏 Sleeping

Shawme-Crowell State Forest　CAMPGROUND $
(☑ 508-888-0351; www.reserveamerica.com; MA 130; tent sites $14) You'll find 285 cool and shady campsites (none with hookups) in this 760-acre pine and oak woodland. It's just one mile from the Cape Cod Canal and is popular with cyclists.

★ Annabelle Bed & Breakfast　　B&B $$
(☑ 508-833-8586; www.annabellebedandbreakfast. com; 4 Grove St; r incl breakfast $170-245; ❋ 🖱) This graceful hilltop inn, sequestered on two manicured acres, manages to feel secluded even though it's just a short walk from the town's attractions. Egyptian cotton sheets, Jacuzzis, evening wine by the fireplace – this is Sandwich at its cushiest. Top choice is the Beach Rose room, which opens to a large deck overlooking the gardens.

Belfry Inne & Bistro　　B&B $$$
(☑ 508-888-8550; www.belfryinn.com; 8 Jarves St; r incl breakfast $149-299; ❋ 🖱) Ever fall asleep in church? Then you'll love the rooms, some with stained-glass windows, in this creatively restored former church, now an upmarket B&B. If, on the other hand, you're uneasy about the angel Gabriel watching over you in bed, Belfry also has two other nearby inns with conventional rooms.

🍴 Eating

Seafood Sam's　　SEAFOOD $$
(www.seafoodsams.com; 6 Coast Guard Rd; mains $8-20; ⊙ 11am-9pm; ⊕) Opposite the Cape Cod Canal Visitor Center, Sam's is a good family choice for fish-and-chips, fried clams and lobster rolls. The $6 kids' menu adds to the appeal, as do the outdoor picnic tables, placed perfectly for watching fishing boats sail by.

Dunbar Tea Room　　CAFE $$
(www.dunbartea.com; 1 Water St; mains $10-24; ⊙ 8am-4:30pm) Tucked amid gardens, a swan pond and period homes, the tea room resembles a Victorian-era movie set. The crumpets, Ceylon tea and classical music just add to the setting. Drop by for a spot of tea or enjoy a leisurely lunch of hearty cheeses, curry salads and finger sandwiches.

Belfry Inne & Bistro　　MODERN AMERICAN $$$
(☑ 508-888-8550; www.belfryinn.com; 8 Jarves St; mains $27-38; ⊙ 5-9pm Wed-Sun) If you like quirky, this restaurant (in the B&B of the same name) occupies the sanctuary of a former church and is one of the Cape's more

ℹ LOCAL LINGO

Cape Codders use a somewhat confusing nomenclature for the Cape's regions. The 'Upper Cape' is nearest to the mainland and includes the towns of Sandwich, Falmouth and Mashpee. 'Mid-Cape' is the midregion, including Barnstable, Dennis and Yarmouth. The 'Lower Cape' generally refers to all points east of that. Also used is 'Outer Cape' to refer to the towns from Orleans north to Provincetown.

SANDWICH BOARDWALK

A local favorite that's missed by most visitors, this wooden-plank boardwalk extends a scenic 1350ft across an expansive marsh to Town Neck Beach. The beach itself is a bit rocky – so-so for swimming but perfect for walks and beach-combing. Once you reach the beach, turn right to make a 1.5-mile loop along the shoreline and then follow the creek back to the boardwalk. There's a $10 parking fee in July and August; at other times it's free. You won't find any signs: to get there, take MA 6A to the center of Sandwich, turn north onto Jarves St at the lights and then bear left onto Boardwalk Rd.

unusual fine-dining spots. The changing menu of New American cuisine strays beyond the predictable, with spicy options like chili-seared yellowfin tuna.

ℹ Information

You'll find visitor information at the **Sandwich Chamber of Commerce** (www.sandwichchamber.com) website.

ℹ Getting There & Away

If you arrive on the Cape via US 6, take exit 2 (MA 130). Water (MA 130), Main and Grove Sts converge in the village center at Shawme Pond. Tupper Rd, off MA 6A, leads to the Cape Cod Canal.

Falmouth

POP 31,530

Crowd-pleasing beaches, a terrific bike trail and the quaint seaside village of Woods Hole are the highlights of the Cape's second-largest town. Falmouth puffs with pride over its favorite daughter, Katharine Lee Bates, who wrote the words to the nation's favorite patriotic hymn, *America the Beautiful*.

◎ Sights & Activities

Old Silver Beach   BEACH
(off MA 28A; 🚻) Deeply indented Falmouth has 70 miles of coastline, none of it finer than Old Silver Beach, off MA 28A in North Falmouth. This long, sandy stretch of beach attracts scores of college students, families and day-trippers from the city. A rock jetty, sandbars and tidal pools provide lots of fun diversions for kids.

The parking lot often fills up on a hot day, so plan on getting there early. Facilities include changing rooms and a snack bar. Parking costs $20 in summer.

South-Side Beaches   BEACH
For a great beach on the sound side, head to Menauhant Beach, off Central Ave from MA 28. It's Falmouth's longest beach, with lots of room for everyone and warm waters that invite a plunge. Surf Drive Beach, on Surf Dr within walking distance of Main St, has full facilities and a straight-on view of Martha's Vineyard. Parking costs $15 in summer at both of these beaches.

Ashumet Holly
Wildlife Sanctuary   NATURE RESERVE
(📋 508-349-2615; www.massaudubon.org; MA 151, East Falmouth; adult/child $3/2; ◎ dawn-dusk) This 45-acre Mass Audubon sanctuary has good birding along a 1.3-mile nature trail through the woods and around a pond. It also has one of the largest collections of holly trees in the region, with 65 varieties of American, Oriental and European hollies growing within the sanctuary.

To get there take MA 151 4 miles east from MA 28 to Currier Rd, which leads into Ashumet Rd; the sanctuary is on the right.

★ **Shining Sea Bikeway**   CYCLING
(🚲) A bright new star among the Cape's stellar bike trails, this 10.7-mile beauty runs along the entire west coast of Falmouth, and offers unspoiled views of salt ponds, marsh and seascapes.

Completed in 2009, the bikeway follows an abandoned railroad bed, taking you places you'd never get a glimpse of otherwise. The entire route is flat, making it well suited for a family outing. To add in a swim, find the ocean beach on the section between Falmouth center and Woods Hole. Bike Zone Rentals (www.bikezonecapecod.com; 13 County Rd; bikes per day $20; ◎ 9am-5pm Mon-Sat, 10am-3pm Sun) rents kids, adult and tandem bicycles at the northern end of the bike path.

✻ Festivals & Events

Independence Day   FIREW
(🚻) The Cape's largest fireworks dis plodes over Falmouth Harbor on ' of July.

LOCAL KNOWLEDGE

CAPE COD FARMERS MARKETS

A homegrown movement of small-scale farms has taken root on Cape Cod. These days you're never far from a farmers market, where you can buy direct from growers. You'll find everything from organic arugula to Cape Cod honey and beach plum jam at the following.

Falmouth (Peg Noonan Park, Main St; ⊘ noon-6pm Thu)

Chatham (1652 Main St; ⊘ 3-6:30pm Tue)

Hyannis (First Baptist Church, 468 Main St; ⊘ 2-6pm Wed)

Orleans (21 Old Colony Way; ⊘ 4-7pm Wed & 8am-noon Sat)

Wellfleet (Wellfleet Preservation Hall, 335 Main St; ⊘ 8am-1pm Sat)

Sandwich (Village Green, 164 MA 6A; ⊘ 9am-1pm Tue)

For more on farms and restaurants that support local agriculture, visit www.buyfresh buylocalcapecod.org.

Barnstable County Fair　　　　FAIR
(www.barnstablecountyfair.org; 1220 MA 151; 🖐) This weeklong old-fashioned agricultural fair, held in the fourth week of July, has farm animals, carnival rides and the usual washed-up bands. Kids and nostalgia freaks will love it.

Falmouth Road Race　　　　SPORTS
(www.falmouthroadrace.com) Thousands compete in this 7-mile race in mid-August that draws international runners.

🛌 Sleeping

**Sippewissett
Campground & Cabins**　　　CAMPGROUND $
(☑ 508-548-2542; www.sippewissett.com; 836 Palmer Ave; campsites/RV sites $43/49, cabins per week $325-1000; 🖐) This family-friendly 13-acre place on the Shining Sea Bikeway has 100 wooded campsites and 11 cabins. The cabins range from one to three rooms and can hold up to eight people. Perks include a free shuttle to the beach and to the Vineyard ferry.

Falmouth Heights Motor Lodge　　MOTEL $$
(☑ 508-548-3623; www.falmouthheightsresort.com; 146 Falmouth Heights Rd; r incl breakfast $129-259; 🖐🖐🖐🖐) Don't be fooled by the name. This tidy operation is no drive-up motor lodge – it's not even on the highway. All 28 rooms, some with kitchenettes, are a cut above the competition. And you can throw your own party: the extensive grounds harbor a picnic grove with gas barbecues.

It's within walking distance of the beach and the Vineyard ferry.

Tides Motel of Falmouth　　　MOTEL $$
(☑ 508-548-3126; www.tidesmotelcapecod.com; 267 Clinton Ave; r $180) It's all about the water. This place is smack on its own private beach, and you could spit into the ocean from your deck. Otherwise, it's straightforward: the same rooms elsewhere would be a yawn. But really, the water is what you came to the Cape for, isn't it?

Between the surf lullaby and million-dollar view, a steady stream of returnees keep the motel busy all summer, so book ahead.

Sea Crest Beach Hotel　　　HOTEL $$$
(☑ 508-540-9400; www.seacrestbeachhotel.com; 350 Quaker Rd; r $199-525; 🖐🖐🖐🖐🖐) Looking for the perfect family beach hotel? Right on the sparkling sands of Old Silver Beach, Sea Crest has indoor/outdoor pools, a kid-friendly beach and a plethora of water-sport activities. Adults will like the bright, freshly renovated rooms, saltwater Jacuzzis and romantic sunset views.

Inn on the Sound　　　　B&B $$$
(☑ 508-457-9666; www.innonthesound.com; 313 Grand Ave S; r incl breakfast $225-275; 🖐🖐) Falmouth's finest inn exudes a clean, contemporary elegance. It's across from the beach, and many of the 10 rooms have private decks with ocean views. Depending on your mood, a gourmet breakfast can be served to you on the beach, in the dining room or in bed – how's that for pampering?

🍴 Eating

Maison Villatte　　　　CAFE $
(☑ 774-255-1855; 267 Main St; snacks $3-10; ⊘ 7am-7pm Wed-Sat, to 5pm Sun) This new bak-

ery-cafe was the buzz of Falmouth before it even opened and it's been packed ever since. A pair of French bakers crowned in toques work the ovens, creating crusty artisan breads, flaky croissants and sinful pastries. Hearty sandwiches and robust coffee make it an ideal lunch spot.

Clam Shack
SEAFOOD $

(☑508-540-7758; 227 Clinton Ave; light meals $6-15; ⏰11:30am-7:30pm) A classic of the genre, right on Falmouth Harbor. It's tiny, with picnic tables on the back deck and lots of fried seafood, as well as burgers and hot dogs. Clams – huge juicy bellies cooked to a perfect crisp – are the place to start. Then eat up the spectacular view. You can bring your own alcohol.

Casino Wharf FX
SEAFOOD $$

(☑508-540-6160; www.casinowharffx.com; 286 Grand Ave; mains $10-30; ⏰11:30am-11pm) This place is so close to the water that you could cast a fishing pole from the deck. But why bother? Just grab a deck table and let the feast begin. The fresh catch is true to its name, and the drinks are poured with a generous hand. There's music, often live and lively, after dark.

Chapoquoit Grill
MEDITERRANEAN $$

(☑508-540-7794; www.chapoquoitgrill.com; 452 Main St; mains $10-22; ⏰5-9pm Mon-Fri, noon-9pm Sat & Sun) At the northwest side of town, this place makes excellent wood-fired piz-zas loaded with everything from artichoke hearts to whole baby clams. The nightly fish specials are a big draw too. Expect to wait in line in summer, but it's worth it.

Glass Onion
MODERN AMERICAN $$$

(www.theglassoniondining.com; 37 N Main St; mains $25-35; ⏰5-9pm Tue-Sat) The place to go to for one of those anniversaries ending in a zero. The menu stars New American cuisine with French and Italian influences. Top billing goes to the lobster strudel brimming with chunks of succulent meat. Service and wine selections are as good as the food.

Drinking & Entertainment

Liam Maguire's Irish Pub & Restaurant
IRISH PUB

(☑508-548-0285; www.liammaguire.com; 273 Main St) Come here for Harp and Murphy's stout on tap, Irish bartenders, live music nightly and boisterous Irish songfests.

Boathouse
CLUB

(☑508-388-7573; 88 Scranton Ave) The place to hit the dance floor, the Boathouse, overlooking Falmouth Harbor, packs with the partying 20-something crowd Thursday through Sunday nights in summer.

College Light Opera Company
THEATER

(☑508-548-0668; www.collegelightoperacompany.com; Highfield Theatre, Highfield Dr) A

WORTH A TRIP

WOODS HOLE

All eyes are on the sea in this tiny village with a huge reputation. Ferries for Martha's Vineyard depart throughout the day, fishing boats chug in and out of the harbor and oceanographers ship off to distant lands from here. Indeed, Woods Hole is home to one of the most prestigious marine research facilities in the world. Research at the Woods Hole Oceanographic Institution (WHOI, pronounced 'hooey') has run the gamut, from exploring the sunken *Titanic* to studying global warming. With 60 buildings and laboratories and 650 employees and visiting scientists, including Nobel laureates, it's the largest oceanographic institution in the US.

Free guided 75-minute tours of **WHOI** (WHOI; ☑508-289-2252; www.whoi.edu; 93 Water St; ⏰tours 10:30am & 1:30pm Mon-Fri Jul & Aug) depart from the information office; reservations are required. You'll also gain insights into scientists' work at the **WHOI Ocean Science Exhibit Center** (15 School St; ⏰10am-4:30pm Mon-Sat) `FREE`.

Woods Hole Science Aquarium (http://aquarium.nefsc.noaa.gov; 166 Water St; ⏰11am-4pm Tue-Sat; 👶) `FREE` has little flash and dazzle, but it does have unusual sea life specimens, local fish and the *Homarus americanus* (aka lobster). Kids will enjoy the touch-tank creatures. The coolest time to come is at 11am or 4pm, when the seals are fed.

Continue with the nautical theme and head over to the drawbridge, where you'll find **Fishmonger Café** (www.fishmongercafe.com; 56 Water St; mains $10-25; ⏰7am-9:30pm), with water views in every direction and an eclectic menu emphasizing fresh seafood.

LOBSTER ICE CREAM, ANYONE?

Lobster mania gets a new twist at **Ben & Bill's Chocolate Emporium** (209 Main St, Falmouth; cones $5; ⊘9am-11pm), where the crustacean has crawled onto the ice cream menu. Forget plain vanilla: step up to the counter and order a scoop of lobster ice cream. Now there's one you won't find with the old 31 flavors, folks.

well-regarded summer theater of college students who hope to make a career in musical theater. Expect Broadway and light opera staples, accompanied by a full pit orchestra. It's consistently a sellout; book early.

Cape Cod Theatre Project   THEATER
(☑508-457-4242; www.capecodtheatreproject.org; Falmouth Academy, 7 Highfield Dr) The Theatre Project brings professional actors together with playwrights to perform staged readings of new works during the month of July. Some of the plays go on to open off-Broadway in New York.

ℹ Information

Falmouth Chamber of Commerce (☑508-548-8500; www.falmouthchamber.com; 20 Academy Lane; ⊘9am-5pm Mon-Fri, 10am-4pm Sat) In the center, just off Main St.

Falmouth Hospital (☑508-548-5300; www.capecodhealth.org; 100 Ter Heun Dr; ⊘24hr) One of the Cape's two hospitals. It's off MA 28 at the north side of town.

Post Office (120 Main St)

ℹ Getting There & Away

Sitting at the southwest corner of the Cape, Falmouth is reached via MA 28, which becomes Main St in the center of town. Ferries to Martha's Vineyard leave from both Falmouth Harbor and Woods Hole (p169).

Barnstable & Hyannis

POP 45,200

Cape Cod's largest town, at 76 sq miles, is so sprawling that it encompasses seven distinct villages. The village of Hyannis is the region's commercial hub. Ferries, buses and planes all converge on Hyannis, so there's a good chance you will, too. In addition to being a jumping-off point for boats to Nan-

tucket and Martha's Vineyard, Hyannis attracts Kennedy fans: JFK made his summer home here and it was at the Kennedy compound that Teddy passed away in 2009. Hyannis Harbor, with its waterfront eateries and ferries, is a few minutes' walk from Main St.

◉ Sights & Activities

Sandy Neck Beach   BEACH
(Sandy Neck Rd, West Barnstable) The barrier beach at Sandy Neck extends 6.5 miles along Cape Cod Bay, backed the entire way by undulating dunes and a scenic salt marsh. It's a destination for all sorts of recreational activities: brisk summer swimming, year-round hiking, and saltwater fishing.

The dunes, which reach heights of 100ft, provide a habitat for red foxes, shorebirds and wildflowers. From four points along the beach, **hiking trails** cross inland over the dunes to a path skirting the salt marsh. Depending on which cross-trail you take, you can make a loop of beach, dunes and marsh in a round-trip hike of 2 to 13 miles. Even the shortest hike, which takes about 90 minutes, is rewarding. Pick up a trail map at the gatehouse; ask about high tide, which affects the marsh trail. Parking is free from September to May, $15 to $20 in season.

Craigville Beach   BEACH
(Craigville Beach Rd, Centerville) Looking for a warm-water swim? Craigville, like other south-side beaches, has much warmer water than those on the north side of the Cape. This mile-long stretch of sand is a great swimming beach that attracts a college crowd.

With 450 parking spaces, the most of any Barnstable town beach, you're unlikely to

A NATIVE AMERICAN FOURTH

The sleepy Cape town of Mashpee is home to the Mashpee Wampanoag, the Native American tribe that welcomed the Pilgrims in 1620. The best time to be in town is during the July 4th weekend, when the tribe sponsors its big three-day **Mashpee Wampanoag Pow Wow** (www.mashpeewampanoagtribe.com), which includes Native American dancing, competitions and a very cool fireball game after the sun sets. Dancers from tribes all over the country come to join in the festivities.

CAPE COD BEACH GUIDE

The crowning glory of the Cape is its stunning beaches. Each has its own personality and there's one that's bound to fit yours. The top beaches for...

➡ Surfing: White Crest Beach (p148) in Wellfleet; Coast Guard Beach (p146) in Eastham

➡ Windsurfing: Kalmus Beach (p133) in Hyannis; West Dennis Beach (p137) in West Dennis

➡ Sunsets: First Encounter Beach (p146) in Eastham; Herring Cove Beach (p153) in Provincetown

➡ Sunrises: Nauset Beach (p144) in Orleans

➡ Tidal flats: Skaket Beach (p145) in Orleans; First Encounter Beach (p146) in Eastham

➡ Fishing: Race Point Beach (p153) in Provincetown; Sandy Neck Beach (p132) in Barnstable

➡ Families: Chapin Memorial Beach (p137) in Dennis; Old Silver Beach (p129) in Falmouth

➡ Singles: Craigville Beach (p132) in Barnstable; Cahoon Hollow Beach in Wellfleet

➡ Seclusion: Long Point Beach (p153) in Provincetown

➡ Long walks: Sandy Neck Beach (p132) in Barnstable; Chapin Memorial Beach (p137) in Dennis

➡ Picnics: Grey's Beach (p137) in Yarmouth Port; Veterans Beach (p133) in Hyannis

➡ Sunbathing: Take your pick!

get shut out even on the sunniest midsummer day. Beach facilities include changing rooms, showers, lifeguards and snack bars, so bring extra sunblock and you can hang out for the whole day. Parking costs $15 or $20 in summer.

Craigville Beach adjoins **Long Beach**, the longest stretch of sand on the south side of town, which makes it ideal for leisurely beach strolls. A walk to the end and back is 3 miles round-trip.

Kalmus Beach　　　　　　　　BEACH
(Ocean St, Hyannis) You'll find plenty of space in which to lay your towel on wide Kalmus Beach, at the south end of Ocean St in Hyannis. Thanks to its steady breezes, it's a haven for windsurfers. The warm summer waters also attract plenty of swimmers. Facilities include a snack bar, lifeguard and changing rooms. Parking costs $15 to $20 in summer.

Veterans Beach　　　　　　　BEACH
(Ocean St, Hyannis; 🚻) The closest beach to Hyannis' Main St, Veterans Beach is a favorite with families thanks to the playground facilities, picnic tables and shallow waters. Parking costs $15 to $20 in summer.

The north side of the beach is also the site of a **memorial to John F Kennedy**, and overlooks the harbor where JFK once sailed. There's free 30-minute parking at the memorial.

John F Kennedy Hyannis Museum　MUSEUM
(☎ 508-790-3077; http://jfkhyannismuseum.org; 397 Main St, Hyannis; adult/child $8/3; ⏰ 9am-5pm Mon-Sat, noon-5pm Sun) The more casual moments of America's 35th president are showcased here through photographs, videos and mementos. The museum also hosts the **Cape Cod Baseball League Hall of Fame**.

**Hyannis Whale
Watcher Cruises**　　　WHALE-WATCHING
(☎ 800-287-0374; www.whales.net; 269 Millway Rd, Barnstable Harbor, Barnstable; adult/child $45/26; 🚼) All whale-watching boat cruises on Cape Cod leave from Provincetown except for this one, which makes for a longer boat ride out to **Stellwagen Bank National Marine Sanctuary**, where the whales hang out. On the plus side, if you're already here, it spares you the hour-long drive to Provincetown. The four-hour boat tours are narrated by well-informed naturalists.

👉 Tours

Hy-Line Cruises　　　　　　CRUISE
(☎ 508-790-0696; www.hylinecruises.com; Ocean St Dock, Hyannis; adult/child $16/8; ⏰ mid-May–Oct; 🚼) Hy-Line, which is best known for its ferries to Martha's Vineyard and Nantucket,

> ### ℹ INTERNET ACCESS
>
> Virtually every town and village on the Cape has a public library with free wi-fi. Most also have online computers that visitors can use for free, though there may be a time limit of 15 to 30 minutes. Find the one nearest you by visiting www.clams.org, the website of the Cape and Islands library association.

rolls out one of its old-fashioned steamboats each summer for harbor tours. These popular one-hour tours include a circle past the compound of Kennedy family homes. Kids will prefer the Sunday afternoon 'ice cream float,' which adds a sundae to the view.

Festivals & Events

Independence Day Celebration   FIREWORKS
The Fourth of July sees a parade down Main St and a big fireworks bash over Hyannis Harbor.

Pops by the Sea   MUSIC
(www.artsfoundation.org) This concert on the village green on the second Sunday in August features the Boston Pops Orchestra and a celebrity guest conductor.

🛏 Sleeping

Cookie-cutter chain hotels line MA 132, the main road connecting Hyannis to US 6. If you want to be in the thick of things, and close to the water, stick with the locally owned hotels in the village center.

HI-Hyannis   HOSTEL $
(☎ 508-775-7990; http://capecod.hiusa.org; 111 Ocean St, Hyannis; dm incl breakfast $32; @ 🛜) 🚲
For a million-dollar view on a backpacker's budget, book yourself a bed at this hostel

overlooking the harbor. It was built in 2010 by adding new wings to a period home and is within walking distance of the Main St scene, beaches and ferries. Now the caveat: there's just 37 beds, so book well in advance.

Captain Gosnold Village   COTTAGES $$
(☎ 508-775-9111; www.captaingosnold.com; 230 Gosnold St, Hyannis; r/cottages from $130/250; 🛜⚌🚲) Captain Gosnold is a little community unto itself and just a sandal-shuffle from the beach. Choose from motel rooms or fully equipped Cape Cod–style cottages. The cottages vary in size, from one to three bedrooms; the smallest sleeps four people, the largest six. Kids will find a playground and plenty of room to romp.

SeaCoast Inn   MOTEL $$
(☎ 508-775-3828; www.seacoastcapecod.com; 33 Ocean St, Hyannis; r incl breakfast $128-168; ❄ @ 🛜) This small, two-story motel offers neat, clean rooms just a two-minute walk from the harbor in one direction and Main St restaurants in the other. OK, there's no view or pool, but the rooms are thoroughly comfy, most have kitchenettes and the price is a deal.

★ Anchor-In   HOTEL $$$
(☎ 508-775-0357; www.anchorin.com; 1 South St, Hyannis; r incl breakfast $179-339; ❄ @ 🛜⚌) This family-run boutique hotel puts the chains to shame. The harbor-front location offers a fine sense of place, and the heated pool is a perfect perch from which to watch fishing boats unload their catch. The rooms are bright and airy, with updated decor and water-view balconies. If you're planning a day trip to Nantucket, the ferry is just a stroll away.

🍴 Eating

Four Seas   ICE CREAM $
(www.fourseasicecream.com; 360 S Main St, Centerville; cones $5; ⏰ 10am-9:30pm;) It ain't sum-

---

ANTIQUING HISTORIC 6A

Nearly anything you can imagine, from nautical antiques to art-deco kitsch, can be found on the tightly packed shelves of Cape Cod's 100-plus antique shops. The key to antiquing on the Cape is to follow MA 6A, also known as the **Old King's Highway**. The oldest continuous stretch of historic district in the USA, the road is lined with old sea captain's homes, many of which have been converted to quality antique shops. You'll find the best hunting on the section between Barnstable and Brewster.

Then there are the auctions. The high roller on the scene, **Eldred's** (www.eldreds.com; 1483 MA 6A, East Dennis), specializes in fine arts and appraised antiques; five-figure bids here barely raise an eyebrow. More homespun is the **Sandwich Auction House** (www.sandwichauction.com; 15 Tupper Rd, off MA 6A, Sandwich), which handles estate sales where you might find anything from antique Sandwich glass to old Elvis albums.

mer till Four Seas opens. This local institution near Craigville Beach has been dispensing homemade ice cream since 1934. Expect lines out the door, since everyone – including the Kennedy clan, whose Hyannisport home is nearby – comes here on hot summer nights.

★ **Bistrot de Soleil** MEDITERRANEAN **$$**
(www.bistrotdesoleil.com; 350 Stevens St, at Main St, Hyannis; mains $10-25; ⊙11:30am-9pm) The hottest new restaurant at this end of the Cape fuses Mediterranean influences with fresh local ingredients. The menu ranges from gourmet wood-fired pizzas to cognac demi-glace filet mignon. The servings are generous, prices more than reasonable. A smart setting, organic wine list and prix fixe menu specials round out the appeal.

Raw Bar SEAFOOD **$$**
(www.therawbar.com; 230 Ocean St, Hyannis; lobster rolls $26; ⊙11am-7pm) Come here for the mother of all lobster rolls: it's like eating an entire lobster in a bun. The view overlooking Hyannis Harbor isn't hard to swallow either. In the unlikely event someone in your party isn't up for lobster rolls, then stuffed quahogs, steamed clams and a raw bar shore up the menu.

Brazilian Grill BRAZILIAN **$$$**
(www.braziliangrill-capecod.com; 680 Main St, Hyannis; lunch/dinner buffets $15/30; ⊙11:30am-9pm) Celebrate the Cape's Brazilian side at this real-deal *rodízio* (steakhouse), where an immense buffet is paired with *churrasco* (barbecued meat on skewers), which are brought to your table by traditionally dressed gauchos. The buffet's a meal in itself, but it's the meat and those hunky gauchos that make the feast an experience.

Eclectic Cafe AMERICAN **$$$**
(☑508-771-7187; www.eclecticcafecapecod.com; 606 Main St, Hyannis; mains $20-34; ⊙5-9pm) Set in a garden courtyard, down a flowery alleyway, Eclectic is an oasis of tranquility on bustling Main St. The food's as pretty as the setting. Comfort food takes a gourmet twist here – as in truffle mac 'n' cheese with lobster or a green salad with raspberries and duck breast.

🍷 Drinking & Entertainment

British Beer Company PUB
(www.britishbeer.com; 412 Main St, Hyannis) On summer nights visitors flock here for grog, pub grub and Red Sox games on monster-

size TVs. There's pop and rock music most nights, too.

Embargo COCKTAIL BAR
(www.embargorestaurant.com; 453 Main St, Hyannis) The upscale place to have a martini with a jazz player in the background.

Cape Cod Melody Tent LIVE MUSIC
(☑508-775-5630; www.melodytent.org; 21 W Main St, Hyannis) It's just that – a giant tent, seating 2300 people – with nobody sitting more than 50ft from the revolving stage. Between June and August it headlines big-name acts such as Willie Nelson and Melissa Etheridge.

ℹ Information

Cape Cod Hospital (☑508-771-1800; www.capecodhealth.org; 27 Park St, Hyannis; ⊙24hr) Near the center of town, this is the Cape's main hospital.

Hyannis Area Chamber of Commerce (☑508-775-2201; www.hyannis.com; 397 Main St, Hyannis; ⊙9am-5pm Mon-Sat, noon-5pm Sun) Provides tourism information for the Town of Barnstable.

Post Office (385 Main St, Hyannis)

ℹ Getting There & Around

AIR

Cape Air (www.flycapeair.com) Flies several times a day to Barnstable Municipal Airport (HYA) from Boston, Martha's Vineyard and Nantucket.

BOAT

The **Steamship Authority** (☑508-477-8600; www.steamshipauthority.com; South St Dock, Hyannis; 🐾) operates **car ferries** (round-trip adult/child/bicycle $35/18/14, 2¼ hours, three to six ferries daily) to Nantucket, but it costs a hefty $450 to bring a car along.

A speedier passenger-only **catamaran service** (round-trip adult/child/bicycle $69/35/14, same-day round-trip Monday to Thursday $50/25/14; one hour; five daily) plies the same route.

STARS OF TOMORROW

The crack of a bat on the ball. The night lights and fireflies. The hopes and dreams of making it big-time.

The Cape Cod Baseball League is the nation's oldest amateur league and most competitive summertime proving ground. The league's slogan – 'Where the stars of tomorrow shine tonight' – isn't far from the truth. One-seventh of all players in the major leagues today played in the Cape League.

Admission is free. However, supporters do pass around the hat between innings to help defray costs. As many of the players are college students, the season runs from mid-June to mid-August. Get the schedule at www.capecodbaseball.org or check the *Cape Cod Times*.

The following are the 10 teams and their home fields:

Bourne Braves Doran Park (Upper Cape Tech, Sandwich Rd, Bourne)

Brewster Whitecaps Stony Brook Elementary School (Underpass Rd, Brewster)

Chatham Anglers Veterans Field (Depot Station, Chatham)

Cotuit Kettleers Lowell Park (Lowell Ave, Cotuit)

Falmouth Commodores Guv Fuller Field (Main St, Falmouth)

Harwich Mariners Whitehouse Field (Oak St, Harwich)

Hyannis Harbor Hawks McKeon Field (High School Rd, Hyannis)

Orleans Firebirds Eldredge Park (MA 28, Orleans)

Wareham Gatemen Clem Spillane Field (US 6, Wareham; just off Cape Cod on the mainland)

Yarmouth-Dennis Red Sox Dennis-Yarmouth Regional High School (Station Ave, South Yarmouth)

Hy-Line Cruises (☑ 508-778-2600; www. hylinecruises.com; Ocean St Dock, Hyannis; 🛜 📶) offers **catamaran journeys** (round-trip adult/child/bicycle $77/51/14, one hour, several daily) to Nantucket.

Hy-Line operates a passenger-only traditional **ferry** (round-trip adult/under 12yr/bicycle $45/free/14, 1¾ hours) to Nantucket that's slower, but cheaper for families.

BUS

Several daily **Plymouth & Brockton** (www.p-b. com) buses depart the **Hyannis Transportation Center** (cnr Main & Center Sts) for Boston's Logan airport ($25, 90 minutes) and various Cape towns, including Provincetown ($10, 80 minutes).

Yarmouth

POP 23,800

There are two Yarmouths, and the experience you have depends on what part of town you find yourself in. The north side of town, along MA 6A, called Yarmouth Port, is green and genteel, with shady trees, antique shops and gracious old homes. The second Yarmouth, to the south, where MA 28 crosses

the villages of West Yarmouth and South Yarmouth, is a flat world of mini-golf, strip malls and endless motels.

⊙ Sights

Captains' Mile HISTORIC BUILDINGS
Nearly 50 historic sea captains' homes are lined up along MA 6A in Yarmouth Port in a 1.5-mile stretch known as Captains' Mile. Most of them are family homes these days, so you'll be doing much of your viewing from the sidewalk.

However, the Historical Society of Old Yarmouth maintains a couple of them, including the **Captain Bangs Hallett House** (☑ 508-362-3021; www.hsoy.org; 11 Strawberry Lane; adult/child $3/50¢; ⊙ 1-4pm Thu-Sun), an 1840 Greek Revival house that was once home to a prosperous seafarer who made his fortune sailing to China and India. The home is just off MA 6A behind Yarmouth Port's post office.

Edward Gorey House MUSEUM
(☑ 508-362-3909; www.edwardgoreyhouse.org; 8 Strawberry Lane, Yarmouth Port; adult/child $8/2; ⊙ 11am-4pm Wed-Sat, noon-4pm Sun) Near the

post office on MA 6A sits the former home of the brilliant and somewhat twisted author and graphic artist Edward Gorey. He illustrated the books of Lewis Carroll, HG Wells and John Updike but is most widely recognized for his offbeat pen-and-ink animations used in the opening of the PBS *Mystery!* series.

Grey's Beach
BEACH

(Center St, Yarmouth Port) Grey's Beach, also known as Bass Hole, is no prize for swimming, but a terrific quarter-mile-long boardwalk extends over a tidal marsh and creek, offering a unique vantage point for viewing all sorts of sea life. It's also a fine spot for picnics and sunsets, and the parking is free. To get there, take Center St off MA 6A, at the playground in the center of the village.

Seagull Beach
BEACH

(Seagull Rd) Long and wide Seagull Beach, off South Sea Ave from MA 28, is the town's best south-side beach. The scenic approach to the beach runs alongside a tidal river that provides habitat for osprey and shorebirds; bring your binoculars. Facilities include a bathhouse and snack bar. Parking costs $15 in summer.

🛏 Sleeping & Eating

Village Inn
B&B $$

(📞508-362-3182; www.thevillageinncapecod.com; 92 MA 6A, Yarmouth Port; r incl breakfast $95-165; ❋🛜) Solid no-frills value, this family-run B&B occupies a 200-year-old house that's on the National Register of Historic Places. Set on an acre lot, the inn provides lots of common space and eight straightforward guest rooms of varying sizes. A hearty country breakfast is served each morning.

The Optimist Cafe
CAFE $

(www.optimistcafe.com; 134 MA 6A, Yarmouth Port; mains $7-12; ⏰7am-4pm) Set in an old sea captain's home, this laid-back cafe offers breakfast fare of the waffles-and-eggs variety until closing. Starting at noon you'll find spicier options, like Thai coconut curry and chipotle fish tacos.

ℹ Information

Yarmouth Chamber of Commerce (📞508-778-1008; www.yarmouthcapecod.com; 424 MA 28, West Yarmouth; ⏰9am-5pm) The staff here are helpful.

Dennis
POP 14,210

Dennis has a distinctly different character from north to south. Heavily trafficked MA 28, which cuts through the villages of West Dennis and Dennisport on the south side of town, is lined with motels, eateries and mini-golf. The classier north side, the village of Dennis, runs along MA 6A with handsome old sea captains' homes sprouting second lives as inns and antique shops.

⦿ Sights

Chapin Memorial Beach
BEACH

(Chapin Beach Rd, Dennis; ♿) Families will love the gently sloping waters at this dune-backed beach. Not only is it ideal for wading, but all sorts of tiny sea creatures can be explored in the tide pools. At low tide, you can walk way out onto the sandy tidal flats – it takes a hike just to reach water up to your knees.

This mile-long beach is also perfect for sunsets and walks under the light of the moon. To get there, take New Boston Rd opposite Dennis Public Market on MA 6A and follow the signs. Parking costs $20 in summer.

West Dennis Beach
BEACH

(Lighthouse Rd, off MA 28, West Dennis) Extending one gorgeous mile along Nantucket Sound, this is the south side's mecca for swimmers, windsurfers and kiteboarders. It's a good

---

STAR PARTIES

What could be more cosmic than being outdoors on a warm summer night and staring up at the stars? How about gaping at Saturn's rings and Jupiter's moons?

Cape Cod Astronomical Society (www.ccas.ws; ♿) FREE welcomes visitors to weekly summer star parties at its 12.5ft Ash Dome observatory (Dennis-Yarmouth Regional High School, 210 Station Ave, South Yarmouth). Peer into the heavens through the observatory's 16in Meade GPS telescope and through smaller scopes set up outdoors on the grounds. Club members put it all in focus and explain the celestial details – and they love to turn on newbies. Star party schedules are online.

bet for finding a parking space on even the sunniest of days, as the parking lot ($20) extends the full length of the beach, with room for 1000 cars.

Scargo Tower
TOWER

(Scargo Hill Rd, Dennis) FREE Built in 1902 on the highest spot in the area – 120ft above sea level – this 38-step, stone tower rising above Scargo Lake gives you grand views of Cape Cod Bay. On clear days you can see all the way to Sandwich and across to Provincetown. To get here, take MA 6A to Scargo Hill Rd.

🏃 Activities

Cape Cod Waterways
BOATING

(📞 508-398-0080; www.capecodwaterways.org; 16 MA 28, Dennisport; rentals from $20; �
8am-8pm) Near MA 134, Cape Cod Waterways can set you up to paddle the scenic Swan River. A 90-minute rental costs $20 for a one-person kayak, $34 for a two-person kayak or canoe.

Lobster Roll Cruises
CRUISE

(📞 508-385-1686; www.lobsterrollcruises.com; 357 Sesuit Neck Rd, Dennis; cruises $27-42; ☉ Jun-Sep) Lobster Roll Cruises provides a different setting for a lobster dinner. Take this cute boat from Sesuit Harbor on a dinner cruise, or go light with the lobster-roll lunch cruise. The food, prepared by nearby Sesuit Harbor Café, is the real deal.

Cape Cod Rail Trail
CYCLING

The exhilarating 22-mile Cape Cod Rail Trail starts in Dennis off MA 134. Barb's Bike Rental (📞 508-760-4723; www.barbsbikeshop.com; 430 MA 134; rentals per half/full day $17/24; ☉ 9am-6:30pm) rents bicycles right at the trailhead.

Air Support Kiteboarding
WATER SPORTS

(📞 508-332-6031; www.kitecod.com; 109 Main St, West Dennis; lessons from $225; ☉ 10am-6pm) If you want to try your hand at kiteboarding, this operation offers lessons for beginners.

🛏 Sleeping

★ Isaiah Hall B&B Inn
B&B $$

(📞 508-385-9928; www.isaiahhallinn.com; 152 Whig St, Dennis; r incl breakfast $120-250; ❋ 🛜) Occupying an 1857 farmhouse, this country-style inn offers homey comforts in a quiet yet central neighborhood. The house has sloping wood floors, canopied beds and a 12ft-long breakfast table ideal for convivial chatter with fellow guests. Prices reflect the size of the room and whether you opt for extras, like balconies or fireplaces.

Scargo Manor
B&B $$$

(📞 508-385-5534; www.scargomanor.com; 909 MA 6A, Dennis; r incl breakfast $170-275; ❋ 🛜) The sea captain who built this grand house in 1895 scored a prime locale on Scargo Lake, and you're free to paddle off in the owner's canoe or kayaks whenever the mood strikes. For places you can't paddle to, you can pedal to, using the inn's loaner bikes. The antiques-laden house has seven rooms, each with its own character.

🍴 Eating

Captain Frosty's
FISH & CHIPS $

(www.captainfrosty.com; 219 MA 6A, Dennis; mains $8-15; ☉ 11am-9pm) Don't be misled by the 1950s ice-cream shack appearance. This simple seafood takeout joint does it right. Forget frozen food – there's none in this kitchen. Order fish-and-chips and you'll be munching on cod caught by day boats in nearby Chatham.

★ Sesuit Harbor Café
SEAFOOD $$

(📞 508-385-6134; 357 Sesuit Neck Rd, Dennis; mains $10-24; ☉ 7am-8:30pm) This is the Cape Cod you won't find on the highway: a little shack tucked into Sesuit Harbor serv-

---

FUN FOR LITTLE ONES

Kids getting restless? Hop in the car and head for Route 28 at the south side of Yarmouth, where you'll find a pair of cool mini-golf courses and a new inflatable water park. **Bass River Sports World** (📞 508-398-6070; www.bassriversportsworld.com; 934 MA 28, South Yarmouth; mini-golf per game $10; ☉ 9am-10pm) sports a pirate-themed 'adventure golf' course, complete with an 8ft-tall skull. **Pirate's Cove** (📞 508-394-6200; www.piratescove.net; 728 MA 28, South Yarmouth; per game adult/child $9/8; ☉ 10am-10pm) has the pedigree to go with its popularity: its caves, footbridges and waterfalls were designed by Disney imagineers. **Cape Cod Inflatable Water Park** (www.capecodinflatablepark.com; 518 Route 28, West Yarmouth; day passes $15; ☉ 10am-6pm) is full of chutes, slides and slippery marine-themed creatures like Wally the Whale. Young tykes will love it.

UP FOR A PEDAL?

The mother of all Cape bicycle trails, the Cape Cod Rail Trail runs 22 glorious miles through forest, past cranberry bogs and along sandy ponds ideal for a dip. A shining example for the rail-to-trail movement, the trail follows an abandoned railway route, given a second life as a bike path in the 1970s. It's had a multimillion-dollar upgrade in recent years, making it one of the finest bike trails in all of New England.

The path begins in Dennis on MA 134 and continues through Nickerson State Park in Brewster, into Orleans and across the Cape Cod National Seashore all the way to South Wellfleet. There's a hefty dose of Old Cape Cod scenery en route, and you'll have opportunities to detour into villages for lunch or sightseeing. If you only have time to do part of the trail, begin at Nickerson State Park and head for the National Seashore – the landscape is unbeatable. Bicycle rentals are available at the trailheads in Dennis and Wellfleet, at Nickerson State Park and opposite the National Seashore's visitor center in Eastham – there's free car parking at all four sites.

ing freshly caught seafood at picnic tables smack on the water. The scrumptious lobster rolls, like everything else, taste like they just crawled onto your plate. BYOB.

Fin SEAFOOD $$$
(☑ 508-385-2096; www.fincapecod.com; 800 MA 6A, Dennis; mains $20-28; ⊙ 5-9pm Tue-Sun) 🍴
Fin embodies the Cape's north-side character. The dining rooms cover two floors of a gracious sea captain's home, creating an intimate dining experience. The chef-owner is a master with all things briny. Start with the rich house chowder, chock-full of Dennis oysters. Then, if sea bass is on the menu, look no further.

Red Pheasant FRENCH $$$
(☑ 508-385-2133; www.redpheasantinn.com; 905 MA 6A, Dennis; mains $25-38; ⊙ 5-9pm Tue-Sun) 🍴 This former ship's chandlery is more than 200 years old, so you can feel as elegant as your surroundings as you tuck into organic salmon gravlax, roast duckling, rack of lamb and other flavorful creations. On chilly nights, when the fireplace is stoked up, it's thoroughly romantic.

🍸 Drinking & Entertainment

Harvest Gallery Wine Bar WINE BAR
(www.harvestgallerywinebar.com; 776 MA 6A, Dennis; ⊙ 1pm-midnight) Tip your glass with class at this combo wine bar and art gallery behind the Dennis village post office. Live jazz and blues several nights a week.

Cape Playhouse THEATER
(☑ 508-385-3911; www.capeplayhouse.com; 820 MA 6A, Dennis; 🚼) The Cape Playhouse is the oldest operating professional summer theater (since 1927) in the US. Bette Davis once worked here as an usher, and some of the biggest names in showbiz have appeared on its stage. It hosts a different production every two weeks – everything from *Hairspray* to Hitchcock – and also has a Children's Theater, with classics, puppetry and more.

Cape Cinema CINEMA
(☑ 508-385-2503; www.capecinema.com; 820 MA 6A, Dennis) On the grounds of the Cape Playhouse, this vintage movie theater shows foreign and independent films. It's a true art house: the entire ceiling is covered in an art-deco mural of the heavens painted by American realist painter Rockwell Kent.

ℹ️ Information

Dennis Chamber of Commerce (☑ 508-398-3568; www.dennischamber.com; 238 Swan River Rd, off MA 28 at MA 134; ⊙ 10am-4pm Mon-Sat)

Brewster

POP 9820

Woodsy Brewster, on the Cape's bay side, makes a good base for outdoorsy types. The Cape Cod Rail Trail cuts clear across town, and there's first-rate camping and water activities. Brewster also has fine restaurants, way out of proportion to the town's small size. Everything of interest is on or just off MA 6A (also called Main St), which runs the length of the town.

⊙ Sights & Activities

Nickerson State Park PARK
(☑ 508-896-3491; 3488 MA 6A; per car $5; ⊙ dawn-dusk; 🚼) The 2000-acre oasis of Nickerson State Park has eight ponds with

sandy beaches ideal for swimming and boating, as well as miles of cycling and walking trails. Bring along a fishing pole to catch your own trout dinner or just pack a lunch and enjoy the park's picnic facilities. **Jack's Boat Rentals** (☑508-349-9808; www.jacksboatrental.com; rentals per hr $25-45; ⊘10am-6pm), within the park, rents canoes, kayaks and sailboats.

Cape Cod Museum of Natural History
MUSEUM

(☑508-896-3867; www.ccmnh.org; 869 MA 6A; adult/child $10/5; ⊘9:30am-4pm; ⊕) a family-friendly museum offering exhibits on the Cape's flora and fauna and has a fine **boardwalk trail** across a salt marsh to a remote beach. The museum sponsors naturalist-led walks, talks and kids' programs.

Brewster Historical Society Museum
MUSEUM

(☑508-896-9521; www.brewsterhistoricalsociety.org; 3171 MA 6A; ⊘1-4pm Thu-Sat) **FREE** Stop here to see just how fine a small-town historical museum can be. Displays include an old barbershop, treasures brought back by sea captains, colonial tools and other bits of Brewster's centuries-old history.

Behind the museum, a pleasant half-mile **trail** leads through a wooded conservation area out to a long sandy **beach**: bring a towel.

Tidal Flats
BEACH

(⊕) When the tide goes out on Cape Cod Bay, the flats – basically giant sandbars – offer opportunities to commune with crabs, clams and gulls, and to take in brilliant sunsets. Best access to the tidal flats is via the Point of Rocks or Ellis Landing Beaches. Parking stickers are required during the summer and cost $15 per day.

🛈 GOLF THE CAPE

For those who never tire of the thrill of knocking a little white ball around a whole mess of greens, Cape Cod has 20 courses open to the public. Many have a distinctively Cape Cod flavor – some perched for spectacular water views, others overlooking cranberry bogs. And there's another 15 or so private courses if you have the right kind of friends. Everything you need to know is online at www.golfoncapecod.com.

Brewster Store
HISTORIC SITE

(☑508-896-3744; www.brewsterstore.com; 1935 MA 6A, at MA 124; ⊘6am-6pm) The Brewster Store, in the heart of town, is a sight in itself. The old-fashioned country store opened in 1866, and it's barely changed since. Penny candy is still sold alongside the local newspaper. Don't miss the half-hidden stairs that lead to the 2nd floor, where you'll discover a stash of museum-quality memorabilia as old as the building.

Cape Cod Rail Trail
CYCLING

The Cape Cod Rail Trail runs through town and across Nickerson State Park. Several places rent bicycles, none more convenient than **Barb's Bike Rental** (☑508-896-7231; www.barbsbikeshop.com; bicycles per half/full day $18/24; ⊘9am-6pm), which has a summer season kiosk at the rail trail parking lot near the entrance to Nickerson.

🛏 Sleeping

★ Nickerson State Park
CAMPGROUND $

(☑877-422-6762; www.reserveamerica.com; campsites $17; yurts $30-40; ⊕) Head here for Cape Cod's best camping, with 418 wooded campsites and a handful of yurts. It often fills up, so reserve your spot early. You can make reservations up to six months in advance.

★ Old Sea Pines Inn
B&B $$

(☑508-896-6114; www.oldseapinesinn.com; 2553 MA 6A; r incl breakfast $85-195; @ 🖧 ⊕) Staying here is a bit like staying at grandma's house: antique fittings, sleigh beds and sepia photographs on the bureau. This former girls' boarding school dating to 1840 has 21 rooms, some small with shared bath, others commodious with claw-foot bathtubs. No TV to spoil the mood. Instead, mosey out to the rocking chairs on the porch and soak up the yesteryear atmosphere.

Brewster by the Sea
B&B $$$

(☑508-896-3910; www.brewsterbythesea.com; 716 MA 6A; r incl breakfast $250-350; ❄ 🖧 ≋) If your idea of a B&B stay is pure pampering, stop the search here. Spend the night in a room with a king-size brass bed, whirlpool bath and fireplace, then wake up to a gourmet farm-fresh breakfast. Spa treatments and deep-tissue massages take it to the next level.

✕ Eating

★ Brewster Fish House
SEAFOOD $$

(www.brewsterfish.com; 2208 MA 6A; mains $14-32; ⊘11:30am-3pm & 5-9:30pm) It's not a real eye-

AFTER DARK

So you're done doing the beach thing for the day and now you think, 'hem...where to head for a little partying?'

Well, if you happen to be at Wellfleet's Cahoon Hollow Beach, lucky you. The Beachcomber (p150) at this beach's former lifeguard station is the Cape's hottest all-round night venue. Big-name bands, surfer dudes, college students working summer jobs – everyone comes to 'Da Coma' to let loose once the sun goes down.

No surprise, Provincetown has the hottest gay and lesbian clubs. Gals will want to head to Pied Bar (p157); guys, to the west end of Commercial St where the A-House (p157) and the Crown & Anchor (p157) hold court.

If you're on the Vineyard, boogie on down to Flatbread Company (p172) out by the airport. On Nantucket, head straight for the Chicken Box (p164).

catcher from the outside, but it's heaven inside for seafood lovers. Start with the lobster bisque, naturally sweet and with chunks of fresh lobster. From there it's safe to cast your net in any direction. Just 11 tables, and no reservations, so think lunch or early dinner to avoid long waits.

Cobie's SEAFOOD $$
(www.cobies.com; 3256 MA 6A; mains $9-23; ⊙11am-9pm) Just off the Cape Cod Rail Trail, this bustling roadside clam shack dishes out fried seafood that you can crunch and munch at outdoor picnic tables.

Chillingsworth FRENCH $$$
(☏508-896-3640; www.chillingsworth.com; 2449 MA 6A; bistro mains $17-33, fixed-price dinners $60-70; ⊙5-9:30pm) The place to celebrate special occasions. The standard here is the seven-course, fixed-price French dinner, with the cost depending on your main course selection. Or take it light and dine à la carte on the restaurant's sunny bistro side. If you come before 6:30pm, you can get a three-course bistro special for just $25 to $30.

❶ Information

Brewster Chamber of Commerce (☏508-896-3500; www.brewstercapecod.org; 2198 MA 6A; ⊙9am-3pm) This office inside Brewster Town Hall has tourist information and sells beach parking stickers.

Harwich

POP 12,250

Things move a little slower here in Harwich, and that's part of the appeal. It has good beaches and restaurants and one of the Cape's most photographed spots – yacht-packed Wychmere Harbor. Most of what you'll need is along MA 28, which runs through the south side of town.

Harwich has fine beaches, although many of them restrict parking to residents. But fret not: to get to **Sea St Beach**, one of the prettiest, park your car for free at the municipal lot behind the tourist office and then walk five minutes to the end of Sea St, which terminates at glistening Sea St Beach.

🛏 Sleeping & Eating

★**Wequassett Inn** LUXURY HOTEL $$$
(☏508-432-5400; www.wequassett.com; Pleasant Bay, East Harwich; r from $595; ❉@🛜🏊) The priciest lodging on the Cape offers pretty much anything you could ask of a full-service resort: flower-filled gardens, private golf course, fine dining and a full menu of watery activities. On the grounds you'll be soothed with gorgeous views of Pleasant Bay. The in-room Jacuzzis and fireplaces spell romance.

Brax SEAFOOD $$
(☏508-432-5515; www.braxlanding.com; 705 MA 28, Harwich Port; mains $10-24; ⊙11:30am-10pm) Head to this casual harborside gem for water-view dining and fresh seafood at honest prices. The menu's broad; stick with the local catch, like the Chatham scrod or the hefty lobster rolls. Grab yourself a seat on the outdoor deck overlooking Saquatucket Harbor for the best drink-with-a-view in town.

Cape Sea Grille SEAFOOD $$$
(☏508-432-4745; www.capeseagrille.com; 31 Sea St, Harwich Port; mains $27-37; ⊙5-9pm) Sit on the glass-enclosed porch of this old sea captain's house and savor some of the Cape's finest seafood. The crispy oysters and

SEAL-WATCHING

Gray and harbor seals gather in amazing hordes in Chatham's waters and haul out on the shoals. There are two ways to see them. When it's low tide, just go down to the Chatham Fish Pier and look due east to spot seals basking on the sandbars. To get closer to the action, join a boat tour with Beachcomber (p144), which leaves from Chatham Harbor.

the seared lobster pancetta are justifiably famous. Landlubbers in the party won't be disappointed with the filet mignon.

❶ Information

Harwich Information Center (☑508-432-1600; www.harwichcc.com; cnr 1 Schoolhouse Rd & MA 28, Harwich Port; ⊗9am-5pm Mon-Fri, 11am-4pm Sat & Sun)

❶ Getting There & Away

Freedom Cruise Line (☑508-432-8999; www.nantucketislandferry.com; 702 MA 28 at Saquatucket Harbor, Harwich Port; round-trip adult/child $70/51) Operates a summer passenger ferry (1 to 1¼ hours) to Nantucket, conveniently scheduled for day-tripping.

Chatham

POP 6125

The patriarch of Cape Cod towns, Chatham has a genteel reserve that is evident along its shady Main St: the shops are upscale; the lodgings, tony. That said, there's something for everyone here – families flock to town for seal-watching, birders migrate to the wildlife refuge. And then there are all those beaches. Sitting at the 'elbow' of the Cape, Chatham has an amazing 60 miles of shoreline along the ocean, sound and countless coves and inlets.

MA 28 leads right to Main St, where the lion's share of shops and restaurants are lined up. Chatham is a town made for strolling. You'll find free parking along Main St and in the parking lot behind the Chatham Squire pub.

◉ Sights

Chatham Light   LIGHTHOUSE
(⊗20min tours 1-3:30pm Wed May-Oct) FREE For dramatic vistas of sand and sea, head to the lighthouse viewing area on Shore Rd. The landmark lighthouse dates to 1878, and its light is visible 15 miles out to sea. No reservations are taken for the tours, so you can just show up.

Beaches   BEACH
Directly below Chatham Light on Shore Rd is **Lighthouse Beach**, an endless expanse of sea and sandbars that offers some of the finest beach strolling on Cape Cod. So many people come here to see the lighthouse view that the parking is limited to 30 minutes; it's only a 15-minute walk from Main St, however, where on-street parking is allowed.

For the warmer waters of Nantucket Sound, the long and sandy **Hardings Beach** (Hardings Beach Rd) is the prize. To reach it, take Bank Hill Rd from MA 28. Parking costs $15 in summer.

Oyster Pond Beach (cnr Pond St & Stage Harbor Rd), on a calm inlet, is smaller but the swimming is good and parking is free.

**Monomoy National Wildlife
Refuge**   WILDLIFE RESERVE
(www.fws.gov/northeast/monomoy) ✈ This 7600-acre wildlife refuge, occupying the uninhabited North Monomoy and South Monomoy Islands, is a haven for shorebirds and seabirds. Nearly 300 species nest here and 10 times that number pass through on migrations. It's one of the most important ornithological stops on the entire Atlantic seaboard. **Monomoy Island Excursions** (☑508-430-7772; www.monomoysealcruise.com; 702 MA 28, Harwich Port; 1½hr tours adult/child $35/30) offers a Monomoy wildlife boat tour.

Chatham Railroad Museum   MUSEUM
(www.town.chatham.ma.us; 153 Depot Rd; ⊗10am-4pm Tue-Sat; ▥) FREE Train buffs won't want to miss the 1910 caboose and assorted memorabilia at Chatham's original 1887 railroad depot. The Victorian building is an architectural treasure worth a visit in itself.

🏃 Activities

Skydive Cape Cod   ADVENTURE SPORTS
(☑508-420-5867; www.skydivecapecod.com; 240 George Ryder Rd; jumps $229) Not all the excitement in Chatham is in the water. These folks will toss you out of a perfectly good airplane, hopefully with a parachute attached, for a lofty tandem jump. The first minute before you pull the chute is the ultimate adrenaline rush. The rest, pure exhilaration. If you can keep your eyes open, the views are stunning.

Monomoy Sail & Cycle
WATER SPORTS

(☎508-945-0811; www.gis.net/~monomoy; 275 MA 28/Orleans Rd, North Chatham; sailboards or kayaks per day $45; ⊙9am-6pm) The waters off Chatham are good for windsurfing and kayaking; the friendly folks here can set you up.

Cape Cod Rail Trail Extension
CYCLING

(🚲) A branch extension of the Cape Cod Rail Trail ends at Chatham, and the town's side streets and shady lanes are well suited to cycling. **Chatham Cycle** (☎508-945-8981; www.brewsterbike.com; 193 Depot St; bicycles per day adult/child $28/22; ⊙9am-6pm) rents quality bikes.

Sleeping

Bow Roof House
B&B $$

(☎508-945-1346; 59 Queen Anne Rd; r incl breakfast $115) It's hard to find places like this anymore. This homey, six-room, c 1780 house is delightfully old-fashioned in price and offerings, and within easy walking distance of the town center and beach. Except for a few modern-day conveniences, like the added private bathrooms, the house looks nearly the same as it did in colonial times.

Chatham Highlander
MOTEL $$

(☎508-945-9038; www.chathamhighlander.com; 946 Main St; r $119-209; ❋☀🚲) The rooms here, about 1 mile from the town center, are straightforward but large and clean. All have a refrigerator and some have kitchenettes. Unlike some stodgier resorts in town that cater to an older set, this motel welcomes families; kids will love the pair of heated pools.

Captain's House Inn
INN $$$

(☎508-945-0127; www.captainshouseinn.com; 369 Old Harbor Rd; r incl breakfast $270-375; ❋🛜🏊) Everything about this place, set in an 1839 Greek Revival house, is gracious. The decor is sumptuous, every guest room has a fireplace, and a gourmet breakfast is served in style overlooking a bubbly fountain.

Carriage House Inn
INN $$$

(☎508-945-4688; www.thecarriagehouseinn.com; 407 Old Harbor Rd; r incl breakfast $189-309; ❋@🛜) An affordable inn by Chatham standards. The rooms are tidy, the queen beds comfy and the breakfast home-cooked. Free use of beach gear adds to its popularity.

✗ Eating

Chatham Cookware Café
CAFE $

(☎508-945-1250; 524 Main St; sandwiches $8; ⊙6:30am-4pm) No, it's not a place to buy pots and pans, but rather *the* downtown spot for a coffee fix, homemade muffins and sandwiches. Order at the counter and take your goodies straight out the back, where you'll find a leafy garden deck.

Red Nun Bar & Grill
BURGERS $

(www.rednun.com; 746 Main St; burgers $9-12; ⊙11:30am-10pm) If burgers are your thing, step up to the bar at this unassuming joint and order the Nun Burger. It starts with a half pound of Black Angus beef placed in an oversize English muffin, which is then piled up with cheddar, bacon, sauteed onions and mushrooms. Burp.

Larry's PX
DINER $

(☎508-945-3964; 1591 Main St; mains $6-14; ⊙6am-2pm) True local flavor, with Formica tables, fishers' hours and service with a sassy smile. Join the townies for omelets and fried seafood. The sign on the door says 'Sorry, we're open.' Gotta love that.

★Chatham Fish Pier Market
SEAFOOD $$

(www.chathamfishpiermarket.com; 45 Barcliff Ave; mains $12-25; ⊙10am-7pm Mon-Thu, to 8pm Fri-Sun) If you like it fresh and local to the core, this salt-sprayed fish shack, with its own sushi chef and dayboats, is for you. The chowder's incredible, the fish so fresh it was swimming earlier in the day. It's takeout, but there are shady picnic tables where you can watch fishermen unload their catch and seals frolic as you savor dinner.

Del Mar
AMERICAN $$

(www.delmarbistro.com; 907 Main St; mains $14-32; ⊙5-9pm Tue-Sun) A welcome addition to the Chatham restaurant scene, the imaginative

---

LOCAL KNOWLEDGE

CHATHAM FISH PIER

In the mid to late afternoon, head to the Chatham Fish Pier, 1 mile north of Chatham Light, to watch the fishing fleet unload its daily catch. This is also a prime time to see seals, which swim around the boats as the haul is brought in. The pier is well worth a visit any day, but if you're lucky enough to be there on a summer weekend you'll likely find seasoned fishers hanging around to regale visitors and locals alike with real-deal fish stories. Park in the upper parking lot on Shore Rd and walk down behind the fish market.

SOUTH & NORTH BEACHES

Want to really get away from it all? The offshore barrier beaches of South Beach and North Beach offer miles of uninhabited sands ideal for sunbathing, ocean dips and long walks. It's common to see seals here: there are so many of them, in fact, that great white sharks, which feed on seals, are now drawn to these waters in summer. The Atlantic sides have surf, while the Chatham-facing bay sides have calm waters. Swimming is occasionally restricted because of the sharks, so check before heading off. There's no shade or facilities, so bring water, snacks and sunscreen.

Beachcomber (☑508-945-5265; www.sealwatch.com; Crowell Rd; North Beach water taxi adult/child $20/10; seal-watching trips adult/child $29/25; ☺10am-5pm) operates a water taxi to North Beach from Chatham Fish Pier.

menu at this stylish bistro swings from fig-and-prosciutto pizza to maple-glazed duck and beyond. A sure winner is the tuna, seared on the outside and sashimi-like inside, plated alongside scrumptious (really!) avocado mashed potatoes.

🍷 Drinking & Entertainment

Chatham Squire   PUB
(☑508-945-0945; www.thesquire.com; 487 Main St; ☺11am-12:15am) The town's favorite watering hole is both a family-friendly pub and an easygoing, boisterous bar. Got an old car license plate on you? It'll find a home with the hundreds of others decorating the walls. Live music on the weekends.

Chatham Bars Inn   COCKTAIL BAR
(www.chathambarsinn.com; 297 Shore Rd) Join the beautiful people here for a martini with a fabulous ocean view.

Monomoy Theatre   THEATER
(☑508-945-1589; www.monomoytheatre.org; 776 Main St) Ohio University students stage musicals, Shakespeare and contemporary plays at this well-known summertime playhouse. They've been at it since 1958.

Kate Gould Park   LIVE MUSIC
(Main St) FREE If you're in town on a Friday night, don't miss the summertime band concerts held under the stars at Kate Gould Park. They're an atmospheric throwback to an earlier era.

🛍 Shopping

Main St is lined with interesting shops and galleries.

Blue Water Fish Rubbings   CLOTHING
(☑508-945-7616; www.bluewaterfishrubbings.com; 505 Main St; ☺10am-5pm) Classy cotton beachwear and T-shirts are painted by a

Chatham artist using rubbings of actual fish, lobsters and seashells. Very cool.

Yankee Ingenuity   GIFTS
(☑508-945-1288; www.yankee-ingenuity.com; 525 Main St; ☺10am-5pm) Full of surprises, from Russian nesting dolls and quirky glass jewelry to elegant pottery and dramatic photos of the Cape.

ℹ Information

Chatham Chamber of Commerce (☑508-945-5199; www.chathaminfo.com; 2377 Main St, cnr MA 28 & MA 137; ☺10am-5pm Mon-Sat, noon-3pm Sun) Stop here for the latest info as you enter town or pick up brochures at the visitor booth (533 Main St) in the town center.

Orleans

POP 5890

To many, Orleans is simply the place where MA 6A and MA 28 converge and US 6 continues onward as the sole road to Provincetown. Others know of the exhilarating surf at Nauset Beach and that untouched Nauset Marsh offers a unique kayaking experience through one of the Cape's richest ecosystems.

Atlantic-facing Nauset Beach is about 3 miles east of Orleans center. Skaket Beach is on the bay side about 1.5 miles west of the town center.

◎ Sights & Activities

Nauset Beach   BEACH
(Beach Rd, East Orleans) Dune-backed and gloriously wide and sandy, this wild barrier beach extends for miles along the open Atlantic. Nauset is one of the Cape's best beaches for surfing, bodysurfing, long walks and just plain partying. You'll find a good clam shack and full facilities. Swing by on

a Monday in July and August for a rocking sunset concert. Parking costs $15 in summer.

Skaket Beach BEACH
(West Rd, off MA 6A) On the bay side, calm Skaket Beach is a magnet for families. Kids love to wade in the shallow waters and dig for hermit crabs. Its generous sands triple in size when the tide goes out, and at low tide you can walk the flats all the way to Brewster and back. Parking costs $15 in summer.

Goose Hummock Outdoor Center BOATING
(508-255-2620; www.goose.com; MA 6A; single/tandem kayaks per 4hr $25/45; 8am-6pm) Right on Town Cove, this outfit rents kayaks for use on the calm waters of Pleasant Bay and Nauset Marsh. It's hard to imagine a prettier place to drop a paddle. Goose also offers kayak tours ($50).

🛏 Sleeping & Eating

Ship's Knees Inn B&B $$
(508-255-1312; www.shipskneesinn.com; 186 Beach Rd, East Orleans; r incl breakfast with shared/private bath from $145/190; ❄@🖥) This place packs in a lot, with solid amenities and appealing period decor. Best of all, it's just a 0.4 mile walk to Nauset Beach. Centered on an old sea captain's home, the 17 rooms have nautical themes. Sea captains were accustomed to close quarters, and some of the rooms are tight on elbow room; others are generous suites.

Cove MOTEL $$
(508-255-1203; www.thecoveorleans.com; 13 MA 28; r $144-229; 🖥) A good choice for those who want to be on the water but within strolling distance of the town center. Rooms are well equipped, but many are built motel-style around a parking lot. Others have a more Cape Cod cottage look, set back overlooking a cove. For the best water views, request rooms 20 to 24.

Hot Chocolate Sparrow CAFE $
(508-240-2230; www.hotchocolatesparrow.com; 5 Old Colony Way; snacks $3-7; 6:30am-9pm Sun-Thu, to 11pm Fri & Sat) The Cape's finest coffee bar brews the headiest espresso around. Or, for a cool treat on a hot day, try the 'frozen hot chocolate.' Panini sandwiches, home-made pastries and fresh-from-the-oven cinnamon buns make perfect accompaniments.

Abba FUSION $$$
(508-255-8144; www.abbarestaurant.com; 89 Old Colony Way; mains $25-36; 5-9pm) Feeling adventurous? This fine-dining restaurant offers superb pan-Mediterranean fare with a hint of Thai thrown in. Start with steamed local mussels in basil and coconut milk and move on to the pan-seared striped bass in mushroom and ginger sauce.

ℹ Information

Orleans Chamber of Commerce (508-255-1386; www.capecod-orleans.com; 44 Main St; 10am-3pm Mon-Fri)

Eastham
POP 5960

Eastham is not only the southern entrance to the Cape Cod National Seashore, but it's also home to the Cape's oldest windmill and some well-known lighthouses. Don't be fooled by the bland commercial development along US 6 – slip off the highway and you'll find an unspoiled world of beaches, marshes and trails.

◎ Sights & Activities

Fort Hill LOOKOUT
(Governor Prence Rd, off US 6) FREE Don't miss the commanding view of expansive Nauset Marsh from Fort Hill. It's a favorite place to be at dawn, but the view is memorable any time of the day. And bring your walking shoes for the 2-mile Fort Hill Trail.

THE FRENCH CONNECTION

Today's telecommunications industry owes a debt of gratitude to Cape Cod's windswept Atlantic shore. The first cable connection between Europe and the US was established here in 1879 by the French Telegraph Company, and until the mid-20th century they transmitted communications via a 3000-mile-long cable between Orleans and Brest, France. Charles Lindbergh's arrival in Paris and Germany's invasion of France were among the messages relayed. The French Cable Station Museum (www.frenchcablestationmuseum.org; 41 S Orleans Rd, cnr Cove Rd & MA 28; 1-4pm Thu-Sun Jul & Aug, 1-4pm Fri-Sun Jun & Sep) FREE in Orleans contains the original equipment.

CAPE COD NATIONAL SEASHORE

Extending some 40 miles around the curve of the Outer Cape, the **Cape Cod National Seashore** (www.nps.gov/caco) encompasses the Atlantic shoreline from Orleans all the way to Provincetown. Under the auspices of the National Park Service, it's a treasure trove of unspoiled beaches, dunes, salt marshes, nature trails and forests. Thanks to the backing of President John F Kennedy, this vast area was set aside for preservation in the 1960s, just before a building boom hit the rest of his native Cape Cod. Access to the park sights is easy: everything of interest is on or just off US 6.

The National Seashore's **Salt Pond Visitor Center** (508-255-3421; 50 Doane Rd, cnr US 6 & Nauset Rd, Eastham; 9am-5pm) **FREE** is the place to start and has a great view to boot. There are first-rate exhibits and short films about the Cape's geology, history and ever-changing landscape. The helpful staff can provide maps to the park's numerous trails, both hiking and cycling, some of which begin right at the visitor center. Call for the daily schedule of interpretive ranger walks, talks, stargazing, campfire programs, and more; most are free.

The Province Lands Visitor Center (p152) in Provincetown is smaller but has similar services and a fab ocean view.

Beach parking permits cost $15 per day or $45 per season and are valid at all National Seashore beaches, so you can use the same permit to spend the morning at one beach and the afternoon at another. The fees are collected only in summer. Between mid-September and mid-June, beach parking is free.

The trail leads down scenic Fort Hill toward the coast and then skirts inland to meander along raised boardwalks over a unique red-maple swamp. It's one of the nicest walks in the National Seashore, especially in fall.

Period Buildings
HISTORIC BUILDINGS

Captain Penniman House (508-255-3421; Governor Prence Rd; 1-4pm Tue-Thu) **FREE** is a mid-19th-century sea captain's house topped with a widow's walk and fronted by an awesome whale-jawbone gate. Hours vary outside of summer; ask at the Salt Pond Visitor Center.

The **Old Schoolhouse Museum** (508-255-0788; www.easthamhistorical.org; cnr Nauset Rd & US 6; 1-4pm Tue & Wed, 10am-4pm Thu & Fri Jul & Aug) **FREE** features a small exhibit on author Henry Beston's year in a cottage on Coast Guard Beach.

Eastham's **windmill** (cnr US 6 & Samoset Rd; 10am-5pm) **FREE** is the oldest structure in town, although it was actually built in Plymouth, Massachusetts, in 1680.

National Seashore Beaches
BEACHES

All roads lead to **Coast Guard Beach**. The main road from the Salt Pond Visitor Center deposits you here, as do cycling and hiking trails. And it's for good reason: this grand beach backed by a classic coast guard station is a stunner that attracts everyone from beachcombers to hard-core surfers. Bird-watchers also flock to Coast Guard Beach for the eagle-eye view of Nauset Marsh. Facilities include rest rooms, showers and changing rooms. In summer, when the small beach parking lot fills up, a shuttle bus runs from a staging area near the visitor center.

Cliff-backed **Nauset Light Beach**, north of Coast Guard Beach, is also the stuff of dreams. Its features and facilities are similar to Coast Guard Beach, but there's a large parking lot right at the beach. Nauset Lighthouse, a picturesque red-and-white-striped tower, guards the shoreline. And don't miss the Three Sisters Lighthouses, a curious trio of 19th-century lighthouses saved from an eroding sea cliff and moved to a wooded clearing just five minutes' walk up Cable Rd from Nauset Light Beach.

Parking at either beach costs $15 in the summer.

First Encounter Beach
BEACH

(Samoset Rd;) First Encounter Beach, where Samoset Rd meets Cape Cod Bay, is a fine place to watch the sunset. With its vast tidal flats and kid-friendly, calm, shallow waters, it offers a night-and-day contrast to the National Seashore beaches on Eastham's wild Atlantic side. Parking costs $15 in summer.

Cape Cod Rail & National Seashore Trails
CYCLING

Eastham has both the Cape Cod Rail Trail and a connecting National Seashore bike trail, the latter traversing a dramatic salt marsh en route to Coast Guard Beach. Rent bikes at **Little Capistrano Bike Shop** (☑508-255-6515; www.capecodbike.com; 30 Salt Pond Rd; bicycles per 8hr adult/child $19/14; ☺9am-6pm), opposite the Salt Pond Visitor Center.

🛏 Sleeping

⭐ Inn at the Oaks
B&B **$$**
(☑508-255-1886; www.innattheoaks.com; 3085 US 6; r incl breakfast $175-305; ❄@🎧🛏🐾) This historic inn has 10 antique-filled guest rooms. There's a room for every taste; some have fireplaces; others open up into family suites. The innkeepers welcome kids (they have several of their own) and are very accommodating: there's a play area for the little ones and family packages that include children's activities.

Eagle Wing Guest Motel
MOTEL **$$**
(☑508-240-5656; www.eaglewingmotel.com; 960 US 6; r incl breakfast $119-179; ❄🎧🛏) Spacious squeaky-clean rooms, comfy beds and quiet grounds are the draw at this boutique motel geared for adults. Opt for one of the rooms with a rear deck and watch the rabbits raid the backyard flowers. You'll have to hop in your car to go anywhere, but the National Seashore is just a 2-mile drive away.

Cove Bluffs Motel
MOTEL **$$**
(☑508-240-1616; www.covebluffs.com; 25 Seaview Rd; r/studios $105/130; ❄) A home-away-from-home kind of place whose extensive grounds include a basketball court and hammocks strung from the trees. You can opt for a motel-style room, but if you swing for the studios to add on a kitchen, you'll save a bundle on restaurant bills.

🍴 Eating

Friendly Fisherman
SEAFOOD **$$**
(☑508-255-6770; www.friendlyfishermaneastham.com; 4580 US 6; meals $12-20; ☺11:30am-7:30pm)

This simple eatery, attached to a fish market, has outdoor picnic tables and serves the perfect lobster roll: huge, overflowing with sweet chunks of claw and tail meat, and with just enough mayo to hold it all together. The fried clams here are impressive, too.

Arnold's Lobster & Clam Bar
SEAFOOD **$$**
(☑508-255-2575; www.arnoldsrestaurant.com; 3580 US 6; meals $10-28; ☺11:30am-8pm) Fried seafood is the staple, but health-conscious diners will also find baked cod, scallops and lobster on the menu. Everything is fresh, and at night this place adds on a raw bar, which separates it from the other counter-service seafood shacks along the highway.

Karoo Kafe
SOUTH AFRICAN **$$**
(www.karookafe.com; 3 Main St; mains $8-18; ☺4-9pm Wed-Sun; 🥗) If you need an alternative to seafood, check out this safari-decor restaurant featuring authentic home-style cooking from South Africa. The ostrich satay's a favorite. Or order the spicy *peri-peri* chicken for a blast of tomato, garlic, onion and chili; it comes in a vegetarian tofu version too.

ℹ Information

Eastham Chamber of Commerce Booth
(☑508-255-3444; www.easthamchamber.com; 1700 US 6, cnr US 6 & Governor Prence Rd; ☺9am-6pm) The ECC maintains this summertime information booth just north of the Fort Hill turnoff.

Wellfleet
POP 2750

Art galleries, primo surfing beaches and those famous Wellfleet oysters lure visitors to this seaside village. Actually, there's not much Wellfleet doesn't have, other than crowds. It's a delightful throwback to an earlier era, from its drive-in movie theater to

BREAK OUT THE S'MORES

That perfect day at the beach doesn't have to end when the sun goes down. Cape Cod National Seashore (p146) allows campfires on the sand at six of its beaches, though you'll need a free permit and there's a run on them in midsummer. Reservations can be made three days in advance at Salt Pond Visitor Center (p146) for Coast Guard, Nauset Light and Marconi Beaches or the **Province Lands Visitor Center** for Race Point, Herring Cove and Head of the Meadow Beaches. Tip: reservations go first to people lined up at the door when it opens at 9am; phone reservations are accepted if there are any left. Four permits are allowed each evening at each beach. Bring firewood (bundles are sold at grocery stores), a bucket to douse the flames, and a big bag of marshmallows!

PEGGY SUE, IS THAT YOU?

For an evening of nostalgia, park at **Wellfleet Drive-In** (☎508-349-7176; www.wellfleet cinemas.com; US 6; adult/child $9/6; 🚻), one of a dwindling number of drive-in theaters surviving in the USA. Built in the 1950s, before the word 'Cineplex' became part of the vernacular, everything except the movie being shown on the giant screen is true to the era. Yep, they still have those original mono speakers that you hook over the car window, there's an old-fashioned snack bar and, of course, it's always a double feature. Plastic – what's that? It's cash-only at the gate.

OK, there are a few accommodations to modern times. So as to not block anyone's view, the lot is now divided into two sections: one for SUVs, the other for cars. And you don't *need* to use those boxy window speakers: you can also listen by tuning your stereo car radio to FM 89.3. But other things remain unchanged. Bring bug spray and a blanket!

Another time-honored throwback is **Wellfleet Flea Market** (☎508-349-0541; admission per car $3; ◷8am-3pm Wed, Thu, Sat & Sun), held in summer at the drive-in. This is the largest flea market on the Cape, with 200 dealers selling everything from antiques to newly made objects, and from treasures to junk.

its unspoiled town center, which has barely changed in appearance since the 1950s.

Most of Wellfleet east of US 6 is part of the Cape Cod National Seashore. To get to the town center, turn west off US 6 at either Main St or School St.

⊙ Sights & Activities

Art Galleries
GALLERIES

You won't have any trouble finding art galleries in central Wellfleet: there are more than 20 of them selling fine art and handcrafted items. Most are within a 10-minute walk of one another on the adjoining Main, Bank and Commercial Sts, but there are galleries sprinkled throughout the town.

At any gallery, pick up the Wellfleet Art Galleries Association map, which has descriptive listings. Hours vary; some are open year-round, others from mid-May to mid-October. Many galleries host receptions with snacks and drinks on Saturday nights in July and August.

Some galleries you shouldn't miss include **Blue Heron Gallery** (☎508-349-6724; www. blueheronfineart.com; 20 Bank St), a gallery with museum-quality art and **Left Bank Gallery** (☎508-349-9451; www.leftbankgallery.com; 25 Commercial St), featuring locally and nationally known artists.

Marconi Beach
BEACH

(off US 6) Part of the Cape Cod National Seashore, Marconi is a narrow Atlantic beach backed by sea cliffs and sand dunes. Facilities include changing rooms, rest rooms and showers. It's named for Guglielmo Marconi,

who sent the first transatlantic wireless message from a station nearby in 1903. Parking costs $15 in summer.

Wellfleet Bay Wildlife Sanctuary
NATURE RESERVE

(☎508-349-2615; www.massaudubon.org; West Rd, off US 6; adult/child $5/3; ◷8:30am-dusk; 🚻) 🐾 Birders flock to Mass Audubon's 1100-acre sanctuary, where trails cross tidal creeks, salt marshes and beaches. The most popular is the Goose Pond Trail (1.5-mile round-trip), which leads out to a remote beach and offers abundant opportunities for spotting marine and bird life. The sanctuary also offers guided walks, seal cruises and kids' programs.

You can walk the sanctuary trails until dusk, but get there before 5pm to see the eco-displays in the solar-powered nature center.

Wellfleet Historical Society Museum
MUSEUM

(☎508-349-9157; www.wellfleethistoricalsociety .com; 266 Main St; ◷10am-4pm Tue-Sat) **FREE** This museum harbors a fascinating mishmash of odds and ends, from a vintage bankteller cage to Native American artifacts.

Surfing Beaches
SURFING

Brought your surfboard, didn't you? The adjacent town-run beaches of **Cahoon Hollow Beach** and **White Crest Beach** offer high-octane surfing. Backed by steep dunes, these long, untamed Atlantic beaches also make for memorable beach walks. Parking at either costs $10 in summer. If you need gear, **SickDay Surf Shop** (☎508-

214-4158; www.sickdaysurf.com; 361 Main St; surfboards per day $25-30; ⊗9am-9pm Mon-Sat) can set you up.

Cape Cod Rail Trail
CYCLING

(🚴) The northern end of the Cape Cod Rail Trail is at Lecount Hollow Rd near its intersection with US 6. You can rent bikes in summer at **Little Capistrano Bike Shop** (📞508-349-2363; www.capecodbike.com; 1446 US 6; bicycles per half-day adult/child $15/11; ⊗9am-4pm), right near the trailhead, and pedal south.

★ Festivals & Events

Wellfleet OysterFest
FOOD

(www.wellfleetoysterfest.org; ⊗mid-Oct) During the Wellfleet OysterFest on a weekend in mid-October, the entire town center becomes a food fair, with a beer garden, an oyster-shucking contest and, of course, belly-busters of the blessed bivalves. It's a wildly popular event and a great time to see Wellfleet at its most spirited.

🛏 Sleeping & Eating

Even'Tide Motel
MOTEL $$

(📞508-349-3410; www.eventidemotel.com; 650 US 6; r from $135, cottages per week $1100-2800; ❄🐕🚴) This 31-room motel, set back from the highway in a grove of pine trees, also has nine cottages that can each accommo-

date four to eight people. Pluses include a large indoor pool, picnic facilities and a playground.

Mac's Seafood Market
SEAFOOD $$

(www.macsseafood.com; 265 Commercial St, Wellfleet Town Pier; mains $7-20; ⊗11am-3pm Mon-Fri, to 8pm Sat & Sun; 🚸) Head here for fish-market-fresh seafood at bargain prices. Fried-fish standards join the likes of oyster po'boys, sushi rolls and grilled striped-bass dinners. You order at a window and chow down at picnic tables overlooking Wellfleet Harbor.

Wicked Oyster
SEAFOOD $$

(📞508-349-3455; www.thewickedo.com; 50 Main St; mains $8-35; ⊗8am-noon & 5-9pm) The 'in' crowd hangs out here for the likes of roasted lamb wrapped in prosciutto, seared scallops with wild-mushroom risotto and, of course, several incarnations of Wellfleet oysters. Although the chef works his magic at dinner, you can also start your day here with a wicked omelet or smoked-salmon bagels.

Bookstore & Restaurant
SEAFOOD $$

(📞508-349-3154; www.wellfleetoyster.com; 50 Kendrick Ave; mains $10-23; ⊗11:30am-8pm) 🚸 This place raises its own oysters and littleneck clams, harvested at low tide in the waters right across the street – can't get fresher than that. Sit out on the deck and

---

LOCAL KNOWLEDGE

BOB PRESCOTT

Director of Mass Audubon's Wellfleet Bay Wildlife Sanctuary, Bob has had the enviable job of running one of the Cape's most spectacular nature sanctuaries for more than 25 years.

'Real Cape Cod' Experience
Getting out on the water in places like Pleasant Bay and Nauset Marsh captures the feeling of what the Cape was like a hundred years ago. It's a timeless feel to be in a kayak out on the marsh. And Fort Hill is a must – you get such a tremendous view of the Atlantic and Nauset Marsh.

Top Wildlife Experiences
Whale watching is a great pastime. I recommend the Dolphin Fleet out of Provincetown – all visitors really should do that. Then there's the thrill of seeing seals inside Chatham Harbor, where kayakers can paddle up close and families with kids can see them on a calm-water boat tour.

Why the Sanctuary Is Special
It's the diversity of habitat, starting at the nature center, out through pine woods to a freshwater pond, then a brackish water pond, along a salt marsh to a coastal heathland community, out across a boardwalk to a barrier beach. In a loop like that you could see 50 species of birds.

OH LÀ LÀ!

A French baker with a Michelin star setting up shop in tiny Wellfleet? You might think he'd gone crazy, if not for the line out the door. **PB Boulangerie & Bistro** (www.pbboulangeriebistro.com; 15 Lecount Hollow Rd; pastries from $3; ⊗7am-7pm Tue-Sun) is set back from US 6 just beyond the Wellfleet tourist office. Walk through the door and scan the glass cases full of flaky fruit tarts and chocolate-almond croissants and you'll think you've died and gone to Paris.

enjoy the view. The menu covers a broad spectrum, from fish sandwiches to seafood Alfredo and prime rib.

Drinking & Entertainment

★Beachcomber   LIVE MUSIC
(☑508-349-6055;   www.thebeachcomber.com; 1120 Cahoon Hollow Rd; ⊗5pm-1am) If you're ready for some serious partying, 'Da Coma' is *the* place to rock the night away. It's a bar. It's a restaurant. It's a dance club. It's the coolest summertime hangout on the entire Cape. Set in a former lifesaving station right on Cahoon Hollow Beach, you can watch the surf action till the sun goes down. And at night some really hot bands – like the Wailers and the Lemonheads – take to the stage.

Wellfleet Harbor Actors Theater   THEATER
(WHAT; ☑508-349-9428; www.what.org; 2357 US 6) WHAT's happening! The Cape's most celebrated theater always has something going on in its state-of-the-art Julie Harris Stage. The contemporary, experimental plays staged here are always lively, occasionally bawdy and often the subject of animated conversation.

ℹ Information

Wellfleet Chamber of Commerce (☑508-349-2510; www.wellfleetchamber.com; 1410 US 6; ⊗9am-6pm) Next to the South Wellfleet post office at Lecount Hollow Rd.

Truro

POP 2000

Squeezed between Cape Cod Bay on the west and the open Atlantic on the east, narrow Truro abounds with views of the water. An odd collection of elements coexist here peacefully: strip motels along the highway, trophy homes in the hills and dales west of US 6, and pine forests and beaches to the east.

To reach Truro's historic sites, which are on the ocean side, take Highland or South Highland Rds off US 6. Or, for fun, just take any winding road off the highway and let yourself get a little lost, soaking in the distinctive scenery.

◎ Sights & Activities

Cape Cod Highland Light   LIGHTHOUSE
(www.capecodlight.org; Light House Rd; admission $4; ⊗10am-5:30pm) Sitting on the Cape's highest elevation (a mere 120ft!), Cape Cod Highland Light dates to 1797 and casts the brightest beam on the New England coast. Admission includes a 10-minute video, an exhibit in the keeper's house and a climb up the lighthouse's 69 steps to a sweeping vista. Children must be at least 48in tall to make the climb.

The adjacent **Highland House Museum** (☑508-487-3397; www.trurohistorical.org; Light House Rd; adult/child $4/free; ⊗10am-4:30pm Mon-Sat) focuses on Truro's farming and maritime past. It's packed with all sorts of vintage goodies, from antique dolls to shipwreck salvage.

Truro Vineyards of Cape Cod   WINERY
(www.trurovineyardsofcapecod.com; 11 Shore Rd, North Truro; ⊗11am-5pm Mon-Sat, noon-5pm Sun) **FREE** This boutique vineyard, the first on the Outer Cape, is worth a stop. Guided tours of the vineyard take place at 1pm and 3pm daily from Memorial Day to Columbus Day. To get there, turn left off US 6 onto Shore Rd; it's a quarter mile from the highway. A huge wine barrel atop a tower marks the spot.

Head of the Meadow Beach   BEACH
(Head of the Meadow Rd, off US 6) Part of the Cape Cod National Seashore, this wide, dune-backed beach has limited facilities, but there are lifeguards in summer. If you happen to be there at low tide, you might catch a glimpse of old shipwrecks that met their fate on the shoals. There are two entrances: the National Seashore beach (parking $15) is to the left, while the town-managed beach (parking $10) is to the right.

Pilgrim Heights   HIKING
(US 6, North Truro) You'll find two short trails with broad views at this historic site within

the Cape Cod National Seashore. Both trails start at the same parking lot, and each takes about 20 minutes to walk. The signposted turnoff into Pilgrim Heights is along the northeast side of US 6.

If you're doing just one hike, opt for the Pilgrim Spring Trail, which makes a loop to the spring where the Pilgrims first found fresh water after landing in the New World in 1620. It also has an overlook with an ideal vantage for spotting hawks as they hunt for rodents in the marsh below.

🛏 Sleeping

Hostelling International Truro　　HOSTEL **$**
(☑508-349-3889; http://capecod.hiusa.org; N Pamet Rd; dm incl breakfast $39; @) Budget digs don't get more atmospheric than this former coast-guard station perched amid undulating dunes. It's so remote that wild turkeys are the only traffic along the road. And it's but a stroll to a quiet beach. There are just 42 beds, so book early to avoid disappointment. It's open from mid-June to early September.

**North of Highland
Camping Area**　　CAMPGROUND **$**
(☑508-487-1191; www.capecodcamping.com; 52 Head of the Meadow Rd, North Truro; tent sites $40) Campers will be pleasantly surprised to find that little Truro harbors one of the most secluded campgrounds on all of Cape Cod, with 237 sites spread around 60 forested acres. And you don't have to worry about setting up your tent next to an RV – this place is only for tent camping.

Days' Cottages　　COTTAGES **$$**
(☑508-487-1062; www.dayscottages.com; 271 Shore Rd/MA 6A, North Truro; cottages per night/week $210/1400) The 23 identical cottages, lined up like ducks in a row, are an architectural landmark dating to 1931. You can't get closer to the water: each cottage is just inches from the shoreline. However, they're very basic inside, with a small kitchen, living room and two bedrooms each with a double bed. Rates cover up to four people.

🍴 Eating

Box Lunch　　SANDWICHES **$**
(www.boxlunch.com; 300 MA 6A; sandwiches $6-10; ☺7am-7pm) Light on the wallet and handy for a quick lunch, this simple roadside operation attached to a farm stand offers an array of roll-up sandwiches, the best of which

is the Californian: a turkey, avocado and tomato combo that hits the mark.

★ BlackFish　　MODERN AMERICAN **$$**
(☑508-349-3399; 17 Truro Center Rd; mains $15-35; ☺5-10pm; ☑) Local ingredients meet urban sophistication at Truro's top dinner restaurant. From the nautical decor to the out-of-the-ordinary menu choices, everything clicks. Perhaps you'll want to start with the rabbit ragout and finish with the blackberry bread pudding and brandy ice cream. There are always some creative vegetarian options as well.

☆ Entertainment

**Payomet Performing
Arts Center**　　PERFORMING ARTS
(☑508-487-5400; www.payomet.org; 29 Old Dewline Rd, North Truro; 🎭) The center's theme of 'national talent on a local stage' rings true, with performances by the likes of guitarist David Bromberg and R&B singer Mavis Staples. The setting, inside a large tent surrounded by woods, is as cool as the performers. Performances of Shakespeare's *Twelfth Night* and children's workshops also take place here in the summer.

ℹ Information

Truro Chamber of Commerce (☑508-487-1288; www.trurochamberofcommerce.com; cnr US 6 & Head of the Meadow Rd, North Truro; ☺10am-4pm)

Provincetown
POP 2950

This is it: Provincetown is as far as you can go on the Cape, and more than just geographically. The draw is irresistible. Fringe writers and artists began making a summer haven here a century ago. Today this sandy outpost has morphed into the hottest gay and lesbian destination in the Northeast. Flamboyant street scenes, brilliant galleries and unbridled nightlife paint the town center. But that's only half the show. Provincetown's untamed coastline and vast beaches also beg exploring. Sail off on a whale watch, cruise the night away, get lost in the dunes – but whatever you do, don't miss this unique, open-minded corner of New England.

◎ Sights

Start exploring on Commercial St, the throbbing waterfront heart of Provincetown, where the lion's share of cafes, galleries and clubs vie for your attention.

★ Provincetown Art Association & Museum
MUSEUM

(PAAM; www.paam.org; 460 Commercial St; adult/child $7/free; ⏰11am-8pm Mon-Thu, to 10pm Fri, to 5pm Sat & Sun) Founded in 1914 to celebrate the town's thriving art community, this vibrant museum showcases the works of hundreds of artists who have found their inspiration on the Lower Cape. Chief among them are Charles Hawthorne, who led the early Provincetown art movement, and Edward Hopper, who had a home and gallery in the Truro dunes.

If you're feeling inspired yourself, PAAM offers a full agenda of workshops in painting, silk-screening, sculpting and other mediums throughout the summer, most lasting three to five days.

★ Pilgrim Monument & Provincetown Museum
MUSEUM

(www.pilgrim-monument.org; High Pole Rd; adult/child $12/4; ⏰9am-7pm Jul & Aug, to 5pm Sep-Jun) Climb to the top of the country's tallest all-granite structure (253ft) for a sweeping view of town, the beaches and the spine of the Lower Cape. At the base of the c 1910 tower is an evocative museum depicting the landing of the *Mayflower* Pilgrims and other Provincetown history.

Stellwagen Bank National Marine Sanctuary
WILDLIFE RESERVE

Provincetown is the perfect launch point for whale-watching since it's the closest port to Stellwagen Bank National Marine Sanctuary, the summer feeding ground for humpback whales. Many of the 300 remaining North Atlantic right whales, the world's most endangered whale species, also frequent these waters.

Province Lands Visitor Center
BEACH

(☎508-487-1256; www.nps.gov/caco; Race Point Rd; ⏰9am-5pm; P) ✏FREE Overlooking Race Point Beach, this Cape Cod National Seashore visitor center has displays on dune ecology and a rooftop observation deck with an eye-popping 360-degree view of the outermost reaches of Cape Cod. The park stays open to midnight so even after the visitor center closes you can still climb to the deck for sunset views and unobstructed stargazing.

The visitor center offers tours ranging from dune walks and forays across the tidal

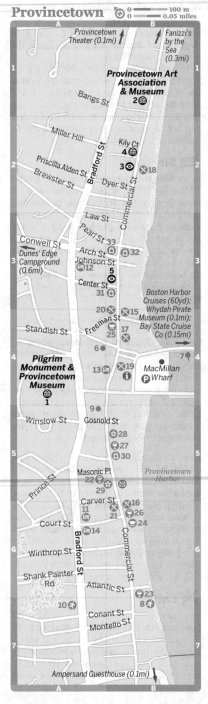

Provincetown

Provincetown

flats to a historical walking tour of downtown Provincetown. Most tours last one to two hours; many are free, and others have a nominal fee.

Race Point Beach   BEACH
(Race Point Rd) On the wild tip of the Cape, this Cape Cod National Seashore beach is a breathtaking stretch of sand, crashing surf and undulating dunes as far as the eye can see. Kick off your sandals, kids – the soft, grainy sand makes a fun run. This is the kind of beach where you could walk for miles and see no one but the occasional angler casting for bluefish. Parking costs $15 in summer.

Herring Cove Beach   BEACH
(Province Lands Rd) Swimmers favor the relatively calm, though certainly brisk, waters of Herring Cove Beach, also part of the National Seashore. The long sandy beach is popular with everyone. Though illegal, nude sunbathers head left to the south section of the beach; families usually break out the picnic baskets closer to the parking lot. The entire beach faces west, making it a spectacular place to be at sunset. Parking costs $15 in summer.

Long Point Beach   BEACH
Home to the Cape's most remote grains of sand, Long Point Beach is reached by a two-hour walk (each way) along the stone dike at the western end of Commercial St. There are no facilities, so bring water. Also time your walk carefully, as the dike is submerged at extreme high tide.

Or do it the easy way and hop on the **Long Point Shuttle** (☑508-487-0898; www.flyers boats.com; MacMillan Wharf; one-way/round-trip $10/15; ⊙10am-5pm), which ferries sunbathers across the bay from June to September.

Art Galleries   GALLERIES
With the many artists who have worked here, it's no surprise that Provincetown hosts some of the finest art galleries in the region. For the best browsing, begin at PAAM and start walking southwest along Commercial St. Over the next few blocks every second storefront harbors a gallery worth a peek.

Galleries you won't want to miss include the **Albert Merola Gallery** (☑508-487-4424; www.albertmerolagallery.com; 424 Commercial St), which showcases works by both contemporary and notable past Provincetown artists; and **Gallery Voyeur** (www.voy-art.com;

DON'T MISS

SHIP IN A...

In a town of quirky attractions, the **Provincetown Public Library** (www.provincetownlibrary.org; 356 Commercial St; ⊙10am-5pm Mon & Fri, to 8pm Tue-Thu, 1-5pm Sat & Sun) might be the last place you'd expect to find a hidden treasure. Erected in 1860 as a church, it was turned into a museum a century later, complete with a replica of Provincetown's famed race-winning schooner *Rose Dorothea*. When the museum went bust, the town converted the building to the library. One catch: the boat, which occupies the building's upper deck, was too big to remove. So it's still there, with bookshelves built around it. Pop upstairs and take a look.

444 Commercial St), which features the vivid paintings of Johniene Papandreas.

Whydah Pirate Museum   MUSEUM
(www.whydah.com; MacMillan Wharf; adult/child $10/8; ⊙10am-5pm) Of the more than 3000 shipwrecks off the coast of the Cape, the *Whydah* is one of the best documented. Captained by 'Black Sam' Bellamy, the *Whydah* sank in 1717 and to this day remains the only authenticated pirate ship ever salvaged.

A local expedition recovered more than 100,000 items of booty – coins, jewelry, weapons – and some of these are on display at this museum on the wharf. Note, however, that many of the prize pieces are being exhibited elsewhere by the National Geographic Society, which aided in the recovery. Argh, matey.

🏃 Activities

⭐ Dolphin Fleet
Whale Watch   WHALE-WATCHING
(📞508-240-3636; www.whalewatch.com; MacMillan Wharf; adult/child $44/29; ⊙Apr-Oct; 🚼) 🏊 Dolphin offers as many as 12 whale-watch tours daily in peak season, each lasting three to four hours. You can expect a lot of splashy fun. Humpback whales have a flair for acrobatic breaching and come surprisingly close to the boats, offering great photo ops.

The naturalists on board not only have all the skinny on these mammoth leviathans but also play a vital role in monitoring the whale population. If you've got kids in tow, ask about the weekend deal in which the first boat out offers free passage to youngsters under 12.

Cape Cod National
Seashore Bike Trails   CYCLING
(www.nps.gov/caco) An exhilarating 8 miles of paved bike trails crisscross the forest and undulating dunes of the Cape Cod National Seashore. Not only is it a fun outing in itself,

but you can cool off with a refreshing swim: the main 5.5-mile loop trail has spur trails leading to both Herring Cove and Race Point Beaches.

The best place to rent bicycles is at **Ptown Bikes** (📞508-487-8735; www.ptownbikes.com; 42 Bradford St; bicycles per day $23; ⊙9am-6pm), though you'll also find bike-rental shops in the center of town on Commercial St.

Flyer's Boat Rental   BOATING
(📞508-487-0898; www.flyersboats.com; 131A Commercial St; rentals per 4hr $30-120; ⊙10am-5pm) Flyer's Boat Rental rents out single and double kayaks, sailboats and other watercraft.

Venture Athletics   BOATING
(📞508-487-9442; www.capeboating.com; 237 Commercial St; 1-/2-person kayaks per 4hr $30/50; ⊙9am-6pm) Venture Athletics rents kayaks and arranges guided kayak tours.

👉 Tours

Provincetown Trolley   GUIDED TOUR
(www.provincetowntrolley.com; Commercial St; adult/child $15/6; ⊙May-Oct) For a 40-minute narrated tour of Provincetown's major sights, hop aboard the Provincetown Trolley, which picks up passengers in front of the town hall throughout the day.

✨ Festivals & Events

Fine Arts Work Center   CULTURE
(www.fawc.org; 24 Pearl St) Talks and presentations by distinguished writers and artists throughout the year; the schedule is online.

**Provincetown International
Film Festival**   FILM
(www.ptownfilmfest.org) A fine excuse for Hollywood to come to Provincetown in mid-June. You can count on director John Waters to show.

Provincetown Portuguese Festival   FIESTA
(www.provincetownportuguesefestival.com) A celebration of the town's Portuguese heritage in late June. Includes the blessing of the fishing fleet and lots of home-cooked food.

Fourth of July Weekend   FIREWORKS
P-town's weekend of gay 'circuit' dance parties and, of course, an Independence Day parade and fireworks, held in early July.

Provincetown Carnival   CARNIVAL
(www.ptown.org/carnival.asp; ⊙3rd week of Aug) Mardi Gras, drag queens, flowery floats: this is the ultimate gay party event in this gay party town, attracting tens of thousands of revelers over the entire third week of August.

🛏 Sleeping

Provincetown has nearly 100 small guesthouses, without a single chain hotel to mar the view. In summer it's wise to book ahead, doubly so on weekends. If you do arrive without a booking, the chamber of commerce keeps tabs on available rooms.

Dunes' Edge Campground   CAMPGROUND $
(☑508-487-9815; www.dunesedge.com; 386 US 6; tent/RV sites $42/54; 🖽) Camp amid the dunes and shady pines at this family-friendly campground on the north side of US 6, between the National Seashore and town. With just 85 sites, it gets booked solid in midsummer, so reserve well in advance.

Race Point Lighthouse   INN $$
(☑508-487-9930; www.racepointlighthouse.net; Race Point; r $155-185) 🌊 Want to *really* get away? If unspoiled sand dunes and a 19th-century lighthouse sound like good company, book one of the three upstairs bedrooms in the old lighthouse-keeper's house. Cool place: totally off the grid, powered by solar panels and a wind turbine, and literally on

the outer tip of the Cape, miles from the nearest neighbor.

Revere Guesthouse   B&B $$
(☑508-487-2292; www.reverehouse.com; 14 Court St; r incl breakfast $155-345; ❄🖥) Tasteful rooms, fresh-baked breakfast goodies and welcoming little touches will make you feel right at home here. The setting is peaceful, yet just minutes from all the action. And if this is your first stay in Provincetown, you can count on the innkeeper to be a treasure trove of in-the-know tips.

Moffett House   GUESTHOUSE $$
(☑508-487-6615; www.moffetthouse.com; 296a Commercial St; r with shared bath $90-159; ❄🖥 🖳) Set back on an alleyway, this guesthouse is not only quiet but has another bonus: every room comes with two bicycles for your entire stay. Rooms are basic – it's more like crashing with a friend than doing the B&B thing – but you get kitchen privileges, bagels and coffee in the morning, and lots of ops to meet fellow travelers.

Ampersand Guesthouse   B&B $$
(☑508-487-0959; www.ampersandguesthouse.com; 6 Cottage St; r incl breakfast $130-200; ❄🖥) Sit on the sundeck and enjoy the water view at this Greek Revival guesthouse on the quieter west end of town. There are 10 rooms in all, each with its own character, some with fireplaces. It's not the fanciest place in town, but it's friendly and cozy and summer rates are a good value.

★Carpe Diem   BOUTIQUE HOTEL $$$
(☑508-487-4242; www.carpediemguesthouse.com; 12 Johnson St; r incl breakfast $229-419; ❄@🖥) Sophisticated yet relaxed, this boutique inn blends a soothing mix of smiling Buddhas, orchid sprays and artistic decor. Each guest room is inspired by a different gay literary genius; the room themed on

---

THE ART OF THE DUNES

On the surface you might think there's not much going on in the dunes of the Cape Cod National Seashore, but **Art's Dune Tours** (☑508-487-1950; www.artsdunetours.com; 4 Standish St; day tours adult/child $27/18, sunset tours adult/child $43/25) will prove you wrong. These 4WD tours are surprisingly informative and scenic. And talk about local – the same family has been running these tours since 1946, so you can bet you'll get the inside scoop. The basic hour-long daytime tour takes you along a remote stretch of beach before heading off to explore the dunes. For more drama, take the sunset tour, which adds time to get out and stroll along the beach as the fiery orb dips into the ocean. Or charter your own tour – perhaps with a little surf-fishing worked in, a beach clambake or even a wedding in the dunes.

poet Raj Rao, for example, has sumptuous embroidered fabrics and hand-carved Indian furniture. The on-site spa includes a Finnish sauna, hot tub and massage therapy.

Brass Key Guesthouse INN $$$

(☑508-487-9005; www.brasskey.com; 67 Bradford St; r from $319; ❋🐾🌊) This adults-only boutique inn sets the standard for gay travelers. The rooms fuse Victorian style with 21st-century comforts, like Jacuzzis and pillow-top mattresses. Other perks include an infinity pool, private sunbathing decks and wine-and-cheese evenings.

✖️ Eating

Provincetown has one of the best dining scenes this side of Boston. Every third building on Commercial St houses some sort of eatery, so that's the place to start.

Cafe Heaven CAFE $

(☑508-487-9639; 199 Commercial St; mains $7-12; ⊗8am-3pm) Light and airy but small and crowded, this art-filled storefront is an easy-on-the-wallet lunch and breakfast place. The menu ranges from sinful croissant French toast to healthy salads. Don't be deterred by the wait: the tables turn over quickly.

Purple Feather Cafe & Treatery CAFE $

(www.thepurplefeather.com; 334 Commercial St; snacks $3-10; ⊗11am-midnight; 🌊🖐) Head to this stylish cafe for killer panini sandwiches, a rainbow of gelatos and decadent desserts all made from scratch. Lemon cupcakes have never looked so lusty. There's no better place in town for light eats and sweet treats. Good mocha lattes too.

Portuguese Bakery BAKERY $

(299 Commercial St; snacks $2-5; ⊗7am-11pm) This old-school bakery has been serving up *malasadas* (sweet fried dough), spicy linguica sandwiches and Portuguese soups for more than a century. True local flavor.

Spiritus Pizza PIZZERIA $

(www.spirituspizza.com; 190 Commercial St; slices/pizzas $3/20; ⊗11:30am-2am) This is the place to pick up a late-night slice, or a late-night date if you haven't been lucky at one of the clubs. While the cruising is top rate, the pizza's just middling. Best bet is to see what's fresh out of the oven and order by the slice.

Cafe Edwidge CAFE $$

(www.edwigeatnight.com; 333 Commercial St; mains $10-32; ⊗8am-1pm & 6-10pm Wed-Mon; 🌊)

New England seafood takes imaginative twists at this lively bistro. For the best breakfast treat on Cape Cod, slip into one of the highback booths, sip a mimosa and order up the lobster benedict. And you needn't get up early: breakfast is served until 1pm.

Fanizzi's by the Sea SEAFOOD $$

(☑508-487-1964; www.fanizzisrestaurant.com; 539 Commercial St; mains $10-25; ⊗11:30am-9:30pm; 🖐) Consistent food, an amazing water view and reasonable prices make this restaurant a local favorite. The extensive menu has something for everyone, from fresh seafood and salads to comfort food; there's even a kids' menu. So why is it cheaper than the rest of the pack? It's less central – about a 15-minute walk northeast of the town center.

★ Mews Restaurant & Cafe MODERN AMERICAN $$$

(☑508-487-1500; www.mews.com; 429 Commercial St; mains $14-35; ⊗5:30-10pm) A fantastic water view, the hottest martini bar in town and scrumptious food add up to Provincetown's finest dining scene. There are two sections. Opt to dine gourmet on tuna sushi and rack of lamb downstairs, where you're right on the sand, or go casual with a juicy Angus burger from the cafe menu upstairs.

Lobster Pot SEAFOOD $$$

(☑508-487-0842; www.ptownlobsterpot.com; 321 Commercial St; mains $22-37; ⊗11:30am-9pm) True to its name, this busy fish house overlooking the ocean is *the* place for lobster. Start with the lobster bisque and then put on a bib and crack open the perfect boiled lobster. Service can be slow. Best way to beat the crowd is to come mid-afternoon.

🍷 Drinking & Nightlife

Streetside cafes and waterfront bars offer an array of options that will sate any thirst and suit any mood.

Patio CAFE

(www.ptownpatio.com; 328 Commercial St; ⊗11am-11pm) Grab yourself a sidewalk table and order up a fresh ginger mojito at this umbrella-shaded cafe hugging the pulsating center of Commercial St.

Bubala's by the Bay CAFE

(☑508-487-0773; www.bubalas.com; 183 Commercial St; ⊗11am-1am) Watch the streetside parade roll by at this sidewalk cafe that bustles night and day.

GAY & LESBIAN PROVINCETOWN

While other cities have their gay districts, in Provincetown the entire town is the gay district. The following are some of the highlights of the scene:

A-House (Atlantic House; www.ahouse.com; 4 Masonic Pl) This landmark club has several faces: the Little Bar, an intimate pub; the Macho Bar; and the Big Room, the town's hottest DJ dance club.

Boatslip Beach Club (www.boatslipresort.com; 161 Commercial St; ⊙4-7pm) Known for its wildly popular afternoon tea dances overlooking the harbor. In summer, it's packed with gorgeous guys.

Crown & Anchor (www.onlyatthecrown.com; 247 Commercial St) The queen of the scene, this multiwing complex has a nightclub, a leather bar and a steamy cabaret that takes it to the limit.

Pied Bar (www.piedbar.com; 193 Commercial St) A popular waterfront lounge that attracts both lesbians and gay men. It's a particularly hot place to be around sunset.

Ross' Grill   BAR
(www.rossgrille.com;237CommercialSt;⊙11:30am-10pm) For a romantic place to have a drink with a water view, head to the bar at this smart bistro.

☆ Entertainment

Provincetown is awash with gay fun, drag shows and cabarets. Gay, straight or in between, everyone's welcome, and many shows have first-rate performers.

Provincetown also has a rich theater history. Eugene O'Neill began his writing career here, and several stars, including Marlon Brando and Richard Gere, performed on Provincetown stages before they hit the big screen. To see tomorrow's stars, take in a show while you're here.

Visit **Provincetown on the Web** (www.provincetown.com) for all the entertainment scoop.

Provincetown Theater   THEATER
(☑508-487-7487; www.provincetowntheater.org; 238 Bradford St) This stellar performing arts center, 1 mile northeast of the town center, always has something of interest happening – sometimes Broadway musicals, sometimes offbeat local shows.

Provincetown Art House   THEATER
(☑508-487-9222; www.ptownarthouse.com; 214 Commercial St) Two state-of-the-art stages featuring a variety of edgy theater performances, drag shows and cabarets.

🛍 Shopping

Commercial St has the most creative and interesting specialty shops on the Cape.

Shop Therapy   ADULT
(www.shoptherapy.com; 346 Commercial St; ⊙10am-10pm) Downstairs, it's patchouli, tie-dyed clothing and X-rated bumper stickers. But everyone gravitates to the upstairs level, where the sex toys are wild enough to make an Amsterdam madam blush. Parents, you'll need to use discretion: your teenagers *will* want to go inside.

Marine Specialties   SOUVENIRS
(☑508-487-1730; www.ptownarmynavy.com; 235 Commercial St; ⊙10am-10pm) This cavernous shop sells kitsch and also really cool stuff: flip-flops, swimsuits, beach and surf wear, army/navy surplus, firefighters' coats, lobster traps and more.

Womencrafts   CRAFT
(www.womencrafts.com; 376 Commercial St; ⊙11am-6pm) The name says it all: jewelry, pottery, books and music by female artists from across America.

Silk & Feathers   FASHION
(www.silkandfeathers.com; 377 Commercial St; ⊙noon-6pm) Beachwear to lingerie, this shop carries clothing that is both artsy and stylish.

ℹ Information

Outer Cape Health Services (☑508-487-9395; Harry Kemp Way) Off Conwell St from US 6; open in summer for walk-ins, and year-round by appointment.

Post Office (www.usps.com; 219 Commercial St)

Provincetown Business Guild (www.ptown.org) This website is oriented towards the gay community.

Provincetown Chamber of Commerce (www.ptownchamber.com; 307 Commercial St; ⊙9am-6pm) The town's helpful tourist office is right at MacMillan Wharf.

Seamen's Bank (221 Commercial St) Has a 24-hour ATM.

Wired Puppy (www.wiredpuppy.com; 379 Commercial St; ⊙6:30am-10pm; 🛜) You can access free online computers for just the price of a coffee at this buzzing cafe.

❶ Getting There & Around

BOAT

Boats connect Provincetown's MacMillan Wharf with Boston and Plymouth. Schedules are geared to day-trippers, with morning arrivals into Provincetown and late-afternoon departures.

Bay State Cruise Co (📞877-783-3779; www.boston-ptown.com; 200 Seaport Blvd, Boston; round-trip adult/child fast ferry $85/62, slow ferry $46/free; ⊙mid-May–mid-Oct) The daily fast ferry (1½ hours) and a Saturday-only slow ferry (three hours) both depart from Boston's World Trade Center Pier.

Boston Harbor Cruises (📞617-227-4321; www.bostonharborcruises.com; round-trip adult/child $85/62; ⊙June–mid-Oct) Daily fast ferry service from Long Wharf in Boston (1½ hours).

Plymouth to Provincetown Express Ferry (📞508-747-2400; www.provincetownferry.com; round-trip adult/child $43/33; ⊙mid-Jun–early Sep) Catamaran fast ferry from Plymouth (1½ hours).

BUS

The **Plymouth & Brockton** (www.p-b.com) bus, which terminates at MacMillan Wharf, runs several times a day from Boston ($35, 3½ hours), stopping at other Cape towns along the way.

From late May to mid-October, **shuttle buses** (www.capecodtransit.org; single trips/day passes $2/6) travel up and down Bradford St, and to MacMillan Wharf, Herring Cove Beach and North Truro. An additional midsummer service heads out to Province Lands Visitor Center and Race Point Beach. Bike racks are available.

CAR

From the Cape Cod Canal via US 6, it takes about 1½ hours to reach Provincetown (65 miles), depending on traffic. Commercial St is narrow and crowded with pedestrians, so you'll want to do most of your driving along the more car-friendly Bradford St.

On-street parking is next to impossible in summer, but you can usually find space in the town's main public parking lot at MacMillan Wharf.

TAXI

Taxi fares are a set $6 per person anywhere within town, $8 between the beach and town. Call **Cape Cab** (📞508-487-2222).

NANTUCKET

One need not be a millionaire to visit Nantucket, but it couldn't hurt. This compact island, 30 miles south of Cape Cod, grew rich from whaling in the 19th century. In recent decades it's seen a rebirth as a summer getaway for CEOs, society types and other well-heeled visitors from Boston and New York.

It's easy to see why. Nantucket is New England at its most rose-covered, cobble-stoned, picture-postcard perfect, and even in the peak of summer there's always an empty stretch of beach to be found. Outdoor activities abound, and there are fine museums, smart restaurants and fun bars.

Nantucket Town

POP 10,170

Nantucket town (called 'Town' by the locals) is the island's only real population center. Once home port to the world's largest whaling fleet, the town's storied past is reflected in the gracious period buildings lining its leafy streets. It boasts the nation's largest concentration of houses built prior to 1850 and is the only place in the US where the entire town is a National Historic Landmark. It's a thoroughly enjoyable place to just amble about and soak up the atmosphere.

There are two ferry terminals: Straight Wharf and Steamboat Wharf. Walk off Straight Wharf and you're on Main St; Steamboat Wharf is just a few blocks north. The majority of restaurants, inns and other visitor facilities are within a 10-minute walk of the wharves.

⊙ Sights

Nantucket Historical Association   HISTORIC SITES
(NHA; 📞508-228-1894; www.nha.org; whaling museum & historic sites adult/child $20/5; historic sites only $6/3; 🚼) The umbrella Nantucket Historical Association maintains eight historical sites covering everything from farming beginnings to the prosperous whaling days.

The NHA's most famous property, the **Nantucket Whaling Museum** (13 Broad St;

adult/child $20/5; ⊙10am-5pm mid-May–Oct, 11am-4pm Nov–mid-May), occupies a former spermaceti candle factory. The evocative exhibits relive Nantucket's 19th-century heyday as the whaling center of the world. A 46ft-long sperm-whale skeleton, a rigged whaleboat and assorted whaling implements tell the story of its history.

A walk through the NHA's **Hadwen House** (96 Main St; adult/child $6/3; ⊙11am-4pm mid-May–mid-Oct), a Greek Revival home built in 1845 by a whaling merchant, provides testimony to just how lucrative the whaling industry was in its heyday.

Built in 1686, the **Jethro Coffin House** (16 Sunset Hill; adult/child $6/3; ⊙11am-4pm mid-May–mid-Oct), 0.4 miles northwest of the town center via W Chester St, is the town's oldest building still on its original foundation. It's in a traditional saltbox style, with south-facing windows to catch the winter sun and a long, sloping roof to protect the home from harsh north winds.

The **Old Mill** (50 Prospect St; adult/child $6/3; ⊙11am-4pm mid-May–mid-Oct) is America's oldest working windmill (c 1746), as game young docents will demonstrate by grinding corn (weather permitting). To see where drunken sailors used to spend the night, visit the **Old Gaol** (15 Vestal St; adult/child $6/3; ⊙11am-4pm mid-May–mid-Oct), the c 1806 jail that served Nantucket for 125 years.

★**Nantucket Atheneum**   HISTORIC SITE
(☑508-228-1110; www.nantucketatheneum.org; 1 India St; ⊙10am-7:30pm Tue & Thu, 10am-5pm Wed, Fri & Sat) **FREE** More than just the public library, this stately Greek Revival edifice is a sight in itself. Just inside the front door you'll find a top-notch **scrimshaw display** from Nantucket's whaling days. The 2nd-floor **Great Hall** has hosted such notables as Ralph Waldo Emerson and abolitionist Frederick Douglass. Nationally known opinion-makers still speak here today; ask about the summer **lecture series**.

★**First Congregational Church**   CHURCH
(☑508-228-0950; 62 Centre St; adult/child $5/1; ⊙10am-4pm Mon-Sat) Everyone comes to this church, which traces its roots to the early 1700s, for the eagle-eye view from the top of the steeple. Well worth the 94-step climb!

African Meeting House   MUSEUM
(☑508-228-9833; www.afroammuseum.org; 29 York St; adult/child $5/free; ⊙11am-3pm Mon-Fri, 11am-1pm Sat, 1-3pm Sun) This worthwhile museum stands as testimony to the influential African American community that thrived on Nantucket in the 19th century. Built in 1820, it's the second-oldest African American meeting house in the nation.

**Nantucket Lightship
Basket Museum**   MUSEUM
(☑508-228-1177; www.nantucketlightshipbasketmuseum.org; 49 Union St; adult/child $5/3; ⊙10am-4:30pm Tue-Sat) What the lighthouse is to the New England coast, the lightship was to the sea – essentially a floating lighthouse to warn of dangerous shoals or sandbars below. Sailors would stay aboard the lightships for weeks on end, and to combat boredom they created beautiful, intricate baskets that have become emblems of the island. This small museum highlights these craftspeople.

In-Town Beaches   BEACH
(🚌) A pair of family-friendly beaches shore up the options close to town. For wilder, less-frequented strands, you'll need to pedal a bike or hop on a bus. Right in town, **Children's Beach**, along S Beach St at the north side of Steamboat Wharf, is heaven for young kids, with gentle water, a fun playground and picnic facilities.

For the nonwading crowd, **Jetties Beach**, 1 mile northwest of town via N Beach St, is the best all-round beach close to town. It's well equipped with changing rooms, a skateboard park and water-sports rentals.

🏃 Activities

Nantucket Community Sailing WATER SPORTS
(☑508-228-5358; www.nantucketcommunitysailing.org; rentals per hr $25-50; ⊙9am-5pm) Rents single and double kayaks, Sunfish sailboats and windsurfing gear at Jetties Beach.

> ### ACK ATTACK
>
> ACK! In Nantucket, the word adorns T-shirts, caps and logos. No, it's not a comment on the island's high cost of living, or reaction to the limerick 'There once was a man from Nantucket.' Instead, ACK is the code for Nantucket Memorial Airport (think 'nAntuCKet') and has been fondly adopted as an insider's moniker for all things Nantucket. Even the website for the island's daily newspaper, the *Inquirer and Mirror*, is www.ack.net.

CAPE COD, NANTUCKET & MARTHA'S VINEYARD NANTUCKET TOWN

Nantucket Island

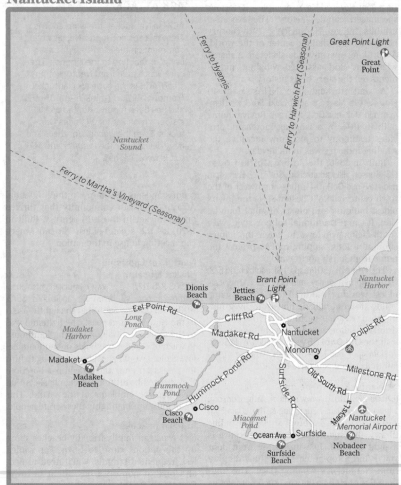

Friendship Sloop Endeavor SAILING
(☎508-228-5585; www.endeavorsailing.com;
Straight Wharf; 1hr sail $40-50; ☺May-Oct) Feel
the wind in your hair on a sail aboard the
Friendship Sloop Endeavor, which runs
numerous daily harbor sails and a sunset
cruise.

Cycling CYCLING
(⬆) Cycling around Nantucket is an unbeatable way to savor the island's natural beauty.
Bike paths connect the town with the main
beaches and the villages of Madaket and
'Sconset – no place is more than an hour's
pedal away. Family-run and family-friendly,

Young's Bicycle Shop (☎508-228-1151; www.
youngsbicycleshop.com; 6 Broad St; bicycles per
day adult/child $30/20; ☺8:30am-5:30pm), near
Steamboat Wharf, rents quality Trek bikes
for adults and kids of all ages.

☞ Tours

Nantucket Island Tours BUS TOUR
(☎800-492-8082; www.nantucketbustours.com;
Straight Wharf; 90-minute tours adult/child $20/7)
A good way to get your bearings around the
island is to hop on a narrated bus tour. Most
convenient are the Nantucket Island Tours,
which dovetail with ferry arrivals.

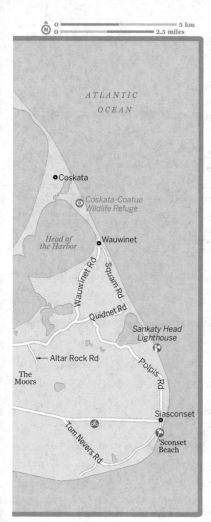

ATLANTIC
OCEAN

● Coskata

Coskata-Coatue
Wildlife Refuge

Head of
the Harbor   ● Wauwinet

Wauwinet Rd

Squam Rd

Quidnet Rd

Sankaty Head
Lighthouse

—— Altar Rock Rd

The
Moors

Polpis Rd

Siasconset

Tom Nevers Rd

'Sconset
Beach

0 ———————— 5 km
0 ———————— 2.5 miles

**Nantucket Historical
Association** WALKING TOURS
(☑508-228-1894; www.nha.org; adult/child $10/
4; ⊙late May-Oct) Interpreters from the
Nantucket Historical Association lead
80-minute history-themed walking tours of
the town twice daily. Pick up schedules and
purchase tickets at the Nantucket Whaling
Museum.

⭐ Festivals & Events

For more information on Nantucket festivals, go to www.nantucketchamber.org.

Daffodil Festival PARADE
The island goes yellow in the last full weekend of April with three million blooms and
antique cars that make their way to 'Sconset
for a tailgate picnic.

Nantucket Film Festival FILM
(www.nantucketfilmfestival.org) A good time to
spot celebrities. Held in mid-June.

Independence Day Celebration FIREWORKS
At high noon on July 4th, island firefighters duke it out – the hook and ladder trucks
versus the fire pumpers. You *will* get wet.
Fireworks at night.

🛏 Sleeping

Unless you've got island friends with a spare
room, a summer stay on Nantucket won't be
cheap. Don't even look for a motel or campground – tony Nantucket is all about inns. In
July and August advance reservations are a
virtual necessity, but between fall and spring
you can practically have the run of the place
for a fraction of the cost.

Harbor Cottages COTTAGES $$
(☑508-228-4485; www.nisda.org; 71 Washington
St; units per night from $180) The Nantucket Is-
land School of Design & the Arts operates
these former fishermen's cottages built in
the 1940s. Rustic by island standards, the
simple studio and one-bedroom cottages
have painted floorboards, exposed rafters
and whitewashed walls. The complex is a
10-minute walk from downtown.

⭐ Centerboard Inn B&B $$$
(☑508-228-2811; www.centerboardinn.com; 8
Chestnut St; r incl breakfast $249-419; ✳@☎)
The pampering provided by the welcoming
innkeeper here – with extras like spa-quality
bath lotions and loaner iPads – give this chic
B&B a leg up on the competition. Rooms
sport an upscale island decor, breakfast includes savory treats and the location is perfect for sightseeing. After a day on the town
slip back to relax over cheese and wine at
afternoon 'tea.'

Sherburne Inn B&B $$$
(☑508-228-4425; www.sherburneinn.com; 10 Gay
St; r incl breakfast $285-415; ✳☎) Sit in the par-
lor by the Victorian fireplace and share trav-
el tips with fellow guests at this gracious inn.
Built in 1838, the inn flawlessly fuses period
appeal with modern amenities, like central
air-con – no boxy air-conditioners hanging
out of windows here. Rooms are comfy, with

Nantucket Town

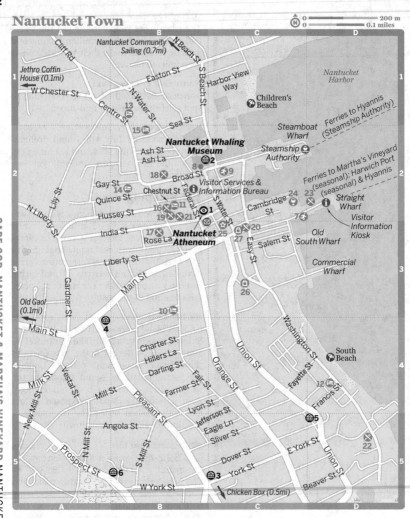

four-poster beds. The street is quiet, yet the inn is just a two-minute stroll from the town center.

Veranda House   BOUTIQUE HOTEL **$$$**
(☏508-228-0695; www.theverandahouse.com; 3 Step Lane; r incl breakfast $319-649; ☎) The Veranda House puts contemporary minimalism into an old New England shell, with striking results, in one of the most stylish inns on the island. Frette linens, cozy comforters and orchid sprays set the tone. Request an upper-floor room for a sweeping harbor view.

Barnacle Inn   B&B **$$$**
(☏508-228-0332; www.thebarnacleinn.com; 11 Fair St; r w/ private/shared bath incl breakfast from $200/140) This is what old Nantucket is all about: folksy owners and simple, quaint accommodations that hearken to earlier times. Rooms in this turn-of-the-19th-century inn don't have phones, TVs or air-con, but they do have good rates, particularly if you opt for a shared bath.

Martin House Inn   B&B **$$$**
(☏508-228-0678; www.martinhouseinn.net; 61 Centre St; s/d incl breakfast from $125/190; ❄☎) In one of the finest homes in a fine neigh-

Nantucket Town

CAPE COD, NANTUCKET & MARTHA'S VINEYARD NANTUCKET TOWN

borhood, this inn has soothing rooms with four-poster beds and stylish period decor. On the downside, some of the bathrooms are barely bigger than a tea towel. Several of the 13 rooms have a fireplace; a couple of the least expensive have a shared bath.

 Eating

Nantucket has lots of exceptional restaurants, especially for fine dining, as well as some solid local eateries that are worth ferreting out.

Bean CAFE $
(☏ 508-228-6215; 29 Centre St; pastries $3-5; ⊗ 6am-7pm; ☎) The place in town to munch on a bagel and get your caffeine fix. If you ask about Starbucks, islanders on Nantucket just might think you're a Melville fan looking for the Whaling Museum!

Black-Eyed Susan's CAFE $$
(www.black-eyedsusans.com; 10 India St; mains $9-30; ⊗ 7am-1pm daily & 6-10pm Mon-Sat) It's hard to find anyone who doesn't adore this quietly gourmet place. Snag a seat on the back patio and try the sourdough French toast topped with caramelized pecans and Jack Daniel's butter. At dinner the fish of the day with black-eyed peas takes top honors. BYOB.

Club Car PUB $$
(www.theclubcar.com; 1 Main St; mains $12-30; ⊗ 11:30am-1am) This converted railroad car,

a vestige of the actual railroad that sank in the sands of Nantucket, dishes up consistently good food, including the best lobster roll in town. The attached piano bar makes a fun place for a drink with the 30-to-40-something set.

Centre Street Bistro CAFE $$
(www.nantucketbistro.com; 29 Centre St; mains $8-30; ⊗ 11:30am-9:30pm Wed-Sat; ☎ 🖉) Settle in at a parasol-shaded sidewalk table and watch the traffic trickle by at this relaxed cafe. The chef-owners, trained at the Culinary Institute of America, make everything from scratch, including delicious warm goat's cheese tarts. A top pick for a healthy lunch at a reasonable price. BYOB.

Brotherhood of Thieves PUB $$
(www.brotherhoodofthieves.com; 23 Broad St; mains $12-25; ⊗ 11:30am-10pm) A longtime favorite of locals who come here for the friendly tavern atmosphere, set off with brick and dark woods, and the island's best burgers. Not in a burger mood? How about a fish taco made with local cod and chipotle cream, or some broiled Nantucket scallops? The craft beers on tap, some island-brewed, go down easy.

Sayle's Seafood SEAFOOD $$
(☏ 508-228-4599; www.saylesseafood.com; 99 Washington St Extension; mains $7-25; ⊗ 10am-8pm Mon-Sat, noon-8pm Sun) For the island's best fried clams, cheapest lobster dinners

GO LANING

Go local, go laning. That's the term Nantucketers coined for wandering about the narrow streets of the town's historic district. For the finest stroll, walk up cobbled Main St, just past the c 1818 Pacific National Bank. There you'll find the grandest whaling-era mansions lined up in a row. Other laning favorites: Gardner and Liberty Sts and the honeycombed lanes between Federal and S Water Sts.

and other seafood treats, head to this combo fish market and clam shack on the south side of town. It's all takeout, but there's outdoor seating where you can enjoy your feast.

 Company of the Cauldron AMERICAN $$$
(☑508-228-4016; www.companyofthecauldron.com; 5 India St; 3-course dinners $70; ☺6:30-10pm Tue-Sun) A splendid choice for a romantic dinner out, this intimate restaurant has attentive service and top-rated food. It's purely reserved seating times and three-course prix-fixe dinners, with the likes of lobster crepe followed by almond-crusted halibut. As the chef concentrates his magic on just one menu each evening, it's done to perfection without distraction.

Straight Wharf Restaurant SEAFOOD $$$
(☑508-228-4499; www.straightwharfrestaurant.com; Straight Wharf; mains $30-44; ☺11:30am-9pm) The best place for fresh-caught seafood served up with a harbor view on the deck of this hot restaurant featuring New American fare. Start with the island-grown squash blossoms sauteed with saffron lobster, then move on to the wild striped bass in lemon aioli.

Tip: if you don't mind shedding the view, you can dine at the bar (serving from the same ace kitchen) for half the price.

Drinking & Entertainment

Gazebo BAR
(☑508-228-1266; Straight Wharf) Great stargazing (both kinds) at this bustling open-air bar right on the wharf. You can keep one eye on who's getting off the ferry and the other on your fizzy drink.

Chicken Box LIVE MUSIC
(☑508-228-5625; www.thechickenbox.com; 16 Dave St) This former fried-chicken shack has evolved into a roadhouse for live jazz and blues. Actually, depending on who's on the island, these days it can cover the full spectrum, especially rock and reggae. The college crowd meets here. It's located 1 mile south of town via Pleasant St.

Starlight Theatre CINEMA
(☑508-228-4435; www.starlightnantucket.com; 1 N Union St) Nantucket's 90-seat theater screens indie and other award-winning films. It's also a venue for live entertainment on summer weekends.

Shopping

Nantucket has dozens of upmarket galleries, antique shops and clothing boutiques, as well as specialty shops that carry the island's signature lightship baskets. You'll find a collection of art galleries lined up like ducks in a row on Old South Wharf.

Four Winds Craft Guild CRAFT
(☑508-228-9623; www.sylviaantiques.com; 15 Main St) Head here for the island's largest selection of Nantucket lightship baskets. Highly prized, they command a premium, with the smallest baskets beginning at $175 and purses running into thousands of dollars.

Artists Association of Nantucket ART
(www.nantucketarts.org; 19 Washington St;) Browse the eclectic works of over 200 Nantucket artists who exhibit at this association gallery. Families with budding artists should inquire about the kids' summer programs.

Information

The public library, Nantucket Atheneum (p159), has free wi-fi 24/7 on its front steps and online computers inside.

Complete Nantucket Island Travel Guide (www.nantucket.net) Private listings of restaurants, housing, arts and recreation.

Inquirer and Mirror (www.ack.net) The island's daily newspaper.

Nantucket Cottage Hospital (☑508-228-1200; 57 Prospect St; ☺24hr) The island's only hospital.

Pacific National Bank (61 Main St)

Police Station (20 S Water St)

Post Office (5 Federal St)

Visitor Services & Information Bureau (☑508-228-0925; www.nantucket-ma.gov; 25 Federal St; ☺9am-5pm) Has everything you'll need, including public rest rooms and a list of available accommodations. The folks here also maintain a summertime **kiosk** (Straight Wharf; ☺9am-5pm Jun–mid-Oct).

ℹ Getting There & Around

AIR

Cape Air (www.flycapeair.com), the island's main carrier, flies from **Boston** (one-way $200, hourly in summer), **Hyannis** (one-way $65, hourly in summer) and **Martha's Vineyard** (one-way $65) to Nantucket Memorial Airport (ACK).

BOAT

The most common way to reach Nantucket is by the Steamship Authority (p135) and Hy-Line Cruises (p136) ferries from Hyannis. Hy-Line Cruises also operates a daily summer ferry between Nantucket and Oak Bluffs in Martha's Vineyard (one-way adult/child/bicycle $36/24/7); travel time is 70 minutes.

BUS

Nantucket Regional Transit Authority (NRTA; www.nrtawave.com; fares $1-2, 1-/3-/7-day passes $7/12/20; ⊘ mid-May–late Sep) runs handy shuttle buses all over the island, connecting Nantucket Town with 'Sconset in the east, Madaket in the west and beach destinations in between. Most routes operate every 30 to 60 minutes throughout the day.

Buses have racks for two bikes and stop at all bike paths along their routes.

CAR

In summer, the center of town is choked with automobiles, so you probably won't want to join the congestion. However, several companies, including **Nantucket Island Rent A Car** (📋 508-228-9989; www.nantucketislandrentacar.com) at the airport and Young's Bicycle Shop (p160) in town, rent cars. Prices start at around $75 per day but can easily be double that in peak season.

TAXI

Taxi rides from Nantucket Town cost $16 to the airport, $25 to 'Sconset. To order a taxi, call **All Point Taxi & Tours** (📋 508-228-5779).

Around Nantucket

Siasconset

Although this village is barely 7 miles from town, it thinks of itself as worlds apart. Nantucket town may seem uncrowded and unhurried compared with the rest of the US, but Siasconset ('Sconset) takes it to another level.

The petite village centers around a pair of cozy cafes, a tiny general store and a stamp-size post office. It's a wonderful place for lunch – but the secret's out, so get there early.

◉ Sights & Activities

The old cottages in this seaside village are a watercolorist's dream, with white-picket fences and climbing pink roses on gray cedar shingles. You'll find some of the loveliest cottages on Broadway, near the village center. Many of them, including the Lucretia M Folger House, at the corner of Main St and Broadway, date to the 18th century. All are private homes now, so do your peeking from a respectful distance.

East-facing 'Sconset Beach gets pounded by the open Atlantic, which has eroded much of the long, narrow beach in recent years. In fact, the erosion has been so severe that in 2007 Sankaty Head Lighthouse, at the north side of the village, was moved inland to prevent it from tumbling over a 90ft bluff.

🛏 Sleeping & Eating

Summer House　　　　　　　　INN $$$
(📋 508-257-4577; www.thesummerhouse.com; 17 Ocean Ave; r incl breakfast $675-1100; 🛜 🖾) A refined getaway of low-key elegance. Stay in one of 'Sconset's signature rose-covered cottages and relax by the pool or just drink in the ocean view. Some rooms have fireplace and Jacuzzi. A piano bar, bistro and fine-dining restaurant round out the facilities.

Sconset Café　　　　　　　　CAFE $$
(📋 508-257-4008; www.sconsetcafe.com; Post Office Sq; mains $8-17; ⊘ 8:30am-3pm) Pedal out for the boursin cheese omelets, homemade quahog chowder and creative salads. Pick up a bottle of wine at the store next door and enjoy it with your meal.

South Shore

The south shore communities of Surfside and Cisco consist almost entirely of private homes, but visitors head here for the long, broad beaches, which are among the island's best.

Surfside Beach, 3 miles from Nantucket town at the end of Surfside Rd, is a top draw with the college and 20-something set. It has full facilities, including a snack shack, and a moderate-to-heavy surf that can make for good body surfing. About 1 mile east of Surfside Beach is Nobadeer Beach, below the flight path of the airport, which attracts surfers and a beach-party crowd.

You'll find some of the most consistently surfable waves at Cisco Beach, at the end of Hummock Pond Rd, where Nantucket

NANTUCKET BREW

Enjoy a hoppy pint of Whale's Tale Pale at the friendliest brewery you'll likely ever see. **Cisco Brewers** (☎508-325-5929; www.ciscobrewers.com; 5 Bartlett Farm Rd; tours $20; ☺10am-7pm Mon-Sat, noon-5pm Sun) is the 'other' Nantucket, a laid-back place where fun banter loosens those stiff upper lips found in primmer quarters. In addition to the brewery, there are casual indoor and outdoor bars and spirited live music of the mountain banjo variety. The brewery tours and entertainment typically happen around 4pm – so let your hair down and plan accordingly.

Island Surf School (☎508-560-1020; www.nantucketsurfing.com; 1hr lessons $50-70, surfboards per half-day $40; ☺9am-5pm) handles everything you'll need for hitting the waves.

🛏 Sleeping & Eating

HI Nantucket　　　　　　　　HOSTEL $
(☎508-228-0433; http://capecod.hiusa.org; 31 Western Ave; dm incl breakfast $35; ☺mid-May–mid-Sep; @) Known locally as Star of the Sea, this cool hostel has a million-dollar setting just minutes from Surfside Beach. It's housed in a former lifesaving station that dates to 1873 and is listed on the National Register of Historic Places.

As Nantucket's sole nod to the budget traveler, the 49 beds here are in high demand, so book as far in advance as possible.

Bartlett's Farm　　　　　　　MARKET $
(☎508-228-4403; www.bartlettsfarm.com; 33 Bartlett Farm Rd; ☺8am-6pm; 🅿) 🍴 From a humble farm stand, this family operation has grown into a huge gourmet market, with salads, tempting desserts and sandwiches. It's the perfect place to grab everything you'll need for a lunch on the beach.

Madaket

There's not a lot to see at this western outpost, but **Madaket Beach**, at the end of the namesake bike path, is the island's ace place to watch sunsets. The strong currents and heavy surf make it less than ideal for swimming, but there's some attractive beach walking to be done.

MARTHA'S VINEYARD

Bathed in scenic beauty, Martha's Vineyard attracts wide-eyed day-trippers, celebrity second-home owners, and urbanites seeking a restful getaway. Its 15,000 year-round residents include many artists, musicians and back-to-nature types. The Vineyard remains untouched by the kind of rampant commercialism found on the mainland – there's not a single chain restaurant or cookie-cutter motel in sight. Instead you'll find cozy inns, chef-driven restaurants and a bounty of green farms and grand beaches. And there's something for every mood here – fine dining in gentrified Edgartown one day and hitting the cotton candy and carousel scene in Oak Bluffs the next.

Martha's Vineyard is the largest island in New England, extending some 23 miles at its widest. Although it sits just 7 miles off the coast of Cape Cod, Vineyarders feel themselves such a world apart that they often refer to the mainland as 'America.'

Getting around is easy by car, though roads are narrow and summertime traffic jams in the main towns are the norm. If you don't have your own wheels, no problem – the extensive public bus system connects every village on the island. Cycling is another great option.

Vineyard Haven

POP 3950

Although it's the island's commercial center, Vineyard Haven is a town of considerable charm. Its harbor has more traditional wooden schooners and sloops than any harbor of its size in New England.

Central Vineyard Haven (aka Tisbury) is just four or five blocks wide and about a half-mile long. Main St, dotted with galleries and boutiques, is the main thoroughfare through town. Steamship Authority ferries dock at the end of Union St, a block from Main St. From the terminal, Water St leads to the infamous 'Five Corners' intersection: five roads come together and no one really has the right of way. Good luck.

🏃 Activities

Wind's Up　　　　　　　　WATER SPORTS
(☎508-693-4252; www.windsupmv.com; 199 Beach Rd; 4hr rentals $35-55; ☺9am-6pm) Vineyard Haven has windsurfing action for all levels. Lagoon Pond, south of the drawbridge between Vineyard Haven and Oak

Bluffs, has good wind and enclosed waters suitable for beginners and intermediates. Vineyard Harbor, on the ocean side, is good for advanced windsurfers. Wind's Up, at the drawbridge, rents windsurfing gear, paddleboards and kayaks.

Martha's Bike Rentals   CYCLING
(☑508-693-6593; www.marthasbikerentals.com; 4 Lagoon Pond Rd; bicycles per day $25; ☺9am-5:30pm) Has a convenient location just 0.1 miles from the ferry terminal.

🛏 Sleeping

Martha's Vineyard Family Campground   CAMPGROUND $
(☑508-693-3772; www.campmv.com; 569 Edgartown Rd; tent/RV sites $53/59, cabins $135-155; ☺mid-May–mid-Oct) This woodsy place offers the island's only camping and has basic cabins that sleep four to six people. Book early, especially for weekends. It's 1.5 miles from the ferry terminal.

Clark House   INN $$
(☑508-693-6550; www.clarkhouseinn.com; 20 Edgartown Rd; r incl breakfast $140-250; ❄@ 🔊📶) This homey colonial inn, close to town, has helpful innkeepers and a nice variety of rooms from small to commodious. Some rooms can accommodate up to four people. As an added perk, guests have access to complimentary bicycles.

Crocker House Inn   INN $$$
(☑508-693-1151; www.crockerhouseinn.com; 12 Crocker Ave; r incl breakfast from $295; ❄🔊) This cozy century-old inn is just a stone's throw from the harbor. Some rooms are small, but otherwise everything about this place is likable. The designer owner has given the eight

rooms a fresh, summery feel – all whites and pastels. And the rockers on the front porch are the perfect place to linger over that second cup of coffee.

🍴 Eating

⭐ Art Cliff Diner   CAFE $$
(☑508-693-1224; 39 Beach Rd; mains $10-16; ☺7am-2pm Thu-Tue) 🌿 Hands-down the best place in town for breakfast and lunch. Chef-owner Gina Stanley, a grad of the prestigious Culinary Institute of America, adds flair to everything she touches, from the almond-encrusted French toast to the fresh fish tacos. The eclectic menu utilizes farm-fresh island ingredients. Expect a line, but it's worth the wait.

Net Result   SEAFOOD $$
(☑508-693-6071; www.mvseafood.com; Tisbury Marketplace, Beach Rd; mains $7-20; ☺9am-7pm) On the west side of town, this fish market is fresh, fresh, fresh, with everything from sushi to award-winning chowder and fish-and-chips. It's takeout, but there are picnic tables outside – or, better yet, take it to the beach.

Black Dog Tavern   AMERICAN $$
(☑508-693-9223; www.theblackdog.com; 20 Beach St Extension; mains $8-35; ☺7am-10pm) These days the Black Dog is more famous for its T-shirts than its food, but this legendary eatery packs a crowd. Just 0.15 miles from the ferry, it's handy for breakfast, with such indulgences as strawberry-and-white-chocolate pancakes.

ℹ Information

Martha's Vineyard Chamber of Commerce
(☑508-693-0085; www.mvy.com; 24 Beach Rd, Vineyard Haven; ☺9am-5pm Mon-Fri) Pick

---

LIGHTHOUSES OF THE VINEYARD

What's more New England than a lighthouse? And which island has the greatest diversity of lighthouses in America? One guess.

West Chop The island's last manned lighthouse dates to 1838 and sits on the west side of Vineyard Haven Harbor.

East Chop This cast-iron structure built in 1875 is an Oak Bluffs landmark.

Edgartown Erected on an island in 1828, shifting sands have since filled in the inlet and it's now connected to Edgartown by land.

Cape Poge Harsh storm erosion has forced the relocation of this Chappaquiddick Island lighthouse four times since 1801.

Gay Head Built in 1844, this red-brick structure on the Aquinnah Cliffs is arguably the most scenic lighthouse on the Vineyard.

Martha's Vineyard

5 km
2.5 miles

Nantucket Sound

Ferry to Nantucket (Seasonal)

Cape Poge Lighthouse

Cape Poge Wildlife Refuge

Cape Poge Bay

Wasque Reservation

Chappaquiddick Rd

Chappaquiddick Island

Katama Bay

Ferry to Falmouth (Seasonal)

Ferry to Hyannis (Seasonal)

Ferry to Falmouth (Seasonal)

Edgartown Harbor

Edgartown Lighthouse

Joseph Sylvia State Beach

Felix Neck Wildlife Sanctuary

Edgartown

Katama Rd

Herring Creek Rd

Katama Beach (South Beach)

Oak Bluffs

Edgartown

Meetinghouse Way

Ferry to Woods Hole (Seasonal)

County Rd

Sengekontacket Pond

Edgartown–Vineyard Haven Rd

Edgartown–West Tisbury Rd

East Chop Lighthouse

Vineyard Haven

Lagoon Pond

Airport Rd

Long Point Wildlife Refuge

Edgartown Great Pond

West Chop Lighthouse

Owen Park

Main St

Beach Rd

Manuel F Correllus State Forest

Martha's Vineyard Airport

Ferry to New Bedford (Seasonal)

Lake Tashmoo

Lamberts Cove Rd

State Rd

Old County Rd

West Tisbury

Tisbury Great Pond

ATLANTIC OCEAN

Tisbury

Lamberts Cove

Indian Hill Rd

State Rd

South Rd

Middle Rd

Cedar Tree Neck Sanctuary

Polly Hill Arboretum

Naushon Island

Vineyard Sound

Tabor House Rd

North Rd

Menemsha Cross Rd

Chilmark

Lucy Vincent Beach

ELIZABETH ISLANDS

Westend Pond

Menemsha Beach

Menemsha

Menemsha Harbor

Menemsha Pond

Buzzards Bay

Pasque Island

Lobsterville Beach

Lobsterville Rd

Squibnocket Pond

Nashawena Island

Aquinnah Cliffs Aquinnah Public Beach

Gay Head Lighthouse

Lighthouse Rd

South Rd

Aquinnah

Moshup Trail

Rhode Island Sound

up a free island-wide guide here or at their summertime visitor center at the ferry dock.

❶ Getting There & Around

AIR

Martha's Vineyard Airport (MVY; ☑ 508-693-7022; www.mvyairport.com), in the center of the island about 6 miles south of Vineyard Haven, has year-round service to Boston, Hyannis and Nantucket. Check **Cape Air** (☑ 508-771-6944; www.flycapeair.com) for fares and schedules.

BOAT

Steamship Authority (☑ 508-477-8600; www.steamshipauthority.com) ferries run from Woods Hole to Vineyard Haven (round-trip adult/child/car $16/8/157, 45 minutes, every one to two hours). Cars should be booked far in advance.

BUS

The **Martha's Vineyard Transit Authority** (www.vineyardtransit.com; 1-/3-day pass $7/15) operates a network of buses from the Vineyard Haven ferry terminal to villages throughout the island. It's a practical way to get around and even serves out-of-the-way destinations such as the Aquinnah Cliffs.

Oak Bluffs

POP 4530

Odds are this ferry-port town, where the lion's share of boats arrive, will be your introduction to the island. Welcome to the Vineyard's summer fun mecca – a place to wander with an ice-cream cone in hand, poke around honky-tonk sights and go clubbing at night.

All ferries dock in the center of town – the Steamship Authority boats along Seaview Ave and the other ferries along Circuit Ave Extension. The two roads connect together as a single loop. The area between the two docks is filled with trinket shops, eateries and bike-rental outlets.

◉ Sights & Activities

Campgrounds & Tabernacle   HISTORIC SITE
Oak Bluffs started out in the mid-19th century as a summer retreat for a revivalist church, whose members enjoyed a day at the beach as much as a gospel service. They first camped out in tents, then built some 300 wooden cottages, each adorned with whimsical filigree trim.

From bustling Circuit Ave, slip into the alley between the Secret Garden and the Tibet store and you'll feel like you've dropped down the rabbit hole. Suddenly it's a world of **gingerbread-trimmed houses**, adorned with hearts and angels and Candy Land colors.

These brightly painted cottages – known as the Campgrounds – surround emerald-green **Trinity Park** and its open-air **Tabernacle** (1879), where the lucky descendants of the Methodist Campmeeting Association still gather for community sing-alongs and concerts.

Flying Horses Carousel   HISTORIC SITE
(www.mvpreservation.org; 15 Lake Ave, at Circuit Ave; rides $2.50; ☉ 10am-10pm; ☝) Take a nostalgic ride on this National Historic Landmark, which has been captivating kids of all ages since 1876. The USA's oldest continuously operating merry-go-round, these antique horses have manes of real horse hair and, if you stare deep into their glass eyes, you'll see neat little silver animals inside.

Oak Bluffs Beaches   BEACHES
Just south of the ferry terminal, a narrow strip of sandy beach runs unbroken for several miles, beginning with **Oak Bluffs Town Beach**. Or continue 1 mile further south to **Joseph Sylvia State Beach** on Beach Rd, which has calm waters suitable for kids. It's also referred to as Bend-in-the-Road Beach as you move toward Edgartown.

Cycling   CYCLING
A scenic **bike trail** runs along the coast connecting Oak Bluffs, Vineyard Haven and Edgartown – it's largely flat, so it makes a good pedal for families. More experienced riders might want to bike the undulating 20 miles to Aquinnah.

Step off the ferry and you'll find a slew of wheelers and dealers renting bicycles. Keep walking until you reach **Anderson's Bike Rentals** (☑ 508-693-9346; www.andersonsbikerentals.com; 1 Circuit Ave Extension; bicycles per day adult/child $18/10; ☉ 9am-6pm), an established family-run operation with well-maintained bikes offered at honest prices.

✦✦ Festivals & Events

Illumination Night   FIREWORKS
(www.mvcma.org) It's all about lights. If you're lucky enough to be in Oak Bluffs on the third Wednesday in August, you'll see the town gather at Trinity Park for the lighting of thousands of Japanese lanterns on Illumination Night. On the Friday of that same week

VINEYARD ROOTS

African Americans have deep, proud roots on the Vineyard. Arriving as slaves in the late 1600s, they broke the yoke here long before slavery ended on the mainland. In 1779 a freed slave named Rebecca Amos became a landowner when she inherited a farm from her Wampanoag husband. Her influence on the island was widespread – Martha's Vineyard's only black whaling captain, William Martin, was one of her descendants.

During the Harlem Renaissance, African American tourism to the Vineyard took off. Writer Dorothy West, author of *The Wedding*, was an early convert to the island's charms. Oak Bluffs soon became a prime vacation destination for East Coast African American movers and shakers.

The cadre of African Americans gathered on the Vineyard during the 1960s was so influential that political activist Joe Overton's Oak Bluffs home became known as the 'Summer White House' of the Civil Rights movement. His guest list ranged from Malcolm X to Jackie Robinson and Harry Belafonte. It was at Overton's home that Martin Luther King Jr worked on his famous 'I Have A Dream' speech. The term 'Summer White House' took on new meaning in 2009 when America's first black president, Barack Obama, took his summer vacation on the Vineyard.

Learn more about the Vineyard's African American heritage at www.mvheritagetrail.org.

is the island's most spectacular **fireworks** display.

🛏 Sleeping

Nashua House INN $$
(📞508-693-0043; www.nashuahouse.com; 30 Kennebec Ave; r with shared bath $99-219; ❀🛜❀) The Vineyard the way it used to be: no phones, no TV, no in-room bathroom. Instead you'll find suitably simple and spotlessly clean accommodations at this small 1873 inn in the town center. Restaurants and pubs are just beyond the front door. It's good value in the summer; in the off-season, when rates drop by nearly half, it's a steal.

Narragansett House B&B $$
(📞508-693-3627; www.narragansetthouse.com; 46 Narragansett Ave; r incl breakfast $150-300; ❀🛜) This charming place comprises two adjacent Victorian gingerbread-trimmed houses on a quiet residential street that's just a stroll from the center. It's old-fashioned without being cloying, and, unlike other places in this price range, all the rooms here have private baths.

Madison Inn INN $$
(📞508-693-2760; www.madisoninnmv.com; 18 Kennebec Ave; r incl breakfast from $169; ❀🛜) OK, the cheaper rooms here are small, but the whole place is tidy, the island-style decor agreeable and the staff as friendly as they come. And you couldn't be more in the thick of things, though on the downside expect to pick up some street noise.

🍴 Eating

Mad Martha's ICE CREAM $
(12 Circuit Ave; cones from $5; ⏱11am-8pm;) If the Obamas are on the island and you want to snag a photo, this is your best paparazzi hang: they'll invariably swing by for a scoop of award-winning homemade ice cream. If you like it rich, order up a scoop of the coconut cream.

MV Bakery BAKERY $
(www.mvbakery.com; 5 Post Office Sq; baked goods $1-3; ⏱7am-5pm) This simple joint serves inexpensive coffee, famous apple fritters and cannoli, but the time to swing by is from 9pm to midnight (when the shop itself is shut), when you can go around the back, knock on the back door and buy hot, fresh doughnuts straight from the baker.

Linda Jean's DINER $
(www.lindajeansrestaurant.com; 25 Circuit Ave; mains $5-15; ⏱6am-10:30pm) The town's best all-around inexpensive eatery rakes in the locals with unbeatable blueberry pancakes, juicy burgers and simple but filling dinners.

Slice of Life CAFE $$
(www.sliceoflifemv.com; 50 Circuit Ave; mains $8-24; ⏱8am-9pm; 🐾) The look is casual; the fare is gourmet. At breakfast, there's kick-ass coffee, portobello omelets and fab potato pancakes. At dinner the roasted cod with sun-dried tomatoes is a savory favorite. And the desserts – decadent crème brûlée and luscious lemon tarts – are as good as you'll find anywhere.

Sweet Life Café   MODERN AMERICAN **$$$**
(☑508-696-0200; www.sweetlifemv.com; 63 Circuit Ave; mains $32-42; ◐5:30-9:30pm) New American cuisine with a French accent is offered by this stylish bistro, which provides the town's finest dining. Local oysters in mango cocktail sauce, wild-mushroom strudel and innovative beef and seafood dishes top the charts.

Drinking & Nightlife

Lampost   CLUB
(www.lampostmv.com; 6 Circuit Ave) Head to this combo bar and nightclub for the island's hottest dance scene. The music is mostly hip-hop, reggae and funk. In the unlikely event you don't find what you're looking for here, keep cruising Circuit Ave where you'll stumble across several dive bars (one actually named the **Dive Bar**, another the **Ritz**), both dirty and nice.

Offshore Ale Co   BREWPUB
(www.offshoreale.com; 30 Kennebec Ave) This popular microbrewery is the place to enjoy a pint of Vineyard ale.

❶ Information

Information Booth (☑508-693-4266; cnr Circuit & Lake Aves; ◐9am-5pm) The town hall staffs this convenient booth near the carousel.
Martha's Vineyard Hospital (☑508-693-0410; 1 Hospital Rd; ◐24hr) The island's only hospital is at the west side of Oak Bluffs, just off the Vineyard Haven–Oak Bluffs road.

❶ Getting There & Around

BOAT
The **Steamship Authority** (☑508-477-8600; www.steamshipauthority.com) runs car ferries from Woods Hole to Oak Bluffs (round trip adult/child/car $16/8/157, 45 minutes, five daily).

From Falmouth Harbor, the passenger ferry **Island Queen** (☑508-548-4800; www.islandqueen.com; 75 Falmouth Heights Rd) sails to Oak Bluffs (round trip adult/child/bike $20/10/8, 40 minutes, seven daily).

Hy-Line Cruises (☑508-778-2600; www.hylinecruises.com; Ocean St Dock; round trip adult/child slow ferry $45/free, fast ferry $72/48) operates a slow ferry (1½ hours, one daily) and a high-speed ferry (55 minutes, several daily) to Hyannis.

Hy-Line also offers a once-daily ferry between Nantucket and Oak Bluffs from July to September.

BUS
Pick up public island buses in front of Ocean Park, 200 yards south of the Oak Bluffs terminal.

Edgartown
POP 4070

Perched on a fine natural harbor, Edgartown has a rich maritime history and a patrician air. At the height of the whaling era, it was home to more than 100 sea captains, whose fortunes built the grand old homes that still line the streets today. Unlike Oak Bluffs and Vineyard Haven, which have substantial ferries carting folks in and out, Edgartown just has a small passenger-only ferry. It's the quietest of the three main towns and the one most geared to upmarket travelers.

All roads into Edgartown lead to Main St, which extends down to the harbor. Water St runs parallel to the harbor. Most restaurants and inns are on or near these two streets.

◉ Sights & Activities

Martha's Vineyard Museum   MUSEUM
(☑508-627-4441; www.marthasvineyardhistory.org; 59 School St; adult/child $7/4; ◐10am-5pm Mon-Sat) This intriguing museum, part of the Martha's Vineyard Historical Society, has a fascinating collection of whaling paraphernalia and scrimshaw. Don't miss the lighthouse display, which includes the huge Fresnel lens that sat in the Gay Head Lighthouse until electrical power arrived in 1952.

Edgartown Beaches   BEACHES
Walk along N Water St in the direction of the Edgartown Lighthouse to reach a pair of beaches on the northeast side of town. Lighthouse Beach, running north from the lighthouse, is a good spot for watching boats putt into Edgartown Harbor. Fuller St Beach, extending north from Lighthouse Beach, is frequented by college students and summer workers taking a break between shifts.

Katama Beach   BEACH
(Katama Rd) Although they're convenient, Edgartown's in-town beaches are just kids' stuff. For the real deal head to Katama Beach, also called South Beach, about 4 miles south of Edgartown center. Kept in a natural state, this barrier beach stretches for three magnificent miles.

Rugged surf will please surfers on the ocean side. Many swimmers prefer the protected salt ponds on the inland side.

Felix Neck Wildlife Sanctuary   NATURE RESERVE
(www.massaudubon.org; Edgartown–Vineyard Haven Rd; adult/child $4/3; ◐dawn-dusk; ▣) Mass

Audubon's sanctuary, 3 miles northwest of Edgartown center, is a birder's paradise, with miles of trails skirting fields, marshes and ponds. Because of the varied habitat, this 350-acre sanctuary harbors an amazing variety of winged creatures, including ducks, oystercatchers, wild turkeys, ospreys and red-tailed hawks. Bring your binoculars. Also offers nature tours of all sorts, from family canoe trips to marine discovery outings.

Cycling
CYCLING

The best bike trails on the Vineyard start in Edgartown. You can pedal on a drippingly scenic bike route along the coastal road to Oak Bluffs; take the bike trail that follows the Edgartown–West Tisbury Rd to Manuel F Correllus State Forest, the island's largest conservation tract; or take the shorter bike path south for a swim at Katama Beach.

Several companies rent bikes in Edgartown, including the family-oriented **Martha's Vineyard Bike Rental** (✓508-627-5928; www.marthasvineyardbike.com; 212 Main St; bikes per day $20-25; ⊙9am-6pm; 🚲), which has quality adults' and children's bikes, and rents baby seats and pull-behind trailers that can hold two toddlers,

🛏 Sleeping

Edgartown Inn
GUESTHOUSE $$

(✓508-627-4794; www.edgartowninn.com; 56 N Water St; r with shared/private bath from $125/175; ❄) The best bargain in town, with 20 straightforward rooms spread across three adjacent buildings. The oldest dates to 1798 and claims Nathaniel Hawthorne and Daniel Webster among its earliest guests. Rooms have changed only a bit since then (no phone or TVs), but most have a private bathroom. Ask about last-minute specials; you might score a discount if things are slow.

Victorian Inn
INN $$$

(✓508-627-4784; www.thevic.com; 24 S Water St; r incl breakfast $260-425; ❄🐾) This is by no means the most expensive place to spend a night in stylish Edgartown, but it is the best. Four-poster beds, freshly cut flowers and a gourmet multicourse breakfast are just part of the appeal at this upscale inn right in the heart of town. And, yes, it's Victorian: it's listed on the National Register of Historic Places.

🍴 Eating

Espresso Love
CAFE $

(✓508-627-9211; www.espressolove.com; 17 Church St; mains $7-12; ⊙6:30am-6pm; 📶) This cafe serves the richest cup o' joe in town, sweet cinnamon rolls and good sandwiches, like curried chicken with walnuts and currants. The shady courtyard is a fine place to enjoy lunch on a sunny day, and the location near the bus terminal is handy.

Among the Flowers Café
CAFE $$

(✓508-627-3233; 17 Mayhew Lane; mains $8-20; ⊙8am-3:30pm; 📶) Join the in-the-know crowd on the garden patio for homemade soups, waffles, sandwiches, crepes and even lobster rolls. Although everything's served on paper or plastic, it's still kinda chichi. In July and August, they add on dinner as well (5:30-9:30pm) and kick it up a notch.

★ **Détente**
FRENCH $$$

(✓508-627-8810; www.detentemv.com; 3 Nevin Sq; mains $30-40; ⊙5:30-10pm) A perky wine bar and a skilled young chef separate this newcomer from the old-money, old-menu places that dominate Edgartown's fine dining scene. Détente's French-inspired fare includes a talk-of-the-town 'ahi tartare served with vanilla-lychee puree. Local organic greens, island-raised chicken and Nantucket bay scallops get plenty of billing on the innovative menu.

🍷 Drinking & Entertainment

Seafood Shanty
BAR

(✓508-627-8622; www.theseafoodshanty.com; 31 Dock St; ⊙11:30am-10pm) For a drink with a view, head to the waterfront deck bar at this harborside restaurant.

★ **Flatbread Company**
LIVE MUSIC

(www.flatbreadcompany.com; 17 Airport Rd; ⊙3pm-late) Formerly the home of Carly Simon's legendary Hot Tin Roof, Flatbread continues the tradition, staging the hottest bands on the island. And they make damn good organic pizzas too. It's adjacent to Martha's Vineyard Airport.

ⓘ Information

Edgartown Visitors Center (29 Church St; ⊙8:30am-6pm) This operation at the bus terminal has rest rooms and a post office.

ⓘ Getting There & Around

The public **bus terminal** is in the town center on Church St, near Main St. Some key buses:

Bus 8 Katama (South) Beach (half-hourly)

Bus 13 Oak Bluffs and Vineyard Haven (half-hourly)

Up Island

The western side of the island – known as Up Island and comprising the towns of West Tisbury, Chilmark and Aquinnah – is a patchwork of rolling hills, small farms and open fields frequented by wild turkeys and deer. Soak up the scenery, take a hike, pop into a gallery, stop at a farm stand, munch, lunch and beach.

West Tisbury

POP 2740

The island's agricultural heart has a white church, calm ponds and a vintage general store, all evoking an old-time sensibility. West Tisbury also has some worthwhile artists' studios and galleries sprinkled throughout.

◉ Sights & Activities

Gathering Places   HISTORIC BUILDINGS

Part food shop, part historic landmark, Alley's General Store (☑508-693-0088; 1041 State Rd; ⊙7am-7pm Mon-Sat, to 6pm Sun) is a favorite local gathering place and has been since 1858.

The 1859 **Grange Hall** (1067 State Rd) is a historic meetinghouse, most visited these days for farmers markets. This post-and-beam structure is also a venue for concerts, lectures and other events.

Art Galleries   GALLERIES

You can't miss the **Field Gallery** (☑508-693-5595; www.fieldgallery.com; 1050 State Rd; ⊙10am-5pm), a field of large white sculptures by local artist Tom Maley (1911–2000) that playfully pose while tourists mill around them. There's an indoor gallery, too, with works by artists of local and national renown.

Master glassblowers turn sand into colorful creations at the **Martha's Vineyard Glassworks** (☑508-693-6026; www.mvglassworks.com; 683 State Rd; ⊙11am-4pm Wed-Mon). If you can stand the heat, you can watch them work their magic.

Cedar Tree Neck Sanctuary   NATURE RESERVE

(www.sheriffsmeadow.org; Indian Hill Rd; ⊙8:30am-5:30pm) **FREE** Cedar Tree Neck's inviting 2.5-mile hike crosses native bogs and forest to a coastal bluff with views of Cape Cod and the Elizabeth Islands. Be sure to take the short detour to Ames Pond to enjoy a meditative moment with painted turtles and peeping tree frogs. To get there, take State Rd to Indian Hill Rd and continue 1.8 miles.

Long Point Wildlife Refuge   NATURE RESERVE

(☑508-693-7392; www.thetrustees.org; off Edgartown–West Tisbury Rd; adult/child $3/free; ⊙9am-5pm) Pond, cove and ocean views all open up on a mile-long trail that leads to a remote beach. Along the way birders can expect to spot nesting osprey and other raptors, from northern harriers to the more common red-tailed hawks. There's a $10 fee to park at the refuge.

Polly Hill Arboretum   NATURE RESERVE

(☑508-693-9426; www.pollyhillarboretum.org; 809 State Rd; adult/child $5/free; ⊙sunrise-sunset) This 60-acre refuge celebrates woodlands and wildflower meadows. It's particularly pretty in the fall. The visitor center is open from 9:30am to 4pm. You can explore on your own or join an hour-long tour; tour times vary.

🛏 Sleeping & Eating

HI Martha's Vineyard   HOSTEL $

(☑508-693-2665; http://capecod.hiusa.org; 525 Edgartown–West Tisbury Rd; dm $35; ⊙mid-May–mid-Oct; @⟩) Reserve early for a bed at this popular purpose-built hostel in the center of the island. It has everything you'd expect of a top-notch hostel: a solid kitchen, bike delivery and no curfew. The public bus stops out front and it's right on the bike path. What more could you ask for?

West Tisbury Farmers Market   MARKET $

(www.westtisburyfarmersmarket.com; 1067 State Rd; ⊙9am-noon Wed & Sat) 🍃 Be sure to head to the Grange Hall in the center of West Tisbury on market days for fresh-from-the-farm produce. The best time to go is Saturday, when it's a full-on community event, with live fiddle music and alpacas for the kids to pet.

Chilmark & Menemsha

POP 870

Occupying most of the western side of the island between Vineyard Sound and the Atlantic, Chilmark is a place of pastoral landscapes and easygoing people. Chilmark's chief destination is the picture-perfect fishing village of Menemsha, where you'll find shacks selling seafood fresh off the boat.

◉ Sights & Activities

Menemsha Harbor   HARBOR

(Basin Rd) Virtually unchanged since it appeared in the movie *Jaws* 40 years ago,

Menemsha is a relaxing outpost to explore. Basin Rd borders a harbor of fishing boats on one side and dunes on the other, ending at the public **Menemsha Beach**. Sunsets here are nothing short of spectacular.

Lucy Vincent Beach   BEACH
(South Rd) Lucy Vincent Beach, off South Rd about half a mile before the junction with Middle Rd, is one of the loveliest stretches of sand on the island, complete with dune-backed cliffs and good, strong surf. The far end of it is popular for nude bathing.

✕ Eating

Bite   SEAFOOD $$
(☑508-645-9239; www.thebitemenemsha.com; 29 Basin Rd; mains $7-20; ⊘11am-dusk) It's a fried-food fest, with fried fish-and-chips, oysters and clams. Forget those wimpy clam strips – big, fat bellies are the specialty at this pint-size clam shack. Take it to the beach or eat here at picnic tables.

Aquinnah

POP 310

Apart from its isolation, the chief attraction of Aquinnah is the windswept cliffs that form a jagged face down to the Atlantic, astonishing in the colorful variety of sand, gravel, fossils and clay that reveal aons of geological history.

Aquinnah also has a rich Native American history, and it's here more than anywhere else on the island that you'll notice the influence of the island's Wampanoag people.

◉ Sights & Activities

Aquinnah Cliffs   BEACH
Also known as the Gay Head Cliffs, these clay cliffs, overlooking a 5-mile-long beach, were formed by glaciers 100 million years ago. Rising 150ft from the ocean, they're dramatic any time of day but are at their very best in the late afternoon, when they glow in the most amazing array of colors.

It's a 10-minute walk down to **Aquinnah Public Beach**, at the base of the cliffs, or if you're more adventurous you can walk 1 mile north along the shore to an area that's popular with nude sunbathers. The clay cliffs are a National Historic Landmark owned by the Wampanoag tribe. To protect them from erosion, it's illegal to bathe in the mud pools that form at the bottom of the cliffs, climb the cliffs, or remove clay from the area. Parking costs $15.

The 51ft, c 1856 brick **Gay Head Lighthouse** (☑508-645-2111; adult/child $5/free; ⊘90min before sunset-30min after sunset Fri-Sun) stands regally at the top of the bluff.

🛏 Sleeping & Eating

★**Outermost Inn**   INN $$$
(☑508-645-3511; www.outermostinn.com; 81 Lighthouse Rd; r incl breakfast $310-430, prix-fixe dinners $80) Be a guest of Hugh Taylor, musician James Taylor's younger brother, at this attractive estate house near Gay Head Lighthouse. The hilltop setting and ocean views are grand, and the Taylors make you feel right at home. Dinner, prepared by the inn's highly regarded chef, is open to the public, but call ahead for reservations.

Central Massachusetts & the Berkshires

Best Places to Eat

➜ Mezze Bistro & Bar (p206)

➜ Nudel (p203)

➜ John Andrews Restaurant (p196)

➜ Chez Albert (p190)

➜ Castle Street Cafe (p196)

➜ Chef Wayne's Big Mamou (p184)

Best Places to Stay

➜ Lord Jeffery Inn (p190)

➜ Stonover Farm B&B (p202)

➜ Canyon Ranch (p202)

➜ Guest House at Field Farm (p205)

Why Go?

The Berkshires draw you in with a tantalizing mix of cultural offerings, verdant hills and sweet farmland. You can ramble through estate homes of the once famous, listen to world-class musicians from a lawnside picnic blanket, and feast on farm-to-table cuisine at chef-driven restaurants. You could easily spend an entire summer hopscotching the patchwork of wilderness areas while taking in a dance festival here, an illustrious music series there and summer theater all over the place.

Head further afield and you'll come across peppy college towns with shady campuses, a wealth of cafes and exceptional art museums. Stretch your quads on hiking trails up Massachusetts' highest mountain and through nature preserves of all stripes. Those lucky enough to be here in autumn will find apples ripe for the picking and hillsides ablaze in brilliant fall foliage.

When to Go
Worcester

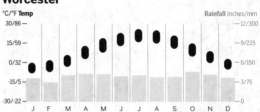

Summer Cultural attractions, summer theater, dance and concert festivals.

Fall A gorgeous time to be here, but avoid weekends, when traffic jams up.

Oct–May During these quieter months you'll find worthy nightlife in the region's college towns.

Central Massachusetts & the Berkshires Highlights

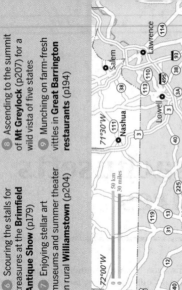

1 Listening to the Boston Symphony as you picnic at **Tanglewood** (p201), Lenox

2 Cruising the cafe and club scene in uber-hip **Northampton** (p185)

3 Rambling about the USA's largest contemporary art museum at **MASS MoCA** (p206), North Adams

4 Relishing the hot dogs at a classic **Worcester diner** (p178)

5 Shooting hoops at Springfield's **Naismith Memorial Basketball Hall of Fame** (p182)

6 Scouring the stalls for treasures at the **Brimfield Antique Show** (p179)

7 Enjoying stellar art museums and summer theater in rural **Williamstown** (p204)

8 Ascending to the summit of **Mt Greylock** (p207) for a wild vista of five states

9 Munching on farm-fresh vittles in **Great Barrington restaurants** (p194)

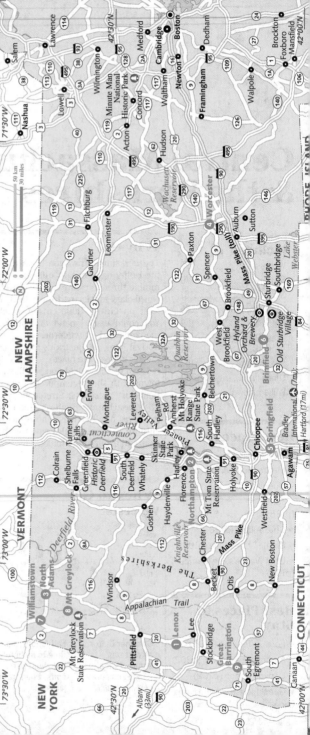

ℹ Getting There & Around

AIR

Worcester has a regional **airport** (ORH; www.massport.com) but it sees very little service. Springfield and the Pioneer Valley towns are served by Bradley International Airport (p438), just over the line in Connecticut.

BUS

Peter Pan Bus Lines (www.peterpanbus.com) connects towns in the region with numerous points in New England.

The **Pioneer Valley Transit Authority** (PVTA; www.pvta.com; ride/day pass $1.25/3) provides bus services to the Five Colleges area (the central part of the Pioneer Valley) and to Springfield. The Northampton–Amherst route has the most frequent service. **Berkshire Regional Transit Authority** (BRTA; www.berkshirerta.com; ride $1.25) runs buses between major Berkshire towns.

CAR

The Massachusetts Turnpike (Mass Pike; I-90) and MA 2 are the major east–west roads connecting Boston with central and western Massachusetts. The Mass Pike is a toll road.

TRAIN

The **Amtrak** (www.amtrak.com) *Lake Shore Limited* departs from Boston, stopping at Worcester, Springfield and Pittsfield before reaching Albany, NY. Its *Vermonter* runs from St Albans, Vermont, to Washington, DC, via Springfield.

CENTRAL MASSACHUSETTS

Also referred to as Worcester County, central Massachusetts marks a boundary between Boston's suburbs to the east and vast swatches of farm and hill country to the west. The city of Worcester (say 'Wooster') dominates the area, offering a worthwhile museum and relic diners to discerning travelers. Another big draw is the recreated Colonial village of Sturbridge, where you can suspend belief and travel back in time with costumed actors.

Worcester

POP 181,000

Welcome to 'Worm Town,' as locals affectionately call their city. A wealthy manufacturing center during the industrial revolution (the place invented and produced barbed wire,

the modern envelope and more), Worcester has struggled mightily since factories began shutting down after WWII, with scant urban renewal victories in recent years. Nonetheless, the city's nine small colleges inject youth and creativity, though the best draw might be the numerous historic diners that have slung blue-collar eggs for generations.

Main St, four blocks west of I-290, is the central drag. The rest of the city sprawls in a confusing mess of streets, and a map will greatly help exploration efforts.

◉ Sights & Activities

Worcester Art Museum MUSEUM
(☑508-799-4406; www.worcesterart.org; 55 Salisbury St; adult/child $14/free; ⊙11am-5pm Wed-Fri & Sun, 10am-5pm Sat; ♿) During Worcester's golden age, its captains of industry bestowed largesse upon the town. The Worcester Art Museum, off Main St (follow the signs), remains a generous and impressive bequest. The museum's comprehensive collection ranges from ancient Egyptian artifacts to European masterworks and contemporary American pieces, including Paul Revere silverwork. It also has a wild collection of Samurai and medieval armor.

EcoTarium MUSEUM
(☑508-929-2700; www.ecotarium.org; 222 Harrington Way; adult/child $14/8; ⊙10am-5pm Tue-Sat, noon-5pm Sun; ♿) ✐ This museum and 'center for environmental exploration' presents an array of exhibits to intrigue young minds. However, the most exciting offerings (tree-canopy walks, planetarium shows, and rides on the one-third-size model steam train) cost extra.

Blackstone River Bikeway CYCLING
(☑508-234-9090; www.blackstoneriverbikeway.com) When it's finished, the Blackstone River Bikeway will offer a mostly off-road bike trail from Union Station in Worcester to Providence, Rhode Island, 48 miles to the south. The trail laces through mill villages and farmland, following remnants of the historic Blackstone River Canal as well as a railroad right-of-way. The construction of the bikeway is reliant upon federal transportation funding, so progress has been slow, with just 13 of the 48 miles done and no completion date yet in sight. Until the bikeway is finished, you can follow the trail on marked roads. Visit the website for updates and maps.

WORCESTER DINERS

Worcester nurtured a great American icon: the diner. Here you'll find a dozen old relics tucked behind warehouses, underneath old train trestles, or steps from dicey bars. Some were made by Worcester Lunch Car Company, which produced 650 prefabricated beauties from 1906 to 1961. Models from the '30s tend to incorporate rich wood-trim and look like old train cars. Those from the '50s shoot for a sleek 'streamlined' aesthetic, with gleaming metal exteriors. Following are among Worcester's finest.

Miss Worcester Diner (☎508-753-5600; 300 Southbridge St; meals $5-9; ⊘6am-2pm Mon-Sat, 7am-2pm Sun) This classic beauty, built in 1948, was used as a showroom diner by Worcester Lunch Car Company, whose now-defunct factory sits across the street. Harleys parked on the sidewalk and Red Sox paraphernalia on the walls set the tone. Enticing selections like banana bread French toast compete with the usual greasy-spoon menu of chili dogs and biscuits with gravy.

Corner Lunch (☎508-799-9866; 133 Lamartine St; meals $4-11; ⊘6am-1pm Wed-Mon) Here you'll find a sweet 1950s prefab replete with silvery metal panels and a big neon sign. Inside, there are fries, club sandwiches and duct-taped vinyl seats.

Boulevard Diner (☎508-791-4535; 155 Shrewsbury St; meals $4-9; ⊘24hr) With its red Formica tables and dark wooden booths, this diner's barely changed a lick since the 1930s. Order breakfast 24/7 or swing for tasty Italian specialties like meatballs and eggplant parmesan.

🛏 Sleeping

Putnam House B&B   B&B $
(☎508-865-9094; www.putnamhousebandb.com; 211 Putnam Hill Rd, Sutton; r/ste $95/105) This hilltop farmstead dates to 1737 and shows its age exceedingly well. Restored by master carpenters, it has large fireplaces, exposed beams and an enormous red centennial barn. The hosts exemplify the term, preparing generous breakfasts. Find the place 10 miles southeast in Sutton.

Beechwood Hotel   HOTEL $$$
(☎508-754-5789; www.beechwoodhotel.com; 363 Plantation St; r $190-310; ❀🕾) This hotel is well known to business travelers for its personal service and pastel-toned luxury rooms. It's a cylinder-shaped building east of the city center along MA 9 near the Massachusetts Biotechnology Park.

🍴 Eating

The core of downtown Worcester is studded with moderately priced lunch spots. A visit to at least one of Worcester's historic diners should be considered mandatory.

Belmont Vegetarian   VEGETARIAN $
(www.belmontvegetarian.com; 157 Belmont St; meals $6-12; ⊘11am-8pm Tue-Sat; 🖉) Proof positive that beautiful flowers can bloom in the most unassuming of places, Belmont offers huge portions of Jamaican-inspired vegetarian fare with enough soulful flavor to convert the most hardened carnivore. Just try the saucy BBQ soy chicken.

Coney Island Hot Dogs   FAST FOOD $
(☎508-753-4362; www.coneyislandlunch.com; 158 Southbridge St; hot dogs $2; ⊘10am-7pm Wed-Mon) A giant neon fist grips a wiener dripping yellow neon mustard in the six-story sign outside this 1918 Worcester institution. Inside, eat dogs in a cavernous space chockfull of wooden booths carved with generations of graffiti.

★ Armsby Abbey   AMERICAN $$
(☎508-795-1012; www.armsbyabbey.com; 144 Main St; mains $8-18; ⊘11:30am-10pm Mon-Fri, 10am-10pm Sat-Sun; 🕾) The Abbey rakes in all sorts of awards for its slow-food menu and stellar selection of local-and-beyond microbrews on tap. Think artesian cheeses, grass-fed beef and comfort food with a gourmet twist. The setting is hip, urban and welcoming.

🍷 Drinking & Entertainment

Pick up the free weeklies **Worcester Mag** (www.worcestermag.com) or the more student-targeted **Pulse** (www.thepulsemag.com) for arts and entertainment listings.

Ralph's Chadwick Square Diner   CLUB
(www.ralphsrockdiner.com; 148 Grove St; ⊘4pm-2am) Hands down the most interesting night

spot in Worcester, this old diner attached to a rock club serves chili dogs, great burgers and cheap booze. But above all come for the sweet gigs, mostly local and often talented. The place attracts college kids, bikers, rockers, goths and yuppies – and everyone gets into the vibe.

MB Lounge   GAY
(☑ 508-799-4521; www.mblounge.com; 40 Grafton St; ⊗ 5pm-2am Mon-Thu, 3pm-2am Fri-Sun; 🛜) Depending on the night, this gay lounge runs the gamut from casual neighborhood bar to bass-thumping dance club.

ⓘ Information

Central Massachusetts Convention & Visitors Bureau (☑ 508-755-7400; www.centralmass. org; 91 Prescott St, Worcester; ⊗ 9am-5pm Mon-Fri) Has the skinny on Worcester and the rest of Central Massachusetts.

ⓘ Getting There & Away

Worcester stands at the junction of four interstate highways. About an hour's drive will bring you here from Boston, Providence or Springfield.

BUS

Peter Pan Bus Lines (☑ 800-343-9999; www. peterpanbus.com; Union Station, 2 Washington Sq) operates buses between Worcester and other destinations throughout New England.

TRAIN

Amtrak trains (www.amtrak.com) stop here en route between Boston and Chicago. **MBTA** (www.mbta.com) runs frequent commuter trains to/from Boston ($10, 80 minutes). Trains for both rails leave from Union Station at 2 Washington Sq.

Sturbridge

POP 9270

Sturbridge can leave a bittersweet taste in the traveler's mouth – here is one of the most visited attractions in New England and a stark example of how far US culture has traveled in less than 200 years in search of the dollar.

The town retained much of its Colonial character until after WWII. When the Mass Pike (I-90) and I-84 arrived in the late 1950s and joined just north of the town, commerce and change came all at once. To take advantage of the handy highway transportation, Sturbridge became host to one of the country's first 'living museums' – Old Sturbridge

Village (OSV). Ironically, the town's effort to preserve an example of a traditional Yankee community at OSV generated a mammoth attraction on whose borders motor inns, fast-food chains, gas stations and roadside shops have sprouted up.

⊙ Sights & Activities

Old Sturbridge Village   MUSEUM
(OSV; ☑ 800-733-1830; www.osv.org; US 20; adult/child $24/8; ⊗ 9:30am-5pm Apr-Oct, off-season hours vary; ➕) Historic buildings from throughout the region have been moved to this site to recreate a New England town from the 1830s, with 40 restored structures filled with antiques. Rather than labeling the exhibits, this museum has 'interpreters' – people who dress in costume, ply the trades of their ancestors and explain to visitors what they are doing.

Although many historians find the layout of the village to be less than accurate, the attention to detail is high. The country store displays products brought from throughout the world by New England sailing ships. Crafters and artisans use authentic tools and materials. The livestock has even been back-bred to approximate the animals that lived on New England farms a century-and-a-half ago. Expect to spend at least three hours here. Admission is good for two days.

Hyland Orchard & Brewery   FARM
(☑ 508-347-7500; www.hylandorchard.com; 195 Arnold Rd; ⊗ noon-7pm Tue-Sun; ➕) **FREE** This 150-acre family-owned farm and craft brewery produces its own Pioneer Pale Ale and a handful of other beers with well water. Try them all at the tasting bar. Lest you think this is no place for the kids, note that Hyland has a **petting farm**, **wagon rides** and ice-cream parlor.

In the fall, **pick apples** while folk bands pick stringed instruments. To find Hyland, go west on Main St/US 20 to Arnold Rd, turn right and go 2 miles north on Arnold Rd.

Brimfield Antique Show   ANTIQUES
(www.brimfieldshow.com; US 20, Brimfield; admission free-$8; ⊗ 6am-dusk) Six miles west of Sturbridge is the Brimfield Antique Show, a mecca for collectors of antique furniture, toys and tools. More than 6000 sellers and 130,000 buyers gather to do business in 23 farmers' fields; it's the largest outdoor antiques fair in North America.

The town has shops open year-round, but the major antiques shows are held in mid-May, early July and early September, usually from Tuesday through Sunday. The more 'premium' fields charge an admission fee of around $8, but most are free.

Sleeping

Along a 1-mile stretch of US 20 just off exit 9 is a procession of chain hotels of the Hampton Inn and Super 8 variety. Keep in mind, many lodgings fill up on weekends in summer and fall. When the Brimfield Antique Show is in progress, prices rise substantially and advance reservations are necessary.

Wells State Park CAMPGROUND $
(☑ 877-422-6762; www.mass.gov/dcr; MA 49; tent sites $12-14, yurts $40) This campground offers 60 wooded sites – some lakefront – on its 1470 acres. It's north of I-90, five miles from Old Sturbridge Village.

Nathan Goodale House B&B $
(☑ 413-245-9228; www.brimfield.org; 11 Warren Rd/MA 19N, Brimfield; r from $90; 🛜) In a large and simple Victorian Italianate house, this B&B has tasteful rooms in residential Brimfield, nicely situated for enjoying the Brimfield Antique Show.

Publick House Historic Inn INN $$
(☑ 508-347-3313; www.publickhouse.com; MA 131; r $99-199; ❄🛜🐾) Here is Sturbridge's most famous historic inn, the 1771 Publick House, near the village common. Three separate buildings make up the property: Country Motor Lodge looks like it sounds, generic and boring, while Chamberlain House offers six suites with decor that is almost nice. Your best bet is the Publick Inn itself, with its canopy beds and 18th-century decor.

Eating

Annie's Country Kitchen BREAKFAST $
(140 Main St/MA 131; mains $3-8; ⏲5am-at least noon; 🚼) If you're big on breakfast and nuts about home fries this local shack is the place to jump-start your day. The omelets are huge, but it's the pancakes – filled with everything from wild blueberries to chocolate chips – that the kids will want.

Thai Place THAI $
(☑ 508-347-2999; 1 Old Sturbridge Villa; mains $5-10; ⏲11:30am-9pm) Here you'll find real-deal homestyle Thai fare with solid options for vegetarians and carnivores alike. Don't be misled by the wallet-friendly prices - everything, including the seafood offerings, is top-of-the-line fresh. For a fiery treat order the spicy ocean curry.

Publick House AMERICAN $$$
(☑ 508-347-3313; www.publickhouse.com; MA 131; mains $18-30; ⏲11:30am-8:30pm) This classic country inn features a formal dining room warmed by fireplaces. Here you can order a traditional Thanksgiving turkey dinner any day of the year, or turn it up a notch with the likes of roast duck in cranberry glaze. It's a staid joint, and while the food is fine, it isn't quite as good as the history.

ℹ Information

Sturbridge Area Tourist Association (☑ 508-347-2761; www.sturbridgetownships.com; 380 Main St/US 20; ⏲9am-5pm Mon-Fri, 10am-4pm Sat & Sun) The helpful information office is conveniently situated opposite the entrance to Old Sturbridge Village.

ℹ Getting There & Away

Most travelers arrive in Sturbridge by car via the Mass Pike, I-90. Take exit 9 onto I-84, and it will

---

DON'T MISS

RUSSIAN ICONS

Since WWII it has been illegal to export icons from Russia, so the collection of 60 rare works preserved at the Russian icon exhibit at **St Anne Shrine** (16 Church St; ⏲10am-5pm) **FREE** is an unusual treasure. Monsignor Pie Neveu, a Roman Catholic Assumptionist bishop, ministered to a diocese in Russia from 1906 to 1936. While at his post, Bishop Neveu collected valuable Russian icons, a hobby no doubt made easier by the collapse of the old order and the advent of secularist communism. The collection was further augmented by acquisitions brought to the USA by the Assumptionist fathers who served as chaplains at the US embassy in Moscow between 1934 and 1941. The collection was installed in 1971 at St Anne Shrine, which is just off US 20 at the western end of Sturbridge. You'll find the icons displayed in a hall at the back side of the church parking lot.

WORTH A TRIP

SALEM CROSS INN

If you haven't had your fill of Colonial reenactment at Old Sturbridge Village, head to **Salem Cross Inn** (📞508-867-2345; www.salemcrossinn.com; 260 W Main St/MA 9, West Brookfield; lunch $10-18, dinner $18-35; 🕐11:30am-9pm Tue-Fri, 5-9pm Sat, noon-8pm Sun), built in 1705 and set on 600 green acres in a bucolic country landscape. The calf's liver with bacon and caramelized onions is a house specialty. In addition to the main dining room there's also the Hexmark Tavern, which cooks up comfort food like chicken pot pie and Yankee pot roast at family-friendly prices. Besides offering traditional New England meals, the inn hosts special events ranging from a Colonial-style fireplace feast cooked on an open hearth to a theatrical murder-mystery dinner. To get there follow US 20 to MA 148 north; 7 miles along, turn left onto MA 9 and go 5 miles.

---

deposit you onto Main St (US 20), not far from the gate of Old Sturbridge Village.

PIONEER VALLEY

With the exception of gritty Springfield, the Pioneer Valley offers a gentle landscape of college towns, picturesque farms and old mills that have been charmingly converted into modern use. The uber-cool burg of Northampton provides the region's top dining, nightlife and street scenes. For visitor information on the entire Pioneer Valley, go to www.valleyvisitor.com.

Springfield

POP 153,000

Springfield has certainly seen better days, but this recession-hit town has some worthy sights, plus one of the best Cajun eateries this side of New Orleans.

Downtown Springfield contains a few reminders of the 19th-century wealth that once caused the city to blossom. They include a handful of quality museums, a grand symphony hall and stately Romanesque Revival buildings at Court Sq. While most of the business types who work here flee promptly at 5pm, Springfield's downtown unexpectedly supports a lively night scene. Up the hill you'll find an intriguing armory dating back to the American Revolution.

As all local grade-schoolers know, basketball originated in Springfield, and that explains how the Hall of Fame got to be here. Springfield is also the birthplace of Theodor Geisel, aka Dr Seuss.

Take I-91 exit 6 northbound or exit 7 southbound, follow it to State St (east) then Main St (north), and you'll be at Court Sq in the heart of Springfield.

◎ Sights & Activities

Museum Quadrangle MUSEUM COMPLEX
(📞800-625-7738; www.springfieldmuseums.org; 21 Edwards St; adult/child $15/8; 🅿) The **Springfield Museums** surround Museum Quadrangle, two blocks northeast of Court Sq. Look for Merrick Park, at the entrance to the quadrangle, and the **Augustus Saint-Gaudens statue** *The Puritan*.

One ticket grants entrance to all five museums. Access to the grounds, and to the **Dr Seuss National Memorial Sculpture Garden**, is free and open 9am to 5pm.

★**George Walter
Vincent Smith Art Museum** MUSEUM
(www.springfieldmuseums.org; 21 Edwards St; 🕐10am-5pm Tue-Sat, 11am-5pm Sun; 🅿) Exterior windows designed by Tiffany Studios and a fine collection of 19th-century American and European paintings, textiles, ceramics and more. The samurai armor collection is among the finest outside of Japan.

★**Museum of Fine Arts** MUSEUM
(www.springfieldmuseums.org; 21 Edwards St; 🕐10am-5pm Tue-Sat, 11am-5pm Sun; 🅿) The 20 galleries of this art deco–style building are filled with lesser paintings of the great European masters and better works of lesser masters. One of the best-known pieces is Erastus Salisbury Field's *The Rise of the American Republic*. The impressionist collection includes works by Pissarro and Renoir. The contemporary gallery includes pieces by Georgia O'Keeffe and Picasso.

★**Museum of Springfield History** MUSEUM
(www.springfieldmuseums.org; 21 Edwards St; 🕐10am-5pm Tue-Sat, 11am-5pm Sun; 🅿) Showcasing the city's heyday, this museum is home to the Esta Mantos **Indian Motocycle collection** and a 1928 Rolls-Royce Phantom

Springfield

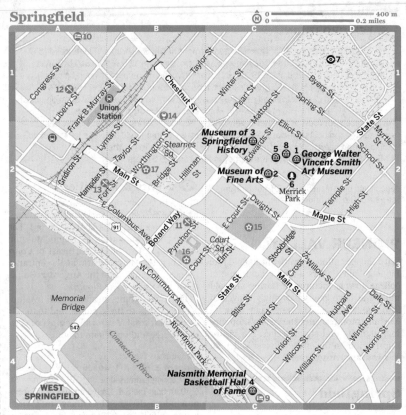

that was – yes, you heard it right – built right here in Springfield. During the Roaring '20s, Rolls-Royce made nearly 2000 vehicles in Springfield before the Great Depression hit and the factory was shut down.

★ Naismith Memorial Basketball Hall of Fame   MUSEUM
(www.hoophall.com; 1000 W Columbus Ave; adult/child $19/14; ⊙10am-5pm; P⋒) Though the emphasis at the basketball hall of fame seems to be more hoopla than hoops – there's an abundance of multiscreened TVs and disembodied cheering – true devotees of the game will be thrilled to shoot baskets, feel the center-court excitement and learn about the sport's history and great players.

One touted figure is James Naismith (1861–1939), inventor of the game, who came to Springfield to work as a physical education instructor at the International YMCA Training School (later Springfield College).

Naismith wanted to develop a good, fast team sport that could be played indoors during the long New England winters. In December of 1891, he had the idea of nailing two wooden peach baskets to opposite walls in the college gymnasium. He wrote down 13 rules for the game (12 of which are still used), and thus basketball was born.

Springfield Science Museum   MUSEUM
(www.springfieldmuseums.org; 21 Edwards St; ⊙10am-5pm Tue-Sat, 11am-5pm Sun; P) Has a respectable, if slightly outdated, range of science and natural-history exhibits. The Dinosaur Hall has a full-size replica of a *Tyrannosaurus rex,* and the African Hall covers evolution and ecology. The Seymour Planetarium has shows daily (adult/child $3/2).

Connecticut Valley Historical Museum   MUSEUM
(www.springfieldmuseums.org; 21 Edwards St; ⊙10am-5pm Tue-Sat, 11am-5pm Sun; P) Focus-

Springfield

ing on the decorative and domestic arts of the Connecticut River Valley from 1636 to the present, this museum has collections of furniture, pewter and glass.

**Springfield Armory
National Historic Site**   HISTORIC SITE
(☎413-734-8551; www.nps.gov/spar; cnr State & Federal Sts; ⊗9am-5pm; ℗) FREE This national historic site preserves what remains of the USA's greatest federal armory, built under the command of General George Washington during the American Revolution. During its heyday in the Civil War, it turned out 1000 muskets a day. A college now occupies many of the former firearm factories, but exhibits in the Main Arsenal recall the armory's golden age.

The site holds one of the world's largest collections of firearms, including Remingtons, Colts, Lugers and even weapons from as early as the 1400s. For the weirdest sculpture you might ever see, don't miss the Or-

gan of Muskets, composed of 645 rifles and made famous in an 1843 anti-war poem by Henry Wadsworth Longfellow.

The armory is a 10-minute walk northeast from Court Sq along State St past Museum Quadrangle. If you are driving, take I-291 exit 3 to Armory St and follow it to Federal St.

✯ Festivals & Events

Big E   FAIR
(www.thebige.com; 1305 Memorial Ave/MA 147; adult/child $15/10; ⊗mid-Sep) Sleepy West Springfield explodes into activity in mid-September, with the annual Eastern States Exposition, better known as the Big E. The fair goes on for 17 days, with farm exhibits and horse shows, carnival rides and parades, mass consumption of food on sticks, a petting zoo and quirky performances by the likes of Hilby the Skinny German Juggle Boy.

Most shows are free once you're in the fairgrounds, though the rides cost extra. It's all a bit hokey, but good fun, and it's the largest event of its kind in New England.

🛏 Sleeping

La Quinta Inn & Suites   HOTEL $
(☎413-781-0900; www.lq.com; 100 Congress St; r incl breakfast from $89; ℗✳︎🛜🛁) The freshly renovated rooms at this hotel offer the best value of any in-town hotel and rates include a hot breakfast.

Naomi's Inn   B&B $$
(☎413-433-6019; www.naomisinn.net; 20 Springfield St; r incl breakfast $135; ℗✳︎🛜) While the house itself appears nice, with a broad porch and shady trees, it overlooks a hospital compound 1.5 miles northwest of the city center. Rooms are ample and comfortable. To get there, follow the signs to Bay State Medical Center; the inn is opposite the hospital.

Hilton Garden Inn   HOTEL $$
(☎413-886-8000; www.hilton.com; 800 W Columbus Ave; r from $145; ℗✳︎🛜🛁♿) Just a hoop toss away from the Naismith Memorial Basketball Hall of Fame, this garden-variety hotel has advantages for families. Not only are the basketball sights right there, but the hall of fame complex also contains pizzerias and other family-friendly eateries. And when you've had your fill of basketball, kids can hop in the swimming pool.

DON'T MISS

DR SEUSS & FRIENDS

The writer and illustrator responsible for such nonsensically sensible classics as *The Cat in the Hat, Horton Hatches the Egg* and *Yertle the Turtle* was born Theodor Seuss Geisel in 1904 in Springfield. Geisel credits his mother for inspiring his signature rhyming style; she would lull him and his sister to sleep by chanting pie lists she remembered from her bakery days back in Germany.

After graduating from Dartmouth College, Geisel made his living primarily as a political cartoonist and ad man. His first children's book, *And to Think That I Saw It on Mulberry Street*, was rejected by dozens of publishers before one bit. Geisel's first major success came with the publication of *The Cat in the Hat*, which he wrote after reading Rudolf Flesch's *Why Johnny Can't Read*, an article that asserted children's books of the day were boring and 'antiseptic,' and called upon people like Geisel (and, er, Walt Disney) to raise the standard of primers for young children. By the time he died in 1991, Geisel had published 44 books and his work had been translated into more than 20 languages. His classic *Green Eggs & Ham* is still ranked as one of the top-selling English-language books to date.

In 2002 the **Dr Seuss National Memorial Sculpture Garden** (www.catinthehat. org; cnr State & Chestnut Sts; 🚶) FREE was completed, featuring bronze pieces made by Geisel's step-daughter, the sculptor Lark Grey Dimond-Cates. Among the works located in the middle of Springfield's Museum Quadrangle are a 10ft-tall 'book' displaying the entire text of *Oh! The Places You'll Go!* – the archetypal graduation gift – and an impish-looking Geisel sitting at his drawing board, the Cat standing by his shoulder. In the opposite corner of the quad, the squat figure of the Lorax looks beseechingly up at passersby, his famous environmental warning engraved at his feet: 'Unless.'

✖ Eating

You'll find the greatest concentration of lunch places, pubs and bistros in the vicinity of Court Sq and Union Station.

★**Chef Wayne's Big Mamou**   CAJUN $$
(www.chefwaynes-bigmamou.com; 63 Liberty St; mains $8-20; ⊘11am-8:30pm Mon-Fri, noon-9:30pm Sat) Don't be fooled by its meager appearance – this hole in the wall serves up fabulous home-style Cajun fare. Highlights include the barbecued pulled pork, crayfish quesadillas and blackened catfish. One caveat: you'll want to get there early at dinner, especially on weekends, when lines form outside the door. Reservations are not taken. You can BYO alcohol.

Cafe Lebanon   MIDDLE EASTERN $$$
(☑413-737-7373; 1390 Main St; mains $8-22; ⊘11:30am-9pm Mon-Fri; 🖉) The upscale setting and eclectic menu attract a business crowd at this downtown restaurant. Choose from traditional Middle Eastern standards like falafels, hummus and kabobs or order fusion fare with an Italian twist. The bruschetta topped with feta and fresh mint makes a zingy starter.

Student Prince Cafe & Fort Restaurant   GERMAN $$$
(☑413-788-6628; www.studentprince.com; 8 Fort St; mains $7-25; ⊘11am-9pm) The Student Prince has been scratching those schnitzel and sauerkraut itches since 1935 and shows no signs of slowing down. Even if you're not in the mood for heavy starches, come by anyway to admire the impressive beer steins (one was owned by a Russian czar) lining the walls. You'll also find some satisfying brews like Spaten Maibock on tap.

🍷 Drinking & Entertainment

Take a walk down Worthington St and you'll find several pubs and clubs crammed into two blocks, one of them likely to suit your taste.

Pick up a copy of the free *Valley Advocate* (www.valleyadvocate.com) for entertainment listings.

Theodore's   BLUES
(☑413-736-6000; www.theobbq.com; 201 Worthington St; ⊘11am-2am Mon-Fri, 5pm-2am Sat & Sun) Truly great blues and jazz acts get booked in this lively bar serving an extensive menu of good barbecue and pub food. A jazzy mural captures its illustrious history

(the Blues Foundation once named Theodore's the best blues club in the country) while softening the cavernous effect of the joint.

Symphony Hall CONCERT VENUE

(☑ 413-788-7033; www.symphonyhall.com; 34 Court St) This imposing edifice, resembling a Greek temple, hosts the reputable Springfield Symphony Orchestra (www.springfieldsymphony.org). Otherwise, the mainstay is musicals of the *Spamalot* and *Grease* genre.

Oz Nightclub GAY

(☑ 413-732-4562; 397 Dwight St; ⊘ 9pm-2am Wed-Sun) This multipurpose gay bar offers everything from a place to shoot pool to DJ dancing – the hottest action is on weekends.

MassMutual Center CONCERT VENUE

(☑ 413-787-6610; www.massmutualcenter.com; 1277 Main St) A major venue for conventions, exhibits and big rock concerts.

❶ Information

Greater Springfield Convention & Visitors Bureau (☑ 413-787-1548; www.valleyvisitor.com; 1441 Main St, Springfield; ⊘ 8:30am-5pm Mon-Fri) A block and a half northwest of Court Sq.

❶ Getting There & Around

BUS

Peter Pan Bus Lines (☑ 800-343-9999, 413-781-2900; www.peterpanbus.com; 1776 Main St) connects Springfield with cities throughout New England. The bus station is a 10-minute walk northwest of Court Sq.

The **Pioneer Valley Transit Authority** (PVTA; ☑ 413-781-7882; www.pvta.com; 1776 Main St; day pass $3), in the Peter Pan terminal, runs routes to 23 communities in the region. Downtown, the 'Green 3' route connects State St and Liberty St via Main St.

TRAIN

Amtrak (www.amtrak.com) operates between Boston and Springfield's **Union Station** (☑ 413-785-4230; 66 Lyman St), which is a 10-minute walk northwest of Court Sq. There's also regular service to New Haven, Connecticut.

Northampton

POP 28,600

In a region famous for its charming college towns, you'd be hard-pressed to find anything more appealing than the crooked streets of downtown Northampton. Old red-brick buildings, buskers and lots of pedestrian traffic provide a lively backdrop as you wander into cafes, rock clubs and bookstores. Move a few steps outside of the picturesque commercial center and you'll stumble onto the bucolic grounds of Smith College.

The presence of college students and their professors gives the town a distinctly liberal political atmosphere. The lesbian community is famously large and outspoken, making Northampton a favorite destination for the gay community.

The center of town is at the intersection of Main St (MA 9) and Pleasant St (US 5). Main St is where you'll find the core of restaurants and shops. Smith College is on the west end of town, where Main St curves right and turns into Elm St.

⊙ Sights & Activities

Smith College COLLEGE CAMPUS

(www.smith.edu; Elm St; Ⓟ) Founded 'for the education of the intelligent gentlewoman' in 1875, Smith College is one of the largest women's colleges in the country, with 2600 students. The verdant 125-acre campus holds an eclectic architectural mix of nearly 100 buildings as well as a pretty pond. Notable

SPRINGFIELD'S MOTO MOJO

When Americans hear 'motorcycle,' they're most likely to think Harley-Davidson. But Springfield-based Indian was the first (1901) and was, many say, the best. Up until it disbanded in 1953, the Indian Motocycle Company produced its bikes in a sprawling factory complex on the outskirts of Springfield. The 'r' in 'motorcycle' was, by the way, dropped as a marketing gimmick. Through the merger of several bike companies, the Indian Motorcycle Corporation was created in 1999 to jumpstart the manufacture of Indians again, but it's widely accepted that the new bikes couldn't hold a candle to the originals.

A mint collection of the original Indian bikes, including a rare 1904 Indian ridden by the company's founder, are now on display in the Museum of Springfield History.

alums of the college include Sylvia Plath, Julia Child and Gloria Steinem.

While most will be pleased with themselves after a stroll around Paradise Pond with its Japanese tea hut, ambitious others might consider a campus tour arranged by the Office of Admissions at 10am, 11am, 1pm and 3pm Monday to Friday.

Smith College Museum of Art   MUSEUM
(☑413-585-2760;   www.smith.edu/artmuseum;
Elm St at Bedford Tce; adult/child $5/2; ☺10am-4pm Tue-Sat, noon-4pm Sun; ℗) This impressive campus museum boasts a 25,000-piece collection. It's particularly strong in 17th-century Dutch and 19th- and 20th-century European and North American paintings, including works by Degas, Winslow Homer, Picasso and James Abbott McNeill Whistler.

Lyman Conservatory   GARDENS
(☑413-585-2740; www.smith.edu/garden; 15 College Lane; ☺8:30am-4pm) FREE Visitors are welcome to explore the college's collection of Victorian greenhouses, which are packed to the brim with odd things in bloom. It's conveniently located opposite Paradise Pond.

Thornes Marketplace   MARKET
(www.thornesmarketplace.com; 150 Main St) You can't miss this urban mall – it's the green-awninged behemoth taking up a large chunk of Main St between Pleasant St and Old South St in the town center. This historic building houses an array of boutiques, student-centered shops and eateries.

NORWOTTUCK RAIL TRAIL

The Norwottuck Rail Trail (nor-wah-tuk; www.mass.gov/dcr/parks/central/nwrt.htm) is a foot and bike path that follows the former Boston & Maine Railroad right-of-way from Amherst to Northampton, a distance of 11 miles. For much of its length, the trail parallels MA 9, passing through open farms and crossing the broad Connecticut River on a historic 1500ft-long bridge. Parking and access to the trail can be found on Station Rd in Amherst and at Elwell State Park on Damon Rd in Northampton. You can rent bikes from Northampton Bicycle (www.nohobike.com; 319 Pleasant St; per day $25; ☺9:30am-7pm Mon-Fri, 9:30am-5pm Sat, noon-5pm Sun) in Northampton.

Dinosaur Footprints   HISTORIC SITE
(☑413-684-0148; www.thetrustees.org; US 5, Holyoke; ☺dawn-dusk) FREE Around 190 million years ago, the Pioneer Valley area was a subtropical swamp inhabited by carnivorous, two-legged dinosaurs, and a large cluster of their footprints is preserved in situ on the west bank of the Connecticut River. The prints here, some 134 in all, represent three distinct species. It's a cool sight and just a two-minute walk from the road.

From Northampton, go south on Pleasant St/US 5 for about 5 miles. The small parking lot is on the left-hand side.

🛏 Sleeping

It's typically easiest to find a room during summer, when school's not in session. At other times, room price and availability depend on the college's schedule of ceremonies and events.

In addition to places to stay in Northampton, there's a run of midrange chain hotels along MA 9 in Hadley midway between Northampton and Amherst.

Starlight Llama B&B   B&B $$
(☑413-584-1703;   www.starlightllama.com;   940 Chesterfield Rd, Florence; r incl breakfast $100) 🌿 Five miles and a world away in neighboring Florence, Starlight offers the ultimate back-to-nature sleep. This off-the-grid solar-powered farm sits amidst 65 acres of llama pastures, hiking trails and friendly barnyard creatures. Owner John Clapp built the house himself along with much of the Shaker-style furniture found in the three guest rooms.

Breakfast centers on the farm's own free-range eggs and organic fruits and veggies.

Autumn Inn   MOTEL $$
(☑413-584-7660;   www.hampshirehospitality.com; 259 Elm St/MA 9; r incl breakfast $115-169; ℗@🛜🏊) Santa should not bring gifts to whoever designed this barn and raised-ranch combination. Despite the weird facade, the rooms are comfortable. It's next to the Smith campus, a 15-minute walk into town.

Hotel Northampton   HISTORIC HOTEL $$$
(☑413-584-3100; www.hotelnorthampton.com; 36 King St; r $185-275; ℗🛜) This old-timer is perfectly situated smack in the center of Northampton and has been the town's best bet since 1927. Some of the 100 rooms are airy and well-fitted, but others rely too much on mass-produced quilts for atmosphere. Even

METACOMET-MONADNOCK TRAIL

The Metacomet-Monadnock Trail (or M&M Trail in local parlance) is 117 miles of a 200-mile greenway and footpath that traverses some of the most breathtaking scenery in western Massachusetts. It extends from Connecticut to New Hampshire's Mt Monadnock and beyond.

The trail, which takes part of its name from the Native American warrior Metacomet, enters Massachusetts from Connecticut near the Agawam/Southwick town line. It proceeds north up the Connecticut River valley, ascends Mt Tom, then heads east along the Holyoke Range, including Skinner State Park, before bearing north again. After entering New Hampshire, the trail ascends Mt Monadnock, where it joins the Monadnock-Sunapee Greenway.

The easiest access for day hikes is in the state parks, where leaflets and simple local trail maps are available. For longer hikes, it's good to have the *Metacomet-Monadnock Trail Guide*, published by the Appalachian Mountain Club. Trail excerpts are posted on the website of the **Appalachian Mountain Club Berkshire Chapter** (www.amc berkshire.org/mmguide).

so, there's a quiet grandeur to the place and mailing a postcard via an antiquated letterbox system always feels good.

🍴 Eating

Whatever cuisine or ambience you're in the mood for, there's probably a restaurant to match.

Haymarket Café   CAFE $
(www.haymarketcafe.com; 185 Main St; items $4-10; ⊙7am-10pm; 📶⏚) Need a place where you can read an entire book in one go? Then try lounging around this bohemian cafe offering espresso, fresh juices, tempeh burgers and an extensive vegetarian menu. If students hunkered down over heated laptops and cooling coffee have snatched all the upstairs tables, look for the steps leading down to the cozy basement.

Green Bean   CAFE $
(www.greenbeannorthampton.com; 241 Main St; mains $6-9; ⊙7am-3pm; 📶) 🌿 Pioneer Valley farmers stock the kitchen at this cute eatery that dishes up organic eggs at breakfast and juicy hormone-free beef burgers at lunch. The scones topped with a dab of jam make the perfect finish. Locavores will love the prices, too, which are surprisingly easy on the wallet.

Herrell's Ice Cream   ICE CREAM $
(☎413-586-9700; Thornes Marketplace, Old South St; cones $3-5; ⊙noon-10:30pm) Steve Herrell began scooping out gourmet ice cream in this place in 1980. Expect unexpected concoctions like apple cider or lemon cake,

though you'll find the usual coffee, chocolate and vanilla flavors too.

Woodstar Cafe   CAFE $
(www.woodstarcafe.com; 60 Masonic St; mains $5-8; ⊙8am-8pm; 📶⏚) Students flock to this family-run bakery/cafe, just a stone's throw from campus, for tasty sandwiches and luscious pastries at bargain prices. Perhaps the smoked salmon and chevre on an organic baguette?

Bela   VEGETARIAN $$
(www.belaveg.com; 68 Masonic St; mains $9-13; ⊙noon-8:30pm Tue-Sat; ⏚⏚) 🌿 This cozy vegetarian restaurant puts such an emphasis on fresh ingredients that the chalkboard menu changes daily depending on what local farmers are harvesting. Think home-cooked comfort food and a setting that welcomes families – there's even a collection of toys for the kids!

Sierra Grille   MODERN AMERICAN $$$
(www.sierragrille.net; 41 Strong Ave; mains $17-29; ⊙3pm-1am) A smart setting, juicy steaks and a knockout brew selection make this the hottest omnivore dinner spot in town. The kitchen also does a stellar job with fish – the grilled tuna topped with cranberry-peach chutney will awaken taste buds you didn't know existed. Reservations are a must on weekends.

Osaka   JAPANESE $$$
(☎413-587-9548; www.osakanorthampton.com; 7 Old South St; mains $10-28; ⊙11:30am-11pm Sun-Thu, 11:30am-midnight Fri & Sat) Osaka's modern dining room is airy and bright, and it serves

SKINNER STATE PARK

Skinner State Park (☏ 413-586-0350; www.mass.gov/dcr; ☉ dawn-dusk) **FREE**, at the summit of Mt Holyoke, offers panoramic views of the Connecticut River and its oxbow curve, the fertile valley and the distant smudge of Mt Greylock to the west. During the fall foliage season, it's a stunner. The 1.5-mile road to the top is open to hikers year-round and to vehicles from May to October. The park is 9 miles southeast of Northampton, off MA 47 in Hadley.

a wide menu of à la carte sushi as well as hibachi, udon and tempura. And if you're looking for top value in the middle of the day, check out the sushi lunch deals offered until 3:30pm. The enclosed porch makes for sunny eating year-round.

India House INDIAN $$$
(☏ 413-586-6344; www.indiahousenorthampton.com; 45 State St; mains $12-22; ☉ 5-10pm Tue-Sun; ☑) Head here for healthy Ayuvedic-style cooking that artfully mixes exotic Eastern spices with fresh local produce and meats. The result is legitimately inspired tandoori, korma and curried dishes. The vegetarian menu is impressive and the kitchen will prepare vegan dishes upon request.

🍷 Drinking & Entertainment

Northampton is the top music destination in the Pioneer Valley. For listings of what's happening, pick up a copy of the free *Valley Advocate* (www.valleyadvocate.com).

Northampton Brewery BREWPUB
(www.northamptonbrewery.com; 11 Brewster Ct; ☉ 11:30am-2am Mon-Sat, noon-1am Sun) The oldest operating brewpub in New England enjoys a loyal summertime following thanks to its generously sized outdoor deck.

Toasted Owl PUB
(www.toastedowl.com; 21 Main St; ☉ 4pm-2am Mon-Fri, noon-2am Sat & Sun) Grab a seat around the oversized oval bar for great people-watching at this peppy joint in the town center. The drinks are poured with a generous hand and the pub grub (especially the barbecued chicken pizza) is reason enough to get toasted here.

Dirty Truth BAR
(☏ 413-585-5999; www.dirtytruthbeerhall.com; 29 Main St; ☉ 4pm-2am Mon-Fri, 1pm-2am Sat & Sun) Slide into a high-top under some decent contemporary art to choose from 50 draft beers available from an impressive chalkboard menu.

Calvin Theatre CONCERT VENUE
(☏ 413-584-0610; www.iheg.com; 19 King St) This gorgeously restored movie house hosts big-name performances with everything from hot rock and indie bands to comedy shows.

Iron Horse Music Hall CONCERT VENUE
(☏ 413-584-0610; www.iheg.com; 20 Center St) The town's prime venue for folk, rock and jazz with performers like Leo Kottke and Tom Rush.

New Century Theatre THEATER
(☏ 413-585-3220; www.newcenturytheatre.org) One of the best regional theater companies in the US stages works by playwrights such as Wendy Wasserstein and Northampton's own Sam Rush. Performances are held at the Mendenhall Center on the Smith College campus.

Academy of Music Theatre THEATER
(☏ 413-584-3220; www.academyofmusictheatre.com; 274 Main St) This gracious, balconied theater is one of the oldest movie houses in the USA (1890), and one of the most beautiful. It shows first-run independent films and books all sorts of music concerts from folk to cabaret as well as theatrical troupes.

Diva's LESBIAN
(www.divasofnoho.com; 492 Pleasant St; ☉ Wed-Sat) Though you can find girl-on-girl action in just about every square inch of Northampton, gals might consider dropping by Diva's, the city's main gay-centric dance club that keeps its patrons sweaty thanks to a steady diet of thumping house music.

ℹ Information

Greater Northampton Chamber of Commerce (☏ 413-584-1900; www.explorenorthampton.com; 99 Pleasant St; ☉ 9am-5pm Mon-Fri; 10am-2pm Sat & Sun) Abounds in all sorts of useful information.

ℹ Getting There & Around

If you're driving, Northampton is 18 miles north of Springfield on I-91. If you don't score a parking spot on Main St, you'll find public parking at Thornes Marketplace (p186) in the town center.

Pioneer Valley Transit Authority (PVTA; www.pvta.com; ride/daypass $1.25/3) provides bus services (with bike racks) throughout the Five College area, with the Northampton–Amherst route having the most frequent service (ride/daily pass $1.25/3).

Amherst

POP 37,800

A quintessential college town, Amherst is home to the prestigious Amherst College, a pretty 'junior ivy' that borders the town green, as well as the hulking University of Massachusetts and the cozy liberal-arts Hampshire College. The town green, where you'll want to start your explorations, is at the intersection of MA 116 and MA 9. Around the green you'll find a few busy streets containing several leftist shops and restaurants, as well as people in tweed reading books on the lawn.

The town centers of Amherst and Northampton are separated by only a few miles, making the sights and amenities in one convenient to the other.

◎ Sights & Activities

The most exciting thing to do is poke around the center of town, browsing through used-book stores and hanging out on the green. Should you grow bored, there are a few other treats in store.

Emily Dickinson Museum   MUSEUM
(☑ 413-542-8161; www.emilydickinsonmuseum.org; 280 Main St; adult/child $10/5; ◎ 10am-5pm Wed-Mon) During her lifetime, Emily Dickinson (1830–86) published only seven poems, but after her death more than 1000 of her poems were discovered and published, and her verses on love, nature and immortality

have made her one of the most important poets in the US.

The museum consists of two buildings, the Dickinson Homestead, where Emily lived in near-seclusion, and the next-door Evergreens, where her brother Austin lived. Unless you're terribly keen on everything Dickinson, you'll want to stick to the shorter Homestead tour. Opening hours vary outside of summer, so call ahead.

**Eric Carle Museum of
Picture Book Art**   MUSEUM
(☑ 413-658-1100; www.carlemuseum.org; 125 W Bay Rd; adult/child $9/6; ◎ 10am-4pm Mon-Fri, 10am-5pm Sat, noon-5pm Sun; ⊕) Cofounded by the author and illustrator of *The Very Hungry Caterpillar,* this superb museum celebrates book illustrations from around the world with rotating exhibits in three galleries, as well as a permanent collection. All visitors (grown-ups included) are encouraged to express their own artistic sentiments in the hands-on art studio.

**Beneski Museum of
Natural History**   MUSEUM
(www.amherst.edu/museums/naturalhistory; 11 Barrett Hill Rd; ◎ 11am-4pm Tue-Sun & 6-10pm Thu) FREE Kids will dig the enormous woolly mammoth and dinosaur skeletons at this museum on the campus of Amherst College.

Atkins Farms Country Market   FARM
(☑ 413-253-9528; www.atkinsfarms.com; 1150 West St/MA 116; ◎ 7am-8pm; ⊕) FREE This farm produce center and local institution, about 3 miles south of Amherst, offers maple sugar products in spring, garden produce in summer and apple picking in the fall. Call about other activities, such as a scarecrow-making workshop in October, that take

---

LOCAL KNOWLEDGE

GHOSTS OF AMHERST

For a peek at Amherst's colorful past, make your way to the West Cemetery, behind Baku's restaurant on N Pleasant St. Here you'll find the graves of Amherst's notables, including Emily Dickinson. To spot her stone, follow the main paved path to the far end of the cemetery; the Dickinson family plot borders the left side of the path.

Somewhat oddly, one of the town's most interesting artworks is also hidden back here, totally out of sight from the road. And lucky you, you'll get to examine it on your return from Dickinson's plot. The ghosts of Amherst come alive on a brilliant mural covering the backside of buildings bordering the cemetery. You'll see, painted larger than life, everyone from local farmer Howard Atkins to famed poet Robert Frost, a professor at Amherst College until his death in 1963. And, of course, Emily herself.

place throughout the year. A deli-bakery sells a full array of picnic supplies.

🛏 Sleeping

Be aware of the college schedules when planning a visit. It's wise to book as far in advance as possible if planning a trip for late August or mid-May. The Amherst Area Chamber of Commerce has a list of more than two dozen member B&Bs.

★ Lord Jeffery Inn   INN $$
(☑ 413-256-8200; www.lordjefferyinn.com; 30 Boltwood Ave; r incl breakfast from $185; ❄ ☎) 🖉 Hands down the finest place in Amherst to lay your head. Fresh off a multimillon-dollar restoration, this Colonial-era inn has reopened as a pampering boutique operation that masterfully fuses traditional fittings with mod conveniences. It hums with college town character, from the organic toiletries and farm-to-table menu to the classic setting overlooking Amherst Green.

Amherst Inn   B&B $$
(☑ 413-253-5000; www.allenhouse.com; 257 Main St; r incl breakfast $105-195; ❄ ☎) A stately, three-story Victorian with handsome Tudor detailing, this classic B&B also offers plenty of appeal in price and comfort. It books heavily with return guests but a nearby sister operation, the Allen House, adds another half-dozen rooms to the mix.

UMass Hotel   HOTEL $$
(☑ 877-822-2110; www.umasshotel.com; 1 Campus Center Way; r from $140; ❄ ☎) Staying at this hotel run by UMass' hospitality program provides all the pluses and minuses of campus life. Guests have plenty of contact with students and are smack in the heart of all the action UMass has to offer. The rooms are pleasant enough, though the cement walls and institutional bedding may leave you feeling like you've stumbled into a dorm.

> ### ⓘ FIVE COLLEGES NIGHT SCENE
>
> To sample from the ever-changing cultural platter served up by the five colleges, pick up a copy of the *Five College Calendar* on any campus, or take a look online at http://calendar.fivecolleges.edu. Many of the lectures, plays, and musical and dance performances are either free or charge just nominal fees.

🍴 Eating

Being a college town, Amherst has many places near the town green peddling pizza, sandwiches, burritos and fresh-brewed coffee. Competition is fierce and quality is high, making the town a fun place to be at lunch time.

Antonio's Pizza by the Slice   PIZZERIA $
(☑ 413-253-0808; www.antoniospizza.com; 31 N Pleasant St; slices $3; ☉ 10am-2am) Amherst's most popular pizza place features excellent slices made with a truly vast variety of toppings. Bizarro as some offerings are, the place comes across as authentic – old brick building, white and red awning.

Lone Wolf   CAFE $
(☑ 413-256-4643; www.thelonewolf.biz; 63 Main St; mains $5-10; ☉ 7am-2pm; 🖉) Thanks to the friendly wait staff and its use of local, organic ingredients, the Lone Wolf has earned itself a strong fan base, especially among vegans, for its superb breakfasts (*huevos rancheros*, crepes, Benedicts) served until closing.

Baku's African Restaurant   AFRICAN $$
(www.bakusafricanrestaurant.com; 197 N Pleasant St; mains $7-14; ☉ noon-8pm Mon-Thu, noon-9pm Fri & Sat) Missing mama's cooking? The flavors may be a bit more exotic here, but with pots simmering on the stove and just five tables, this is real home cooking, Nigerian style. Chef-owner Chichi Ononibaku whips up everything from scratch. Think black-eyed peas with plantains, melon-seed soup and curried goat meat – oh, mama!

★ Chez Albert   FRENCH $$$
(☑ 413-253-3811; www.chezalbert.net; 188 N Pleasant St; lunch $10-14, dinner mains $24-26; ☉ 11:30am-2pm Tue-Fri, 5-9pm Mon-Sat) Want to impress a date? Take a seat at one of the coppertop tables at this chic bistro serving up the best French fare in the valley. The menu changes to take advantage of seasonal fare but includes all the traditional mainstays like escargot, pâté and Boulonnais seafood stew, expertly prepared.

The A-team also manages the kitchen at lunch, offering tempting midday deals that don't slack.

🍷 Drinking & Entertainment

With nearly 30,000 college students letting off steam when Friday rolls around, the pubs in Amherst overflow on the weekends.

PEACE PAGODA

The world could certainly do with a little more peace these days, and a group of monks, nuns and volunteers are doing their part from the top of a hill outside the pea-sized town of Leverett.

There are over 80 so-called peace pagodas all over the globe, and their mission is simple – to spread peace. The Leverett Peace Pagoda (☑413-367-2202; www.new englandpeacepagoda.com; 100 Cave Hill Rd) was the first in the western hemisphere, and is run by members of the nonproselytizing Nipponzan Myohoji sect of Buddhism. But no matter what your spiritual inclination, a visit to this scenically set peace pagoda will leave you feeling profoundly serene.

The centerpiece is a stupa – a 100ft-tall white bell-shaped monument to Buddha, meant to be circumambulated, not entered.

To get here from Amherst, take MA 9 west until MA 116 north, then turn onto MA 63 north and follow it 7 miles. Turn right onto Jackson Hill Rd and then right onto Cave Hill Rd. Parking is about half a mile up the road. The last half-mile is accessible only by foot.

Moan & Dove   BAR
(☑413-256-1710; www.moananddove.com; 460 West St; ☺3pm-1am Mon-Fri, 1pm-1am Sat & Sun) The folks at this small, dark saloon near Hampshire College sure know their beer, and their 150 bottled and 20 draft beers are top-notch – try a Belgian lambic, the only type of commercially available beer made with wild yeast.

Black Sheep Café   LIVE MUSIC
(www.blacksheepdeli.com; 79 Main St; ☺7am-9pm) This bustling deli cafe typically has live music Thursday through Sunday, and not necessarily at night. If lucky, you might knock back some coffee and a bagel while a bluegrass band helps you through Sunday morning.

UMass Fine Arts Center   PERFORMING ARTS
(http://fac.umass.edu; UMass campus) The region's largest concert hall is on the University of Massachusetts campus. It offers a full program of classical and world-music concerts, theater and dance.

❶ Information

Amherst Area Chamber of Commerce
(☑413-253-0700; www.amherstarea.com; 28 Amity St; ☺8:30am-4:30pm Mon-Fri) In the heart of town, just around the corner from Pleasant St and the town common.

❶ Getting There & Around

BUS
The Pioneer Valley Transit Authority (p177) provides bus service around Amherst and to Northampton, Springfield and other nearby towns. Pick up a day pass for $3.

Deerfield

POP 5125

While the modern commercial center is in South Deerfield, it's Historic Deerfield 6 miles to the north that history buffs swarm to, where zoning and preservation keep the rural village looking like a time warp to the 18th century – sleepy, slow and without much to do other than look at the period buildings.

The main (OK, the only) street of Historic Deerfield is simply called the Street, and it runs parallel to US 5/MA 10. Follow the signs from I-91.

◉ Sights & Activities

Historic Deerfield Village   HISTORIC BUILDINGS
(☑413-774-5581; www.historic-deerfield.org; the Street; adult/child $12/5; ☺9:30am-4:30pm) The main street of Historic Deerfield Village escaped the ravages of time and now presents a noble prospect: a dozen houses dating from the 1700s and 1800s, well preserved and filled with period furnishings that reflect their original occupants. It costs nothing to stroll along the Street and admire the buildings from outside.

Buying a ticket allows you to go inside and take half-hour tours of several of the buildings. Guides in the houses provide insightful commentary.

LOCAL KNOWLEDGE

MONTAGUE BOOKMILL

You gotta love a place whose motto is 'books you don't need in a place you can't find.' Luckily, both claims are slightly exaggerated. On an unassuming road in the sleepy town of Montague lies the **Montague Bookmill** (☑ 413-367-9206; www.montaguebookmill.com; 440 Greenfield Rd; ⊙ 10am-6pm Sun-Wed, 10am-8pm Thu-Sat), a converted cedar gristmill from 1842 whose multiple rooms contain oodles of used books and couches on which to read them. Its westward-facing walls are punctuated by large windows that overlook the roiling Sawmill River and its waterfall.

An art gallery, antiques shop and casual cafe share the same awesome river view – making it a fun place to join locals whiling away a lazy afternoon.

From Amherst, take MA 63 to the Montague Center exit. Take a left off the exit and turn right onto Main St. Continue through the town center, bearing left after the village green onto Greenfield Rd; the mill is on the left.

Quinnetukut II Riverboat Cruise   BOAT TOUR
(⊙ late Jun–mid-Oct; 🚗) For a junket on the Connecticut River, catch a riverboat cruise on the *Quinnetukut II*. A lecturer fills you in on the history, geology and ecology of the river during the 12-mile, 1½-hour ride, and you'll pass under the elegant French King Bridge. Cruises are run from late June to mid-October by the **Northfield Mountain Recreation & Environmental Center** (☑ 800-859-2960; www.firstlightpower.com/northfield/riverboat.asp; MA 63; adult/child $12/6; ⊙ cruises 11am, 1:15pm & 3pm Fri-Sun).

To get to the departure point, take I-91 north to exit 27, then MA 2 east, then MA 63 north. Call ahead for reservations.

🛏 Sleeping & Eating

Deerfield Inn   INN $$$
(☑ 413-774-5587; www.deerfieldinn.com; the Street; r incl breakfast $220-315; ❄ 🕸 🐾) This establishment, smack in the heart of the historic district, has 24 modernized, spacious rooms. The inn, built in 1884, was destroyed by fire and rebuilt in 1981. During the tourist season, the inn's tavern serves lunch fare.

ℹ Information

Hall Tavern Visitor Center (☑ 413-775-7133; www.historic-deerfield.org; the Street; ⊙ 9:30am-4:30pm) In town, across from the Deerfield Inn, this center has maps, brochures and handles the ticket sales.

Shelburne Falls

POP 1890

This artisan community's main drag (Bridge St) is tiny and charming, only three blocks long but with a passel of interesting galleries and craft shops. Forming the background are mountains, the Deerfield River and a pair of picturesque bridges that cross it – one made of iron, the other covered in flowers.

Shelburne Falls is just off MA 2 on MA 116.

👁 Sights & Activities

Bridge of Flowers   BRIDGE
FREE Shelburne Falls lays on the hype a bit thick, yet one can't deny that its bridge of flowers makes for a photogenic civic centerpiece. Volunteers have been maintaining it since 1929. Over 500 varieties of flowers, shrubs and vines flaunt their colors on the 400ft-long span from early spring through to late fall. Access to the bridge is from Water St.

Glacial Potholes   RIVER
(Deerfield Ave) **FREE** Stones trapped swirling in the roiling Deerfield River have been grinding into the rock bed at this location ever since the ice age. The result: 50 near-perfect circles in the riverbed, including the largest known glacial pothole (39ft diameter) in the world.

A hydroelectric dam overlooking this site now controls the flow of the river over the potholes, so it's possible that on your visit the water will be completely obscuring the holes. Either way it's worth a look – if the flow is a trickle, you readily see the circles; if it's raging, you'll feel like you're at Niagara Falls. The potholes are at the end of Deerfield Ave.

Deerfield Valley Canopy Tours   ADVENTURE SPORTS
(☑ 800-532-7483; www.deerfieldzipline.com; 7 Main St/MA 2, Charlemont; zip $94; ⊙ 10am-5pm)

Ready to fly? This zip line lets you unleash your inner Tarzan on a treetop glide above the Deerfield River Valley. The three-hour outing includes three rappels and 11 zips that get progressively longer. The hardest part is stepping off the first platform – the rest is pure exhilaration!

Children are welcome to join in the fun as long as they are at least 10 years old and weigh a minimum of 70 pounds. Charlemont is 7 miles west of Shelburne Falls.

Zoar Outdoor RAFTING
(🖉800-532-7483; www.zoaroutdoor.com; 7 Main St/MA 2, Charlemont; tours from $30; ⊗9am-5pm; 🖈) This outfitter offers all sorts of splashy fun from white-water rafting to canoeing and kayaking the Deerfield River. No experience? No problem. Zoar's enthusiastic guides adeptly provide newbies with all the ABCs. It's a family-friendly scene with several activities geared especially for kids.

🛌 Sleeping

Dancing Bear Guest House GUESTHOUSE $$
(🖉413-625-9281; www.dancingbearguesthouse. com; 22 Mechanic St; r incl breakfast $129; 🕸🛜) Everything the town has to offer is within easy walking distance of this c 1825 guesthouse. The owners are welcoming, the breakfast home-cooked and the rooms squeaky clean. It's like staying with old friends – a perfect choice for travelers who want a truly local experience.

★Kenburn Orchards B&B B&B $$$
(🖉413-625-6116; www.kenburnorchards.com; 1394 Mohawk Trail/MA 2; r incl breakfast $139-249; 🕸) Foodies take note: if a gourmet home-cooked breakfast is as important as the

room, then this country farmhouse takes top billing. The host lays out a candlelit three-course spread that begins with fresh-baked breads and homemade jams from berries grown here on the farm.

Devoid of the floral excess that typifies so many New England B&Bs, the three comfortable guest rooms have an agreeable simplicity. It's 3 miles west of exit 26 on I-91, convenient to both Deerfield and Shelburne Falls.

🍴 Eating

West End Pub PUB $$
(🖉413-625-6246; www.westendpubinfo.com; 16 State St; mains $8-15; ⊗11am-9pm Tue-Sun) Shelburne Falls' favorite place for a drink also serves an expanded menu of tasty pub fare. Best of all, it has a fantastic deck jutting out above the Deerfield River and directly overlooking the Bridge of Flowers.

Gypsy Apple Bistro FUSION $$$
(🖉413-625-6345; 65 Bridge St; mains $20-30; ⊗5-9pm Wed-Sun) When a place starts you off with warm bread and olive-caper tapenade you know it's gonna be good. The menu showcases French-inspired fare with a New England twist, like rainbow trout in sherry butter or gnocchi with local mushrooms. Seating is limited, so call ahead for reservations.

🍷 Drinking & Entertainment

Mocha Maya's CAFE
(🖉413-625-6292; www.mochamayas.com; 417 Bridge St; ⊗6:30am-5pm, later some Fri & Sat; 🛜) 🖉 No matter what your thirst, Mocha Maya's is the place, pouring everything from organic fair-trade coffee to blackberry

---

MASSACHUSETTS LEAF PEEPS

Mohawk Trail For the finest fall foliage drive in Massachusetts, head west on MA 2, from Greenfield to Williamstown (p206) on this 63-mile route. The lively Deerfield River slides alongside, with roaring, bucking stretches of white water that turn leaf-peeping into an adrenaline sport for kayakers.

Mt Greylock State Reservation (p207; www.mass.gov/dcr/parks/mtGreylock) The drive to the summit is long and steep, with gasp-inducing views. The road winds ever upward into a colorful tapestry as it approaches Massachusetts' highest peak. At the top you'll be rewarded with a stunning scene of reds and yellow and a vista that stretches well into New Hampshire, Vermont and New York.

Northern Berkshire Fall Foliage Parade (www.fallfoliageparade.com) If you're in the area for the leaves, catch this festival in North Adams on the first Sunday in October. Music, food and fun.

martinis. Occasional live music and poetry readings as well.

Information

Shelburne Falls Visitor Center (☑413-625-2544; www.shelburnefalls.com; 75 Bridge St; ⊙10am-4pm Mon-Sat, noon-3pm Sun) Helps with accommodations in the area.

THE BERKSHIRES

Few places in America combine culture with rural countryside as deftly as the Berkshire hills, home to Tanglewood, Jacob's Pillow and the Massachusetts stretch of the Appalachian Trail. Extending from the highest point in the state – Mt Greylock – southward to the Connecticut state line, the Berkshires have been a summer refuge for more than a century, when the rich and famous arrived to build summer 'cottages' of grand proportions, many of which now survive as inns or performance venues. On summer weekends when the sidewalks are scorching in Boston and New York, crowds of city dwellers jump in their cars and head for the Berkshire breezes.

Great Barrington & Around

POP 7100

Main St used to consist of Woolworth's, hardware stores, thrift shops and a run-down diner. These have given way to artsy boutiques, antique shops, coffeehouses and restaurants, so much so that locals are beginning to call their town 'Little SoHo,' perhaps to appeal to the many city travelers who are now stopping to shop and eat at the best selection of restaurants in the region. The Housatonic River flows through the center of town just east of Main St/US 7, the central thoroughfare.

◉ Sights & Activities

Most of your time in town will be spent strolling along the pedestrian-scaled Main St, with its mild bustle, handful of shops and dozen or so restaurants. After an hour or two's rest in small-town America, you might consider a hike in the hills.

Bartholomew's Cobble NATURE RESERVE
(☑413-229-8600; www.thetrustees.org; US 7; adult/child $5/1; ⊙sunrise-sunset) Ten miles

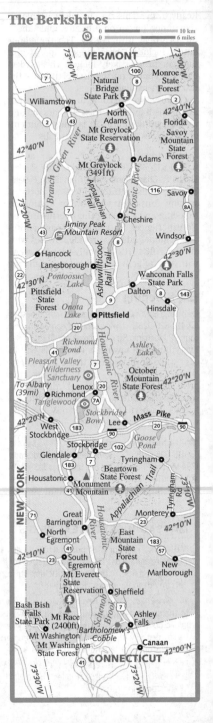

The Berkshires

south of Great Barrington along US 7 and MA 7A toward Ashley Falls brings you to Bartholomew's Cobble, a 'cobble' being a high, rocky knoll of limestone, marble or quartzite. The highly alkaline soil of this 329-acre reservation supports an unusual variety of trees, flowers, moss and especially ferns. Five miles of hiking trails provide routes for enjoying the cobble and the woods, which are set beneath a flyway used by over 200 species of birds. Try the Ledges Trail that weaves along the Housatonic River.

Monument Mountain
NATURE RESERVE

(📞413-298-3239; www.thetrustees.org; US 7; ⊙sunrise-sunset) **FREE** Less than 5 miles north of Great Barrington center on US 7 is Monument Mountain, which has two hiking trails to the 1642ft summit of Squaw Peak. From the top you'll get fabulous views all the way to Mt Greylock in the northwestern corner of the state and to the Catskills in New York.

Windy Hill Farm
FARM

(📞413-298-3217; www.windyhillfarminc.com; 686 Stockbridge Rd/US 7; ⊙9am-5pm) If you hop in the car and drive, you're bound to find several farms where you can pick seasonal produce at harvest times. The setting can be overwhelmingly beautiful in the fall. A favorite is Windy Hill Farm, about 5 miles north of Great Barrington, where more than a score of apple varieties, from pucker-sour to candy-sweet, are yours for the autumn picking. Summer is the blueberry-picking season.

🛏 Sleeping

Beartown State Forest
CAMPGROUND $

(📞413-528-0904; www.mass.gov/dcr; 69 Blue Hill Rd, Monterey; tent sites $16-19) It's mostly backpackers who stay at this quiet campground on the Appalachian Trail, 8 miles east of Great Barrington via MA 23. It has 12 basic sites that overlook 35-acre Benedict Pond.

Mt Washington State Forest
CAMPGROUND $

(📞413-528-0330; www.mass.gov/dcr; East St, Mt Washington; tent sites $14-17) The forest contains the glorious Bash Bish Falls as well as 30 miles of trails. Some 15 wilderness campsites are available for the adventurous.

Lantern House Motel
MOTEL $$

(📞413-528-2350; www.thelanternhousemotel. com; 256 Stockbridge Rd/MA 7, Great Barrington; r incl breakfast $55-200; ❇🛜🛏🐕) The decor's a bit dated, but the cheerful operators of this independent family-run motel keep everything spotlessly clean and the beds are damn comfortable. After all, that's what you stopped for, right? Most of the rooms are spacious, too, so if you've got kids with you they won't be tripping all over each other here.

The 3-acre backyard with its saltwater pool and playground gear offer kid-centric diversions.

Wainwright Inn
B&B $$$

(📞413-528-2062; www.wainwrightinn.com; 518 S Main St, Great Barrington; r incl breakfast $149-249; ❇🛜) Great Barrington's finest place to lay your head, this c 1766 inn exudes historical appeal from its wraparound porches and spacious parlors to the period room decor. Most of the eight guest rooms come with working fireplaces. Breakfast is a decadent experience. The inn is a short walk from the center of town on a busy road.

Old Inn on the Green & Thayer House
INN $$$

(📞413-229-7924; www.oldinn.com; 134 Hartsville New Marlborough Rd/MA 57, New Marlborough; r incl breakfast $260-385; ❇) Once a relay stop on a post road, the Old Inn, c 1760, is exactly what most people picture when they think New England country inn. The dining rooms are lit entirely by candlelight, antiques furnish each of the five rooms and some have fireplaces.

Ask about dinner-and-lodging specials that add a three-course dinner for less than the regular room rates. The innkeepers also operate the Thayer House, a stone's throw

> ### ℹ BERKSHIRES SCOOP
>
> **Berkshire Grown** (p196) Online directory of pick-your-own orchards, farmers markets and restaurants offering organic local ingredients.
>
> **Berkshires Visitors Bureau** (📞413-743-4500; www.berkshires.org; 3 Hoosac St; ⊙10am-5pm) Has the scoop on accommodations and activities.
>
> **Berkshires Week** (www.berkshire eagle.com/berkshiresweek) Look at this newspaper's site for updated arts and theater listings.
>
> **See the Berkshires** (www.berkshires. com) Extensive recommendations for dining, lodging, activities, galleries and more.

away and equally atmospheric, but quieter since it doesn't have a restaurant.

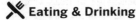 Eating & Drinking

Surrounded by farms and favored by back-to-earthers, Great Barrington is a natural for the eat-local movement. Any excuse to be here at mealtime will do.

Berkshire Co-op Market Cafe   CAFE $
(www.berkshire.coop; 42 Bridge St; meals $6-10; ⊙8am-8pm Mon-Sat, 10am-8pm Sun; ⏲) ✎ You don't need to spend a bundle to eat green, wholesome and local. This cafe inside the Berkshire Co-op Market, just off Main St, has a crunchy farm-fresh salad bar, generous made-to-order sandwiches (both meat and veggie) and fair-trade coffees.

Gypsy Joynt   CAFE $$
(www.gypsyjoyntcafe.net; 293 Main St; mains $8-15; ⊙11am-midnight Wed-Sun, 11am-4pm Mon; ⏳⏲) This is a family affair, with three generations pitching in to serve innovative pizzas, beefy sandwiches and bountiful salads. Almost everything is organic and locally sourced. The Gypsy Joynt also throws in great coffee, live music and a super boho atmosphere.

Barrington Brewery   BREWPUB $$
(www.barringtonbrewery.net; 420 Stockbridge Rd; mains $8-20; ⊙11:30am-9:30pm; ⏳) ✎ Solar-powered microbrews – you know you're in Great Barrington! The dark, hoppy brews are the star of the show here but the grass-fed beef burgers make a decent complement and the outdoor seating takes it up a notch on a balmy summer night.

Allium   MODERN AMERICAN $$$
(⏺413-528-2118; www.alliumberkshires.com; 42 Railroad St; mains $12-28; ⊙5-9pm) ✎ For an atmospheric date, try the New American cuisine in this stylish restaurant, which manages to combine a repurposed barn door, a pretty jigsaw-esque panel of wooden shingles, flower boxes and modern Scandinavian influences without being heavy-handed. Ilium subscribes to the slow-food movement with a seasonal menu that gravitates towards fresh organic produce, cheeses and meats.

⭐**Castle Street Café**   MODERN AMERICAN $$$
(⏺413-528-5244; www.castlestreetcafe.com; 10 Castle St; mains $21-29; ⊙5-9pm Wed-Mon; ⏲) ✎ The menu reads like a who's who of local farms: Ioka Valley Farm grass-fed natural beef, Rawson Brook chevre and Equinox Farm mesclun greens. Chef-owner Michael Ballon's preparations range from innovative vegetarian fare to classics like rack of lamb.

The setting is as engaging as the food, with both a jazzy bar with a pub menu and an art-filled dining room. Prime time to dine is on Friday or Saturday, when there's live jazz.

⭐**John Andrews Restaurant**   MODERN AMERICAN $$$
(⏺413-528-3469; www.jarestaurant.com; 224 MA 23, Egremont; mains $24-35; ⊙5-9pm Thu-Tue) ✎ Celebrated chef Dan Smith turns out organic mountain lamb, a daily risotto and a fine Italian–New American menu with most items grown on nearby farms. The setting, a rustic 19th-century farmhouse overlooking a garden, makes a perfect match for the menu. Excellent desserts and wine selection, too.

The $30 prix fixe specials on Sundays are absolutely worth the 6-mile trek west from Great Barrington.

☆ Entertainment

For up-to-date entertainment listings, pick up a copy of the free *Berkshires Week* at bars and restaurants.

ⓘ THINGS FROM FARMS

Undeniably, part of the joy of a drive through the Berkshires – or any part of rural New England, for that matter – is stumbling unexpectedly on a small farm stand and stopping to chat for a while with the farmer who grew those apples or blueberries herself.

But if you don't want to leave it all to chance, or are curious about which restaurants in the region stock their kitchens with farm-fresh vittles, pick up or check out online the Berkshire Grown (www.berkshiregrown.org), a guide to locally grown food, as well as other hand-crafted or hand-raised goodies such as cheeses, maple syrup and meats.

The seasonally published directory lists pick-your-own farms, farmers markets and member restaurants like Castle Street Café in Great Barrington and Mezze Bistro & Bar in Williamstown. Special events – agricultural fairs, farm dinners and garden tours – are announced as well.

BASH BISH FALLS

In the very southwest corner of the state, near the New York state line, is Bash Bish Falls (www.mass.gov/dcr; Falls Rd, Mt Washington; ☉ sunrise-sunset) FREE, the largest waterfall in Massachusetts. The water feeding the falls runs down a series of gorges before the torrent is sliced in two by a massive boulder perched directly above a pool. There it drops as a picture-perfect double waterfall. These 60ft-high falls are a popular spot for landscape painters to set up their easels.

To get there from Great Barrington, take MA 23 west to South Egremont. Turn right onto MA 41 south and then take the immediate right onto Mt Washington Rd (which becomes East St) and continue for 7.5 miles. Turn right onto Cross Rd, then right onto West St and continue 1 mile. Turn left onto Falls Rd and follow that for 1.5 miles. The parking lot and trailhead will be on your left. The hike takes about 20 minutes.

Mahaiwe Performing Arts Center
PERFORMING ARTS

(www.mahaiwe.org; 14 Castle St) Culture vultures will find an eclectic menu of events at this classic theater, from David Bromberg concerts to Chinese opera and modern dance.

Guthrie Center
LIVE MUSIC

(☑ 413-528-1955; www.guthriecenter.org; 4 Van Deusenville Rd; ☉ May-Sep) The old church made famous in Arlo Guthrie's *Alice's Restaurant* hosts folk concerts by the likes of Tom Paxton, Country Joe McDonald and, of course, local boy Arlo himself. It's a cozy setting with just 100 seats, so book in advance.

ℹ Information

Southern Berkshire Chamber of Commerce
(☑ 413-528-1510; www.southernberkshire
chamber.com; 362 Main St; ☉ 10am-6pm Thu-Mon) Maintains a kiosk in front of the town hall that's well stocked with maps, restaurant menus and accommodations lists.

ℹ Getting There & Away

Most travelers arrive by car on US 7, which runs through the center of town. Otherwise, **Peter Pan** (www.peterpanbus.com) buses can drop you off in the center of town.

Tyringham

POP 330

The village of Tyringham, between Lee and Monterey, is the perfect destination for an excursion into the heart of the countryside. Once the home of a Shaker community (1792–1874), Tyringham is now famous for its Gingerbread House, an architectural fantasy designed at the beginning of the 20th century by sculptor Henry Hudson Kitson, whose best-known work – a statue of Captain Parker as a minuteman – graces the Lexington Green. Kitson's fairy-tale thatched-roofed cottage is at 75 Main St on the north side of the village; it's readily visible from the road, though the interior is not open to the general public.

After leaving Tyringham bear west at the fork in the road toward Monterey and continue your journey snaking over gentle hills and past farmland along the scenic back road into Great Barrington. En route you'll discover some woodsy places to hike, a roadside pond that begs a dip and a couple of art studios.

Stockbridge

POP 1950

Take a good look down Stockbridge's wide Main St. Notice anything? More specifically, notice anything missing? Not one stoplight stutters the view, not one telephone pole blights the picture-perfect scene – it looks very much the way Norman Rockwell might have seen it.

In fact, Rockwell did see it – he lived and worked in Stockbridge during the last 25 years of his life. The town attracts summer and fall visitors en masse, who come to stroll the streets, inspect the shops and sit in the rockers on the porch of the historic Red Lion Inn. And they come by the busload to visit the Norman Rockwell Museum on the town's outskirts. All that fossilized picturesqueness bears a price. Noticeably absent from the village center is the kind of vitality that you find in the neighboring towns of Great Barrington and Lenox.

The center of Stockbridge is at the intersection of MA 102 and MA 7. In town, MA 102 becomes Main St. The town center is compact, just a few blocks long and easily explored on foot.

◉ Sights & Activities

Norman Rockwell Museum   MUSEUM
(☑ 413-298-4100; www.nrm.org; 9 Glendale Rd/MA 183; adult/child $16/5; ☉ 10am-5pm) Norman Rockwell (1894–1978) was born in New York City, and he sold his first magazine cover illustration to the *Saturday Evening Post* in 1916. In the following half-century he did another 321 covers for the *Post,* as well as illustrations for books, posters and many other magazines on his way to becoming the most popular illustrator in US history.

His sense of humor can be seen in Triple Self Portrait (1960), where an older Rockwell looks in a mirror, only to paint a much younger version of himself.

The museum has the largest collection of Rockwell's original art and also hosts exhibitions of other wholesome, feel-good artists such as David Macaulay, of The Way Things Work fame. The grounds contain Rockwell's studio, too, which was moved here from behind his Stockbridge home.

To find the museum follow MA 102 west from Stockbridge and turn left (south) on MA 183.

Naumkeag   HISTORIC ESTATE
(www.thetrustees.org; 5 Prospect St; adult/child $15/free; ☉ 10am-5pm late May–mid-Oct) Designed by the renowned architect Stanford White in 1885, this 44-room Gilded Age 'cottage' was the summer retreat of Joseph Hodges Choate, a former US ambassador to England. The estate retains so much of its original character that you almost expect Choate to be sitting at the breakfast table.

The influence of Choate's travels abroad are visible not only in the home's rich and eclectic interior but also in the acres of surrounding **formal gardens** with their fountains, sculpture and themed plantings. The prominent landscape architect Fletcher Steele spent some three decades laying them out and establishing the plantings. Strolling through the gardens alone is worth the price of admission.

To get there, follow Pine St from the Red Lion Inn to Prospect St.

Chesterwood   MUSEUM
(☑ 413-298-3579; www.chesterwood.org; 4 Williamsville Rd; adult/child $16/free; ☉ 10am-5pm late May–mid-Oct) This pastoral 122-acre plot was 'heaven' to its owner Daniel Chester French (1850–1931), the sculptor best known for his great seated statue of Abraham Lincoln in the Lincoln Memorial in Washington, DC. French lived in New York City but spent most summers after 1897 here at Chesterwood, his gracious Berkshire estate.

French's more than 100 great public works, mostly monumental, made him a wealthy man. His house and studio are substantially as they were when he lived and worked here, with nearly 500 pieces of sculpture, finished and unfinished, in the barnlike studio. The space and the art have a way of beguiling even those who aren't sculpture enthusiasts.

To get there take MA 138 south 0.75 miles past the Norman Rockwell Museum, go right onto Mohawk Lake Rd and left onto Willow St, which becomes Williamsville Rd.

Mission House   HISTORIC BUILDING
(www.thetrustees.org; 19 Main St; adult/child $6/3; ☉ 10am-5pm) Swing by this classic c 1739 Colonial home, a National Historic Landmark, if just to view it from the outside. It was home to John Sergeant, the first missionary to the region's native Mohicans. The interior contains a collection of 18th-century American furniture and decorative arts.

Mission House is on the corner of Main and Sergeant Sts, a five-minute walk west of the Red Lion Inn.

🛏 Sleeping

Red Lion Inn   HISTORIC HOTEL $$
(☑ 413-298-5545; www.redlioninn.com; 30 Main St; r with shared bath $155-195, with private bath $245-345; @ 🛜 ⊠ ✷) This aging white-frame hotel is at the very heart of Stockbridge village, marking the intersection of Main St and MA 7. It's been the town's focal point since 1773, though it was completely rebuilt after a fire in 1897. Many rooms in the main building have fireplaces, old print wallpaper, classic moldings and white linens.

Stockbridge Country Inn   INN $$$
(☑ 413-298-4015; www.stockbridgecountryinn.com; 26 Glendale Rd/MA 183; r incl breakfast $199-349; 🛜 ✷) Occupying a 19th-century estate house, this is the closest inn to the Norman Rockwell Museum. Antique fittings, four-poster beds and 4 acres of pretty grounds set the tone. But it's the full country breakfast served on a sunny porch overlooking flowery gardens that sets it apart.

CULTURE & FESTIVALS

Aston Magna (www.astonmagna.org) Listen to Bach, Brahms and other early classical music in Great Barrington during June and July.

Big E (p183) You will probably want to hang out with some carnies at New England's largest agriculture fair in West Springfield during September.

Brimfield Antique Show (p179) The world's biggest outdoor antique extravaganza would like you to buy some 19th-century tooth powder. It's held near Sturbridge throughout summer.

Jacob's Pillow (☑ 413-243-9919; www.jacobspillow.org; 385 George Carter Rd; ⊘ Jun-Aug) Most cities' best troupes can't top the stupefying and ground-breaking dance of Jacob's Pillow, which runs from mid-June through August near Lee.

Shakespeare & Company (p203) Relive the Gilded Age at a Shakespearian play performed on the grounds of The Mount in Lenox in July and August.

Tanglewood Music Festival (p201) For many, the Berkshires' most famous festival and its outstanding orchestral music is reason enough to return to Lenox each summer.

Williamstown Theatre Festival (☑ 413-597-3400; www.wtfestival.org; 1000 Main St, Williamstown; ⊘ late Jun–late Aug) If you've seen better summer theater, then you're dead and heaven apparently has different seasons.

✖ Eating

Lion's Den   PUB $$
(☑ 413-298-1654; www.redlioninn.com; mains $10-13; ⊘ 4-10pm Mon-Fri, noon-10pm Sat & Sun) Downstairs at the Red Lion Inn, this cocktail lounge serves daily pub specials like chicken pot pie. In fair weather you can dine in the courtyard out back.

Once Upon a Table   AMERICAN $$$
(☑ 413-298-3870; www.onceuponatablebistro. com; 36 Main St; mains $10-30; ⊘ 11am-3pm & 4:30-8:30pm) This bright spot in the Mews shopping arcade serves upscale fare in a sunny dining room. It's the best place in town for lunch, with choices like smoked-salmon-and-chevre omelets. The dinner menu features reliably delicious treats such as pecan-crusted rainbow trout and fine dessert pastries.

Red Lion Inn   AMERICAN $$$
(☑ 413-298-5545; www.redlioninn.com; 30 Main St; mains $10-35; ⊘ 7am-9pm Mon-Fri, 7:30am-9:30pm Sat & Sun) The Red Lion Inn is the main eating venue in Stockbridge. On the stodgy side is the formal dining room, where you can indulge in a roasted native turkey while sitting under a crystal chandelier. More relaxed is the Widow Bingham Tavern, a rustic Colonial pub that serves gourmet sandwiches and many variations on cow.

❶ Information

Stockbridge Chamber of Commerce (www. stockbridgechamber.org; 50 Main St; ⊘ 9am-5pm Mon, Wed & Fri) You can also pick up brochures at the small kiosk opposite the library on Main St in the town center. It's often unstaffed, but the door's always open.

Lee

POP 5950

Welcome to the towniest town in the Berkshires. A main street, both cute and gritty, runs through the center, curving to cross some railroad tracks. On it you'll find a hardware store, a bar and a few places to eat including a proper diner favored by politicians desiring photo ops with working-class folks. Most travelers pass through Lee simply because it's near a convenient exit off the Mass Pike. The main draw is the prestigious Jacob's Pillow dance festival on the outskirts of town.

Lee, just off exit 2 of I-90, is the gateway to Lenox, Stockbridge and Great Barrington. US 20 is Lee's main street, and leads right into Lenox, about a 15-minute drive away.

⊙ Sights

October Mountain State Forest   FOREST
(www.mass.gov/dcr; Center St) **FREE** Most out-of-towners who venture to the Berkshires head to the Mt Greylock State Reservation to see the state's highest peak, and thus leave

October Mountain State Forest, a 16,127-acre state park and the largest tract of green space in Massachusetts, to the locals.

Hidden amid the hardwoods, Buckley Dunton Reservoir – a small body of water stocked with bass – is a great spot for canoeing. For hikers, a 9-mile stretch of the Appalachian Trail pierces the heart of the forest through copses of hemlocks, spruces, birches and oaks. To get there from Lee, follow US 20 west for 3 miles and look for signs.

✫ Festivals & Events

★ Jacob's Pillow   DANCE FESTIVAL
(☑ 413-243-0745; www.jacobspillow.org; 358 George Carter Rd, Becket; ☺ mid-Jun–Aug) Founded by Ted Shawn in an old barn in 1932, Jacob's Pillow is one of the premier summer dance festivals in the USA. Through the years, Alvin Ailey, Merce Cunningham, the Martha Graham Dance Company and other leading interpreters of dance have taken part.

A smorgasbord of free shows and talks allows even those on tight budgets to join in the fun. The festival theaters are in the village of Becket, 8 miles east of Lee along US 20 and MA 8.

🛏 Sleeping

Motels in Lee are clustered around I-90 exit 2, on heavily trafficked US 20. For a list of area accommodations visit www.leelodging.org.

October Mountain State
Forest   CAMPGROUND $
(☑ 877-422-6762; www.mass.gov/dcr; Center St; tent sites $12-14) This state forest campground, near the shores of the Housatonic River, has 47 sites with hot showers. To find the campground, turn east off US 20 onto Center St and follow the signs.

Jonathan Foote 1778 House   B&B $$
(☑ 413-243-4545; www.1778house.com; 1 East St; r incl breakfast $150-245; ✳ 🛜) An old Georgian farmhouse set in spacious grounds with shady maple trees and stone walls. Stay here for antiquated fireplaces, appropriately decorated rooms and hearty breakfasts.

✗ Eating

While Joe's Diner is the main draw, you'll also find a Chinese joint, a good bakery and a health food store in the center of town.

Joe's Diner   DINER $
(☑ 413-243-9756; 85 Center St; mains $4-9; ☺ 5:30am-9pm Mon-Fri, 5:30am-3:30pm Sat, 7am-1pm Sun) There's no better slice of blue-collar Americana in the Berkshires than Joe's Diner, at the north end of Main St. Norman Rockwell's famous painting of a policeman sitting at a counter talking to a young boy, *The Runaway* (1958), was inspired by this diner. Take a look at the repro of it above the counter.

Joe's has barely changed a wink, and not just the stools – think typical bacon-and-eggs diner fare.

❶ Information

Lee Chamber of Commerce (☑ 413-243-0852; www.leechamber.org; 3 Park Pl; ☺ 10am-4pm Mon-Sat) Maintains an information booth on the town green in summer.

Lenox

POP 5025

This gracious, wealthy town is a historical anomaly: its charm was not destroyed by the industrial revolution, and then, prized for its bucolic peace, the town became a summer retreat for wealthy families with surnames like Carnegie, Vanderbilt and Westinghouse, who had made their fortunes by building factories in other towns.

As the cultural heart of the Berkshires, Lenox's illustrious past remains tangibly present today. The superstar among its attractions is the Tanglewood Music Festival, an incredibly popular summer event drawing scores of visitors from New York City, Boston and beyond.

The center of Lenox is compact and easy to get around on foot. Tanglewood is 1.5 miles west of Lenox's center along West St/ MA 183.

◉ Sights & Activities

The Mount   HISTORIC ESTATE
(www.edithwharton.org; 2 Plunkett St; adult/child $18/free; ☺ 10am-5pm May-Oct) Almost 50 years after Nathaniel Hawthorne left his home in Lenox (now part of Tanglewood), another writer found inspiration in the Berkshires. Edith Wharton (1862–1937) came to Lenox in 1899 and proceeded to build her palatial estate, The Mount. When not writing, she would entertain literary friends here, including Henry James.

TANGLEWOOD MUSIC FESTIVAL

Dating from 1934, the Tanglewood Music Festival (☎ 888-266-1200; www.tanglewood. org; 297 West St/MA 183, Lenox; ☉ late Jun-early Sep) is among the most esteemed summertime music events in the world. Symphony, pops, chamber music, jazz and blues are performed from late June through early September. Performance spaces include the 'Shed,' which is anything but – a 6000-seat concert shelter with several sides open to the surrounding lawns.

The weekend Boston Symphony Orchestra concerts pack the largest crowds. Most casual attendees – up to 8000 of them – arrive three or four hours before concert time, staking out good listening spots on the lawn outside the Shed, then break out picnics until the music starts. Some people just spread out a blanket on the lawn, but those with chairs will get a better view.

You can count on renowned cellist Yo-Yo Ma, violinist Joshua Bell and singer James Taylor to perform each summer, along with a run of world-class guest artists and famed conductors.

Concert tickets range from $19 per person for picnic space on the lawn to around $100 for the best seats at the most popular concerts. Lawn tickets for children age 17 and younger are free.

Families should check out Kids' Corner, offered on weekends, where children can participate in musical, arts and crafts projects.

As for food, many people bring prepacked picnic baskets and wine from the gourmet markets in the area. Or with advance notice you can order a picnic basket from the on-site Tanglewood Cafe (☎ 413-637-5240), which also serves a menu of salads and light fare.

Tanglewood is easy to find – just follow the car in front of you! From Lenox center, head west on West St/MA 183 for about 1.5 miles. Ample free concert parking is available, but remember that parking – and, more importantly, unparking – 6000 cars can take time. If your lodging is close, consider walking.

Besides such novels as *The Age of Innocence*, Wharton penned *The Decoration of Houses*, which helped legitimize interior decoration as a profession in the USA. Wharton was also a keen horticulturist and many visitors come here just to wander the magnificent formal gardens. Thanks to a $3 million restoration effort, the gardens have regained much of their original grandeur. And you needn't worry about pesticides and other nasty sprays – as was the case in Edith's day, the gardens are once again maintained using organic practices.

The Mount is on the southern outskirts of Lenox at US 7 and Plunkett St.

Jiminy Peak Mountain Resort   SKIING
(☎ 413-738-5500; www.jiminypeak.com; 37 Corey Rd, Hancock; ☉ 9am-10pm) ∕ In keeping with the Berkshires' ecofriendly green vibe, Jiminy Peak proudly claims title to being the first wind-power-operated ski resort in the country. Its 253ft wind turbine generates up to half the resort's electrical usage. And with 45 trails, and a Left Bank run of 2 miles, Jiminy offers the area's finest skiing.

There are a slew of pricing categories but expect a one-day ski pass to cost around $60 on weekdays, a bit more on weekends. It's an activity center in summer as well, when mountain biking, a ropes course and Segway tours take over the slopes. Jiminy Peak is 18 miles north of Lenox via US 7.

Kripalu Center   YOGA
(☎ 413-448-3400; www.kripalu.org; West St/MA 183) ∕ The premier yoga institute in the northeast, Kripalu breathes tranquility. Set on a lush estate overlooking a calm cerulean lake, this former Jesuit monastery and its new environmentally green annex offer a great opportunity for those wanting to take some time off to pursue inner peace.

Although serious students spend weeks here at a time, the center offers visitor-friendly flexibility. You could get a day pass and join the yoga class, meditation sessions and other holistic offerings for $120, vegetarian meals included. Or you could stay the night for an additional fee, and use Kripalu as a base during your Lenox stay.

Pleasant Valley Wilderness Sanctuary
NATURE RESERVE

(📞413-637-0320; www.massaudubon.org; 472 W Mountain Rd; adult/child $5/3; ⊗ dawn-dusk) This 1300-acre wildlife sanctuary has 7 miles of pleasant walking trails through forests of maples, oaks, beeches and birches. It's not uncommon to see beaver here if you come at dawn or dusk. A nature center is open daily, and you can arrange canoe trips on the Housatonic from here.

To reach the sanctuary, go north on US 7 or MA 7A. Three-quarters of a mile north of the intersection of US 7 and MA 7A, turn left onto W Dugway Rd and go 1.5 miles to the sanctuary.

Arcadian Shop
OUTDOORS

(📞413-637-3010; www.arcadian.com; 91 Pittsfield Rd/US 7; ⊗ 9:30am-6pm Mon-Sat, 11am-5pm Sun) Kennedy Park, just north of downtown Lenox on US 7, is popular with mountain bikers in summer and cross-country skiers in winter. You might also explore the Berkshires' many miles of stunning back roads or paddle down the Housatonic River. The Arcadian Shop rents high-end mountain and road bikes ($35 to $45), kayaks ($35), skis ($25) and snowshoes ($20). Rates are per day.

Berkshire Scenic Railway Museum
MUSEUM

(📞413-637-2210; www.berkshirescenicrailroad.org; 10 Willow Creek Rd; ⊗ 9am-4pm Sat & Sun late May-Oct; 🅰) **FREE** This museum of railroad lore is set up in Lenox's 1903 vintage railroad station. Its model-railroad display is a favorite with kids, and there are toy trains they can play with. The museum is 1.5 miles east of Lenox center, via Housatonic St.

🛏 Sleeping

Lenox has no hotels and only a few motels, but it does have lots of inns. The Tanglewood festival means that many inns require a two- or three-night minimum stay on Friday and Saturday nights in summer. Many thrifty travelers opt to sleep in lower-priced towns like Great Barrington. But if you can afford them, Lenox's inns provide charming digs and memorable stays.

Days Inn
MOTEL $$$

(📞413-637-3560; www.daysinn.com; 194 Pittsfield Rd/US 7; r incl breakfast $90-210; ❋ 🖥 ☒) Shoring up the budget end, this two-story motel on the northern outskirts of Lenox offers a comfortable, if bland, room at an affordable price.

Hampton Inn & Suites Berkshires-Lenox
MOTEL $$$

(wwwl.berkshirehampton.com; 445 Pittsfield Rd/US 7; r incl breakfast $169-249; @ 🖥 ☒) Top choice among the area's motels, the Hampton Inn sits in a quiet location 2 miles north of town.

Cornell in Lenox
B&B $$$

(📞413-637-4800; www.cornellbb.com; 203 Main St; r incl breakfast $145-265; @ 🖥) Spread across three historic houses, this B&B offers good value in a pricey town. When not full, the manager might even bargain a little – so ask about specials. It's no gilded mansion, but the rooms are cozy with the expected amenities and the staff is friendly.

Bordering Kennedy Park at the north side of town, it's well suited for hikers and guests itching for a morning jog before breakfast.

Birchwood Inn
INN $$$

(📞413-637-2600; www.birchwood-inn.com; 7 Hubbard St; r incl breakfast $200-375; ❋ 🖥 ☒) A pretty hilltop inn a couple of blocks from the town center, Birchwood occupies the oldest (1767) home in Lenox. The 11 spacious rooms vary in decor; some swing with a vintage floral design, others are more country classic. Several of the rooms have fireplaces.

Home-cooked breakfasts, perhaps fondue florentine soufflé or blueberry cheese blintzes, served in a fireside dining room stoke up the appeal.

★ Stonover Farm B&B
B&B $$$

(📞413-637-9100; www.stonoverfarm.com; 169 Under Mountain Rd; ste incl breakfast $385-575; ❋ @ 🖥) If you're looking for a break from musty Victorians with floral wallpaper, you'll love this contemporary inn wrapped in a century-old farmhouse. The three suites in the main house groan with unsurpassed, yet casual, luxury. Oversized Jacuzzis, marble bathrooms, wine and cheese in the evening – this is pampering fitting its Tanglewood neighborhood setting.

There are also two very private standalone cottages. One's in a converted 1850s schoolhouse that's ideal for a romantic getaway. The other features an atmospheric stone fireplace, views of a duck pond and enough space for a small family.

Canyon Ranch
SPA RETREAT $$$

(📞413-637-4100; www.canyonranchlenox.com; 165 Kemble St; r incl meals per person from $800;

⊞ ≋ ≋) The well-heeled come from around the world to unwind and soak up the spa facilities at this famed resort. All-inclusive rates include healthy gourmet meals (including vegetarian options), Ayurvedic bodywork, candlelit Euphoria treatments and oodles of saunas, pools and quiet paths.

Should you feel the need to ever leave the grounds, just sign out one of the bicycles and hit the mountain trail.

✖ Eating & Drinking

The following places to eat are on or within a block of Church St, Lenox's main restaurant row.

Haven Cafe & Bakery
CAFE **$$**

(www.havencafebakery.com; 8 Franklin St; mains $7-15; ⊘7am-3pm Mon-Sat, 7am-2pm Sun; ☎ ✐) It looks like a cafe, but the sophisticated food evokes a more upscale experience. Try inventive egg dishes for breakfast or fancy salads and sandwiches for lunch – all highlighting local organic ingredients. Definitely save room for something sweet from the bakery counter.

Nejaime's Wine Cellar
PICNIC BASKETS **$$**

(☑413-637-2221; www.nejaimeswine.com; 60 Main St; picnic basket for two people $53; ⊘9am-9pm Mon-Sat) You can order a Tanglewood picnic basket here, or just pick up a few bottles of wine and some gourmet cheeses to get started on your own creation.

★ Nudel
AMERICAN **$$$**

(☑413-551-7183; www.nudelrestaurant.com; 37 Church St; mains $22-25; ⊘5:30-9:30pm Tue-Sat) A driving force in the area's sustainable-food movement, just about everything on Nudel's menu is seasonally inspired and locally sourced. The back-to-basics approach rings through in dishes like heritage-bred pork chops and the spaetzle pasta with rabbit,

leeks and white beans. Incredible flavors. Nudel has a loyal following and doesn't take reservations, so arrive early to avoid a long wait.

Bistro Zinc
FRENCH **$$$**

(☑413-637-8800; www.bistrozinc.com; 56 Church St; mains $15-30; ⊘11:30am-3pm & 5:30-10pm) The postmodern decor here is all metal surfaces and light woods, with doors made of wine crates. The tin ceiling and black and white floors add to the LA feel. The cuisine features tempting New French offerings like veal cordon bleu with grilled asparagus. Or just slip in after dinner for a glass of wine and style points.

Olde Heritage Tavern
PUB

(www.theheritagetavern.com; 12 Housatonic St; mains $7-15; ⊘11:30am-12:30am Mon-Fri, 8am-12:30am Sat & Sun; ☛) Come to this upbeat tavern for local microbrews on tap and pub fare a cut above the usual. The menu spreads broad and wide: waffles, quesadillas, pizza and steaks. The shady outdoor tables make it a family-friendly option as well.

☆ Entertainment

Shakespeare & Company
THEATER

(☑413-637-1199; www.shakespeare.org; 70 Kemble St; ⊘Tue-Sun) One enjoyable feature of a Berkshires summer is taking in a show by Shakespeare & Company. The repertoire features the Bard's plays as well as contemporary performances. The company stages plays at a variety of locations, including The Mount, Edith Wharton's former estate.

❶ Information

Lenox Chamber of Commerce (☑413-637-3646; www.lenox.org; 18 Main St; ⊘11am-4:30pm Tue-Sat) This office, inside the public library, is a clearinghouse of information on everything from inns to what's going on.

CYCLING THE HOOSIC

When the Boston & Maine Railroad gave up on the corridor between Lanesborough and Adams in 1990, citizens agitated to have it paved over and recast as the 11-mile **Ashuwillticook Rail Trail** (☑413 442 8928; www.mass.gov/dcr). The trail closely follows the Hoosic River and the Cheshire Reservoir through glorious wetlands, with many benches along the way and a handful of rest facilities. It's a fabulous place for cycling, in-line skating or just taking a stroll.

The southern access is on the eastern outskirts of Pittsfield. At the intersection of MA 9 and MA 8, continue 1.5 miles north on MA 8 to the Lanesborough–Pittsfield line. Turn left at the Berkshire Mall Rd entrance to reach the rail trail parking. The northern access is behind the Berkshires Visitors Bureau at 3 Hoosac St in Adams.

ℹ Getting There & Away

The nearest airports are Bradley International in Connecticut and Albany International in New York. **Peter Pan Bus Lines** (www.peterpanbus. com; 5 Walker St) operates between Lenox and Boston. Amtrak trains stop in nearby Pittsfield. If you're driving, Lenox is on MA 7A, just off US 7.

Pittsfield

POP 44,800

The lame jokes about the name of this town are easy to make and not without a modicum of accuracy. Welcome to the service city of the Berkshires, where the trains stop and where one finds the biggest stores. Travelers pause here for the Hancock Shaker Village and the nearby Crane Museum of Papermaking. For information on Pittsfield and the rest of the Berkshires, contact the **Berkshire Chamber of Commerce** (☑ 413-499-4000; www.berkshirechamber.com; 66 Allen St, Pittsfield; ☺ 9am-5pm Mon-Fri).

You'll find something for everyone at the surprisingly impressive **Berkshire Museum** (www.berkshiremuseum.org; 39 South St; adult/child $13/6; ☺ 10am-5pm Mon-Sat, noon-5pm Sun; ⏢), which has a solid collection of Hudson River School artworks and a permanent Alexander Calder exhibit, as well as kid-friendly attractions like a touch-tank aquarium and a hands-on science center.

Since 1879 every single American bill has been printed on paper made by Crane & Co, based in the small mill town of Dalton. This 'Champagne of papers' is made from 100% cotton rag rather than wood, and so is wonderfully strong and creamy as well as environmentally sound. The **Crane Museum of Papermaking** (☑ 413-684-7780; www.crane.

com; 40 Pioneer St, Dalton; ☺ 1-5pm Mon-Fri Jun–mid-Oct) **FREE**, housed in the original stone mill room built in 1844, traces the history of Zenas Crane's enterprise, which is still family-run after seven generations. The videos – on Crane's papermaking process and on counterfeit detection – are fascinating. To get to the museum from Pittsfield, take MA 9 northeast for 5 miles.

While there aren't many places of interest to eat in Pittsfield, **Elizabeth's** (☑ 413-448-8244; 1264 East St; mains $20; ☺ 5-8:30pm Wed-Sat) is a shocking exception. Don't be put off by its location across the street from a vacant General Electric plant, nor by its deceptively casual interior – chefs travel from New York and Boston to sample Tom and Elizabeth Ellis' innovative Italian dishes.

Pittsfield is 7 miles north of Lenox on US 7 at the intersection with MA 9. **Peter Pan** (www.peterpanbus.com) buses operate out of the **Pittsfield Bus Terminal** (1 Columbus Ave). Amtrak trains going to Boston or Albany, New York, stop here.

Williamstown

POP 7750

Home to Williams College, an elite liberal arts college, this small town lies nestled within the heart of the Purple Valley, so named because the surrounding mountains often seem shrouded in a lavender veil at dusk. In it you'll find plenty of green spaces on which to lie and a friendly town center (two blocks long) where everyone congregates. You'll also find a pair of exceptional art museums and one of the most respected summer theater festivals in the northeast.

WORTH A TRIP

HANCOCK SHAKER VILLAGE

If you're ready for a soulful diversion, head 5 miles west from the town of Pittsfield on US 20 to **Hancock Shaker Village** (☑ 413-443-0188; www.hancockshakervillage.org; US 20; adult/child $18/free; ☺ 10am-5pm mid-Apr–Oct; ⏢). This evocative museum illustrates the lives of the religious sect that founded the village in 1783. The Shakers believed in communal ownership, the sanctity of work and celibacy, the latter of which proved to be their demise. Known as the City of Peace, the village was occupied by Shakers until 1960. At its peak in 1830, the community numbered some 300 members.

Twenty of the original buildings have been restored and are open to view, most famously the **Round Stone Barn** (1826). During summer, you're free to wander about on your own, watch demonstrations of Shaker crafts, visit the heirloom gardens and hike up to Mt Sinai where the Shakers went to meditate. The rest of the year, guided tours are given once or twice daily; call for details.

US 7 and MA 2/Main St intersect on the western side of town. The small central commercial district is off Main St on Spring St. Williamstown is the ultimate college town, with the marble-and-brick buildings of Williams College filling the town center.

⊙ Sights & Activities

★ Clark Art Institute MUSEUM

(☑ 413-458-2303; www.clarkart.edu; 225 South St, Williamstown; adult/child Jun-Oct $15/free, Nov-May free to all; ⊙ 10am-5pm, closed Mon Sep-Jun) The Sterling & Francine Clark Art Institute is a gem among US art museums. Even if you're not an avid art lover, don't miss it. The collections are particularly strong in the impressionists, with significant works by Monet, Pissarro and Renoir. Mary Cassatt, Winslow Homer and John Singer Sargent represent contemporary American painting.

Robert Sterling Clark (1877–1956), a Yale engineer whose family made a fortune in the sewing machine industry, began collecting art in Paris in 1912. He and his wife eventually housed their impressive collection in Williamstown in a white marble temple built expressly for the purpose. 'The Clark,' as everyone in town calls it, is less than 1 mile south of the intersection of US 7 and MA 2.

Williams College Museum of Art MUSEUM

(☑ 413-597-2429; www.wcma.org; 15 Lawrence Hall Dr, Williamstown; ⊙ 10am-5pm Tue-Sat, 1-5pm Sun) FREE This sister museum of the Clark Art Institute graces the center of town and has an incredible collection of its own. Around half of its 13,000 pieces comprise the American Collection, with substantial works by notables such as Edward Hopper (*Morning in a City*), Winslow Homer and Grant Wood, to name only a few.

The photography collection is also noteworthy, with representation by Man Ray and Alfred Stieglitz.

To find the museum, look for the huge bronze eyes embedded in the front lawn on Main St.

🛏 Sleeping

In addition to what follows, you'll find several motels on the outskirts of town on MA 2 east and US 7 north.

Clarksburg State Park CAMPGROUND $

(☑ 877-422-6762; www.mass.gov/dcr; 1199 Middle Rd, Clarksburg; tent sites $12-14) For the closest camping, follow MA 2 to MA 8 to reach these 45 campsites near the lovely and swimmable Mauserts Pond.

River Bend Farm B&B B&B $$

(☑ 413-458-3121; www.riverbendfarmbb.com; 643 Simonds Rd/US 7, Williamstown; r incl breakfast with shared bath $120; ✳ 🐾) A Georgian tavern in revolutionary times, River Bend Farm owes its painstaking restoration to hosts Judy and Dave Loomis. Four doubles share two bathrooms here. Despite the name it's not on a farm but along US 7 on the north side of the little bridge over the Hoosic River. River Bend is a seasonal operation, open from April to October.

Maple Terrace Motel MOTEL $$

(☑ 413-458-9677; www.mapleterrace.com; 555 Main St, Williamstown; r incl breakfast $121-157; 🐾 🏊) The Maple Terrace is a simple, yet cozy 15-room place on the eastern outskirts of town. The Swedish innkeepers have snazzed up the grounds with gardens that make you want to linger. In winter ask about discounted lift tickets to Jiminy Peak ski resort.

★ Guest House at Field Farm INN $$$

(☑ 413-458-3135; www.thetrustees.org/field-farm; 554 Sloan Rd; r incl breakfast $195-295; @ 🐾 🏊) This one-of-a-kind inn offers an artful blend of mid-20th-century modernity and timeless mountain scenery. It was built in 1948 in spare, clean-lined Bauhaus style on 300 acres of woods and farmland facing Mt Greylock. The original owners, art collectors Lawrence and Eleanor Bloedel, bequeathed the estate to the Trustees of Reservations, which now operates it.

The six rooms are spacious and fitted with handcrafted furnishings that reflect the modernist style of the house. The sculpture-laden grounds feature miles of lightly trodden walking trails and a pair of Adirondack chairs set perfectly for unobstructed star gazing.

🍴 Eating & Drinking

If you're just looking for a quick meal, a good place to start is Spring St, the main shopping street.

Tunnel City Coffee CAFE

(www.tunnelcitycoffee.com; 100 Spring St; snacks $2-6; ⊙ 6am-6pm; 🐾) A bustling den of cramming students and mentoring professors. Besides liquid caffeine, some seriously delicious desserts like triple-layer chocolate mousse cake will get you buzzing.

Pappa Charlie's Deli
DELI $

(☑413-458-5969; 28 Spring St; mains $5-9; ⊙7:30am-8pm) Here's a welcoming breakfast spot where locals really do ask for 'the usual.' The stars themselves created the lunch sandwiches that bear their names. The Richard Dreyfuss is a thick pastrami and provolone number. Or order a Politician and get anything you want on it.

Moonlight Diner & Grille
DINER $

(☑413-458-3305; 408 Main St, Williamstown; mains $6-10; ⊙7am-8:30pm Mon-Thu, to 9:30pm Fri & Sat) This old-school diner on the east side of town dishes up all the classics at honest prices. Think retro-1950s decor and huge burgers and cheesy omelets that will sate any appetite.

★ Mezze Bistro & Bar
FUSION $$$

(☑413-458-0123; www.mezzerestaurant.com; 777 Cold Spring Rd/US 7, Williamstown; mains $20-30; ⊙5-9pm) East meets West at this chic restaurant where chef Joji Sumi masterfully blends contemporary American cuisine with classic French and Japanese influences. Situated on 3 acres, Mezze's farm-to-table approach begins with an edible garden right on site. Much of the rest of the seasonal menu, from small-batch microbrews to organic meats, is locally sourced as well.

The setting is as pretty as the food.

☆ Entertainment

Williamstown Theatre Festival
THEATER

(☑413-597-3400; www.wtfestival.org; ⊕) Stars of the theater world descend upon Williamstown every year from the third week in June to the third week in August. While many summer-stock theaters offer cheese, the Williamstown Theatre Festival bucks the trend, and was the first summer theater to win the Regional Theatre Tony Award.

The festival mounts the region's major theatrical offerings with a mix of classics and contemporary works by up-and-coming playwrights. Kevin Kline, Richard Dreyfuss and Gwyneth Paltrow are but a few of the well-known thespians who have performed here. Besides the offerings on the Main Stage and Nikos Stage, there are cabaret performances in area restaurants and family nights when kids can attend performances for free.

ℹ Information

Williamstown Chamber of Commerce (☑413-458-9077; www.williamstownchamber.com; 100 Spring St; ⊙11am-6pm Mon-Sat) Oper-ates an information booth in the B&L Building in summer.

North Adams
POP 13700

At first glance, North Adams' beautiful and bleak 19th-century downtown seems out of sync with the rest of the Berkshires. But those who allow their gaze to settle will be confronted with an exemplary contemporary art museum of staggering proportions.

◉ Sights

MASS MoCA
MUSEUM

(☑413-662-2111; www.massmoca.org; 1040 Mass Moca Way, North Adams; adult/child $15/5; ⊙10am-6pm Jul & Aug, 11am-5pm Wed-Mon Sep-Jun; ⊕) Welcome to MASS MoCA, which sprawls over 13 acres of downtown North Adams, or about one-third of the entire business district. After the Sprague Electric Company packed up in 1985, more than $31 million was spent to modernize the property into 'the largest gallery in the United States.'

The museum encompasses 222,000 sq ft and over 25 buildings, including art construction areas, performance centers and 19 galleries. One gallery is the size of a football field, giving installation artists the opportunity to take things into a whole new dimension. Bring your walking shoes!

In addition to carrying the bread-and-butter rotation of description-defying installation pieces, the museum has evolved into one of the region's key venues for theater, documentary films and avant-garde dance performances. Families with budding artists should check out the museum's Kidspace, where children can create their own masterpiece.

🛏 Sleeping

Savoy Mountain State Forest
CAMPGROUND $

(☑413-663-8469; www.mass.gov/dcr; 260 Central Shaft Rd; tent sites/cabins $14/30) This wooded campground has 45 sites and four very rustic log cabins in one of the best state parks for mountain biking. From the center of town, head south on MA 8 and east on MA 116.

Porches
BOUTIQUE HOTEL $$$

(☑413-664-0400; www.porches.com; 231 River St, North Adams; r incl breakfast $189-285; ❄ ⓦ ≋ ❅) Across the street from MASS MoCA, the artsy rooms here combine well-considered color palettes, ample lighting and French doors into a pleasant sleeping experience.

Eating

Lickety Split
CAFE $

(☏413-346-4560; 1040 Mass Moca Way; mains $7-10; ☺8:30am-6pm) A convenient place for museumgoers to eat is at this pretty cafe inside MASS MoCA. Surprisingly good homemade soups and sandwiches, as well as breakfast fare and free-trade coffee.

Public Eat & Drink
PUB $$

(www.publiceatanddrink.com; 34 Holden St, North Adams; mains $10-22; ☺5-9pm; ☏) With exposed brick walls and big windows overlooking the street, this cozy pub is the most popular dinner spot in North Adams. Come for an excellent selection of craft beers and gourmet pub fare, like brie burgers, flatbread pizzas and bistro steak. Some decent vegetarian options as well.

Mt Greylock State Reservation

At a modest 3491ft, the state's highest peak can't hold a candle altitude-wise to its western counterparts, but a climb up the 92ft-high War Veterans Memorial Tower at its summit rewards you with a panorama stretching up to 100 verdant miles, across the Taconic, Housatonic and Catskill ranges, and over five states. Even if the weather seems drab from the foot, a trip to the summit may well lift you above the gray blanket, and the view with a layer of cloud floating between tree line and sky is simply magical.

Mt Greylock State Reservation (☏413-499-4262; www.mass.gov/dcr/parks/mtGreylock; ☺visitor center 9am-5pm) FREE has some 45 miles of hiking trails, including a portion of the Appalachian Trail. Frequent trail pull-offs on the road up – including some that lead to waterfalls – make it easy to get at least a little hike in before reaching the top of Mt Greylock. There are a few primitive campsites in the park that are not accessible by car; call for information and reservations.

Bascom Lodge (☏413-743-1591; www.bascomlodge.net; 1 Summit Rd; dm/r $37/125, mains $7-10; ☺restaurant 8am-10am & 11am-4:30pm), a truly rustic mountain hostelry, was built as a federal work project in the 1930s at the summit of Mt Greylock. From June to mid-October, it provides beds for 34 people. The lodge's restaurant serves straightforward fare like sirloin burgers and three-egg omelets.

You can get to Mt Greylock from either Lanesborough (follow the signs 2 miles north of town) or North Adams (from MA 2 west, and again, follow the signs). Either way, it's 10 slow miles to the summit. The visitor center is halfway up via the Lanesborough route. There's a $2 fee to park at the summit.

Rhode Island

☑ 401 / POP 1.05 MILLION

Best Places to Eat

➜ birch (p216)

➜ Chez Pascal (p217)

➜ Matunuck Oyster Bar (p232)

➜ Fluke Wine Bar (p230)

➜ Hotel Manisses (p239)

Best Places to Stay

➜ Stone House (p222)

➜ The Attwater (p230)

➜ Fishermen's Memorial State Park (p232)

➜ The Richards (p233)

➜ Sea Breeze Inn (p237)

Why Go?

The smallest of the US states, Rhode Island might only take 45 minutes to drive across but it packs over 400 miles of coastline into its tiny boundaries. Quite a lot of this coastline takes the form of white sandy beaches, arguably the finest places for ocean swimming in the northeast. Otherwise there are islands to explore, seaside cliffs to walk along and isolated lighthouses where you can either indulge in brooding melancholia or maybe hold someone's hand.

Rhode Island's cities (OK, its *only* city) brim with fantastic museums and galleries, gorgeous old neighborhoods and excellent restaurants and bars, all set within a beautiful and walkable urban fabric. Along the coast, you'll find seaside towns with cobblestone streets, colonial-era buildings, extravagant summertime resorts and Gilded Age (and contemporary) mansions. No wonder the Vanderbilts and their friends decamped here for summer balls and swimming. You'd be wise to follow suit.

When to Go
Providence

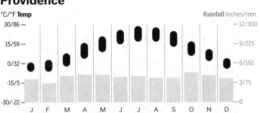

Jun This is the Ocean State, so hit the beach. In Newport, Rosecliff hosts the flower show.

Jul & Aug Newport's festival season is in full swing with classical, jazz and folk music.

Dec Providence's Federal Hill comes alive for the Christmas holiday.

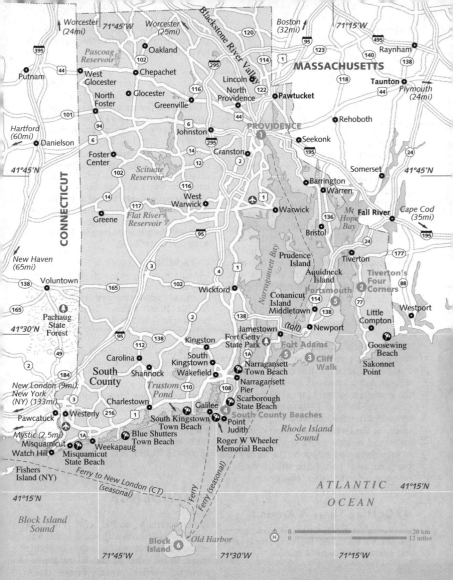

Rhode Island Highlights

1 Experiencing Providence's artsy side at **AS220** (p218) and the monthly art shindig, **Gallery Night** (p214)

2 Driving or cycling the scenic East Bay with stops for shopping and a quality coffee cabinet at Tiverton's **Four Corners** (p221)

3 Wiping ocean spray from your glasses while standing between the roaring Atlantic and Gilded Age mansions on the **Cliff Walk** (p226)

4 Slurping oysters on **Point Judith Pond** and beach-hopping along **South County beaches** (p232)

5 Kicking back with a glass of bubbly at the Portsmouth polo or a keg of locally brewed beer at the Folk Festival in **Fort Adams** (p228)

6 Getting back to nature: bird-watching, hiking and fishing on **Block Island** (p236)

History

Ever since it was founded in 1636 by Roger Williams, a religious outcast from Boston, Providence has enjoyed an independent frame of mind. Williams' guiding principle, the one that got him ostracized from Massachusetts, was that all people should have freedom of conscience. He put his liberal beliefs into practice when settling Providence, remaining on friendly terms with the local Narragansett Native Americans after purchasing from them the land for a bold experiment in tolerance and peaceful coexistence.

Williams' principles would not last long. As Providence and Newport grew and merged into a single colony, competition and conflict with area tribes sparked several wars, leading to the decimation of the Wampanoag, Pequot, Narragansett and Nipmuck peoples. Rhode Island was also a prolific slave trader and its merchants would control much of that industry in the years after the Revolutionary War.

The city of Pawtucket birthed the American industrial revolution with the establishment of the water-powered Slater Mill in 1790. Industrialism impacted the character of Providence and surrounds, particularly along the Blackstone River, creating urban density. As with many small east coast cities, these urban areas went into a precipitous decline in the 1940s and '50s as manufacturing industries (textiles and costume jewelry) faltered. In the 1960s, preservation efforts salvaged the historic architectural framework of Providence and Newport. The former has emerged as a lively place with a dynamic economy and the latter, equally lively, survives as a museum city.

❶ Getting There & Around

Providence has excellent transportation options. Elsewhere in the state, things can be tricky unless you have your own wheels.

AIR

TF Green State Airport (PVD; www.pvdairport.com; I-95, exit 13, Warwick) The state's main airport is in Warwick.

Westerly State Airport (☑596 23 57; www.pvdairport.com; 56 Airport Rd, Westerly) For flights to Block Island.

BOAT

Block Island Express (p240) Runs seasonal ferries from New London, Connecticut, to Block Island between May and September.

Block Island Ferry (p240) From mid-May to October, ferries run between Newport and Galilee to Block Island.

BUS

Providence and Newport are well serviced, and some buses depart direct from TF Green airport.

Greyhound (www.greyhound.com) Operates services throughout New England. Most depart from Providence, including frequent departures for New York City ($45, 3½ hours).

Peter Pan (www.peterpanbus.com) Slightly cheaper regional operator with a greater variety of routes. Also, runs to New York ($40, 3¾ hours) and Boston ($8, one hour).

Rhode Island Public Transit Authority (RIPTA; www.ripta.com) Rhode Island's regional transport network links Providence's Kennedy Plaza with the rest of the state for $2. A day/week pass costs $6/$23.

CAR & MOTORCYCLE

I-95 cuts diagonally across the state, providing easy access from coastal Connecticut to the south and Boston to the north. From Worcester take Rte 146 to Providence. Cars are easily rented in Providence and at TF Green airport.

TRAIN

Amtrak (www.amtrak.com) trains stop in Westerly (five daily), Kingston (eight daily) and Providence (eight daily) and connect with Boston and New York. The additional high-speed Acela Express train stops only in Providence.

Massachusetts Bay Transportation Authority (MBTA; www.mbta.com) operates a commuter train between Providence and Boston ($10, one hour), and Providence and TF Green airport ($5.50, 1½ hours).

PROVIDENCE

POP 178,000

Rhode Island's capital city, Providence presents its visitors with some of the finest urban strolling this side of the Connecticut River. In the crisp air and falling leaves of autumn, wander through Brown University's green campus on 18th-century College Hill and follow the Riverwalk into downtown. Along the way you'll have opportunities to lounge in the sidewalk cafe of an art-house theater, dine in a stellar restaurant and knock back a few pints in a cool bar. At night, take in a play at the Trinity Repertory, pass out in a club or eat some 3am burgers aboard the mobile Haven Brothers Diner.

Providence contains several high-profile universities and colleges plus a correspondingly large student population, helping to keep the city's social and arts scenes lively and current. The most notable of these schools are Brown University and the Rhode Island School of Design (RISD). Johnson & Wales University, one of the nation's best culinary arts programs, ensures that you'll find excellent restaurants in all price ranges throughout the city.

⊙ Sights

★Rhode Island State House
GOVERNMENT BUILDING

(✐401-222-2357; www.rilin.state.ri.us; Smith St; ⊙tours by appointment) **FREE** Designed by McKim, Mead and White in 1904, the Rhode Island State House rises above the Providence skyline, easily visible from miles around. Modeled in part on St Peter's Basilica in Vatican City, it has the world's fourth-largest self-supporting marble dome and houses one of Gilbert Stuart's portraits of George Washington, which you might want to compare to a dollar bill from your wallet.

Inside the public halls are the battle flags of Rhode Island military units and a Civil War cannon, which sat here for a century loaded and ready to shoot until someone thought to check whether it was disarmed. The giant half-naked guy standing on top of the dome is the Independent Man, continuously struck by lightning.

★Rhode Island School of Design (RISD)
ACADEMIC INSTITUTION

(✐401 454 6300; www.risd.edu) Perhaps the top art school in the United States, RISD's imprint on Providence is easily felt. From public statuary to film performances, the creativity of the school's students extends across the small cityscape. Not least in the extraordinary collections at its **Museum of Art** (✐401-454-6500; www.risdmuseum.org; 224 Benefit St; adult/child $12/3; ⊙10am-5pm Tue-Sun, to 9pm Thu; ♿) which include 19th-century French paintings; classical Greek, Roman and Etruscan art; medieval and Renaissance works; and examples of 19th- and 20th-century American painting, furniture and decorative arts.

Kids love staring at the mummy, while others will be impressed to see the works of Manet, Matisse and Sargent. The museum stays open until 9pm on the third Thursday of the month, when admission is free after 5pm. It's also free the last Saturday of the month and Sunday from 10am to 1pm.

★Brown University
ACADEMIC INSTITUTION

(www.brown.edu) Dominating the crest of the College Hill neighborhood on the East Side, the campus of Brown University exudes Ivy League charm. **University Hall**, a 1770 brick edifice used as a barracks during the Revolutionary War, sits at its center. To explore the campus, start at the wrought-iron gates opening from the top of College St and make your way across the green toward Thayer St.

Free tours of the campus begin from the **Brown University Admissions Office** (✐401-863-2378; Corliss Brackett House, 45 Prospect St). Call or drop by for times.

College Hill
NEIGHBORHOOD

East of the Providence River, College Hill, headquarters of Brown University and RISD, contains over 100 Colonial, Federal and Revival houses dating from the 18th century. Stroll down **Benefit Street's** 'Mile of History' for the best of them. Amidst them you'll find the clean lines of William Strickland's 1838 **Providence Athenaeum** (✐401-421-6970; www.providenceathenaeum.org; 251 Benefit St; ⊙9am-7pm Mon-Thu, 9am-5pm Fri & Sat, 1-5pm Sun) **FREE**, inside which plaster busts of Greek gods and philosophers preside over a collection that dates to 1753.

The cheap eateries and used-record stores that nourish college types are on **Thayer St**, College Hill's main commercial drag.

Fox Point
NEIGHBORHOOD

South of College Hill is Fox Point, the waterfront neighborhood where the city's substantial Portuguese population resides. Though gentrification has brought influxes of Brown University professors and artists,

DON'T MISS

EAST BAY BICYCLE PATH

Starting at India Point Park on the Narragansett Bay waterfront in Providence, the scenic path winds its way for 14.5 miles south along a former railroad track. The mostly flat, paved route follows the shoreline to the pretty seaport of Bristol. State parks along the way make good spots for picnics.

The **State Department of Transport** (www.dot.ri.gov/bikeri) maintains a website devoted to bicycling in Rhode Island, which has a downloadable map of bikeways throughout the state and other useful information.

Providence

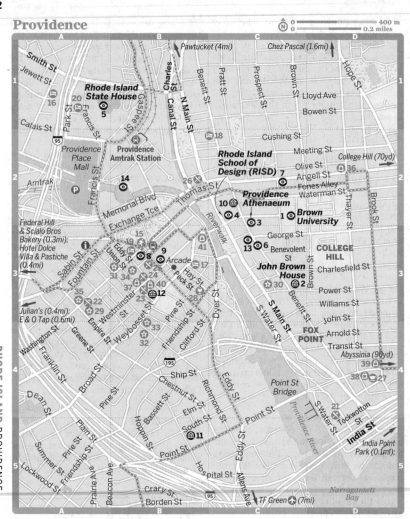

you can still find an old world–style grocery like the **Friends Market** (📞401-861-0345; 126 Brook St) tucked in among the trendy coffeehouses, salons and galleries. Most activity in Fox Point centers on Wickenden St.

Culinary Arts Museum MUSEUM
(📞401-598-2805; www.culinary.org; 315 Harborside Blvd; adult/child $7/2; ⊙10am-5pm Tue-Sun; 🅿) Johnson & Wales' oddity of a museum displays about 300,000 objects connected in some way to the culinary arts. Ogle a cookbook collection dating back to the 15th century, resist fingering presidential cutlery and

peruse over 4000 menus from around the world. To reach the museum, it's a straight shot south on Rte 1 toward Pawtuxet.

Sol Koffler GALLERY
(📞401-277-4809; 169 Weybosset St; ⊙noon-5pm Wed-Sat) **FREE** RISD maintains several fine galleries. Sol Koffler serves as the main exhibition space for graduate students, where you can see work in a range of media. Hours vary on the weekend.

Federal Hill NEIGHBORHOOD
Among the most colorful of Providence's neighborhoods is fervently Italian Federal

Providence

Hill (when Tony Soprano's crew needed a special job done, they came here). West of the center, it's a great place to wander, taking in the aromas of sausages, peppers and garlic from neighborhood groceries such as Tony's Colonial Food (p218). Many of Providence's best restaurants are on Atwells Ave.

Roger Williams Park   PARK
(1000 Elmwood Ave) **FREE** In 1871, Betsey Williams, great-great-great-granddaughter of the founder of Providence, donated her farm to the city as a public park. Today this 430-acre expanse of greenery, only a short drive south of Providence, includes lakes and ponds, forest copses and broad lawns, picnic grounds and a **Planetarium and Museum of Natural History** (✆401-785-9457; museum $2, planetarium $4; ◷10am-4pm, planetarium shows 2pm Sat & Sun; 🚼).

The park's main attraction is the **zoo** (✆401-785-3510; www.rogerwilliamsparkzoo. org; adult/child $14.95/9.95; ◷9am-4pm; P🚼), which is home to more than 600 animals (polar bear, giraffes, lemurs) and performs some interesting conservation work.

Providence Children's Museum   MUSEUM
(✆401-273-5437; www.childrenmuseum.org; 100 South St; admission $9; ◷9am-6pm Tue-Sun, daily Apr-Labor Day; P) This well-designed, hands-on museum genuinely delights its intended guests, who can enter a giant kaleidoscope, do experiments with water fountains, pretend to be a veterinarian or play with marionettes made by some renowned puppeteers. It's aimed at kids aged one to 11.

🏃 **Activities**

Providence Rink   ICE-SKATING RINK
(www.providencerink.com; 2 Kennedy Plaza, Bank of America City Center; adult/child $6/3, skate rental $4; ◷10am-10pm Mon-Fri, 11am-10pm Sat & Sun mid-Nov–mid-Mar; 🚼) This outdoor rink at the Bank of America City Center occupies prime downtown real estate. While the Biltmore hotel and Fleet Building provide a nice architectural backdrop, you might have to skate to some seriously loud pop songs. College students skate for three bucks on Wednesday night.

PROVIDENCE ARCHITECTURE

Come to Providence and you'll find an urban assemblage of unsurpassable architectural merit – at least in the States. It's the only American city to have its *entire* downtown listed on the National Registry of Historic Places. The beaux arts **City Hall** (25 Dorrance St) makes an imposing centerpiece to Kennedy Plaza, and the stately white dome of the Rhode Island State House remains visible from many corners of the city. The **Arcade** is modeled after Parisian antecedents. These impressive buildings, along with the art deco **Industrial Trust building** (Fleet Bldg; 55 Exchange Pl) – note the third-story friezes of industrial progress on the Westminster St facade – are only a few of many showcase buildings. The more ordinary 19th-century brick structures that fill in the space between their more famously designed neighbors work together to create an extraordinary landscape of harmonious scale, beauty and craftsmanship.

Immediately east of downtown, you'll find College Hill, where you can see the city's colonial history reflected in the multihued 18th-century houses that line **Benefit Street** on the East Side. These are, for the most part, private homes, but many are open for tours one weekend in mid-June during the annual Festival of Historic Homes (p215). Benefit St is a fitting symbol of the Providence renaissance, rescued by local preservationists in the 1960s from misguided urban-renewal efforts that would have destroyed it. Its treasures range from the 1708 **Stephen Hopkins House** (✆ 401-421-0694; 15 Hopkins St; donations accepted; ☷ 1-4pm Wed-Sat May-Oct, otherwise by appointment), named for the 10-time governor and Declaration of Independence signer, to the clean Greek Revival lines of William Strickland's 1838 Providence Athenaeum (p211). This is a library of the old school, with plaster busts and oil paintings filling in spaces not occupied by books. Edgar Allen Poe used to court ladies here.

Also on College Hill, the brick **John Brown House** (✆ 401-273-7507; www.rihs.org; 52 Power St; adult/child $8/4; ☷ tours 1:30pm & 3pm Tue-Fri, 10:30am, noon, 1:30pm & 3pm Sat Apr-Dec), called the 'most magnificent and elegant mansion that I have ever seen on this continent' by John Quincy Adams, was built in 1786.

Providence Bicycle   BICYCLE RENTAL
(✆ 401-331-6610; www.providencebicycle.com; 725 Branch Ave; per day $30; ☷ 9:30am-8pm Mon-Thu, to 6pm Fri & Sun) The closest rental outlet is 2.5 miles north of Brown University off Rte 146. The rental cost includes the use of a helmet and bike lock.

☞ Tours & Courses

RISD CE   COURSE
(✆ 401-454-6200; ce.risd.edu) Unsurprisingly the school of design runs a whole host of courses under the 'Continuing Education' banner. They range from day classes in pastry sculpture to month-long glass workshops and three month courses in art history, digital photography and design. Prices range from $50 to $675 and courses must be booked in advance.

**Rhode Island
Historical Society**   WALKING TOUR
(RIHS; ✆ 401-273-7507; www.rihs.org; tours $5-14; ☷ Jun-Oct) The historical society runs four guided tours a day of College Hill's premier historic home, the John Brown House Museum (adult/child $10/6). Other tours include Benefit Street's 'Mile of History,' an informed amble on Riverwalk and summer walks along South Main St. All tours leave from outside the John Brown House.

Savoring Rhode Island   FOOD TOUR
(✆ 401-934-2149; www.savoringrhodeisland.com; tour $50; ☷ tours start 9am) Meet the chefs, bakers and ravioli makers of Federal Hill's historic restaurant row on chef Cindy Salvato's three-hour, behind-the-scenes walking tour. See the tiny kitchen where Venda Ravioli hand-craft hundreds of their namesake ravioli and visit Scialo Brothers Bakery who make their *sfogliatelle* pastries from scratch each day. Take along a cooler so you can shop as you go and don't be afraid to ask Cindy for Italian recipe tips.

✯ Festivals & Events

Gallery Night   ART
(www.gallerynight.info) Held every third Thursday of the month from March to November from 5pm to 9pm. Twenty-three galleries and museums around the city open their

doors for free viewings. Check out the website before you go and find out where to hop on the shuttle, hook up with a guide or sign up for a free celebrity guided tour.

Festival of Historic Homes   ARCHITECTURE

(www.ppsri.org) Tour some of the East Side's fabulous 18th-century homes during this annual shindig in June.

Rhode Island
International Film Festival   FILM

(www.film-festival.org) For five days in August, cool kids from RISD and beyond screen hundreds of independent shorts and feature-length films.

🛏 Sleeping

Providence is devoid of hostels and has a limited number of midrange options. The summer months represent peak season, while the big universities' parents' weekends and graduations fill rooms up to a year in advance.

★Hampton Inn &
Suites Providence Downtown   HOTEL $$

(📞401-608-3500; www.hamptoninn.hilton.com; 58 Weybosset St; s $110-205, d $189-225; 🅿🤶) Occupying the historic Old Colony House on Weybosset St, the Hampton Inn is the best-located hotel in Providence. Although the standard rooms are comfortable enough, it's the suites that are the winners here, set up like one-bedroom apartments. And you might want to bring your cookbook: each suite has a full refrigerator and microwave. Got a little work to do? Complimentary wi-fi and free local calls await. Little wonder travelers love it.

Hotel Dolce Villa   HOTEL $$

(📞401-383-7031; www.dolcevillari.com; 63 De-Pasquale Sq; ste $169-269; 🅿🤶) Three of this hotel's 14 suites have balconies perched directly over Federal Hill's DePasquale Sq, a lively plaza covered with terrace seating for nearby restaurants. Slick, contemporary rooms overwhelm visitors with whiteness – everything from bedding to furniture to the tile floors gleams in a bright, colorless void. Gay friendly and with full kitchens.

Christopher Dodge House   B&B $$

(📞401-351-6111; www.providence-hotel.com; 11 W Park St; r incl breakfast $120-180; 🅿) This 1858 Federal-style house is furnished with early American reproduction furniture and marble fireplaces. Austere on the outside it has elegant proportions, large, shuttered windows and wooden floors.

Old Court B&B   HISTORIC INN $$

(📞401-751-2002; www.oldcourt.com; 144 Benefit St; r $145-215) Well positioned among the historic buildings of College Hill, this three-story, 1863 Italianate home has stacks of charm. Enjoy eccentric wallpaper, good jam at breakfast and occasional winter discounts.

Providence Biltmore   HISTORIC HOTEL $$$

(📞401-421-0700; www.providencebiltmore.com; 11 Dorrance St; r/ste $146/279; 🅿🤶) The grand-daddy of Providence's hotels, the Biltmore dates to the 1920s. The lobby, both intimate and regal, nicely combines dark wood, twisting staircases and chandeliers, while well-appointed rooms stretch many stories above the old city. Ask for one of the 292 rooms that are on a high floor.

RHODE ISLAND PROVIDENCE

DON'T MISS

WATERFIRE

Particularly during summer, much of downtown Providence transforms into a carnivalesque festival thanks to the exceedingly popular WaterFire (www.waterfire.org) art installation created by Barnaby Evans in 1994. Marking the convergence of the Providence, Moshassuck and Woonasquatucket Rivers, 100 anchored, flaming braziers illuminate the water, overlooked by crowds of pedestrians strolling over the bridges and along the landscaped riverside.

All the gazing and making out is accompanied by live (and canned) music, outdoor stages hosting theatrical performances, public ballroom dancing (you can join in) and a few ostentatious gondolas that drift by the pyres. The landscaped cobblestone paths of the Riverwalk lead along the Woonasquatucket River to Waterplace Park's (Memorial Blvd) central pool and fountain, overlooked by a stepped amphitheater.

WaterFire occurs about 15 times a year from May to October and begins at sunset. A schedule is posted on the website. Occasionally there's a lighting around Christmas or the New Year.

Renaissance Providence Hotel
HISTORIC HOTEL $$$

(☑ 401-276-0010; www.marriott.com; 5 Ave of the Arts; r $189-259; P✳🐾🛜) Built as a Masonic temple in 1929, this monster stood empty for 77 years before it opened in 2007 as a hotel. Some rooms overlook the State House and are decorated in forceful colors that attempt, with limited success, to evoke Masonic traditions. The graffiti artist who once tagged the vacant building was hired to do his thing in the 'Masonic' hotel bar. Wi-fi costs an additional $10.

🍴 Eating

Both RISD and Johnson & Wales University have top-notch culinary programs that annually turn out creative new chefs who liven up the city's restaurant scene. The large student population on the East Side ensures that plenty of good, inexpensive places exist around College Hill and Fox Point. To experience old Providence, head over to the restaurant district along Atwells Ave in Federal Hill.

Red Fez, AS220 and Cable Car Cinema also serve food.

Haven Brothers Diner
DINER $

(Washington St; meals $5-10; ⊗5pm-3am) Parked next to City Hall, this diner sits on the back of a truck that has rolled into the same spot every evening for decades. Legend has it that the business started as a horse-drawn lunch wagon in 1893, giving it the dubious title of oldest food cart in the country. Climb up a rickety ladder to get basic diner fare alongside everyone from prominent politicians to college kids pulling an all-nighter to drunks. The murder burger ($4) comes highly recommended.

Flan y Ajo
SPANISH $

(☑ 401-432-6656; 225a Westminster St; tapas $3-7; ⊗6-11pm) This BYOB tapas bar serves lipsmacking *pintxos* – or 'bites' – like singleshell on prawn with *salsa verde*, mussels in white wine and succulent *lomito* (pork tenderloin). Barely more than a hole in the wall on Westminster St, come early, buy a bottle of wine from Eno Fine Wines next door and be prepared to be sociable.

If you can't get a stool here or prefer more refined surroundings head for their wine bar, Bodega Malasaña (186 Union St; meals $25-30; ⊗noon-1am Mon-Fri, 3pm-1am Sat, 5pm-1am Sun), round the corner on Union St.

Scialo Bros Bakery
ITALIAN $

(☑ 401-421-0986; www.scialobakery.com; 257 Atwells Ave; sweets $1-3; ⊗8am-7pm Mon-Thu & Sat, to 8pm Fri, to 5pm Sun) Since 1916, the brick ovens at this Federal Hill relic have turned out top-notch butterballs, *torrone* (a nougat and almond combo), amaretti and dozens of other kinds of Italian cookies and pastries. Avoid the mediocre cannoli.

Abyssinia
ETHIOPIAN $$

(☑ 401-454-1412; www.abyssinia-restaurant.com; 333 Wickenden St; meals $20; ⊗11am-10pm; ☑) From the plum colored banquettes to the roaring (or is that smiling) Lion of Judah on the wall, get ready to experience the heady flavors, textures and temperatures of Ethiopian cooking. Vegetarian lentils and split pea curries tempt the tastebuds before the spicy onslaught of chicken Doro Wat and beef Key Wot. All dishes come spread out on a spongy expanse of *injera*, the Ethiopian sour-dough flatbread made from the smallest grain in the world, *teff*.

Julian's
NEW AMERICAN $$

(☑ 401-861-1770; www.juliansprovidence.com; 318 Broadway; brunch $6-12, meals $15-25; ⊗9am-1am; 🛜☑🍴) A messy combination of neon, exposed brick and ductwork in Federal Hill; come here for tattooed cooks preparing a stellar brunch (served until 5pm) with changing blackboard specials (goat's cheese, caper, tomato and mushroom hash) along with a variety of poached eggs and plenty of vegetarian- and vegan-friendly options.

New Rivers
NEW AMERICAN $$$

(☑ 401-751-0350; 7 Steeple St; meals $30-40; ⊗5:30-10pm Mon-Sat) Every bit as good as they say, this New American bistro has a seasonal menu featuring dishes like rabbit loin with sweet pea sauce, roasted sole, and beef tenderloin with mushrooms and pearl onions. With soft lighting, walls painted in rich hues of green, red and yellow, and a well-conceived wine list, it's worth a splurge.

★ birch
NEW AMERICAN $$$

(☑ 401-272-3105; www.birchrestaurant.com; 200 Washington St; meals $25-35; ⊗5pm-midnight Thu-Tue) With a background at Noma in Copenhagen and the fabulous Dorrance at the Biltmore, chef Benjamin Sukle and his wife, Heidi, now have their own place, understated, but fabulously good birch. The intimate size and style (seating is around a U-shaped bar) of the place means attention to detail is exacting in both the decor and the food, which focuses on underutilised, small-batch and hyper-seasonal produce.

Take the humble pea: simmered in a butter broth made from the shells, clams and lemons, and then served with jasmine rice and green strawberries. Utterly exquisite.

★**Chez Pascal**　　　　　　　FRENCH $$$
(☎401-421-4422; www.chez-pascal.com; 960 Hope St; meals $40-60, 3-course bistro menu $35; ⊘5:30-9pm Mon-Thu, to 10pm Fri & Sat, wurst kitchen 11:30am-2:30pm Tue-Sat) This friendly French bistro welcomes diners warmly with inspiring homemade pâtés and charcuterie, escargots à la Bourguignon and slow-roasted duck with a golden raisin and red wine sauce. Sourcing ingredients from local growers like Arcadian Fields Organic Farm and Little City Growers, you can tuck in safe in the knowledge that you'll not only eat well but keep it in the neighborhood.

At lunchtime keep it real with a housemade hotdog ($8) from the Wurst Window.

Al Forno　　　　　　　　　ITALIAN $$$
(☎401-273-9760; www.alforno.com; 577 S Main St; meals $35-50; ⊘5-10pm Tue-Sat; P) Our most recent visit featured scallops with blackened bacon so perfect that they were celestial. Also enjoy wood-grilled leg of lamb, handmade cavatelli with butternut squash and prosciutto, and incredible desserts (such as limoncello cake with candied citrus peel). Budget-minded folks can order wood-fired pizzas ($20) big enough for two to split. Make a reservation.

🍸 Drinking & Nightlife

Cafes

Coffee Exchange　　　　　COFFEEHOUSE
(☎401-273-1198; 201 Wickenden St; ⊘6:30am-11pm; 🛜) Drink strong coffee at one of the many small tables in this college-town coffeehouse, with thick layers of flyers tacked to the walls and a large roaster lurking behind bean bins (there are 40 or so varieties available).

Pastiche　　　　　　　　　　　　CAFE
(☎401-861-5190; www.pastichefinedesserts.com; 92 Spruce St; cakes $3-6; ⊘8:30am-11pm Tue-Thu, 8:30am-11:30pm Fri & Sat, 10am-10pm Sun) Warmed by a fire in winter, this tiny cafe in Federal Hill has a robin's-egg-blue facade, an ultra-friendly staff and an impressive seasonal dessert menu. In summer, its fruit tarts are to die for.

Bars & Clubs

★**Avery**　　　　　　　　　　　　BAR
(18 Luongo Memorial Sq; ⊘4pm-midnight Mon-Fri, 5pm-midnight Sat & Sun) Tucked into a quiet residential neighborhood in West Providence, the Avery is easy to miss. But once inside there's a jaw-droppingly gorgeous varnished wood interior, with backlit art nouveau wood cuttings and an elegant, curved bar that's lit from beneath and lined with black vinyl stools.

The Salon　　　　　　　　BAR, CLUB
(www.thesalonpvd.com; 57 Eddy St; ⊘5pm-1am Mon-Fri, 7pm-2am Sat) A few handy steps from the Haven Brothers Diner, the Salon mixes ping-pong tables and pinball machines with '80s pop and pickleback shots (whiskey with a pickle juice chaser) upstairs, and live shows, open mic, DJs and dance parties downstairs. If you get hungry there are PB&J sandwiches or dash out to the Haven Brothers (p216).

E & O Tap　　　　　　　　　　　BAR
(289 Knight St; ⊘4pm-midnight) E & O is brighter, louder and more raucous than other Providence night spots, with a pool table, a rockin' jukebox and a clientele that tends toward the hip and hipper still. Think girls with Betty Paige 'dos and dudes with bushy beards and tattooed sleeves. But the crowd is unpretentious and the drinks are cheap.

Red Fez　　　　　　　　　　　BAR
(☎401-272-1212; 49 Peck St; ⊘4pm-1am Tue & Wed, to 2am Thu-Sat) Packed full of Hasbro copywriters who work on the packaging for Transformers action figures and RISD girls with interesting hair, this dark, spooky, red-lit bar makes stiff drinks and fantastic grilled cheese sandwiches.

Mirabar　　　　　　　　　　　GAY
(☎401-331-6761; www.mirabar.com; 35 Richmond St; ⊘3pm-1am Sun-Thu, to 2am Fri & Sat) This venerable gay nightclub attracts devoted regulars, many on a first-name basis with the bartenders. It's got two floors – the 2nd, a sort of promenade, overlooks the action of the main level's dance floor. If Mirabar isn't your thing, there are a half-dozen other gay clubs clustered between Washington and Weybosset Sts downtown.

⭐ Entertainment

Check the 'Lifebeat' section in the *Providence Journal* or the *Phoenix* for listings of live-music performers, venues and schedules.

AS220
CLUB

(☑ 401-831-9327; www.as220.org; 115 Empire St; ⊙ 5pm-1am) A longstanding outlet for all forms of Rhode Island art, AS220 (say 'A-S-two-twenty') books experimental bands (Lightning Bolt, tuba and banjo duos), hosts readings and provides gallery space for a very active community. If you need a cup of coffee, vegan cookie or spinach pie, it also operates a cafe and bar. Hours above are for the bar, but the gallery opens at midday Wednesday through Saturday, and the cafe closes at 10pm.

Trinity Repertory Company
THEATER

(☑ 401-351-4242; www.trinityrep.com; 201 Washington St; tickets $30-60) Trinity offers classic and contemporary plays *(Some Things are Private, A Christmas Carol)* in the stunning and historic Lederer Theater downtown. It's a favorite try-out space for Broadway productions, and it's not unusual for well-known stars to turn up in a performance. Student discounts available.

Providence Performing Arts Center
PERFORMING ARTS

(☑ 401-421-2787; www.ppacri.org; 220 Weybosset St) This popular venue for touring Broadway musicals and other big-name performances is in a former Loew's Theater dating from 1928. It has a lavish art deco interior.

Lupo's Heartbreak Hotel
MUSIC

(☑ 401-331-5876; www.lupos.com; 79 Washington St) This legendary music venue occupies digs in a converted theater, whose age adds historic charm. It hosts national and international acts (Bloc Party, Tiger Army, Blonde Redhead) in a relatively small space.

Cable Car Cinema
CINEMA

(☑ 401-272-3970; www.cablecarcinema.com; 204 S Main St; tickets $9) This theater screens offbeat and foreign films. Inside, patrons sit on couches. The attached sidewalk cafe brews excellent coffee and serves sandwiches and baked goods. It's a good place to hang out, even if you aren't catching a flick.

🔒 Shopping

Brown University Bookstore
BOOKS

(☑ 401-863-3168; 244 Thayer St; ⊙ 9am-6pm Mon-Fri, 10am-6pm Sat, 11am-5pm Sun) Providence's most comprehensive bookstore.

Craftland
CRAFT

(☑ 401-272-4285; www.craftlandshop.com; 235 Westminster St; ⊙ 11am-6pm; 🖝) Craftland is a great place to shop for souvenirs given that its inventory consists of one-of-a-kind finds from over 150 local artists. Ceramics and jewelry sit side-by-side with handmade soap, prints and kids toys. Classes and workshops are offered from time to time. Check out the website for details.

Queen of Hearts
FASHION

(☑ 401-421-1471; www.queenofheartsri.com; 222 Westminster St; ⊙ 11am-6pm Mon-Wed, 11am-8pm Thu-Sat, noon-5pm Sun) Feel the love amid the vibrant and stylish threads in Queen of Hearts, where pieces with individuality and personality are the order of the day. Owned by designer Karen Beebe, the boutique stocks unique footwear (like the hot-pink Adele gladiator sandal), super cute dresses, sunglasses and belts, many of them locally made and all well priced.

risd|works
ARTWORKS, HOMEWARES

(☑ 401-277-4949; www.risdworks.com; 10 Westminster St; ⊙ 10am-5pm Tue-Sun; 🖝) RISD maintains several fine galleries. A design showcase is risd|works, a shop displaying an assortment of goods (jewelry, photographic prints, flatware, coffee tables, children's books) made by faculty and alumni.

★ Curatorium
GIFTS

(☑ 401-453-4080; www.thecuratorium.com; 197 Wickenden St; ⊙ 10am-6pm Mon-Wed & Fri-Sat, to 8pm Thu and 5pm Sun) Matt Bird's treasure trove of miscellany is the place to shop if you like to bask in the gratitude of a well-received gift. From books on haunted house architecture to that essential framed tarantula and squirrel wall hanging, you'll find it in the Curatorium. Staff are knowledgeable and clearly enjoy working here, too.

Tony's Colonial Food
DELI

(☑ 401-621-8675; www.tonyscolonial.com; 311 Atwells Ave; ⊙ 8:30am-6pm) Wander Federal Hill and take in the aromas of sausages, peppers and garlic from neighborhood groceries such as Tony's. Imported olive oil, gourmet pastas and specialty cheeses have kept housewives happy since 1952.

ℹ Information

The daily newspaper for Providence and indeed all of Rhode Island is the **Providence Journal** (www.providencejournal.com). The *Providence Phoenix*, which appears on Thursday, is the city's free alternative weekly. Find it in record stores and cafes on Thayer and Wickenden Sts.

Visitor's Center (www.goprovidence.com; 1 Sabin St; ⊙9am-5pm Mon-Sat)

❶ Getting There & Around

Providence is small, pretty and walkable, so once you arrive you'll probably want to get around on foot.

AIR

TF Green State Airport (p210) is in Warwick, about 20 minutes south of Providence. Green is served by most major airlines.

Aero-Airport Limousine Service (✆401-737-2868; per person $11; ⊙5am-11pm) runs an hourly shuttle to most downtown Providence hotels. Taxi services include **Airport Taxi** (✆401-737-2868; www.airporttaxiri.com) and **Checker Cab** (✆401-273-2222; www.checker-cabri.com).

RIPTA (p440) buses 12, 20 and 66 ($2, 20 to 30 minutes) run to the Intermodal Transportation Center in Providence. Service is frequent on weekdays until 11pm. On Saturday and Sunday it is significantly reduced.

BUS

All long-distance buses and most local routes stop at the central **Intermodal Transportation Center** (Kennedy Plaza; ⊙6am-8pm). RIPTA, **Greyhound** (www.greyhound.com) and **Peter Pan** (www.peterpanbus.com) all have ticket counters inside, and there are maps outlining local services.

RIPTA operates two 'trolley' routes. The Green Line runs from the East Side through downtown to Federal Hill. The Gold Line runs from the Marriott hotel south to the hospital via Kennedy Plaza, and stops at the Point St Ferry Dock.

Bonanza Bus Lines (✆401-751-8800, 888-751-8800; www.peterpanbus.com), operated by Peter Pan, connects Providence and TF Green State Airport with Boston's South Station ($8, one hour, 12 daily) and Boston's Logan International Airport ($20, 70 minutes, 12 daily).

Greyhound buses depart for Boston ($10.80 to $18, 70 minutes, five daily), New York City ($35 to $45, 3½ to six hours, six daily) and elsewhere.

CAR & MOTORCYCLE

With hills, two interstates and two rivers defining its downtown topography, Providence can be a confusing city to find your way around. Parking can be difficult downtown and near the train station. For a central lot, try the huge garage of the Providence Place Mall and get a merchant to validate your ticket. On the East Side, you can usually find street parking easily.

Most major car-rental companies have offices at TF Green State Airport in Warwick. **Avis** (✆401-521-7900; www.avis.com; Providence Biltmore, 1 Dorrance St; ⊙8am-6pm Mon-Fri,

8am-4:30pm Sat, 9am-5pm Sun) has an office downtown as well.

TRAIN

Amtrak (www.amtrak.com; 100 Gaspee St) trains connect Providence with Boston ($15, 50 minutes) and New York ($62 to $107, three hours). High-speed Acela trains also service Boston ($35, 45 minutes) and New York ($123 to $177, 2¾ hours), although the Boston run isn't good value.

MBTA commuter rail (www.mbta.com) connects to Boston ($7, 70 minutes).

BLACKSTONE VALLEY

This attractive river valley in the northeast corner of the state is named for its first European settler, the Rev William Blackstone, who arrived here in 1635. But it wasn't until the invention of the water-powered spinning jenny, which was brought to the area in the 1790s, that the region really began to boom. Fueled by the Blackstone River, small wool and cotton textile mills proliferated, becoming the valley's dominant industry.

Slater Mill (www.slatermill.org; 67 Roosevelt Ave, Pawtucket; adult/child 6-12 $12/8.50; ⊙10am-4pm Tue-Sun May-Oct) has been dubbed the 'Birthplace of the Industrial Revolution' – with good cause. It was here that, in 1793, Samuel Slater built the first successful water-powered cotton-spinning mill in North America. After the decline of the Rhode Island textile plants, the area fell on hard economic times. Only in recent years, through a concerted effort to repair the natural beauty of the region, has the Blackstone become an attractive destination for outdoor enthusiasts.

The Blackstone Valley Visitor Center (✆401-724-2200; www.tourblackstone.com; 175 Main St, Pawtucket; ⊙10am-5pm Mon-Fri, to 4pm Sat & Sun) is a good resource for information on the area, including events, maps and information on the 48-mile Blackstone River Bikeway, which will eventually lead all the way to Worcester, Massachusetts.

A short drive (or bike ride) north of Providence, Lincoln Woods State Park (www.riparks.com/lincoln.htm; 2 Manchester Print Works Rd, Lincoln; ⊙sunrise-sunset) has 627 acres of beautifully maintained grounds, extensive hiking trails, 92 picnic sites and two game fields. The lake-sized Olney Pond has a wide sandy beach and rocky outcroppings for diving into the water or lounging in the

PRUDENCE ISLAND

Idyllic Prudence Island sits in the middle of Narragansett Bay, an easy 25-minute ferry ride from Bristol. Originally used for farming and later as a summer vacation spot for families from Providence and New York, who traveled here on the Fall River Line Steamer, the island now has only 88 inhabitants. There are some fine Victorian and beaux-arts houses near Stone Wharf, a lighthouse and a small store, but otherwise it's wild and unspoiled. Perfect for mountain biking, barbeques, fishing and paddling.

Between mid-June and Labor Day, regular ferries shuttle between Bristol and Prudence Island (www.prudenceferry.com; adult/child $6.60/2.90).

sun. There are also boat and kayak rentals and a lifeguard on duty during swimming season. In winter, ice skating, snowmobiling and ice fishing are popular.

THE EAST BAY

Rhode Island's jagged East Bay captures the early American story in microcosm, from the graves of early settlers in Little Compton, to the farmsteads and merchant homes of whalers and farmers in Warren and Barrington, and the mansions of slave traders in Bristol.

This corner of the state was settled as early as 1621, when Pilgrim Fathers from Plymouth crossed the Sakonnet River and purchased some farmland from the Wampanoag tribe. But when the chief's first son, Wamsutta, died mysteriously in a row over hunting rights, his brother Metacom (aka King Philip) vowed to avenge him and precipitated one of New England's bloodiest Indian Wars in 1675. Despite the involvement of tribes from as far afield as central Massachusetts and Maine, the war ended in 1676 with the massacre of Metacom's Narragansett allies and his own death at the hands of a treacherous fellow tribesman. After which his East Bay lands fell to the colonists.

Aside from Barrington's historic and picturesque Tyler Point Cemetery, set between the Warren and Barrington Rivers, and Warren's clutch of early stone and clapboard churches (built in the 18th and 19th centuries), the most interesting of the three communities is Bristol. Further south is Sakonnet, the Wampanoag's 'Place of Black Geese,' a rural landscape of pastures and woods centred around the two tiny communities of Tiverton and Little Compton.

Bristol

One fifth of all slaves transported to America were brought in Bristol ships and by the 18th century the town was one of the country's major commercial ports. The world-class Herreshoff Marine Museum (www.herreshoff.org; 1 Burnside St; adult/child $10/free; ⊙10am-5pm May-Oct; ⊕) showcases some of America's finest yachts, including eight built for the America's Cup. You can climb aboard a number of the boats, the best being Harvard's gorgeous mahogany-decked launch.

Local resident Angustus Van Wickle bought a 72ft Herreshoff yacht for his wife Bessie in 1895, but having nowhere suitable to moor it, he then had to build Blithewold Mansion (www.blithewold.org; 101 Ferry Rd; adult/child $11/3; ⊙10am-4pm Tue-Sun mid-Apr–Oct; P). The Arts & Crafts mansion sits in a peerless position on Narragansett Bay and is particularly lovely in spring, when the daffodils life the shore. Other local magnates included slave trader General George DeWolf who built Linden Place (✆401-253-0390; www.lindenplace.org; 500 Hope St; adult/child $8/6; ⊙10am-4pm Thu-Sat May-Oct; P), famous as the film location for Jack Clayton's 1974 The Great Gatsby.

Bristol's Colt State Park (www.riparks.com; RI-114; ⊙8:30am-4:30pm) is Rhode Island's most scenic park, with its entire western border fronting Narragansett Bay, fringed by 4 miles of cycling trails and shaded picnic tables.

Tiverton

The community of Tiverton stretches alongside the Sakonnet River, with views of distant sailing vessels and Aquidneck Island. The further south you explore on Rte 77, the prettier the landscape gets with ramshackle farm stands selling fresh produce and rolling fields extending in all directions.

On the north stretch of Rte 77, you'll find gray-shingled Evelyn's Nanaquaket Drive-In (☎ 401-624-3100; www.evelynsdrivein.com; 2335 Main Rd, Tiverton; chowder & cakes $3.99-7.50, mains $6.99-20; ☺ 11:30am-8pm; ℗ ♿ ❃), a traditional roadside eatery from another era. Park on the crushed-shell driveway and eat amazing lobster rolls (cool, mildly spiced claw and tail meat on a hotdog bun). The place sits next to a blue inlet with a handful of bobbing dinghies. There's a children's menu for the kiddies.

A little further south, stop in Sakonnet Vineyards (☎ 401-635-8486; www.sakonnetwine.com; 162 West Main Rd; ☺ 11am-5pm) for free daily wine tastings and guided tours. Shortly after, a rare traffic light marks Tiverton's historic Four Corners (www.tivertonfourcorners.com). This crossroads represents the hub of the community where shops, restaurants and provision stores cluster. Stop in at Gray's Ice Cream (☎ 401-624-4500; www.graysicecream.com; 16 East Rd; ice creams $3-5; ☺ 7am-7pm) for a coffee cabinet (milkshake with ice cream), as beachgoers have been doing since 1923. Otherwise, head to Provender (☎ 401-624-8084; cnr Main & Neck Rds; sandwiches $6-8) for a gourmet sandwich or giant homemade cookies.

Tiverton is an artists' colony so it also offers some of the best shopping in the state, including handwoven Shaker-style rugs from Amy C Lund (www.amyclundhandweaver.com; 3964 Main Rd; ☺ 10am-5pm Wed-Sat, noon-5pm Sun), local deli delicacies at Milk & Honey Bazaar (www.milkandhoneybazaar.com; 3838 Main Rd; ☺ 10am-5pm Wed-Sat, noon-5pm Sun) and museum-quality art from Gallery 4 (www.gallery4tiverton.com; 3848 Main Rd; ☺ 11am-4:30pm Wed-Sat, noon-4:30pm Sun).

Little Compton

Continue south into Little Compton and the smell of the sea will soon emerge. Here, large wood-framed homes become older, grayer and statelier just as an increasing number of stone walls crisscross the green landscape. One of them, 17th-century Wilbor House (☎ 401-635-4035; www.littlecompton.org; 548 West Main Rd; adult/child $6/3; ☺ 1-5pm Thu-Mon Apr-Oct, 9am-3pm Tue-Fri Nov-Mar), belonged to early settler Samuel Wilbor, who crossed the Sakonnet River from Portsmouth in 1690 and built this big square house, which served his family for eight generations.

The rest of Little Compton, from the hand-hewn clapboard houses to the white-steepled United Congregational Church overlooking the Old Commons Burial Ground, is one of the oldest and most quaint villages in all of New England. Elizabeth Padobie, daughter of the Mayflower pilgrims Priscilla and John Alden and the first settler born in New England, is buried here.

Though many are content just driving or biking around town, a pair of beaches also competes for your attention. To find them, turn right after arriving at the United Congregational Church, continue to Swamp Rd and make a left. Make a second left onto South Shore Rd, at the end of which you'll find South Shore Beach (parking $10; ☺ dawn-dusk) and, across a small tidal inlet, the more remote and appealing Goosewing Beach. The latter is part of a pristine coastal preserve and bird-breeding sanctuary managed by the Nature Conservancy (www.nature.org). In 2010 CNN voted it one of the most eco-friendly beaches in the world. The Benjamin Family Environmental Center, located atop a hill within the conservancy,

---

LOCAL KNOWLEDGE

COFFEE MILK & CABINETS

In 1993, two popular beverages battled each other for the honor of becoming Rhode Island's official state drink: coffee milk and Del's frozen lemonade.

Though Del's tastes great, no one really doubted that coffee milk would come out on top. Rhode Island kids have guzzled this mixture of coffee syrup and milk since before the Great Depression. To try it, head to a grocery store, pick up a bottle and go to town.

While we've got your attention, please note this crucially important distinction: in Rhode Island, a milkshake is traditionally syrup and milk blended together without ice cream. Rhode Islanders call the version with ice cream a 'cabinet' or 'frappe.' (The term 'cabinet' is pretty much specific to Rhode Island, while 'frappe' gets thrown around by folks as far away as Boston.)

offers stunning views of the beach, as well as summer programs for kids of all ages and seasonal nature walks. Check out the website for details.

If you fancy staying for a few days amid this rural tranquillity, you can't do better than checking in to Stone House (☑401-635-2222; www.stonehouse1854.com; 122 Sakonnet Point; r $275-425; ☺May-Oct; 🅿🛜), a granite block and sandstone villa surrounded by a frilly porch with views across Round Pond.

NEWPORT

POP 24,700

Established by religious moderates fleeing persecution from Massachusetts Puritans, 'new port' flourished to become the fourth-richest city in the newly independent colony and the harbor remains one of the most active and important yachting centres in the country. Downtown the Colonial-era architecture is beautifully preserved along with notable landmarks such as Washington Square's Colony House, where Rhode Island's declaration of independence was read in May 1776.

Fascinating as Newport's early history is, it struggles to compete with its own latter-day success when, bolstered by the boom in shipping, wealthy industrialists made it their summer vacation spot and built opulent country 'cottages' down lantern-lined Bellevue Avenue. Modelled on Italianate palazzos, French chateaux and Elizabethan manor houses, and decorated with priceless furnishings and artwork, they remain the town's premier attraction alongside a series of summer music festivals – classical, folk, jazz – which are among the most important in the US.

👁 Sights

👁 Downtown

Downtown Newport's main north–south commercial streets are America's Cup Ave and Thames (that's 'thaymz,' not 'temz') St, which teems with restaurants, bars and weekend crowds. There are public toilets at the entrance to the parking lot at Bowen's Wharf. While downtown, be sure to notice the lanterns on Pelham St, the first street in the USA illuminated by gas (1805).

Bowen's Wharf & Bannister's Wharf   OUTDOOR MALLS
(Map p224) These wharves typify Newport's transformation from working city-by-the-sea to a tourist destination. Fishing boats and pleasure vessels sit around the periphery of fudge shops and clothing stores (some local, some chain), all housed in an outdoor mall on a former wharf meant to blend into the old city by virtue of the liberal use of grey shingles. Nearby Bannister's Wharf is a smaller-scale version of the same thing.

Wanton-Lyman-Hazard House   HISTORIC SITE
(Map p224; ☑401-841-8770; www.newporthistorical.org; 17 Broadway; tours $8) For some serious timber framing, visit the oldest surviving house in Newport, constructed c 1697. Used as a residence by colonial governors and well-to-do residents, it's now a museum of colonial Newport history operated by the Newport Historical Society. Check the online schedule for guided tours.

Touro Synagogue National Historic Site   SYNAGOGUE
(Map p224; ☑401-847-4794; www.tourosynagogue.org; 85 Touro St; adult/child $12/free; ☺10am-4pm Sun-Fri Jul-Sep, 10am-2pm Sun-Fri Sep-Oct, noon-1.30pm Sun-Fri May-Jun, noon-1.30pm Sun Nov-Apr) Designed by Peter Harrison (architect of the Athenaeum and King's Chapel, Boston), this synagogue is the finest example of 18th-century Georgian architecture in Newport. Its large glass windows illuminate an interior that treads the line between austere and lavish. Built by the nascent Sephardic Orthodox Congregation Yeshuat Israel in 1763, it has the distinction of being North America's oldest synagogue.

Inside, a letter to the congregation from President George Washington, written in 1790, hangs in a prominent spot. There's a historic cemetery just up the street. The synagogue opens for worship only on Saturday.

Trinity Church   CHURCH
(Map p224; ☑401-846-0660; www.trinitynewport.org; Queen Anne Sq; suggested donation $5; ☺10am-4pm Mon-Fri, to 3pm Sat mid-Jun–mid-Oct, 11am-2pm May–mid-Jun) On Queen Anne Sq, Trinity follows the design canon of Sir Christopher Wren's Palladian churches in London. Built between 1725 and 1726, it has a fine wineglass-shaped pulpit, Tiffany stained glass, traditional box pews (warmed by the bottoms of many celebrity guests including George Washington, Queen Eliza-

Newport Area

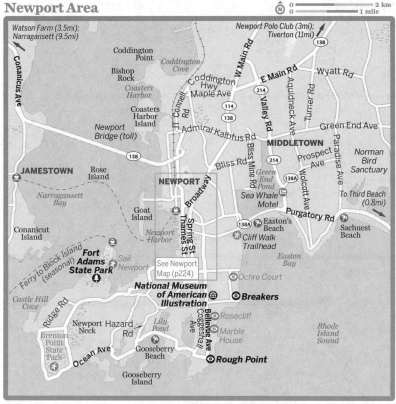

beth II and Archbishop Desmond Tutu) and an organ once played by Handel.

Tours also run year-round right after the Sunday service (around 11am).

Whitehorne Museum   MUSEUM
(Map p224; ☎ 401-324-611; www.newportrestoration.org; 416 Thames St; guided/self-guided tour/child $12/6/free; ⊗ 11am-3pm Thu-Mon May-Oct) A few decades ago, colonial Newport was decaying and undervalued. Enter Doris Duke, who used her huge fortune to preserve many of the buildings that now attract people to the city. One of them is Whitehorne, a Federal period estate. Rooms contain a collection of extraordinary furniture crafted by Newport's famed cabinetmakers, including pieces by Goddard and Townsend.

Museum of Yachting   MUSEUM
(MoY; Map p224; ☎ 401-848-5777; www.iyrs.edu; 449 Thames St; ⊗ noon-5pm Tue-Sat May-Oct) Want to look at some boats? Head inside

this bad-boy museum inside the 1831 Aquidneck Mill for a collection of model yachts, a handful of craft being restored by an on-site restoration school and pictures of the New York Yacht Club winning the America's Cup regatta for 130 consecutive years until Australia ruined sporting history's longest winning streak in 1983.

Perched on the top floor, the museum commands great views over Newport harbor. Call ahead to check that the museum is open during summer break (May to September).

Bellevue Avenue

During the 19th century, the wealthiest New York bankers and business families chose Newport as their summer resort, building their fabulous mansions along Bellevue Ave. Eleven of the mansions (not including Rough Point or Ochre Court) are under the management of the **Preservation Society**

Newport

N

0 — 400 m
0 — 0.2 miles

Battery Park

20 Cherry St

Braman Cemetery

Island Cemetery

St Mary's Cemetery

Chestnut St

Walnut St

Common Ground Cemetery

Warner St

Gould St

Powell Ave

Broadway

Kingston St

Everett St

Poplar St

15 Elm St

3rd St

Bridge St

Storer Park

Washington St

America's Cup Ave

Farewell St

31

Broadway

Mann Ave

Mt Vernon St

Causeway

Goat Island Connector

28

Bull St

Long Wharf

P i

Touro St 11

30

9

Kay St 18

HISTORIC HILL

6

Thames St

Touro St

Bellevue Ave

Interstate Navigation

29 32

Spring St

Perotti Park

13

3

Queen Anne Square 10

25

Church St

14

22

33

Mill St

Pelham St

Touro Park

1

Redwood Athenaeum

Old Beach Rd

Commercial Wharf

27

23

Prospect Hill

21

Hammett's Wharf

Christie's Landing

Ann St

William St

Memorial Blvd

17

16

12

Aquidneck Park

Jones St

4

Howard's Wharf

19

7

Bowery St

5

Newport Harbor

Pope St

E Bowery St

Berkeley St

Dearborn St

Perry St

Bellevue Ave

Thames St

Dean St

Spring St

The Elms 2

Parker Ave

Clay St

King Park

Lee Ave

McAlister St

Wellington Ave

Narragansett Ave

24

26

8

Newport

(Map p224; ☑ 401-847-1000; www.newportmansions.org; 424 Bellevue Ave; 5-site ticket adult/child $49/19) and are open seasonally between June and November. Combination tickets are better value if you intend visiting several of the properties, and some tours require advance booking, which is advisable anyway during high season. Tickets can be purchased online or on-site. The society also offers a range of food- and wine-themed events.

Alternatively, hire a bike and cruise along Bellevue Ave enjoying the view of the mansions and their grounds or saunter along the famed Cliff Walk, a pedestrian path that runs along the headland between the mansions and their sea view.

★ **Redwood Athenaeum** LIBRARY
(Map p224; ☑ 401-847-0292; www.redwoodlibrary.org; 50 Bellevue Ave; ⊙ 9:30-5:30pm Mon-Wed & Fri-Sat, to 8pm Thu, 1-5pm Sun; P) FREE Founded by Abraham Redwood in 1747 as an important archive of American history and architecture, the neo-classical structure was built by Peter Harrison, who the library honors with a room devoted to priceless American portraiture. There's also a gallery with revolving exhibits, a quiet reading room and a series of genteel concerts and garden parties.

Guided tours run at 2pm every day (adult/child $5/free).

International Tennis Hall of Fame MUSEUM
(Map p224; ☑ 401-849-3990; www.tennisfame.com; 194 Bellevue Ave; adult/child $12/free; ⊙ 9:30am-5pm) To experience something of the American aristocracy's approach to 19th-century leisure, visit this museum. It lies inside the historic Newport Casino building (1880), which served as a summer club for Newport's wealthiest residents. The US National Lawn Tennis Championships (forerunner of today's US Open tennis tournament) was held here in 1881. A scavenger hunt, available at reception gets kids engaged with eight centuries of tennis.

If you brought your whites, playing on one of its 13 grass courts (closed in winter) remains a delightful throwback to earlier times ($110 for two people for one hour). Otherwise have a drink lawnside at the La Forge Casino Restaurant (lunch menu $30 to $35).

Kingscote MANSION
(Map p224; ☑ 401-847-1000; 253 Bellevue Ave; adult/child $14.50/5.50; ⊙ 10am-5pm Jul–mid-Oct;

CLIFF WALK

In 1975, eager to protect their privacy, Newport's mansion-owners sought to close **Cliff Walk** (www.cliffwalk.com), the public footpath that snakes along the cliff top overlooking their front lawns. The move was prevented by local fishermen and the 3.5 mile path was designated a National Recreation Trail. The best section runs from Ledge Rd near Rough Point to the Forty Steps (each one named for someone lost at sea) on Narragansett Ave, although the southernmost tip (between Ledge Rd and Ruggles Ave) was closed at the time of writing due to damage from Hurricane Sandy.

You can park for free on Narragansett Ave from 6am to 9pm (there's a four-hour limit). Many favor this entry point because it shaves the first half-mile off the walk (which is pretty, but lacks mansions).

P) An Elizabethan fantasy complete with Tiffany glass, Kingscote was Newport's first 'cottage' strictly for summer use, designed by Richard Upjohn in 1841 for George Noble Jones of Savannah, Georgia. It was later bought by China-trade merchant William H King, who gave the house its name.

★The Elms   MANSION
(Map p224; www.newportmansions.org; 367 Bellevue Ave; adult/child $14.50/5.50, servant life tour adult/child $15/5; ☺10am-5pm Apr-mid-Oct, hours vary mid-Oct–Mar; P⃞) Designed by Horace Trumbauer in 1901, the Elms is a replica of Château d'Asnières, built near Paris in 1750. Here you can take a 'behind-the-scenes' tour which will have you snaking through the servants' quarters and up onto the roof. Along the way you'll learn about the activities of the army of servants and the architectural devices that kept them hidden from the view of those drinking port in the formal rooms.

Taking the regular tour in addition to the behind-the-scenes variant will give you the best idea of how a Newport mansion functioned, although it is exhausting. Advance reservations are required.

Ochre Court   MANSION
(Map p223; ☎401-847-6650; www.salve.edu; 100 Ochre Point Ave; ☺9am-4pm Mon-Fri) FREE De-signed by Richard Morris Hunt and built in 1892, Ochre Court offers a grand view of the sea from its soaring three-story hallway. Elsewhere you can find a rainbow of stained glass, pointed arches, gargoyles and other emblems of an architecture inspired by a medieval (and mythical) French Gothic. Ochre Court now houses the administration of Salve Regina University, and as such provides an interesting example of the repurposing of a Newport mansion.

You can visit much of the main floor anytime during opening hours. In summer there are guided tours.

★National Museum of
American Illustration   MUSEUM
(Map p223; ☎401-851-8949; www.americanillustration.org; 492 Bellevue Ave; adult/child $18/8; ☺11am-5pm Thu-Mon May-Sep, 11am-5pm Fri & by reservation Mon-Thu Oct-Apr; P) This acclaimed museum features an impressive collection of Maxfield Parrish's impossibly luminous works in color, NC Wyeth prints, Norman Rockwell's nostalgia and the illustrations of other American graphic heavyweights. If you can, take the free guided tour on Friday (3pm; available year-round) which sheds light on the stories behind the images and how they moulded American culture through the decades.

The museum is housed within the palatial Vernon Court (yet another mansion, this one from 1898) set within Olmstead-designed grounds.

★Breakers   MANSION
(Map p223; 44 Ochre Point Ave; adult/child $19.50/5.50; ☺9am-5pm Apr–mid-Oct, hours vary mid-Oct–Mar; P) A 70-room Italian Renaissance megapalace inspired by 16th-century Genoese palazzos, Breakers is the most magnificent Newport mansion. At the behest of Cornelius Vanderbilt II, Richard Morris Hunt did most of the design (though craftsmen from around the world perfected the decorative program). The building was completed in 1895 and sits at Ochre Point, on a grand oceanside site. The furnishings, most made expressly for the mansion, are all original. Don't miss the **Children's Cottage** on the grounds.

The Breakers' Stable & Carriage House, also designed by Hunt, sits on the west side of Bellevue Ave. It is now a museum of Vanderbilt family memorabilia, much of which provides a detailed look at the lifestyle of one of the USA's wealthiest families at the turn of the 19th century.

Rosecliff
MANSION

(Map p223; 548 Bellevue Ave; adult/child $14.50/5.50; ⊙ 10am-5pm Apr–mid-Oct, hours vary mid-Oct–Mar; P) Stanford White designed Rosecliff to look like the Grand Trianon at Versailles, and its palatial ballroom (Newport's largest) and landscaped grounds quickly became the setting for some truly enormous parties. Houdini entertained at one. Rosecliff was built for Mrs Hermann Oelrichs, an heiress of the Comstock Lode silver treasure.

If the building seems oddly familiar during your visit, that might be because it has appeared in films such as the 1974 *Great Gatsby*, *Amistad* and *High Society*. In June the Newport Flower Festival is held here.

Marble House
MANSION

(Map p223; 596 Bellevue Ave; adult/child $14.50/5.50; ⊙ 10am-5pm; P 🚻) Designed by Richard Morris Hunt and built in 1892 for William K Vanderbilt, the younger brother of Cornelius II, the gaudy Marble House – built of many kinds of garishly colored marble – is a whorish building whose inspiration was drawn from the palace of Versailles and comes complete with custom furnishings styled after the era of Louis XIV.

★ Rough Point
MANSION

(Map p223; www.newportrestoration.com; 680 Bellevue Ave; adult/child $25/free; ⊙ 10am-2pm Thu-Sat mid-Apr–mid-May, 10am-3.45pm Tue-Sat mid-May–mid-Nov; P) While the peerless position and splendor of the grounds alone are worth the price of admission, this faux-English manor house also contains heiress and philanthropist Doris Duke's impressive art holdings, including medieval tapestries, furniture owned by French emperors, Ming dynasty ceramics and paintings by Renoir and Van Dyck.

Built in 1889 by Frederick W Vanderbilt on a rocky bluff jutting out into the ocean, Rough Point was later purchased by tobacco baron James B Duke, and passed to his only daughter, Doris (then aged 12) in 1925 along with his $80 million fortune. Throughout her teenage years Doris spent her summers here, and as an adult Rough Point was one of her favorite houses.

The contents of the house are exactly as she left them at the time of her death in 1993, when she bequeathed the house to the Newport Restoration Society (which she founded) with the directive that it be opened as a museum. Particularly interesting is a glassed-in sunroom containing just about the only pedestrian furniture (the couch appears to be from a department store). Also on hand are mannequins wearing some of Duke's eight decades of bizarro clothing.

🏃 Activities

Newport is a fine town for biking, with only a few gentle slopes. A scenic and satisfying ride is the 10-mile loop around Ocean Ave, which includes Bellevue Ave and its many beautiful mansions.

★ Fort Adams State Park
PARK

(Map p223; www.fortadams.org; Harrison Ave; fort tours adult guided/self-guided $12/6, child $6/3; ⊙ sunrise-sunset) Fort Adams is America's

---

NEWPORT BEACH GUIDE

Newport's public beaches are on the eastern side of the peninsula along Memorial Blvd. All are open 9am to 6pm in summer and charge a parking fee of $10/20 on weekdays/weekends (except for Gooseberry Beach, which charges $20 all week for parking).

Easton Beach (First Beach; Memorial Blvd) This is the largest beach with a pseudo-Victorian pavilion containing bathhouses and showers, a snack bar and a large carousel. You can rent umbrellas, chairs and surf boards at the pavilion.

★ **Sachuest Beach** (Second Beach; ☑ 401-846-6273) The most beautiful beach on Aquidneck Island, curves around Sachuest Bay and is backed by the 450-acre Norman Bird Sanctuary.

Third Beach (☑ 401-847-1993) Popular with families because it is protected from the open ocean. Third Beach also appeals to windsurfers because the water is calm and the winds steady.

Gooseberry Beach (130 Ocean Ave; ⊙ 9am-5pm) This beach has calm waters, white sand and a restaurant.

largest coastal fortification and is the centerpiece of this gorgeous state park, which juts out into Narragansett Bay. It's the venue for the Newport jazz and folk festivals and numerous special events. A beach, picnic and fishing areas and a boat ramp are open daily.

To explore the fort in greater detail join one of the tours, which take you deep into its underground tunnels and up onto the ramparts for fabulous views of Newport Harbor and the bay.

Brenton Point State Park   PARK

(Map p223; ☑ summer only 401-849-4562; Ocean Ave; ☺ dawn-dusk) At the opposite end of the peninsula, due south of Fort Adams on Ocean Ave, this park is a prime place for standing on rocky outcroppings to watch the ocean and flying kites.

Ten Speed Spokes   BICYCLE RENTAL

(Map p224; ☑ 401-847-5609; www.tenspeed spokes.com; 18 Elm St; hybrid per hr/3 days/week $7/70/100; ☺ 10am-6pm Mon-Sat, 10am-5pm Sat, noon-5pm Sun, shorter hours winter) Rents regular bikes as well as hybrids and offers free use of helmets and locks.

🎓 Courses

★ Sail Newport   SAILING

(Map p223; ☑ 401-846-1983; www.sailnewport.org; 60 Fort Adams Dr; 1-/2-week sessions $365/475, sailboat rental per 3hr $73-138; ☺ 9am-7pm; ⊕) As you'd expect in the hometown of the prestigious America's Cup, the sailing in breezy Newport is phenomenal. Sail Newport offers intermediate and advanced youth and adult courses. The minimum age is seven years.

🧭 Tours

If you'd rather go on your own, the historical society has erected 26 self-guided walking-tour signs on the sidewalks of Historic Hill describing many of the prominent and historic buildings found there.

Newport History Tours   WALKING TOUR

(☑ 401-841-8770; www.newporthistorytours.org; Brick Market Museum & Shop, 127 Thames St; tours adult/child $12/5; ⊕) Will guide you on a walking tour of Historic Hill. Periodically, the society offers themed heritage tours, where you'll learn about 'Pirates & Scoundrels,' Jewish or African American history. Tours begin at 10am or 11am at the **Museum of Newport History** (Map p224; 127 Thames St).

★ America's Cup Charters   YACHT TOURS

(Map p224; ☑ 401-846-9886; www.americacup charters.com; 49 America's Cup Ave, Newport Harbor Hotel Marina; sunset tour per person $70; ☺ May-Sep; ⊕) Take the ultimate waterborne tour aboard a 12m, America's Cup racing yacht. Ticketed, two-hour sunset sails and private charters are available daily in season and offer an unforgettably thrilling experience.

Classic Cruises of Newport   BOAT TOUR

(Map p224; ☑ 401-847-0299; www.cruisenewport. com; Bannister's Wharf; adult/child $25/20; ☺ mid-May–mid-Oct) Runs excursions on the *Rum Runner II*, a Prohibition-era bootlegging vessel, and *Madeleine*, a 72ft schooner. The narrated tour will take you past mansions and former speakeasies.

🎆 Festivals & Events

If you plan to attend any of Newport's major festivals make sure you reserve accommodation and tickets in advance (tickets usually go on sale in mid-May). For a full schedule of events, see www.gonewport.com.

Newport Music Festival   MUSIC

(www.newportmusic.org; tickets $20-42; ☺ mid-Jul) In mid-July, this internationally regarded festival offers classical music concerts in many of the great mansions.

International Tennis Hall of Fame Championships   SPORTS

(☑ 401-849-6053; www.halloffametennischampion ships.com; tickets $50-105) For a week in July, Wimbledon comes to Newport with top athletes competing on the famed grass courts.

Newport Folk Festival   MUSIC

(www.newportfolkfest.net; Fort Adams State Park; 1-/3-day pass $49/120, parking $12; ☺ late Jul) In late July, big-name stars and up-and-coming groups perform at Fort Adams State Park and other venues around town. Bring sunscreen.

Newport Jazz Festival   MUSIC

(www.newportjazzfest.net; Fort Adams State Park; tickets $47.50-100; ☺ early Aug) This classic festival usually takes place on an August weekend, with concerts at the Newport Casino and Fort Adams State Park. Popular shows can sell out a year in advance.

Newport International Boat Show   NAUTICAL

(www.newportboatshow.com; Newport Yachting Center, 4 Commercial Wharf; adult $18-27, child free,

POLO IN PORTSMOUTH

Drab though the urban environs may seem, in-the-know locals rate Portsmouth as a family-friendly destination. Not least because the polo matches hosted at Glen Farm make for a great family day out. Home to the **Newport Polo Club** (www.nptpolo.com; 715 East Main Rd, Portsmouth; lawn seats adult/child $12/free; ⊙ gates open 1pm), the 700 acre 'farm' was assembled by New York businessman Henry Taylor, who sought to create a gentleman's country seat in the grand English tradition. Every Saturday between June and September, the farm is host to the club's polo matches, which are a perfect way to enjoy the property and get an authentic taste of Newport highlife.

Bring a picnic basket for a fieldside tailgate and watch the US team take on Egypt, Jamaica and other Olympic-caliber squads. Crowds aren't large and you'll be close enough to hear snorting horses and walloping mallets.

---

parking $15) Held in mid-September, this is one of the largest in-water boat shows in the country featuring 850 exhibitors.

🛏 Sleeping

Expensive in summer (particularly on weekends) and discounted off season, the inns and harborside hotels in the center of town often require a two-night minimum on summer weekends, and a three-night minimum on holidays.

As rooms can be scarce in summer, you might want to use a reservation service. **B&B of Newport** (☑ 800-800-8765, 401-846-1828; www.bbnewport.com; 33 Russell Ave, Newport) and **Taylor-Made Reservations** (☑ 401-847-6820; www.citybythesea.com) together represent about 400 establishments in the Newport area.

★ **Newport International Hostel** HOSTEL $
(William Gyles Guesthouse; Map p224; ☑ 401-369-0243; www.newporthostel.com; 16 Howard St; dm with shared bath incl breakfast $35-119; ⊙ Apr-Dec; 🛜) Welcome to Rhode Island's only hostel, run by an informal and knowledgeable host. Book as early as you can. The tiny guesthouse contains fixings for a simple breakfast, a laundry machine and spare, clean digs in a dormitory room. Private rooms are available but you need to enquire by email.

Sea Whale Motel MOTEL $$
(Map p223; ☑ 888-257-4096; www.seawhale. com; 150 Aquidneck Ave, Middletown; d $109-179; P🛜♿) This owner-occupied motel is a lovely place to stay with rooms facing Easton's Pond and flowers hung about the place everywhere. Rooms have little style, but are comfortable and neat with fridges, microwaves and tea and coffee provided. Everything is within easy walking distance

and the owner is a fount of information and recommendations.

Stella Maris Inn INN $$
(Map p224; ☑ 401-849-2862; www.stellamarisinn. com; 91 Washington St; r incl breakfast $125-225; P) This quiet, stone-and-frame inn has numerous fireplaces, heaps of black-walnut furnishings, Victorian bric-a-brac and some floral upholstery. Rooms with garden views rent for less than those overlooking the water. The owner can be a bit gruff, but the prices are good (for Newport, that is). Oddly, it doesn't accept credit cards.

★ **Marshall Slocum Guest House** B&B $$$
(Map p224; ☑ 401-841-5120; www.marshallslocu-minn.com; 29 Kay St; d $79-275; 🛜) This clapboard colonial house, a former parsonage, is situated in a quiet residential street between Historic Hill and downtown Newport. The period feel is wonderfully preserved in gorgeous rooms featuring canopy beds, cool linen bed sheets, wide wooden floorboards and shuttered windows. Book well in advance.

Admiral Fitzroy Inn INN $$$
(Map p224; ☑ 401-848-8000; www.admiralfitzroy. com; 398 Thames St; r $105-325; P❄) Though named for Fitzroy (he invented the barometer and sailed with Darwin) and decorated with 19th-century maps that imply a personal connection, it's doubtful the admiral spent any time in this 1854 building. Nevertheless, the inn offers good value, nautically themed rooms in a central position on Thames St. While noise from emptying bars can be disruptive, the rooftop terrace offers sweeping water views.

Francis Malbone House HISTORIC INN $$$
(Map p224; ☑ 401-846-0392; www.malbone.com; 392 Thames St; d incl breakfast May-Oct $275-350,

Nov-Apr $150-195; P 🛜) This grand brick mansion was designed by the Touro Synagogue's architect and built in 1760 for a shipping merchant. Now beautifully decorated and immaculately kept with a lush garden, it is one of Newport's finest inns. Some guest rooms have working fireplaces, as do the public areas. Afternoon tea is included.

★ **The Attwater** BOUTIQUE HOTEL $$$
(Map p224; ☑ 401-846-7444; www.theattwater. com; 22 Liberty St; r $180-309; P ✳ 🛜) Newport's newest hotel has the bold attire of a mid-summer beach party with turquoise, lime green and coral prints, ikat headboards and snazzily patterned geometric rugs. Picture windows and porches capture the summer light and rooms come furnished with thoughtful luxuries like iPads, Apple TV and beach bags.

There's no in-house restaurant, but the bistro serves French Press coffee all day and the breakfast buffet is heaped with brioche au chocolat, corn muffins and ginger molasses cookies.

✗ Eating

From June through September make reservations and show up on time or lose your spot. Many Newport restaurants don't accept credit cards; ask about payment when you reserve. The widest selection of restaurants is along lower Thames St.

Franklin Spa DINER $
(Map p224; ☑ 401-847-3540; 229 Spring St; meals $3-10; ◷ 6am-2pm; 🖶) This old-school joint slings hash, eggs and grease for cheap. It's locally loved and opens early. Enjoy freshly squeezed orange juice, homemade turkey noodle soup or coffee cabinet at a Formica-topped table on a worn white-and-red tiled floor.

★ **Rosemary & Thyme Cafe** BAKERY, CAFE $
(Map p224; ☑ 401-619-3338; www.rosemary andthymecafe.com; 382 Spring St; baked goods $2-5, sandwiches & pizza $5.95-7.95; ◷ 7.30am-3pm Tue-Sat, to 11.30am Sun; 🖶) With a German baker in the kitchen its hardly surprising that the counter at Rosemary & Thyme is piled high with buttery croissants, apple and cherry tarts and plump muffins. At lunchtime gourmet sandwiches feature herbed goat's cheese and Tuscan dried tomatoes, an Alsatian cheese mix and a Havana Cuban pork loin outlier. A children's menu is also thoughtfully provided.

Mamma Luisa ITALIAN $$
(Map p224; ☑ 401-848-5257; www.mammaluisa. com; 673 Thames St; mains $14-25; ◷ 5-10pm Thu-Tue) This cozy restaurant serves authentic Italian fare to its enthusiastic customers, who recommend this low-key pasta house as a place to escape the Newport crowds. There are classic pasta dishes (cheese ravioli with fava beans, spaghetti *alle vongole*), as well as meat and fish entrees. Upstairs feels like eating at grandma's house.

The Mooring SEAFOOD $$$
(Map p224; ☑ 401-846-2260; www.mooringrestau rant.com; Sayer's Wharf; meals $15-40; ◷ 11:30am-10pm) A harborfront setting and a menu brimming with fresh seafood make this an unbeatable combination for seaside dining. Tip: if it's packed, take the side entrance to the bar, grab a stool and order the meaty clam chowder and a 'bag of doughnuts' (tangy lobster fritters).

★ **Fluke Wine Bar** SEAFOOD $$$
(Map p224; ☑ 401-849-7778; flukewinebar.com; 41 Bowen's Wharf; meals $40-60; ◷ 5-11pm Wed-Sat Nov-Apr, daily in summer) The Scandinavian-inspired dining room, with its blond wood and picture windows, offers an accomplished seafood menu featuring roasted monkfish, seasonal striped sea bass and plump scallops. Upstairs, the bar serves a rock-and-roll cocktail list.

Thames St Kitchen MODERN AMERICAN $$$
(Map p224; ☑ 401-846-9100; www.thamesstreet kitchen.com; 677 Thames St; meals $30-50; ◷ 5:30-11pm Tue-Sat) 🍴 This BYOB restaurant is the baby of two New York chefs who are devoted to field-to-fork dining and craft their limited menu with exciting seasonal ingredients and unexpected flavor combinations like monkfish and grapefruit, skirt steak with seaweed salad and lots of bright, fresh greens. Portions are small and flavors are big so savor them slowly.

White Horse Tavern TAVERN $$$
(Map p224; ☑ 401-849-3600; www.white horsetavern.us; 26 Marlborough St; meals $30-60; ◷ 11:30am-9pm) If you'd like to eat at a tavern opened by a 17th-century pirate that once served as an annual meeting place for the colonial Rhode Island General Assembly, try this historic, gambrel-roofed beauty. It opened in 1673, making it one of America's oldest taverns. Menus for dinner (at which men should wear a jacket) might include

baked escargot, truffle-crusted Atlantic halibut or beef Wellington. Service is hit-or-miss.

Drinking

This is a resort town, and in July and August it teems with crowds looking for a good time, which is why Thames St often feels like either a cobblestone obstacle course or an out-of-control sorority party. For what's going on, check out the 'Lifebeat' section in the *Providence Journal*.

Coffee Grinders COFFEEHOUSE
(Map p224; ☑ 401-847-9307; 33 Bannister's Wharf; ⊗ 6:30am-11pm summer, call in winter) Enjoy espresso and a pastry on some benches at this small shingled shack at the end of Bannister's Wharf. You'll be surrounded by water, with great views over yacht activity and crustaceans being unloaded at the Aquidneck Lobster Company.

Fastnet BAR
(Map p224; www.thefastnetpub.com; 1 Broadway; ⊗ 11am-1am) Named for a lighthouse off the coast of Cork, this pub serves classics like bangers and mash and fish and chips, beside an ever-flowing river of Guinness. There's live Irish music every Sunday night.

Brick Alley Pub PUB
(Map p224; ☑ 401-849-6334; www.brickalley.com; 140 Thames St; meals $10-20; ⊗ 11.30am-9pm Sun-Thu, to 10pm Fri & Sat) With wood-paneled booths, exposed-brick wall and vintage memorabilia, the Brick Alley Pub is a fun and friendly place. Lounge on the large patio and order one of Newport's locally brewed beers or a frozen Mudslide (equal parts vodka, Kahlua and Baileys). If the munchies strike their lobster rolls once won an award from *Bon Appetit* for best in the US.

Salvation Café BAR
(Map p224; www.salvationcafe.com; 140 Broadway; ⊗ 5pm-midnight) With its outdoor Tiki lounge, corduroy velvet couches, stylish Formica tables and wood-paneled walls, this bar-cum-restaurant is indeed a salvation from Newport's tourist hordes. Here, you'll find creative cocktails served alongside grass-fed hanger steak frites, organic tandoori chicken (entrees $18 to $24) and the like.

☆ Entertainment

Newport Blues Café CLUB
(Map p224; ☑ 401-841-5510; www.newportblues.com; 286 Thames St) This popular rhythm and blues bar and restaurant draws top acts to

an old brownstone that was once a bank. It's an intimate space with many enjoying quahogs, house-smoked ribs or pork loins at tables adjoining the small stage. Dinner is offered 6pm to 10pm; the music starts at 9:30pm.

Jane Pickens Theater CINEMA
(Map p224; ☑ 401-846-5252; www.janepickens.com; 49 Touro St) This beautifully restored one-screen art house used to be an Episcopalian church, built around 1834. Simple, pretty and old, the theater contains an organ and a balcony. It screens both popular and art-house films.

ⓘ Information

Newport Visitor Center (Map p224; ☑ 401-845-9123; www.gonewport.com; 23 America's Cup Ave; ⊗ 9am-5pm) Offers maps, brochures, local bus information, tickets to major attractions, public restrooms and an ATM. There's free parking for 30 minutes adjacent to the center.

ⓘ Getting There & Around

BICYCLE
Scooter World (☑ 401-619-1349; www.scooterworldri.com; 11 Christie's Landing; per day $30; ⊗ 9am-7pm) Scooters are available by the hour ($30 for first hour, $10 each additional hour) or by the day ($125), as are bicycles ($7/30 per hour/day), kayaks ($25/50 per hour/half-day) and jet skis ($145 per hour).

BOAT
Interstate Navigation (Map p224; www.blockislandferry.com; Perotti Park, 39 America's Cup Ave; one-way adult/child/bike $25.50/13/6) Between June and September ferries depart three times daily from a dock near Fort Adams to Block Island.

BUS
Bonanza Bus Lines (☑ 401-846-1820; www.peterpanbus.com) Operates buses to Boston ($27, 1¾ hours, four to five daily) from the visitor center.

RIPTA (www.ripta.com) Bus 60 serves Providence ($2, one hour) almost every hour. For the South Kingstown Amtrak station, take bus 64 or 66 ($2, 90 minutes, five buses Monday to Friday, three on Saturday). Bus 14 serves TF Green airport (70 minutes) in Wickford.

Most RIPTA buses arrive and depart from the visitor center.

CAR & MOTORCYCLE
Parking is tough in Newport. The very lucky might find free parking on the street, though

most nonmetered spots are reserved for Newport residents. The most convenient garage is at the Newport Gateway Transportation & Visitor Center, which gives you the first half-hour for free, the next for $3 and $24.50 per day.

Around Newport

More rural than its prosperous neighbor Newport, Conanicut Island's first inhabitants were Quaker farmers, shepherds and pirates. Captain Kidd spent considerable time here and is said to have buried his treasure on the island.

These days, the real treasure of the island's center, **Jamestown**, is the peace and quiet. The waterfront is undeveloped and you can walk along Conanicut Ave and take a bench overlooking the harbor. The island also makes a good day trip for families who can explore Rhode Island's last operational windmill and wander around **Watson Farm** (☑401-423-0005; www.historicnewengland.org; 455 North Rd; adult/child $4/free; ☺1-5pm Tue, Thu & Sun Jun–mid-Oct; ℗), a 200-year-old working farm that continues to practice traditional farming methods, grazing Red Devon cattle across its seaside pastures. A self-guided walking map is provided.

At the southernmost tip of Conanicut Island is **Beavertail State Park**, where you can enjoy one of the best vistas – and sunsets – in the Ocean State. Many vacationers bring lawn chairs, barbecues and picnics and spend all day enjoying the walking trails and clifftop views. At the point, picturesque **Beavertail Lighthouse** (1749; www.beavertaillight.org), one of the oldest along the Atlantic coast, still signals ships into Narragansett Bay.

West, across Mackerel Cove (the site of Jamestown's protected family beach), you'll find the quiet **Fort Getty park** and campground (☑401-423-7211; www.jamestownri.net/parks/ftgetty.html; tent/RV sites $25/40) with 25 tent and 100 RV sites. The views from here are fabulous but the facilities and shade are minimal.

The Jamestown ferry sails to Newport with stops at Fort Adams and Rose Island. It is the best deal going for a harbor tour. To cross the bridge into Newport you have to pay a $4 toll each way.

NARRAGANSETT & POINT JUDITH

Named after one of the most powerful Native American tribes in New England, Narragansett, meaning literally 'People of the Small Point,' is the essence of Rhode Island. Surrounded by miles of sandy beaches and punctuated by salt ponds and mudflats it became a popular beach resort at the end of the 19th century. Large oceanfront hotels were constructed, a holiday **pier** (rebuilt in the 1970s) and a Stanford White–designed Towers Casino, of which only the **twin towers** (www.thetowersri.com) remain standing on Ocean Dr. But you're not here for the architecture. Head out of town in almost any direction, beach umbrella in hand, or make your way south along RI 108 to Point Judith to catch the ferry for Block Island. John Casey's award-winning novel, *Spartina*, is set nearby in **Galilee**, Rhode Island's major fishing port.

Fronted by commercial warehouses and the takeout Shuckintruck, Point Judith is a great place to eat. Head for the deck at **Champlin's Seafood** (☑401-783-3152; 256 Great Rd; dishes $3-15; ☺11am-9pm summer, shorter hours off-season) for lobster rolls, stuffed clams, snail salad or one of many breaded and fried sea critters. The swaying masts of rusty fishing vessels keep you company. On Point Judith Pond, **Matunuck Oyster Bar** (www.rhodyoysters.com; 629 Succotash Rd, Matunuck; meals $20-30; ☺11:30am-9pm) serves up bivalves raised in its own farm at Potter Pond Estuary. The oyster sampler ($20) lets you try 12 varieties.

★**Fishermen's Memorial State Park** (☑401-789-8374; www.riparks.com; 1011 Point Judith Rd; tent sites RI residents/nonresidents $14/20; ☺May-Oct) in Galilee is so popular that many families return year after year to the same site. There are only 180 campsites, so it's wise to reserve early through the RI

LOCAL KNOWLEDGE

DIY BAY CRUISES

The Jamestown ferry sails to Newport with stops at Fort Adams and Rose Island. It is the best deal going for a harbor cruise. If you want to make more of a stop on Rose Island, landing fees are adult/child $5/4 and you can spend the day beachcombing, fishing, touring the lighthouse and swimming, before being picked up on the return journey.

State Parks website (www.riparks.com). Alternatively, book into the English Gothic Manor, **The Richards** (401-789-7746; www.therichardsbnb.com; 144 Gibson Ave, Narragansett; incl breakfast r $165-185, ste $200-240;), in Narragansett, or press on to the beachy town of **Matunuck** for the **Admiral Dewey Inn** (800-457-2090, 401-783-2090; www.admiraldeweyinn.com; 668 Matunuck Beach Rd, South Kingstown; r incl breakfast $120-170;), an 1898 National Historic Register building with 10 rooms with sea views.

If heading to Manutuck don't miss sundowners at **Ocean Mist** (401-782-3740; www.oceanmist.net; 145 Matunuck Beach Rd; 10-1am), where the outdoor deck extends so close to the sea that an offshore breeze can knock the head off your beer.

Activities

All-day parking in all of the beach lots costs $10.

Narragansett Town Beach   BEACH
(39 Boston Neck Rd; single entry/season pass $6/25; admission office 8:30am-5:30pm) This mile-long stretch of beach tends to be crowded because it's an easy walk from Narragansett Pier. Its popular with surfers thanks to its soft curling waves, and is serviced by two pavilions, changing rooms and restrooms. It's the only beach in Rhode Island that charges a per-person admission fee on top of parking.

Scarborough State Beach   BEACH
(970 Ocean Rd) Scarborough (sometimes written as 'Scarboro') is considered by many to be the best in the state. A massive, castle-like pavilion, generous boardwalks, a wide and long beachfront, on-duty lifeguards and great, predictable surf make Scarborough special. On a hot summer day, expect hordes of beachgoers.

Roger Wheeler State Beach   BEACH
(100 Sand Hill Cove Rd) Locally known as Sand Hill Cove, the Roger W Wheeler Memorial Beach, just south of Galilee, is the spot for families with small children. Not only does it have a playground and other facilities, it also has an extremely gradual drop-off and little surf because of protection afforded by the rocky arms of the Point Judith breakwater.

Information

Narragansett Chamber of Commerce (401-783-7121; www.narragansettri.com/chamber;

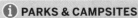

PARKS & CAMPSITES

The Rhode Island Division of Parks & Recreation (p433) manages a collection of beaches and campsites throughout the state. You can make reservations through the website, which gives full information on facilities and pitches.

36 Ocean Rd, Narragansett) For information on the town of Narragansett and its vicinity. It also operates a very useful free shuttle from an out-of-town parking lot to the downtown and pier areas during summer weekends.

South County Tourism Council (800-548-4662; www.southcountyri.com) For in-depth coverage of the entire South County area, including beaches and attractions, contact this office.

SOUTHERN RHODE ISLAND

South of Matunuck the tribal lands of the Narragansett Nation spread south across 1800 acres of woods and fields encompassing Charlestown on the coast and, to the north, Richmond with its white-clapboard mill villages of Carolina and Shannock. In the westernmost corner of the state, Westerly sits on the Pawcatuck River, which marks the boundary between Rhode Island and Connecticut. Once a wealthy 19th-century town, it's now a quiet commuter community, upstaged by the wealthy Watch Hill resort.

Charlestown

POP 7800

Situated on the coast, Charlestown is framed by beaches and salt ponds rich in crabs and quahogs. The largest of these, Ninigret (or Charlestown) Pond is surrounded by the 1711-acre **Ninigret State Conservation Area** (50 Bend Rd, Charlestown;), a coastal lagoon bounded by barrier beaches and fed by freshwater springs. A 2.5 mile beach (known as East Beach) fronts the ocean and offers fishing (striped bass, flounder, bluefish and tautog), a 10-speed bicycle course and well-marked walking trails, while the **Ninigret Wildlife Refuge** shelters deer and birds.

At the southern end of the pond, the **Blue Shutters Beach** is a good choice for families

FANTASTIC UMBRELLA FACTORY

A sprawling collection of farm buildings and wild gardens, the **Fantastic Umbrella Factory** (☑401-364-6616; www.fantasticumbrellafactory.com; 4820 Old Post Rd, Charlestown; ⊙10am-6pm), a former commune, got its start as one of Rhode Island's strangest stores in 1968. You can find almost anything in a series of shacks and sheds filled with a wide variety of gift items: from flower bulbs and perennials to greeting cards, toys, handmade jewelry and scads of stuff hippies favor like drums and hemp clothing. The cafe serves sandwiches and carrot cake. Exotic birds and farm animals walk all over the place, much to the delight of children.

with convenient facilities, a watchful staff lifeguard and mild surf.

Burlingham State Park Campsites (☑401-322-7337; www.riparks.com; off US 1 N; tent sites RI residents/nonresidents $14/20) has more than 750 spacious wooded sites near crystal-clear Watchaug Pond. The park occupies 3100 acres. First-come, first-served is the rule. It's open mid-April to mid-October.

Westerly

POP 22,800

Westerly sits on Rhode Island's western border sharing the banks of the Pawcatuck River with Connecticut. In the 19th century it was a town of some wealth thanks to its high-grade granite quarries and textile mills. That heyday is long gone, although local **Misquamicut State Beach** still draws huge weekending crowds who favor its scenic situation on Winnapaug Pond. It offers families low prices and convenient facilities for changing, showering and eating. Another plus is that it's near an old-fashioned amusement area, **Atlantic Beach Park** (☑401-322-0504; www.atlanticbeachpark.com; 321-338 Atlantic Ave, Misquamicut), which ranges between charming and derelict. Here you'll find plenty to enjoy or avoid – miniature golf, batting cages and kiddie rides.

New England Airlines (p240) flies from Westerly airport to Block Island.

Watch Hill

POP 154

One of the tiniest summer colonies in the Ocean State, Watch Hill occupies a spit of land at the southwesternmost point of Rhode Island. Drive into the village along winding RI 1A, and the place grabs you: huge, shingled and Queen Anne summerhouses command the rolling landscape from their perches high on rocky knolls. Though they were built around the turn of the 19th century, contemporaneously with Newport's mansions, they aren't flashy palaces. Perhaps partly because of that, Watch Hill's houses are still in private hands – previous and current residents include Clarke Gable, Henry Ford and Taylor Swift.

Summertime parking in downtown Watch Hill is a real hassle. Most curb parking is vigorously reserved for town residents. If you're lucky, you can snag a free spot (strict three-hour limit) on Bay St. Otherwise, expect to shell out $10 to $15 at one of several lots.

Visitors spend their time at the beach and browsing in the shops along the two-block-long main drag, Bay St. For children, an ice-cream cone and a twirl on the carousel provide immediate gratification and fodder for fond memories. For adults, there is next to nothing to do at night.

◉ Sights & Activities

Flying Horses Carousel CAROUSEL

(Bay St; rides $1; ⊙11am-9pm Mon-Fri, 10am-9pm Sat & Sun) The antique ride dates from 1883. Besides being perhaps the oldest carousel in the country, it boasts a unique design: its horses are suspended on chains so that they really do 'fly' outward as the carousel spins around. The flying horses have a mane of real horsehair and real leather saddles. No riders over 12 years old.

East Beach BEACH

FREE This fine beach is in front of the Ocean House Hotel. It stretches for several miles from the Watch Hill lighthouse all the way to Misquamicut, with the open ocean crashing on one side and large, gray-shingled homes rising behind grassy dunes on the other. The public access path to the beach is on Bluff Ave near Larkin Rd and neighboring property owners are vigilant about restricting beachgoers to the public area below the high-tide line.

⭐ Napatree Point   WALK

For a leisurely beach walk, the half-mile stroll to the westernmost tip of Watch Hill is unbeatable. With the Atlantic on one side and the yacht-studded Little Narragansett Bay on the other, Napatree is a protected conservation area, so walkers are asked to stay on the trails and off the dunes.

Watch Hill Beach   BEACH

(adult/child $6/4; ☺ 10am-7pm Mon-Fri, 9am-6pm Sat & Sun) This small beach is behind the Flying Horses Carousel.

🛏 Sleeping

The high season (summer) sees massive price increases for accommodations – and weekends are higher still. Midweek prices are often discounted 25% or more, while low-season rates bring the price down another 25% or so.

Grandview B&B   B&B $$

(☎ 401-596-6384; www.grandvinebandb.com; 212 Shore Rd/RI 1A, Westerly; r incl breakfast $115-140, ste incl breakfast $250; 🛜) Within the town limits of Westerly, but close to the beach town of Weekapaug, this modestly furnished guesthouse boasts a stone porch and a proprietor full of local knowledge. Rooms in the front catch a bit of traffic noise.

Watch Hill Inn   HISTORIC INN $$$

(☎401-348-6300; www.watchhillinn.com; 38 Bay St; r incl breakfast $200-375; P❄🛜) The wood-floored rooms of this mostly modern (and well-equipped) inn contain Victorian-ish furnishings and overlook the bobbing boats floating out in the harbor across the street. It sells out early and hosts a lot of wedding parties. In 2007, a new annex was added, which offers studios and one- and two-bedroom apartments right on the beach.

⭐ Ocean House   LUXURY HOTEL $$$

(☎401-584-7000; www.oceanhouseri.com; 1 Bluff Ave; r from $495; P❄🛜⛱) This visually striking hotel sits like a frosted yellow wedding cake, dominating the bluffs above East Beach. Though designed to emulate the grandeur of a previous era, the Ocean House is a recent construction with ultra-luxe modern amenities, including fireplaces, private terraces, Italian-woven linens and on and on. All rooms include complimentary 'resort activities' from yoga to cooking classes.

✕ Eating

In addition to the following, you'll find an espresso joint and virtually nothing else. For a wider selection of grub, head to neighboring Westerly.

⭐ St Clair's Annex   ICE CREAM $

(☎ 401-348-8407; www.stclairannex.com; 41 Bay St; cones from $2; ☺ 7:45am-9pm summer, 8am-5pm winter) This ice-cream shop has been run by the same family since 1887, and features several dozen flavors of homemade ice cream. On top of traditional light breakfast fare (omelets and the like), it serves seaside specialties like lobster rolls, hot dogs and lemonade.

The Cooked Goose   CAFE $

(www.thecookedgoose.com; 92 Watch Hill Rd, Westerly; lunches $7-11; ☺ 7am-7pm May-Sep, to 3pm Oct-Apr) With its appealing selection of Benedicts, omelets, baked goods (pain au chocolate, house-made donuts) and exotic sandwiches (consider the Nirvana, with baked tofu, honey ginger dressing, cheddar cheese and sprouts on whole wheat), this is a favorite of the Watch Hill elite. Prices are reasonable and the location, across from the harbor, is good for watching the boats.

Olympia Tea Room   BISTRO $$$

(☎ 401-348-8211; www.olympiatearoom.com; 74 Bay St; meals $12-40; ☺ 11:30am-9pm) The most atmospheric restaurant in town is an authentic 1916 soda-fountain-turned-bistro. Varnished wooden booths, pink walls,

---

THEATRE BY THE SEA

For over 60 years, **Theatre By the Sea** (☎ 401-782-8587; www.theatrebythe sea.biz; Cards Pond Rd, South Kingstown; tickets $39-59; 🎭) has entertained families with Broadway musicals and new plays. Recent hits have included *Hair*, *Annie* and Andrew Lloyd-Weber's *Cats*, which featured an all-singing, all-dancing cast accompanied by an in-house orchestra. Go early to enjoy the lovely flower-filled grounds and take dinner in the restaurant after the show. It's a great family evening out and a unique piece of history – the weathered, shingle building is one of the oldest barn theaters in the US.

In July they offer a two-week theater camp for kids. Check online for details.

black-and-white checkered tiles on the floor and the antique marble-topped soda fountain help to ease calf livers, broiled flounder and little necks and sausages past your esophagus.

84 High Street Café AMERICAN, ITALIAN $$$
(☑ 401-596-7871; www.84highstreet.com; 84 High St, Westerly; meals $16-35; ⊙ 11am-late Mon-Sat, 9am-3pm Sun) For big plates of well-prepared Italian-influenced American classics (seafood Parmesan, for example, or baked Ritz cracker-stuffed shrimp), 84 High prides itself on massive portions of hearty, heavy but delicious fare. The lounge bar hosts local bands on Friday and Saturday nights.

ⓘ Getting There & Away

Though the Shore Route Amtrak trains between Boston and New York stop in Westerly, you really need a car to efficiently get to the beaches. Distances are not great: Westerly to Wakefield is only about 21 miles.

Traffic to and from the South County beaches can be horrendous on hot summer weekends. Come early, stay late.

BLOCK ISLAND

POP 1050

From the deck of the summer ferry, you'll see a cluster of mansard roofs and gingerbread houses rising picturesquely from the commercial village of **Old Harbor**, where little has changed since about 1895. Yes, they've added lights and toilets, but – especially if you remain after the departure of the masses on the last ferry – the scale and pace of the island will seem distinctly pre-modern.

The island's attractions are simple. Stretching for several miles to the north of Old Harbor is a lovely beach. Otherwise, bike or hike around the island's rural, rolling farmland, pausing to admire a stately lighthouse or one of the many species of birds that make the island their home. During off-season, the island landscape has the spare, haunted feeling of an Andrew Wyeth painting, with stone walls demarcating centuries-old property lines and few trees to interrupt the ocean views. At this time, the island's population dwindles to a few hundred.

Block Island doesn't use normal US street addresses. Because the place is so small, each house is assigned a fire number, useful if you're trying to deliver mail or track down

a blaze, but not if you're a traveler trying to find your hotel. Grab an island map before you disembark, which shows the location of all hotels.

◉ Sights

You're apt to find Block Island's **Old Harbor** hub simultaneously charming and annoying (at least during peak season). Antiquated buildings form the backdrop of a very lively scene, with pedestrian traffic spilling off sidewalks and inexperienced moped riders wobbling around them. If you're keen to acquire some saltwater taffy, souvenir T-shirts or some beach sandals, you'll find a dozen crowded shops amid all the restaurants and hotels. On a slow day, it's nice to grab a drink on one of several verandas and watch the ferries come and go.

Southeast Light LIGHTHOUSE
You'll likely recognize the red-brick lighthouse called Southeast Light from postcards of the island. Set dramatically atop 200ft red-clay cliffs called Mohegan Bluffs south of Old Harbor, the lighthouse had to be moved back from the eroding cliff edge in 1993. With waves crashing below and sails moving across the Atlantic offshore, it's probably the best place on the island to watch the sunset. Just south of it a steep stairway descends to a narrow beach backed by the bluffs.

North Light LIGHTHOUSE
(⊙ museum 10am-5pm Jun-Labor Day) At **Sandy Point**, the northernmost tip of the island, scenic North Light stands at the end of a long sandy path lined with beach roses. The 1867 lighthouse contains a small **maritime museum** with information about famous island wrecks. As you travel there along Corn Neck Rd, watch for lemonade stands. If riding a bike on a hot day, you'll pray that one is open.

🏃 Activities

Bicycles as well as mopeds are available for rental at many places in Old Harbor. Most islanders resent the noise and hazards caused by mopeds, so you'll get friendlier greetings (and exercise) if you opt for a bicycle. A dozen outfits compete for your attention all with similar prices.

Bird-watching opportunities abound, especially in spring and fall when migratory species make their way north or south along the Atlantic Flyway.

Block Island State Beach   BEACH

The island's east coast, north of Old Harbor, is lined with this glorious, 3-mile beach. The southern part, **Benson Town Beach**, sits closest to Old Harbor; and is supplied with changing and showering stalls, a snack stand and umbrella and boogie board rentals. Heading north, you'll next hit **Crescent Beach**, then **Scotch Beach** and finally **Mansion Beach**.

If you're wandering up the beach from town looking for a picnic spot, be patient. The further north you walk the beach gets wider, the dunes and cliffs get higher and the crowds dwindle.

★ Greenway Trail   HIKING

Explore Block Island's unique ecosystems (dune fields, morainal grasslands, salt ponds and kettle hole ponds) along 15 miles of Greenway walking trails. The trails meander over the southern half of the island through Nathan Mott Park, the Enchanted Forest and Rodman's Hollow. Access can be found on Lakeside Dr, and along Old Mill, Cooneymus, West Side and Beacon Hill Rds.

Rodman's Hollow Natural Area   HIKING

(entrance off Cooneymus Rd) In the south of the island, this 100-acre wildlife refuge is laced with trails that end at the beach – perfect for a picnic.

Clay Head Nature Trail   HIKING

(off Corn Neck Rd) To the north of Old Harbor, this trail follows high clay bluffs along the beachfront, then veers inland through a mazelike series of paths cut into low vegetation that attracts dozens of species of bird.

Block Island Fishworks   FISHING

(☑ 401-466-5392; www.bifishworks.com; Ocean Ave, New Harbor; half-day/full-day charters $350/750) Fishing charters on a small boat with Coast Guard–licensed captain. Possible prey includes striped bass, bluefish, bonito, false albacore, tuna, shark, scup, sea bass and fluke.

🛏 Sleeping

Many places have a two- or three-day minimum stay in summer and close between November and April. Advance reservations are essential. Peak season runs roughly from mid-June to Labor Day. Off-season prices can be far cheaper than those listed here. Camping is not allowed on the island.

The visitor center near the ferry dock keeps track of vacancies, and will try to help

---

ℹ BLOCK ISLAND FERRY SERVICE

Block Island Ferry (p240) offers both traditional and high-speed ferries (return fare per adult/child $25.55/12.50 and $35.85/19.50 respectively) from Point Judith to Old Harbor, although the high-speed service only runs from Memorial Day to mid-October. There are between four and five services daily.

You don't need a car to get around Block Island and, aside from hotel parking lots, there aren't many places to put one. You'll save a ton of money by leaving it behind in the well-organised parking lots at Point Judith ($10 per day). Besides, why mess with the island's pristine ecology and laid-back, bike-riding vibe (there are tons of bike and scooter rentals on the island). If you simply can't live without your car, a one-way ticket costs $38.95, excluding driver. Bike tickets cost $3.20.

---

you should you make the mistake of arriving without a reservation.

★ Sea Breeze Inn   INN $$

(☑ 401-466-2275; www.seabreezeblockisland.com; Spring St, Old Harbor; r $230-310, with shared bath $150-180; P 🐾) Some rooms in these charming hillside cottages have uninterrupted views over a tidal pond and the ocean beyond. Others face inward towards a country garden. Inside, airy rooms have eccentric, rustic furnishings, cathedral ceilings and no electronic distractions like TVs and clocks. Breakfast comes served in a basket, which can be enjoyed on the porch.

Gables Inn   INN $$

(☑ 401-466-2213; www.gablesinnbi.com; Dodge St, Old Harbor; r $135-200) A wood-framed Victorian, the friendly Gables features high beds and small rooms with a variety of lace and wallpaper, often of a vivid floral pattern. Guests have free access to beach supplies (towels, chairs, coolers, umbrellas) and a parlor of velvet furniture. No water view. There's wi-fi at Juice 'n' Java (p240) across the street.

1661 Inn   INN $$$

(☑ 401-466-2063; www.blockislandresorts.com; Spring St, Old Harbor; r $120-450; P 🐾) Set on a sunset-facing hill overlooking the sea, the

RHODE ISLAND BLOCK ISLAND

Block Island

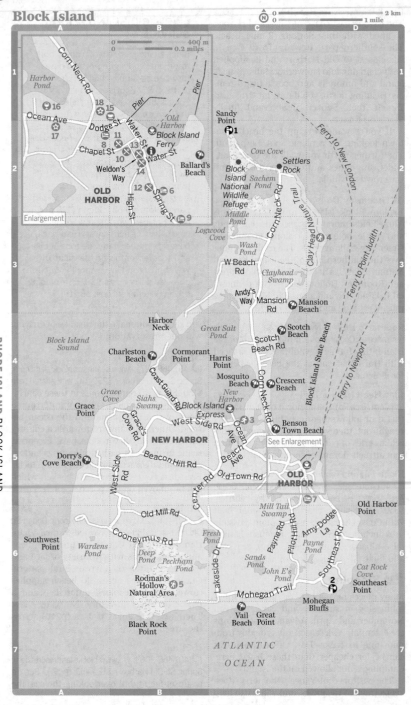

Block Island

1661 inn has one of the best locations on the island. Its nine rooms are decorated in antique style with charming floral wallpaper, brass and four-poster beds and some stunning private decks. You can just walk across the road for one of the island's finest dinners.

Atlantic Inn   HISTORIC INN **$$$**
(☑ 401-466-5883; www.atlanticinn.com; High St, Old Harbor; d low season $185-225, high season $215-320; P) This 1879 establishment overlooks the town center from a gentle perch on a grassy hilltop. The views over ocean and town are commanding and beautiful. The gracefully appointed Victorian inn features a wide porch, a fine-dining restaurant and Adirondack chairs strewn across a spacious lawn. The 21 rooms vary in size, with some on the small side, but all are quaintly decorated with quilts and lace curtains.

✘ Eating

Most places are open for lunch and dinner during summer; many close off-season. Make dinner reservations in the high season or risk hour-long waits.

Aldo's Bakery & Homemade Ice Cream   ICE CREAM **$**
(www.aldosbakery.com; 130 Weldon's Way; ⊙ 6am-11pm May–mid-Oct; ⊕) Family friendly Aldo's has been serving homemade ice cream and pastries, including the delicious Portuguese sweetbread, to Block Island tourists for over 40 years. They even operate a 'pastry boat' so you can have fresh baked muffins delivered right to your deck.

Rebecca's   SEAFOOD **$$**
(☑ 401-466-5411; Water St, Old Harbor; sandwiches $4-7, fried fish $6-13; ⊙ 7am-2am Thu-Mon, to 8pm Tue & Wed) This snack stand serves burgers, chowder, grilled-cheese sandwiches, grease and deep-fried clams, fish, scallops and more to hungry tourists seated at picnic tables under umbrellas.

Mohegan Cafe & Brewery   BREWPUB **$$**
(☑ 401-466-5911; Water St, Old Harbor; meals $10-20; ⊙ 11:30am-9pm Sun-Thu, to 10pm Fri & Sat) Besides brewing its own beer, this atmospheric pub with large picture windows offers a select menu of local fish specials alongside more standard pub fare of steaks and barbecued brisket. The lunchtime lobster bisque and Cajun catfish sandwiches go down nicely with a hand-crafted beer.

Finn's Seafood   SEAFOOD **$$$**
(☑ 401-466-2473; www.finnsseafood.com; 212 Water St, Old Harbor; meals $10-30; ⊙ 11:30am-10pm) Finn's is an island institution, its bunting-draped deck the first cheerful sight that greets arrivals at the ferry dock. Come here for New England style chowder, clams, lobster rolls, steamers and broiled fish that still taste of the ocean. There's a take-out window, too.

★ Eli's   NEW AMERICAN **$$$**
(☑ 401-466-5230; www.elisblockisland.com; 456 Chapel St, Old Harbor; meals $20-40; ⊙ from 5:30pm; ✐) The locally caught sea-bass special (tender fillets over scallions, grapes and beans) tastes so fresh and mildly salty and sweet that its memory will haunt you for weeks. For real. The room is cramped, crowded and casual with lots of pine wood and some well-conceived art.

Hotel Manisses   NEW AMERICAN **$$$**
(☑ 401-466-2421; Spring St, Old Harbor; meals $25-50; ⊙ 5:30-9:30pm) Dine in either the Gatsby

Room, a tall-ceilinged space with old light fixtures and wicker, or on a fine patio surrounded by flowers and bubbling statuary. The menu features local seafood, vegetables from the hotel's garden and homemade pastas. Have flaming coffees and outrageous desserts in the parlor.

Drinking

The fiercely beating heart of Block Island's nightlife scene centers on the crossroads between Ocean Ave and Corn Neck Rd. Here, in quick succession you'll find **Captain Nick's** (☑ 401-466-5670; www.captainnicks.com; 34 Ocean Ave; Old Harbor; ☺ 4pm-1am) rock-and-roll bar, **Poor People's Pub** (☑ 401-466-8533; www.pppbi.com; 33 Ocean Ave; ☺ 11:30am-late) with its barbecue, beer and bands, and down Corn Neck Rd, **McGovern's Yellow Kittens** (☑ 401-466-5855; www.mcgoverns yellowkittens.com; Corn Neck Rd; ☺ 11am-late) with a rowdy crowd, pool table and table tennis. There's live music at one of them virtually every night of the week in season.

★ Oar
BAR, RESTAURANT

(☑ 401-466-8820; Jobs Hill Rd, New Harbor; sushi $7-15; ☺ mid-May–Columbus Day; 🖐🍴) Sitting on the lawn, cold Mudslide in hand, overlooking the boats bobbing in the Great Salt Pond, The Oar is quintessential Block Island and its open-sided, wraparound bar can't be beat. What's more it serves a surprisingly decent sushi menu (although remember this is Block Island, not New York) alongside regular plates of fish and burgers. Work up an appetite with competitive Baggo on the lawn.

Juice 'n' Java
COFFEEHOUSE

(☑ 401-466-5220; 235 Dodge St, Old Harbor; ☺ 6:30am-7pm Mon-Sat, 8am-6pm Sun; @ 🛜) This popular coffee shop serves smoothies – something you'll be very thankful for after last night's encounter with a 2lb lobster with butter. There are also healthy sandwiches, many of them vegetarian, plus there's wi-fi internet access.

ⓘ Information

Visitor Center (www.blockislandchamber.com; Water St, Old Harbor; ☺ 9am-5pm summer, shorter hours other times) Next to the ferry dock, where you'll also find public restrooms.

ⓘ Getting There & Around

AIR

New England Airlines (☑ 800-243-2460; www. block-island.com/nea; 56 Airport Rd, Westerly; one way/round trip $49/95) Flies between Westerly State Airport, on Airport Rd off RI 78, and Block Island State Airport (12 minutes). Westerly is served by Amtrak from Boston and New York.

BOAT

Block Island Ferry (☑ 401-783-4613; www. blockislandferry.com; adult/child round trip ferry $25.55/12.50, high-speed $35.85/19.50) Provides a year-round ferry service from Point Judith to Block Island (55 minutes). This is the only ferry that carries cars for which a reservation is essential. Cars and bikes are carried for $38.95 and $3.20 one way, excluding driver/cyclist.

They also run a high-speed service from Memorial Day to mid-October, which docks in Old Harbor in under 30 minutes.

Block Island Newport Ferry (www.block islandferry.com; round trip adult/child $50/26) Three services daily from Newport's Pirotti Park to Old Harbor run between July and August (one hour).

Block Island Express (www.goblockisland. com; one way/return adult $25/45, child $12.50/22.50) Services from New London, Connecticut, to Old Harbor (75 minutes) between May and September.

CAR & MOTORCYCLE

Island Moped and Bike Rentals (☑ 401-741-2329; www.bimopeds.com; 41 Water St, Old Harbor; per day bikes/mopeds $20/115; ☺ 9am-8pm) Mountain bikes, tandems, hybrids and mopeds as well as beach chairs and umbrellas.

TAXI

Mig's Rig Taxi (☑ 401-480-0493; www. migsrigtaxi.com) A friendly and reliable taxi service that also offers island tours.

Connecticut

📞 860, 203 / POP 3.5 MILLION

Best Places to Eat

➡ Frank Pepe's Pizzeria (p266)

➡ The Whelk (p269)

➡ River Tavern (p252)

➡ Ford's Lobster (p260)

➡ Sharpe Hill (p261)

Best Places to Stay

➡ Inn at Stonington (p262)

➡ Chez Fiona (p270)

➡ Stanton House Inn (p271)

➡ Inn at Kent Falls (p275)

➡ Hopkins Inn (p273)

Why Go?

On the far southern edge of New England, Connecticut is often seen as a bedroom community to nearby New York City and a mere stepping stone to the 'real thing' to the north. Ironically, the comparative lack of tourist interest has saved the state – three quarters of which is rural – from the overexposure of its more 'New Englandy' neighbors.

The Litchfield Hills, with lakes, vineyards and hiking trails, and the Quiet Corner, with its orchards and rolling meadows, capture Connecticut as it's been for centuries. The pristine scenery of the Connecticut River Valley began luring artists in the 1900s, and it's easy to see what inspired them. Dense with historical attractions, don't be fooled into thinking Connecticut is all about the past, the state has an impressive record of innovations from the revolver and the nuclear submarine to one of the nation's first public museums and the cutting-edge Mystic Aquarium, where Dr Robert Ballard (discoverer of the *Titanic*) resides.

When to Go
Hartford

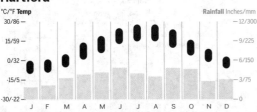

Jun Enjoy New Haven's Arts & Ideas Festival and beachgoing along the coast.

Aug Hit the great outdoors in the Litchfield Hills – and take in the Litchfield Jazz Festival in Kent.

Fall Norwalk Oyster Festival in September and fall foliage in October.

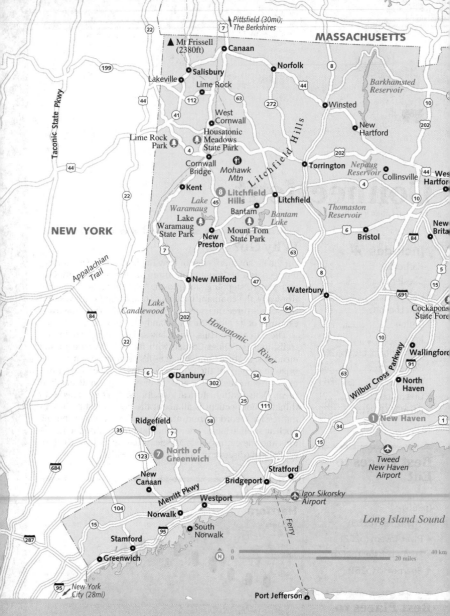

Connecticut Highlights

1 Exploring the excellent museums, bars, galleries and thriving food scene in **New Haven** (p262)

2 Discovering Mark Twain's penchant for fine furnishings

and browsing fine art at the Wadsworth Atheneum in **Hartford** (p244)

3 Scoffing down lobster dock side at Ford's Lobster shack in **Noank** (p260)

4 Casting off amid the salt marshes and paddling for miles in utter tranquillity in the swampy acreage of Stonington's **Barn Island** (p261)

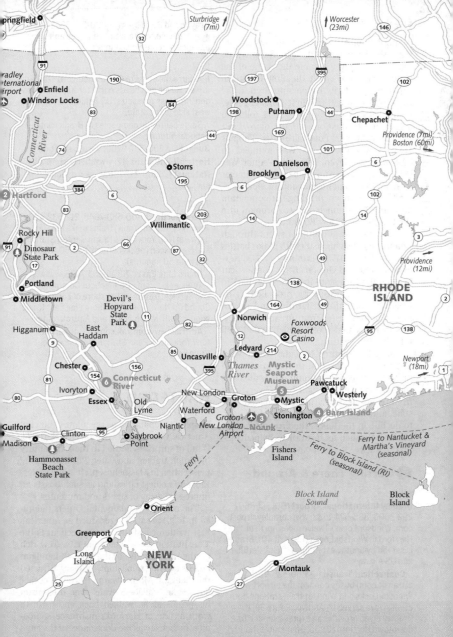

⑤ Appeasing budding mariners with a day, or days, of sailing, boat-building and exploring at Mystic's marvellous **Mystic Seaport Museum** (p257)

⑥ Taking the slow boat or a vintage steam train up or down the **Connecticut River** (p252) for views of castles and eagles

⑦ Discovering shockingly avant garde architecture and art amid centuries-old scenery **north of Greenwich** (p271)

⑧ Bedding down in country inns, hiking forested hills and fly fishing in the Housatonic in the **Litchfield Hills** (p272)

History

A number of Native American tribes (notably the Pequot and the Mohegan, whose name for the river became the name of the state) were here when the first European explorers, primarily Dutch, appeared in the early 17th century. The first English settlement was at Old Saybrook in 1635, followed a year later by the Connecticut Colony, built by Massachusetts Puritans under Thomas Hooker. A third colony was founded in 1638 in New Haven. After the Pequot War (1637), the Native Americans were no longer a check to colonial expansion in New England, and Connecticut's English population grew. In 1686, Connecticut was brought into the Dominion of New England.

The American Revolution swept through Connecticut, leaving scars with major battles at Stonington (1775), Danbury (1777), New Haven (1779) and Groton (1781). Connecticut became the fifth state in 1788. It embarked on a period of prosperity, propelled by its whaling, shipbuilding, farming and manufacturing industries (from firearms to bicycles to household tools), which lasted well into the 19th century.

The 20th century brought world wars and the depression but, thanks in no small part to Connecticut's munitions industries, the state was able to fight back. Everything from planes to submarines was made in the state, and when the defense industry began to decline in the 1990s, the growth of other businesses (such as insurance) helped pick up the slack.

ℹ Getting There & Around

AIR

Bradley International Airport (BDL; ☑ 860-292-2000, 888-624-1533; www.bradleyairport.com; Windsor Locks) Twelve miles north of Hartford in Windsor Locks (I-91 exit 40), Bradley is served by Southwest Airlines, Delta, JetBlue and US Airways.

Connecticut Transit (☑ 860-525-9181; www.cttransit.com) buses connect the airport with Windsor Locks and Windsor train stations both of which are served by Amtrak. Route 30, the Bradley Flyer, provides an express service to downtown Hartford ($1.30, 30 minutes, hourly).

BUS

Peter Pan Bus Lines (☑ 800-343-9999, 413-781-3320; www.peterpanbus.com) operates routes across New England with services connecting Hartford with New Haven ($15, one hour) and Boston ($17, two to 2½ hours).

Greyhound Bus Lines (☑ 800-231-2222; www.greyhound.com) offers similar prices and some advance purchase discounts.

CAR

I-95 hugs the coast of Connecticut. I-91 starts in New Haven and heads north through Hartford and into Massachusetts. US 7 shimmies up the west side of the state.

Some car-rental companies at Bradley International Airport:

Budget (☑ 800-527-0700; www.budget.com)

Hertz (☑ 800-331-1212; www.hertz.com)

National (☑ 800-217-7368; www.nationalcar.com)

TRAIN

Metro-North (☑ 800-638-7646, 212-532-4900; www.new.mta.info/mnr) trains make the run between New York City's Grand Central Station and New Haven (peak/off-peak $20.50/15.50, one hour 50 minutes).

Shore Line East (☑ 800-255-7433; www.shorelineeast.com), Connecticut Commuter Rail Service, travels up the shore of Long Island Sound. At New Haven, the Shore Line East trains connect with Metro-North and Amtrak routes.

Amtrak (www.amtrak.com) trains depart New York City's Penn Station for Connecticut on three lines.

HARTFORD

POP 124,900

Despite its reputation as the 'filing cabinet of America,' Connecticut's capital city, Hartford, is full of surprises. Settled in the 17th century by Dutch traders and, later, Puritans fleeing persecution in Massachusetts, it is one of New England's oldest cities and as such boasts an impressive array of sights and museums.

The colony's Fundamental Orders (adopted in 1639) are widely regarded as America's first written constitution; Connecticut is the 'Constitution State.' Later the city grew rich on the manufacture of the Colt .45 handgun and its thriving publishing industry attracted the likes of Mark Twain, Harriet Beecher Stowe and Wallace Stevens, who dreamt up his poems as he walked back and forth to work at one of Harford's insurance companies. In fact, it was the dominance of the city's gray-suited insurance industry (which was invented here after a city resident insured his house against fire in 1794) that helped flood the city with money, art and culture in the 19th century leaving a legacy of historic attractions worthy of any travel itinerary.

⊙ Sights & Activities

The easiest way to take in most of the Hartford attractions is on foot.

From Main St, it's also an easy walk down to the riverfront, where the not-for-profit **Riverfront Recapture** (☑ 860-713-3131; www.riverfront.org) project encompasses landscaped walkways through a series of interlinked parks. Along here you can wander through the **Lincoln Financial Sculpture Park**, take rowing lessons or join one of the **riverboat cruises** (☑ 800-979-3370; www.hartfordbelle.com). Check out the website for details.

★**Wadsworth Atheneum**   MUSEUM
(☑ 860-278-2670; www.thewadsworth.org; 600 Main St; adult/child $10/free; ⊙ 11am-5pm Wed-Fri, 10am-5pm Sat & Sun) The nation's oldest public art museum, the Wadsworth Atheneum houses nearly 50,000 pieces of art in a castle-like Gothic Revival building. On display are paintings by members of the Hudson River School, including some by Hartford native Frederic Church; European Old Masters, 19th-century Impressionist works; 18th-century New England furniture; sculptures by Connecticut artist Alexander Calder; and a small yet outstanding array of surrealist works.

Barely known outside art circles, the Wadsworth was founded by generous Hartford art lover Daniel Wadsworth, scion of one of the oldest settler families in Connecticut. His father made the family fortune in trade, manufacturing, banking and insurance, and Daniel bolstered the family's reputation with his marriage to Faith Trumbull, niece of celebrated artist John Trumbull. The museum was built on the site of the family home and Daniel donated its first Hudson River School paintings. Where Daniel left off, Elizabeth Hart Jarvis Colt, widow of Samuel Colt, picked up. In 1905 she bequeathed the museum more than 1000 items, purchased from the sale of Colt's weapons to the military.

As if the mind-blowing array of the permanent exhibits isn't enough, the **Amistad Foundation Gallery** has an outstanding collection of African American art and historical objects and the **Matrix Gallery** features works by contemporary artists. The museum's art deco **Aetna Theater** (☑ 860-278-4171; adult/senior & student $9/8; ⊙ Jun-Sep) shows independent and art films during the summer months.

On the first Thursday of the month the museum stays open until 8pm. Most evenings there are also lectures, which are open to the public and free.

★**Connecticut Science Center**   MUSEUM
(www.ctsciencecenter.org; 250 Columbus Blvd; adult/child $19/14, movie $7/6; ⊙ 10am-5pm; ℗) Designed by Italian architect Cesar Pelli, Connecticut's Science Center is both an exciting architectural space and an absorbing museum for adults and kids alike. Innovative, interactive exhibits and programs abound, there's a dedicated KidsZone on the first floor and temporary exhibits include internationally acclaimed shows like 'Bodies Revealed,' an exhibit of 200 forensically flayed human bodies in action.

You could easily spend a whole day here, but it's best to arrive after 2pm when the school groups clear out. In July, the museum hosts a special barbecue evening during Riverfest which gets you a front row spot on the terrace for the fireworks display.

Teachers are eligible for significant discounts.

★**Mark Twain House & Museum**   MUSEUM
(☑ 860-247-0998; www.marktwainhouse.org; 351 Farmington Ave; adult/child $16/10; ⊙ 9:30am-5:30pm Mon-Sat, noon-5:30pm Sun) For 17 years, encompassing the most productive period of his life, Samuel Langhorne Clemens (1835–1910) and his family lived in this striking orange-and-black brick Victorian house, which then stood in the pastoral area of the city called Nook Farm. Architect Edward Tuckerman Potter lavishly embellished it with turrets, gables and verandas, and some of the interiors were done by Louis Comfort Tiffany.

Though Twain maintained that it was difficult to write in the house, it was here that he penned some of his most famous works, including *The Adventures of Tom Sawyer, The Adventures of Huckleberry Finn* and *A Connecticut Yankee in King Arthur's Court.* A tour, which focuses largely on the house's beautifully restored interior design, is included in the admission fee.

State Capitol   HISTORIC BUILDING
(☑ 860-240-0222; www.cga.ct.gov/capitoltours; cnr Capitol Ave & Trinity St; ⊙ hourly tours 9:15am-1:15pm Mon-Fri Sep-Jun, and 2:15pm Jul-Aug) **FREE** Built of New England granite and white marble and topped by an ostentatious gold-leaf dome, the Gothic palace that is Connecticut's

Hartford

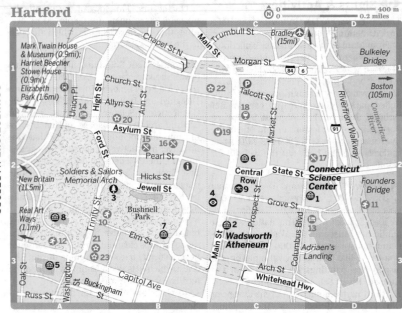

State Capitol (1879) was designed by Richard Upjohn and took over a decade to complete. Because of the variety of architectural styles it reflects, it's been called 'the most beautiful ugly building in the world' (Frank Lloyd Wright dismissed it as 'ridiculous'), but in true Hartford form it is insured for a cool $200,000,000 rebuild value.

Guided tours depart from the southwest entrance of the **Legislative Office Building** (Capitol Ave, near Broad St).

Museum of Connecticut History MUSEUM
(📞860-757-6535; www.museumofcthistory.org; 231 Capitol Ave; ⊘9am-4pm Mon-Fri, 9am-2pm Sat) **FREE** While you're on Capitol Hill, have a look at this museum housed in the **Connecticut State Library**. Nationally known for its genealogy library, it also holds Connecticut's royal charter of 1662, a collection of Colt firearms (which were manufactured in Hartford), coins and the table at which Abraham Lincoln signed the Emancipation Proclamation.

Bushnell Park PARK
(📞tour 860-232-6710; www.bushnellpark.org; tours by donation; ⊘dawn-dusk, tour noon Thu May-Oct) The Capitol overlooks the 37-acre Bushnell Park, the first public park in the US built with taxpayers money. It was designed by

Jacob Weidenmann and opened in 1861. Weidenmann's unique vision – an informal, natural style – broke from the traditional New England central green, and included 157 varieties of trees and shrubs from around North America, Europe and East Asia.

Over time, additions were made to the park, including the Gothic **Soldiers & Sailors Memorial Arch**, which frames the Trinity St entrance and is accessible only by tour. The Tudor-style **Pump House Gallery** (📞860-757-4895; 60 Elm St) features exhibits by local artists and the **Bushnell Park Carousel** (rides $1; ⊘May–mid-Oct; 🚻) delights children with a vintage 1914 merry-go-round designed by Stein and Goldstein.

Center Church RELIGIOUS
(📞860-249-5631; www.centerchurchhartford.org; 60 Gold St; ⊘10am Sun) Established by the Reverend Thomas Hooker when he came to Hartford from the Massachusetts Bay Colony in 1632, this church still holds services each Sunday. The present building dates from 1807 and was modeled on St Martin-in-the-Fields in London. In the **Ancient Burying Ground** behind the church lie the remains of Hooker and Revolutionary War patriots Joseph and Jeremiah Wadsworth. Some headstones date from the 17th century.

Hartford

Travelers Tower   LOOKOUT
(📞860-277-4208; 1 Tower Sq; ⊙10am-3pm mid-May–Oct) **FREE** The best views of the city and the Connecticut River can be found on the observation deck of the 34-story Travelers Tower, named after its tenant, the Travelers Insurance Company. When it was built, in 1919, the tower was the tallest in New England and the seventh tallest in the United States. To reach the observation deck, you have to climb 70 steps along a spiral staircase from the elevator to the deck.

Old State House   HISTORIC BUILDING
(📞860-522-6766; www.ctoldstatehouse.org; 800 Main St; adult/child $6/3; ⊙10am-5pm Tue-Sat 4 Jul-Columbus Day, Mon-Fri Columbus Day-4 Jul; ♿) Connecticut's original capitol building (from 1797 to 1873) was designed by Charles Bulfinch, who also designed the Massachusetts State House in Boston, and was the site

of the trial of the *Amistad* prisoners. Gilbert Stuart's famous 1801 portrait of George Washington hangs in the senate chamber. The newly expanded space houses interactive exhibits aimed at kids, as well as a **Museum of Curiosities** that features a two-headed calf, a narwhal's horn and a variety of mechanical devices.

Harriet Beecher Stowe House   MUSEUM
(📞860-522-9258; www.harrietbeecherstowe.org; 77 Forest St; adult/child $9/6; ⊙9:30am-4:30pm Tue-Sat, noon-4:30pm Sun) As well as literary titan Mark Twain, Hartford was also home to Harriet Beecher Stowe, author of the antislavery book *Uncle Tom's Cabin*. Upon meeting Stowe, Abraham Lincoln is alleged to have said, 'So this is the little lady who made this big war.' Built in 1871, the Stowe house reflects the author's strong ideas about decorating and domestic efficiency, as she expressed in her bestseller *American Woman's Home,* which was nearly as popular as her famous novel.

Elizabeth Park Rose Gardens   GARDENS
(📞860-231-9443; www.elizabethpark.org; cnr Prospect Ave & Asylum Ave; ⊙dawn-dusk) Known for its collection of 15,000 rose bushes, the 102-acre Elizabeth Park was donated to the city by a wealthy industrialist, who asked that it be named for his wife. Planted with more than 900 varieties the gardens are covered in blooms in June and July, but they flower, if less profusely, well into fall. During the summer months, **concerts** (⊙6:30pm Wed late Jul-late Aug) are held at the park.

🛏 Sleeping

Nearly all the hotels in downtown Hartford are on the upper end of the price spectrum (and all charge extra for parking); sadly, quality also tends to be underwhelming. Call **Nutmeg B&B Agency** (📞860-236-6698, 800-727-7592; www.nutmegbb.com/hartford.htm) for a list of area B&Bs.

Holiday Inn Express   HOTEL **$$**
(📞860-246-9900; www.hiexpress.com; 440 Asylum St; d/ste incl breakfast $110/120; ℗⊚⊛) The best value downtown, this straightforward high-rise hotel has a great location around the corner from the train station and admirable views of the Capitol. Parking is $13 per night.

**Hartford Marriott
Downtown**   BUSINESS HOTEL **$$**
(📞866-373-9806, 860-249-8000; www.marriott.com; 200 Columbus Blvd; d/ste $159/299;

P @ 🛜 ▣) This colossal Marriott hotel is in the Adriaen's Landing District overlooking the Connecticut River and linked to the convention center. There are 401 stylish rooms spread over 22 stories alongside an indoor rooftop pool and fitness center. There's also an affiliated spa, an upscale Mediterranean restaurant and a slick bar on the ground floor.

Internet access is an additional $10, and parking will put you back $20 per night.

Eating

The annual **Taste of Hartford** (www.ct.com; ☺ Jul-Aug) event is a great time to explore what's current in the local dining scene.

Tisane Euro Asian Cafe   CAFE $$
(www.mytisane.com; 537 Farmington Ave; mains $15-25; ☺ 7:30am-1am Mon-Thu, 7:30-2am Fri, 8am-2am Sat, 8am-1pm Sun) This odd – and locally loved – coffeehouse-cum-restaurant-cum-bar, somehow manages to morph from one beast to another throughout its long business day. In the mornings, it serves strong espressos and fresh pastries; for lunch and dinner there are Asian noodle dishes alongside Italian-style flatbreads and American-style hamburgers. Later still, Tisane becomes a full-service bar, serving cocktails until last call.

Bin 228   WINE BAR $$
(☑ 860-244-9463; www.bin228winebar.com; 228 Pearl St; paninis & small plates $8-12; ☺ 11:30am-10pm Mon-Thu, to midnight Fri, 4pm-midnight Sat) This wine bar serves Italian fare – paninis, cheese platters, salads – alongside its expansive all-Italian wine list. For those eager to avoid the larger, louder late-night eateries, this is a good option on weekends, when the kitchen stays open until midnight (later for drinks).

★ ON20   FUSION $$$
(☑ 860-722-5161; www.ontwenty.com; 400 Columbus Blvd; meals $30-60; ☺ noon-3pm Mon-Fri, 4-7pm Wed, 4pm-10:30pm Thu-Fri) On the 20th floor of the Hartford Steam Boiler Inspection and Insurance Co, contemporary ON20 serves an elegant fusion menu with peerless views of the city. Dishes, such as lemongrass-scented loin with white bean chilli and laughing bird shrimp with roasted grape, are executed with precision and are beautifully presented with bright drizzles, micro greens and flowers.

The bar menu offers more democratically priced small bites ($4 to $12) to accompany a damn fine house martini among other cocktails. On Wednesday only the bar menu is served in the evening.

Max Downtown   AMERICAN $$$
(☑ 860-522-2530; www.maxrestaurantgroup.com/downtown; 185 Asylum St; meals $50-80; ☺ lunch & dinner Mon-Fri, dinner Sat & Sat) With its swinging tunes, 'pre-Prohibition' cocktails and retro-luxe look – a piano lounge with a long, curved wooden bar, massive wrought-iron chandeliers and leather-upholstered chairs in the white-tablecloth dining room – this is downtown's new hot spot for the professional and political classes. The menu includes classic chophouse fare, like coffee-rubbed 'cowboy cut' beef-rib chop and peach-glazed sockeye salmon. Bookings are advisable.

🍷 Drinking

City Steam Brewery Café   BREWPUB
(☑ 860-525-1600; 942 Main St; ☺ 11:30am-midnight Mon-Thu, 11:30am-1am Fri & Sat, 4pm-10pm Sun) This big and boisterous place has house-made beers on tap. The Naughty Nurse Pale Ale is a bestseller, but the seasonals are also worth a try. The brewery's basement is home to the **Brew Ha Ha Comedy Club** (tickets Thu $10, Fri & Sat $15), where you can yuk it up with visiting comedians from New York and Boston.

Vaughan's Public House   PUB
(☑ 860-882-1560; www.irishpublichouse.com; 59 Pratt St; pub fare $9-16; ☺ 11:30am-1am) This popular Irish pub serves a full pub menu – including beer-battered cod and chips, Guinness lamb stew and farmhouse pie – at a long wooden bar. There are also two taps of Guinness, an excellent happy hour (3pm to 7pm, $3 for 16oz pints) and an amusing mural celebrating famous Irish men and women, including James Joyce and Sinéad O'Connor.

☆ Entertainment

Pick up a free copy of the **Hartford Advocate** (www.hartfordadvocate.com) for weekly entertainment listings.

Black-Eyed Sally's BBQ & Blues   LIVE MUSIC
(☑ 860-278-7427; www.blackeyedsallys.com; 350 Asylum St; cover $4-12; ☺ 11am-10pm Mon-Thu, to 11pm Fri & Sat, bar open late) This blues palace drags in local and national acts. There's live music Wednesday through Saturday, and Sunday and Monday are all-you-can-eat barbecue nights.

Bushnell
CONCERT VENUE

(☑ 860-987-5900; www.bushnell.org; 166 Capitol Ave; tickets $37-70) Hosting over 500 events a year, Bushnell plays a major role in the state's cultural life. Its historic building is where you go for most ballet, symphony, opera and chamber music performances. Among the annual biggies are the **Greater Hartford Festival of Jazz** (www.jazzhartford.org), held over the third weekend in July, and the Monday Night Jazz Series, the oldest jazz series in the country. For current shows contact the **Greater Hartford Arts Council** (☑ 860-525-8629; www.letsgoarts.org). The well-respected **Hartford Symphony** (☑ 860-244-2999; www.hartfordsymphony.org) stages performances year-round.

Hartford Stage
THEATER

(☑ 860-527-5151; www.hartfordstage.org; 50 Church St; tickets $20-60) Staging six major productions and one or two summer productions each season, this respected theater has brought recognized actors (Ellen Burstyn, Angela Bassett, Calista Flockhart) into Hartford. Plays include classic dramas and provocative new works. Venturi & Rauch designed the striking theater building of red brick with darker red zigzag details.

Real Art Ways
GALLERY, CINEMA

(RAW; ☑ 860-232-1006; www.realartways.org; 56 Arbor St; cinema tickets adult/senior & student $9/6.25; ☺ gallery 2-10pm Tue-Thu & Sun, 2pm-11pm Fri & Sat) Contemporary works in all kinds of media find an outlet at this consistently offbeat and adventurous gallery/cinema/performance space/lounge. You can sip wine or beer while watching the drag-queen documentary, listen to an all-female chamber-rock quintet or connect with Hartford's art community at the **Creative Cocktail Hour** (admission $10; ☺ 6-10pm, 3rd Thu of the month).

ⓘ Information

Greater Hartford Welcome Center (☑ 860-244-0253; www.letsgoarts.org/welcomecenter; 100 Pearl St; ☺ 9am-5pm Mon-Fri) The bulk of tourist services can be found at this centrally located office.

Library (www.hplct.org; 500 Main St; ☺ 10am-8pm Mon-Thu, 10am-5pm Fri & Sat) The central library offers free internet access, as well as other resources.

ⓘ Getting There & Around

Centrally located **Union Station** (☑ 860-247-5329; www.amtrak.com; 1 Union Pl), at Spruce St, is the city's transportation center and the place to catch trains, airport shuttles, intercity buses and taxis.

AIR
Bradley International Airport (p244) is in Windsor Locks. The Bradley Flyer connects the airport with downtown Hartford ($1.30, 30 minutes, hourly).

BUS
Connecticut Transit (p244) operates city-wide bus services. A general all-day bus pass costs $3.25.

CAR
By car, interstates connect Hartford to Boston (102 miles), New Haven (36 miles), New York (117 miles) and Providence (71 miles).

TAXI
For cabs, check the taxi stand outside Union Station, or call **Yellow Cab Co.** (☑ 860-666-6666; www.theyellowcab.com)

TRAIN
Amtrak (☑ 800-872-7245) trains connect Hartford to Boston ($65, four hours via New Haven) and New York Penn Station ($40 to $57, two hours 45 minutes).

AROUND HARTFORD

New Britain
POP 73,260

Not technically a part of the Connecticut River Valley, and not really a suburb of Hartford either, New Britain is hard to situate and easy to miss. Indeed, this small formerly industrial city has seen better days. Even so, the city's truly wonderful art museum is reason enough to visit.

The **New Britain Museum of American Art** (www.nbmaa.org; 56 Lexington St; adult/child/student $10/free/8; ☺ 11am-5pm Tue, Wed & Fri, 11am-8pm Thu, 10am-5pm Sat, noon-5pm Sun) has a fine, contemporary interior, but it's the pieces themselves that really stand out at this little-known wonder. Part of that is the museum's storytelling approach to presentation, which groups works according to 'schools' – the Hudson River School, the Ash Can School and the American Scene Painters – and contextualizes each one, giving a fantastic overview of the development of modern American art. What's more the collection is small and features some outstanding pieces such as Thomas Benton's stunning *Arts of Life* murals painted at the height of the Great Depression.

Hungry? Stop in at **Capitol Lunch** (☎860-229-8237; www.capitollunch.com; 510 Main St; hot dogs $1.80, meals $5; ⊗10am-8pm Mon-Sat, 11am-6pm Sun) for some of the best hotdogs you'll find anywhere. Going strong for over 80 years, this is no gourmet sausage shop, but get the famous dog with mustard, onions and secret homemade sauce and you'll see immediately what all the fuss is about.

Nearby **Avery's** (☎860-224-0830; www.averysoda.com; 520 Corbin Ave; ⊗8:30am-5:30pm Tue & Wed, 8:30am-7pm Thu, 8:30am-6pm Fri, 8:30am-3pm Sat) offers 30-plus flavors of sodas and seltzers, still made with 1950s technology in the original red barn where it all started back in 1904. If your group is at least four strong, be sure to call ahead to arrange a make-your-own-soda tour.

CONNECTICUT RIVER VALLEY

Snaking its way from Long Island Sound up through Connecticut and into Massachusetts before forming the border between Vermont and New Hampshire, the Connecticut River covers over 400 miles. It is easily New England's longest river. Mercifully, it escaped the bustle of industry and commerce that marred many of the northeast's rivers.

Today, well-preserved historic towns grace the river's banks, notably Old Lyme, Essex, Ivoryton, Chester and East Haddam. Together, they enchant visitors with gracious country inns, fine dining, train rides and river excursions that allow authentic glimpses back into provincial life on the Connecticut.

Dinosaur State Park

Connecticut's answer to Jurassic Park, **Dinosaur State Park** (☎860-529-8423; www.dinosaurstatepark.org; 400 West St, Rocky Hill I-91 exit 23; adult/6-12yr $6/2; ⊗9am-4:30pm Tue-Sun; Ⓟ) lets you view dinosaur footprints left 200 million years ago on mudflats near Rocky Hill, 10 miles due south of Hartford along I-91. The tracks hardened in the mud and were only uncovered by road-building crews in the early 20th century. Today, they're preserved beneath a geodesic dome and you can tour an 80ft-long diorama that shows how the tracks were made. The park also has a picnic area and 2 miles of interesting nature trails.

Connecticut River Valley

Outside, there are several on-site dino prints where visitors can make plaster casts. The casting site is free, open from May through October, and the park provides everything you need except the plaster of paris, 25 pounds of which is recommended to make several decent-sized casts.

East Haddam

POP 9150

Looming on one of the Seven Sisters hills above East Haddam is **Gillette Castle** (☎860-526-2336; www.ct.gov/dep/gillettecastle; 67 River Rd; adult/child $6/2; ☉10am-4:30pm late May–mid-Oct; **P**), a turreted mansion made of fieldstone. Built in 1919 by eccentric actor William Gillette, who made his fortune in the role of Sherlock Holmes, the folly is modeled on the medieval castles of Germany's Rhineland and the views from its terraces are spectacular. The surrounding 125 acres are a designated state park and are open year-round but the interior is only open for tours from late May through mid-October.

With residents like Gillette and banker William Goodspeed, East Haddam became a regular stopover on the summer circuit for New Yorkers, who travelled up on Goodspeed's steam ship. North of Gillette Castle stands the **Goodspeed Opera House** (☎860-873-8668; www.goodspeed.org; 6 Main St;

tickets $45-70; ☉performances Wed-Sun Apr-Dec), an elegant 1876 Victorian music hall dedicated to preserving and developing American musicals. The shows *Man of La Mancha* and *Annie* premiered at the Goodspeed before going on to national fame.

Also in East Haddam is the **Nathan Hale Schoolhouse** (☎860-873-9547; Main St; ☉by appointment) **FREE**, behind St Stephen's Church in the center of town. Hale (1755–76) is famous for his patriotic statement, 'I only regret that I have but one life to lose for my country,' as he was about to be hanged for treason by the British.

If you're in town for the opera, make a weekend of it and stay at the elegant **Boardman House Inn** (☎860-873-9233; www.boardmanhouse.com; 8 Norwich Road; r incl breakfast $195-295, ste $225-350; **P**❋✿) in the light-filled garden suite. The house is a spectacular 1860 Second Empire mansion with a deep porch, tall French windows and a rose-filled garden.

Chester

POP 4000

Cupped in the valley of Pattaconk Brook, Chester is another sedate river town. A general store, post office, library and a few shops pretty much account for all the activity in the village. Most visitors come either for fine dining or to browse in the antique

---

INTO THE WILD

Connecticut has a bevy of wonderful – and undervisited – parks which are looked after by the **Department of Environmental Protection** (☎860-424-3200; www.ct.gov/deep). Some of them, such as the Essex Steam Train & Riverboat Ride and Dinosaur State Park stand out for their cultural or historical interest as well.

Many Nutmeggers (people from the state of Connecticut) head to Watch Hill, Rhode Island, when they crave serious ocean action, but there are several fine beach state parks where you can view the sunset over Long Island Sound. Hammonasset Beach State Park in Madison and Rocky Neck State Park in East Lyme are two of the best, though summer weekends can see big crowds. For weekend adventure in the rough, the Lower Connecticut River Valley has several options:

Cockaponset State Forest (☎860-663-2030; Haddam) The second-biggest state forest in Connecticut offers fishing, hiking and swimming, horseback riding and more.

Devil's Hopyard State Park (☎860-873-8566; off CT 82, East Haddam) Chapman Falls tumbles more than 60ft over a series of steps. The 860 acres that surround it are popular for mountain biking and hiking.

Haddam Meadows State Park (☎860-663-2030; Haddam) Once a Connecticut River floodplain and agricultural land, this park is now a fine place to picnic on the riverbank.

Hurd State Park (☎860-526-2336; Rte 151 & Hurd Park Rd, East Hampton) This car-free park is beloved by boaters for its riverside camping.

🛈 CHESTER-HADLYME FERRY

In summer you can cross the Connecticut River on the Chester-Hadlyme Ferry (☑860-443-3856; car/pedestrian $3/1; ☻7am-6:45pm Mon-Fri & 10:30am-5pm Sat & Sun Apr-Nov). The short, five-minute river crossing on the *Selden III* is the second-oldest ferry in America and began service in 1769. The ferry ride affords great views of the river and Gillette Castle and deposits passengers at the foot of the castle in East Haddam. In the opposite direction it's a fun way to link up with the Essex Steam Train, which runs between Chester and Essex.

shops and boutiques on the town's main street.

The Connecticut River Artisans (☑860-526-5575; www.ctriverartisans.com; 5 W Main St; ☻noon-6pm daily) artists co-op offers one-of-a-kind craft pieces including clothing, folk art, furniture, jewelry, paintings, photographs and pottery. Hours are shorter during the off-season, so it's a good idea to call ahead.

On any itinerary up or down the river valley, plan to lunch in Chester where Main St is lined with great options. For family-friendly and casual opt for Simon's Marketplace (☑860-526-8984; www.simonsmarketplacechester.com; 17 Main St; ☻8am-6pm; 🖰) a cafe-cum-deli-cum-store. Further along bistro dining is available at the wood-paneled River Tavern (☑860-526-9417; www.rivertavernrestaurant.com; 23 Main St; meals $17-30; ☻11:30am-9:30pm Mon-Thu & Sun, to 10:30pm Fri & Sat) and for something more romantic reserve a table at Restaurant L&E (☑860-526-5301; www.restaurantfrench75bar.com; 59 Main St; meals $25-35; ☻5-9pm Tue-Sun), an intimate French restaurant with a small wine bar serving classics such as coquille St Jacques and braised oxtail.

Essex

POP 6700

Tree-lined Essex, established in 1635, stands as the chief town of the region and features well-preserved Federal-period houses, legacies of rum and tobacco fortunes made in the 19th century. Coming into the town center from CT 9, you'll eventually find yourself deposited onto Main St.

At the end of Main St is the Connecticut River Museum (☑860-767-8269; www.ctrivermuseum.org; 67 Main St; adult/child $8/5; ☻10am-5pm Tue-Sun; 🅿), next to Steamboat Dock. Its meticulous exhibits recount the history of the area. Included among them is a replica of the world's first submarine, the *American Turtle*, a wooden barrel-like vessel built here by Yale student David Bushnell in 1776 and launched at nearby Old Saybrook. The museum runs summer river cruises (adult/child $26/16, June to October) and weekend eagle-watch tours between February and mid-March ($40 per person, Friday to Sunday).

Another good way to experience the river is to take the Essex Steam Train & Riverboat Ride (☑860-767-0103; www.essexsteamtrain.com; 1 Railroad Ave; adult/child $17/9, with cruise $26/17; 🖰), which rumbles slowly north to the town of Deep River. There you can connect with a riverboat for a cruise up to the Goodspeed Opera House before heading back down to Deep River and returning to Essex via train. The round-trip train ride takes about an hour; with the riverboat ride, the excursion takes 2½ hours. The depot is on the west side of CT 9 from the main part of Essex. Take CT 9 exit 3A.

★ Griswold Inn (☑860-767-1776; www.griswoldinn.com; 36 Main St; r incl breakfast $110-190, ste $190-305; 🅿🛜🖰) is one of the oldest continually operating inns in the country, and has been Essex's physical and social centerpiece since 1776. The inn's buffet-style Hunt Breakfast (served 11am to 1pm Sunday) is a tradition dating to the War of 1812, when British soldiers occupying Essex demanded to be fed.

Old Lyme

POP 7590

Near the mouth of the Connecticut River and perched on the smaller Lieutenant River, Old Lyme (I-95 exit 70) was home to some 60 sea captains in the 19th century. Since the early 20th century, however, Old Lyme has been known as the center of the Lyme Art Colony, which cultivated the nascent American impressionist movement. Numerous artists, including William Chadwick, Childe Hassam, Willard Metcalfe and Henry Ward Ranger, came here to paint, staying in the mansion of local art patron Florence Griswold.

Her house, which her artist friends decorated with murals (often in lieu of paying rent), is now the Florence Griswold Museum (☑860-434-5542; www.flogris.org; 96 Lyme

St; adult/child $10/free; ⊙10am-5pm Tue-Sat, 1-5pm Sun; Ⓟ) and contains a fine selection of both impressionist and Barbizon paintings. The estate consists of her Georgian-style house, the Krieble Gallery, the Chadwick studio and Griswold's beloved gardens.

The neighboring **Lyme Academy of Fine Arts** (☑860-434-5232; www.lymeacademy.edu; 84 Lyme St; ⊙10am-4pm Mon-Sat) FREE features rotating drawing, painting and sculpture exhibits by students.

★**Bee & Thistle Inn & Spa** (☑860-434-1667; www.beeandthistleinn.com; 100 Lyme St; r $180-280; Ⓟ🅪), a butter-yellow 1756 Dutch Colonial farmhouse, has well-tended gardens that stretch down to the Lieutenant River, and all nine antique-filled rooms feature a canopy or a four-poster bed. Its romantic dining room is the perfect setting for superlative New American cuisine. Lunch and dinner (meals $30 to $60) are served Wednesday to Sunday, often enhanced by a harpist. Reservations essential.

In East Lyme, well-developed **Rocky Neck State Park** (☑860-739-5471; 244 West Main St/CT 156; sites CT resident/nonresident $20/30; ⊙May-Sep) has 160 sites with showers, concession stands and picnic tables. There's hiking, fishing, horseback riding and a beach for swimming. Take exit 72 off the I-95.

EAST OF THE CONNECTICUT RIVER

The southeastern corner of Connecticut is home to the state's number one tourist attraction and the country's largest maritime museum, Mystic Seaport. Built on the site of a former shipbuilding yard in 1929, the museum celebrates the areas seafaring heritage when fishermen, whalers and clipper ship engineers broke world speed records and manufactured gunboats and warships for the Civil War.

To the west of Mystic, you'll find the submarine capital of America, Groton where General Dynamics built World War II subs and across the Thames River, New London. To the east is the historic fishing village of Stonington, extending along a narrow mile-long peninsula into the sea. It's one of the most charming seaside villages in New England, where Connecticut's only remaining commercial fleet operates and yachties come ashore in summer to enjoy the charming restaurants on Water St.

New London

POP 27,600

During its golden age in the mid-19th century, New London was home to some 200 whaling vessels, second only to New Bedford in Massachusetts as the biggest whaling center along the coast (Nantucket was third). But with the discovery of crude oil in Pennsylvania in 1858, whale oil ceased to be a lucrative commodity and the subsequent decline of New London's commercial port sent the city into an extensive period of decline. More recently the port has been refurbished for sightseeing and cruise liners have started to dock at the State Pier between May and November. Still, New London retains strong links with its seafaring and military past (the US Coast Guard Academy and one of America's five military academies are based here) and has a blue-collar grittiness that places it in stark contrast to the unrelenting cuteness of Mystic and Stonington.

HAMMONASSET BEACH STATE PARK

Though not off the beaten path by any means, the two full miles of flat, sandy beach at **Hammonasset Beach State Park** (☑203-245-2785; www.ct.gov/deep; 1288 Boston Post Rd, I-95 exit 62; residents $9-13, nonresidents $15-22; ⊙8am-sunset; Ⓟ), located midway between Old Lyme and New Haven, handily accommodate summer crowds. Backed by pines the 1100-acre sanctuary offers superb swimming, excellent facilities (including showers) and a long wooden boardwalk.

Stroll all the way to **Meigs Point** at the tip of the peninsula and visit the **Nature Center** (☑203-245-8743; ⊙10am-5pm Tue-Sat Apr-Oct, to 4pm Nov-Mar) before heading out on a trail that meanders through saltwater marshes. There's excellent bird-watching here.

The massive park **campground** (☑203-245-1817; www.ct.gov/deep; sites residents/nonresidents $20/30, with electric hook-up $35/45) sits on the coast between Madison and Clinton. Despite its whopping 550 sites, it's often full in high summer. Reserve early.

🔾 Sights & Activities

The area of greatest interest to visitors is the Historic Waterfront District where you'll find the visitors center, the City Pier and the Ferry Terminal (from where ferries to Block Island depart in summer). Several blocks back from the waterfront, on Huntington St, is Whale Oil Row lined with four white mansions (Nos 105, 111, 117 and 119) built for whaling merchants in 1830. More historic houses line Starr St, between Eugene O'Neill Dr and Washington St.

At the southern end of Ocean Ave is a beach (www.ocean-beach-park.com; 1225 Ocean Ave; adult/child $5/3) and amusement area with waterslides, miniature golf, an arcade and a swimming pool. The parking fee ($15/20 weekdays/weekends) includes admission for everyone in your car, or else it's $5 for adults and $3 for kids. Entrance to the pool is $7.

Hempsted Houses　　　HISTORIC BUILDINGS
(📞 860-443-7949; www.ctlandmarks.org; 11 Hempstead St; adult/child $7/4; ⊙1-4pm Thu-Sun Jul-Aug, 1-4pm Sat & Sun May-Jun & Sep-Oct) Part of a well-laid-out walking tour are two Hempsted Houses; the wood-framed older one (1678) is one of the oldest 17th-century houses in New England and the oldest in New London. It was maintained by the descendants of the original owners until 1937, having survived the burning of New London by Benedict Arnold and the British in 1781.

Custom House Maritime Museum　MUSEUM
(📞 860-447-2501; www.customhousemaritimemuseum.org; 150 Bank St; adult/child $7/5; ⊙10am-4pm Tue-Sat, noon-4pm Sun May-Dec, 10am-4pm Sat & noon-4pm Sun Jan-Apr) Near the ferry terminal, this 1833 building is the oldest operating customhouse in the country, in addition to functioning as a museum. Its front door is made from the wood of the USS *Constitution*.

Hygienic Art　　　GALLERY
(📞 860-443-8001; www.hygienic.org; 79 Bank St; ⊙11am-3pm Sun, Tue-Wed, 11am-6pm Thu-Sat) Done up in a Greek Revival style replete with a sculpture garden, mural plaza, fountains and a large performance area, Hygienic Art is a nonprofit art space featuring 10 to 12 mixed-media exhibits each year. It hosts poetry readings, film screenings, a summer concert series and an annual art show attracting nearly 500 artists. The gardens and amphitheater are open during daylight hours.

Monte Cristo Cottage　　LIBRARY, MUSEUM
(📞 860-443-0051; www.theoneill.org/monte-cristo-cottage; 325 Pequot Ave; adult/senior & student $7/5; ⊙noon-4pm Thu-Sat, 1-3pm Sun; Ⓟ) This cottage was the boyhood summer home of Eugene O'Neill, America's only Nobel Prize–winning playwright. Near Ocean Beach Park in the southern districts of the city (follow the signs), the Victorian-style house is now a research library for dramatists. Many of O'Neill's belongings are on display, including his desk. You might recognize the living room: it was the inspiration for the setting for two of O'Neill's most famous plays, *Long Day's Journey into Night* and *Ah, Wilderness!*

Fort Trumbull State Park　　　FORT
(www.ct.gov/deep/forttrumbull; 90 Walbach St; tours adult/child $6/2; ⊙park 8am-sunset, fort 9am-5pm Wed-Sun mid-May–Columbus Day) FREE The best view of New London is to be had from the enormous Fort Trumbull, which has stood at the mouth of the Thames River since 1839. It was an integral part of the coastal defense system and an early home for the US Coast Guard Academy. Now winding walking paths, a fishing pier and fort tours make it a great place to take kids.

Lyman Allyn Art Museum　GALLERY, MUSEUM
(📞 860-443-2545; www.lymanallyn.org; 625 Williams St; adult/child $10/free; ⊙10am-5pm Tue-Sat, 1-5pm Sun) This neoclassical building contains exhibits that span the 18th, 19th and 20th centuries, including impressive collections of early American silver and Asian, Greco-Roman and European paintings. Among the highlights are the American impressionists gallery and the charming doll and toy exhibit. There's also a self-guided children's art park on the grounds.

US Coast Guard Academy　MILITARY ACADEMY
(📞 860-444-8270; www.cga.edu; 15 Mohegan Ave; ⊙11am-5pm) FREE Visitors here can stroll the grounds of one of the four military academies in the country. Pick up a self-guided walking tour booklet at the museum.

✴️ Festivals & Events

Sailfest　　　ENTERTAINMENT
(www.sailfest.org) This three-day festival in July features live entertainment, tall ships, amusement rides and fireworks over the Thames.

🛏 Sleeping

There's just no other way to say it: pickings here are slim. There are a couple of overpriced, chain hotels near the freeway exits, otherwise the only downtown option is the **Holiday Inn** (☎860-443-7000; www.holidayinn.com/newlondonct; 35 Governor Winthrop Blvd; ☺d $102-119; P❄☎☎☎) (previously the Plaza), which received a complete renovation in 2013. It's well situated for exploring the historic district. Alternatively, base yourself in Old Lyme or Mystic, which are just a short drive away.

✗ Eating

New London is short on fancy restaurants, but you'll find a number of mediocre cafes and bars along Bank St.

Muddy Waters Cafe CAFE $
(☎860-444-2232; 42 Bank St; sandwiches $4.50-8.50; ☺7am-4pm Mon-Fri, 9am-3pm Sat & Sun) This friendly coffee bar is the heart of the downtown lunchtime scene, serving a full coffee menu alongside generous sandwiches and pastries. The outdoor deck overlooks the river and there are stacks of board games, magazines and books scattered around the couches.

★**Captain Scott's Lobster Dock** SEAFOOD $$
(☎860-439-1741; www.captscotts.com; 80 Hamilton St; meals $10-20; ☺11am-9pm May-Oct; ☻) The Coast Guard knows a thing or two about the sea, and you'd be remiss if you didn't follow students of its academy to *the* place for seafood in the summer. The setting's just a series of picnic tables by the water, but you can feast on succulent (hot or cold) lobster rolls, followed by steamers, fried whole-belly clams, scallops or lobsters.

Recovery Room PIZZA $$
(☎860-443-2619; www.therecoveryroomnl.com; 445 Ocean Ave; meals $9-18; ☺11:30am-9pm Mon-Sat) The family-run Recovery Room has New London's best pizza – thin crusted and one-sized – with a variety of topping options. Some of the less-traditional toppings, like barbecue chicken or sour cream, might not suit every taste. But this still makes for a decent stop en route from a day at Ocean Beach Park.

On the Waterfront SEAFOOD $$$
(☎860-444-2800; www.onthewaterfront.com; 250 Pequot Ave; meals $25-50; ☺3-9pm Mon-Tue, 11:30am-9pm Wed, Thu & Sun, 11:30am-10pm Fri & Sat; ☻) Seafood specials such as bourbon tuna with wasabi mash and fried whole clams are served up with lovely marina views from a multitude of windows. A kids

menu is also provided and the bar is a popular spot for pre-dinner drinks before a show at the Garde Arts Center.

☙ Drinking & Entertainment

Part of New London's charm is its rough edges. That charm can wear thin at some of the town's hard-boozing bars. The more raucous bars are on the river side of Bank St. During the day, they are worth a visit for their enviable decks overlooking the river.

Dutch Tavern PUB
(☎860-442-3453; www.dutch-tavern.com; 23 Green St) Raise a cold one to Eugene O'Neill at the Dutch, the only surviving bar in town that the playwright frequented (though back in the day it was known as the Oak). It's a good honest throwback to an earlier age, from the tin ceiling to the century-old potato salad recipe.

Garde Arts Center THEATER
(www.gardearts.org; 325 State St) The centerpiece of this arts complex is the 1472-seat Garde Theater, a former vaudeville house, built in 1926, with a restored Moroccan interior. Today, the theater presents everything from Broadway plays to operas to national music acts and film screenings.

❶ Information

The municipal website (www.ci.new-london.ct.us) has information on accommodation and transport.
New London Mainstreet (newlondonmainstreet.org; 147 State St; ☺9am-5pm Mon-Fri) This downtown revitalization organization has a useful website and a downloadable downtown map and brochure.

❶ Getting There & Away

New London's transport hub is **Union Station** (www.amtrak.com; 47 Water St), which is served by Amtrak; the bus station is in the same building and the ferry terminal (for boats to Long Island, Block Island and Fishers Island) is next door.

BOAT

Cross Sound Ferry (p439) operates car ferries (adult/child $15.20/6.29) and high-speed passenger ferries (adult/child $21.22/9.43) year-round between Orient Point, Long Island, New York and New London, a 1½-hour run on the car ferry, 40 minutes on the high-speed ferry. From late June through Labor Day, ferries depart each port every hour on the hour from 7am to 9pm (last boats at 9:45pm). The 'auto and driver' fare is $53.45, for bicycles $4.25.

Fishers Island Ferry (p439) runs cars and passengers from New London to Fishers Island, New York, several times a day year-round.

Block Island Express (p440) operates summer-only services between New London and Block Island, Rhode Island.

CAR & MOTORCYCLE

For New London, take I-95 exit 84, then go north on CT 32 (Mohegan Ave) for the US Coast Guard Academy, or take I-95 exits 82, 83 or 84 and go south for the city center. The center of the commercial district is just southwest of Union station along Bank St. Follow Ocean Ave (CT 213) to reach Ocean Beach Park.

TRAIN

Amtrak (☑ 800-872-7245; www.amtrak.com; 27 Water St) trains between New York ($49 to $71, 2½ hours) and Boston ($36 to $52, 1½ hours) stop at New London.

Groton

POP 40,050

Just across the river from New London, Groton is the proud home to the **US Naval Submarine Base**, the first and the largest in the country, and General Dynamics Corporation, a major naval defense contractor.

Unsurprisingly, both claims to fame are vigorously off-limits to the public.

You can get into the spirit of things with a visit to the **Historic Ship Nautilus & Submarine Force Museum** (☑ 860-694-3174, 800-343-0079; www.ussnautilus.org; 1 Crystal Lake Rd; ☺ 9am-5pm Wed-Sun; P) FREE, on the Naval Submarine Base. It's home to *Nautilus*, the world's first nuclear-powered submarine and the first sub to transit the North Pole. The brief audio tour is fascinating. Other museum exhibits feature working periscopes and sounds of the ocean.

Groton's other unconventional attractions are the oceonography and seal watching tours run by **Project Oceonology** (☑ 860-445-9007; www.oceanology.org; 1084 Shennecossett Rd; cruises adult/child $25/20; ☺ reservations 9am-4pm Mon-Fri). Established by a group of teachers in the 1970s the project has now developed into a fully fledged marine-science program. In summer months families are invited aboard for research cruises (June to August), seal watches (February to March) and lighthouse expeditions. It is also the only organization with permission to bring visitors to the **New London Ledge Lighthouse**, which features incredible views from the middle of Long Island Sound.

CONNECTICUT'S CASINOS

Rising above the forest canopy of Great Cedar Swamp, north of Mystic, the gleaming towers of **Foxwoods Resort Casino** (☑ 800-369-9663; www.foxwoods.com; 350 Trolley Line Blvd, CT 2) are an alien vision in turquoise and lavender. Built on the ancestral land of the Mashantucket Pequot Tribal Nation (www.mashantucket.com), aka 'the fox people', the casino is a remarkable symbol of the resilience of a tribe that was nearly annihilated by colonists in King Philip's 1637 war and which fought a long and dispiriting legal battle against attempts to declare the reservation abandoned in the 1970s and '80s. Their tenacity paid off, and in 1986 they were granted permission to open a high-stakes bingo hall. The casino and its success rejuvenated the tribe which now numbers around 900 members.

The resort features the world's largest bingo hall, nightclubs with free entertainment, cinemas, rides and video-game and pinball parlors for children. There are about 2266 luxury **guest rooms** (☑ 800-369-9663; d $169-288; P ❄ ☎) in four hotels (the Grand Pequot Tower, Great Cedar Hotel, MGM Grand and Two Trees Inn).

Visitors to Foxwoods interested in the tribe behind the casino should definitely set aside a few hours to see the **Mashantucket Pequot Museum & Research Center** (☑ 800-411-9671; www.pequotmuseum.org; 110 Pequot Trail, off CT 214; adult/child $20/12; ☺ 9am-5pm Wed-Sun Jun-Sep, 10am-4pm Oct-May). This ultramodern museum devoted to an ancient people features dioramas, films and interactive exhibits, highlighted by a very effective simulated glacial crevasse and a recreated 16th-century Pequot village. Shuttles run every 20 minutes between the museum and Foxwoods.

To reach Foxwoods, take I-95 to exit 92, then follow CT 2 west; or take I-395 to exit 79A, 80, 81 or 85 and follow the signs for the 'Mashantucket Pequot Reservation.'

The **Mohegan Sun Casino** (☑ 888-226-7711; www.mohegansun.com; 1 Mohegan Sun Blvd), at I-395 exit 79A, is a smaller version of Foxwoods operated by the Mohegan tribe on its reservation.

On the south side of the bridge, **Fort Griswold Battlefield State Park** (☑860-445-1729; 57 Fort St; ☺10am-5pm daily late May-early Sep, 10am-5pm Sat & Sun early Sep–mid-Oct) **FREE** is centered on a 134ft obelisk that marks the place where colonial troops were massacred by Benedict Arnold and the British in 1781 in the Battle of Groton Heights. The battle saw the death of colonial Colonel William Ledyard and the British burning of Groton and New London.

Mystic

POP 4200

A skyline of masts greets you as you arrive in town on US 1. They belong to the vessels bobbing ever so slightly in the postcard-perfect harbor. There's a sense of self-satisfied calm and composure in the air – until suddenly a heart-stopping steamer whistle blows, followed by the cheerful cling of a drawbridge bell. You know you've arrived in Mystic.

From simple beginnings in the 17th century, the village of Mystic grew to become a prosperous whaling center and one of the great shipbuilding ports of the East Coast. In the mid-19th century, Mystic's shipyards launched clipper ships, gunboats and naval transport vessels, many from the George Greenman & Co Shipyard, now the site of Mystic Seaport Museum, Connecticut's largest tourist attraction.

⊙ Sights & Activities

★**Mystic Seaport Museum** MUSEUM
(☑860-572-5315; www.mysticseaport.org; 75 Greenmanville Ave/CT 27; adult/child $24/15; ☺9am-5pm mid-Feb–Oct, to 4pm Nov-Dec; ℗) More than a museum, Mystic Seaport is the recreation of an entire New England whaling village spread over 17 acres of the former George Greenman & Co Shipyard. To recreate the past, 60 historic buildings, four tall ships and almost 500 smaller vessels are gathered along the Mystic River. Interpreters staff the site and are glad to discuss traditional crafts and trades. Most illuminating are the demonstrations on such topics as ship-rescue, oystering and whaleboat launching.

Visitors can board the *Charles W Morgan* (1841), the last surviving wooden whaling ship in the world; the *LA Dunton* (1921), a three-masted fishing schooner; or the *Joseph Conrad* (1882), a square-rigged training ship. The museum's exhibits include a replica of the 77ft schooner *Amistad*, the slave ship on which 55 Africans cast off their chains and sailed to freedom. (In the Steven Spielberg movie *Amistad*, the museum was used to stage many of the scenes that actually took place in colonial New London.)

At the **Henry B DuPont Preservation Shipyard**, you can watch large wooden boats being restored. Be sure not to miss the **Wendell Building**, which houses a fascinating collection of ships' figureheads and carvings. Close by is a small 'museum' (more like a playroom) for children seven and under. The seaport also includes a small boat shop, jail, general store, chapel, school, pharmacy, sail loft, shipsmith and ship chandlery.

If the call of the sea beckons during your visit, you can visit the Boathouse and captain your own sailboat. Alternatively, take a trip on the **Sabino** (☑860-572-5351; 30-/90-minute cruise adult $5.50/13, child $4.50/11; ☺May-Oct), a 1908 steamboat, which takes visitors on excursions up the Mystic River. Rides are also available on the 20ft Crosby catboat *Breck Marshall* ($6); and full-day charters to **Fishers Island** are possible aboard the 33ft Herreshoff auxiliary ketch *Araminta* ($350 per person, June to October). Weeklong teen charters, sailing programs and boat-building workshops are regular summer sell-outs so book well in advance.

Check the online calendar for hosted events throughout the year.

★**Mystic Aquarium & Institute for Exploration** AQUARIUM
(☑860-572-5955; www.mysticaquarium.org; 55 Coogan Blvd; adult/child 3-17 $29.95/21.95; ☺9am-5pm Apr-Oct, to 4pm Nov & Mar, 10am-4pm Dec-Feb; ♿) This state-of-the-art aquarium boasts more than 6000 species of sea creatures (including three beluga whales), an outdoor viewing area for watching seals and sea lions below the waterline, a penguin pavilion and the 1400-seat Marine Theater for dolphin shows. There's even an 'immersion' theater that involves a live underwater web feed of places like the Monterey Bay Marine Sanctuary.

Argia Mystic Cruises CRUISE
(☑860-536-0416; www.argiamystic.com; 15 Holmes St; adult/child $44/35) There's no shortage of outfits in Mystic ready to whisk you away on a watery adventure. This outfit offers two- to three-hour daytime or sunset cruises down the Mystic River to Fishers' Island Sound on the authentic 19th-century replica schooner *Argia*.

CONNECTICUT MYSTIC

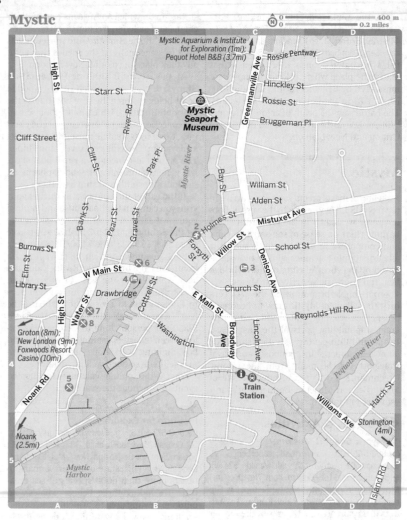

Mystic Aquarium & Institute for Exploration (1mi); Pequot Hotel B&B (3.7mi)

Mystic Seaport Museum

Groton (8mi); New London (9mi); Foxwoods Resort Casino (10mi)

Noank (2.5mi)

Mystic Harbor

Train Station

Stonington (4mi)

✦✦ Festivals & Events

Lobster Days FOOD
An old-fashioned lobster bake held at Mystic Seaport on Memorial Day weekend.

**Antique & Classic
Boat Rendezvous** PARADE
Vintage vessels parade down a 3-mile stretch of Mystic River in late July.

Mystic Outdoor Arts Festival ARTS & CRAFTS
In mid-August, Mystic hosts 300 international arts and crafts people on downtown's streets.

🛏 Sleeping

As a bustling tourism boomtown, Mystic has an array of accommodations. The town runs an excellent website (www.mystic.org) with information. Reservations are recommended in peak season (July and August). Outside of that time, prices drop by 20% and are significantly less midweek.

★ **Mermaid Inn** B&B $$
(☎ 860-536-6223; www.mermaidinnofmystic.com; 2 Broadway Ave; d incl breakfast $175-225; P) This quirky, mermaid-themed Italianate B&B sits on a quiet street within walking distance

of the town center. Its three rooms each have a private bathroom (with bidet and granite bath), TV and special touches such as fresh flowers and Italian chocolates. In warm weather, guests enjoy breakfast on the porch.

Pequot Hotel B&B B&B $$
(☏860-572-0390; www.pequothotelbandb.com; 711 Cow Hill Rd; d $90-175; P ⛱) Once a stagecoach stop, this beautiful property (no children under 8 permitted) is nestled in the countryside north of Mystic and has a wide, screened porch and three luxury guest rooms, two of which have fireplaces. To reach it, head west out of Mystic on US 1 and turn north onto CT 614. After 2.6 miles you'll find the B&B on your right-hand side.

★**Steamboat Inn** INN $$$
(☏860-536-8300; www.steamboatinnmystic.com; 73 Steamboat Wharf; d incl breakfast $160-295; P✳⛱) Located right in the heart of downtown Mystic, the 11 rooms of this historic inn have wraparound water views and luxurious amenities, including two-person whirlpool tubs, cable TV, free local calls and fireplaces. Antiques lend the interior a romantic, period feel and service is top-notch with baked goods for breakfast, complimentary bikes, boat docks and gym facilities.

✖ **Eating & Drinking**

There are several places to grab a snack within Mystic Seaport Museum, but most of Mystic's restaurants are in or near the town center, close to the drawbridge. Among the town's claims to fame is Mystic Pizza, an otherwise unexceptional pizza place that shares its name with one of Julia Roberts' first films. The place might have inspired the movie, but sadly, the food will inspire only the movie's most devoted fans.

Mystic Drawbridge Ice Cream ICE CREAM $
(www.mysticdrawbridgeicecream.com; 2 W Main St; cones $4, panini $7.50; ⊙9am-11pm; ⛱) Strolling through town is best done with an ice cream cone in hand. Some of the more quirky flavors, such as pumpkin pie and southern peach, are seasonal, but on any given day there will be something innovative to try. This perpetually buzzing parlor also serves some light fare, including paninis, salads and quiche.

Pizzetta PIZZA $
(www.pizzettamystic.com; 7 Water St; pizzas $11-19; ⊙11.30am-9pm Sun-Thu, to 10pm Fri & Sat; ⛱) Skip Mystic Pizza and head to this stylish spot down the street, where excellent thincrust pizza is served with toppings ranging from the quintessentially Connecticut (white clam) to the inventive (mac 'n' cheese and chicken fajita). There's also a good wine and beer selection and a pleasant backyard dining area.

★**Captain Daniel Packer Inne** AMERICAN $$
(☏860-536-3555; www.danielpacker.com; 32 Water St; meals $14-24; ⊙11am-10pm) This 1754 historic house has a low-beam ceiling, creaky floorboards and a casual (and loud) pub downstairs. On the lower level, you'll find regulars at the bar, a good selection of beer on tap and no need for reservations. Upstairs, the dining room has river views and an imaginative American menu, including the likes of petite filet mignon with Gorgonzola sauce and walnut demi-glace. Reservations are recommended.

Oyster Club SEAFOOD $$$
(☏860-415-9266; www.oysterclubct.com; 13 Water St; Noank oysters $2, meals $12-35; ⊙4-9pm Mon-Thu, 11am-2pm & 4-9pm Fri-Sun) A little off the main drag, this is the place locals come for oysters served grilled or raw on the deck out back. Classics like chowder and cherrystone clams satisfy traditionalists, while mussels steamed in lemongrass and coconut milk and yellowfin tuna with sweet soy and ginger tempt more adventurous palates.

ℹ **Information**

Greater Mystic Chamber of Commerce
(☏860-572-1102; www.mysticchamber.org; 2 Roosevelt Ave; ⊙9am-4:30pm) The best stop for tourist information in town, located in the train depot.

WHERE THE LOCALS EAT LOBSTER

Locals know that the best place to head for fresh, fresh seafood is the tiny fishing village of Noank, situated on Morgan Point between Mystic and Groton. Almost the entire village is listed on the National Register of Historic Places thanks to its 18th- and 19th-century houses and shipyards, but the real treat in Noank is its seafood shacks. In fact, the quaint marine-side lobster-shack covered in rainbow-colored buoys featured in the film *Mystic Pizza* is Noank's Ford's Lobster (☑ 860-536-2842; 15 Riverview Ave, Noank; meals $10-20; ⊘ 11.30am-9pm Wed-Sat). Here you can sit at an outdoor bar literally framing the dock and devour delicious buttered lobster rolls, clam chowder and mussels in white wine.

To reach Noank from Mystic, take Water St/Rte 215 southwest. When you reach a stop sign take a left (Mosher Ave) and stay right when it divides. Turn left onto Main St and right onto Riverview Ave. BYO beer or wine.

❶ Getting There & Away

Mystic train station (2 Roosevelt Ave) is served by **Amtrak** (☑ 800-872-7245; www.amtrak.com) trains to New York ($52 to $75; 2½ hours) and Boston ($32 to $56; one-1½ hours). It's less than a mile south of Mystic Seaport Museum.

Peter Pan Bus Lines (☑ 800-243-9560; www.peterpanbus.com) operate buses to New York City ($30, three hours).

Take I-95 exit 90 for the Mystic Seaport Museum and town center.

Stonington

POP 930

Five miles east of Mystic on US 1, Stonington is Connecticut's oldest 'borough' and one of the most appealing towns on the coast. Compactly laid out on a peninsula that juts into Long Island Sound, the town offers complete streetscapes of 18th- and 19th-century houses, many of which were once sea captains homes. At the southern end of Water St is the 'point' or tip of the peninsula, with a park and the tiny Du Bois beach.

◉ Sights & Activities

The best way to explore town is by foot. Walk down Water St toward its southern end, climb the lighthouse tower for a panoramic view and then head back north on Main St, the other major north–south street, one block east of Water St.

Old Lighthouse Museum　　MUSEUM
(☑ 860-535-1440; 7 Water St; adult/child $9/6; ⊘ 10am-5pm daily Thu-Tue May-Oct) Climb the winding iron staircase of this squat, granite lighthouse for 360-degree views from the lantern room. Afterwards browse the small museum, which recounts unsuccess-

ful British assaults on the harbor during the American Revolution and the War of 1812, as well as hosting exhibits on whaling, Native American artifacts and curios from the China trade.

Included in the Old Lighthouse Museum ticket is admission to the 16-room Captain Nathaniel Palmer House (☑ 860-535-8445; 40 Palmer St; ⊘ 1-5pm Wed-Sun), one of the finest houses in town and the former home of the first American to see the continent of Antarctica (at the tender age of 21, no less).

Portuguese Holy Ghost Society Building　　HISTORIC BUILDING
(www.holyghostclub.com; 26 Main St) Built in 1836, the club building of the Portuguese Holy Ghost Society is a reminder of the contributions Portuguese whalers have made to Stonington since they settled in the village in the 19th century. Although the club is not open to the public, the society continues its century-long, open-house tradition of spring and autumn Friday fish fries (11:30am to 7:30pm). In August, the Holy Ghost Festival offers an opportunity for a weekend-long feast of traditional food and music.

The festival dates back to the 16th century and commemorates Queen Isabel (1271-1336) and her act of kindness during the great famine of 1293, when she offered her crown to the church in exchange for a miracle to feed her starving people. She was canonised by Pope Urban VIII in 1625. Check out the society's website for details.

★ Saltwater Farm Vineyard　　WINERY
(☑ 860-415-9072;　www.saltwaterfarmvineyard.com; 349 Elm St; tastings $10; ⊘ 11am-5pm Wed, 11am-7pm Thu, 11am-3pm Fri-Sun) Housed in a visually striking, 1930s aluminium airport

hangar, Saltwater Farm is one of the newest vineyards in Connecticut. Surrounded by tidal marshes and cooled by salty coastal breezes the cabernet franc, merlot, chardonnay and sauvignon blanc vintages benefit from a unique microclimate and are only sold locally. But the real joy here is sampling wines on terraces overlooking lush green vines and Wequetequock Cove.

Unsurprisingly, it's outrageously popular as a wedding venue so always check hours in advance. In August they host live band sessions on Thursday evenings.

Barn Island Wildlife Management Area
PARK

(Palmer Neck Rd) **FREE** Canoeists, kayakers, hikers and birders come to enjoy over 300 acres of unique salt- and freshwater marshes at Barn Island. Inhabited by hundreds of species of birds, four miles of hiking trails snake between placid pools and reed beds and offer beautiful views over Little Narragansett Bay and Wequetequock Cove.

🛏 Sleeping

Stonington is the area's quaintest – and most pricey – place to stay. Rates are generally lower out of season and on weekdays.

Stonington Motel
MOTEL **$**

(📞 860-599-2330; www.stoningtonmotel.com; 901 Stonington Rd/US 1; d $55-70; 🅿 ❄ 🛜 📶 🐾) This owner-run, old-school motel is Stonington's most affordable accommodation and is simple, convenient and quaint. The no-frills 13 rooms have cable TV, microwaves and fridges. It's an easy and pleasant bike ride into town and is well located for Saltwater Farm and Barn Island.

WORTH A TRIP

THE QUIET CORNER

Wedged between the Quinebaug and Shetucket Rivers valley, Connecticut's Quiet Corner is known locally as 'the last green valley' between Boston and Washington. The 12 miles of CT 169 between Brooklyn and Woodstock induce sighs of contentment and frequent pullovers. To get to 169 from New London, take I-395 north; from Stonington take CT-2 through Norwich.

From Norwich pick up CT 169 to Canterbury, where the **Prudence Crandall House Museum** (www.cultureandtourism.org; 1 South Canterbury Rd; adult/child $3/2; ⊘ 10am-4pm Wed-Sun May-Nov) records the heroic attempt of a Baptist schoolmistress to offer the daughters of free African American farmers an equal education in 1832 and was arrested for her efforts. Then head on through bucolic Brooklyn where families will want to stop in at the Creamery Brook Bison Farm to pet the bison and stock up on farm shop treats. Come evening, dinner at the **Golden Lamb Buttery** (📞 860-774-4423; 499 Wolf Den Rd, Brooklyn; lunch $30-40, prix fixe dinner menu $75; ⊘ noon-2.30pm & 7-10pm Fri & Sat, noon-2.30pm Tue-Thu; 🅿 📶) 🍴 isn't just a meal, but an award-winning prix fixe dinner with a hayride thrown in.

In Pomfret, quaint accommodation at **Chickadee Cottage** (📞 806-963-0587; 70 Averill Rd; cottages $175-210; 🅿 📶 🐾) allows for further exploration of the region. The carriage house sits on the edge of the 500-acre Audubon preserve and neighbors the Air Line State Park scenic hiking and biking path. Homemade ice creams from **We-Li-Kit Farm** (www.welikit.com; 728 Hampton Rd; scoops from $3.50; ⊘ 11am-8pm Mon-Thu, to 9pm Fri & Sat; 📶) round off perfect summer days.

Detour to Abington for wine tastings and scenic dining amid the vineyards of **Sharpe Hill** (📞 860-974-3549; sharpehill.com; 649 108 Wade Rd; tastings $12, meals $40-55; ⊘ 11am-5pm Fri-Sun). This is arguably Connecticut's finest vineyard, with over 250 medals for its signature Chardonnay Ballet of Angels. Take a walk through the vines before sitting down to a gourmet farm-to-table meal at the vineyard's Fireside Tavern.

Finally end your tour in Woodstock in the flourishing gardens of the **Roseland Cottage-Bowen House** (www.historicnewengland.org; 556 Rte 169; adult/student $8/4; ⊘ 11am-5pm Wed-Sun Jun-Oct) followed by English tea and scones at Mrs Bridge's Pantry. And before heading home, stock up on blueberries and apples at the old-fashioned **Woodstock Orchards** (📞 860-928-2225; 494 CT 169, Woodstock; ⊘ 9am-6pm).

For detailed area information check the **Northeast Connecticut Visitor Guide** (📞 860-779-6383; www.visitnect.com).

Inn at Stonington INN $$$
(☎ 860-535-2000; www.innatstonington.com; 60 Water St; d incl breakfast $185-445; P❄@☎) Well deserving of its recommendation in *Distinguished Inns of North America*, the Inn at Stonington has an easy sophistication and is deeply romantic. From windows overlooking Stonington Harbor you can watch the sunrise and in the evening yachties tie-up at the hotel dock. Country-style rooms are furnished with plump sofas, four-posters, Jacuzzi tubs and fireplaces, and complimentary bikes and kayaks are available for use.

✖ Eating

Stonington's handful of restaurants are within a couple blocks of each other along Water St. On Saturday morning you'll find a farmers market down at the Town Dock selling local honey, veg and cheese.

Noah's CAFE $$$
(www.noahsfinefood.com; 115 Water St; meals $15-30; ⏱ 7.45am-9pm Tue-Sun; 🚸) Noah's is a popular, informal place on Church St, with two small rooms topped with original stamped-tin ceilings. It's famous for its seafood (especially chowder and scallops) and pastries, like the mouthwatering apple spice and sour cream coffee cakes. Lunchtime is a family-friendly affair, while dinner is more formal. Book ahead at weekends.

Water St Cafe NEW AMERICAN $$$
(☎ 860-535-2122; www.waterst-cafe.com; 143 Water St; meals $10-35; ⏱ 5-10pm Tue-Sat, 9am-9pm Sun) North of Grand St, this crimson-walled cafe set in a post-and-beam house offers a creative, modern menu. The restaurant's seafood dishes, often with Asian-influenced preparations (think black bean roast salmon and miso glazed halibut), are the big draw, but basics – like the shoestring fries – also stand out.

❶ Getting There & Away

The only way to reach Stonington is by car (off of I-95). It's also possible to take an Amtrak train to Mystic, then hop a cab from there.

NEW HAVEN

POP 129,600

Much maligned for decades as a decayed urban seaport notable only for being an uneasy home to the venerable Yale University, Connecticut's second-largest city is shaking off its negative reputation with its growing urban sophistication and thriving arts scene.

At the city's center stands tranquil New Haven Green, laid out by Puritan settlers in the 1600s and dotted with white-steepled churches. Around it, the 300-year-old ivied Yale campus offers visitors a wealth of architectural and artistic attractions, from world-class museums and galleries to a lively concert program and walking-tour tales of secret societies.

While Yale may have put New Haven on the map, there's much to savor beyond campus. Well-aged dive bars, ethnic restaurants, barbecue shacks and cocktail lounges make the area almost as lively as Cambridge's Harvard Square – but with better pizza.

◉ Sights

Most of New Haven's sites and museums cluster around its stage-set green. Due south is Long Wharf and the city's harbor, and further south still, in West Haven, is the 7.5-mile long public beach and the Bradley Point boardwalk.

★ **Yale University** UNIVERSITY
(www.yale.edu) Each year, thousands of high-school students make pilgrimages to Yale, nursing dreams of attending the country's third-oldest university, which boasts such notable alums as Noah Webster, Eli Whitney, Samuel Morse, and Presidents William H Taft, George HW Bush, Bill Clinton and George W Bush. You don't need to share the students' ambitions in order to take a stroll around the campus, just pick up a map at the **Visitors Center** (www.yale.edu/visitor; cnr Elm & Temple Sts; ⏱ 9am-4:30pm Mon-Fri, 11am-4pm Sat & Sun) or join a free, one-hour guided tour.

The tour does a good job of fusing historical and academic facts and gives you the fascinating background of James Pierpont's 1702 religious college, which was moved to New Haven in 1717 in response to a generous grant by Elihu Yale, for whom the university later changed its name in 1887. You'll also pass by several standout architectural flourishes including **Phelps Gate** on College St, the modernist Beinecke Rare Book & Manuscript Library and Yale's tallest building the 216ft **Harkness Tower** from which a carillon peals at appropriate moments throughout the day.

Although the tour overflows with tidbits about life at Yale, the guides refrain from mentioning the tombs (secret socie-

YALE UNIVERSITY MUSEUMS

★ **Yale University Art Gallery** (☎203-432-0600; artgallery.yale.edu; 1111 Chapel St; ⊗10am-5pm Tue-Fri, 11am-5pm Sat & Sun) FREE This outstanding museum was Kahn's first commission and houses the oldest university collection in the country, including masterpieces by Frans Hals, Peter Paul Rubens, Manet, Picasso and van Gogh. In addition there are displays of American silver from the 18th century and art from Africa, Asia, the pre- and post-Columbian Americas and Europe. Between September and June the gallery stays open until 8pm on Thursday.

Yale Center for British Art (☎203-432-2800; ycba.yale.edu; 1080 Chapel St; ⊗10am-5pm Tue-Sat, noon-5pm Sun) FREE Architect Louis Kahn's last commission and the setting for the largest collection of British art outside the UK. Spanning three centuries from the Elizabethan era to the 19th century, and arranged thematically as well as chronologically, the collection gives an unparalleled insight into British art, life and culture.

Peabody Museum of Natural History (☎203-432-5050; www.yale.edu/peabody; 170 Whitney Ave; adult/child $9/5; ⊗10am-5pm Mon-Sat, noon-5pm Sun; P ⋒) Has a vast collection of animal, vegetable and mineral specimens, including wildlife dioramas, meteorites and minerals. The Great Hall of Dinosaurs illuminates the museum's fossil collection against the backdrop of the Pulitzer Prize–winning mural *The Age of Reptiles*.

CONNECTICUT NEW HAVEN

ties) scattered around the campus. The most notorious of them, the **Skull & Bones Club**, founded in 1832 is at 64 High St. Its list of members reads like a 'who's who' of high-powered judges, financiers, politicians, publishers and intelligence officers. Stories of bizarre initiation rites and claims that the tomb is full of stolen booty like Hitler's silverware and the skulls of Apache warrior Geronimo and Mexican general Pancho Villa further fuel popular curiosity.

New Haven Green PARK
New Haven's spacious green has been the spiritual center of the city since its Puritan fathers designed it in 1638 as the prospective site for Christ's second coming. Since then it has held the municipal burial grounds – graves later moved to Grove St Cemetery – several statehouses and an array of churches, three of which still stand.

The 1816 **Trinity Church** (Episcopal) resembles England's Gothic York Minster, featuring several Tiffany windows. The Georgian-style 1812 **Center Church on the Green** (United Church of Christ), a fine New England interpretation of Palladian architecture, harbors many colonial tombstones in its crypt. The 1814 **United Church** (also United Church of Christ), at the northeastern corner of the green, is another Georgian-Palladian work.

Across Church St, the 14ft bronze **Amistad Memorial** stands in front of City Hall on the spot where 55 kidnapped African slaves,

who sought their freedom and seized control of the slave-ship *Amistad*, were imprisoned in 1839 while awaiting one of a series of trials that would ultimately release them.

Beinecke Rare Book & Manuscript Library LIBRARY
(www.library.yale.edu/beinecke; 121 Wall St; ⊗9am-7pm Mon-Thu, 9am-5pm Fri) FREE Built in 1963, this extraordinary piece of architecture is the largest building in the world designed for the preservation of rare manuscripts. The windowless cube has walls of Danby marble which subdue the effects of light, while inside glass towers display sculptural shelves of books, including one of only 48 surviving Gutenberg Bibles (1455) and original manuscripts by Charles Dickens, Benjamin Franklin and Goethe.

In the center a sunken courtyard contains sculptures by Isamu Noguchi representing time (the pyramid), the sun (the circle) and chance (the cube).

Grove Street Cemetery CEMETERY
(www.grovestreetcemetery.org; 227 Grove St; ⊗9am-4pm) Three blocks north of the green, this cemetery holds the graves of several famous New Havenites behind its grand Egyptian Revival gate, including rubber magnate Charles Goodyear, the telegraph inventor Samuel Morse, lexicographer Noah Webster and cotton-gin inventor Eli Whitney. It was the first chartered cemetery in the country in 1797 and the first to arrange graves by family plots. Around the turn of the 19th

New Haven

century, Yale medical students would sneak in at night to dig up bodies for dissection, but you can simply join the free walking tour at 11am on Saturdays.

John Slade Ely House   GALLERY
(☎ 203-625-8055; www.elyhouse.org; 51 Trumbull St; ☺ 11am-4pm Wed-Fri, 2-5pm Sat & Sun) FREE Housed in a Elizabethan-style 1905 building in the Audubon Arts District, this nonprofit Center for Contemporary Art hosts three to five thematic group exhibitions of contemporary regional artists each year.

🏃 Activities

Leitner Family Observatory & Planetarium   STAR-GAZING
(☎ 203-285-8840; astro.yale.edu/observatory; 355 Prospect St; ☺ 7pm & 8pm Tue Apr-Oct, 6pm & 7pm Tue Nov-Mar) A little-known attraction, Yale University's observatory hosts an hour-long planetarium show every Tuesday evening after which the observatory's telescopes are open for viewings of planets, nebulae and star clusters.

Shore Line Trolley   TROLLEY RIDE
(☎ 203-467-6927; www.shorelinetrolley.com; 17 River St, East Haven; adult/child $10/6; ☺ 10:30am-4:30pm daily Jun-Aug, Sat & Sun May, Sep & Oct; 🚼) For a unique take on East Haven's shoreline take a ride on this open-sided antique trolley along 3 miles of track which takes you from River St in East Haven to Short Beach in Branford. Bring a picnic lunch.

Bradley Point Park   BEACH
(Beach St, West Haven; ☺ 9am-sunset) Bradley Point is the best family-friendly sandy beach within striking distance of New Haven. Bicycle trails and a 3.5-mile long walkway link Bradley with Morse Beach and Sandy Point to the northeast with views of Long Island Sound en-route. Parking costs $10, or $5 after 4pm.

New Haven

🍴 Courses

Creative Arts Workshop   ARTS CENTER
(✆203-562-4927; www.creativeartsworkshop.
org; 80 Audubon St; classes & workshops $150-
250; ⊙9:30pm-5:30pm Mon-Fri, 9am-noon Sat)
New Haven's Audubon Arts District is between Church and Orange Sts. In the midst
of the Audubon Arts District, the Creative
Arts Workshop acts as a gallery, a cultural
resource center and an art school. Classes
are available in all manner of skills from
sculpture and painting to pottery and jewelry making.

🎊 Festivals & Events

New Haven has a number of annual festivals, many of which include free public
events. Check out Info New Haven (www.
infonewhaven.com) for a calendar.

International Festival of Arts & Ideas ARTS
(www.artidea.org) A city-hosted, two-week
festival held in mid- to late June, featuring
tours, lectures, performances and master
classes by artists and thinkers from around
the world.

Music on the Green   MUSIC
(www.infonewhaven.com/mog; ⊙6pm opening
act, 7pm headliner) This free outdoor concert
series (mid- to late July) has presented the
likes of Soul Asylum, Regina Belle and Los
Lobos.

**New Haven
Symphony Orchestra**   CLASSICAL MUSIC
(www.newhavensymphony.com) In late July,
crowds flock to this annual concert series
(featuring Beethoven, Tchaikovsky and
Mendelssohn) on the Green clutching lawn
chairs.

City-Wide Open Studios   ARTS
(www.artspacenh.org) Organized by Artspace
(50 Orange St; admission free; ⊙noon-6pm Tue-
Thu, noon-8pm Fri & Sat), this annual fall event
sees city artists open their doors to the public for a peek inside the workspaces of some
of New Haven's up-and-coming talent.

🛏 Sleeping

Area accommodations fill up – and prices
rise – during the fall move-in and spring
graduation weekends for local colleges. It's
best to reserve well in advance if you plan to
be in town during those periods.

Hotel Duncan   HISTORIC HOTEL $
(✆203-787-1273; www.hotelduncan.net; 1151
Chapel St; s/d $60/80; ﷽) Though the shine
has rubbed off this fin-de-siècle New Haven
gem – with stained carpets, unstable water
pressure and exfoliating towels – it's the enduring features that still make a stay here a
pleasure, like the handsome lobby and the
hand-operated elevator with uniformed attendant. There are 65 rooms rented on a
long-term basis, plus 35 for nightly rental.
Check out the wall in the manager's office
filled with autographed pictures of celebrity guests like Jodie Foster and Christopher
Walken.

Farnam Guesthouse
B&B $$

(📞203-562-7121; www.farnamguesthouse.com; 616 Prospect St; r $149-199; P ✳ 🛜) The Farnams have a long association with Yale as alums, donors and professors, and you can stay in their grand Georgian Colonial mansion in the best neighborhood in town. Expect old-world ambience, with Chippendale sofas, wingback chairs, Victorian antiques and plush oriental carpets.

Omni New Haven Hotel
BUSINESS HOTEL $$

(📞860-772-6664; www.omnihotels.com; 155 Temple St; d $161-219; P ✳ 🛜) At this enormous, 306-room hotel you get all the smart amenities you'd expect, including a 24-hour fitness center and a restaurant on the top floor. Ask for a room with a view of either the sound or the Green.

Study at Yale
HOTEL $$$

(📞203-503-3900; www.studyhotels.com; 1157 Chapel St; r $219-359; P 🛜) The Study at Yale manages to evoke a mid-century modern sense of sophistication (call it 'Mad Men chic') without being over-the-top or intimidating. Ultra-contemporary touches include in-room iPod docking stations and cardio machines with built-in televisions. There's also an in-house restaurant and cafe, where you can stumble for morning snacks.

🍴 Eating

The Chapel Sq area – just south of Yale's campus, between York and Church Sts – makes up a restaurant district in which cuisines from far-flung parts of the globe are represented. New Haven is also the pizza capital of New England, if not the entire East Coast. The city's most revered parlors are found in what was traditionally the city's traditional Italian neighborhood, Wooster Sq, due east of downtown on Chapel St.

Mamoun's Falafel Restaurant
MIDDLE EASTERN $

(85 Howe St; dishes $4-13; ⊙11am-3am) This hole-in-the-wall Middle Eastern joint serves fresh, cheap, delicious food in a simple restaurant with loads of character (and characters).

Claire's Corner Copia
VEGETARIAN $

(📞203-562-3888; 1000 Chapel St; meals $7-10; ⊙8am-9pm Mon-Thu & Sun, 9am-10pm Fri & Sat; 🛜🍴) Bright, airy and always packed, this has been the best vegetarian restaurant in town for over 30 years. Soups, salads and quiches are excellent, though sandwiches can be a bit anemic. Try something off the Mexican section of the menu, or a sweet treat like the Lithuanian coffeecake ($3.60).

Caseus Fromagerie Bistro
CHEESE SHOP $$$

(📞203-624-3373; www.caseusnewhaven.com; 93 Whitney Ave; meals $10-30; ⊙11:30am-2:30pm Mon-Tue, 11:30am-2:30pm & 5:30-9pm Wed-Sat) With a boutique cheese counter piled with locally sourced labels and a concept menu devoted to *le grand fromage*, Caseus has hit upon a winning combination. After all, what's not to like about a perfectly executed mac 'n' cheese or the dangerously delicious poutine (pommes frites, cheese curds and velouté). There's also European-style pavement seating.

DON'T MISS

NEW HAVEN PIZZA

Pizza fiends from around the country know about New Haven's Wooster St, where Neapolitan pizza pies have been crafted in coal-fired brick ovens since the 1920s when Frank Pepe arrived in town. In 1938, Frank's nephew did a bunk and opened Sally's Apizza just down the street. These days competition has proliferated but the lines at Frank's and Sally's don't seem to get any shorter. Why not do the rounds and find a favorite for yourself:

★ **Frank Pepe Pizzeria** (📞203-865-5762; www.pepespizzeria.com; 157 Wooster St; pizza $7-20; ⊙11:30am-10pm) The granddaddy of the New Haven pizza scene since 1925.

Sally's Apizza (📞203-624-5271; www.sallysapizza.com; 237 Wooster St; pizza $7-16; ⊙5-10pm Tue-Fri, to 11pm Sat & Sun) Some say Sal's spicier sauce puts his pies ahead of the competition.

Modern Apizza (📞203-776-5306; www.modernapizza.com; 874 State St; pizzas $9-18; ⊙11am-11pm Tue-Sat, 3-10pm Sun) Modern has been slinging its Italian Bomb since 1934.

Zuppardi's Apizza (📞203-934-1949; www.zuppardisapizza.com; Union Ave, West Haven; pizza $7.50-30.50; ⊙11am-9:30pm Mon-Sat, noon-8:30pm Sun) Another octogenarian, Zuppardi's is in the quieter neighbourhood of West Haven.

Soul de Cuba
CUBAN $$$

(203-498-2822; www.souldecuba.com; 283 Crown St; meals $15-25; 11:30am-10pm) With its peach-colored walls, Afro-Caribbean soundtrack and spirit-rousing cocktails, Soul de Cuba is warm and inviting. Aside from the enormous and excellent value Cuban sandwiches the menu is packed with sunshine flavors from fried chicken with Spanish olives, to oxtail cooked in red wine and red snapper simmered with tomato, cilantro and garlic.

ZINC
NEW AMERICAN $$$

(203-624-0507; www.zincfood.com; 964 Chapel St; meals $15-35; noon-2:30pm & 5-9pm Tue-Fri Tue-Sat, 5-10pm Sat) Whenever possible, this trendy bistro's ingredients hail from local organic sources, but the chef draws inspiration from all over, notably Asia and the Southwest. There's a constantly changing 'market menu,' but for the most rewarding experience, share several of the small plates for dinner, like the smoked duck nachos or the *prosciutto Americano crostini*. Reservations are advised.

Atticus Bookstore Café
CAFE, BOOKSHOP

(203-776-4040; www.atticusbookstorecafe.com; 1082 Chapel St; 7am-6pm Mon, 7am-8pm Tue-Thu, 7am-9pm Fri & Sat, 8am-8pm Sun) Offers both great coffee and a great range of books.

Union League Café
BISTRO $$$

(203-562-4299; 1032 Chapel St; meals $25-40; 11:30am-9:30pm Mon-Sat) Here's an upscale French bistro in the historic Union League building. Expect a menu featuring continental classics like *cocotte de joues de veau* (organic veal cheeks with sautéed wild mushrooms, $25) along with those of nouvelle cuisine. If your budget won't stretch to dinner, slip in for a sinful dessert like *crêpe soufflé au citron* (lemon crêpes) washed down with a glass from the exquisite wine list. Date place par excellence.

🍷 Drinking & Nightlife

Whether you're in the mood for an artisanal cocktail in a chic setting or a local beer in an old-school dive bar, New Haven has no shortage of nightspots.

116 Crown
BAR

(203-777-3116; www.116crown.com; 116 Crown St; 5pm-1am Tue-Sun) Upscale contemporary design, DJ sets, expertly mixed cocktails and an international wine list draw the style crowd to this Ninth Sq bar. Small plates and a raw bar keep you from toppling off your stool, but style this chic doesn't come cheap. Bartender John Ginnetti runs cocktail classes ($45 per person), if you'd like to learn the art of that perfect pisco sour for yourself.

★ Anchor
BAR

(203-865-1512; 272 College St; 11-2am) Sure, you can score the standard pub-grub burgers here, but you're much better off strolling in later on for a drink in one of the blue vinyl booths. The clientele represents a real cross-section of folks. Throw some tunes on the classics-heavy jukebox, get a drink from the full bar and settle into your vinyl booth.

Blue State Coffee
COFFEEHOUSE

(84 Wall St; 7am-midnight Mon-Fri, 8am-midnight Sat, 9am-midnight Sun;) This small chain of coffeehouses has three outlets in New Haven and they are always packed. Aptly named, these shops donate money to your cause of choice with each purchase. Whether Blue State's popularity speaks to Yale's ideological bent or the fact that Blue State serves strong coffee, delicious and affordable cafe fare is anyone's guess. Free wifi. The other branches are at 276 York St and 320 Congress Ave.

BAR
CLUB

(203-495-1111; www.barnightclub.com; 254 Crown St; 11:30-1am Wed-Sun, 5pm-1am Mon-Tue) This restaurant/club/pub encompasses the Bru Room (New Haven's first brewpub), the Front Room, the video-oriented BARtropolis Room and other enclaves. Taken in toto, you're set for artisanal beer and brick-oven pizza, a free pool table and either live music or DJs spinning almost every night of the week.

☆ Entertainment

New Haven has a vibrant cultural life. On any given night you'll be spoilt for choice, from acoustic coffeehouse warbling to world-class theater performances. Check the **New Haven Advocate** (www.newhavenadvocate.com) for weekly entertainment listings.

Live Music

Café Nine
LIVE MUSIC

(www.cafenine.com; 250 State St; cover free-$20) An old-school beatnik dive with a roadhouse feel, this is the heart of New Haven's local music scene (it dubs itself the 'musician's living room'). It's an odd place where banjo-playing hippies rub shoulders with rockabillies, all in the name of good music.

Toad's Place   MUSIC

(☎ 203-624-8623; www.toadsplace.com; 300 York St) Toad's is arguably New England's premier music hall, having earned its rep hosting the likes of the Rolling Stones, U2 and Bob Dylan. These days, an eclectic range of performers work the intimate stage, including They Might Be Giants and Martin & Wood.

Theater & Classical Music

Yale Repertory Theatre   THEATER

(☎ 203-432-1234; www.yale.edu/yalerep; 1120 Chapel St) Performing classics and new works in a converted church, this Tony-winning repertory company has mounted more than 90 world premiers. Its varied program is presented by graduate student actors from the Yale School of Drama (Meryl Streep and Sigourney Weaver are alums) as well as professionals.

Long Wharf Theatre   THEATER

(☎ 203-787-4282; www.longwharf.org; 222 Sargent Dr) This nonprofit regional theater mounts modern and contemporary productions, from comedy troupes to the likes of Tom Stoppard and Eugene O'Neill, in a converted warehouse off I-95 (exit 46, on the waterfront).

Shubert Theater   THEATER

(☎ 203-562-5666; www.shubert.com; 247 College St) Dubbed 'Birthplace of the Nation's Greatest Hits,' since 1914 the Shubert has been hosting ballet and Broadway musicals on their trial runs before heading off to New York City. In recent years, it has expanded its repertoire to include a broader range of events, including a series of interviews and musical performances.

New Haven
Symphony Orchestra   CLASSICAL MUSIC

(☎ 203-776-1444; www.newhavensymphony.org; cnr College & Grove Sts; tickets $10-55) Yale's Woolsey Hall is home to most performances by this orchestra, whose season runs from October through April. The Pops series performs on Friday evenings.

ℹ Information

INFO New Haven (☎ 203-773-9494; www. infonewhaven.com; 1000 Chapel St; ◷ 10am-9pm Mon-Sat, noon-5pm Sun) This downtown bureau offers maps and helpful advice.

ℹ Getting There & Around

AIR

Tweed New Haven Airport (☎ 203-466-8833; www.flytweed.com; I-95 exit 50) is served by several commuter airlines to Boston or New York. However, flights out of airports in New York City or Hartford are significantly less expensive, and ground transportation to both cities is easy and inexpensive. **Connecticut Transit** (☎ 203-624-0151) bus G gets you to the airport ($3.25, 10 minutes). A taxi costs $15 to $20.

BUS

Peter Pan Bus Lines (☎ 800-343-9999; www. peterpanbus.com) connects New Haven with New York City ($22, 2½ hours, four daily), Hartford ($15, one hour, four daily) and Boston ($33, four hours, two daily), as does **Greyhound Bus Lines** (☎ 203-772-2470, 800-221-2222; www. greyhound.com), inside New Haven's **Union Station** (☎ 203-773-6177; 50 Union Ave).

Connecticut Limousine (☎ 800-472-5466; www.ctlimo.com) runs buses between New Haven and Bradley airport ($50 per person), and New Haven and New York City's airports (La Guardia and JFK, plus Newark) for around $68 to $92 per person. Pick-up and drop off is at Union Station.

CAR & MOTORCYCLE

New Haven is 141 miles southwest of Boston, 36 miles south of Hartford, 75 miles from New York and 101 miles from Providence via interstate highways. **Avis**, **Budget** and **Hertz** rent cars at Tweed airport.

TRAIN

Metro-North (☎ 800-638-7646, 800-223-6052, 212-532-4900; new.mta.info/mnr) trains make the run between Union Station (p268) and New York City's Grand Central Terminal ($15.50 to $20.50, 1½ hours) almost every hour from 7am to midnight. On weekends, trains run about every two hours.

Shore Line East (☎ 800-255-7433) runs **Commuter Connection buses** that shuttle passengers from Union Station (in the evenings) and from State St Station (in the mornings) to New Haven Green. Regional services travel up the shore of Long Island Sound.

Amtrak trains (☎ 800-872-7245; www.amtrak.com) run from New York City's Penn Station to New Haven's Union Station ($39 to $56, 80 minutes), but at a higher fare than Metro-North. Shore Line East travels up the shore of Long Island Sound to Old Saybrook ($6.25, 45 minutes) and New London ($9, 70 minutes).

THE GOLD COAST

The southwestern corner of Connecticut, otherwise known as the Gold Coast, was once home to potato farmers and fishermen until 19th-century railroads brought New Yorkers north. With their blue-chip companies they transformed Fairfield County into one of the wealthiest regions in America with the affluent town of Greenwich at its heart. Now financial firms, yacht clubs and gated communities line the shore. You must ply further north to New Canaan, Ridgefield and Redding for the original Colonial flavor of the area although the perfectly clipped lawns and spotless clapboards are tell-tale signs that many New Yorkers also have second homes here.

Further north along the coast, Stamford, once a stage-coach stop on the New York–Boston post road, is the area's commercial and industrial hub while Norwalk and Westport have quietly thriving cultural communities with radically different characters.

Westport

POP 26,600

Traveling south from New Haven, you enter Fairfield County via affluent Westport, otherwise known as Beverly Hills East for its popularity as a retreat for artists, writers and film stars. Joanne Woodward lives here; she and her late husband Paul Newman established the august and well-respected Westport Country Playhouse ([phone] 203-227-4177; www.westportplayhouse.org; 254 South St; tickets $30-50); while Martha Stewart built her media empire from her Westport drawing room.

Although there aren't any conventional tourist sights, Westport has a lovely location beside the Saugatuck River (perfect for kayaking) and Main St is lined with fancy boutiques and good restaurants, which make it a good alternative to underserved neighboring Norwalk. The Westport Arts Center ([phone] 203-222-7070; www.westportartscenter.org; 51 Riverside Ave; classes $10-60, exhibits free; ⊙10am-5pm Mon-Thu, 10am-2pm Fri, noon-4pm Sat & Sun) is right on the river and has a busy schedule of changing exhibits, kids classes and performances. Also by the river is Downunder Fitness & Surf (www.downunderkayaking.com; 575 Riverside Ave; kayaks half-/full-day $65/95, paddleboard $80/110; ⊙9am-6pm Mon-Thu, 9am-8pm Fri, 8am-6pm Sat & Sun May-Sep, 9am-5pm Sep-Dec & Apr) a one-stop shop for kayaks, paddleboards and surf shorts. You can launch off the dock (fee $15) just below the shop.

Just south of Westport (Exit 18 on I-95) Sherwood Island State Park (www.ct.gov/deep; Exit 18, I-95; weekdays resident/non-resident $13/22, weekends resident/non-resident $9/15;

⊙8am-sunset) is the largest (1.5 miles) beach within 45 minutes drive of New York City. The gentle surf and shallow waters make it ideal for families. Out-of-season (October to March), parking is free and dogs are permitted on the beach.

Food-wise, Westport has a great range of eateries from the Black Dog Cafe ([phone] 203-227-7978; 605 Riverside Ave; meals $10-20; ⊙11:30am-11pm) houseboat, star of *Diners, Drive-ins and Dives*, and Bobby Q's ([phone] 203-454-7800; www.bobbyqsrestaurant.com; 42 Main St; meals $10-20; ⊙11:30am-9pm Mon-Thu & Sun, 11:30am-10:30pm Fri & Sat; ⊕) surprisingly credible barbecue joint (where there's live music at weekends) to the fabulous terrace of chinos-and-boaters favorite The Boathouse (Saugatuck Rowing Club; [phone] 203-221-7475; www.saugatuckrowing.com; 521 Riverside Ave; meals $30-40; ⊙12:30-3pm Mon, 11:30am-10pm Tue-Fri & Sun, 5-10pm Sat) at the Saugatuck Rowing Club and the latest riverside seafood restaurant from the talented chef, Bill Taibe, The Whelk ([phone] 203.557.0902; www.thewhelkwestport.com; 575 Riverside Ave; meals $15-45; ⊙4:30pm-10pm Tue-Sat).

The in-house gourmet restaurant at the Playhouse, the Dressing Room ([phone] 203-226-1114; www.dressingroomrestaurant.com; 25 Powers Ct; meals $15-30; ⊙5:30pm-10pm Tue-Sun & 11:30-2:30pm Sat & Sun; ⓟ), is headed by chef Michel Nischan.

Norwalk

POP 86,500

Straddling the Norwalk River and encrusted with the salt spray of Long Island Sound, Norwalk is fiercely proud of its maritime tradition. The area supported a robust oystering industry in the 18th and 19th centuries, and is still the state's top oyster producer.

The past decade has seen the redevelopment of the crumbling waterfront in South Norwalk, where a clutch of small galleries, funky boutiques and restaurants have opened around Washington, Main and Water Sts, earning the area the 'SoNo' moniker. Thanks to the fast and easy Metro-North train line, it's possible to get from Manhattan to Norwalk in about an hour – and be kayaking around the Norwalk Islands soon after.

◉ Sights & Activities

Maritime Aquarium   AQUARIUM
([phone] 203-852-0700; www.maritimeaquarium.org; 10 N Water St, S Norwalk; adult/3-12yr $19.95/12.95;

⊘ 10am-5pm, to 6pm Jul-Aug) This aquarium focuses on the marine life of Long Island Sound, including sand tiger sharks, loggerhead turtles and harbor seals, whose daily feedings at 11:45am, 1:45pm and 3:45pm are a real treat. IMAX movies are also shown throughout the day for an additional fee ($11.50/9.50 adult/child).

For a more hands-on experience, take a 2½-hour cruise on the research vessel *Oceanic* (per person $20.50). Cruises depart at 1pm daily in July and August, and on weekends in April through June and September.

Stepping Stones
Museum for Children   MUSEUM
(☑ 203-899-0606; www.steppingstonesmuseum.org; Mathews Park, 303 West Ave; admission $15; ⊘ 10am-5pm Wed-Sun, 1-5pm Tue; P) This museum is bursting with interactive, instructive fun, from the weather cycle to gravity to the principles of conservation. The Toddler Terrain is a hit with the under-three crowd. Across the parking lot from the museum is **Devon's Place**, a playground designed with mentally and physically challenged children in mind, but it holds appeal for all.

Lockwood-Mathews
Mansion Museum   HISTORIC SITE
(☑ 203-838-9799; www.lockwoodmathewsmansion.com; Mathews Park, 295 West Ave; adult/8-18yr $10/6; ⊘ tours 1pm, 2pm & 3pm Wed-Sun Apr-Dec; P) This is one of the best surviving Second Empire–style country houses in the nation, so it's no wonder the 62-room mansion was chosen as the set for the 2004 version of *The Stepford Wives*. The 2nd floor houses the Music Box Society International's permanent collection of music boxes, which you can view and listen to on the tour.

Norwalk Islands   ISLANDS
The Norwalk Islands lie a half-mile off the coast of SoNo, and are the playground of a menagerie of gawk-worthy coastal birds. Admission to the historic **Sheffield Island Lighthouse**, activated in 1868, is included in the price of the summer-only **ferry** (☑ 203-838-9444; adult/4-12yr/3yr & under $23.76/13.41/6.17), which departs from the dock outside the aquarium. Or if you want to take matters into your own hands, you can kayak there. The **Small Boat Shop** (☑ 203-854-5223; www.thesmallboatshop.com; 144 Water St; tours $85-105; ⊘ 9:30am-5pm Mon-Sat, 10am-4pm Sun) rents kayaks and small boats, and leads trips to the islands in the summer.

✯ Festivals & Events

Oyster Festival   FOOD
(www.seaport.org) Held in mid-September, Norwalk's oyster festival is a big deal, with skydivers, fireworks, bands and plenty of bivalves.

⌂ Sleeping

There are relatively few hotels in Norwalk. Perhaps because of the town's proximity to nearby New York, many visitors arrive as day-trippers.

★ Chez Fiona   B&B $$
(☑ 203 434 0493; www.chezfiona.com; 8 Lori Lane; d incl breakfast $100-180; P 🛜 🐾 ❄) A short drive north towards Cranbury, Chez Fiona sits prettily amid a dappled forest. With hanging chairs, an outdoor terrace and a climbing frame and slide the house is wonderfully family friendly while maintaining four luxurious, contemporary rooms. Host Fiona provides a slap-up English breakfast and you can even indulge in a spot of yoga on the broad green lawn.

✕ Eating

Swanky Franks   HOTDOG STAND $
(www.theoriginalswankyfranks.com; 182 Connecticut Ave; meals $2.50-7.50; ⊘ 10:30am-4pm; P) A classic Connecticut roadside hotdog stand with checkered floors, photos of locals papering the walls and some fine diner grub, this is the place to grab an affordable bite for the kids on the way to nearby museums. Try a dog topped with the award-winning chili.

The Brewhouse   AMERICAN $$$
(☑ 203-853-9110; www.sonobrewhouse.com; 13 Marshall St; meals $8-30; ⊘ 11:30am-9pm Mon-Wed & Sun, to 10:30pm Thu-Sat; 🚼) Convenient for the aquarium, this 1920s converted brewery is a popular stop for families thanks to its easy-going menu of burghers, beer-steamed mussels and fish and chips. True to its brewhouse past the menu features lots of local microbrews, including the former occupant's Atlantic Amber. A children's menu is also available.

Pasta Nostra   ITALIAN $$$
(☑ 203-854-9700; www.pastanostra.com; 116 Washington St, South Norwalk; meals $25-40; ⊘ 6pm-10pm Wed-Sat) You can feel the love at this black-and-white-tiled restaurant, where chef Joe Bruno has been wowing diners since 1984 with his handmade pastas and exquisite attention to detail. Freshness be-

ing paramount, even the meat is butchered on site. Reservations required.

ℹ Getting There & Away

Norwalk is about 32 miles south of New Haven on I-95.

Metro-North (p244) serves Norwalk South Station from New York's Grand Central Station ($21, one hour) and trains continue to Westport.

Greenwich

POP 62,800

In the early days exclusive Greenwich shipped oysters and potatoes to nearby New York. But with the advent of passenger trains and the first cashed-up commuters, the town became a haven for Manhattanites in search of country exclusivity.

Robert Moffat Bruce, one of Greenwich's wealthiest 19th-century inhabitants, was a textile tycoon who lived in what is now the **Bruce Museum** (✆203-869-0376; www.bruce museum.org; 1 Museum Dr; adult/student & senior $7/6; ✆10am-5pm Tue-Sat, 1-5pm Sun). Its galleries house a natural science collection, a permanent display of impressionist works by the Cos Cob art colony, as well as hosting more than a dozen art exhibits a year. For more on the Cos Cob colony head to the **Bush-Holley Historic Site** (✆203-869-6899; www.hstg.org; 39 Strickland Rd; adult/child $10/free; ✆noon-4pm Wed-Sun), a saltbox built in 1732, which was run as a boardinghouse for artists between 1890 and 1925. It features a wealth of antique furnishings and a recreation of artist Elmer MacRae's studio. Admission is by guided tours run by the Greenwich Historical Society (www.hstg.org).

For a real glimpse of monied Greenwich head across Cos Cob Harbor to the exclusive enclave of **Old Greenwich**, which preserves the feel of the 1800s summer colony in its shingled Victorians and neatly landscaped, 24-acre **Binney Park** with its ponds and tennis courts. The bigger jewel, though, is **Greenwich Point Park** (www.greenwichct. org; Shore Rd, Old Greenwich; day pass $6, parking $20; ✆6am-sunset), whose 147 acres sweep across the promontory and since 2001 has been opened up to the public. Passes (which must be displayed from May to October) are available to buy at the Greenwich Town Hall.

Sadly, the dining scene in Greenwich is a huge disappointment with plenty of slick-looking restaurants offering over-priced menus and sub-standard fare. For a quick bite, **Meli-Melo** (✆203-629-6153; www.meli melogreenwich.com; 362 Greenwich Ave; crêpes $3-15; ✆7am-10pm Mon-Fri, 8am-10pm Sat & Sun) on the main drag, serves salads, soups, crêpes and sandwiches. The excellent value **Stanton House Inn** (✆203-869-2110; www. stantonhouseinn.com; 76 Maple Ave; d incl breakfast $159-195; P❄🖥🐾🖨) provides genteel country-house accommodation in an early-1900s mansion in one of Greenwich's best neighborhoods.

Being only 28 miles from Grand Central Terminal, Greenwich is less than an hour by train. If you're driving, avoid heading north for Greenwich anywhere around evening rush hour, or south into town during the morning commute.

North of Greenwich

The only Gold Coast town without a shoreline, **New Canaan** (pop 19,800) is characterized by big clapboard houses, grand Georgian mansions and, unusually, one of the most famous modern houses in the world: the 1949 **Philip Johnson Glass House** (✆866-811-4111; www.philipjohnsonglasshouse.org; 199 Elm St; house/site tour $30/$45; ✆Wed-Mon May-Nov). Inspired by Mies van der Rohe, this icon of mid-century modern architecture was the home of late Pritzker Prize winner, Philip Johnson, and his art collector partner, David Whitney. Johnson added 13 other structures to the 47-acre site during this life there and daily tours allow you to explore a selection of them along with the stunning gardens. Tours must be reserved and visitors assemble at the visitors center across the street from the New Canaan train station.

Twelve miles further north, **Ridgefield** (pop 24,700) serves as the poster-boy for a Norman Rockwell painting with its old Yankee charm and cultural sophistication. Tree-lined Main St is fronted by stately 18th- and 19th-century mansions and quaint local shops. At No 258 swing into the parking lot of a spotless white clapboard, which was once the town store and is now the shockingly good **Aldrich Contemporary Art Museum** (✆203-438-4519; www.aldrichart.org; 258 Main St; adult/child $10/free; ✆noon-5pm Tue-Sun; P). Photography, sculpture, painting and mixed-media installations are displayed in cutting-edge temporary exhibitions which have previously featured notable names such as Cy Twombly, Robert Rauschenberg, Anslem Kiefer and Tom Sachs. Workshops for children are held downstairs in light-filled rooms and the museum also runs summer camps.

Green ROCKS Inn (☑203-894-8944; www.greenrocksinn.com; 415 Danbury Rd; d incl breakfast $200-285, ste $295-450; P 🛜 🐾) 🐾 offers fabulous, eco-friendly bed and breakfast accommodation in a striking, shingled farmhouse. You'll find it 2 miles north of Main St on the Danbury Rd.

THE HOUSATONIC VALLEY

North of the Gold Coast, the Housatonic River Valley unfurls languidly between forested mountain peaks, picturesque ponds and rural Colonial villages. The area is anchored by industrial Danbury in the south, but beyond that city's sprawling suburbs Connecticut's prettiest rural landscape lines the valley's main north–south byway, scenic US 7. The centerpiece of the region is the Litchfield Hills with its centuries old farms, winding country roads, abundant autumn fairs and hospitable country inns.

Lake Candlewood

With a surface area of 8.4 square miles Lake Candlewood is the largest lake in Connecticut. Created in the 1920s with water from

---

WORTH A TRIP

ANTIQUES CAPITAL

At the southern border of the Litchfield Hills **Woodbury** is justifiably famous as the 'antiques capital' of Connecticut, boasting over 40 dealerships and 20 stores along its historic, mile-long Main St. **Woodbury Antiques Dealers Association** (www.antiqueswoodbury.com) publishes an online guide. While you're in Woodbury don't forget to stop by Carole Peck's **Good News Café** (☑20 3-266-4663; www.good-news-cafe.com; 649 Main St S/US 6; meals $15-30; ☉11:30am-10pm Mon & Wed-Sat, noon-10pm Sun; P 🛜) 🐾. Considered the Alice Waters of the East Coast, this cafe is a magnet for celebrities and lovers of fine food who come for the locally sourced farm food and inventive, seasonal menus.

---

the Housatonic River, the four towns of Brookfield, New Milford, Sherman and New Fairfield share its shoreline.

On the western shore the **Squantz Pond State Park** (☑203-312-5013; www.ct.gov/deep; 178 Shortwoods Rd, New Fairfield; residents $9-13, nonresidents $15-22; ☉8am-sunset; 🐾) is popular with leaf-peepers, who come to amble the pretty shoreline. In Brookfield and Sherman, quiet vineyards with acres of gnarled grapevines line the hillsides. Stop in at **White Silo Farm Winery** (☑860-355-0271; www.whitesilowinery.com; 32 CT 37; tastings $7; ☉11am-6pm Fri-Sun Apr-Dec; 🐾) for a unique tasting of specialty wines made from farm-grown fruit. In September and October the fields are also open for blackberry and raspberry picking.

For the ultimate bird's-eye view of the foliage though, consider a late afternoon hot-air-balloon ride with **GONE Ballooning** (☑203-262-6625; www.flygoneballooning.com; 88 Sylvan Crest Dr; adult/under 12yr $250/125; 🐾) in nearby Southbury.

Litchfield Hills

The rolling hills in the northwestern corner of Connecticut are sprinkled with lakes and dotted with forests and state parks rich in waterfalls. Historic Litchfield is the hub of the region, but lesser-known villages such as Bethlehem, Washington, Preston, Warren, Kent and Norfolk boast similarly illustrious lineages and are just as photogenic.

Because of an intentional curb on development that guarantees the preservation of the area's rural character there is limited accommodation. Contact the **Western Connecticut Convention & Visitors Bureau** (☑800-663-1273; www.litchfieldhills.com) for detailed itineraries and listings of the region's hard-to-find B&Bs.

Volunteers staff a useful **information booth** on Litchfield's town green from June to November.

Lake Waramaug

Of the dozens of lakes and ponds in the Litchfield Hills, Lake Waramaug, north of New Preston, stands out. Gracious inns dot its shoreline, parts of which are a state park. As you make your way around the northern shore of the lake on North Shore Rd, you'll come to the **Hopkins Vineyard** (☑860-868-7954; www.hopkinsvineyard.com; 25 Hopkins Rd;

10am-5pm Mon-Sat, 11am-5pm Sun May-Dec). The wines are made mostly from French-American hybrid grapes and are eminently drinkable, and the vineyard hosts wine tastings with views of the lake from its bar. Call ahead during the low season.

★ **Hopkins Inn** (860-868-7295; www.thehopkinsinn.com; 22 Hopkins Rd, Warren; r from $120-135, apt $150; P), next door to the winery, has a variety of lodging options, from simple rooms with shared bathrooms to lake-view apartments. Its restaurant (meals $15 to $20) specializes in contemporary Austrian cuisine. In good weather, there's something magical about sitting on the porch overlooking the lake and hills. The restaurant is closed January through March.

Around the bend in the lake is the **Lake Waramaug State Park** (860-868-0220; www.ct.gov/deep; 30 Lake Waramaug Rd; sites $17-$27), with 77 campsites, both wooded and open, and many lakeside. There's a snack bar in the park and a small beach for swimming.

Heading east from the lake towards Litchfield you'll find an unassuming, low-slung building on your right along the Litchfield Turnpike. Don't drive by or you'll miss the best brunch in the area at **Community Table** (860-868-9354; www.communitytablect.com; 223 Litchfield Turnpike/US 202; brunch $10-18, meals $35-45; 5-9pm Mon-Tue, noon-2pm & 5-10pm Fri & Sat, 10am-2pm & 5-9pm Sun; P). Everything here is locally sourced from the citrus-cured salmon to the melt-in-your mouth brioche with spiced apple butter.

Bethlehem

Bethlehem is Connecticut's 'Christmas Town' and every year thousands of visitors come for the **Christmas Fair** (www.ci.bethlehem.ct.us) and to have their Christmas mail hand-stamped in the village post office.

The town's religious history extends to the founding of the first theological seminary in America by local resident Rev Joseph Bellamy. His home, the **Bellamy-Ferriday House & Garden** (203-266-7596; www.ctlandmarks.org; 9 Main St North; adult/child $7/4; noon-4pm Thu-Sun May-Sep, noon-4pm Sat & Sun Oct), a 1750s clapboard mansion, is a treasure trove of Delftware, Asian art and period furnishings. Equally exquisite is the garden, the design of latter-day owner Caroline Ferriday, who designed it to resemble an Aubusson Persian carpet, it's geometrical box hedges infilled with frothing peonies, lilacs and heirloom roses.

LOCAL KNOWLEDGE

BANTAM CINEMA

Locals know that one of the best things to do on rainy days is book in to see a film at the **Bantam Cinema** (860-567-1916; www.bantamcinema.com; 115 Bantam Lake Rd, Bantam). Housed in a converted former red barn on the shores of Lake Bantam it's the oldest continuously operating movie theatre in Connecticut and is a real Litchfield experience. The well-curated screenings focus on independent and foreign films and the 'Meet the Filmmaker' series features guest directors, actors and producers.

Bethlehem is also the location of one of the area's best restaurants, the quietly sophisticated **Woodward House** (203-266-6902; www.thewoodwardhouse.com; 4 The Green; meals $45-60; 5-9pm Wed-Sun), a 1740s saltbox with its original wainscoting and hand-hewn beams serving a modern American menu.

Litchfield

POP 8420

Litchfield is Connecticut's best-preserved late-18th-century town and the site of the nation's first law school. The town converges on a long oval green, and is surrounded by lush swaths of protected land just aching to be hiked through and picnicked on.

Founded in 1719, Litchfield prospered from 1780 to 1840 (by 1810 it was the state's fourth-largest town) on the commerce brought through the town by stagecoaches en route between Hartford and Albany, NY. In the mid-19th century, railroads did away with the coach routes, and industrial water-powered machinery drove Litchfield's artisans out of the markets, leaving the town to languish in faded gentility.

◉ Sights & Activities

A walk around town starts at the information kiosk, where you should ask for the walking-tour sheets. Just north across West St is the town's **historic jail**. Stroll along North St to see the fine houses. More of Litchfield's well-preserved **18th-century houses** are along South St. Set well back from the roadway across broad lawns and behind tall trees, the houses take you back visually to Litchfield's golden age.

Tapping Reeve House & Law School
HISTORIC SITE

(860-567-4501; www.litchfieldhistoricalsociety.org; 82 South St; adult/child $5/free; 11am-5pm Tue-Sat, 1-5pm Sun mid-Apr–Nov) In 1775, Tapping Reeve established the English-speaking world's first law school at his home. When attendance overwhelmed his own house, he built the meticulously preserved one-room schoolhouse in his side yard. John C Calhoun and 130 members of Congress studied here.

Litchfield History Museum
MUSEUM

(7 South St; 11am-5pm Tue-Sat, 1-5pm Sun mid-Apr–Nov) This museum's small permanent collection includes a modest photographic chronicle of the town and a dress-up box with colonial clothes for children to try on, plus some local-interest rotating exhibits. Admission is included in the ticket to Tapping Reeve House & Law School.

Topsmead State Forest
FOREST

(860-567-5694; www.ct.gov/deep; 8am-sunset) This forest was once the estate of Edith Morton Chase. You can visit her grand Tudor-style summer home (free guided tours are available between June and October, but hours vary, so call ahead), complete with its original furnishings. Then spread a blanket on the lawn and have a picnic while enjoying the view at 1230ft. Topsmead is 2 miles east of Litchfield.

White Memorial Conservation Center
PARK

(860-567-0857; www.whitememoriallcc.org; US 202; park free, museum adult/child $6/3; park sunrise-sunset, museum 9am-5pm Mon-Sat, noon-5pm Sun) Made up of 4000 supremely serene acres, this park has two dozen trails (0.2 miles to 6 miles long) that crisscross the center, including swamp paths on a raised boardwalk. The center also manages three campgrounds and there's a small **nature museum**. The center is 2 miles west on 202 from Litchfield.

Mount Tom State Park
PARK

(860-567-8870; US 202; resident/nonresident per car $9/15; 8am-sunset) The best swimming in the Litchfield Hills is at this state park, 3.5 miles west of Bantam. The not-even-1-mile 'tower trail' leads to the stone Mt Tom Tower at the summit. Fees are reduced during weekdays.

Lee's Riding Stable
HORSEBACK RIDING

(860-567-0785; www.windfieldmorganfarm.com; 57 East Litchfield St, off CT-118; trail ride $40; 9am-5pm) What better way to see the rolling hills around Litchfield than on a trail ride from local riding stable Lee's. Sweet-natured ponies and horses make for gentle rides with experienced guide Heather. The stable caters to children seven years and up and also offers lessons in its indoor and outdoor schools ($35 for 30 minutes).

✕ Eating

★ Peaches n'Cream
ICE CREAM $

(632 Torrington Rd; scoops $2; 11am-10pm) This old-fashioned ice-cream parlor with peppermint trim on the road to Torrington has been serving up homemade ice cream for decades. Seasonal flavors include the eponymous peaches n'cream, but also cashew cream, maple walnut and kahlua chocolate. They also make a neat ice-cream sandwich.

West Street Grill
MODERN AMERICAN $$$

(860-567-3885; weststreetgrill.com; 43 West St; meals $25-40; 11:30am-2:30pm Mon-Tue, 11:30am-2:30pm & 5:30-9pm Wed-Sun) This Parisian-style bistro on Litchfield's historic green is one of the state's top restaurants. Over the years its inventive modern American cooking has earned it nods from *Gourmet* magazine and the *New York Times*. The shrimp salad with orange and fennel is delightful.

The Village
AMERICAN $$$

(www.village-litchfield.com; 25 West St; dinner mains $18-28; 11.30am-9.30pm Wed-Sun) This restaurant-cum-taproom on Litchfield's town green manages to do what few can: it's both a casual, welcoming hometown pub and – if eating in the dining room – a place to go for a special-occasion meal. The menu has something for everyone, from well-composed salads, to burgers and sandwiches, to lobster-stuffed sole with buerre blanc. There's even a children's menu and an excellent sangria for the liquid-lunch crowd.

ℹ Information

Volunteers staff an **information booth**, open on a 'catch-as-you-can' basis from June through November, on the town green.

ℹ Getting There & Away

Litchfield lies 34 miles west of Hartford and 36 miles south of Great Barrington, MA, in the Berkshires. The town green is at the intersection of US 202 and CT 63.

No buses stop in Litchfield proper, but **Bonanza Bus Lines** (800-343-9999; www.

CONNECTICUT LEAF PEEPS

Kent has previously been voted *the* spot in all of New England for fall foliage viewing. But the fact is the whole of the densely wooded Housatonic River Valley offers numerous opportunities for leaf peeping:

⇒ **Squantz Pond** Shoreline walks with views of bristling mountains carpeted with forests plunging straight down to the pond.

⇒ **Lake Waramaug** For fabulous foliage reflected twice over in the mirror-like expanse of the lake.

⇒ **Boyd Wood Audubon Sanctuary, Litchfield** For gentle walks through deciduous woodland alongside Wigwam Pond and milkweed meadow.

⇒ **Kent Falls State Park** For a leaf-framed waterfall and Technicolor mountain views from Macedonia State Park.

⇒ **West Cornwall** For a red covered bridge set against the tree-lined Housatonic River.

peterpanbus.com) will get you to Torrington, the closest major town, from where you'll need your own wheels.

Kent

POP 3000

During summer and fall, weekenders (often starting on Thursday) throng to Kent's small but respected clutch of art galleries and its August **Jazz Festival** (litchfieldjazzfest.com). The small town on the banks of the Housatonic River is also a popular stop for hikers on the **Appalachian Trail** (www.appalachian trail.org), which intersects CT 341 about 2 miles northwest of town. Unlike much of the trail, the Kent section offers a mostly flat 5-mile river walk alongside the Housatonic, the longest river walk along its entire length.

Two miles north of town, the quirky, **Sloane-Stanley Museum** (☑ 860-927-3849; www.cultureandtourism.org; US 7; adult/child $3/1.50; ⊗ 10am-4pm Wed-Sun May-Oct) is a barnful of early American tools and implements – some dating from the 17th century – lovingly collected and arranged by artist and author Eric Sloane, who painted the cloud-filled sky mural at the Smithsonian Air and Space Museum.

At **Kent Falls State Park**, about 5 miles north of town, the water drops 250ft over a quarter mile before joining up with the Housatonic River. Hike the easy trail to the top of the cascade, or just settle into a sunny picnic spot at the bottom near a red covered bridge. More extensive hiking trails (over 80 miles of them) can be found in **Macedonia State Park** (www.ct.gov/deep; 159 Macedonia Brook Rd; residents/nonresidents $14/24; ⊗ mid-Apr–Sep; 🛇) cresting the rocky ridges of

Cobble Mountain and affording panoramic views of the valley. The 51 camping sites here are much in demand in summer.

You can rent bikes at **Bicycle Tour Company** (☑ 888-711-5368; www.bicycletours.com; 9 Bridge St), or it can customize a guided ride for you around the area.

🛏 Sleeping & Eating

Inn at Kent Falls   HISTORIC INN $$$
(☑ 860-927-3197; www.theinnatkentfalls.com; 107 Kent-Cornwall Rd/US 7; r $215-350; P 🛜 🛋) This historic inn dates back to the early 1900s. Original floorboards, three generous lounges with open fireplaces and a grand piano make for a home-away-from-home atmosphere. Breakfast is a communal affair with homemade pancakes and fresh baked croissants.

Gifford's   MODERN AMERICAN $$$
(☑ 860-592-0262; www.jpgifford.com; 9 Maple St; meals $20-35; ⊗ 5-9pm Wed-Sat, 4-8pm Sun) From Gifford's successful micromarket, bakery and deli to a new rousingly acclaimed restaurant on Maple St, Michael Moriarty and James Neunzig are definitely on the up. As you'd expect from experienced specialty provenders the secret is in the ingredients: meat from Mountain Products Smokehouse, golden-hued chicken from FreeBird and Connecticut harvested clams. On top of that the stylish contemporary interiors painted in sunshine blocks of color and the covered terrace make for a truly memorable dining experience.

West Cornwall

The village of West Cornwall is just one of six Cornwall villages in Connecticut, but it is the most famous thanks to its picturesque covered bridge. The bridge was known as the 'Kissing Bridge,' because its long span allowed horse-drawn carriages to slow down inside it and allowing their passengers some complimentary canoodling.

Otherwise the area attracts nature lovers, birders and hikers who come to hike, fish and boat on the lazy Housatonic River. Housatonic Meadows State Park (☏860-927-3238; www.ct.gov/deep; US 7; ☺8am-sunset) is famous for its 2-mile-long stretch of water set aside exclusively for fly-fishing. Its campground (☏860-672-6772; sites CT residents/nonresidents $17/27; ☺mid-Apr–mid-Oct) has 97 sites on the banks of the Housatonic. Housatonic River Outfitters (www.dryflies.com; 24 Kent Rd, Cornwall Bridge) run guided fishing trips with gourmet picnics.

In winter the nearby Mohawk Mountain Ski Area (www.mohawkmtn.com; 42 Great Hollow Rd, Cornwall) is the largest ski resort in the state with 24 slopes and trails. On Labour Day weekend, in the nearby town of Goshen, you can visit the Goshen Fair (www.goshenfair.org), one of Connecticut's best old-fashioned fairs with ox-pulling and wood-cutting contests.

The tranquil, 14-room Cornwall Inn (☏860-672-6884; www.cornwallinn.com; 270 Kent Rd/US 7, Cornwall Bridge; r $159-199, ste incl breakfast $239-219; P☏☁) offers rustic accommodation and straightforward country cuisine (meals $12 to $30, dinner Thursday to Sunday).

Lakeville

A quiet and remote corner of the Litchfield hills, the rolling farmland around Lakeville is home to millionaires and movie luminaries such as Meryl Streep. Better still from May to September motor races, including a series of vintage car races, take place at the venerable Lime Rock Race Track (www.limerock.com; 497 Lime Rock Rd; ☺Apr-Nov). Paul Newman raced here and thought its seven-turn, 1.5 mile track the most beautiful racing track in America.

Nearby in teeny-tiny Falls Village you'll find the gorgeous Falls Village Inn (☏860-824-0033; www.thefallsvillageinn.com; 33 Railroad St; d/ste $209/299; P☏), which once served railroad workers on the Housatonic Railroad. These days the inn sports interiors style by decorator Bunny Williams and the Tap Room is a hangout for Lime Rock racers. In Lakeville itself the Inn at Iron Masters (☏860-435-9844; www.innatironmasters.com; 229 Main St/US 44, Lakeville; d incl breakfast $159-216; P✱☏☁) is a bargain for this blue-chip town. Although it may look like a Florida motel at first glance, inside is all New England (quilts, cutesy flower motifs) and the grounds feature gardens and gazebos.

Tea lovers will want to check out Mary O'Brien's shop Chaiwalla (☏860-435-9758; 1 Main St/US 44, Salisbury; items $3-10; ☺10am-6pm Wed-Sun) in next-door Salisbury, which serves a variety of tea, especially unblended Darjeelings, as well as traditional accompaniments. Try Mary's famous tomato pie.

Norfolk

Norfolk's bucolic scenery and cool summers have long attracted prosperous New Yorkers. They built many of the town's fine mansions, its well-endowed Romanesque Revival library and its Arts & Crafts–style town hall, now the Infinity Music Hall & Bistro (☏box office 866-666-6306; www.infinityhall.com; 20 Greenwoods Rd W; ☺11am-9pm Wed-Sun). This beautiful beaux-arts building with its original stage brings top acoustic, blues, jazz and folks acts to Norfolk from New York and beyond.

Opposite the Infinity is the opulent Whitehall, the summer estate of Ellen and Carl Battell Stoeckel, passionate and monied music lovers who established the Norfolk Music Festival (www.norfolkmusic.org; Ellen Battell Stoeckel Estate, US 44; tickets $25-100; ☺Jul-Aug). These extravagant affairs – the couple brought the 70-piece New York Philharmonic orchestra to perform – were among the most popular summer events in New England and on her death, in 1939, Ellen Stoeckel bequeathed the redwood 'Music Shed' to Yale University Summer School of Music, ensuring the tradition continues today.

Vermont

📞 802 / POP 626,000

Best Places to Eat

➡ American Flatbread (p309)
➡ Hen of the Wood (p318)
➡ Skunk Hollow Tavern (p295)
➡ Pangaea (p289)
➡ Mint (p302)

Best Places to Stay

➡ Inn at Shelburne Farms (p308)
➡ Forty Putney Road B&B (p282)
➡ Inn at Round Barn Farm (p302)
➡ Inn at Mountain View Farm (p323)
➡ Parker House Inn (p294)

Why Go?

Whether seen under blankets of snow, patchworks of blazing fall leaves or the exuberant greens of spring and summer, Vermont's blend of bucolic farmland, mountains and picturesque small villages make it one of America's most appealing states. Hikers, bikers, skiers and kayakers will find four-season bliss here, on the expansive waters of Lake Champlain, the award-winning Kingdom Trails Network, the 300-mile Long and Catamount Trails and the fabled slopes of Killington, Stowe and Sugarbush. Foodies will love it here too: small farmers have made Vermont a locavore paradise, complemented by America's densest collection of craft brewers. But most of all, what sets Vermont apart is its independent spirit: the first state to endorse same-sex civil unions, the only one to elect a socialist senator in the 21st century, and the only one without a McDonald's in its capital city, remains a haven of quirky creativity unlike any other place in America.

When to Go
Burlington

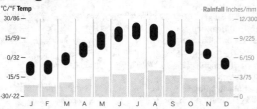

| Dec–Mar Plummet down snow-covered pistes at New England's paramount ski resorts. | Jun–Aug Kayak in Lake Champlain, climb a mountain or frolic with fireflies at a Vermont state park. | Sep–Oct Pick apples, choose pumpkins and gawk at the colors during leaf season. |

Vermont Highlights

1 Cruise past green meadows, sculpture gardens and dazzling Mt Mansfield views on Stowe's gorgeous riverside **Recreation Path** (p315)

2 Explore a 19th-century lighthouse, a one-room schoolhouse and dozens of other historic buildings at the **Shelburne Museum** (p303)

3 Survey your next black-diamond run or simply gawk at the foliage from the nation's sole surviving single chairlift at **Mad River Glen** (p301)

4 Celebrate the apple and pumpkin harvest, make friends with pretty brown cows or hop aboard a horse-drawn sleigh at **Billings Farm & Museum** (p293) in Woodstock

5 Catch a taste of Vermont's thriving locavore food culture at the **Brattleboro Farmers Market** (p280)

6 Soak up the sun and enjoy a six-glass beer sampler on the riverside deck at **Long Trail Brewery** (p297) near Killington

7 Shop or bar-hop your way through lively **Church Street Marketplace** (p303), Burlington's multiblock pedestrian paradise

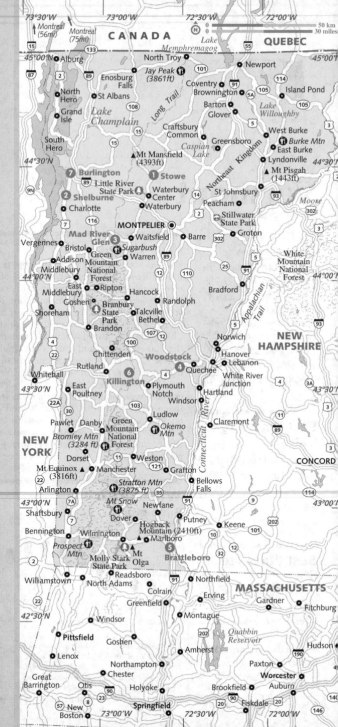

ℹ️ Information

Vermont Chamber of Commerce (www.visitvt.com) Distributes a wealth of information about the state.

Vermont Division of Tourism and Marketing (☏802-828-3237, 800-837-6668; www.vermontvacation.com; 1 National Life Dr, Montpelier) Maintains a fabulous Welcome Center on I-91 near the Massachusetts state line, one on VT 4A near the New York state line and three others along I-89 between White River Junction and the Canadian border. Produces a free, detailed road map and camping guide.

Vermont Public Radio (VPR; www.vpr.net) Vermont's statewide public radio station features superb local programming, including 'Vermont Edition' (weekdays at noon) for coverage of Vermont current events, and the quirky, information-packed 'Eye on the Sky' weather forecast.

Vermont Ski Areas Association (☏802-223-2439; www.skivermont.com) Helpful information for planning ski trips, as well as summer adventures at Vermont ski resorts.

ℹ️ Getting There & Around

AIR

Vermont's major airport is in Burlington (p438), served by Continental, Delta, JetBlue, Northwest, United and US Airways. Cape Air also flies from Boston to the smaller commercial airports in **Rutland** (RUT; ☏ 802-786-8881; www.flyrutlandvt.com) and **Lebanon, NH** (LEB; flyleb.com), just across the Vermont/New Hampshire state line.

BOAT

Lake Champlain Ferries (p311) runs ferries between Plattsburgh, New York and Grand Isle; between Port Kent, New York and Burlington; and between Essex, New York and Charlotte.

The teeny-tiny **Fort Ti Ferry** (www.forttiferry.com; per car/bike/motorcycle $9/2/5; ☉May-Oct) runs from Larrabees Point in Shoreham, Vermont, to Ticonderoga Landing, New York.

BUS

Greyhound (www.greyhound.com) provides limited long-distance bus service to and from Vermont. The most convenient schedules serve Brattleboro (from Boston, New York City and points in between) and Burlington (from Boston and Montreal).

CAR

Vermont is not particularly large, but it is mountainous. Although I-89 and I-91 provide speedy access to certain areas, the rest of the time you must plan to take it slow and enjoy the winding roads and mountain scenery.

VERMONT FRESH NETWORK

Finding locavore food in Vermont is a piece of cake. The farm and chef partnership **Vermont Fresh Network** (www.vermontfresh.net) 🍴 identifies restaurants that focus on sustainable, locally sourced produce, cheese and meats. Just look for the green-and-white square sticker with a plate and silverware – you'll see it proudly displayed at farms and eateries throughout the state.

TRAIN

Amtrak operates two trains in Vermont. The *Ethan Allen Express* (www.amtrak.com/ethan-allen-express-train) departs New York City and stops in Fair Haven and Rutland. The more scenic **Vermonter** (www.amtrak.com/vermonter-train) heads from Washington, DC, and New York City to Brattleboro, Bellows Falls, Windsor, White River Junction, Randolph, Montpelier, Waterbury, Burlington–Essex Junction and St Albans. If you're a cyclist, you can buy one ticket on the *Vermonter* and get on and off as many times as you like, as long as you reserve a space for yourself and your bicycle ahead of time.

SOUTHERN VERMONT

White churches and inns surround village greens throughout historic southern Vermont, a region that's home to several towns that predate the American Revolution. In summer the roads between the three 'cities' of Brattleboro, Bennington and Manchester roll over green hills; in winter, they wind their way toward the ski slopes of Mt Snow, southern Vermont's cold-weather playground. For hikers, the Appalachian and Long Trails pass through the Green Mountain National Forest here, offering a colorful hiking experience during the fall foliage season.

Brattleboro

POP 12,000

Perched at the confluence of the Connecticut and West Rivers, Brattleboro is a little gem that reveals its facets to those who stroll the streets and prowl the dozens of independent shops and eateries. An energetic mix of aging hippies and the latest crop of pierced and tattooed hipsters fuels the town's sophisticated eclecticism, keeping the downtown scene percolating and skewing its politics decidedly leftward.

Whetstone Brook runs through the south end of town, where a wooden stockade dubbed Fort Dummer was built in 1724, the first European settlement in Vermont (theretofore largely a wilderness populated exclusively by Native Americans). The town received its royal charter a year later, named for Colonel William Brattle Jr of the King's Militia, who never set foot in his namesake

At the Old Town Hall (location of the current Main Street Gallery), many celebrated thinkers and entertainers, including Oliver Wendell Holmes, Horace Greeley and Will Rogers, held forth on the concerns of the day. Rudyard Kipling married a Brattleboro woman in 1892, and while living here he wrote *The Jungle Book*.

◉ Sights & Activities

While most of Brattleboro's action is easily found in the downtown commercial district, the surrounding hillsides are well salted with farms, cheesemakers and artisans, all awaiting discovery on a pleasant back-road ramble.

★ **Brattleboro Farmers Market**   MARKET
(www.brattleborofarmersmarket.com; ⏲10am-2pm Wed early Jun–mid-Oct, 9am-2pm Sat early May–mid-Oct) 🐾 Offering a crash course in Vermont food, the market has more than 50 local vendors selling cheese, free-range beef and lamb, honey, pastries, maple syrup, fruit and veggies. Live music and a lively crafts scene round out the experience. Saturday's market is located just west of town by the Creamery Bridge; Wednesday's is held on the Whetstone Pathway off Main St.

Brattleboro Museum & Art Center   MUSEUM
(www.brattleboromuseum.org; 10 Vernon St; adult/child $8/4; ⏲11am-5pm Sun, Mon, Wed & Thu, 11am-7pm Fri, 10am-5pm Sat) Located in a 1915 railway station, this museum hosts a wealth of inventive exhibits by local artists in a variety of media. It also has a rotating multimedia exhibition program of contemporary art.

Robb Family Farm   FARM
(☎888-318-9087; www.robbfamilyfarm.com; 827 Ames Hill Rd; ⏲10am-5:30pm Mon-Fri, to 2pm Sat; 🚼) 🐾 Run by the same family for more than a century, this 400-acre farm hosts maple-sugaring demonstrations in early spring; they also offer free sugarhouse tours and sell maple products and organic beef in the gift shop year-round. From Brattleboro, follow VT 9 west to Greenleaf St, then continue 3 miles up Ames Hill Rd and look to the right.

Gallery Walk   GALLERIES
(☎802-257-2616; www.gallerywalk.org; ⏲5:30-8:30pm first Fri of month) On the first Friday

Brattleboro

DON'T MISS

VERMONT LEAF PEEPS

Here are a few spots to see Vermont's famous fall foliage at its best:

Mt Mansfield Vermont's highest peak is gorgeous when draped in fall colors, especially when an early snowfall dusts the summit white. The best panoramic perspectives are from Stowe, Jeffersonville, Cambridge and Underhill. Hikers can also experience the full sweep of color from the mountaintop; one of the prettiest routes is the Sunset Ridge Trail in Underhill State Park.

Grafton (p284) Villages don't get any cuter than Grafton, which looks like it was airlifted in from an earlier century. The white clapboard buildings are even more photogenic when contrasted against fiery leaves and a brilliant blue sky.

Lake Willoughby (p323) The technicolor majesty of changing maples looks especially dramatic on the steep slopes surrounding this fjordlike lake in Vermont's Northeast Kingdom.

Killington K1 Gondola (p296) The same lift that whisks skiers and mountain bikers to the mountaintop in winter and summer also affords spectacular panoramic views for fall leaf peepers.

Vermont Rte 100 A road-tripper's dream, this classic driving route through the heart of the Green Mountains shows off Vermont's farm country in its full autumnal splendor.

Merck Forest (p292) Climb to the barn meadow at this environmental education center in southwestern Vermont for breathtaking vistas of the Taconic Mountains in bright rainbow colors.

---

of each month, join like-minded folk on the immensely popular Gallery Walk. Since the early 1990s, galleries and businesses have opened their walls to artists from an ever-increasing geographic reach and level of renown. A free monthly publication, available throughout town and on the website, maps the locations for this self-guided tour.

Brattleboro Bicycle Shop BICYCLE RENTAL
(📞800-272-8245, 802-254-8644; www.bratbike.com; 165 Main St; bicycles per day/week $25/150; ⊙10am-6pm Mon-Fri, 10am-5pm Sat, noon-4pm Sun) Rents hybrid bicycles and dispenses plenty of advice about where to use them, including the West River Trail (westrivertrail.org), which opened at the north end of town in 2012.

Vermont Canoe Touring CANOEING
(📞802-257-5008; Veterans Memorial Bridge, 451 Putney Rd; canoes/kayaks per day $45/40; ⊙late Apr–mid-Oct) Rents kayaks and canoes. While away an afternoon by bird-watching in the estuaries or visiting an unofficial nude sun-bathing spot up the White River.

🎎 Festivals & Events

Strolling of the Heifers PARADE
(www.strollingoftheheifers.com; 👪) This fun-spirited June celebration of agriculture and community begins with flower-garlanded heifers mooing their way down Main Street. Then come the bagpipes, 4H-ers, Vermont politicians, bad cow jokes from the parade's commentators, some excrement-scooping superheroes (complete with capes!), antique tractors and synchronized shopping-cart performances by the local food co-op. Don't miss the crowning of Miss Ver-mooont, prettiest heifer of them all!

Marlboro Music Fest MUSIC
(📞215-569-4690, 802-254-2394; www.marlboromusic.org; tickets $5-37.50) A delight for lovers of chamber music, this summer festival is held on weekends from early July to mid-August at Marlboro College, 12 miles west of Brattleboro. Founded in 1951, it regularly draws big names in classical music, with performances held in an intimate 700-seat auditorium. Reserve ahead; many concerts sell out almost immediately.

🛏 Sleeping

If all you're after is a cheap sleep, there are plenty of motels on Putney Rd north of town; take Exit 3 off I-91.

Latchis Hotel HOTEL $$
(📞800-798-6301, 802-254-6300; http://hotel.latchis.com; 50 Main St; tw $80-100, d $105-180,

ste $160-210; 🛜) You can't beat the location of these 30 reasonably priced rooms and suites, in the epicenter of downtown and adjacent to the historic theater of the same name. The hotel's art-deco overtones are refreshing, and wonderfully surprising for New England.

Meadowlark Inn
INN $$

(☎ 802-257-4582, 800-616-6359; meadowlarkinnvt.com; Orchard St; r incl breakfast $139-239; 🛜) You'll find exquisite peace here, where you can relax on the porch or escape to one of the eight thematically decorated rooms. The innkeepers are culinary-school graduates and serve breakfast and treats just like you wish your mamma used to. It's 3 miles northwest of downtown Brattleboro via VT 9 and Orchard St.

Artist's Loft B&B
B&B $$

(☎ 802-257-5181; www.theartistsloft.com; 103 Main St; ste $158, incl breakfast $188; 🛜) In the heart of downtown, this B&B has only one room, but what a room! Innkeepers (and artists) Patricia Long and William Hays rent a spacious 3rd-floor suite (the size of a large one-bedroom apartment) that overlooks the Connecticut River and the seasonally changing canvas of Wantastiquet Mountain.

★ Forty Putney Road B&B
B&B $$$

(☎ 800-941-2413, 802-254-6268; www.fortyputneyroad.com; 192 Putney Rd; r incl breakfast $159-329; @🛜) This 1930 B&B with a small cheery pub is a sweet spot just north of town. It has a glorious backyard, four rooms and a separate, self-contained cottage. Overlook-

ing the West River estuary, it also offers boat and bike rentals that are just a five-minute walk away. Request a room at the back if you want peace and quiet.

🍴 Eating

Amy's Bakery Arts Cafe
BAKERY, CAFE $

(113 Main St; sandwiches & salads $7-12; ⏰ 8am-6pm Mon-Sat, 9am-5pm Sun) Of the many bakeries in town that inspire poetic accolades, this one garners the most. Enjoy breakfast breads, pastries and coffee with views of the river. Lunchtime offerings include salads, soups and sandwiches, and rotating exhibitions of art (all for sale) by local artists cover the walls.

Brattleboro Food Co-op
DELI $

(www.brattleborofoodcoop.com; 2 Main St; ⏰ 7am-9pm Mon-Sat, 9am-9pm Sun) 🌱 The perfect place to load up your picnic basket with whole-food groceries, organic produce, and local cheeses, this thriving community co-op also has a juice bar and a great deli full of healthy treats; don't miss local favorite Chai Wallah chai, one of the tastiest hot drinks in Vermont.

Whetstone Station
PUB $$

(www.whetstonestation.com; 36 Bridge St; mains $10-20; ⏰ 11:30am-10pm Sun-Thu, to 11pm Fri & Sat) This pub opened to universal acclaim in 2012. The kudos were not just for its dozen-plus craft brews on tap and excellent pub fare, but also for its outstanding roof deck with a bird's-eye view of the Connecticut River. It's the ideal spot for a beer and a bite at sundown.

Marina Restaurant
AMERICAN $$

(☎ 802-257-7563; www.vermontmarina.com; US 5/Putney Rd; mains $10-22; ⏰ 11:30am-9pm Mon-Wed, 11:30am-10pm Thu-Sat, 10am-9pm Sun) The spirited atmosphere and a sublime location on the banks of the West River make this one of Brattleboro's most pleasant places to grab a bite. The varied menu features burgers, seafood, salads, pasta and sandwiches, and there's a killer Sunday brunch. The outdoor deck is a perennial favorite for summertime sundowners. It's a mile north of downtown Brattleboro, on the west side of US 5.

TJ Buckley's
AMERICAN $$$

(☎ 802-257-4922; www.tjbuckleys.com; 132 Elliot St; mains $40; ⏰ 5:30-9pm Thu-Sun) 🌱 Chef-owner Michael Fuller founded this exceptional, upscale little eatery in an authentic 1927 diner over 30 years ago. Ever since, he's been offering a verbal menu of four nightly-changing items, sourced as much as possible from local farms. Locals rave that the food here is Brattleboro's best. The diner seats just 18 souls, so reserve ahead. No credit cards.

 Drinking & Entertainment

Mocha Joe's   CAFE
(☑802-257-7794; www.mochajoes.com; 82 Main St; ⊙7:30am-8pm Sun-Thu, to 10pm Fri & Sat; 🛜) Before your eyes spy this ultrahip, subterranean space, your nose will locate the exceptionally rich brews and excellent pastries.

McNeill's Brewery   PUB
(☑802-254-2553; www.mcneillsbrewery.com; 90 Elliot St; ⊙4pm-2:30am Mon-Thu, 1pm-2:30am Fri-Sun) This classic pub is inhabited by a lively, friendly local crowd. With 10 varieties, plus a few seasonal options, there's a beer for every taste here. Offerings include its namesake microbrew, McNeill's, its flagship Firehouse Amber and award-winning Pullman Porter.

Latchis Theater   CINEMA
(☑802-254-6300; http://theater.latchis.com; 50 Main St) The nicely restored, art-deco Latchis Building houses this theater, where you can see mainstream and indies on three screens nightly, catch live music performances (such as a string quartet) or catch New York City's Metropolitan Opera broadcast live on the screens.

ℹ️ **Information**

Brattleboro Chamber of Commerce (☑877-254-4565, 802-254-4565; www.brattleborochamber.org; 180 Main St; ⊙9am-5pm Mon-Fri)
Brattleboro Chamber of Commerce Information Booth (☑802-257-1112; ⊙variable hours mid-May–mid-Oct) On the town green just north of downtown.

ℹ️ **Getting There & Around**

While Brattleboro is very easy to get around on foot, you can call **Brattleboro Taxi** (☑802-254-6446; www.brattleborotaxi.com) for transportation beyond its limits.

BUS

Greyhound (www.greyhound.com) runs several buses to and from Brattleboro; those from NYC stop in Northampton, MA, and other New England cities en route. There's one bus daily to each of the cities listed here. Southbound buses leave Brattleboro at 10:20am, northbound buses at 11:05am. Prices quoted are full, refundable fares. Check Greyhound's website for advance-purchase and internet discounts.

GRAFTON VILLAGE CHEESE COMPANY & RETREAT PETTING FARM

Just outside Brattleboro lies the cheesemaking facility of **Grafton Village Cheese Company** (www.graftonvillagecheese.com; 400 Linden St/VT30; ⊙10am-6pm), where you can see the sublime cheddars being made, taste and discover your favorite, and pick up a chunk to take with you. The shop also sells wine and local beer. Next door is the **Retreat Petting Farm** (theretreatfarm.com; adult/child under 12yr $6/5; ⊙10am-4pm Wed-Sat, noon-4pm Sun late May–mid-Oct; ♿) ✈, where you can say hello to farm animals and walk the farm's network of recreational trails. Look for the large cluster of red barns (or listen for the goats).

Boston $44, four hours, one daily (10:20am)
Burlington $60, 3¾ hours, one daily (11:05am)
Montpelier $49, three hours, one daily (11:05am)
New York City $65, 5¼ hours, one daily (10:20am)
Northampton $19.50, one hour, one daily (10:20am)

CAR

By car, the scenic 40-mile drive across VT 9 from Brattleboro to Bennington takes about an hour.

From Brattleboro to Northampton, Massachusetts, it's a 45-minute, 40-mile cruise along I-91.

TRAIN

Amtrak's scenic daily **Vermonter train** (www.amtrak.com/vermonter-train) connects Brattleboro with points north and south, including Montpelier (from $26, 2½ hours), Burlington (from $26, 3¼ hours), New York City (from $55, six hours) and Washington, DC (from $84, 10 hours). See Amtrak's website for details.

Around Brattleboro

Newfane

POP 1730

Vermont is rife with pretty villages, but Newfane is near the top of everyone's list. All the postcard-perfect sights you'd expect in a Vermont town are here: tall old trees,

MAPLE SUGARING

Ranking first among states in maple syrup production, Vermont regularly produces more than one million gallons of the sweet stuff per year – 40% of America's entire output. This is particularly impressive considering almost 40 gallons of sap must be tapped from maple trees for a mere quart of syrup. Demonstrations can be seen and samples tasted at the Robb Family Farm (p280), Shelburne Farms (p303), and dozens of other farms around Vermont during Maple Open House Weekend (www.vermontmaple.org), held in late March, when the sap is flowing.

white high-steepled churches, adorable inns and gracious old houses. In spring Newfane is busy making maple sugar; in summer, the town buzzes around its flea market; fall lures leaf peepers; and winter brings couples seeking cozy rooms in warm hideaways.

A short stroll exposes Newfane's core: you'll see the stately Congregational Church (1839), the Windham County Courthouse (1825), built in Greek Revival style, and a few antique shops.

Newfane is on VT 30, just 12 miles northwest of Brattleboro and 19 miles northeast of Wilmington.

Grafton

POP 680

The must-see village of Grafton is graceful, but it's not that way by accident. In the 1960s the private Windham Foundation established a restoration and preservation program for the entire village, and it has been eminently successful. The foundation's initiatives included burying all electrical and telephone lines, which helps account for Grafton's ultra-picturesque, lost-in-time appearance.

In the heart of the village, visit the brand-new retail shop of local success story Grafton Village Cheese Company (☑802-843-1062; www.graftonvillagecheese.com; 56 Townshend Rd; ☺10am-5pm) . The shop offers free samples of Grafton's many mouthwatering, nose-tingling cheddar varieties, which you can also purchase here along with wine and beer. The maple-smoked and stonehouse cheddars regularly win awards at interna-

tional cheese festivals. Tours of the actual cheese-production facility, half a mile down the street at 533 Townshend Rd, are sometimes available; ask for a schedule at the shop.

Just south of the village, Grafton Ponds Outdoor Center (☑802-843-2400; graftonponds.com) offers year-round recreation on mountain-biking, hiking and cross-country ski trails, along with canoeing, swimming, snow tubing and adventure camps for kids.

The double porch at The Grafton Inn (Old Tavern at Grafton; ☑800-843-1801, 802-843-2231; www.old-tavern.com; 92 Main St; r/ste incl breakfast from $165/235; ☎) is Grafton's landmark, and the inn has played host to such notable guests as Rudyard Kipling, Theodore Roosevelt and Ralph Waldo Emerson. While the original brick inn is quite formal, many of the 45 guest rooms and suites, scattered around houses within the village, are less so. The inn has tennis courts, a sand-bottomed swimming pond and cross-country skiing trails. The dining room (mains $21 to $29) is New England formal, and the cuisine is refined New American with a seasonal menu. Its casual on-site pub, Phelps Barn (www.graftoninnvermont.com/dining/phelps-barn; ☺4-10pm Tue-Sun), has live music every Saturday night and serves light pub food and a wide range of Vermont microbrews; or pop in for Flatbread Fridays, when it serves pizza cooked in 'Big Red,' its beloved pizza oven.

Grafton lies at the junction of VT 121 and VT 35, about 15 miles north of Newfane.

Wilmington & Mt Snow

POP 1880

Nestled in the upper Deerfield River valley, Wilmington is the gateway to Mt Snow, one of New England's best ski resorts and an excellent summertime mountain-biking and golfing spot. Many restaurants and stores cater to families, who are the resort's main clientele.

Wilmington was clobbered with massive flooding during Tropical Storm Irene in August 2011. Some downtown businesses were wiped out completely and many more were closed for months, but the town has been rebuilding and is largely back in business as this book goes to press.

The state's central north–south highway, VT 100, goes north from Wilmington past Haystack and Mt Snow. Wilmington's main street is VT 9, the primary route across southern Vermont.

◉ Sights & Activities

Mt Snow SKIING
(☑800-245-7669; www.mountsnow.com; VT 100, West Dover; adult lift ticket midweek/weekend $75/85) Southern Vermont's biggest ski resort features varied, family-friendly terrain, with 132 trails (20% beginner, 60% intermediate, 20% expert) and 23 lifts, plus a vertical drop of 1700ft and the snowmaking ability to blanket 85% of the trails. Area cross-country routes cover more than 60 miles; other winter activities include tubing and snowmobile tours.

Come summer, Mt Snow hosts one of the best mountain-biking schools in the country. The mountain's 3-mile, lift-served introductory downhill trail, the Gateway, was opened in 2012 and is the longest of its kind in eastern US.

To reach Mt Snow/Haystack from Wilmington, travel 10 miles north of town on VT 100. The free bus service **MOOver** (www.moover.com) offers free hourly transport from Wilmington to the slopes of Mt Snow between 7am and 6pm year-round, with extra service added on weekends and throughout the ski season.

🛏 Sleeping & Eating

Old Red Mill Inn INN $
(☑877-733-6455, 802-464-3700; www.oldredmill.com; 18 N Main St; d $65-95; 🛜) Squeezed between VT 100 and the Deerfield River's north branch, this converted sawmill in the heart of town has simple rooms (chunky wood furnishings, checkered bedspreads) at bargain prices. In summer, the attached Jerry's Deck Bar & Grill offers outdoor seating with pleasant river views.

Nutmeg Country Inn INN $$
(☑855-868-8634, 802-464-3907; www.nutmeginn.com; VT 9; r/ste incl breakfast from $119/209; 🛜) Just west of Wilmington, this 18th-century farmhouse has 10 rooms and four suites with antiques and reproduction pieces. Most luxurious is the Grand Deluxe King Suite, with skylights and a marble bath.

White House of Wilmington INN $$$
(☑866-774-2135, 802-464-2135; www.whitehouseinn.com; VT 9; r/ste incl breakfast from $170/240; 🛜🏊) Perched on a hillside east of town, this white Colonial Revival mansion has great cross-country trails and 16 luxury rooms, some with Jacuzzi and fireplace. Enhancing the inn's romantic appeal are an excellent restaurant (mains $28 to $34) complete with fireplace, wood paneling and views of the Deerfield Valley; an on-site spa; and a convivial tavern.

Wahoo's Eatery AMERICAN $
(VT 9; sandwiches $5-10; ⊙11am-8pm May-Sep) 'We welcome your business and relish your buns' reads the sign at this friendly, family-run roadside snack shack less than a mile east of Wilmington on VT 100. A long-standing local institution, it whips up quality burgers ($2 extra for grass-fed Vermont beef), along with hand-cut fries, handmade

---

DON'T MISS

COVERED BRIDGES

Vermont has more covered bridges per square mile than any state in the union. Here's a trivia-lover's guide to some of our favorites throughout the state:

Bartonsville (southern Vermont) The original 19th-century bridge here was famously swept away in Hurricane Irene's floodwaters in 2011 (search for remarkable footage on YouTube), but in classic Vermont fashion, locals rallied to have a replica reconstructed. The bridge reopened to the public in January 2013. It's 7 miles northeast of Grafton.

Northfield Falls (northern Vermont) This small town 8 miles south of Montpelier has a unique claim to fame: three covered bridges in a row! Turn west off VT 12 onto Cox Brook Rd and you'll see Station Bridge, Newell Bridge and Upper Bridge – all within a few hundred feet of each other.

Montgomery (northern Vermont) This village near the Jay Peak ski area has a whopping seven covered bridges, more than any other town in Vermont.

Windsor (central Vermont) Spanning the Connecticut River from Windsor, VT, to Cornish, NH, the 449-ft Cornish–Windsor Bridge is the longest historical covered bridge in America still open to automobile traffic.

CHEESEMAKING

Local cheesemakers have been around since Colonial times in Vermont, but it's only in the last few decades that artisanal cheese has come into vogue and become more widely available. Sheep's and goat's milk are now used in addition to cow's milk, adding variety to the traditional staples of cheddar and Colby. **Vermont Cheese Council** (www.vtcheese.com) lists nearly four dozen cheese producers on its online Cheese Trail map; two of the best and easiest to visit are Shelburne Farms (p303) and the Grafton Village Cheese Company (p284). Serious cheese connoisseurs can learn more about the state's smaller producers in Ellen Ecker Ogden's *The Vermont Cheese Book*. You'll also find a huge selection of local cheeses at places like the Brattleboro Food Co-op (p282) and City Market (p308) in Burlington.

conch fritters, wraps, sandwiches, hot dogs, salads and ice cream.

Dot's   DINER $$
(☑ 802-464-7284; www.dotsofvermont.com; 3 E Main St; dishes $5-16; ⊘ 5:30am-8pm Sun-Thu, to 9pm Fri & Sat) Devastated by flooding in 2011, Wilmington's venerable down-home diner was rebuilt from scratch and reopened in September 2013. Its spicy Jailhouse Chili, covered with melted cheese, is renowned throughout New England. With a **second location** (VT 100) near the slopes in Dover, it's justly popular with locals and skiers in search of cheap sustenance like steak and eggs for breakfast.

❶ Information

Mt Snow Valley Chamber of Commerce
(☑ 877-887-6884, 802-464-8092; www.visitvermont.com; 21 W Main St; ⊘ 8:30am-4:30pm Mon-Wed, 8:30am-6pm Thu & Fri, 10am-4pm Sat & Sun) Has information on accommodations and activities.

❶ Getting There & Away

Wilmington is 20 miles west of Brattleboro and 20 miles east of Bennington; it's a winding half-hour drive to either town along the mountainous VT 9.

Bennington

POP 15,800

Bennington is a mix of historic Vermont village (Old Bennington), workaday town (Bennington proper) and college town (North Bennington). It is also home to the famous Bennington Monument, which commemorates the crucial Battle of Bennington during the American Revolution. Had Colonel Seth Warner and the local 'Green Mountain Boys' not helped weaken British defenses

during this battle, the colonies might well have been split.

The charming hilltop site of colonial Old Bennington is studded with 80 Georgian and Federal houses (dating from 1761 – the year Bennington was founded – to 1830). The poet Robert Frost is buried here and a museum in his old homestead pays eloquent tribute.

As Bennington is within the bounds of the Green Mountain National Forest, there are many hiking trails nearby, including the granddaddies of them all: the Appalachian and Long Trails.

◎ Sights & Activities

Old First Church   HISTORIC SITE
(cnr Monument Ave & VT 9) Gracing the center of Old Bennington, this historic church was built in 1805 in Palladian style. Its churchyard holds the remains of five Vermont governors, numerous American Revolution soldiers and poet Robert Frost (1874–1963), the best-known, and perhaps best-loved, American poet of the 20th century, buried beneath the inscription 'I Had a Lover's Quarrel with the World.'

Bennington Battle Monument   HISTORIC SITE
(www.benningtonbattlemonument.com; 15 Monument Circle; adult/child $3/1; ⊘ 9am-5pm mid-Apr–Oct) Vermont's loftiest structure offers an unbeatable 360-degree view of the countryside with peeks at covered bridges and across to New York. And you won't have to strain hamstrings climbing this 306ft-tall obelisk: an elevator whisks you painlessly to the top.

Bennington
Battlefield Historic Site   HISTORIC SITE
To reach the actual battle site, 6 miles from the Bennington Battle Monument, follow

the 'Bennington Battlefield' signs along back roads and through a historic covered bridge to North Bennington, then continue west on VT 67. Admission is free, and picnic tables are provided.

Park-McCullough House Museum   MUSEUM

(☑ 802-442-5441; www.parkmccullough.org; 1 Park St, North Bennington; adult/under 12yr/student $10/free/7; ☺ hourly tours 10am-3pm Fri mid-May–mid-Oct) Just off VT 67A in North Bennington, this magnificent 35-room mansion, built in 1865, is filled with period furnishings and a fine collection of antique dolls, toys and carriages. Stroll the grounds during daylight hours or visit the house on a guided tour (Fridays only). The house is also open for seasonal celebrations in November or December.

Robert Frost Stone House Museum   MUSEUM

(☑ 802-447-6200; www.frostfriends.org; 121 VT 7A, Shaftsbury; adult/under 18yr $5/2.50; ☺ 10am-5pm Wed-Sun May-Oct) When he moved his family to Shaftsbury (4 miles north of Bennington), poet Robert Frost was 46 years old and at the height of his career. This modest museum opens a window into the poet's life, with one entire room dedicated to his most famous work, 'Stopping by Woods on a Snowy Evening,' which he penned here in the 1920s.

Bennington Museum   MUSEUM

(☑ 802-447-1571; www.benningtonmuseum.org; 75 Main St; adult/child $10/free; ☺ 10am-5pm daily Jul-Oct, Thu-Tue Nov, Dec & Feb-Jun, closed Jan) Between downtown and Old Bennington, this museum has an outstanding collection of early Americana that includes furniture, glassware, Bennington pottery, Colonial paintings, dolls, military memorabilia and the world's oldest surviving American Revolutionary flag. There's also a noteworthy collection of works by 'Grandma Moses' (1860–1961). Perhaps the country's most famous folk artist, she's known for her lively, natural depictions of farm life that she painted between the ages of 70 and 100.

Norman Rockwell Exhibition   MUSEUM

(☑ 802-375-6747; www.normanrockwellexhibit.com; VT 7A, Arlington; adult/child $3/free; ☺ 9am-5pm May-Dec) In Arlington, a 10-mile drive north of Bennington, a tiny maple syrup shop (the sweet stuff is made on site) houses this exhibition of 500 of Rockwell's *Saturday Evening Post* covers and prints. It also shows a short film about the artist, who lived in this town from 1939 to 1953.

Bennington Center for the Arts   ARTS CENTER

(☑ 802-442-7158; www.thebennington.org; cnr Gypsy Lane & VT 9; adult/under 12yr $9/free; ☺ 10am-5pm Wed-Mon) Half a mile west of Bennington's Old First Church, this arts

VERMONT BENNINGTON

HIKING VERMONT'S LONG LONG TRAIL

Built between 1912 and 1930 as America's first long-distance hiking trail, the Long Trail of Vermont follows the south–north ridge of the Green Mountains for 264 miles, from Massachusetts to Canada. A little less than half of the trail is located inside the Green Mountain National Forest (☑ 802-747-6700).

Often only 3ft wide, the trail traverses streams and forests, skirts ponds and weaves up and down the mountains to bare summits like Mt Abraham, Mt Mansfield and Camel's Hump. From up top, hikers will enjoy exceptional vistas, with wave after wave of hillside gently rolling back to a sea of green dotted with the occasional pasture or meadow.

Three excellent guides to the trail – *Long Trail Guide*, the *Day Hiker's Guide to Vermont* and *The Long Trail End-to-Ender's Guide* – are published by the venerable Green Mountain Club, which originally constructed the trail and still maintains it. All three guides are packed with nitty-gritty details on equipment sales and repairs, mail drops and B&Bs that provide trailhead shuttle services.

The GMC maintains more than 60 rustic lodges and lean-tos along the trail, all spaced at 5- to 7-mile intervals. Hikers can easily walk from one shelter to the next in a day, but it's imperative to bring a tent as shelters often fill up.

While the trail is wonderful for multiday excursions, it's also popular for day hikes. Call or drop by the Green Mountain Club Visitors Center (☑ 802-244-7037; www.greenmountainclub.org; 4711 Waterbury-Stowe Rd, Waterbury Center; ☺ 9am-5pm Jun-Aug), or visit the website for information and itinerary planning advice.

center has a hodgepodge of offerings, including the Great Outdoors gallery of wind sculptures and whirligigs, a Covered Bridge museum and other galleries devoted to fine art, Native American art and rotating contemporary exhibitions.

BattenKill Canoe   BOATING
(☏ 802-362-2800; www.battenkill.com; 6328 VT 7A, Arlington; ⊙ 9am-5:30pm daily May-Oct, Wed-Fri Nov-Apr) These outfitters 4 miles north of Arlington rent paddling equipment and organize trips for one or more days on the lovely Battenkill River.

Prospect Mountain Cross-Country Ski Touring Center   SKIING
(☏ 802-442-2575; www.prospectmountain.com; VT 9, Woodford; ⊙ 9am-5pm) About 7 miles east of Bennington, Prospect Mountain has more than 40km of groomed trails. It offers ski rentals and lessons as well as snowshoe rentals.

🛏 Sleeping

Camping on the Battenkill   CAMPGROUND $
(☏ 800-830-6663, 802-375-6663; www.campingonthebattenkillvt.com; tent sites $25-31, RV sites with/without hookups from $34/32, lean-tos $33-38; ⊙ late Apr–mid-Oct) Fishing is the forte at this campground just north of Arlington, which has 100 sites split between forest, meadow and open areas. Call early to reserve the popular riverside sites. Multiday stays are required during peak periods.

Greenwood Lodge & Campsites   HOSTEL, CAMPGROUND $
(☏ 802-442-2547; www.campvermont.com/greenwood; VT 9, Prospect Mountain; 2-person tent/RV site $27/35, dm/d from $29/70; ⊙ mid-May–late Oct) Nestled in the Green Mountains in Woodford, this 120-acre space with three ponds is home to one of Vermont's best-sited hostels. Accommodations include 17 budget beds and 40 campsites. You'll find it easily, 8 miles east of Bennington on VT 9 at the Prospect Mountain ski area. Facilities include hot showers and a game room.

South Shire Inn   INN $$
(☏ 888-201-2250, 802-447-3839; www.southshire.com; 124 Elm St; r/ste incl breakfast from $125/185; ☎) This centrally located, antique-filled Victorian inn has plush, high-ceilinged rooms, including some with fireplaces, scattered across a main house and carriage house. Complimentary afternoon teas held in the mahogany library enhance the sense of luxury.

Four Chimneys Inn   INN $$$
(☏ 802-447-3500; www.fourchimneys.com; 21 West Rd; r incl breakfast $129-299; ☎) Old Bennington's only B&B, this grand white 1910 mansion surrounded by 11 acres of manicured lawns has a variety of spacious rooms, many with fireplaces and porches. The best suite is a two-story revamped former ice house with a spiral staircase. The attached restaurant, open August to October, has seated such guests as Walt Disney, Richard Burton and Elizabeth Taylor.

🍴 Eating & Drinking

Crazy Russian Girls   BAKERY $
(443 Main St; sandwiches $7-9; ⊙ 7am-6pm)   A family-run venture with deep community roots, this turquoise-walled bakery started as a humble street cart, but popular demand soon nudged it into a full-time business. The owner, whose Russian grandmother fled Stalin's regime and came to the US, mixes American and Russian baked goods with whimsical sandwiches. 'International' days include Russian Fridays, with homemade pierogi. Yum!

Blue Benn Diner   DINER $
(☏ 802-442-5140; 314 North St; mains $5-12; ⊙ 6am-4:45pm Mon-Fri, 7am-3:45pm Sat & Sun) This classic 1950s-era diner serves breakfast all day and a healthy mix of American, Asian and Mexican fare – including vegetarian options. Enhancing the retro experience are little tabletop jukeboxes where you can play Willie Nelson's 'Moonlight in Vermont' or Cher's 'Gypsies, Tramps and Thieves' till your neighbors scream for mercy.

South Street Café   CAFE $
(☏ 802-447-2433; South St; ⊙ 7am-7pm Mon-Thu, 7am-9pm Fri & Sat, 9am-5pm Sun; ☎) Sink into a velvet sofa and sip a cup of locally roasted joe in this inviting, high-ceilinged cafe with warm orange walls and vintage patterned tinwork. Located smack in Bennington's center at the corner of VT 9 and US 7, it's an oasis for soups, sandwiches, quiche, bakery treats and warm mugs of deliciousness.

Madison Brewing Co Pub & Restaurant   PUB $$
(☏ 802-442-7397; www.madisonbrewingco.com; 428 Main St; mains $8-16; ⊙ 11:30am-9pm Sun-Thu, to 10pm Fri & Sat; 🏠) With six to eight of its own brews on tap, this bustling two-level pub features fare ranging from sandwiches and burgers to steak, meatloaf, salads and

WESTON & THE VERMONT COUNTRY STORE

On the Green Mountains' eastern slopes, Weston (population 630) is one of Vermont's most pristine towns. Built along the banks of the West River and anchored by a grassy common graced with towering maples and a bandstand, the village is home to Vermont's oldest professional theater, the Weston Playhouse (☑802-824-5288; www.westonplayhouse.org; tickets $22-45; ☺performances late Jun-early Sep).

Weston also draws fans from far and wide to its famed Vermont Country Store (☑802-463-2224; www.vermontcountrystore.com; VT 100), a time warp from a simpler era when goods were made to last, and quirky products with appeal (but not a mass-market appeal) had a home. Here you'll discover plastic, electronic yodeling pickles (because everyone needs one, right?), taffeta slips, Tangee lipstick, three kinds of shoe stretchers with customizable bunion and corn knobs, personal care items and clothing – in short, everything you didn't know you needed. Additionally, it carries small toys and games of yesteryear Americana (think wooden pick-up-sticks and vintage tiddlywinks). The store also contains entire sections filled with candy jars and cases of Vermont cheese.

Weston is on VT100, 20 miles northwest of Grafton and 22 miles east of Manchester.

pasta. The small upstairs deck is a popular summertime hang-out.

★**Pangaea** INTERNATIONAL $$$
(☑802-442-7171; www.vermontfinedining.com; 1 Prospect St, North Bennington; lounge mains $11-23, restaurant mains $30-39; ☺lounge 5-9pm daily, restaurant 5-9pm Tue-Sat) Whether you opt for the tastefully decorated dining room, the intimate lounge or the small riverside terrace, you'll be served exceptional food here. The menu is full of fresh ingredients and international influences; try the Thai shrimp on organic udon noodles in a curry peanut sauce or the Herbes de Provence–rubbed Delmonico steak topped with gorgonzola. One of Vermont's finest restaurants.

🛍 Shopping

Bennington Potters CERAMICS
(www.benningtonpotters.com; 324 County St; ☺9:30am-6pm Mon-Sat, 10am-5pm Sun) The artisans at this factory store are maintaining Bennington's strong tradition of handmade stoneware manufacturing, which dates back to the 1700s. Take a self-guided tour through the manufacturing area, which reveals how much hand work still goes into the company's mass-produced items.

ℹ Information

Bennington Area Chamber of Commerce
(☑800-229-0252, 802-447-3311; www.bennington.com; 100 Veterans Memorial Dr; ☺9am-5pm) Offers current and historical information and a self-guided walking tour of historic Old Bennington. It's just north of downtown, on the east side of US 7.

ℹ Getting There & Away

Bennington is 40 miles west of Brattleboro via VT 9, or 25 miles south of Manchester via US 7.

Manchester

POP 4400

Manchester has been a fashionable resort town for almost two centuries. These days, the draw is mostly winter skiing and upscale outlet shopping (there are more than 100 shops, from Armani to Banana Republic).

Two families put Manchester on the map. The first was native son Franklin Orvis (1824–1900), who became a New York businessman but returned to Manchester to establish the Equinox House Hotel (1849). Franklin's brother, Charles, founded the Orvis Company, makers of fly-fishing equipment, in 1856. The Manchester-based company now has a worldwide following.

The second family was that of Abraham Lincoln (1809–65). His wife, Mary Todd Lincoln (1818–82), and their son Robert Todd Lincoln (1843–1926), came here during the Civil War, and Robert returned to build a mansion, Hildene, a number of years later.

◉ Sights

★**Hildene** HISTORIC SITE
(☑800-578-1788, 802-362-1788; www.hildene.org; 1005 Hildene Rd/VT 7A; adult/child $16/5, tours $5/2; ☺9:30am-4:30pm) Outside Manchester, the 24-room Georgian Revival mansion of Robert Todd Lincoln, son of Abraham and Mary Lincoln, is a national treasure. Lincoln family members lived here until 1975,

when it was converted into a museum and filled with many of the family's personal effects and furnishings. These include the hat Abraham Lincoln probably wore when he delivered the Gettysburg Address, and remarkable brass casts of his hands, the right one swollen from shaking hands while campaigning for the presidency.

Guided tours of the mansion depart at 11am and 1pm from June to September; at other times visitors can take a self-guided tour. The museum ticket includes access to the surrounding grounds, which are home to 8 miles of walking, skiing and snowshoeing trails, an observatory with a telescope, the Cutting and Kitchen Garden (a pretty herb and vegetable garden), the Hoyt Formal Garden (an exquisite flower garden designed to resemble a stained-glass window), and an agricultural center with a solar-powered barn where you can see the goats that produce Hildene cheese (watch it being made here, and purchase it at the museum gift shop).

Hildene also has a packed calendar of concerts and lectures; check its website for up-to-date listings.

Southern Vermont Arts Center   MUSEUM
(☑802-362-1405; www.svac.org; West Rd; adult/child $6/3; ⊙galleries 10am-5pm Tue-Sat, noon-5pm Sun) In addition to excellent outdoor sculptures, this center's 10 galleries of classic and contemporary art feature touring shows of sculpture, paintings, prints and photography. Other attractions include walking trails, the on-site Garden Cafe, lectures, and numerous musical events, including jazz concerts and the Manchester Music Festival, where classical is the focus.

American Museum of
Fly Fishing & Orvis   MUSEUM
(www.amff.com; 4070 Main St; adult/child $5/3; ⊙10am-4pm Tue-Sun Jun-Oct, Tue-Sat Nov-May) This museum has perhaps the world's best display of fly-fishing equipment. This includes fly collections and rods used by Ernest Hemingway, Bing Crosby and several US presidents, including Herbert Hoover. If you can believe it, the latter penned the tome *Fishing for Fun & To Wash Your Soul.*

🏃 Activities

Mt Equinox   SCENIC DRIVE, HIKE
(☑802-362-1114; www.equinoxmountain.com; car & driver $15, each additional passenger $5; ⊙9am-dusk May-Oct as snow allows) For exceptional views, climb the insanely steep 5-mile private toll road to the summit of 3816ft Mt Equinox; it's just off VT 7A, south of Manchester. Alternatively, hike to the summit via Burr and Burton and Lookout Rock Trails (five hours, 2918ft elevation gain). Hiking information is available at the Equinox hotel and resort, where the trail begins.

Appalachian Trail   HIKING, BIKING
The Appalachian Trail passes just east of Manchester, and in this area follows the same route as Vermont's Long Trail. Shelters pop up about every 10 miles; some are staffed from June to early October. Good day hikes include one to the summit of Bromley Mountain and another to Stratton Pond. For details and maps, visit the Green Mountain National Forest ranger station (☑802-362-2307; 2538 Depot St; ⊙8am-4:30pm Mon-Fri), about 3 miles east of Manchester Center. The Chamber of Commerce also has detailed printouts.

Stratton Mountain   SKIING
(☑802-297-4000, 800-787-2886; www.stratton.com; VT 30, Bondville) All-season recreational playground 16 miles southeast of Manchester, with 90 trails and 100 acres of glade- and tree-skiing terrain, 13 lifts (including a summit gondola) and a vertical drop of more than 2000ft on a 3875ft mountain, plus 20 miles of cross-country trails. Summer activities include golf, tennis, swimming, hiking, horseback riding, mountain biking and more.

Bromley Mountain   SKIING
(☑800-865-4786, 802-824-5522; www.bromley.com; VT 11, Peru; ⊕) Approximately 5 miles east of Manchester, 3284ft Bromley Mountain is a family-oriented resort featuring 43 downhill ski runs and 10 chairlifts. Summer attractions include the Alpine Slide (North America's longest), the Sun Mountain Flyer (a new half-mile-long zip line), an aerial adventure park, a climbing wall, trampolines, a water slide, a children's adventure park and access to the Long/Appalachian Trail.

Battenkill Sports
Bicycle Shop   BICYCLE RENTAL
(☑802-362-2734, 800-340-2734; www.battenkillsports.com; 1240 Depot St; mountain/road bikes per day $30/40; ⊙9:30am-5:30pm) One mile east of Manchester Center, this bike shop rents road, mountain and hybrid bikes.

✦ Festivals & Events

Manchester Music Festival   MUSIC
(www.mmfvt.org) This series of seven to eight classical-music concerts takes place from

early July to late August at the Southern Vermont Arts Center.

Concerts on the Green
MUSIC

(Manchester Town Green, Depot St) Each Tuesday evening between 6pm and 8pm from mid-July to mid-August you can catch live music performances (mainly local folk bands) al fresco at the town green.

Sleeping

Casablanca Motel
MOTEL, CABINS $

(800-254-2145, 802-362-2145; www.casablanca motel.com; cabins $72-150; ❄@🛏) This tidy collection of cabins on the northern fringes of town has units with microwaves, fridges and coffee-makers, each decorated in a different country theme.

Inn at Manchester
INN $$

(800-273-1793, 802-362-1793; www.innat-manchester.com; 3967 Main St/VT 7A; r/ste incl breakfast from $155/205; ❄@🛏🏊) This restored inn and carriage house offers rooms and suites with comfy quilts and country furnishings, each named after an herb or flower. There's a big front porch, afternoon teas with fresh-baked goodies, an expansive backyard and comfortable common rooms, one with a wee pub.

Barnstead Inn
INN $$

(800-331-1619, 802-379-5069; www.barnstead-inn.com; 349 Bonnet St; r $135-195, ste $210-275; 🛏🏊) Barely a half mile from Manchester Center, this converted 1830s hay barn exudes charm and is in a good location. Rooms have refrigerators and homey braided rugs, while the porch has wicker rockers for watching the world pass by.

Inn at Ormsby Hill
INN $$$

(800-670-2841, 802-362-1163; www.ormsbyhill. com; 1842 Main St/VT 7A; r incl breakfast $205-535; 🛏) Just southwest of Manchester, Ormsby Hill is arguably one of the most welcoming inns in all of New England. Fireplaces, two-person Jacuzzis, flat-screen TVs, antiques, gracious innkeepers and 2.5 acres of lawn are among the features that draw repeat guests. The inn's breakfast is without equal (from bacon-and-egg risotto to pancakes baked in the shape of a top hat).

Equinox
RESORT $$$

(802-362-4747; www.equinoxresort.com; 3567 Main St; r $259-689; @🛏🏊) Manchester's most famous resort encompasses many worlds: cottages with wood-burning fire-places, luxury town houses with full kitchens, the main house's elegant suites, and the Federal-style 1811 House's antique-filled rooms, canopied beds and oriental rugs. High-end extras abound: an 18-hole golf course, two tennis courts, a state-of-the-art fitness center, a full-service spa and endless activities, including falconry, archery and snowmobiling.

Eating & Drinking

Spiral Press Café
CAFE $

(cnr VT 11 & VT 7A; mains $6-10; 7:30am-7pm; 🛏) Attached to Manchester Center's fabulous Northshire Bookstore, this cozy cafe buzzes with locals and tourists alike who flock here for good coffee, flaky croissants and delicious panini sandwiches.

Little Rooster Cafe
CAFE $$

(802-362-3496; VT 7A; dishes $7-11; 7am-2:30pm Thu-Tue) This colorful spot serves an eclectic mix of dishes, including pan-seared salmon, roast leg of lamb, spinach salad, and focaccia sandwiches with tasty ingredients like roasted portobello mushrooms and grilled eggplant. It's also popular for its delicious breakfast entrees, like the trademark Cock-A-Doodle-Doo (poached eggs with smoked salmon and dill-mustard-caper sauce on an English muffin).

Bistro Henry
INTERNATIONAL $$$

(802-362-4982; www.bistrohenry.com; VT 11/30; mains $25-35; 5-9pm Tue-Sun) This casual, chef-owned bistro serves creative French- and Italian-inspired cuisine highlighting fresh seafood, aged meats and produce from local farms. Its acclaimed wine selection features eclectic and hard-to-find labels. Complementing the regular menu, weekly specials include barbecue on Slow Smoke Sundays, small dishes for $9.99 on Thursday, and early-bird three-course meals for $25 on Tuesday between 5pm and 6pm.

Perfect Wife
INTERNATIONAL $$$

(802-362-2817; www.perfectwife.com; 2594 Depot St; mains tavern $12-25, restaurant $26-32; restaurant 5-10pm Mon-Sat, tavern 4pm-late Mon-Sat) In the hills east of town, this cozy eatery serves international fare, such as sesame-crusted salmon and filet mignon, in its cobblestone-walled restaurant half. The adjoining Other Woman Tavern offers pub fare and is an excellent evening hang-out, with live music two or three nights a week (mainly rock, blues and folk).

VERMONT MANCHESTER

OFF THE BEATEN TRACK

MERCK FOREST & FARM CENTER

Hidden away on a gorgeous hilltop that's only a 25-minute drive from Manchester but a world apart from the village hustle and bustle, this sprawling **farm and environmental education center** (802-394-7836; www.merckforest.org; 3270 VT 315;) is a blissful place to experience Vermont's natural beauty and agricultural heritage. Over 2700 acres of high-country meadow and forest have been preserved here; the park's centerpiece is a working organic farm with animals, organic vegetable gardens, renewable energy installations and a sugar house where you can watch maple syrup being produced during sugaring season. The center offers a wide range of hikes, environmental education programs and events such as sheepdog trials. It also rents out cabins and tent sites, which are spread all over the property. Sales of produce and syrup, coupled with voluntary contributions, help sustain the nonprofit foundation at the heart of it all.

To get here from Manchester, take VT 30 northwest 8 miles to East Rupert, then turn left on VT 315, travel 2½ miles and look for signs on your left at the top of the hill.

Ye Olde Tavern AMERICAN $$$
(802-362-0611; www.yeoldetavern.net; 5183 Main St; mains $17-34; 5-9pm) Hearthside dining at candlelit tables enhances the experience at this gracious roadside 1790s inn. The menu is wide-ranging, but the 'Yankee favorites' like traditional pot roast cooked in the tavern's own ale, New England scrod baked with Vermont cheddar, and local venison (a regular Friday special) seal the deal.

Mistral's FRENCH $$$
(802-362-1779; www.mistralsattollgate.com; 10 Toll Gate Rd; mains $28-40; 6-10pm Thu-Tue Jul-Oct, Thu-Mon Nov-Jun) Nestled deep in the woods (off VT 30 and VT 11 east of town) and overlooking the rushing waters of Bromley Brook, Mistral's offers fine dining on filet mignon, Norwegian salmon or roast duck in an incredibly intimate setting.

ⓘ Information

Manchester & the Mountains Regional Chamber of Commerce (802-362-6313, 800-362-4144; www.visitmanchestervt.com; 39 Bonnet St; 9am-5pm Mon-Fri, 10am-4pm Sat, 11am-3pm Sun;) This spiffy new tourist office, with free wi-fi and tons of brochures, is just west of the VT 30/VT 7A junction in Manchester Center. Staff can help visitors find rooms and provide printouts for hikes of varying difficulty within the Green Mountain National Forest.

ⓘ Getting There & Away

Manchester sits 25 miles north of Bennington and 65 miles south of Middlebury on US 7. For a scenic alternate route to Middlebury, take VT 30 through Dorset and Pawlet.

Around Manchester

Manchester's a terrific base for visiting quintessential Vermont towns, whether they are pristine like Dorset or more workaday like Pawlet.

Dorset

POP 2030

Six miles northwest of Manchester along VT 30, Dorset is a pristinely beautiful Vermont village, originally settled in 1768, with a stately inn (the oldest in Vermont), a lofty church and a village green. The sidewalks and many other buildings are made of creamy marble from the nearby **quarry**, about a mile south of the village center on VT 30. Dorset supplied much of the marble for the grand New York Public Library building and numerous other public edifices. These days the quarry is filled with water and makes a lovely place to picnic.

Dorset is best known as a summer playground for well-to-do city folks (a role it has played for over a century) and the home of a renowned theater the **Dorset Playhouse** (802-867-5777; www.dorsetplayers.org; 104 Cheney Rd), which draws a sophisticated audience for the annual **Dorset Theatre Festival** (www.dorsettheatrefestival.org; midJun–late Aug). On Fridays and Saturdays in summer, the playhouse features tapas and music in the Gallery Café from 6:30pm until showtime; the cafe also hosts art exhibitions throughout the summer season – check the website for details.

Vermont's oldest continuously operating inn (in business since 1796), the **Dorset Inn** (802-867-5500; www.dorsetinn.com; cnr Church

& Main Sts; r incl breakfast $165-475; 🛜) is still going strong. Just off VT 30 facing the village green, this traditional but plush inn has 35 guest rooms and suites, some with fireplaces and Jacuzzis. The front-porch rockers provide a nice setting for watching the comings and goings of this sleepy Vermont town. The on-site restaurant, serving bistro food and locally sourced items (mains $15 to $29), is highly regarded, or pop into the spa for some pampering.

Innkeepers Jean and Jim Kingston greet travelers at the tidy 1800s **Dovetail Inn** (📞802-867-5747, 888-867-5747; www.dovetailinn. com; VT 30; r incl continental breakfast $99-265; ✳🛜), which faces the village green. Breakfast is served in the comfort of the 11 well-kept guest rooms in two houses.

Dorset Union Store (www.dorsetunion-store.com; 31 Church St; ⏰7am-7pm Mon-Sat, 8am-6pm Sun) sells all manner of edible Vermont items, especially high-end gourmet goodies and picnic fixings, including cheese (of course); it also has a well-stocked wine room, a deli and a freezer full of gourmet take-and-bake treats, including its award-winning mac-and-cheese.

CENTRAL VERMONT

Vermont's heart features some of New England's most bucolic countryside. Cows begin to outnumber people just north of Rutland (Vermont's second-largest city, with a whopping 16,500 residents). Lovers of the outdoors make frequent pilgrimages to central Vermont, especially to the resort areas of Killington, Sugarbush and Mad River Glen, which attract countless skiers and summer hikers. For those interested in indoor pleasures, antique shops and art galleries dot the back roads between picturesque covered bridges.

Woodstock & Quechee Village

POP 3050

Chartered in 1761, Woodstock has been the highly dignified seat of scenic Windsor County since 1766. It prospered in this role. The townspeople built many grand houses surrounding the oval village green, and four of Woodstock's churches can claim bells cast by Paul Revere. Senator Jacob Collamer, a friend of Abraham Lincoln's, once observed,

'The good people of Woodstock have less incentive than others to yearn for heaven.'

Today Woodstock is still very beautiful and very wealthy. Spend some time walking around the green, surrounded by Federal and Greek Revival homes and public buildings, or along the Ottauquechee River, spanned by three covered bridges. The Rockefellers and the Rothschilds own estates in the surrounding countryside, and the well-to-do come to stay at the grand Woodstock Inn & Resort. Despite its high-tone reputation, the town also offers some reasonably priced lodging and meal possibilities.

About five minutes east of Woodstock, small, twee Quechee Village is home to Quechee Gorge – Vermont's answer to the Grand Canyon – as well as some outstanding restaurants.

◉ Sights

★**Quechee Gorge**   CANYON
Lurking beneath US 4, less than a mile east of Quechee Village, the gorge is a 163ft-deep scar that cuts about 3000ft along a stream that you can view from a bridge or easily access by footpaths from the road. A series of well-marked, undemanding trails, none of which should take more than an hour to cover, cut away from the stream.

Just upstream from the gorge, the tranquil water of Dewey's Mill Pond is another lovely spot; bordered by a pretty expanse of reeds and grasses, the pond is named for AG Dewey, who set up a prosperous woolen mill here in 1869.

Billings Farm & Museum   FARM
(📞802-457-2355; www.billingsfarm.org; 69 Old River Rd, Woodstock; adult/child $12/6; ⏰10am-5pm daily May-Oct, to 3:30pm Sat & Sun Nov-Feb; 🚼) 🐾 A mile north of the village green, this historic farm founded by 19th-century railroad magnate Frederick Billings delights children with hands-on activities related to old-fashioned farm life. Farm animals, including pretty cows descended from Britain's Isle of Jersey, are abundant. Family-friendly seasonal events include wagon and sleigh rides, pumpkin and apple festivals and old-fashioned Halloween, Thanksgiving and Christmas celebrations.

Marsh-Billings-Rockefeller National Historical Park   PARK
(📞802-457-3368; www.nps.gov/mabi; Woodstock; mansion tours adult/child $8/free, trails free; ⏰10am-5pm late May–Oct) Built around the

historic home of early American conservationist George Perkins Marsh, Vermont's only national park examines the relationship between land stewardship and environmental conservation. The estate's 20 miles of trails and carriage roads are free for exploring on foot, cross-country skis or snowshoes. There's an admission fee to the mansion itself, where tours are offered every 30 minutes.

Sugarbush Farm
FARM

(📞800-281-1757, 802-457-1757; www.sugarbush-farm.com; 591 Sugarbush Farm Rd, Woodstock; ☉8am-5pm Mon-Fri, 9am-5pm Sat & Sun; 🚼) **FREE** While this working farm at the end of a bucolic road also collects maple sap, cheddar's the king here. See how it's made and sample the 14 varieties – from the mild sage cheddar to the jalapeño and cayenne pepper variety to the prize-winning hickory and smoked cheddar. Wax-coated bars of cheese are sold and travel well.

Vermont Institute of Natural Science
SCIENCE CENTER

(VINS; 📞802-359-5000; www.vinsweb.org; US 4, Quechee; adult/child $13/11; ☉10am-5:30pm; 🚼) 🐾 This science center near Quechee houses two dozen species of raptors, ranging from the tiny, 3oz saw-whet owl to the mighty bald eagle. The birds that end up here have sustained permanent injuries that prevent them from returning to the wild. On offer are regular educational presentations and three self-guided nature trails, delightful for summer hiking and winter snowshoeing.

🏃 Activities

Suicide Six
SKIING

(📞802-457-6663, 800-448-7900; www.suicide6.com; VT 12, Pomfret; ☉mid-Dec–Mar) In 1934 Woodstockers installed the first mechanical ski tow in the USA, and skiing is still important here. Three miles north of Woodstock, this resort is known for challenging downhill runs. The lower slopes are fine for beginners, though. There are 23 trails (30% beginner, 40% intermediate, 30% expert) and three lifts.

Woodstock Ski Touring Center
SKIING

(📞802-457-6674; www.woodstockinn.com/Activities/Nordic-Skiing; VT 106, Woodstock) Just south of town, rents equipment and has 50 miles of groomed touring trails, including one that takes in 1250ft Mt Tom.

Woodstock Sports
BICYCLE RENTAL

(📞802-457-1568; 30 Central St, Woodstock; ☉8:30am-5:30pm Mon-Sat) Rents bicycles and provides maps of good local routes.

👉 Tours

Discovery Bicycle Tours
BICYCLE TOUR

(📞800-257-2226; discoverybicycletours.com) This family-run, Woodstock-based company (formerly known as Bike Vermont) operates two- to five-night bike tours in the area, including inn-to-inn tours.

🛏 Sleeping

Quechee State Park
CAMPGROUND $

(📞802-295-2990; www.vtstateparks.com/htm/quechee.htm; 5800 US 4, Quechee; tent & RV sites/lean-tos $20/27; ☉mid-May–mid-Oct) Eight miles east of Woodstock and 3 miles west of I-89 along US 4, this 611-acre spot has 45 pine-shaded campsites and seven lean-tos a short stroll from Quechee Gorge.

Silver Lake State Park
CAMPGROUND $

(📞802-234-9451; www.vtstateparks.com/htm/silver.htm; 20 State Park Beach Rd, Barnard; tent & RV sites/lean-tos $20/27; ☉late May–early Sep) This 34-acre park (off VT 12) is 10 miles north of Woodstock and has 47 sites (with seven lean-tos), a beach, boat and canoe rentals and fishing.

Ardmore Inn
B&B $$

(📞802-457-3887; www.ardmoreinn.com; 23 Pleasant St, Woodstock; r incl breakfast $155-230; 🛜) This congenial, centrally located inn in a stately 1867 Victorian–Greek Revival building has five antique-laden rooms with oriental rugs and private marble bathrooms. The owners are especially helpful, and the breakfasts are seemingly never-ending.

Shire Riverview Motel
MOTEL $$

(📞802-457-2211; www.shiremotel.com; 46 Pleasant St/US 4, Woodstock; r $128-228; 🌐🛜) Set within walking distance of the town center on US 4, this motel is located on the Ottauquechee River, which visitors can mull over from rockers on a wraparound porch while sipping a mug of their complimentary coffee or tea. It has 42 comfortable rooms, some with fireplaces and most with river views.

⭐ Parker House Inn
INN $$$

(📞800-295-6077, 802-295-6077; www.theparkerhouseinn.com; 1792 Main St, Quechee; r incl breakfast $195-275; 🌐🛜) A Victorian-style redbrick house built in 1857 for former Vermont senator Joseph Parker, this antique-laden inn has seven large guest rooms and a riverside porch. It's just 100 yards from one of the Ottauquechee River's covered bridges and a waterfall. The on-site restaurant (mains $24 to $29)is excellent.

Woodstock Inn & Resort   RESORT $$$
(☑888-338-2745, 802-457-1100; www.woodstockinn.com; 14 The Green, Woodstock; r $240-450, ste $350-700; ❀☞☲) One of Vermont's most luxurious hotels, this resort has extensive grounds, a formal dining room, an 18-hole golf course, tennis courts, cross-country skiing, a fitness center, a spa and an indoor sports center. A fire blazes in the huge stone fireplace during chilly periods, enhancing the welcoming ambiance. Rooms are done up in soft, muted colors and Vermont-crafted wood furnishings.

Village Inn of Woodstock   INN $$$
(☑800-722-4571, 802-457-1255; www.villageinnofwoodstock.com; 41 Pleasant St, Quechee; r incl breakfast $150-350; ❀☞) The eight guest rooms in this lovely Victorian mansion, situated on a 40-acre estate, have four-poster feather beds, down comforters and period details like oak wainscoting and tin ceilings. Enjoy the welcoming terrace or the cozy tavern (open only to guests), with its stained-glass windows and full bar. The luscious breakfast includes granola, pastries and breads, all made on site.

🍴 Eating & Drinking

If you have a picnic lunch, take it to Teagle's Landing, a tiny streamside hideaway with picnic tables just below the Central St bridge.

White Cottage Snack Bar   AMERICAN $
(462 Woodstock Rd, Woodstock; mains $5-15; ☺11am-10pm) A Woodstock institution, this glorified snack shack by the river has been serving loyal locals fried clams, burgers and ice cream by the riverside since 1957.

★ Skunk Hollow Tavern   AMERICAN $$
(☑802-436-2139; www.skunkhollowtavern.com; 12 Brownsville Rd, Hartland Four Corners; mains $13-25; ☺5pm-late Wed-Sun) Few Vermont eateries are as atmospheric as this tiny 200-year-old crossroads tavern 8 miles south of Woodstock, with worn wooden floors that ooze history. Enjoy burgers, fish-and-chips or rack of lamb downstairs at the bar or in the more intimate space upstairs. Friday evenings, when there's live music and the band takes up half the room, are a special treat.

Osteria Pane e Salute   ITALIAN $$
(☑802-457-4882; www.osteriapaneesalute.com; 61 Central St, Woodstock; mains $16-23; ☺6-10pm Thu-Sun, closed Apr & Nov) Book ahead at this very popular downtown bistro where you can enjoy classic northern Italian dishes, plus thin-crust Tuscan pizza in winter, complemented by an extensive wine list that focuses on Italian wines from small boutique vineyards. The owners regularly travel to Italy in their months off, gathering inspiration for new recipes and wine selections.

Prince & the Pauper   AMERICAN $$$
(☑802-457-1818; www.princeandpauper.com; 24 Elm St, Woodstock; bistro mains $16-23, prix-fixe menu $49; ☺6-9pm) Woodstock's elegant New American bistro serves a sublime three-course fixed-price menu, including appetizer, salad and main courses such as applewood-smoked ruby trout with grilled corn cake and crème fraîche. The lighter à la carte bistro fare is an enticing option for smaller appetites, offered every evening except Saturday.

★ Simon Pearce Restaurant   NEW AMERICAN $$$
(☑802-295-1470; www.simonpearce.com; 1760 Main St, Quechee; lunch mains $13-18, dinner mains $23-35; ☺11:30am-2:45pm & 5:30-9pm) Be sure to reserve a window table in the dining room, which is suspended over the river in this converted brick mill. Local ingredients are used to inventive effect here to produce such delicacies as crab and cod melt or the seared chicken (with roasted-corn mascarpone polenta). The restaurant's beautiful stemware is blown by hand in the Simon Pearce Glass workshops, also in the mill. This place is difficult to leave.

🔒 Shopping

Shackleton Thomas   FURNITURE, CERAMICS
(☑802-672-5175; www.shackletonthomas.com; The Mill, VT 4, Bridgewater; ☺10am-5pm Mon-Sat, 11am-4pm Sun) Charles Shackleton and Miranda Thomas run this lovely shop and gallery in the Bridgewater Mill, a three-story converted 1820s mill on the Ottauquechee River 6 miles west of Woodstock. The shop specializes in designer furniture, pottery, textiles and accessories. A few other artisans, including a jeweler, a gilder and a weaver, also have studio space here.

Simon Pearce Glass
GLASS, CERAMICS

(☑ 802-295-2771; www.simonpearce.com; 1760 Main St, Quechee; ☺ 10am-9pm) At this exceptional studio and shop, visitors can watch artisans produce distinctive pieces of original glass.

ℹ Information

Woodstock Area Chamber of Commerce Welcome Center (☑ 802-432-1100; www.woodstockvt.com; Mechanic St, Woodstock; ☺ 10am-4pm Mon-Fri, 9am-5pm Sat & Sun) Woodstock's welcome center is housed in a lovely red building on a riverside backstreet, two blocks from the village green. There's also a small information booth on the village green itself. Both places can help with accommodations.

ℹ Getting There & Away

Burlington (1¾ hours, 95 miles) is a straight shot from Woodstock via US 4 east and I-89 north.

For Killington (20 miles, 30 minutes), take US 4 west.

Greyhound buses (www.greyhound.com) and the Amtrak **Vermonter train** (www.amtrak.com/vermonter-train) stop at nearby White River Junction. From either station, you'll need to take a taxi to Woodstock, a distance of 15 miles.

Killington Mountain
POP 810

The largest ski resort in the east, Killington spans seven mountains, dominated by 4241ft Killington Peak, the second-highest in Vermont, and operates the largest snowmaking system in North America. Although upwards of 20,000 people can find lodging within 20 miles, its numerous outdoor activities are centrally located on the mountain. Officially, the mountain town is Killington Village, but all the action can be found along Killington Rd on the way up the mountain.

◉ Sights & Activities

Killington Resort
SKIING

(☑ 802-422-6200; www.killington.com; adult/senior/youth lift ticket weekend $88/75/68, midweek $80/68/62) Known as the 'Beast of the East,' Vermont's prime ski resort is enormous, yet runs efficiently enough to avoid overcrowding (it has five separate lodges, each with a different emphasis, as well as 32 lifts). The ski season runs from early November through early May, enhanced by the largest snowmaking system in America.

K-1 Lodge boasts the Express Gondola, which transports up to 3000 skiers per hour in heated cars along a 2.5-mile cable and is the highest lift in Vermont. **Snowshed Lodge** is an ideal base for adults looking for lessons or refresher courses. Free-ride enthusiasts should check out **Bear Mountain Lodge** for pipe action, tree skiing or rail jibbing, not to mention the double black-diamond Outer Limits, the steepest mogul run in the East. **Ramshead Lodge** caters to children and families, as well as those looking for easier terrain, w hile **Skyeship Lodge** is the home of the Skyeship Gondola, a two-stage gondola with quick and direct access to Skye Peak. Each lodge has food courts, restaurants, bars and ski shops.

Two hundred runs snake down Killington's seven mountains (4241ft Killington Peak, 3967ft Pico Mountain, 3800ft Skye Peak, 3610ft Ramshead Peak, 3592ft Snowdon Peak, 3295ft Bear Mountain and 2456ft Sunrise Mountain), covering 1215 acres of slopes. A quarter are considered easy, a third moderate and the rest difficult. Snowboarders will find six challenging parks, including superpipes with 18ft walls.

Mountain Bike & Repair Shop
MOUNTAIN BIKING, HIKING

(☑ 802-422-6232; Killington Rd; mountain bikes per day $70; ☺ late Jun–mid-Oct) This shop rents mountain bikes. Serious riders will want to take the 1.25-mile K-1 gondola ride to the top of Killington Mountain and find their way down along the 45 miles of trails. Mountain-bike trail access costs $5 daily or $35 for trail and gondola access. Hikers can also ride the gondola to the top (1/2/3/4 people $10/17/24/27) and hike down. The shop has an excellent free map of 14 self-guided nature hikes.

🛏 Sleeping

Killington Motel
MOTEL $

(☑ 800-366-0493, 802-773-9535; www.lodgingkillington.com; 1946 US 4, Killington; r incl breakfast $68-164; ✳ 🐾 🛜) This clean, well-maintained motel just west of the VT 100/US 4 junction has some of the best rates in town.

Gifford Woods State Park
CAMPGROUND $

(☑ 802-775-5354; www.vtstateparks.com/htm/gifford.htm; Gifford Woods Rd, Killington; tent & RV sites $20, lean-tos/cabins $27/48; ☺ mid-May–mid-Oct) A half mile north of US 4 and VT 100, this park has four cabins, 20 lean-tos, and 22 tent/trailer sites set on 114 acres.

Added bonuses are the playground, fishing in Kent Pond, and hiking trails, including an easy access to the Appalachian Trail.

Inn at Long Trail   INN **$**
(☎ 800-325-2540, 802-775-7181; www.innatlongtrail.com; 709 US 4, Killington; r/ste incl breakfast from $79/110; 🐾) The first hotel built (in 1938) expressly as a ski lodge, the inn is also temporary home to hikers pausing along the nearby Long Trail. The rustic decor makes use of tree trunks (the bar is fashioned from a single log), the rooms are cozy and suites include fireplaces.

Inn of the Six Mountains   INN **$$**
(☎ 802-422-4302, 800-228-4676; www.sixmountains.com; 2617 Killington Rd, Killington; r incl breakfast $109-134; @🐾) Well situated a third of the way up the mountain, this hotel has all the modern conveniences, in addition to a Jacuzzi, exercise rooms, tennis courts and a spa.

✖ Eating

Long Trail Brewing Company   BREWERY, PUB
(☎ 802-672-5011; www.longtrail.com; cnr US 4 & VT 100A, Bridgewater; mains $6-10; ⏱ 10am-7pm) Halfway between Killington and Woodstock, the brewer of 'Vermont's No 1 Selling Amber' draws crowds for free brewery tours and a sunny riverside deck where you can enjoy sandwiches, burgers, salads and, of course, beer. Order a sampler of six 4oz glasses ($7) and taste 'em all: hearty stout, blackberry wheat ale and more.

Sunup Bakery   BAKERY **$**
(☎ 802-422-3865;   www.sunupbakery.com; 2250 Killington Rd, Killington; light meals $4-8; ⏱ 6:30am-5pm) Fresh muffins and bagels are baked daily along with yummy breakfast sandwiches, great soy lattes and an emphasis on friendly (ie not fast) service. It makes great box lunches to go.

Sushi Yoshi   JAPANESE, CHINESE **$$**
(☎ 802-422-4241; www.vermontsushi.com; 1807 Killington Rd, Killington; mains $12-33; ⏱ 11:30am-10pm Nov–mid-Apr) A gourmet Chinese restaurant that has successfully added Japanese food to its repertoire, Sushi Yoshi is one of the more exotic restaurants on the main drag. Its eight hibachi tables are extremely popular.

♟ Drinking & Entertainment

With over 25 clubs, and lively bars in many restaurants, Killington is where the après-ski scene rages. Many of these nightspots are on Killington Rd, the 4-mile-long access road to the ski resort.

Jax Food & Games Bar   BAR, LIVE MUSIC
(☎ 802-422-5334; www.supportinglocalmusic.com; 1667 Killington Rd; ⏱ 3pm-late Mon-Fri, 11am-late Sat & Sun) Combines an indoor game room/bar with live music, burgers, a good beer selection and an outdoor deck.

Pickle Barrel   BAR, LIVE MUSIC
(☎ 802-422-3035; www.picklebarrelnightclub.com; 1741 Killington Rd; ⏱ 4pm-late Sep–mid-Apr) With four bars, three levels and two stages, this popular club showcases great rock-and-roll bands.

McGrath's Irish Pub   PUB, LIVE MUSIC
(☎ 802-775-7181;   www.innatlongtrail.com/McGraths_Irish_Pub.html; Inn at Long Trail, US 4; ⏱ 11:30am-11pm Sun-Thu, to 1am Fri & Sat) Guinness on tap, Vermont's largest selection of Irish whiskies, and live Irish music on Friday and Saturday evenings.

Wobbly Barn   BAR, LIVE MUSIC
(☎ 802-422-6171; www.wobblybarn.net; 2229 Killington Rd; ⏱ 3:30pm-late Nov–mid-Apr) Has dancing, blues, and rock and roll.

❶ Information

Killington Central Reservations (☎ 800-621-6867; www.killington.com; US 4, Killington; ⏱ 8am-9pm Nov-May) Advice on accommodations, including package deals.

Killington Chamber of Commerce (☎ 800-337-1928, 802-773-4181; www.killingtonchamber.com; 2046 US 4, Killington; ⏱ 10am-4:30pm Mon-Fri, 9am-1pm Sat) General tourist information, conveniently located on US 4.

❶ Getting There & Away

To reach Killington from Burlington (1¾ hours, 95 miles), take US 7 south to VT 4 east.

> ### ❶ SEASONAL HOURS IN KILLINGTON
>
> Unlike other resort towns in Vermont, Killington hibernates outside of ski season. Many restaurants, shops and hotels close down altogether between mid-April and November; others only remain open on weekends. We've listed details in individual reviews where applicable, but outside of winter, it's still best to call in advance to confirm hours.

From Manchester (70 minutes, 45 miles), take US 7 north and VT 4 east.

Middlebury

POP 8500

Standing at the nexus of several state highways, aptly named Middlebury was built along the falls of Otter Creek at the end of the 18th century. In 1800 Middlebury College was founded, and it has been synonymous with the town ever since. Poet Robert Frost (1874–1963) owned a farm in nearby Ripton and co-founded the college's renowned Bread Loaf School of English in the hills above town. The college is also famous for its summer foreign-language programs, which have been drawing linguists here for nearly a century. Middlebury's history of marble quarrying is evident in the college's architecture: many buildings are made with white marble and gray limestone.

◎ Sights

University of Vermont Morgan Horse Farm   FARM

(☑802-388-2011; www.uvm.edu/morgan; 74 Battell Dr, Weybridge; adult/child $5/2; ☉9am-4pm May-Oct; ⊕) See registered Morgan horses and tour their stables at this farm 3 miles north of Middlebury. Known for their strength, agility, endurance and longevity, and named after Justin Morgan, who brought his thoroughbred Arabian colt to Vermont in 1789, these little horses became America's first native breed, useful for heavy work, carriage draft, riding and even war service.

Otter Creek Brewing   BREWERY

(☑802-388-0727; www.ottercreekbrewing.com; 793 Exchange St; ☉11am-6pm) One of New England's best, this brewery makes several fine craft beers, including its trademark Copper Ale, Stovepipe Porter and the organic Wolaver's line. Stop by for a free self-guided tour, then stick around for a pint and a bite at the recently opened brewpub.

Champlain Orchards   FARM

(www.champlainorchards.com; Shoreham; ⊕) ✍ One of many orchards near Middlebury, this century-old operation has pick-your-own cherries, peaches, plums and berries starting in June. Its busiest season is fall, when apples are ripe for the picking and twin October festivals (Harvest Festival and Ciderfest) fill the air with fiddle tunes and family fun. It's 16 miles southwest of Middlebury via VT 30 and VT 74.

Middlebury College Museum of Art   MUSEUM

(☑802-443-5007; http://museum.middlebury.edu; S Main St; ☉10am-5pm Tue-Fri, noon-5pm Sat & Sun) FREE Small but diverse museum with rotating exhibitions alongside a fine permanent collection that includes an Egyptian sarcophagus, Cypriot pottery, 19th-century European and American sculpture, and works by such luminaries as Pablo Picasso, Salvador Dalí, Alice Neel and Andy Warhol.

🏃 Activities

Undulating with rolling hills and farms, the pastoral countryside around Middlebury makes for great cycling. Nearby Green Mountain National Forest is also home to some great ski areas.

Middlebury College Snow Bowl   SKIING

(☑802-443-7669; www.middlebury.edu/about/facilities/snow_bowl; VT 125; ☉9am-4pm Mon-Fri,

---

THE ROBERT FROST INTERPRETIVE TRAIL

In 1920 Robert Frost moved from New Hampshire to Vermont seeking 'a better place to farm and especially grow apples.' For almost four decades Frost lived in the Green Mountain State, growing apples and writing much of his poetry in a log cabin in Ripton, a beautiful hamlet set in the Vermont mountains 10 miles southeast of Middlebury.

The Ripton area in the Green Mountain National Forest has been designated Robert Frost Country. You can visit his cabin (from the outside, at least) on foot from the **Robert Frost Wayside** picnic area on Hwy 125 or on skis from the nearby Rikert Nordic Center (p299).

Along the same stretch of VT 125 you'll find the **Bread Loaf School of English**, which Frost helped found while teaching at Middlebury College, and the **Robert Frost Interpretive Trail**. Roughly three quarters of a mile, the circular trail is marked by half a dozen of his poems, while the surrounding woods and meadows are highly evocative of his work. To get here from Middlebury, take US 7 south for 4 miles, then continue 6 miles east on VT 125 and look for the trail on the right side.

8:30am-4pm Sat & Sun; 🚡) One of Vermont's most affordable, least crowded ski areas, this college-owned facility has only three lifts, but with trails for all levels, nonexistent lift lines, and prices half of what you'd pay elsewhere, who's complaining? Middlebury's 'graduation on skis' takes place here each February: graduates slalom down the slopes in full valedictory regalia, their dark robes fluttering amid the snowflakes.

Blueberry Hill Ski Center   SKIING
(📞802-247-6735; www.blueberryhillinn.com/skicen ter.html; 1307 Goshen-Ripton Rd, Goshen; ⏱9am-5pm; 🚡) With 50km of cross-country skiing and snowshoe trails threading through the national forest, this low-key nordic center 15 miles southeast of Middlebury is a great place to get away from it all. Trails connect to the statewide Catamount Trail system, and the cozy Blueberry Hill Inn (singles/doubles $169/199) is right here if you decide to stay overnight.

Rikert Nordic Center   SKIING
(📞802-443-2744; www.middlebury.edu/about/facilities/rikert; VT 125, Ripton; ⏱8:30am-4:30pm; 🚡) Middlebury College's cross-country ski center offers 50km of trails in Green Mountain National Forest, in a gorgeous mountain setting along VT 125, an easy 12-mile drive from Middlebury.

🛏 Sleeping

Branbury State Park   CAMPGROUND $
(📞802-247-5925; www.vtstateparks.com/htm/branbury.htm; VT 53; campsite/lean-to $20/27; ⏱late May–mid-Oct; 🚡) Ten miles south of Middlebury at the foot of the Green Mountains, this family-friendly 96-acre lakeside park has 37 campsites and seven lean-tos. The small beach, which offers swimming and rental boats, is backed by a grassy lawn with playground and barbecue facilities. Hiking trails climb to the pretty Falls of Lana and Silver Lake in Green Mountain National Forest.

Inn on the Green   INN $$
(📞888-244-7512, 802-388-7512; www.innonthe green.com; 71 S Pleasant St; r incl breakfast $159-299; ❄@🛜) Lovingly restored to its original stateliness, this 1803 Federal-style home has spacious rooms and suites in the main house and in an adjoining carriage house (where the rooms are more modern). One of its signature treats is breakfast served in bed each morning.

Waybury Inn   INN $$
(📞800-348-1810, 802-388-4015; www.waybury inn. com; VT 125, East Middlebury; r/ste incl breakfast from $130/280; 🛜) A favorite of Robert Frost, this former stagecoach stop 5 miles southeast of Middlebury has a wood-paneled restaurant and sumptuous guest rooms. The inn's exterior was featured in the 1980s TV show *Newhart* (though Bob's never actually been here). Laze away a summer afternoon in the nearby swimming hole or warm yourself in the pub on a wintry evening.

Swift House Inn   INN $$
(📞866-388-9925, 802-388-9925; www.swift houseinn.com; 25 Stewart Lane; r incl breakfast $139-279; 🛜) Two blocks north of the town green, this grand white Federal mansion (1814) is surrounded by fine formal lawns and gardens. Luxurious standard rooms in the main house and adjacent carriage house are supplemented by suites that have fireplaces, sitting areas and Jacuzzis. Other welcome luxuries include a steam room and sauna, a cozy pub, a library and a sun porch.

Middlebury Inn   INN $$
(📞800-842-4666, 802-388-4961; www.middle buryinn.com; 14 Court Sq, VT 7; r $139-279; 🛜) Directly opposite the town green, this inn's fine old main building (1827) has beautifully restored formal public rooms with wide hallways, and its charming guest rooms have all the modern conveniences. The adjacent Porter Mansion, with Victorian-style rooms, is also full of attractive architectural details. Lower-priced units in the modern annex out back are considerably less appealing.

🍴 Eating & Drinking

Middlebury Bagel & Deli   BAKERY $
(11 Washington St; breakfast $5-8; ⏱6am-1pm) Since 1979, the Rubright family has been showing up at 4am daily to bake some of New England's finest doughnuts and bagels. Skiers on their way to the slopes, workers en route to the job site and professors headed for class all converge here for warm-from-the-oven apple fritters, doughnuts and bagel sandwiches, along with omelettes and other breakfast treats.

⭐ American Flatbread   PIZZERIA $$
(📞802-388-3300; americanflatbread.com/restaurants/middlebury-vt; 137 Maple St; flatbreads $14-20; ⏱5-9pm Tue-Sat) 🌿 In a cavernous old marble building with a blazing fire that keeps things cozy in winter, this is one of

FREE BLUEBERRIES & A VIEW TOO!

About 15 miles southeast of Middlebury, an unpaved forest service road leads to one of central Vermont's best-kept secrets: the Green Mountain National Forest Blueberry Management Area. This vast hillside patch of wild blueberries is ripe (and free) for the picking between late July and early August, and the view over the surrounding mountains is fantastic. From VT 125, just east of Ripton, follow the unpaved Goshen Rd past Blueberry Hill Inn, then look for signs for the Blueberry Management Area on your left.

Middlebury's most beloved eateries. The menu is limited to farm-fresh salads and custom-made flatbreads (don't call it pizza or they'll come after you with the paddle) topped with locally sourced organic cheeses, meat and veggies, accompanied by Vermont microbrews on tap.

51 Main INTERNATIONAL $$

(☑802-388-8209; www.go51main.com; 51 Main St; mains $9-24; ⏱5pm-late Tue-Sat; 🛜) Overlooking Otter Creek, this high-ceilinged restaurant, lounge and live-music venue was started by a few Middlebury College students as a fun social space where people could dine, perform and generally hang out. It features a convivial, casual bar and serves an eclectic international menu: Brazilian shrimp stew, cider-glazed pork chops and gourmet mac-and-fromage – made with Vermont cheddar, of course.

Storm Cafe CAFE $

(☑802-388-1063; www.thestormcafe.com; 3 Mill St; mains $6-25; ⏱11:30am-2:30pm & 5-10pm Tue & Wed, 7:30am-2:30pm & 5-10pm Thu-Sat, 7:30am-2:30pm Sun) In the basement of Frog Hollow Mill, this creekside cafe serves breakfast, followed by soups, salads and sandwiches at lunchtime. In good weather, the more substantial dinner offerings are best enjoyed out on the terrace overlooking the falls of Otter Creek; some consider this to be the most imaginative menu in town.

ℹ Information

Addison County Chamber of Commerce (☑802-388-7951; www.addisoncounty.com;

93 Court St; ⏱9am-5pm Mon-Fri) About half a mile south of the town green, this place dispenses plenty of information.

Green Mountain National Forest District Office (☑802-388-4362; 1007 US 7; ⏱8am-4:30pm Mon-Fri) Drop by this ranger station 2 miles south of town for information about the many good day hikes in the region.

ℹ Getting There & Away

Middlebury is right on US 7. To get here from Burlington (50 minutes, 35 miles), take US 7 south; from Manchester (1½ hours, 65 miles), take US 7 or VT 30 north.

Mad River Valley & Sugarbush

POP 1700 (WARREN); 1720 (WAITSFIELD)

North of Killington, VT 100 is one of the finest stretches of road in the country: a bucolic mix of rolling hills, covered bridges, white steeples and farmland so fertile you feel like jumping out of the car and digging your hands in the soil. Forty miles (or an hour) north of Killington, you'll land in the Mad River Valley, a virtual advertisement for Vermont. Nestled in the valley are the pretty villages of Waitsfield and Warren, as well as two major ski areas, Sugarbush and Mad River Glen. Both feature the New England skiing of yore, a time when trails were cut by hand and weren't much wider than a hiking path.

The 'gap roads' that run east to west over the Green Mountains offer some of the most picturesque views of the region: VT 73 crosses Brandon Gap (2170ft) from Brandon to Rochester and Talcville; VT 125 crosses Middlebury Gap (2149ft) from East Middlebury to Hancock; and VT 17 crosses Appalachian Gap (2356ft) from Bristol to Irasville and Waitsfield.

Highest, steepest and perhaps prettiest of all is the narrow local road, unpaved in sections, that crosses Lincoln Gap (2424ft) from Bristol to Warren (closed in wintertime due to heavy snowfall). Stop at the top for the scenic 3-mile hike along the Long Trail to Mt Abraham (4017ft), fifth-highest peak in Vermont.

🏃 Activities

Winter skiing is the big draw here, but canoeing and kayaking are prime on the Mad River (along VT 100 near Waitsfield) and White River (along VT 100 near Hancock) in April, May and early June, and on the larger

Winooski River (along I-89) in the spring, summer and fall.

★ **Mad River Glen** SKIING
(☎802-496-3551; www.madriverglen.com; VT 17; adult lift ticket weekend/midweek $71/55) Subaru wagons (Vermont's unofficial state car) often bear bumper stickers that present this dare: 'Mad River Glen, Ski It If You Can.' The most rugged lift-served ski area in the east, Mad River is also one of the quirkiest. Managed by an owner cooperative, not a major ski corporation, it largely eschews artificial snowmaking, prohibits snowboarding, and proudly continues to use America's last operating single chairlift, a vintage 1948 model! It's 6 miles west of Waitsfield.

Sugarbush SKIING
(☎800-537-8427, 802-583-6300; www.sugarbush. com; 1840 Sugarbush Access Rd, Warren; adult lift ticket weekend/midweek $89/84, 10% discount if purchased online) Lincoln Peak (3975ft) and Mt Ellen (4083ft) are the main features of this large resort 6 miles southwest of Waitsfield. In all, the two afford skiers 111 trails, includling backcountry runs like Paradise and Castlerock that hurtle through a rolling tapestry of maple, oak, birch, spruce, pine and balsam. There are 508 acres for skiing overall, and snowboarding is also available.

Clearwater Sports BICYCLE RENTAL, WATER SPORTS
(☎802-496-2708; www.clearwatersports.com; 4147 Main St/VT 100, Waitsfield; boat rentals per day $59-89, bicycles per day $25, boat trips incl lessons per person per day from $125; ☺9am-6pm Mon-Sat, 10am-5pm Sun) This friendly shop rents river-floating tubes ($28/18 per person with/without shuttle service), canoes, kayaks, in-line skates, bicycles, snowshoes, telemark demo gear and many other types of sports equipment. Clearwater also organizes kayak tours, family overnight tours and one- or two-day guided boating trips, including lessons.

Vermont Icelandic Horse Farm HORSEBACK RIDING
(☎802-496-7141; www.icelandichorses.com; 3061 N Fayston Rd, Fayston; 1-3hr rides $55-105, full day incl lunch $195; ☺by appointment; ⊞) Explore the scenic hills above Waitsfield on beautiful, gentle and easy-to-ride Icelandic horses. Rides range from hour-long jaunts to five-day inn-to-inn treks.

Sugarbush Soaring GLIDING
(☎802-496-2290; www.sugarbush.org; 15/20/30min rides $99/129/169; ☺10am-5pm May-Oct) This outfit can take you soaring quietly through the skies, far above the mountains and river valleys, in a glider, which is kept aloft by updrafts of warm air. It's especially beautiful in early October, when central Vermont's trees are fully ablaze.

Ole's Cross Country Ski Center SKIING
(☎802-496-3430; www.olesxc.com; 2355 Airport Rd, Warren; ☺9am-5pm) A local center with 30 miles of groomed cross-country ski trails and 10 miles of snowshoe trails, Ole's also offers an innovative rental program that allows visitors to explore on skis for half the day and snowshoes the other half.

🛏 Sleeping

Because the Sugarbush area is primarily active in the winter ski season, there are no campgrounds nearby. Many accommodations are condos ($130 to $850 per day) marketed to the ski trade. The largest selection is rented by **Sugarbush Village** (☎800-451-4326; www.sugarbushvillage.com), right at the ski area.

Inn at Mad River Barn INN $
(☎800-631-0466, 802-496-3310; www.madriver barn.com; VT 17, Waitsfield; s/d incl breakfast from $75/90; ☎⊞) Built in the 1940s, this is one of the last of the old-time Vermont lodges, with rustic wood panelling, bright quilts and steam-heated bathrooms in some rooms. The lodge's historic charm is preserved with a massive stone fireplace, deep leather chairs and a deck overlooking landscaped gardens. A pool hidden in a birch grove welcomes guests in summer.

> **LOCAL KNOWLEDGE**
>
> ### SWIMMING HOLE HEAVEN
>
> Where do locals head when the mercury starts hitting devilish highs? One popular spot is **Bartlett Falls**, a heavenly swimming hole hidden just off the main road near Bristol, halfway between Warren and Middlebury. This gorgeous natural pool sits at the foot of a pretty waterfall, flanked by cliffs that make a popular jumping-off point for local youths. With shallow and deep sections and plenty of forested shade, it's perfect for all ages. Look for the parked cars along Lincoln Gap Rd, a half mile east of VT 116.

Waitsfield Inn INN $$

(☑ 800-758-3801, 802-496-3979; www.waits-fieldinn.com; 5267 Main St/VT 100, Waitsfield; d incl breakfast $125-170; ☎) This converted parsonage has 12 tastefully decorated rooms as well as various nooks and dining areas to unwind in. All rooms have private bathrooms, and some have four-poster beds. The inn also offers dinner (New England comfort fare) on weekend evenings and has a tiny, on-site pub that serves home-flavored fruit vodkas (blueberry or raspberry mixed with pineapple).

★ Inn at Round Barn Farm INN $$$

(☑ 802-496-2276; www.roundbarninn.com; 1661 E Warren Rd, Waitsfield; r/ste incl breakfast from $175/295; ☎⊠) This inn gets its name from the adjacent 1910 round barn – among the few authentic examples remaining in Vermont. The decidedly upscale inn has antique-furnished rooms with mountain views, gas fireplaces, canopy beds and antiques. All overlook the meadows and mountains. In winter guests leave their shoes at the door to preserve the hardwood floors. The country-style breakfast is huge.

✖ Eating

Skiers' taverns abound in this area. Restaurants are busy in the ski season, but rather sleepy at other times. Outside of winter, call ahead to verify opening hours: they change frequently.

★ Warren Store SANDWICHES $

(☑ 802-496-3864; www.warrenstore.com; Main St, Warren; light meals $5-9; ⊙ 8am-7pm Mon-Sat, to 6pm Sun) This atmospheric country store serves the area's best sandwiches along with delicious pastries and breakfasts. In summer, linger over coffee and the *New York Times* on the front porch, or eat on the deck overlooking the waterfall, then descend for a cool dip among river-sculpted rocks. Browsers will love the store's eclectic collection of clothing, toys, jewelry, cheeses and wines.

★ Mint VEGETARIAN $$

(☑ 802-496-5514; www.mintvermont.com; 4403 Main St, Waitsfield; mains $15-19; ⊙ 5-8:30pm Wed-Sun; ✑) With a short, sweet menu that's big on flavor, this stylish vegan- and vegetarian-friendly spot serves sandwiches, salads, soups and desserts: think falafel, vegetable bowls and the signature salad (spinach, arugula, pears, toasted almonds, shaved parme-

san and cranberries, tossed in a mint vinaigrette). Save room for homemade desserts (tofu-pumpkin pie, anyone?) and a wide selection of loose-leaf teas.

ℹ Information

Mad River Valley Chamber of Commerce (☑ 800-828-4748, 802-496-3409; www.madrivervalley.com; 4061 Main St, Waitsfield; ⊙ 8am-5pm Mon-Fri) Staff here can assist with lodging and the latest skiing info. The office also opens on Saturday during holiday weekends, and has 24-hour public restrooms.

ℹ Getting There & Away

From Waitsfield, take VT 100 to Stowe (40 minutes, 24 miles); for Montpelier (30 minutes, 19 miles), take VT 100B north and US 2 east.

NORTHERN VERMONT

Home to the state capital, Montpelier, northern Vermont is also home to the state's largest city, Burlington. Never fear, though: this area still has all of the rural charms found elsewhere. Even within Burlington, cafe-lined streets coexist with scenic paths along Lake Champlain. Further north, the pastoral Northeast Kingdom offers a full range of outdoor activities, from skiing to biking, in the heart of the mountains.

Burlington

POP 42,400

Vermont's largest city would be a small city in most other states, but Burlington's size is one of its charms. With the University of Vermont (UVM) swelling the city by 13,400 students, and with a vibrant cultural and social life, Burlington has a spirited, youthful character. And when it comes to nightlife, this is Vermont's epicenter. Just due south of Burlington is Shelburne, an upscale village that's home to the crown jewel of the area, Shelburne Museum. The village is considered more of an extension of Burlington rather than a separate suburb – people think nothing of popping down to one of its fine restaurants for an evening meal.

Perched on the shore of Lake Champlain, Burlington is less than an hour's drive from Stowe and other Green Mountain towns. In fact, the city can be used as a base for exploring much of northwestern Vermont.

LAKE CHAMPLAIN ISLANDS

Unfolding like a forgotten ribbon just north of Burlington lie the Champlain Islands, a 27-mile-long stretch of three largely undeveloped isles – South Hero, North Hero and Isle La Motte – all connected by US 2 and a series of bridges and causeways. It's an easy day trip from Burlington, perfect for aimless meandering. Below are a few highlights.

Snowfarm Winery (☑802-372-9463; www.snowfarm.com; 190 W Shore Rd, South Hero; ⊙10am-5pm May-Oct) Vermont's first vineyard has a sweet tasting room and a free summer **concert series** (⊙6:30-8:30pm Jun-Aug) on the lawn beside the vines.

Allenholm Orchards (www.allenholm.com; 150 South St, South Hero; ⊙9am-5pm late May–Christmas Eve; ⊕) Pick-your-own apples, plus a petting zoo and playground for kids.

Grand Isle State Park (www.vtstateparks.com/htm/grandisle.htm; Grand Isle; tent & RV sites $20, lean-tos/cabins $27/48) Waterfront living in four cabins, 36 lean-tos and 117 tent/trailer sites.

Hyde Log Cabin (☑802-372-4245, 802-828-3051; www.historicvermont.org; US2, Grand Isle; adult/child $3/free; ⊙11am-5pm Fri-Sun Jun–mid-Oct) One of the oldest (1783) log cabins in the US.

Hero's Welcome (www.heroswelcome.com; 3537 Hwy 2, North Hero; ⊙6:30am-6:30pm Mon-Sat, 7am-6pm Sun) A quirky, jam-packed general store with a good deli and dockside seating out front.

North Hero House (☑802-372-4732; www.northherohouse.com; US2, North Hero; r from $140; 🔊) A country inn with incomparable, front-row lake views of the water and a fantastic restaurant, **Steamship Pier Bar & Grill** (sandwiches $10-18; ⊙noon-8pm Thu-Sun), serving kebabs, burgers, lobster rolls and cocktails on the pier.

◎ Sights

Waterfront　　　　　　　　　WATERFRONT
A five-minute walk from downtown, Burlington's delightfully uncommercialized waterfront is a scenic, low-key promenade with a 7.5-mile bike path, a pier for Lake Champlain **boat trips**, the Echo Lake aquarium and the Discovery Landing, a modern **observatory** with a cafe that's great for watching the sunset over the lake.

Church Street Marketplace　PEDESTRIAN MALL
(⊕) Burlington's pulse can often be taken along this four-block pedestrian zone running from Pearl to Main St. When the weather's good, buskers (now licensed by the town), food and craft vendors, soapbox demagogues, restless students, curious tourists and kids climbing on rocks mingle in a vibrant human parade.

★ Shelburne Museum　　　　　　MUSEUM
(☑802-985-3346; www.shelburnemuseum.org; US 7, Shelburne; adult/child $22/11, after 3pm $15/7; ⊙10am-5pm mid-May–Oct; ⊕) The extraordinary 45-acre Shelburne Museum, 9 miles south of Burlington, showcases the priceless Americana collections of Electra Havemeyer Webb (1888–1960) and her parents:

150,000 objects in all. The mix of folk art, decorative arts and more is housed in 39 buildings, most of them moved here from other parts of New England to ensure their preservation.

Structures include a sawmill (1786), a one-room brick schoolhouse (1840), a covered bridge (1845), a lighthouse (1871), a luxury rail coach (1890), a classic round barn (1901), a railroad station (1915), the Lake Champlain side-wheeler steamship *Ticonderoga* (1906) and a 1920s carousel. There's also an entire building (Owl Cottage) filled with books, games and activities for kids. Allow at least half a day for your visit.

Shelburne Farms　　　　　　　　FARM
(☑802-985-8686; www.shelburnefarms.org; 1611 Harbor Rd, Shelburne; adult/child $8/5; ⊙9am-5:30pm mid-May–mid-Oct, 10am-5pm mid-Oct–mid-May; ⊕) ✎ In 1886 William Seward Webb and Lila Vanderbilt Webb built themselves a magnificent country estate on the shores of Lake Champlain. The 1400-acre farm, designed by landscape architect Frederick Law Olmsted (who also designed New York's Central Park and Boston's Emerald Necklace), was both a country house for the Webbs and a working farm, with stunning

Burlington

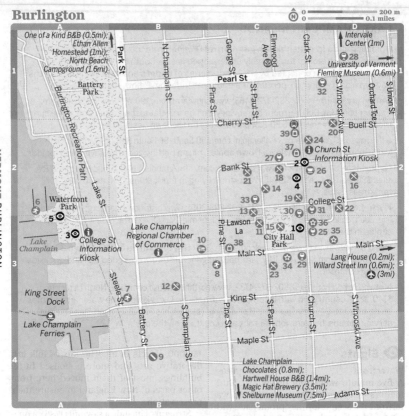

One of a Kind B&B (0.5mi);
Ethan Allen
Homestead (1mi);
North Beach
Campground (1.6mi)

Intervale
Center (1mi)

University of Vermont
Fleming Museum (0.6mi)

lakefront perspectives. The grand, 24-bedroom English-style country manor (completed in 1899), now an inn, is surrounded by working farm buildings inspired by European romanticism.

Today, visitors to Shelburne Farms can buy some of the cheese, maple syrup, mustard and other items produced here, hike miles of walking trails, visit the animals in the children's farmyard or take a guided 1½-hour tour from a truck-pulled open wagon. The farm is 8 miles south of Burlington, off US 7.

Ethan Allen Homestead   HISTORIC HOUSE
(☏802-865-4556; www.ethanallenhomestead.org; adult/child $7/3; ◷10am-4pm Thu-Mon mid-May–mid-Oct) American Revolution hero Ethan Allen lived in this 18th-century colonial homestead, 1 mile north of Burlington on VT 127. Be sure to take the guided tour (included in entrance fee; tour times vary) of the historic house. The center features multimedia

exhibits documenting the exploits of Allen's Green Mountain Boys and also has walking trails behind the house.

**University of Vermont
Fleming Museum**   MUSEUM
(☏802-656-3131; www.uvm.edu/~fleming; 61 Colchester Ave; adult/student & senior $5/3; ◷10am-4pm Tue-Fri, noon-4pm Sat & Sun Sep-Jun) A mile east of City Hall Park, on the verdant campus of UVM (New England's fifth-oldest university, chartered in 1791), this museum has an international collection of over 20,000 objects, from African masks to samurai armor. The American collection includes works by Alfred Stieglitz, Winslow Homer and Andy Warhol.

Burlington City Arts   ARTS CENTER
(BCA; www.burlingtoncityarts.com) This local arts organization mounts regular installations and organizes a range of arts-related programs. Its **BCA Center** (☏802-865-7166;

Burlington

www.burlingtoncityarts.org/BCACenter; 135 Church St; ⊙11am-5pm Sun & Tue-Thu, to 8pm Fri & Sat) is an exciting locus for exhibitions, workshops, classes and discussions; check online to see what's going on during your visit.

Frog Hollow Craft Center ARTS CENTER
(www.froghollow.org; 85 Church St) FREE This excellent contemporary and traditional craft center feels more like a museum gallery than the retail store that it is. A rigorous jury process screens artisans for acceptance.

Echo Lake Aquarium & Science Center SCIENCE CENTER
(☑802-864-1848; www.echovermont.org; 1 College St; adult/child $13.50/10.50; ⊙10am-5pm; ⋒) This kid-friendly lakeside museum examines the colorful past, present and future of Lake Champlain. A multitude of aquariums wiggle with life, and nature-oriented displays invite inquisitive minds and hands to splash, poke, listen and crawl. Regular rotating exhibits focus on scientific themes – from windpower to giant insects, and dinosaurs to cadavers – with plenty of hands-on activities.

Vermont Teddy Bear Factory FACTORY
(☑802-985-3001; www.vermontteddybear.com; 6655 Shelburne Rd, Shelburne; adult/under 13yr $4/free; ⊙9am-6pm Jul–mid-Oct, to 5pm mid-Oct–Jun; ⋒) Tours of this thriving, touristy factory demonstrate the entire teddy bear life cycle, from designers' sketches, to stuffing and stitching, to the bear 'hospital,' that patches up tattered beasts for their devoted owners.

Magic Hat Brewery BREWERY
(☑802-658-2739; www.magichat.net; 5 Bartlett Bay Rd, South Burlington; ⊙10am-6pm Mon-Sat, noon-5pm Sun) Drink in the history of one of Vermont's most dynamic microbreweries on the fun, free, self-guided 'Artifactory' tour (once you see the whimsical labels, this name makes perfect sense) and learn all the nuances of the beer-making process. Afterwards, sample a few experimental brews from the four dozen taps in the on-site Growler Bar, or grab a six-pack to go. The brewery is located 3.5 miles south of downtown Burlington, on the west side of US 7.

LOCAL KNOWLEDGE

BURLINGTON'S SECRET GARDEN

You'd never guess it standing on a busy Burlington street corner, but one of Vermont's most idyllic green spaces is less than 2 miles from the city center. Tucked among the lazy curves of the Winooski River, Burlington's Intervale Center (www.intervale.org; 180 Intervale Rd) FREE encompasses a dozen organic farms and a delightful trail network, open to the public 365 days a year for hiking, biking, skiing, berry picking and more; check the website for details. From downtown, follow N Willard St until it curves right to join Riverside Ave, then look for the Intervale signs on your left.

Shelburne Vineyard Tasting Room WINERY
(☑ 802-985-8222; www.shelburnevineyard.com; 6308 Shelburne Rd, Shelburne; 8-wine tastings $5; ⊙11am-6pm May-Oct, to 5pm Nov-Apr) One of Vermont's best tasting rooms, this converted barn offers samples of Shelburne's award-winning whites and reds and free tours of the energy-efficient winery building.

🏃 Activities

Boating & Water Sports

Approximately 120 miles long and 12 miles wide, Lake Champlain is the largest freshwater lake in the country after the Great Lakes. Consistently good wind, sheltered bays, lack of boat traffic, hundreds of islands and scenic anchorages combine to make this one of the Northeast's top boating spots.

The departure point for boat cruises and rentals is Burlington Community Boathouse (☑ 802-865-3377; www.enjoyburlington. com; foot of College St, at Lake Champlain; ⊙mid-May–mid-Oct), a popular hang-out fashioned after Burlington's original 1900s yacht club. It's easy to spot on the waterfront's 8-mile recreational path.

There's no finer way to enjoy Lake Champlain than on a multiday paddling trip on the Lake Champlain Paddlers' Trail (☑ 802-658-1414; www.lakechamplaincommittee. org) 🛶. Paddlers are encouraged to join the ecofriendly Lake Champlain Committee ($45 per year), for which they receive an essential guidebook that details the trails, campsites and rules of the nautical road.

Whistling Man Schooner Company SAILING
(☑ 802-598-6504; www.whistlingman.com; Boathouse, College St, at Lake Champlain; 2hr cruises adult/child $40/25; ⊙3 trips daily late May-early Oct) Sail around Lake Champlain with the breeze in your hair and a Vermont microbrew in your hand on the 'Friend Ship,' a classic 43ft New England beauty that holds up to 17 passengers. Captains are knowledgeable about the area, and encourage passengers to bring food and drink on board. Private charters are also available (from $370 for two hours). Reserve ahead.

Spirit of Ethan Allen II CRUISE
(☑ 802-862-8300; www.soea.com; boathouse, foot of College St, at Lake Champlain; day cruises adult/child $16/6.50, sunset cruises adult/child $22/14; ⊙mid-May–mid-Oct) In addition to lunch and dinner cruises, this ship plies the lake with 1½-hour scenic, narrated day cruises at 10am, noon, 2pm and 4pm, and a 2½-hour sunset cruise at 6:30pm.

Diving

Throughout the 18th and 19th centuries, Lake Champlain was the site of military battles as well as a major commercial thoroughfare between the St Lawrence Seaway and the Hudson River. Over this period, many military and merchant ships, victims of cannonballs or bad weather, sank to the lake's bottom. Of the 200 wrecks discovered, nine are accessible to divers, preserved by the state of Vermont as underwater historical sites.

All divers must obtain a free permit, available at the Burlington Community Boathouse; the limited permits are available on a first-come basis.

Waterfront Diving Center DIVING
(☑ 800-283-7282, 802-865-2771; www.waterfrontdiving.com; 214 Battery St; ⊙9am-6:30pm Mon-Fri, 8:30am-5:30pm Sat & Sun late May–mid-Oct) This dive shop offers rentals, charters, instruction and a full line of snorkeling, swimming, scuba and underwater photography gear.

🎉 Festivals & Events

First Friday Art Walk ART
(www.artmapburlington.com; ⊙5–8pm) The First Friday Art Walk takes place on the first Friday of each month.

Discover Jazz Festival JAZZ
(www.discoverjazz.com) Burlington plays host to jazz in early June at the waterfront and various venues around town.

Vermont Brewers Festival   BEER
(vtbrewfest.com) Meet Vermont's artisan craft brewers and sample their wares, in mid-July, on the waterfront.

First Night   NEW YEAR
(www.firstnightburlington.com; ✦) A very big and family-friendly New Year's Eve festival featuring a parade, an ice- and snow-sculpture exhibition, music and lots more.

🛏 Sleeping

Burlington's budget and midrange motels are on the outskirts of town. Many chain motels lie on Williston Rd east of I-89 exit 14; there's another cluster along US 7 north of Burlington in Colchester (take I-89 exit 16). The best selection is along Shelburne Rd (US 7) in South Burlington.

North Beach Campground   CAMPGROUND $
(✆802-862-0942; www.enjoyburlington.com; 60 Institute Rd; tent/RV site $26/36; ⊙ May–mid-Oct; 🛜) Campers should make a beeline for this wonderful spot on Lake Champlain, with 69 tent sites on 45 wooded acres near the city center. From Burlington's downtown waterfront, follow Battery St and North Ave (VT 127) north, turning left on Institute Rd. All sites have picnic tables, fire rings, and access to hot showers, a playground, beach and bike path.

Hartwell House B&B   B&B $
(✆802-658-9242, 888-658-9242; www.vermontbedandbreakfast.com; 170 Ferguson Ave; r incl breakfast $90; @🛜🏊) Linda Hartwell offers two clean rooms (with shared bathroom) in her welcoming home in a residential neighborhood just five minutes' drive from the center of town. A pool is available in good weather, as is the deck for continental breakfasts.

Lang House   B&B $$
(✆802-652-2500; www.langhouse.com; 360 Main St; r incl breakfast $145-245; ❉🛜) Burlington's most elegant B&B occupies a centrally located and tastefully restored 19th-century Victorian home and carriage house with 11 spacious rooms, some with fireplaces. Pampering touches include wine glasses and robes in each room, and sumptuous breakfasts served in an alcove-laden room that is decorated with old photographs of the city. Reserve ahead for one of the 3rd-floor rooms with lake views.

Willard Street Inn   INN $$
(✆802-651-8710; www.willardstreetinn.com; 349 S Willard St; r incl breakfast $150-265; 🛜) Perched on a hill within easy walking distance of UVM and the Church St Marketplace, this mansion, fusing Queen Anne and Georgian Revival styles, was built in the late 1880s. It has a fine-wood and cut-glass elegance, yet radiates a welcoming warmth. Many of the guest rooms overlook Lake Champlain.

One of a Kind B&B   B&B $$
(✆802-862-5576; www.oneofakindbnb.com; 53 Lakeview Tce; ste incl breakfast $175-250, cottage

---

BIKING YOUR WAY AROUND BURLINGTON

Burlington's core is pedestrian central. You could also spend your whole Burlington vacation on a bike – if you're staying for a number of days during the non-snowy months, consider renting a bike for your entire stay (you'll fit in well with the ever-so-green locals, who passionately use bikes as a primary mode of transport). Bike paths cover the entire city and most suburbs, and vehicles generally give cyclists plenty of breathing space.

The **Burlington Recreation Path**, a popular 7.5-mile route for walking, biking, in-line skating and general perambulating, runs along the waterfront through the Waterfront Park and promenade. Rent bikes (or in-line skates or roller-skis for that matter!) at **Ski Rack** (✆802-658-3313; www.skirack.com; 85 Main St; bicycles per 1/4/24hr $18/23/28; ⊙May-Nov) or North Star Sports (p311).

Local Motion (✆802-652-2453; www.localmotion.org; 1 Steele St; bicycles per day $30; ⊙10am-6pm; ✦) 🚲, a nonprofit group with its own trailside center downtown, spearheads ongoing efforts to expand bike trails and sustain existing ones. It also offers encyclopedic advice on where to cycle in the local area, along with bike rentals, maps, tours and refreshments. Highly recommended is the 12-mile **Island Line Trail**. It combines with the waterfront bike path, beginning just south of the boathouse and extending onto the narrow Colchester causeway that juts 5 miles out into the lake. You can even extend your adventure at trail's end by catching Local Motion's summer **bike ferry** ($8) north to the Champlain Islands.

$175-250; ☎) In the quiet Lakeview Terrace neighborhood north of downtown, this two-unit place offers a suite at the back of a creatively renovated 1910 house, with a cozy sofa, colorful artwork, Lake Champlain–Adirondack views and a delicious breakfast. There's also a cottage set apart from the main house, with a full kitchen and your own tiny garden to loll about in.

Sunset House B&B
B&B $$

(✒ 802-864-3790; www.sunsethousebb.com; 78 Main St; r with shared bath $119-169; ☎) This sweet B&B has four tidy guest rooms and a small common kitchen. This is the only B&B smack in the center of downtown (within easy walking distance of Church St Marketplace and the waterfront), and the congenial owners make you feel like you are part of the family.

★ Inn at Shelburne Farms
INN $$$

(✒ 802-985-8498; www.shelburnefarms.org/stay-dine; 1611 Harbor Rd, Shelburne; r with private/shared bath from $289/169, cottage $289-430, guesthouse $436-926; ☎) One of New England's top 10 places to stay, this inn, 7 miles south of Burlington off US 7, was once the summer mansion of the wealthy Webb family. It now welcomes guests, with rooms in the gracious, welcoming country manor house by the lakefront, as well as four independent, kitchen-equipped cottages and guesthouses scattered across the property.

Relive the Webbs' opulent lifestyle by taking tea (served every afternoon), eating in the inn's fabulous restaurant (most of the menu is built around produce from the surrounding 1400-acre farm), or chill out playing billiards or relaxing in one of the common areas, complete with elegant, original furnishings. If you're feeling more energetic, the hiking trails, architect-designed barns and vast grounds are also worthy of several hours' exploration.

✖ Eating

A large cluster of eateries is located on and near the Church St Marketplace. But if you explore just a little bit further out, your taste buds will be richly rewarded.

★ Penny Cluse Cafe
CAFE $

(www.pennycluse.com; 169 Cherry St; mains $7-11; ⊙ 6:45am-3pm Mon-Fri, 8am-3pm Sat & Sun) ✐ In the heart of downtown, one of Burlington's most popular breakfast spots whips up pancakes, biscuits and gravy, breakfast burritos, omelettes and tofu scrambles along with sandwiches, fish tacos, salads and the best chile relleno you'll find east of the Mississippi. Expect an hour's wait on weekends: best bet is to put your name down, grab a coffee and take a pre-meal wander.

¡Duino! (Duende)
INTERNATIONAL $

(10 N Winooski Ave; mains $5-12; ⊙ 10am-midnight Sun-Thu, to 1am Fri & Sat) This funky round-the-world street food–inspired spot has everything from falafel to Baja fish tacos, Jamaican jerk chicken, Belgian *frites* (fries) and Cuban pork sandwiches. It's all served in a chill space with dark tables and crimson walls.

City Market
MARKET $

(www.citymarket.coop; 82 S Winooski Ave; ⊙ 7am-11pm) ✐ If there's a food co-op heaven, it must look something like this. Burlington's gourmet natural foods grocery is chock-full of local produce and products (with over 1600 Vermont-based producers represented), a huge takeout deli section, a massive microbrew-focused beer section and a 'Hippie Cooler,' where you'll find all the tofu and tempeh you could dream of.

Stone Soup
VEGETARIAN $

(www.stonesouppvt.com; 211 College St; buffet per lb $9.75, light meals $5-10; ⊙ 7am-9pm Mon-Fri, 9am-9pm Sat; ☎✐) Best known for its excellent vegetarian- and vegan-friendly buffet, this longtime local favorite also has homemade soups, sandwiches on home-baked bread, a salad bar, pastries and locally raised meats.

Henry's Diner
DINER $

(✒ 802-862-9010; henrysdiner1925.com; 155 Bank St; mains $5-12; ⊙ 6am-4pm) A Burlington fixture since 1925, this homey diner has breakfast all day and a variety of weekend specials.

August First Bakery & Cafe
BAKERY $

(www.augustfirstvt.com; 149 S Champlain St; sandwiches $5-9; ⊙ 7:30am-5pm Mon-Fri, 8am-3pm Sat) This bakery-cafe is a hot spot for a cup of coffee, baked goods and sandwiches – not to mention its famous breads, served by the loaf.

Uncommon Grounds
CAFE $

(www.ugvermont.com; 42 Church St; baked goods $2-5; ⊙ 7am-9pm Mon-Thu, 7am-10pm Fri, 8am-10pm Sat, 9am-9pm Sun; ☎) Take your newspaper, order a cup of joe and a muffin, grab a sidewalk table and people-watch in good weather. And muse about how good life is.

Burlington Farmers' Market
MARKET $

(www.burlingtonfarmersmarket.org; cnr St Paul & College Sts; ⊙8:30am-2pm Sat May-Oct) ✦ Every Saturday from May through October, City Hall Park bursts into life with this busy farmers market; during the rest of the year, the market moves indoors to the Memorial Auditorium (250 Main St). It's enormously popular and all vendors must grow or make precisely what they sell: expect fresh produce, prepared food, cheeses, breads, baked goods and crafts.

★ American Flatbread
PIZZERIA $$

(www.americanflatbread.com/restaurants/burlington-vt; 115 St Paul St; flatbreads $14-23; ⊙restaurant 11:30am-2:30pm & 5-10pm, taproom 11:30am-late) ✦ Central downtown location, bustling atmosphere, great microbrews on tap, and some of the best flatbread (thin-crust pizza) you'll find anywhere in the world are reason enough to make this one of your first lunch or dinner stops in Burlington. Throw in an outdoor terrace in the alleyway out back in summer, and you've got one of Vermont's very best eateries.

Bluebird Tavern
INTERNATIONAL $$

(☎802-540-1786; www.bluebirdtavern.com; 86 St Paul St; mains $15-28; ⊙11:30am-2:30pm & 4-10pm Tue-Fri, 4-11pm Sat) ✦ Nominated for a James Beard award within its first year, this wildly experimental locavore eatery offers an ever-changing menu of small and large plates, from pork belly with snow peas and horseradish to carrot soup with local apples and smoked cinnamon cream. A bar with exquisite libations and live music on the weekends are just icing on the cake.

Single Pebble
CHINESE $$

(☎802-865-5200; www.asinglepebble.com; 133 Bank St; mains $10-23; ⊙11:30am-1:45pm & 5-11pm; ✐) This spacious restaurant – the brainchild of a local chef who mastered Szechuan and Cantonese cuisine while living in China – sprawls over two adjoining clapboard houses and offers up sumptuous MSG-free fare to the strains of traditional Chinese music. The dim sum is particularly satisfying – be sure to try the mock eel.

Daily Planet
INTERNATIONAL $$

(☎802-862-9647; www.dailyplanet15.com; 15 Center St; mains $11-20; ⊙4-11pm daily plus 10am-2pm Sun; ☎✐) This long-established downtown haunt serves a changing, varied menu that ranges from burgers with exotic trimmings (sauteed mushrooms, pickled mango, gor-

gonzola) to barbecued duck confit to PEI mussels to pecan-crusted rainbow trout. The bar stays open nightly till 2am, and there's a good Sunday brunch.

Blue Cat Cafe & Wine Bar
INTERNATIONAL $$$

(☎802-363-3639; www.bluecatvt.com; 1 Lawson Lane; mains $22-32; ⊙4:30-10pm Mon-Thu, to midnight Fri & Sat, to 9pm Sun) Tucked down an alley opposite City Hall Park, this upscale but far-from-stuffy wine bar and restaurant serves serious gourmet fare whipped up with expertise and love: think huge steaks (from grass-fed, local cows), seafood and wine from a lengthy wine list. The bar is a popular hang-out for those seeking a quiet glass of wine and an appetizer.

Leunig's Bistro
FRENCH $$$

(☎802-863-3759; www.leunigsbistro.com; 115 Church St; lunch mains $10-17, dinner mains $21-32; ⊙11am-10pm Mon-Fri, 9am-10pm Sat & Sun) 'Live well, laugh often and love much' advises the sign over the bar at this stylish and convivial Parisian-style brasserie with an elegant, tin-ceilinged dining room. A longstanding Burlington staple, it's as much fun for the people-watching (windows face the busy Church St Marketplace) as it is for the excellent wine list and food.

Trattoria Delia
ITALIAN $$$

(☎802-864-5253; www.trattoriadelia.com; 152 St Paul St; mains $17-35; ⊙5-10pm) A longtime favorite, this dimly lit Italian restaurant with a large stone fireplace serves homemade pastas and specialties like *ossobuco alla milanese* (wine-and-herb-braised veal shank with saffron risotto), coupling them with selections from its award-winning wine list.

🍷 Drinking & Nightlife

Burlington's student-fueled nightlife usually revolves around live music and mugs of beer. The city's social epicenter is Church St Marketplace (the pedestrian mall), thick with restaurants and sidewalk cafes. Late at night on summer weekends, the south end (by Main St) feels like one massive outdoor bar.

For nightlife and entertainment listings, look no farther than *Seven Days* (p311), a free, energetic tabloid that tells all with a sly dash of attitude.

Dobra Tea
TEAHOUSE

(☎802-951-2424; dobrateavt.com; 80 Church St; ⊙10am-10pm Sun-Tue, to 11pm Wed-Sat) This

Czech-owned tearoom offers more than 50 varieties – some seasonal, all hand-selected directly from their regions of origin. Sit at a table, an up-ended tea box, or on cushions around a small, low pedestal.

Splash at the Boathouse
BAR

(802-658-2244; www.splashattheboathouse.com; College St; 11:30am-2am) Perched atop Burlington's floating boathouse is this sometimes low-key, sometimes raucous restaurant-bar with stellar views over Lake Champlain. It serves a full menu, but that's really not the point. Come here to kick back with an evening cocktail or microbrew and watch the boats lolling about the lake, preferably at sunset when yellow and purple shadows dance across the water.

Radio Bean
BAR, CAFE

(www.radiobean.com; 8 N Winooski Ave; 8am-2am;) This is the social hub for the arts and music scene. The Radiator, a low-power FM radio station (105.9) beams over the airwaves from this funky cafe-bar. Espressos, beer and wine keep things jumping, and grilled sandwiches and baked goods ($4 to $7) feed the soul. Live performances nightly include jazz, acoustic music and poetry readings.

1/2 Lounge
COCKTAIL BAR

(136½ Church St; 6pm-late) Step downstairs to this cavelike speakeasy for cocktails, boutique wines and occasional live music. It's sophisticated and sheltered from the raucous scene that unfolds upstairs on Church St on weekend evenings. Its martini list is excellent, and it serves light tapas until the wee hours.

Vermont Pub & Brewery
MICROBREWERY

(www.vermontbrewery.com; 144 College St; mains $6-16; 11:30am-1am Sun-Wed, to 2am Thu-Sat) This large pub's specialty and seasonal brews are made on the premises, including weekly limited releases. Try the Burly Irish Ale, the highly popular Dogbite Bitter and the acclaimed Karlswalde Russian Imperial Stout. There's also plenty of British pub fare to accompany the pints.

Farmhouse Tap & Grill
PUB

(www.farmhousetg.com; 160 Bank St; 11am-late) This place labels itself a gastropub, which translates in this instance to a farm-to-table bar and grill, with most food sourced locally. A cozy interior 'parlor' and an outdoor beer garden pack 'em in every night.

Three Needs
BAR

(802-658-0889; 185 Pearl St; 4pm-2am) Whatever *your* needs, this small college hang-out doles out fabulous suds from its microbrewery. The crowd gravitates toward the pool table in the back, which can get pretty raucous on weekends.

Rasputin's
CLUB

(www.rasputinsvt.com; 163 Church St; 4pm-2am) A popular UVM hangout with pool tables, oodles of TVs, regular DJ nights and occasional live music.

Rí Rá The Irish Pub
PUB

(802-860-9401; www.rira.com/burlington; 123 Church St; 11:30am-2am) Part of an Irish-American chain that imports architectural elements from authentic historic Irish pubs and brings them to the US, this one was restored in Ireland, dismantled and then

---

DON'T MISS

VERMONT'S MICROBREWERIES

The same easy access to fresh ingredients and commitment to local craftsmanship that defines the state's restaurants also fuel its microbreweries – as does a simple, honest love of beer. With more craft breweries per capita than any other state (roughly one beermaker for every 28,000 people), Vermont pours an acclaimed and diverse array of beers.

Some of our favorite microbreweries include Alchemist Brewery (p313), Long Trail Brewing Company (p297), Magic Hat Brewery (p305) and Otter Creek Brewing (p298). Other good choices:

Switchback Brewing Company (802-651-4114; www.facebook.com/SwitchbackBrewingCompany; 160 Flynn Ave, Burlington)

Harpoon Brewery (802-674-5491; www.harpoonbrewery.com; 336 Ruth Carney Dr, Windsor)

Most microbreweries offer free tours and/or samples; see their websites for details.

shipped to Burlington. Pints of Guinness are accompanied by regular live music (mainly folk).

Sweetwaters BAR
(☑ 802-864-9800; www.sweetwatersvt.com; 120 Church St; ☺ 11:30am-midnight Sun-Thu, to 1:30am Fri & Sat) Drenched in heavily nouveau-Victorian decor, this local watering hole attracts the young and upwardly mobile.

☆ Entertainment

★ Flynn Center for the Performing Arts PERFORMING ARTS
(☑ 802-863-5966; www.flynncenter.org; 153 Main St) Broadway hits, music, dance and theater grace the stage at this art-deco masterpiece. Expect anything from the Khmer Arts Ensemble to Liza Minnelli.

Nectar's LIVE MUSIC
(www.liveatnectars.com; 188 Main St; ☺ 7pm-2am Sun-Tue, 5pm-2am Wed-Sat) Indie darlings Phish got their start here and the joint still rocks out with the help of aspiring acts. Grab a vinyl booth, chill at the bar or dance upstairs at **Club Metronome**, which hosts a slew of theme nights (every Friday is '80s night) along with larger live acts.

Red Square LIVE MUSIC
(www.redsquarevt.com; 136 Church St; ☺ 4pm-late Sun-Thu, 2pm-late Fri & Sat) With a stylish SoHo-like ambience, this is where Vermonters in the know go to sip martini or wine, munch on good bar food (including sandwiches) and listen to Burlington's best roadhouse music.

🛍 Shopping

Lake Champlain Chocolates CHOCOLATE
(☑ 802-864-1807; www.lakechamplainchocolates.com; 750 Pine St; ☺ 9am-6pm Mon-Sat, 11am-5pm Sun; hourly tours 10am-2pm Mon-Fri) No, you can't run through the chocolate waterfall, but Burlington's home-grown chocolate factory offers tours, plus a store where you can purchase chocolate truffles, bars, coins and gift baskets. There's also a cafe serving luscious homemade ice cream. If all you're after is the chocolates, check out LCC's second, more conveniently located store and cafe (65 Church St; ☺ 10am-8pm Mon-Thu, to 9pm Fri & Sat, to 6pm Sun) in Church St Marketplace.

Outdoor Gear Exchange OUTDOOR EQUIPMENT
(☑ 888-547-4327, 802-860-0190; www.gearx.com; 37 Church St; ☺ 10am-8pm Mon-Thu, to 9pm Fri & Sat, to 6pm Sun) This place rivals major outdoor-gear chains for breadth of selection, and trumps them on price for a vast array of used, closeout and even new gear and clothing. Name the outdoor pursuit and staff can probably outfit you.

North Star Sports OUTDOOR EQUIPMENT
(☑ 802-863-3832; www.northstarsportsvt.com; 100 Main St; ☺ 10am-7pm Mon-Fri, 10am-6pm Sat, 11am-5pm Sun) Head to this friendly, laid-back local favorite for an unusually complete selection of clothing, gear and bikes specifically designed for women. Don't worry, guys; there's plenty here for you too. For winter fun, it offers Nordic skis, snowshoes and outerwear.

ℹ Information

One of the best resources for getting a comprehensive idea of what's going on in the area is **Seven Days** (www.7dvt.com). This hip, free tabloid is piled in stacks just about everywhere around town.

BTV Information Center (☑ (802) 863-1889; www.vermont.org; Burlington International Airport; ☺ 9am-midnight) This helpful office in Burlington's airport is staffed by the Lake Champlain Regional Chamber of Commerce. It keeps longer hours than the downtown branch.

Church St Information Kiosk (Church St; ☺ 10am-5pm daily mid-Jun–late Aug, Sat & Sun mid-May–mid-Jun & late Aug–mid-Oct)

College St Information Kiosk (College St; ☺ 10am-5pm daily mid-Jun–late Aug, Sat & Sun mid-May–mid-Jun & late Aug–mid-Oct)

Lake Champlain Regional Chamber of Commerce (☑ 877-686-5253, 802-863-3489; www.vermont.org; 60 Main St; ☺ 8am-5pm Mon-Fri, 9am-5pm Sat & Sun) Staffed tourist office in the heart of downtown.

ℹ Getting There & Around

AIR

A number of national carriers, including JetBlue, serve Burlington International Airport (p438), 3 miles east of the city center. You'll find all the major car-rental companies at the airport.

BOAT

Lake Champlain Ferries (☑ 802-864-9804; www.ferries.com; King St Dock; adult/child/car $8/3.10/30) runs scenic, summer-only car ferries (one way car and driver/adult/child $30/8/3, 70 minutes, eight daily mid-June to August, four daily in September) between Burlington and Port Kent, New York.

The company also operates ferries from Charlotte, Vermont (south of Burlington) to Essex, New York, for as long as the lake stays unfrozen; and 24-hour, year-round service from Grand Isle, Vermont (north of Burlington), to Plattsburgh, New York. See the website for fare and schedule details.

BUS

Greyhound (☑ 800-231-2222; www.greyhound. com; 219 S Winooski St) runs multiple buses daily to Montreal, Canada ($31, 2½ hours) and Boston ($45, 4½ to 5½ hours).

Chittenden County Transportation Authority (CCTA; ☑ 802-864-2282; www.cctaride. org) operates its free College St shuttle bus (route 11) every 15 to 30 minutes between the UVM campus and Waterfront Park near the Burlington Boathouse, with a stop at Church St Marketplace. Local fares around Burlington are $1.25 for adults, 60¢ cents for children and seniors.

CCTA also operates buses from its Cherry St terminal to the following destinations throughout the region. See the website for fares and schedules. There are no services on major holidays.

Burlington International Airport route 1 (20 to 30 minutes, half-hourly, less frequent on Sunday)

Essex Junction route 2 (40 minutes, every 15 to 30 minutes Monday to Saturday, no service Sunday)

Middlebury routes 46 and 76

Montpelier route 86

Shelburne route 6

> **WORTH A TRIP**
>
> ### CAMEL'S HUMP
>
> The distinctive form of Camel's Hump – the state's third-highest mountain – is a familiar image to Vermonters: its silhouette is visible on the Vermont state quarter, from suburban Burlington and along I-89. Yet it remains one of the state's wildest spots, one of the few significant Vermont peaks not developed for skiing. To get here, detour south off I-89 at Richmond (between Burlington and Waterbury), take US 2 east to Richmond's main stop light, then drive south 10 miles to Huntington Center, where you'll turn left (east) 3 miles, dead-ending at the trailhead for the 6-mile Burrows–Forest City loop to the summit. After climbing through forest, the final ascent skirts rock faces above the treeline, affording magnificent views.

CAR

To get here from Boston (3½ hours, 216 miles), take I-93 to I-89. It's another 1¾ hours (97 miles) north from Burlington to Montreal. All of Burlington's car-rental companies (Hertz, Avis, Enterprise, National, Thrifty, Budget and Alamo) are located at Burlington International Airport (there are no downtown locations). The best option for Amtrak passengers arriving in Essex Junction is to take a taxi 5 miles to the airport and rent a car there. **Green Cab VT** (☑ 802-864-2424; greencabvt.com), recommended for its fuel-efficient fleet, can shuttle people from Essex Junction to the airport for about $15.

TRAIN

Amtrak's daily **Vermonter train** (☑ 800-872-7245; www.amtrak.com/vermonter-train), which provides service as far south as New York City and Washington DC, stops in Essex Junction, 5 miles from Burlington.

Stowe & Around

POP 4310 (STOWE)

In a cozy valley where the West Branch River flows into the Little River and mountains rise to the sky in all directions, the quintessential Vermont village of Stowe (founded in 1794) bustles quietly. The town's long-standing reputation as one of the East's classiest mountain resorts continues to draw well-heeled urbanites from Boston, New York and beyond. A bounty of inns and eateries lines the thoroughfares leading up to stunning Smuggler's Notch, a narrow rock-walled pass through the Green Mountains just below Mt Mansfield (4393ft), the highest point in Vermont. More than 200 miles of cross-country ski trails, some of the finest mountain biking and downhill skiing in the east, and world-class rock and ice climbing make this a natural mecca for adrenaline junkies and active families.

Waterbury, on the interstate highway 10 miles south, is the gateway to Stowe. Its attractions include a pair of standout restaurants, a beloved brewery and the Ben & Jerry's world-renowned ice cream factory.

◉ Sights

★ **Ben & Jerry's Ice Cream Factory**   FACTORY
(☑ 802-882-1240; www.benjerrys.com; 1281 VT 100, Waterbury; adult/child $4/free; ◎ 9am-9pm Jul–mid-Aug, 9am-7pm mid-Aug–Oct, 10am-6pm Nov–Jun; ⊕) In 1978 Ben Cohen and Jerry Greenfield took over an abandoned Burlington gas station and launched the outlandish flavors

that forever changed America's ice-cream culture. Time and corporate takeovers have forever changed the company, but this legendary factory, north of I-89 between Waterbury and Stowe, still draws crowds for tours that include a campy moo-vie and a taste tease of the latest flavor. Behind the factory, a mock cemetery holds 'graves' of Holy Cannoli and other long-forgotten flavors. The factory is 10 miles south of Stowe via VT 100.

Alchemist Brewery BREWERY
(www.alchemistbeer.com; 35 Crossroad, Waterbury; ☺11am-7pm Mon-Sat) One of Vermont's most beloved breweries, the Alchemist lost its venerable Waterbury brewpub to Hurricane Irene in 2011. Thankfully, the brand-new production facility they had just opened the same week (on higher ground near Ben & Jerry's, 10 miles south of Stowe via VT 100) is still going strong, inviting visitors in for self-guided tours, free 2oz samples and a chance to buy their very limited production of canned homebrew.

Helen Day Art Center ARTS CENTER
(☎802-253-8358; www.helenday.com; 90 Pond St; ☺noon-5pm Wed-Sun) FREE In the heart of the village, this gently provocative community art center has rotating exhibitions of traditional and avant-garde work. It also sponsors 'Exposed,' an annual townwide outdoor sculpture show that takes place from mid-July to mid-October.

West Branch Gallery & Sculpture Park GALLERY
(☎802-253-8943; www.westbranchgallery.com; 17 Towne Farm Lane; ☺11am-6pm Tue-Sun Jul-Oct, 10am-5pm Tue-Sun Nov-Jun) A captivating collection of contemporary sculpture, paintings, photography and fountains fill this gallery and sculpture park 1 mile up Mountain Rd from Stowe village. Don't miss the winding, sculpture-filled paths along the river's edge.

Boyden Valley Winery WINERY
(☎802-644-8151; www.boydenvalley.com; 64 VT 104, at VT 15, Cambridge; ☺10am-5pm daily May-Dec, Fri-Sun only Jan-Apr) Winery and maple-syrup producer set on a gorgeous farm at the foot of the Green Mountains, 19 miles north of Stowe along VT 108. Take a free winery tour (twice daily) and sample award-winning varietals – including an exquisite ice wine. Annual events include the mid-September Harvest Festival and the Maple Sugar Festival in late March.

VERMONT SKI & SNOWBOARD MUSEUM

Located in an 1818 meeting house that was rolled to its present spot by oxen in the 1860s, this museum (www.vtssm.com; 1 S Main St; suggested donation $3-5; ☺noon-5pm Wed-Mon) is an inspired tribute to skiing and snowboarding history. It holds much more than an evolution of equipment (including 75 years of Vermont ski lifts) and a chance to chuckle at what was high slope-side fashion in the '70s. A huge screen shows ski footage so crazy that you can hardly keep your footing. The most moving exhibit tells the tale of the famous 10th Mountain Division of skiing troops from WWII – it inspires wonder at how they held out with the (then cutting-edge) canvas- and leather-based gear.

VERMONT STOWE & AROUND

🏃 Activities
Downhill Skiing

Stowe Mountain Resort SKIING
(☎888-253-4849, 802-253-3000; www.stowe.com; 5781 Mountain Rd) This venerable resort encompasses two major mountains, Mt Mansfield (which has a vertical drop of 2360ft) and Spruce Peak (1550ft). It offers 48 beautiful trails, 16% of which are earmarked for beginners, 59% for middle-of-the-roadies and 25% for hard-core backcountry skiers – many of whom get their adrenaline rushes from the 'front four' runs: Starr, Goat, National and Liftline.

Smugglers' Notch Resort SKIING
(☎802-644-8851, 800-419-4615; www.smuggs.com; VT 108; 🦽) Consistently less crowded than Stowe, this family-oriented resort on the west side of Smugglers' Notch is spread over Sterling (3010ft), Madonna (3640ft) and Morse (2250ft) mountains. It has incredible alpine and cross-country skiing (78 trails and 14 miles' worth), dogsled rides, a lit tubing hill, nightly family entertainment, and the only learn-to-ski program for two- to five-year-olds in the country.

Cross-Country Skiing & Snowshoeing
Stowe has the second-largest cross-country skiing network in the country (200 miles of groomed and backcountry trails), which links a handful of ski areas, including four of

Stowe & Around

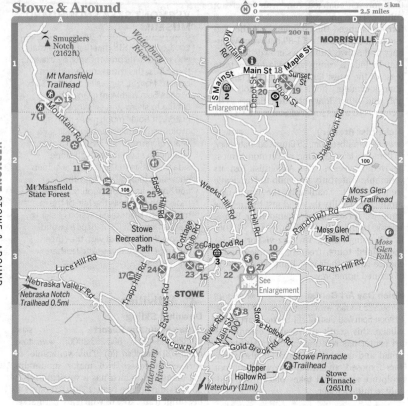

the top ski touring centers in the state. The network includes groomed trails as well as tough backcountry ski runs.

XC Touring Center   CROSS-COUNTRY SKIING
(☎800-621-0284, 802-253-7371; www.edsonhill-manor.com; 1500 Edson Hill Rd) Tucked up a side road 4 miles northwest of Stowe village, this off-the-beaten-track cross-country ski center (attached to the inn of the same name) offers 25km of trails for all skill levels, with connections to Vermont's 300-mile-long Catamount Trail.

Stowe Mountain Resort Touring Center   CROSS-COUNTRY SKIING
(☎800-253-4754, 802-253-3688; www.stowe.com/ski-ride/xc; 5281 Mountain Rd, Stowe) Adjacent to Stowe's venerable downhill ski resort, this cross-country center features 45km of groomed trails and 30km of backcountry skiing options.

Trapp Family Lodge   CROSS-COUNTRY SKIING
(☎800-826-7000, 802-253-8511; www.trappfamily.com/activities/cross-country-skiing; 700 Trapp Hill Rd) America's oldest cross-country ski center, with 100km of trails.

Hiking

The **Green Mountain Club** (☎802-244-7037; www.greenmountainclub.org; 4711 Waterbury-Stowe Rd/VT 100) ✍, 5 miles south of Stowe, was founded in 1910 to maintain the Long Trail. The club publishes some excellent hikers' materials, available here or by mail. Staff also lead guided hiking, biking, boating, skiing and snowshoeing day trips.

Several excellent day hikes around Stowe:

Moss Glen Falls (easy, 1 mile, 45 minutes) Follow VT 100 for 3 miles north of Central Stowe and bear right onto Randolph Rd. Go 0.3 miles and turn right for the parking area, then walk along the obvious path to reach a deep cascade and waterfalls.

Stowe & Around

Mt Mansfield (difficult, 7 miles, five hours) Follow VT 108 west from Stowe to the Long Trail parking area, 0.7 miles past Stowe Mountain Resort ski area. Mt Mansfield is thought by some to resemble a man's profile in repose, so follow the Long Trail to the 'chin,' then go south along the summit ridge to Profanity Trail; follow that aptly named route to Taft Lodge, then take the Long Trail back down. An alternate route, the Sunset Ridge Trail, leads up the west side of the mountain from Underhill State Park.

Nebraska Notch (moderate, 3.2 miles, 2½ hours) Take VT 100 south of Stowe and turn west onto River Rd, which becomes Moscow Rd. Continue for 5.8 miles to Lake Mansfield Trout Club. The trail follows an old logging road for a while and then ascends past beaver dams and grand views to join the Long Trail at Taylor Lodge.

Stowe Pinnacle (moderate, 2.8 miles, three hours) Follow VT 100 south of Stowe and turn east onto Gold Brook Rd, proceeding for 0.3 miles; cross a bridge and turn left to continue along Gold Brook Rd. About 1.6 miles later, you come to Upper Hollow Rd; turn right and go to the top of the hill, just past Pinnacle Rd, to find the small parking area on the left. The hike to Stowe Pinnacle (2651ft), a rocky outcrop offering sweeping mountain views, is short but steep.

Cycling

Cyclists of all ages and abilities will love the well-maintained, traffic-free Stowe Recreation Path. Those looking for greater challenges are spoiled for choice, with scenic roads fanning out in all directions. Several bike shops can supply you with information and wheels for everything from light cruising to backwoods exploration.

★ **Stowe Recreation Path** OUTDOORS
(www.stowe-village.com/BikePath; ♿) ✦ The flat to gently rolling 5½-mile Stowe Recreation Path, which starts from the pointy-steepled Stowe Community Church in the village center, offers a fabulous four-season escape for all ages. It rambles through woods, meadows and outdoor sculpture gardens along the West Branch of the Little River, with sweeping views of Mt Mansfield unfolding in the distance. Bike, walk, skate or ski – and swim in one of the swimming holes along the way.

Canoeing & Kayaking

Umiak Outdoor Outfitters OUTDOORS
(☏802-253-2317; www.umiak.com; 849 S Main St; ⊙9am-6pm) This place rents canoes and sport kayaks, gives kayak and stand-up paddleboard lessons and offers a variety of guided and self-guided tours on local rivers, including the Lamoille and the Winooski. In winter, it also rents snowshoes and telemark skis, and offer moonlit snowshoe tours.

THE CATAMOUNT CROSS-COUNTRY SKI TRAIL

Vermont's magnificent Catamount Trail (802-864-5794; www.catamount-trail.org) is the longest cross-country ski trail in the United States, a 300-mile-long route that runs the length of Vermont. Starting in southern Vermont at Readsboro, it winds along the flanks of the Green Mountains all the way to North Troy on the Canadian border. In between lies some of the finest skiing in the east, from backcountry trails on Mt Mansfield to 11 ski touring centers – some, including Blueberry Hill (p299) and Mountain Top Inn & Resort (800-445-2100, 802-483-2311; www.mountaintopinn.com; Mountaintop Rd, Chittenden), offer lodging within the Green Mountain National Forest.

Equipment Rentals

AJ's Ski & Sports EQUIPMENT RENTAL
(800-226-6257, 802-253-4593; www.stowesports.com; 350 Mountain Rd; 10am-6pm) In the village center, near the south end of the recreation path. Rents bikes, kayaks and ski and snowboard equipment.

Nordic Barn EQUIPMENT RENTAL
(802-253-6433; www.nordicbarnvt.com; 4081 Mountain Rd) Near the north end of the recreation path. Rents bikes and skis.

Skiershop EQUIPMENT RENTAL
(800-996-8398, 802-253-7919; www.skiershop.com; 580 Mountain Rd; bicycles per day $26-32; 9am-6pm Mon-Sat, to 5pm Sun) Rents bikes and skis (but not boots).

Sleeping

Stowe has a wide variety of lodging, with dozens of inns, motels and B&Bs; many are along Mountain Rd. The Stowe Area Association (p318) helps with reservations.

Smugglers Notch State Park CAMPGROUND $
(802-253-4014; www.vtstateparks.com/htm/smugglers.htm; 6443 Mountain Rd; tent & RV sites $20, lean-tos $27; mid-May–mid-Oct) This 35-acre park, 8 miles northwest of Stowe, is perched up on the mountainside. It has 81 tent and trailer sites and 20 lean-tos and walk-in sites.

Fiddler's Green Inn INN $
(800-882-5346, 802-253-8124; www.fiddlers-greeninn.com; 4859 Mountain Rd; r incl breakfast midweek/weekend $90/125;) A throwback to simpler times, this unembellished 1820s farmhouse is less than a mile from the lifts and has rustic pine walls, a fieldstone fireplace and seven very simple guest rooms. The best rooms and the breakfast area overlook the river out back, within earshot of the rushing water. Guests congregate around the hearth in winter; it's all quite homey.

Inn at Turner Mill INN $
(800-992-0016, 802-253-2062; www.turnermill.com; 56 Turner Mill Lane; r/apt from $75/110;) Hidden on 9 acres next to Notch Brook, this streamside inn is just a sweet 1-mile ski from Stowe's lifts. It's a rustic place with only two rooms and two small apartments, but it makes up for lack of quantity with the innkeepers' encyclopedic knowledge of local outdoor activities.

Brass Lantern Inn B&B B&B $$
(800-729-2980, 802-253-2229; www.brasslanterninn.com; 71 Maple St/VT 100; r incl breakfast $105-245;) Just north of the village, this beautiful inn has spacious antique-laden rooms with handmade quilts. Some have fireplaces and views of Mt Mansfield.

Sun & Ski Inn INN $$
(800-448-5223, 802-253-7159; www.sunandskiinn.com; 1613 Mountain Rd; r $115-169, ste $188-260;) A nicely landscaped inn adjacent to the river and the recreation path. The 25-room lodge has a fireplace, Jacuzzi and covered pool with retractable roof. It also rents a pair of basic two- and three-bedroom condos up the road.

Stowe Motel & Snowdrift MOTEL, APARTMENT $$
(800-829-7629, 802-253-7629; www.stowemotel.com; 2043 Mountain Rd; r $85-200, ste $182-240, apt $162-250;) In addition to the efficiency rooms (with kitchenettes), suites, apartment and two- to six-bedroom houses (rates highly variable; call to inquire), this motel set on a generous 16 acres offers a tennis court, hot tubs, badminton and lawn games. You can also borrow bikes or snowshoes to use on the recreation path.

Topnotch at Stowe RESORT $$$
(800-451-8686, 802-253-8585; www.topnotchresort.com; 4000 Mountain Rd; r $275-$550;) Fresh off a major renovation, Stowe's most lavish resort dazzles guests

with amenities: indoor and outdoor pools, tennis courts, fine dining, a skating rink, a ski touring center and a legendary spa. The stylishly modern Roost pub, with cathedral windows overlooking Mt Mansfield, was added in 2013. Accommodations range from comfortable standard rooms to immaculate two- and three-bedroom houses.

Trapp Family Lodge LODGE $$$
(☑800-826-7000, 802-253-8511; www.trappfamily.com; 700 Trapp Hill Rd; r from $275; @ 🛜 ⛆) With wide-open fields and mountain vistas, this hilltop lodge 3km southwest of town boasts Stowe's best setting. The Austrian-style chalet, built by Maria von Trapp of *The Sound of Music* fame, houses traditional lodge rooms. Alternatively, you can rent one of the modern villas or cozy guesthouses scattered across the property. The 2700-acre spread offers stupendous hiking, snowshoeing and cross-country skiing.

 Eating

Depot Street Malt Shoppe DINER $
(☑802-253-4269; 57 Depot St; dishes $6-9; ⊗11:30am-9pm) Burgers, fries, onion rings,

chocolate sundaes and old-fashioned malteds reign at this fun, 1950s-themed restaurant. The egg creams hit the spot in any season.

Harvest Market MARKET $
(www.harvestatstowe.com; 1031 Mountain Rd; ⊗7am-7pm) Before you head for the hills, stop in at this market for morning coffee, delicious pastries, Vermont cheeses, sandwiches, gourmet deli items and a wide array of wines and local microbrews.

Black Cap Coffee & Townsend Gallery CAFE $
(144 Main St; baked goods $5-7; ⊗7am-5pm Mon-Wed, 7am-7pm Thu-Sat, 8am-5pm Sun; 🛜) Unwind at this cafe in the heart of the village, which serves baked goods and coffee concoctions in an inviting old house with armchairs, couches and a small but delightful front porch.

Gracie's Restaurant BURGERS $$
(☑802-253-8741; www.gracies.com; 18 Edson Hill Rd; mains $11-35; ⊗5-9:30pm) Dogs are the theme at this animated burger joint halfway between the village and the mountain. Go

---

DON'T MISS

VERMONT'S STATE PARKS

With more than 150,000 acres of protected land set aside in more than 50 state parks, Vermont isn't called the Green Mountain State for nothing! Finding an exceptional and often underutilized state park in Vermont is about as easy as breathing. Whether you're interested in swimming, hiking, snowshoeing, cross-country skiing, camping or fishing, you'll find plenty of places that fit the bill.

Many great state-park campgrounds are reviewed throughout this chapter. Here are some of our favorites that are more off the beaten track:

Burton Island State Park (www.vtstateparks.com/htm/burton.htm; 2714 Hathaway Point Rd, St Albans; 🚹) Only accessible by ferry, this island state park in the middle of Lake Champlain has lakeside campsites and lean-tos, walking trails, boat rentals, a cafe and a nature center.

Seyon Lodge State Park (☑802-584-3829; www.vtstateparks.com/htm/seyon.htm; 2967 Seyon Pond Rd, Groton; ⊗Jan-Mar & mid-Apr–mid-Nov) The only park of its kind in Vermont, offering private rooms in its rustic lodge on the shores of Noyes Pond and serving meals, including three-course dinners made with locally sourced produce. Great fly-fishing in the pond and hiking or skiing on the network of trails just outside the front door.

Jamaica State Park (☑802-874-4600; www.vtstateparks.com/htm/jamaica.htm; 48 Salmon Hole Lane, Jamaica) With campsites directly adjacent to the rushing West River, this is one of only two riverside state parks in Vermont. It's especially popular with kayakers and rafters for its annual whitewater weekends in late September.

Underhill State Park (www.vtstateparks.com/htm/underhill.htm; 352 Mountain Rd, Underhill) This teeny park on the western slopes of Mt Mansfield is the perfect jumping-off point for a climb to the summit via the Sunset Ridge Trail.

For complete details on all state parks, contact Vermont State Parks (p433).

Mexican with 'South of the Border Collie,' or stick to big burgers, hand-cut steaks, Waldorf salad and garlic-laden shrimp scampi. Try the famous 'Doggie Bag' dessert: a white-chocolate 'bag' filled with chocolate mint mousse and hot fudge.

Pie-casso
PIZZERIA $$

(☑802-253-4411; www.piecasso.com; 1899 Mountain Rd; mains $9-22; ☺11am-9pm) Going far beyond the simple pie, this pizzeria serves up organic arugula, chicken salad, and portobello panini alongside more traditional offerings like hand-tossed pesto pizza. There's a bar and live music too.

Trattoria La Festa
ITALIAN $$

(☑802-253-8480; www.trattoriastowe.com; 4080 Mountain Rd; mains $15-25; ☺5pm-late Mon-Sat) In business for three decades, this Italian-owned trattoria serves family-style Italian fare inside an old barn. It also has an award-winning (mainly Italian) wine list.

★ Hen of the Wood
AMERICAN $$$

(☑802-244-7300; www.henofthewood.com; 92 Stowe St, Waterbury; mains $18-32; ☺5-10pm Mon-Sat) 🖉 Arguably the finest dining in northern Vermont, this chef-driven restaurant in Waterbury gets rave reviews for its innovative farm-to-table cuisine. Set in a historic grist mill, the ambience is as fine as the food, which features densely flavored dishes like smoked duck breast and sheep's-milk gnocchi.

The Bistro at Ten Acres
FUSION $$$

(☑802-253-6838; www.tenacreslodge.com; 14 Barrows Rd; mains $18-30; ☺5-10pm Wed-Sat) The brainchild of Scottish immigrant Linda Hunter and Stowe native Marc Fucile, this new venture in a plank-floored 1820s farmhouse blends cozy atmosphere with delicious food from New York–trained chef Gary Jacobsen (think *steak frites*, lobster with polenta, or slow-roasted orange duck). The attached bar serves a good selection of cocktails and draft beers, plus a cheaper burger-centric menu.

Michael's on the Hill
INTERNATIONAL $$$

(www.michaelsonthehill.com; 4182 Waterbury-Stowe Rd, Waterbury Center; mains $27-43, tasting menus $45-67; ☺5:30-9pm Wed-Mon) 🖉 A 10-minute drive south of Stowe, this is one of the area's standout eateries. A seasonally changing menu built on locally sourced ingredients is served in a pair of interior dining rooms and on an intimate wrap-around porch.

Blue Moon Café
INTERNATIONAL $$$

(☑802-253-7006; www.bluemoonstowe.com; 35 School St; mains $16-32; ☺6-9pm Tue-Sun) In a converted house with a little sun porch, this intimate bistro is one of Stowe's top restaurants. Mains change monthly, but the contemporary cuisine usually includes something like crab cakes, salmon dishes, steak with chipotle and jicama or dishes utilizing locally foraged mushrooms. The cheese plate, compiled from local artisan varieties, is exquisite.

🍷 Drinking & Entertainment

Vermont Ale House
PUB

(www.facebook.com/vtalehouse; 294 Mountain Rd; ☺4pm-1am Tue & Wed, 11:30am-1am Thu-Sun) With two dozen different craft brews and a rotating menu of pub fare, this relative newcomer to Stowe's drinking scene has already won a loyal following since opening in 2013.

Charlie B's
PUB

(☑802-253-7355; www.stoweflake.com/charliepub.aspx; Stoweflake Inn & Resort, 1746 Mountain Rd; ☺noon-1am) If you're searching for a standard après-ski scene with a bit more class, basic pub fare and occasional live music, head to this place.

Matterhorn Bar & Grill
BAR, LIVE MUSIC

(☑802-253-8198; www.matterhornbar.com; 4969 Mountain Rd; cover free-$15; ☺5pm-late daily late Nov–mid-Apr, Thu-Sat mid-Apr–late Nov) Near the top of Mountain Rd, this place starts hopping at 5pm, when skiers start hobbling off the slopes. Top draws include brick-oven pizzas and the lower-level sushi bar, which has a view of the river out back. Bands play Friday and Saturday nights during ski season.

❶ Information

Stowe Area Association (☑802-253-7321; www.gostowe.com; 51 Main St; ☺9am-5pm Mon-Sat, to 8pm Jun-Oct & Jan-Mar) This association is well organized and can help you plan your trip, including making reservations for rental cars and local accommodations.

❶ Getting There & Around

BUS

GMTA (gmtaride.org) operates a couple of useful buses for those without a vehicle.

The **Mountain Road Shuttle** runs every half-hour daily during ski season from Stowe village,

VILLAGES FROZEN IN TIME

Many Vermont villages have a lost-in-time quality, thanks to their architectural integrity and the state's general aversion to urban sprawl. Some, like Grafton, Newfane, Woodstock and Dorset, are covered prominently in this chapter. Others are further off the beaten track.

Brownington (Northeast Kingdom)

This sleeping beauty 40 miles north of St Johnsbury is full of 19th-century buildings reposing under the shade of equally ancient maple trees. The **Old Stone House Museum** (www.oldstonehousemuseum.org; 109 Old Stone House Rd; adult/child $8/3; ⊙11am-5pm Wed-Sun mid-May–mid-Oct) here pays tribute to educational trailblazer Alexander Twilight. The first African American college graduate in the US, he built Brownington's boarding school and ran it for decades.

Peacham (Northeast Kingdom)

This idyllically sited village 15 miles southwest of St Johnsbury was originally a stop on the historic Bayley–Hazen Military Rd – intended to help Americans launch a sneak attack on the British during the Revolutionary War. These days it's just a pretty spot to admire pastoral views over the surrounding countryside.

Plymouth Notch (Central Vermont)

President Calvin Coolidge's boyhood home, preserved as the **Calvin Coolidge State Historic Site** (www.historicvermont.org/coolidge; 3780 Rte 100A; adult/child/family $7.50/2/20; ⊙9:30am-5pm late May–mid-Oct), looks much as it did a century ago, with a church, one-room schoolhouse, cheese factory and general store gracefully arrayed among old maples on a bucolic hillside. It's 15 miles southwest of Woodstock.

along Mountain Rd, to the ski slopes. Pick up a schedule and list of stops at your inn or the Stowe Area Association's information office.

On weekdays, the **Route 100 Commuter** also offers limited service between Stowe and Waterbury, where you can connect to the Montpelier LINK Express bus to Montpelier or Burlington.

CAR
To get to Burlington (45 minutes, 37 miles), head south on VT 100, then north on I-89.

TRAIN
The Amtrak **Vermonter train** (☏800-872-7245; www.amtrak.com/vermonter-train) stops daily at Waterbury. Some hotels and inns will arrange to pick up guests at the station. The **Route 100 Commuter** is the only bus service between Waterbury and Stowe, but it doesn't make good connections with Amtrak. **Stowe Taxi** (☏802-253-9490, www.stowetaxi.com) offers taxi service for $28.

Montpelier & Around
POP 7860 (MONTPELIER)

Montpelier (pronounced mont-*peel*-yer) would qualify as nothing more than a large village in most places. But in sparsely populated Vermont it's the state capital – the smallest in the country (and the only one without a McDonald's, in case you were wondering). Surprisingly cosmopolitan for a town of 8000 residents, its two main thoroughfares – State St and Main St – make for a pleasant wander, with some nice bookstores and boutiques, and a few top-notch eateries.

Montpelier's smaller, distinctly working-class neighbor Barre (pronounced *bear*-ee), which touts itself as the 'granite capital of the world,' is a 10-minute drive from the capital.

◎ Sights

State House   HISTORIC BUILDING
(www.vtstatehouse.org; 115 State St; ⊙tours 10am-3:30pm Mon-Fri, 11am-2:30pm Sat Jul-Oct) **FREE** Montpelier's main landmark, the gold-domed capitol building, is open for self-guided audio tours year-round, or free guided tours in summer, when the legislature is not in session. The front doors are guarded by a massive statue of American Revolutionary hero Ethan Allen, and the base supporting the gold dome was built of granite quarried in nearby Barre in 1836.

Vermont History Museum MUSEUM

(☎802-828-2291; www.vermonthistory.org/visit/vermont-history-museum; 109 State St; adult/child $5/3; ⊙10am-4pm Tue-Sat) The Pavilion Building houses an excellent museum that recounts Vermont's history with exhibits, films and re-creations of taverns and Native American settlements.

Rock of Ages Quarries QUARRY

(☎802-476-3119; www.rockofages.com; 560 Graniteville Road, Graniteville; guided tours adult/child $5/2.75; ⊙tours 9:15am-3:35pm Mon-Sat May-Aug, daily Sep–mid-Oct) The world's largest granite quarries, four miles southeast of Barre off I-89 exit 6, cover 50 acres, tapping a granite vein that's a whopping 6 miles long, 4 miles wide and 10 miles deep. Most fascinating is the 35-minute guided minibus tour of the active quarry, where you can gaze down on seemingly ant-size workers in hard hats extracting massive granite blocks at the bottom of a 600ft-deep pit.

The beautiful, durable, granular stone, formed more than 330 million years ago, is used for tombstones, building facades, monuments, curbstones and tabletops. The quarry tour also includes a short video, historical exhibits and a trip to the factory, where you can watch granite products being made – some with an accuracy that approaches 25 millionths of an inch.

Hope Cemetery CEMETERY

Barre's cemetery, 1 mile north of US 302 on VT 14, celebrates the artistic prowess of generations of local stone carvers. The whimsical tombstones here include a man and his wife sitting up in bed holding hands, smiling for eternity; a granite cube balanced precariously on a tombstone's corner; a giant soccer ball and a small airplane. If a cemetery can ever be a work of art, this one is! It's open to the living all the time.

🛏 Sleeping

Betsy's Bed & Breakfast B&B $$

(☎802-229-0466; www.betsysbnb.com; 74 E State St; r incl breakfast $85-190; 🕾) This restored Victorian house on a residential street leading to Vermont College has gracefully appointed rooms and suites decorated with period antiques. Updated amenities include phone and TV; the suites come with kitchens. Despite the feeling of seclusion, you are a quick walk from the middle of town.

Inn at Montpelier INN $$$

(☎802-223-2727; www.innatmontpelier.com; 147 Main St; r incl continental breakfast $165-205, ste $235-250; ❄🐾🕾) Good enough for repeat visitor Martha Stewart, this first-rate inn made up of two refurbished Federal houses sits smack in the heart of town. All the rooms are luxuriously furnished, including some deluxe units with wood-burning fireplaces; the wicker rocking chairs on the wraparound veranda make it a perfect spot to while away a lazy afternoon.

🍴 Eating

You can eat well in Montpelier, thanks to the presence of the New England Culinary Institute (NECI), one of America's finest cooking schools. Graduates often stick around town to start restaurants of their own.

La Brioche CAFE, BAKERY $

(www.neci.edu/labrioche; 89 Main St; pastries & sandwiches $2-8; ⊙7am-5pm Mon-Fri, to 3pm Sat) NECI's first restaurant, this casual bakery and cafe serves delicious pastries and coffee drinks for breakfast, followed by soups, salads and sandwiches on homemade bread at lunchtime. It starts running out of sandwich fixings around 2pm, so time it right if you're hungry!

★ Threepenny Taproom PUB $$

(www.threepennytaproom.com; 108 Main St; mains $9-18; ⊙11am-late Mon-Fri, noon-late Sat, noon-5pm Sun) With the names of two dozen microbrews from Vermont and beyond scrawled on the blackboard every evening, this pub is a perennial late-night favorite. But it also has a fabulous lineup of snacks and light meals, including cheeses, house-cured salmon and smoked trout, salads, sandwiches, flatbreads and bistro classics such as *moules frites* (mussels with French fries).

NECI on Main AMERICAN, MEDITERRANEAN $$$

(☎802-223-3188; www.neci.edu/neci-on-main; 118 Main St; lunch mains $10-13, dinner mains $20-29; ⊙11:30am-9pm Tue-Sat, 10am-2pm Sun) 🐾 NECI's multilevel signature restaurant focuses on farm-to-table locavore food. There's an open window to the kitchen, allowing you to watch student chefs at work, and a lovely outdoor patio for summer dining. Menu highlights include Mediterranean tapas and a superb Sunday brunch ($20), considered one of the best brunches in all of New England.

ℹ Information

Capitol Region Visitors Center (☏802-828-5981; cri.center@state.vt.us; 134 State St; ☺6am-5pm Mon-Fri, 9am-5pm Sat & Sun) Opposite the Vermont state capitol building.

ℹ Getting There & Away

Burlington (40 minutes, 39 miles) is an easy drive on I-89 .

Amtrak's daily **Vermonter train** (☏800-872-7245; www.amtrak.com/vermonter-train) runs from Montpelier to points north and south, including Brattleboro ($26, 2½ hours) and Burlington's Essex Junction station ($10, 40 minutes). The Amtrak station is 1.7 miles southwest of downtown Montpelier, at 299 Junction Rd in the Montpelier Junction neighborhood

Northeast Kingdom

When Senator George Aiken noted in 1949 that 'this is such beautiful country up here. It ought to be called the Northeast Kingdom of Vermont,' locals were quick to take his advice. Today, the Northeast Kingdom connotes the large wedge between the Quebec and New Hampshire borders. Less spectacular than spectacularly unspoiled, the landscape is a sea of green hills, with the occasional small village and farm spread out in the distance.

Here, inconspicuous inns and dairy cows contrast with the slick resorts and Morgan horses in the southern part of the state; the white steeples are chipped, the barns in need of a fresh coat of paint. In a rural state known for its unpopulated setting (only Wyoming contains fewer people), the Kingdom is Vermont's equivalent to putting on its finest pastoral dress, with a few holes here and there. It's a region that doesn't put on any airs about attracting tourists, and locals speak wryly of its 'picturesque poverty.'

While St Johnsbury is easily reached by I-91 or I-93 (a three-hour drive from Boston through New Hampshire), the rest of the Northeast Kingdom is spread out. Use I-91 as your north–south thoroughfare, and then use smaller routes like VT 5A to find dramatically sited Lake Willoughby, or VT 14 to find picturesque Craftsbury Common.

◉ Sights

St Johnsbury Athenaeum   MUSEUM
(☏802-748-8291; www.stjathenaeum.org; 1171 Main St, St Johnsbury; ☺10am-5:30pm Mon-Fri, to 3pm Sat) **FREE** Home to the country's oldest

LYNDONVILLE FREIGHTHOUSE

It's tough to throw a label on the Lyndonville Freighthouse (☏802-626-1174; www.thelyndonfreighthouse.com; 1000 Broad St, Lyndonville; mains $8-12; ☺7am-5:30pm)✐. The authentic 1870 railroad freighthouse houses a family restaurant serving organic, locally sourced American fare – including many items grown on the owner's farm (anything from omelettes to burgers to veggie plates); a deli and ice-cream counter; a country store (selling Vermont cheeses, trinkets and maple syrups); and a local art gallery (all pieces for sale). But head upstairs for the most important of all: the tiny railroad museum, which is really a small section of the shop with miniature train track (push the button and watch it whistle its way along the track).

art gallery still in its original form, the athenaeum was initially founded as a library by Horace Fairbanks in 1871. Comprising some 9000 finely bound books of classic world literature, the library was soon complemented by the gallery, built around its crown jewel, Albert Bierstadt's 10ft-by-15ft painting, *Domes of the Yosemite*. The collection also includes other large-scale dramatic landscapes by Bierstadt's fellow Hudson River School artists such as Asher B Durand, Worthington Whittredge and Jasper Crospey.

Fairbanks Museum & Planetarium MUSEUM
(☏802-748-2372; www.fairbanksmuseum.org; 1302 Main St, St Johnsbury; adult/child & senior $8/6; ☺9am-5pm Mon-Sat, 1-5pm Sun, closed Mon Nov-Mar) In 1891, when Franklin Fairbanks' collection of stuffed animals and cultural artifacts from across the globe grew too large for his home, he built the Fairbanks Museum of Natural Science. This massive stone building with a 30ft-high barrel-vaulted ceiling still displays more than half of Franklin's original collection, including a 1200lb moose, a Bengal tiger and a bizarre collection of 'mosaics' made entirely from dead bugs. The attached planetarium offers shows ($5 per person) throughout the year.

🏃 Activities

Not surprisingly, this sylvan countryside is the perfect playground for New England outdoor activities, including skiing, mountain biking and boating.

Skiing

Jay Peak   SKIING

(☎802-988-2611; www.jaypeakresort.com; VT 242, Jay) Even when Boston is balmy, you can still expect a blizzard at Vermont's northernmost ski resort. Only 10 miles south of the Quebec border. Jay gets more snow than any other ski area in New England (about 350 inches of powder). The mountain has plenty of easy and intermediate runs, but natural off-trail terrain also offers some of America's most challenging backcountry snowboarding and skiing.

Burke Mountain   SKIING

(☎802-626-7300; www.skiburke.com; 223 Sherburne Lodge Rd, East Burke) Off US 5 in East Burke, Burke Mountain is relatively unknown to out-of-staters, even though nearby Burke Mountain Academy has been training Olympic skiers for decades. Locals enjoy the challenging trails and empty lift lines. Burke has 55 trails (10% beginner, 45% intermediate, 45% expert) and six lifts, including three quad chairs and one with a vertical drop of 2000ft.

Craftsbury Outdoor Center   SKIING

(☎802-586-7767; www.craftsbury.com; 535 Lost Nation Rd, Craftsbury Common; ♿) Cross-country skiers adore this full-service resort just out-side the village of Craftsbury Common, 38 miles northwest of St Johnsbury. The 80 miles of trails – 50 of them groomed – roll over meadows and weave through forests of maples and firs, offering an ideal experience for all levels. In summer, the center is also a Mecca for runners and boaters.

Highland Lodge   SKIING

(☎802-533-2647; www.highlandlodge.com; Crafts-bury Rd, Greensboro) Has 40 miles of trails that slope down to the shores of Caspian Lake and connect with the trails of Craftsbury Outdoor Center. The Lodge was for sale at press time; check the website for current status.

Mountain Biking

On VT 114 off I-91, East Burke is a terrific place to start a mountain-bike ride.

★ Kingdom Trails   CYCLING

(www.kingdomtrails.com; day passes adult/child $15/7, year-round passes $75; ♿) ⚲ In the summer of 1997, a group of dedicated locals linked together more than 200 miles of single and double tracks and dirt roads to form this astounding, award-winning trail network. Riding on a soft forest floor dusted with pine needles and through century-old farms makes for one of the best mountain-biking experiences in New England. Passes can be purchased at the Kingdom Trails

---

WORTH A TRIP

THE BREAD & PUPPET MUSEUM

Rolling though the Northeast Kingdom, it's easy to become jaded at the sight of yet another barn. One in Glover definitely warrants a detour though – not for its livestock but for the cosmological universe of the Bread & Puppet Museum (☎802-525-3031; breadandpuppet.org/museum; 753 Heights Rd, Glover; donations welcome; ⊙10am-6pm) FREE, lurking within.

Formed in New York City by German artist Peter Shumann in 1963, the Bread & Puppet Theater is a collective-in-training that presents carnivalesque pageants, circuses, and battles of Good and Evil with gaudy masks and life-size (even gigantic) puppets. The street theater of its early performances gave voice to local rent strikes and anti–Vietnam War protests as well as an epic parade down Fifth Ave in the early '80s to protest nuclear proliferation. By then, it had moved its operation to Glover, where it currently occupies two barns.

The first barn is a two-floor space crammed with puppets and masks from past performances. The high-ceilinged top floor is especially arresting, with its collection of many-headed demons, menacing generals, priests, bankers, everyday people and animals, and an array of gods (some as large as 15ft). A second barn features performances in July and August – Bread & Puppet is on tour the rest of the year – for which Schumann bakes the bread that gives the enterprise half its name.

To get here, take I-91 to exit 24, then take a right onto VT 122 and continue 13 miles.

Welcome Center (478 VT 114, East Burke; ☺8am-5pm Sun-Thu, 8am-6pm Fri & Sat).

East Burke Sports   BICYCLE RENTAL
(☎802-626-3215; www.eastburkesports.com; 439 VT 114, East Burke; bicycles per day from $30; ☺9am-6pm) Supplies maps and rents bikes, including top-of-the-line models for serious mountain bikers.

Hiking
The stunning beauty of Lake Willoughby will leave even a jaded visitor in awe. The lake sits sandwiched between Mt Hor and Mt Pisgah, where the cliffs plummet more than 1000ft to the glacial waters below and create, in essence, a landlocked fjord.

The scenery is best appreciated on the hike (three hours) to the summit of Mt Pisgah. From West Burke, take VT 5A for 6 miles to a parking area on the left-hand side of the road, just south of Lake Willoughby. The 1.7-mile (one way) South Trail begins across the highway. It's about a 35-minute drive from St Johnsbury.

🛏 Sleeping

Rodgers Country Inn   INN $
(☎800-729-1704, 802-525-6677; 582 Rodgers Rd, West Glover; d incl breakfast from $80, cabins per week $600) Not far from the shores of Shadow Lake, Jim and Nancy Rodgers offer five guest rooms in their 1840s farmhouse, plus two independent cabins. Hang out on the front porch and read, or take a stroll on this 350-acre former dairy farm. This inn appeals to people who really want to feel what it's like to live in rural Vermont.

★**Inn at Mountain View Farm**   INN $$
(☎800-572-4509, 802-626-9924; www.innmtnview.com; 3383 Darling Hill Rd, East Burke; r/ste incl breakfast $175/275; 🐾) Built in 1883, this spacious, elegant farmhouse is set on a hilltop with stunning views, surrounded by 440 acres that are ideal for mountain biking, cross-country skiing or simply taking a long stroll on the hillside. There's also an on-site animal sanctuary, which is a rescue center for large farm animals; guests are encouraged to visit.

✕ Eating

Miss Lyndonville Diner   DINER $
(☎802-626-9890; 686 Broad St/US 5, Lyndonville; mains $5-12; ☺6am-8pm Mon-Thu, 6am-9pm Fri & Sat, 7am-8pm Sun) Five miles north of St Johnsbury and popular with locals, this place offers friendly, prompt service and a tantalizing display of pies. Large breakfasts are cheap, as are the sandwiches, but for a real steal try the tasty homemade dinners like roast turkey with all the fixings.

Trout River Brewery   BREWERY, PIZZERIA $$
(☎802-626-9396; www.troutriverbrewing.com; Hwy 5, Lyndonville; pizzas from $12; ☺4-9pm Fri & Sat) This roadside artisanal brewery is a great hang-out on Friday and Saturday nights, when pints of beer are accompanied by gourmet sourdough pizzas; one local classic is Smokin' Hot Trout, with smoked trout, dill, scallions and capers.

River Garden Cafe   INTERNATIONAL $$$
(☎802-626-3514; www.rivergardencafe.com; 427 Main St/VT 114, East Burke; mains $15-27; ☺11:30am-2pm & 5-9pm Wed-Sun) A summer patio within earshot of the river and a back-porch dining area that's open year-round set the mood of casual elegance at this popular eatery. The wide-ranging menu includes chicken marsala, filet mignon, rainbow trout, lamb chops, duck breast and steaks, along with pasta dishes and salads. Don't miss the cinnamon rolls at Sunday brunch.

ℹ Information
Northeast Kingdom Chamber of Commerce (☎802-748-3678; www.nekchamber.com; Ste 11, 2000 Memorial Dr, St Johnsbury; ☺8:30am-5pm mid-Jun–mid-Oct) Plentiful regional information, 3 miles north of town in the Green Mountain Mall just off US5.

ℹ Getting There & Away
To get to St Johnsbury from Montpelier (55 minutes, 38 miles), take US 2 east; from Burlington, I-89 to US 2 (1½ hours, 76 miles).

To get to Brattleboro (two hours, 122 miles), take a straight shot south down I-91.

The only way to get around the Northeast Kingdom is with your own wheels.

New Hampshire

🔌 603 / POP 1.3 MILLION

Includes ➡

Best Places to Eat

➡ Black Trumpet (p330)

➡ The Lone Oak (p333)

➡ White Mountain Cider Co (p362)

➡ Wolfetrap Grill & Raw Bar (p347)

➡ Burdick Chocolate (p337)

Best Places to Stay

➡ Ale House Inn (p329)

➡ Snowflake Inn (p362)

➡ Proctor's Lakehouse Cottages (p343)

➡ Omni Mt Washington Hotel & Resort (p364)

Why Go?

New Hampshire bleeds jagged mountains, scenic valleys and forest-lined lakes – they lurk in all corners of this rugged state. It all begs you to embrace the outdoors, from kayaking the hidden coves of the Lakes Region to trekking the upper peaks surrounding Mt Washington. Each season yields a bounty of adrenaline and activity: skiing and snowshoeing in winter, magnificent walks and drives through autumn's fiery colors, and swimming in crisp mountain streams and berry-picking in summer. Jewel-box colonial settlements like Portsmouth buzz a sophisticated tune, while historic attractions and small-town culture live on in pristine villages like Keene and Peterborough.

But there's a relaxing whiff in the air too – you're encouraged to gaze out at a loon-filled lake, recline on a scenic railway trip or chug across a waterway on a sunset cruise – all while digging into a fried-clam platter or a lobster roll, of course.

When to Go
Concord

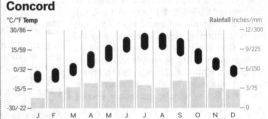

Dec Glide across trails on a horse-driven sleigh ride.

Jul Watch Exeter's American Independence Festival.

Oct See jack-o'-lanterns at Keene's annual Pumpkin Festival.

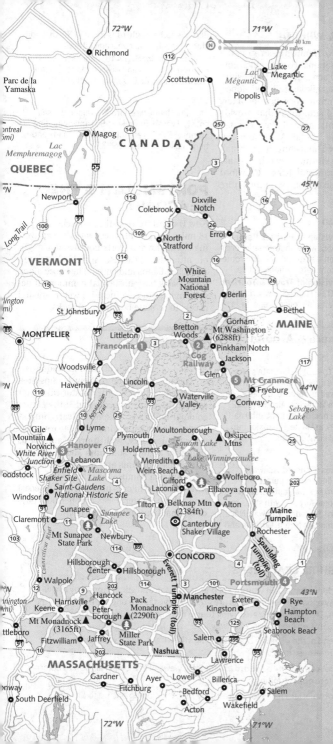

New Hampshire Highlights

❶ Walk in the footsteps of Robert Frost at his former farm in **Franconia** (p356)

❷ Trundle up the second-steepest railway track in the world along Mt Washington's **cog railway** (p363)

❸ Take a free walking tour at **Dartmouth College** (p338) in Hanover and discover renowned Mexican muralist José Clemente Orozco's riveting mural in the depths of the library

❹ Kayak your way around Portsmouth Harbor and do yoga on the beach with **Portsmouth Kayak Adventures** (p328)

❺ Tube down the snowy slopes at **Mt Cranmore Resort** (p359)

State Parks & Wildlife

The feather in New Hampshire's cap is the White Mountain National Forest, which covers nearly 800,000 acres in New Hampshire and Maine. It boasts hiking trails, ski slopes, campgrounds, swimming beaches and a few carefully controlled auto roads that provide access to this gigantic natural playground.

Aside from the White Mountain National Forest, New Hampshire has a small but exceedingly well-run network of state parks, including Franconia Notch, Crawford Notch and Echo Lake, along with the entire seacoast.

ⓘ Information

New Hampshire Division of Parks & Recreation (☑603-271-3556; www.nhstateparks.org) Offers information on a statewide bicycle route system and a very complete camping guide.
New Hampshire Division of Travel & Tourism Development (☑603-271-2665; www.visitnh.gov) Ski conditions and fall foliage reports, among other things.

ⓘ Getting There & Around

AIR

Manchester Airport (p438) is the state's largest airport and offers direct flights to 16 other American cities as well as Toronto, Canada. The smaller Lebanon Municipal Airport (p342) serves Hanover. The nearby Portland International Jetport (p369), in Maine, is a major hub and offers additional flight options.

BUS

Concord Coach Lines (Concord Trailways; www.concordcoachlines.com) operates a bus route to and from Boston South Station and Logan International Airport, with stops in Manchester, Concord, Meredith, Conway, North Conway, Jackson, Pinkham Notch, Gorham and Berlin. Another route runs through North Woodstock/Lincoln, Franconia and Littleton.

Dartmouth Coach (p440) offers services from Hanover, Lebanon and New London to Boston South Station and Logan International Airport.

CAR & MOTORCYCLE

The New Hampshire Turnpike (along the seacoast), Everett Turnpike (I-93) and Spaulding Turnpike (NH 16) are toll roads. For road conditions, call ☑800-918-9993.

PORTSMOUTH & THE SEACOAST

New Hampshire's coastline stretches for just 18 miles but provides access to the captivating coastal town of Portsmouth and a length of attractive beaches, sprinkled around rocky headlands and coves. The shore along these parts has substantial commercial development, but also includes well-regulated access to its state beaches and parks.

Portsmouth

POP 20,600

Perched on the edge of the Piscataqua river, Portsmouth is one of New Hampshire's most elegant towns, with a historical center set with tree-lined streets and 18th-century colonial buildings. Despite its early importance in the maritime industry, the town has a youthful energy, with tourists and locals filling its many restaurants and cafes. The numerous museums and historic houses allow visitors a glimpse into the town's multilayered past, while its proximity to the coast brings both lobster feasts and periodic days of fog that blanket the waterfront.

DON'T MISS

NEW HAMPSHIRE LEAF PEEPS

In fall the White Mountains turn vibrant shades of crimson and gold, capped by rocky peaks. Already awesome when the trees are green, the vistas are unparalleled when the leaves turn color. The classic foliage driving tour is the Kancamagus Hwy, a gorgeous mountain road between Lincoln and Conway.

➡ The western end of the highway boasts **Franconia Notch**, where you can marvel at the colors on numerous trails.

➡ Ride the gondola up **Cannon Mountain** for lofty views of the great rainbow of colors and fantastic photo opportunities.

➡ **Crawford Notch** offers hikes for more hardy types, including one up to Mt Washington.

True to its name, Portsmouth remains a working port town, and its economic vitality has been boosted by the Naval Shipyard (actually located across the river in Maine) and by the influx of high-tech companies.

⊙ Sights

Strawbery Banke Museum   MUSEUM
(📞603-433-1100; www.strawberybanke.org; cnr Hancock & Marcy Sts; adult/child $17.50/10; ⊙10am-5pm May-Oct) Spread across a 10-acre site, the Strawbery Banke Museum is an eclectic blend of period homes that date back to the 1690s. Costumed guides recount tales that took place among the 40 buildings (10 furnished). Strawbery Banke includes **Pitt Tavern** (1766), a hotbed of American revolutionary sentiment, **Goodwin Mansion**, a grand 19th-century house from Portsmouth's most prosperous time, and **Abbott's Little Corner Store** (1943). The admission ticket is good for two consecutive days.

Market Square   SQUARE
(📞603-436-3680; cnr Congress & Pleasant Sts) The heart of Portsmouth is this picturesque square, set neatly beneath the soaring white spire of the North Church. Within a few steps of the square are open-air cafes, colorful storefronts and tiny galleries where banjo-playing buskers entertain the tourists and locals that drift past on warm summer nights.

Prescott Park   PARK
(📞603-436-3680; 105 Marcy St) Overlooking the Piscataqua River, this small, grassy park makes a pleasant setting for a picnic. More importantly, it's the leafy backdrop for the **Prescott Park Arts Festival** (www.prescottpark.org) which means free music, dance, theater and food festivals throughout June, July and August. Separate one-day music festivals showcase jazz, folk and Americana; other highlights include the clam-chowder and chili festivals.

Albacore Park   PARK, MUSEUM
Just north of the old town center, this park serves as a maritime museum and host to the **USS Albacore** (📞603-436-3680; http://ussalbacore.org; 600 Market St; adult/child $6/3; ⊙9:30am-5pm Jun–mid-Oct, to 4pm Thu-Mon mid-Oct–May), a 205ft-long US Navy submarine, now open to the public. The *Albacore* was launched from the Portsmouth Naval Shipyard in 1953 and, with a crew of 55, it was piloted around the world for 19 years without firing a shot.

John Paul Jones House   HISTORIC ESTATE
(📞603-436-8420; www.portsmouthhistory.org; 43 Middle St; adult/child $6/free; ⊙11am-5pm May-Oct) This former boardinghouse is where America's first great naval commander resided in Portsmouth. Jones, who uttered, 'I have not yet begun to fight!' during a particularly bloody engagement with the British, is believed to have lodged here during the outfitting of the *Ranger* (1777) and the *America* (1781). The marvelous Georgian mansion with gambrel roof is now the headquarters of the Portsmouth Historical Society.

Wentworth Gardner House   HISTORIC ESTATE
(📞603-436-4406; www.wentworthgardnerandlear.org; 50 Mechanic St; adult/child $5/2; ⊙12-4pm Thu-Sun mid-Jun–mid-Oct) This 1760 structure is one of the finest Georgian houses in the US. Elizabeth and Mark Hunking Wentworth were among Portsmouth's wealthiest and most prominent citizens, so no expense was spared in building this home, which was a wedding gift for their son.

Tobias Lear & Moffatt-Ladd House   HISTORIC ESTATE
(📞603-436-8221; www.moffattladd.org; 154 Market St; adult/child $6/2.50, gardens admission $2; ⊙11am-5pm Mon-Sat & 1-5pm Sun Jun-Oct) Originally owned by an influential ship captain, the Georgian Moffatt-Ladd House was later the home of General William Whipple, a signer of the Declaration of Independence. The 18th-century chestnut tree and the old-fashioned **gardens** behind the house are delightful. Prices include admission to the **Tobias Lear House** (50 Mechanic St; adult/child $5/2; ⊙1-4pm Wed), the hip-roofed Colonial residence that was home to the family of George Washington's private secretary.

Wentworth-Coolidge Mansion   HISTORIC ESTATE
(📞603-436-6607; www.wentworthcoolidge.org; 375 Little Harbor Rd; adult/child $5/3; ⊙10am-4pm Wed-Sun late Jun-early Sep) This 42-room place south of the town center was home to New Hampshire's first royal governor and served as the colony's government center from 1741 to 1766. The lilacs on its grounds are descendants of the first lilacs planted in America, which were brought over from England by Governor Benning Wentworth.

Portsmouth

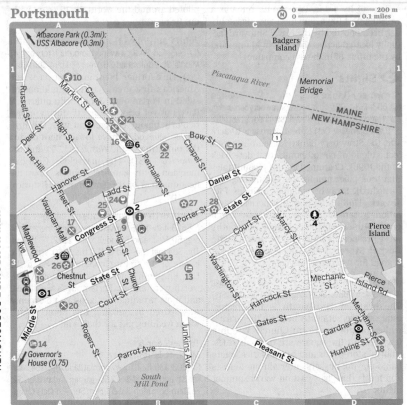

Children's Museum of New Hampshire
MUSEUM

(www.childrens-museum.org; 6 Washington St, Dover; admission $9; ⏱10am-5pm Mon-Sat, 12-5pm Sun, closed Mon early Sep–late May) Just 12 miles north of Portsmouth, this children's museum teaches and entertains, with interactive exhibits like the Dino Detective (where kids can be a paleontologist for a day and excavate through mini digs) or climb into the Yellow Submarine (a simulated deep dive). The focus is on having fun while learning.

🏃 Activities

Portsmouth Kayak Adventures
KAYAKING

(📞603-559-1000; www.portsmouthkayak.com; 185 Wentworth Rd; tours $40-75, kayak rental $45-64; ⏱9am-5pm) This outfitter offers a range of peaceful kayaking tours out on the harbors near Portsmouth, including an eco-tour (learn about the local ecosystem from a naturalist), a sunset tour and a combined kayaking/yoga-on-the-beach experience.

Isles of Shoals Steamship Co
CRUISE

(📞603-431-5500; www.islesofshoals.com; 315 Market St; adult/child $28/18; 👶) From mid-June to October the company runs an excellent tour of the harbor and the historic Isles of Shoals aboard a replica 1900s ferry. Look into the all-day whale-watching and shorter sunset, hip-hop and dinner cruises.

Portsmouth Harbor Cruises
CRUISE

(📞800-776-0915, 603-436-8084; www.portsmouthharbor.com; Ceres St Dock; adult $16-21, child $9-12) Cruises on the *Heritage* go around the harbor or to the Isles of Shoals. One unique option is cruising up an inland river and through the Great Bay tidal estuary. This cruise is particularly popular in fall when the foliage is colorful.

☞ Tours

Harbor Trail WALKING TOUR
(☏603-436-3988; Market Sq; adult/child $12/8; ◷10:30am Mon-Sat, 1:30pm Sun Jun–mid-Oct) A guided walking tour of the historic downtown and waterfront. The tour takes you past nine historic houses listed in the national register of historic buildings such as the Moffat-Ladd House (where a signer of the Declaration of Independence lived) and the Warner House, one of the few remaining brick mansions in the downtown area.

Legends & Ghosts WALKING TOUR
(☏207-439-8905; www.newenglandcuriosities.com; tours $12-25) New England Curiosities runs a variety of walking tours, visiting old graveyards, an abandoned prison, the 'haunted' pubs of Portsmouth and other locales where history and mystery collide. Call or check the website for meeting places and times.

Red Hook Brewery BREWERY
(☏603-430-8600; www.redhook.com; 35 Corporate Dr; tours $1; ◷hours vary) For the chance to see the crafting of a fine ale, book one of Red Hook's daily tours (hours highly variable – call for details). On site is also the Cataqua Public House (open for lunch and dinner daily), which serves pub fare alongside the signature brews. It's roughly 4 miles northwest of the town center.

🛏 Sleeping

Portsmouth is expensive in season. Oodles of cheaper (but less atmospheric) motels and hotels cluster at I-95 exits 5 and 6, around the Portsmouth (Interstate) traffic circle.

Great Bay Camping CAMPGROUND $
(☏603-778-0226; www.greatbaycamping.com; 56 NH 108, Newfields; tent sites $32; ◷May-Sep; 🐾) About 13 miles from Portsmouth, this family-oriented campground has numerous sites along a tidal river.

Ale House Inn INN $$
(☏603-431-7760; www.alehouseinn.com; 121 Bow St; r $150-280; P🔊) This former brick warehouse for the Portsmouth Brewing Company is now Portsmouth's snazziest boutique, fusing contemporary design with comfort. Rooms are modern, with clean lines of white, flat-screen TVs and, in the suites, plush tan sofas. Deluxe rooms feature an in-room iPad. Rates include use of vintage cruising bikes.

Inn at Strawbery Banke B&B $$
(☏603-436-7242; www.innatstrawberybanke.com; 314 Court St; r incl breakfast $170-190; P🔊) Set amid the historic buildings of Strawbery Banke, this colonial charmer has seven small but attractive rooms, each uniquely set with quilted bedspreads and brass or canopy beds.

Governor's House HOTEL $$$
(☏866-427-5140, 603-427-5140; www.governorshouse.com; 32 Miller Ave; r incl breakfast $200-240; P@🔊) This stately Georgian house is named for New Hampshire governor Charles Dale, who lived here in the mid-20th century. It has only four wood-floored guest rooms, each exquisitely fitted out with

NEW HAMPSHIRE PORTSMOUTH

ANNABELLE'S NATURAL ICE CREAM

Locals line up in droves for the best scoop in town: the homemade concoctions at **Annabelle's** (49 Ceres St; ⊘11am-10pm Tue-Sat, to 9pm Sun & Mon) include regional nods like New Hampshire Pure Maple Walnut and Pumpkin Pie, traditional varieties like Dutch Chocolate and Lemon Sorbet, and eclectic faves like Yellow Brick Road (vanilla, pralines, roasted pecans and caramel swirls).

unique period furnishings, private bathroom with hand-painted tiles and elegant decor. Rates include use of touring bikes.

Sise Inn
INN $$$

(☑877-747-3466, 603-433-1200; www.siseinn.com; 40 Court St; r/ste incl breakfast $200/280; ⓟ@⬚) A short walk from the city center, this elegant, Queen Anne–style inn dates from 1881 and has beautiful common areas with original wood details and antiques. Its 28 large, carpeted rooms and six suites have period furnishings coupled with modern comforts; some of the larger suites have Jacuzzis.

✖ Eating

Geno's
SEAFOOD $

(177 Mechanic St; mains $6-16; ⊘11am-4pm Mon, 8:30am-4pm Tue-Sat) For more than 40 years, this family-owned no-frills place has been a local institution for homemade chowder and lobster rolls. Its outdoor deck overlooks Portsmouth Harbor.

Friendly Toast
DINER $

(113 Congress St; mains $7-12; ⊘7am-10pm Sun-Thu, to 2am Fri & Sat; ⬚✎) Fun, whimsical furnishings set the scene for filling sandwiches, omelets, Tex-Mex and vegetarian fare at this retro diner. The breakfast menu is huge and is served around the clock: good thing since weekend morning waits can be long.

Savario's
PIZZERIA $

(☑603-427-2919; 278 State St; slices $1.50-3; ⊘noon-2pm & 5-9pm Mon-Fri) This tiny, family-run takeout pizza shop serves tasty pizzas and calzones, and remains something of a Portsmouth secret – despite winning 'best in town' awards for its homemade pies.

Oar House
SEAFOOD $$

(☑603-436-4025; 55 Ceres St; mains $11-34; ⊘11:45am-2:30pm & 5-10pm) One of Portsmouth's best seafood restaurants, this elegant place has a dark, cozy interior as well as an outdoor deck (across the street) overlooking the harbor.

Poco's Bow Street Cantina
AMERICAN $$

(☑603-431-5967; www.pocosbowstreetcantina.com; 37 Bow St; mains $12-23; ⊘noon-3pm & 4-11pm) Southwestern dishes arrive with New England flair at this lively waterfront spot. Blackened red snapper, fish tacos and jerk chicken quesadillas are among the mouthwatering favorites.

★ Black Trumpet Bistro
INTERNATIONAL $$$

(☑603-431-0887; www.blacktrumpetbistro.com; 29 Ceres St; mains $17-38; ⊘5:30-9pm) With brick walls and a sophisticated ambience, this bistro serves unique combinations – anything from house-made sausages infused with cocoa beans to seared haddock with *yuzu* (an Asian citrus fruit) and miso. The full menu is also available at its wine bar upstairs, which whips up equally inventive cocktails.

Jumpin' Jays Fish Cafe
SEAFOOD $$$

(☑603-766-3474; www.jumpinjays.com; 150 Congress St; mains $20-28; ⊘5:30-10pm) This exceptional seafood cafe offers fresh catches of the day simply grilled or seared (with a choice of six sauces, like tamarind and guava, or citrus and dijon), plus unconventional twists like bouillabaisse with lemongrass and coconut or haddock Piccata (whitefish sliced and sauteed in butter, olive oil and white wine). Add a raw bar, a huge warm and cold appetizer menu plus a buzzing modern space, and Jumpin' Jays wins on all counts.

Library
STEAKHOUSE $$$

(401 State St; mains $15-39; ⊘11:30am-2pm Mon-Sat, 8am-2pm Sun, 5-10pm Thu-Sun) In a palatial and opulent home built by a prominent judge in 1785, the Library is among New Hampshire's top steakhouses, serving juicy prime rib and rack of lamb in a dapper wood-paneled dining room.

🍷 Drinking & Nightlife

Portsmouth Brewery
MICROBREWERY

(www.portsmouthbrewery.com; 56 Market St; ⊘11:30am-12:30am; ⬚) Classically set with tin ceilings and exposed brick walls, this airy brewpub serves excellent homegrown pilsners, porters and ales. Come for the beer, not for the pub fare.

Thirsty Moose Taphouse
PUB

(www.thirstymoosetaphouse.com; 21 Congress St; bar snacks $3-11, brunch $10-17; ⊘11:30-1am Mon-Sat, 10:30am-1pm Sun) This convivial spot has more than 100 beers – leaning heavily towards New England brews – on tap and a staff that can walk you through most of them (it's impressive). Bites include *poutine* (a Montreal fave: fries drenched in cheese and gravy), corn dogs and a handful of salads. A fine spot to kick back and relax.

☆ Entertainment

Press Room
LIVE MUSIC

(☑603-431-5186; 77 Daniel St; ⊘4pm-midnight Mon-Fri, noon-midnight Sat) Between the nightly live music (jazz to blues to folk, from 6pm to 9pm), the tasty pub fare and the wooden booths, this is one of Portsmouth's best watering holes. The Tuesday Night Hoot (open-mic night, from 9pm) is renowned for being, well, a hoot.

Music Hall
PERFORMING ARTS

(☑603-436-2400; www.themusichall.org; 28 Chestnut St; tickets $22-65) For a small-town theater, this venue hosts a surprising array of performances, including dance, theater, opera and other music. Musicians, comedians and theater companies from around the country make appearances here.

Seacoast Repertory Theater
THEATER

(☑603-433-4472; www.seacoastrep.org; 125 Bow St; tickets $23-34) This theater is housed in a cool, converted building on Portsmouth's industrial riverfront and stages numerous musicals, plus the occasional comedian.

Red Door
LIVE MUSIC

(www.reddoorportsmouth.com; 107 State St; ⊘11:30am-midnight) Marked only by a red door, this casual, low-key lounge has nightly DJs or live music and a luscious martini list. There's often a cover charge; the amount changes according to who's spinning or performing.

ⓘ Information

Greater Portsmouth Chamber of Commerce
(☑603-436-3988; www.portsmouthchamber. org; 500 Market St; ⊘8:30am-5pm Mon-Fri) Also operates an information kiosk in the city center at Market Sq.

ⓘ Getting There & Away

Portsmouth is equidistant (57 miles) from Boston and Portland, Maine. It takes about 1¼ hours to reach Portland and roughly 1½ hours to reach Boston, both via I-95. Rush-hour and high-season traffic can easily double or triple this, however.

Greyhound (www.greyhound.com) runs several daily buses to Boston (one-way $22), Bangor, Maine ($48), and Bar Harbor, Maine ($52).

EXETER & INDEPENDENCE DAY

Exeter, founded 1638, is utterly quiet on the Fourth of July. But on the second Saturday after the 4th, this small town celebrates Independence Day two weeks after the rest of the country. The spirited American Independence Festival brings out the whole town (seemingly) dressed up in Colonial garb. The procession, led by George Washington, and the reading of the Declaration of Independence take center stage. But there are loads of other events, from Colonial cooking to militia drills to gunpowder races. Add fireworks and a night of rock and roll and you'll be reminded that reenactments are fun.

The town's specially designated meetinghouse, unique in these parts, played a crucial role in 1774, when British governor John Wentworth dissolved the provincial assembly that met in Portsmouth in an attempt to prevent the election of a continental congress. The revolutionary councils then began to gather at the meetinghouse in Exeter, which effectively became the seat of government.

Exeter's early history is best viewed at the American Independence Museum (☑603-772-2622; www.independencemuseum.org; 1 Governor's Lane; adult/under 6yr $5/free; ⊘10am-4pm Wed-Sat mid-May–Oct). Among the highlights of this National Landmark Property are the furnishings and possessions of the Gilman family, who lived here from 1720 to 1820, along with a document archive, including two original drafts of the US Constitution and personal correspondence of George Washington.

To reach Exeter, take I-95 to exit 2, then NH 101 west. Turn left on Portsmouth Ave (NH 108) and right on Water St.

ART 'ROUND TOWN

A small collection of galleries pepper Portsmouth's historical center. The majority feature the oil paintings, watercolors and woodblock prints of local artists, but national and international artists also make an appearance now and again. Between 6pm and 8pm on the first Friday of each month, many galleries, including leading spaces like Nahcotta (603 433 1705; www.nahcotta.com; 110 Congress St) and Three Graces Gallery (603 436 1988; www.threegracesgallery.com; 105 Market St), open their doors for a gallery walk. Most galleries treat the evening like an art-opening reception, with nibbles and wine. For a complete list, visit www.artroundtown.org, or pick up a brochure at the chamber of commerce.

Buses stop either in front of Mainely Gourmet at 55 Hanover St or at the **C&J Trailways Center** (603-430-1100; www.ridecj.com; 185 Grafton Dr), 3.5 miles west of downtown (off NH 33). C&J Trailways runs similar routes at like prices.

❶ Getting Around

The **Coast Trolley Downtown Loop** (rides 50¢, 3-day passes $2; ⊙10:30am-2:30pm & 3-5pm late Jun-late Aug) provides shuttle service between public parking lots, Market Sq and the major historic sights around town. Pick up a schedule and route map at the Market Sq information kiosk.

Hampton Beach & Around

POP 15,100

Littered with summer clam shacks, motels, fried-dough stands and arcades full of children, Hampton Beach isn't the classiest stretch of New England coastline, but it has New Hampshire's only sandy beach – a wide, inviting stretch of shore that gives pasty sunseekers their fix. North of Hampton Beach, the tacky beach fun transitions into rolling greenswards and serpentine private drives in Rye, where oceanfront mansions and sprawling 'summer cottages' show a different side of the coastline.

◎ Sights & Activities

Hampton Beach State Park   BEACH, PARK
(603-926-3784) The beach actually begins south of the state line, on the north bank of the Merrimack River at Salisbury Beach State Reservation in Massachusetts. Take I-95 exit 56 (MA 1A) and head east to Salisbury Beach, then north along NH 1A to Hampton Beach State Park, a long stretch of sand shielded by dunes. Facilities include a promenade, bathhouses and a band shell with an amphitheater.

Rye Beaches   BEACH
As NH 1A enters Rye, parking along the road is restricted to vehicles with town parking stickers, but **Jenness State Beach** has a small metered parking lot that's open to the general public. Further north near **Rye Harbor** you're allowed to park along the roadway. Climb over the seawall of rubble and rocks to get to the gravel beach. It lacks facilities but is much less crowded than anything further south. Continuing northward, **Wallis Sands State Beach** has a wide sandy beach with views of the Isles of Shoals. Besides the bathhouses, there are grassy lawns for children's games, making this the top spot for families with smaller kids.

Seacoast Science Center   SCIENCE CENTER
(603-436-8043; www.seacoastsciencecenter.org; 570 Ocean Blvd, Rye; adult/child $7/3; ⊙10am-5pm April-Oct, closed Tue-Fri Nov-Mar) Undersea videos, huge aquariums and a hands-on 'touch tank' are the highlights of this family favorite. The center hosts lots of special activities, such as trail walks, lighthouse tours and concerts.

🛏 Sleeping & Eating

Hampton Beach and – to a lesser degree – Rye have no shortage of roadside motels, scattered along NH 1A. Wherever you stay, you'll need reservations in the summer months.

Lamie's Inn & Tavern   INN $$
(603-926-0330; www.lamiesinn.com; 490 Lafayette Rd, Hampton; r incl breakfast $135-155; @🕏) To escape the din and tack of Hampton Beach, head inland to this colonial manor in downtown Hampton. The graceful guest rooms have exposed brick walls, four-poster beds and lace curtains. The Old Salt, the inn's restaurant (mains $9 to $20), has a cozy dining room and fresh seafood.

Galley Hatch   AMERICAN $$
(603-926-6152; 325 Lafayette Rd/US 1, Hampton; sandwiches $8-11, mains $17-26; ⊙noon-10pm; 🕏) Located in Hampton proper, Galley Hatch is a longtime favorite for its wide menu of

fresh fish, sandwiches, steaks, pastas, pizzas and veggie dishes.

ℹ Information

Hampton Beach Area Chamber of Commerce (☑603-926-8718; www.hamptonbeach.org; 169 Ocean Blvd, Hampton Beach; ☺10am-5pm) Offers information on tourist attractions.

ℹ Getting There & Around

There is no public transportation servicing the Hampton Beach area. Once you arrive, however, ditch your car and utilize the free **Beach Trolley** (☺noon-9:30pm Jun-Aug), which circles the beach.

MERRIMACK VALLEY

Although New Hampshire is noted more for mountains than for cities, Concord, the state's tidy capital, is a pleasant – if not overly exotic – place to spend a day. It sits along the mighty Merrimack River.

Concord

POP 42,500

New Hampshire's capital is a trim and tidy city with a wide Main St dominated by the striking State House, a granite-hewed 19th-century edifice topped with a glittering dome. The stone of choice in 'the granite state' appears in other fine buildings about Concord's historical center, cut from the still-active quarries on Rattlesnake Hill, just north of town. Concord is worth an afternoon visit and also makes a good base for visiting the idyllic Canterbury Shaker village.

⊙ Sights

McAuliffe-Shepard Discovery Center   SCIENCE MUSEUM
(www.starhop.com; 2 Institute Dr; adult/3-12yr $10/7; ☺10am-5pm Sun-Thu, to 9pm Fri) This science center is named after and dedicated to two New Hampshire astronauts. Christa McAuliffe was the schoolteacher chosen to be America's first teacher-astronaut – she and her fellow astronauts died in the tragic explosion of the *Challenger* spacecraft in 1986 – and Alan B Shepard was a member of NASA's elite *Mercury* corps and became America's first astronaut in 1961. Exhibits chronicle the life and story of these two icons. You can also view a life-size replica of a NASA rocket and the *Mercury* capsule that transported Shepard to space, play the role of a TV weather forecaster, and learn about space travel to Mars and the power of the sun.

State House
(107 N Main St; ☺8am-4:30pm Mon-Fri) FREE
The handsome 1819 New Hampshire State Capital House is the oldest capitol building in the US, and the state legislature still meets in the original chambers. Self-guided tour brochures point out the highlights of the building and its grounds, including the **Memorial Arch**, which commemorates those who served in the nation's wars. The capitol building's **Hall of Flags** holds 103 flags that New Hampshire military units carried into battle in various wars, including the Civil and Vietnam wars. Portraits and statues of New Hampshire leaders, including a mural of the great orator Daniel Webster, line its corridors and stand in its lofty halls.

🛏 Sleeping & Eating

Unlike the rest of the state, Concord is devoid of any remarkable B&Bs or homey inns. For cozier accommodations, consider staying in the Merrimack Valley, the Lakes

> ### DON'T MISS
>
> ### THE LONE OAK
>
> Locals swear by this no-frills **roadside spot** (175 Milton Rd/NH 125/Spaulding Turnpike/Rte 16 exit 12, Rochester; scoops $3.25-5.25, sandwiches $3-11, mains $9.50-18; ☺11am-10pm), which has been serving up the best lobster rolls and fried fish in the area since 1962. Others come for the homemade ice cream, made right on the premises. Like many New England snack shacks, there's no interior seating, just a scatterng of picnic tables sheltered by a makeshift roof. It's a satisfying pit stop conveniently located in Rochester (21 miles north of Portsmouth), just off the Spaulding Turnpike, the major thoroughfare running north from Portsmouth. There's a second **Lone Oak** (74 Lafayette Rd, Rye; sandwiches $3-11; seafood plates $9.50-18; ☺noon-10pm) in Rye (6 miles north of Portsmouth), off Rte 1.

NEW HAMPSHIRE CONCORD

NEW HAMPSHIRE'S FAVORITE STONE

New Hampshire will forever be known as 'the granite state.' This refers not merely to the tough, take-no-bullshit attitude of the locals but also to the state's enormous granite quarries, which still yield vast amounts of this very solid stone. They've also played a pivotal role in some of the country's most important structures: New Hampshire granite was used in Boston's Quincy Market, the Brooklyn Bridge, the Pentagon and even the Library of Congress.

Region, Portsmouth or the seacoast and visiting the capital on a day trip.

Centennial Inn   INN $$
(☑ 603-227-9000, 800-360-4839; www.thecentennialhotel.com; 96 Pleasant St; r $165-220; ⓟ🛜) This turn-of-the-20th-century turreted manse has 32 luxurious rooms and suites. Stylish minimalism prevails inside the Victorian landmark, with subdued earth tones, deluxe bedding, trim furnishings, black-and-white artwork and vessel-bowl sinks in the granite bathrooms. Several rooms are set in the turret, while the best have private outdoor porches. The hotel and its fine-dining, New American restaurant, the Granite (www.graniterestaurant.com; mains $12-24) is popular among business travelers.

Hermanos Cocina Mexicana   MEXICAN $$
(☑ 603-224-5669; www.hermanosmexican.com; 11 Hills Ave; mains $7-18; ⊘noon-11pm) Just off Main St in a historic brick building, Hermanos serves authentic and creative Mexican dishes, from pork *taquitos* (minitacos) to chimichangas. The menu also has more than 25 versions of nachos. Head to the upstairs lounge for excellent margaritas and live jazz (6.30pm to 9pm Sunday to Thursday, 7:30pm to 10pm Saturday).

ℹ Information

The **Greater Concord Chamber of Commerce** (☑ 603-224-2508; www.concordnhchamber.com; 40 Commercial St; ⊘9am-5pm Mon-Fri, 9am-3pm Sat) is quite helpful, and there's also a small, seasonal information kiosk in front of the State House on N Main St. Caveat: both keep unreliable hours.

ℹ Getting There & Away

Concord Coach Lines (Concord Trailways; www.concordcoachlines.com) has frequent daily services from the **Trailways Transportation Center** (☑ 800-639-3317, 603-228-3300; 30 Stickney Ave, I-93 exit 14) to Boston ($15, 1½ hours).

MONADNOCK REGION

In the southwestern corner of the state the pristine villages of Peterborough and Jaffrey Center (2 miles due west of Jaffrey) anchor Mt Monadnock (moh-NAHD-nock; 3165ft). 'Mountain That Stands Alone' in Algonquian, Monadnock is relatively isolated from other peaks, which means hikers to the summit are rewarded with fantastic views of the surrounding countryside. The trail, however, is anything but lonely. Monadnock is one of the most climbed mountains in the world.

For a list of inns and B&Bs in the Monadnock region, visit www.nhlodging.org.

Peterborough & Around

POP 6200

The picturesque town of Peterborough is a charming village of redbrick houses and tree-lined streets, with the idyllic Nabanusit River coursing through its historic center. Nestled between Temple Mountain to the east and Mt Monadnock to the west, Peterborough is a gateway to some captivating countryside, and its restaurants and B&Bs draw plenty of visitors in their own right.

Peterborough is something of an arts community, an impression left deeply by the nearby MacDowell Colony (www.macdowellcolony.org). Founded in the early 1900s, the country's oldest art colony has attracted a diverse and dynamic group of poets, painters, composers and playwrights. Aaron Copland composed parts of *Appalachian Spring* at the colony; Virgil Thomson worked on *Mother of Us All;* Leonard Bernstein completed his Mass; and Thornton Wilder wrote *Our Town,* a play that was openly inspired by Peterborough. Milton Avery, James Baldwin, Barbara Tuchman and Alice Walker are but a few of the luminaries that have passed this way.

More than 200 poets, composers, playwrights, architects, filmmakers, painters and photographers still come to Peterborough each year. They come for inspiration from the serene beauty of the countryside, from one another, and from the MacDowell legacy of creative collaboration that endures to this day. The colony is open to visitors just once a year, in the second weekend in August.

◉ Sights & Activities

Mariposa Museum
MUSEUM

(www.mariposamuseum.org; 26 Main St; adult/child $6/4; ☺11am-5pm daily, closed Mon & Tue Sep–mid-Jun) 'Please touch!' implores this museum, which exhibits folk art and folklore from around the world. It's a wonderful place for kids, who are invited to dive into the collections to try on costumes, experiment with musical instruments, play with toys and make their own art. Periodic performances feature musicians and storytellers who lead interactive performances.

Sharon Arts Center
GALLERY

(☎603-924-2787; www.sharonarts.org; 30 Grove St) FREE This arts center consists of two parts: a fine-art exhibition space with a rotating array of paintings and crafts by some of the region's many artists, and a gallery-shop selling art, jewelry and pottery made by local artisans. There's a second entrance at 20-40 Depot St.

Miller State Park
PARK

(☎603-924-3672; www.nhstateparks.org; NH 101; adult/child $4/2; ☺9am-5pm late May-Oct, limited access Nov-late May) New Hampshire's oldest state park, Miller is the site of Pack Monadnock, a 2290ft peak not to be confused with its better-known neighbor, Mt Monadnock. The park has three easy-to-moderate paths to the summit of Pack Monadnock; you can also access the 21-mile Wapack trail here. Miller State Park is about 4.5 miles east of Peterborough along NH 101. A self-service pay box (where you can pay the park fee by putting money in the slot) exists for days and times outside the standard hours.

⌂ Sleeping

Greenfield State Park
CAMPGROUND $

(☎603-271-3628; www.nhsstateparks.org; tent sites $26-28; ☺late May-early Oct) Twelve miles northeast of Peterborough, off NH 136, this 400-acre park has over 250 pine-shaded campsites. There's fine swimming and hiking, as well as canoe and kayak rental.

Apple Gate B&B
B&B $$

(☎603-924-6543; 199 Upland Farm Rd; r incl breakfast $95-140) This 1832 colonial is nestled among apple orchards, and its four cozy guest rooms are each named after a variety of apple. It has an incredible parlor with crackling fireplace and a reading room warmed by a wood stove.

✗ Eating & Drinking

Nonie's
CAFE $

(☎603-924-3451; 28 Grove St; mains $5-12; ☺6am-2pm Mon-Sat, 7am-1pm Sun) A longtime Peterborough favorite, Nonie's serves excellent breakfasts as well as fresh bakery items. In the summer grab a table in the tiny front garden.

Harlow's Pub
PUB

(☎603-924-6365; www.harlowspub.com; 3 School St; ☺noon-midnight Wed-Sat, noon-5pm Sun,

NEW HAMPSHIRE PETERBOROUGH & AROUND

WORTH A TRIP

LAKE SUNAPEE

Lake Sunapee is a worthwhile detour any time of year. In summer, head to the lake situated within Mount Sunapee State Park (Newbury; adult/child $4/2; ☺8:30am-6pm mid-Jun–mid-Oct, 9am-5pm Mon-Fri, 8:30am-6pm Sat & Sun mid-May–mid-Jun), off NH 103, for hiking, picnicking, swimming and fishing. The wide sandy beach has a pleasant grassy sitting area. Canoes and kayaks are available for rental. From I-89 take exit 9, NH 103 to Newbury.

In winter, alpine skiing is the attraction at Mt Sunapee Resort (☎603-763-2356; www.mtsunapee.com; Newbury; adult/child Mon-Fri $62/37, Sat & Sun $66/41; ☺9am-4pm). Mt Sunapee has a vertical drop of 1510ft – the biggest in southern New Hampshire. It's not much to compete with Cannon or Loon Mountain, but it offers some challenging skiing all the same. Rentals, lessons and childcare are available. Coming from Hanover or Concord, take exit 12A off I-89 and turn right on Rte 11. In the town of Sunapee, turn left onto Rte 103B. Coming from the south, take exit 9 and follow NH 103 through Bradford and Newbury to Mt Sunapee.

CANTERBURY SHAKER VILLAGE

The Canterbury Shaker Village (📞603-783-9511; www.shakers.org; 288 Shaker Rd, Canterbury; adult/child $17/8; ⏰10am-5pm mid-May–Oct) is now preserved as a nonprofit trust to present Shaker history. Members of the United Society of Believers in Christ's Second Appearing were called 'Shakers' because of the religious ecstasies they experienced during worship. This particular Shaker community was founded in 1792 and was occupied for two centuries. Sister Ethel Hudson, last member of the Shaker colony here, died in 1992 at the age of 96.

The national historic landmark has 'interpreters' in period garb who perform the tasks and labors of community daily life: fashioning Shaker furniture and crafts (for sale in the gift shop) and growing herbs and producing herbal medicines. Families with kids will appreciate the family tour, which includes singing and dancing in the Dwelling House Chapel and allows kids to touch reproduction Shaker items like bonnets and woodworking tools. Each December, the village opens for two consecutive Saturdays and has resplendent seasonal decorations, candlelight strolls and horse-drawn sleigh rides.

The Canterbury Shaker Village is 15 miles north of Concord on MA 106. Take I-93 to exit 18.

4-10pm Mon) This local pub has a good selection of draught beers, including New England brews. It also serves Mexican and pub fare until 9pm, but the real reason to come here is for the convivial wooden bar and to catch live music.

☆ Entertainment

Peterborough Folk Music Society　　　　　LIVE MUSIC
(📞603-827-2905; www.pfmsconcerts.org; Peterborough Players, Hadley Rd; tickets $17-22) This active group attracts nationally known folk musicians to perform in a wonderful barn-style theater about 3.5 miles from Peterborough center. Recent shows have included the Jonathan Edwards Trio and Boston folk scene hero Ellis Paul.

ℹ Information

Greater Peterborough Chamber of Commerce (📞603-924-7234; www.peterborough chamber.com; NH 101, at NH 123; ⏰9am-5pm Mon-Fri year-round, 10am-3pm Sat Jun-Oct)

ℹ Getting There & Away

Peterborough is at the intersection of US 202 and NH 101 (roughly 1 hour southeast of Concord and 15 minutes northeast of Jaffrey Center). No public transportation is available.

Jaffrey Center

Two miles due west of bigger, less interesting Jaffrey, Jaffrey Center is a tiny, picture-perfect village of serene lanes, 18th-century homes and a dramatic white-steepled meetinghouse.

All of Jaffrey Center's sights are clustered around the village's wee historic district, located on both sides of Gilmore Pond Rd off NH 124. The most intriguing sights include the frozen-in-time Little Red School House and the Melville Academy, which houses a one-room museum of rural artifacts. Both are open from 2pm to 4pm on weekends in summer. For a deeper look at local history, wander the Old Burying Ground behind the meetinghouse. Willa Cather, a frequent visitor who wrote portions of her novels in Jaffrey (including *My Ántonia* and *One of Ours*), is buried here (a quotation from *My Ántonia* graces her tombstone). Jaffrey Town Green often hosts free concerts on Wednesday nights in July and August.

🛏 Sleeping & Eating

Currier House　　　　　B&B $
(📞603-532-7670; www.thecurrierhouse.com; 5 HarknessRd; r incl breakfast $95-110; 🛜) Outfitted with simple quilts and antiques, this B&B (which has views of Mt Monadnock from its tranquil porch) near town is a steal. Book early to snag one of its three rooms.

Monadnock Inn　　　　　INN $$
(📞603-532-7800; www.monadnockinn.com; 379 Main St; r $110-190) This family affair has 11 unique guest rooms, each with its own color scheme and decorative style. Beautifully maintained grounds and wide porches grace the home's exterior. The on-site restaurant

(mains $17 to $22) serves bistro fare (many with a local influence, like lobster pie or cider house scallops), and the adjacent pub dishes up small bites like sandwiches and comfort food.

Kimball Farm ICE CREAM, SEAFOOD **$$**
(☑603-532-5765; NH 124; mains $9-23; ☺11am-10pm May-Oct) This dairy has achieved more than local fame for its sinfully creamy ice cream that comes in 40 flavors and unbelievable portion sizes. It also serves excellent sandwiches and fried seafood, but those in the know get the famous lobster rolls.

ℹ Information

Jaffrey Chamber of Commerce (☑603-532-4549; www.jaffreychamber.com; Main St, cnr NH 124 & NH 202, Jaffrey; ☺10am-1pm & 1:30-4pm Mon-Fri, 9am-noon Sat late May-early Oct) Pick up a walking-tour brochure here.

ℹ Getting There & Away

Jaffrey is at the intersection of US 202 and NH 124, while quaint Jaffrey Center is 2 miles west on NH 124. No public transportation is available.

Mt Monadnock State Park

This 3165ft **peak** (www.nhstateparks.org; NH 124; adult/child $4/2) can be seen from 50 miles away in any direction and is the area's spiritual vertex. With a visitor center (where you can get good hiking information), 12 miles of ungroomed cross-country ski trails and over 40 miles of hiking trails (6 miles of which reach the summit), this state park is an outdoor wonderland. The White Dot Trail (which turns into the White Cross Trail) from the visitor center to the bare-topped peak is about a 3½-hour hike round trip.

Well placed for a sunrise ascent up the mountain, Gilson Pond campground (☑603-532-8862, reservations 603-271-3556; 585 Dublin Rd/NH 124; tent sites $25) has 35 peaceful, well-shaded sites. It's open year-round, but from November until mid-May there is no water and the road in may not be plowed.

To reach Peterborough and Jaffrey from Portsmouth, take I-95 south to NH101. Then head south and take east on NH 101. Expect the trip to take about 1½ to 2 hours. It also makes sense to visit the region on the way to or from Brattleboro, Vermont.

NEW HAMPSHIRE MT MONADNOCK STATE PARK

SCENIC DRIVE: MONADNOCK VILLAGES

The region surrounding Mt Monadnock is a web of narrow winding roads connecting classic New England towns, and one could easily spend a few days exploring this picturesque countryside.

➡ **Fitzwilliam**, south of the mountain on NH 119, has a town green surrounded by lovely old houses and a graceful town hall with a steeple rising to the heavens.

➡ **Harrisville**, northwest of Peterborough via NH 101, is a former mill village that looks much as it did in the late 1700s, when the textile industry in these parts was flourishing. Today its brick-and-granite mill buildings have been converted into functionally aesthetic commercial spaces.

➡ **Hancock**, north of Peterborough on NH 123, is another quintessential New England village. The town's showpiece is one of the oldest continuously operating inns in New England: Hancock Inn (☑800-525-1789, 603-525-3318; www.hancockinn.com; 33 Main St, Hancock; r incl breakfast $180-300; 🛜), New Hampshire's oldest inn, has 15 rooms, each with its own unique charms. Dome ceilings (in rooms that used to be part of a ballroom), fireplaces and private patios are some of the features. The cozy dining room is open for breakfast and dinner.

➡ **Hillsborough Center**, 14 miles north of Hancock on NH 123, is another classic, not to be confused with Hillsborough Lower Village and Upper Village. Steeped in the late 18th and early 19th centuries, the trim little town has a number of art studios.

➡ **Walpole**, northwest of Keene along NH 12, is another gem. Locals descend from surrounding villages to dine at Burdick Chocolate (☑603-756-9058; 47 Main St, Walpole; mains $5-30; ☺7am-6pm Mon, 7am-9pm Tue-Sat, 7:30am-5pm Sun). Originally a New York City chocolatier, Burdick opened this sophisticated cafe to showcase its desserts. Besides rich chocolaty indulgences, the lively bistro has a full menu of creative new American dishes, plus artisanal cheeses and top-notch wines.

LOCAL KNOWLEDGE

NEW HAMPSHIRE'S WINE & CHEESE TRAIL

Watch out, Vermont. New Hampshire's small cheese producers are multiplying, and small wineries are popping up left and right. The tourism board put together an excellent leaflet, *New Hampshire Wine & Cheese Trails*, detailing three itineraries across 21 farms and wineries, including a few cider producers. Pick it up from any tourist office or download it from the web at http://agriculture.nh.gov/publications/documents/winecheesepdf.pdf.

UPPER CONNECTICUT RIVER VALLEY

The Connecticut River, New England's longest, is the boundary between New Hampshire and Vermont. The Upper Connecticut River Valley extends from Brattleboro, Vermont, in the south to Woodsville, New Hampshire, in the north, and includes towns on both banks. The river has long been an important byway for explorers and traders. Today it is an adventure destination for boaters and bird-watchers, canoeists and kayakers. The region's largest population center is Lebanon, while the cultural focal point is prestigious Dartmouth College in Hanover.

Hanover & Around

POP 11,400

Hanover is the quintessential New England college town. On warm days, students toss Frisbees on the wide college green fronting Georgian ivy-covered buildings, while locals and academics mingle at the laid-back cafes, restaurants and shops lining Main St. Dartmouth College has long been the town's focal point, giving the area a vibrant connection to the arts.

Dartmouth was chartered in 1769 primarily 'for the education and instruction of Youth of the Indian Tribes.' Back then, the school was located in the forests where its prospective students lived. Although teaching 'English Youth and others' was its secondary purpose, in fact Dartmouth College graduated few Native Americans and was soon attended almost exclusively by colonists. The college's most illustrious alumnus is Daniel Webster (1782–1852), who graduated in 1801 and went on to be a prominent lawyer, US senator, secretary of state and perhaps the USA's most esteemed orator.

Hanover is part of a larger community that includes Lebanon in New Hampshire, as well as Norwich and White River Junction in Vermont. When looking for services (especially accommodations), consider all of these places, not just Hanover. Unless otherwise stated, the listings in this section are in Hanover proper.

◉ Sights

Baker Berry Library　　　　　　LIBRARY

(☎603-646-2560; http://library.dartmouth.edu; 25 N Main St; ☺8am-midnight Mon-Thu, 8am-10pm Fri, 10am-10pm Sat, 10am-midnight Sun) On the north side of the green is Dartmouth College's central Baker Berry Library. The reserve corridor on the lower level houses an impressive mural called *Epic of American Civilization*, by José Clemente Orozco (1883–1949). The renowned Mexican muralist taught and painted at Dartmouth from 1932 to 1934. The mural follows the course of civilization in the Americas from the time of the Aztecs to the present.

Go upstairs and enjoy the view of the campus from the **Tower Room** on the 2nd floor. This collegiate wood-paneled room is one of the library's loveliest.

The adjacent **Sanborn House** also has ornate woodwork, plush leather chairs and books lining the walls, floor to ceiling, on two levels. It is named for Professor Edwin Sanborn, who taught for almost 50 years in the Department of English. This is where students (and you!) can enjoy a **traditional teatime** (☺4pm Mon-Fri).

Dartmouth College Green　　　　UNIVERSITY

The green is the focal point of the campus, both physically and historically. Along the east side of the green, picturesque **Dartmouth Row** (College St) consists of four harmonious Georgian buildings: **Wentworth**, **Dartmouth**, **Thornton** and **Reed**. Dartmouth Hall was the original college building, constructed in 1791. Just north of Dartmouth Row, **Rollins Chapel** (College St) is a fine example of Richardsonian architecture and a peaceful place to collect your thoughts.

Throughout the year undergraduate students lead free guided **walking tours** (☎603-646-2875; www.dartmouth.edu) of the Dartmouth campus. Reservations are not required, but call to confirm the departure times, which change seasonally.

Hood Museum of Art
MUSEUM

(☎603-646-2808; E Wheelock St; ☺10am-5pm Tue-Sat, to 9pm Wed, noon-5pm Sun) FREE Shortly after the university's founding in 1769, Dartmouth began to acquire artifacts of artistic or historical interest. Since then the collection has expanded to include nearly 70,000 items, which are housed at the Hood Museum of Art. The collection is particularly strong in American pieces, including Native American art. One of the highlights is a set of Assyrian reliefs from the Palace of Ashurnasirpal that date to the 9th century BC. Special exhibitions often feature contemporary artists.

Enfield Shaker Museum
MUSEUM

(☎603-632-4346; www.shakermuseum.org; 447 NH 4A; adult/child $12/free; ☺10am-5pm Mon-Sat, noon-5pm Sun Jun–mid-Oct, noon-2pm Mon, Wed & Fri-Sun mid-Oct–May) Set in a valley overlooking Mascoma Lake, the entire Enfield Shaker site dates back to the late 18th century and grew into a small but prosperous community of Shaker farmers and craftspeople in the early 1800s. The museum centers on the Great Stone Dwelling, the largest Shaker dwelling house ever built.

Exhibition galleries contain Shaker furniture, tools, clothing and photographs, and visitors can explore the herb and flower gardens, browse the crafty gift shop and hike to the Shaker Feast Ground, which offers spectacular views (particularly in autumn) over the former village and Mascoma Lake.

At its peak, some 300 members (divided into several 'families') lived in Enfield, farming 3000 acres of land. They built a handful of impressive wood and brick buildings in the area, and took in converts, orphans and children of the poor – who were essential for the Shaker future, since sex was not allowed in the pacifist, rule-abiding community. By the early 1900s the community had gone into decline, with the last remaining family moving out in 1917. Enfield is 11 miles southeast of Dartmouth.

Saint-Gaudens National Historic Site
GARDENS

(☎603-675-2175; www.nps.gov/saga; 139 St Gaudens Rd, Cornish; adult/child $5/free; ☺buildings 9am-4:30pm year-round, grounds 9am-dusk May-Oct, 9am-4:15pm Mon-Fri Nov-Apr) In the summer of 1885, the sculptor Augustus Saint-Gaudens rented an old inn near the town of Cornish and came to this beautiful spot in the Connecticut River Valley to work. He

Hanover

N 0 ——— 200 m
0 ——— 0.1 miles

Hanover

DON'T MISS

HAVE PUMPKIN, WILL TRAVEL

One of New Hampshire's quirkiest annual gatherings, the Keene Pumpkin Festival (www.pumpkinfestival.org) brings to the tiny town of Keene some 80,000 visitors (more than three times its population). They come for the magnificent tower of jack-o'-lanterns rising high above Central Sq.

The event started in 1991 when local merchants, eager to keep shoppers in the area on weekend nights, displayed hundreds of pumpkins around Main St. Since then the event has exploded as, each year on the third Saturday in October, Keene attempts to better its record of nearly 29,000 in 2003. (This was a Guinness world record for the most jack-o'-lanterns lit in the same place at the same time – until Boston copied the event and trumped Keene with 30,000 or so in 2006.)

In addition to gazing into the eyes of the plump, artfully carved orange fruit, you can enjoy a craft fair, a costume parade, seed-spitting contests and fireworks. Live bands play on the surrounding streets as local merchants dish up clam chowder, fried sausages, mulled cider and plenty of pumpkin pie. Following the festival, all those brightly lit gourds become pearls before swine as area farmers spread a feast before their pumpkin-loving piggies.

If you plan to go, don't forget your pumpkin, and if you're keen to stay in Keene, try the Carriage Barn Guest House (☑603-357-3812; www.carriagebarn.com; 358 Main St; s/d incl breakfast from $110; 🛜) for a comfy stay.

Greyhound (www.greyhound.com) serves Keene from Boston (transfer required; $45, four hours) and Brattleboro ($14.75, 30 minutes). The bus stops at 67 Main St, in front of Corner News.

returned summer after summer, and eventually bought the place in 1892. The estate, where he lived until his death in 1907, is now the Saint-Gaudens National Historic Site.

Saint-Gaudens is best known for his public monuments, such as the Sherman Monument in New York's Central Park and the Adams Memorial in Rock Creek Park, Washington DC. Perhaps his greatest achievement was the Robert Gold Shaw Memorial across from the State House in Boston. Recasts of all of these sculptures are scattered around the beautiful grounds of the estates.

In addition to seeing Saint-Gaudens' work, you can tour his home and wander the grounds and studios, where artists-in-residence sculpt. The visitors center shows a short film about the artist's life and work. You can catch a summer concert series in the Little Studio on Sunday between 2pm and 4pm in July and August. The site is just off NH 12A in Cornish, 21 miles south of Dartmouth.

🏃 Activities

Gile Mountain　　　　　　　　HIKING
Just over the river in Norwich, about 7 miles from Hanover, the mountain is a popular destination for Dartmouth students looking for a quick escape from the grind. A half-hour hike – and a quick climb up the fire tower – rewards adventurers with an incredible view of the Connecticut River Valley.

Cross the river into Norwich and take Main St through town to Turnpike Rd. Stay left at the fork and straight on Lower Turnpike Rd, even as it turns to gravel. Look for the old farmhouse on the right and the sign for parking on the left.

✨ Festivals & Events

Winter Carnival　　　　　　STUDENT FESTIVAL
(www.dartmouth.edu/~sao/events/carnival) Each February, Dartmouth celebrates the week-long Winter Carnival, featuring special art shows, drama productions, concerts, an ice-sculpture contest and other amusements. The festival is organized by the Student Activities Office.

🛏 Sleeping

Storrs Pond Recreation Area　CAMPGROUND $
(☑603-643-2134; www.storrspond.com; NH 10; tent/RV sites $28/36; 🕑late May–early Sep; 🛜) In addition to 37 woodsy sites next to a 15-acre pond, this private campground has tennis courts and two sandy beaches for swimming. From I-89 exit 13, take NH 10 north and look for signs.

Norwich Inn INN $$
(☎802-649-1143; www.norwichinn.com; 325 Main St, Norwich; r $145-210; 📶) Just across the Connecticut River in Norwich, Vermont, this is both a historic inn and a microbrewery. Rooms in the main house are decorated with Victorian antiques and traditional country furniture, and the two adjacent buildings include modern furnishings and gas fireplaces in each room.

At least four of its beers (its signature ales have won multiple awards) are on tap at its brewpub, Jasper Murdock's Alehouse, and the wine list includes more than 2000 wines from its on-site wine cellar.

Six South Street Hotel HOTEL $$$
(☎603-643-0600; www.sixsouth.com; 6 E South St; r $200-320; @📶) This 69-room upscale boutique hotel in downtown Hanover is sleek, modern and stylish. It's an excellent choice if you're done with frilly B&Bs and don't require the full New England vibe.

Hanover Inn INN $$$
(☎800-443-7024, 603-643-4300; www.hanoverinn.com; cnr W Wheelock & S Main Sts; r from $280; 📶) Owned by Dartmouth College, Hanover's loveliest guesthouse has nicely appointed rooms with elegant wood furnishings. It has a wine bar and an award-winning restaurant on site.

Eating & Drinking

Lou's DINER $
(www.lousrestaurant.net; 30 S Main St; mains $6-12; ⌚6am-3pm Mon-Fri, 7am-3pm Sat & Sun) A Dartmouth institution since 1947, this is Hanover's oldest establishment, always packed with students meeting for a coffee or perusing their books. From the retro tables or the Formica-topped counter, order typical diner food like eggs, sandwiches and burgers. The bakery items are also highly recommended.

Mai Thai THAI $$
(☎603-643-9980; 44 S Main St; lunch buffet $8.50, mains $11-16; ⌚11:30am-10pm Mon-Sat) This popular 2nd-floor place has an excellent-value lunch buffet and pleasantly upscale environs. Six kinds of curry and five versions of pad Thai make this a spicy delight.

Canoe Club PUB
(www.canoeclub.us; 27 S Main St; mains $10-27) Not your typical college nightlife scene, this upscale pub features live music seven nights a week – usually jazz or folk, with a little bit of bluegrass. An excellent menu of charcuterie, sandwiches and organic fare, such as seared salmon with Vermont butternut squash, adds to the appeal.

Murphy's on the Green PUB
(☎603-643-4075; 11 S Main St; mains $8-18; ⌚11am-12:30am) This classic collegiate tavern is where students and faculty meet over pints (it carries more than 10 beers on tap, including local microbrews like Long Trail Ale) and satisfying pub fare. Stained-glass windows and church-pew seating enhance the cozy atmosphere.

☆ Entertainment

Hopkins Center for the Arts PERFORMING ARTS
(☎603-646-2422; www.hop.dartmouth.edu; 2 E Wheelock St) A long way from the big-city lights of New York and Boston, Dartmouth hosts its own entertainment at this outstanding performing arts venue. The season brings everything from movies to live performances by international companies.

WORTH A TRIP

MOOSILAUKE RAVINE LODGE

About 50 miles north of Hanover and 15 miles west of North Woodstock, the **Moosilauke Ravine Lodge** (☎603-764-5858; www.dartmouth.edu/~doc/moosilauke/ravinelodge; 1 Ravine Rd, Warren; dm adult $25-32, child $15-20, linens $8, meals $8-14; ⌚May-Oct) is a rustic lodging owned and maintained by the Dartmouth Outing Club but open to the public. The lodge is set in the midst of wooded hills and pristine countryside, and 30 miles of hiking trails connect it to the summit of Mt Moosilauke and other trailheads. (For information on hiking, regional history and trail maps visit www.mtmoosilauke.com.) Accommodations at Moosilauke are basic bunks and shared baths, but the price is right. Delicious, hearty meals are served family-style in the dining hall.

To reach Moosilauke from Woodstock, take NH 118 west. From Hanover, take NH 10A north to NH 25. Head north on NH 25 and turn right at the junction with NH 118. Moosilauke Ravine Lodge is north of NH 118; follow the signs from the turn-off.

ℹ Information

Hanover Area Chamber of Commerce
(☑603-643-3115; www.hanoverchamber.org; 53 S Main St, Suite 216; ⏱9am-4pm Mon-Fri) On the second floor of the Nugget Building. The chamber of commerce also maintains an information booth on the village green from July to mid-September.

ℹ Getting There & Around

At **Lebanon Municipal Airport** (www.flyleb. com), 6 miles south of Hanover, **Cape Air** (www. capeair.com) links Lebanon with Boston, New York and Philadelphia.

Dartmouth Coach (www.dartmouthcoach. com) operates five daily shuttles from Hanover to Logan International Airport and South Station in Boston (one-way adult/child $38/20, three hours).

Advance Transit (www.advancetransit.com) provides a free service to White River Junction, Lebanon, West Lebanon and Norwich. Bus stops are indicated by a blue-and-yellow AT symbol.

It's a three-hour drive to Hanover from Boston; take I-93 to I-89 to I-91. From Hanover to Burlington, Vermont, it's an additional 2½ hours north via I-89.

LAKES REGION

Vast Winnipesaukee, with an odd mix of natural beauty and commercial tawdriness, is the centerpiece of one of New Hampshire's most popular holiday destinations. Here, forest-shrouded lakes with beautiful sinuous coastlines stretch for hundreds of miles. The roads skirting the shores and connecting the lakeside towns are a riotous spread of small-town Americana: amusement arcades, go-cart tracks, clam shacks, junk-food outlets and boat docks.

Lake Winnipesaukee has 183 miles of coastline, more than 300 islands and excellent salmon fishing. Catch the early-morning mists off the lakes and you'll understand why the Native Americans named it 'Smile of the Great Spirit.' The prettiest stretches are in the southwest corner between Glendale and Alton (on the shoreline Belknap Point Rd), and in the northeast corner between Wolfeboro and Moultonborough (on NH 109). Stop for a swim, a lakeside picnic or a cruise. Children will enjoy prowling the video arcades, bowl-a-dromes and junk-food cafes of Weirs Beach.

Weirs Beach & Around

Called 'Aquedoctan' by its Native American settlers, Weirs Beach takes its English name from the weirs (enclosures for catching fish) that the first European settlers found along the small sand beach. Today Weirs Beach is the honky-tonk heart of Lake Winnipesaukee's childhood amusements, famous for video-game arcades and fried dough. The vacation scene is completed by a lakefront promenade, a small public beach and a dock for small cruising ships. A water park and drive-in theater are also in the vicinity. Away from the din on the waterfront, you will notice evocative Victorian-era architecture – somewhat out of place in this capital of kitsch.

South of Weirs Beach lie Laconia, the largest town in the region but devoid of any real sights, and lake-hugging Gilford, another excellent lodging base.

CRUISING LAKE WINNIPESAUKEE

With 183 miles of coastline, Lake Winnipesaukee is prime cruising territory.

The classic **MS Mount Washington** (☑603-366-5531; www.cruisenh.com; 11 Lakeside Ave, Weirs Beach; adult/child $29/12) steams out of Weirs Beach on relaxing 2½-hour scenic lake cruises twice a day in July, August and late September to mid-October (reduced schedule May, June and early September). Special events include the Sunday champagne brunch cruise and evening sunset, fall foliage and theme cruises ('70s dance fever, lobsterfest etc) running throughout the summer and fall ($40 to $50).

The **MV Sophie C** (adult/child $25/12) is a veritable floating post office. This US mail boat delivers packages and letters to quaint ports and otherwise inaccessible island residents across four to five islands. Between mid-May and early September, 1½-hour runs depart at 11am and 2pm Monday to Saturday from Weirs Beach.

The **MV Doris E** (adult/child from $23/12) offers one- and two-hour cruises of Meredith Bay and northern Lake Winnipesaukee from 10:30am to 7:30pm from late June to August. It leaves from Weirs Beach and also stops at Meredith.

CASTLE IN THE CLOUDS

Perched up high like a king surveying his territory, Castle in the Clouds (www. castleintheclouds.org; NH 171, Moultonborough; adult/child $16/6; ⊘10:30am-4:30pm daily mid-Jun–late Oct, Fri & Sat May–mid-Jun) wows with its stone walls and exposed-timber beams, but it's the views of lakes and valleys that draw the crowds: in autumn, the kaleidoscope of rust, red and yellow beats any postcard. The 5500-acre estate has gardens, ponds and a path leading to a small waterfall. Admission includes the castle and stories about the eccentric millionaire Thomas Plant, who built it. From June to August there are Monday-morning walks and talks on anything from birds to wild food. On Thursdays 'Jazz at Sunset' concerts (admission $10) start at 5:30pm in the carriage house. The Castle is 2 miles east of NH 109.

◉ Sights & Activities

Winnipesaukee Scenic Railroad   TRAIN
(☑603-279-5253; www.hoborr.com; adult/child $15/12) The touristy Scenic Railroad offers one- or two-hour lakeside rides aboard 1920s and '30s train cars departing from Weirs Beach and Meredith. The train travels to Lake Winnipesaukee's southern tip at Alton Bay before making a U-turn. Kids love the ice-cream parlor car; for an extra $2 you can ride in the caboose.

Ellacoya State Park   PARK
(☑603-293-7821; www.nhstateparks.org; adult/child $4/2; ⊘9am-5pm Mon-Fri, 8:30-6pm Sat & Sun May-Oct) Many lakeshore lodgings have water access, but if your place does not, head for Ellacoya State Park, which has a 600ft-wide beach with lovely views across to the Sandwich and Ossipee mountains. This is an excellent place for swimming, fishing and canoeing.

Belknap Mountain   MOUNTAIN
At 2384ft, Belknap Mountain is the highest peak in the Belknap range, with numerous hiking trails. The most direct route to the summit is from the Belknap Carriage Rd in Gilford. From NH 11A, take Cherry Valley Rd and follow the signs for the Belknap Fire Tower.

Three marked trails lead from the parking lot to the summit of Belknap Mountain, a one-hour trek. The white-blazed trail leads to the summit of nearby Piper Mountain (2030ft).

Within the Belknap Mountain State Forest, the Mt Major Summit Trail is a good 2-mile trek up that 1780ft peak. The summit offers spectacular views of all corners of Lake Winnipesaukee. The trailhead is a few miles south of West Alton on NH 11; park just off the road.

🛏 Sleeping

Some of the nicer moderately priced area motels lie on US 3 (Weirs Blvd) between Gilford and Weirs Beach.

Paugus Bay Campground   CAMPGROUND $
(☑603-366-4757; www.paugusbaycampground. com; 96 Hilliard Rd; tent/RV sites $42/45; ⊘mid-May–mid-Oct; ⊞) Off US 3, Paugus has 170 wooded sites overlooking the lake. The campground has a private beach as well as other recreation facilities and regularly holds fun family-friendly events like pancake breakfasts and ice-cream socials.

★**Proctor's**
Lakehouse Cottages   APARTMENTS $$
(☑603-366-5517; www.lakehousecottages.com; NH 3; apt & ste $170-230; ⊗⊞) This family-owned collection of cottages and suites, all with kitchens, is blissful. The more modern suites clustered in the main structure feature porches, while cottages exude old-school New England with original wood walls and rustic (but well-kept) furnishings. All have views of the lake (there's a tiny beach and deck), and every unit comes with its own lakeside grill.

Cozy Inn & Cottages   INN, APARTMENT $$
(☑603-366-4310; www.cozyinn-nh.com; 12 Maple St; r without/with bath $69/99, ste $165-255, cottages $130-235; ⊗) Cozy is the truth here: rooms and suites in the two main houses come with quilts and antiques and have access to a common lounge and kitchen. Typical New Hampshire standalone cottages (one to two rooms) have full kitchens – many include decks overlooking the lake. Also on offer is the sprawling, three-bedroom Tower Street House ($1300 per week), with a huge deck and balcony. Weekly rates

are also available for the other units. Cozy is right up the hill from the promenade.

Ferry Point House B&B
B&B $$

(☑603-524-0087; www.ferrypointhouse.com; 100 Lower Bay Rd, Winnisquam; r incl breakfast $160-195, ste from $270; ☜) Overlooking Lake Winnisquam, this picturesque Victorian B&B has nine cozy and uniquely furnished rooms set with antiques. The rooms range in size from small to spacious; some of them have lake views and one suite has a large Jacuzzi.

Bay Side Inn
INN $$

(☑603-875-5005; www.bayside-inn.com; NH 11D, Alton Bay; r $160-195; ☜) The attractive guest rooms here sit right on the Winnipesaukee waterfront. Guests enjoy a private beach that is excellent for fishing and swimming. Motorboats (with skis) and kayaks are available for rental. Two-bedroom efficiency suites (and weekly rates) are available for longer-term guests.

Lighthouse Inn B&B
B&B $$

(☑603-366-5432; www.lighthouseinnbb.com; 913 Scenic Rd; r incl breakfast $135-210; ☜) Set on five acres of fields and forest, this charming B&B has attractively designed guest rooms, all with fireplaces and homey touches. Complimentary tea is served in the afternoon, and the breakfasts are superb.

KELLERHAUS

Kellerhaus (www.kellerhaus.com; NH 3; sundaes $4-13, breakfasts $10-25; ☺10am-10pm Mon-Fri, 8am-10pm Sat & Sun) is home to the ice-cream sundae of your childhood dreams. They've been making homemade ice cream here for over a century, but it's the over-the-top, self-service ice-cream sundae buffet featuring 12 toppings that packs them in. Chow down under the groovy-kitsch light fixtures next to the jukebox blaring oldies and pray your trousers will fit later. In summer, it serves breakfast on weekend mornings: it's known for its waffles with – you guessed it – unlimited toppings. The rest of the exposed-timber building houses a candy and chocolate shop (also with homemade wares) and gift shops stuffed with every frilly, silly gift item under the sun.

✗ Eating & Drinking

Cruise the promenade for an abundance of heart-attack-inducing snack shops.

Weirs Beach Lobster Pound
SEAFOOD $$

(☑603-366-2255; 70 N Endicott St; mains $11-25; ☺10am-10pm Mon-Fri, 8am-10pm Sat & Sun; ☻) A Weirs Beach institution for more than 40 years, this place serves a broad menu, from staples like clam chowder, lobsters and barbecue to bouillabaisse and maple Dijon salmon. Popular children's menu.

NazBar & Grill
BAR

(www.naswa.com; 1086 Weirs Blvd; mains $12-16; ☺Jun-Sep) This colorful lakeside bar is recommended because it's a scene. This is Weirs Beach, after all. Watch boats pull up to the dock as you sip your cocktail beside – or in – the lake. The menu includes nachos, wraps and burgers.

ℹ Information

Lake Winnipesaukee Home Page (www.winnipesaukee.com) A great independent site with lots of resources, webcams and news.

Lakes Region Chamber of Commerce (☑603-524-5531; www.lakesregionchamber. org; 383 S Main St, Laconia ; ☺8:30am-4:30pm Mon-Fri) The Greater Laconia/Weirs Beach Chamber of Commerce supplies information on the area.

Weirs Beach Information Booth (www.laconia-weirs.org; 513 Weirs Blvd; ☺10am-5pm Fri & Sat Jun-Oct) Useful for same-day accommodations.

ℹ Getting There & Around

Weirs Beach is on the west side of Lake Winnipesaukee. From I-93 take exit 20 (from the south) or 24 (from the north) to US 3.

The **Greater Laconia Transit Agency** (all-day passes adult/child $3/2; ☺Jul-early Sep) runs shuttle trolleys through town to Weirs Beach and Meredith.

Meredith & Around

POP 6700

More upscale than Weirs Beach, Meredith is a lively lakeside town with a long commercial strip stretching along the shore. Its few backstreets are set with attractive colonial and Victorian homes. There are no sights per se, but it's a convenient base for exploring the Lakes Region and offers a slew of accommodations and dining options. US 3, NH 25 and NH 104 converge here.

🛏 Sleeping

Long Island Bridge Campground
CAMPGROUND **$**

(☑ 603-253-6053; www.ucampnh.com; Moulton-boro Neck Rd; tent/RV sites $25/27; ⊙ mid-May–mid-Oct) Located 13 miles northeast of Meredith near Center Harbor, this camping area overlooking the lake has popular tent and RV sites and a private beach. Water-front sites are more expensive, and in July and August there's a three-night minimum stay. To get here, follow NH 25 east for 1.5 miles from Center Harbor, then go south on Moultonborough Neck Rd for 6.5 miles.

White Lake State Park
CAMPGROUND **$**

(☑ 603-323-7350; www.nhstateparks.org; 1632 White Mountain Hwy, Tamworth; tent sites with/without water views $34/26; ⊙ mid-May–mid-Oct) This campsite, 22 miles northeast of Me-redith off NH 16, has 200 tent sites on over 600 acres, plus swimming and hiking trails. The park has some of New Hampshire's fin-est swimming in White Lake, a pristine gla-cial lake. (During the last ice age, glacial ice formed in the site of White Lake. After the ice melted, a depression formed and gradu-ally filled with water.)

Tuckernuck Inn
INN **$$**

(☑ 603-279-5521, 888-858-5521; www.thetuck ernuckinn.com; 25 Red Gate Lane; r incl breakfast $145-168) Tuckernuck has five cozy, quiet rooms (one with a fireplace) with stenciled walls and handmade quilts. From Main St, head inland along Water St, then turn right (uphill) onto Red Gate Lane.

Meredith Inn B&B
INN **$$**

(☑ 603-279-0000; www.meredithinn.com; Main St; r incl breakfast $140-190) This delightful Vic-torian inn has eight rooms outfitted with antique furnishings and luxurious bedding; several rooms also have Jacuzzis, gas fire-places or walk-out bay windows.

🍴 Eating

Waterfall Cafe
CAFE **$**

(Mill Falls Marketplace, 312 Daniel Webster Hwy; mains $8-10; ⊙ 6:30am-1pm) A sweet, friendly space on the top floor of the Mill Falls Mar-ketplace (part of a former working mill), this cafe dishes up mainly breakfast food like omelets, buttermilk pancakes and eggs Ben-edict with lunch items like salads and sand-wiches. Country tables flank a spectacular wall mural depicting Lake Winnipesaukee and the surrounding rolling hills.

Mame's
SEAFOOD, AMERICAN **$$**

(☑ 603-279-4631; 8 Plymouth St; mains $13-28; ⊙ 11:30am-2pm & 5-10pm; 🛜) Tucked inside an 1825 brick mansion on one of Meredith's backstreets, Mame's serves a broad selection of seafood and classic American fare in its pine-floored, antique-filled dining rooms. Steak au poivre, baked stuffed shrimp and lobster crab cakes are top dinner choices, while sandwiches, salads and flat-bread piz-zas round out the lunch menu.

Lago
ITALIAN **$$**

(☑ 603-279-2253; www.thecman.com; 1 US 25; mains $14-25; ⊙ 11:30am-3pm & 5-9pm) Inside the Inn at Bay Point, the stylishly rustic Lago serves oven-roasted salmon with arti-choke salsa, lasagne with roasted eggplant and zucchini, and traditional pastas such as spaghetti carbonara. There's also a wine bar with extensive selections by the glass.

Lakehouse
SEAFOOD, AMERICAN **$$**

(☑ 603-279-5221; cnr US 3 & NH 25, Church Land-ing; mains $18-32; ⊙ 5-10:30pm) At the Inn at Church Landing, this classy restaurant is part of the statewide 'Common Man' fam-ily of restaurants. The wide-ranging menu focuses on seafood and steaks, usually prepared with some creative international twist. Enjoy your dinner on the breezy lake-side deck.

ℹ Information

Meredith Chamber of Commerce (☑ 603-279-6121; www.meredithcc.org; US 3, at Mill St; ⊙ 9am-5pm Mon-Fri year-round, 9am-5pm Sat, 9am-2pm Sun May-Oct)

ℹ Getting There & Away

Concord Coach Lines (Concord Trailways; www.concordcoachlines.com) stops in Meredith at a Mobil gas station (NH 25) en route between Boston and Berlin.

Concord (one way $12, one hour)

Boston South Station (one way $24, 2½ hours)

Logan International Airport (one way $30, 2½ hours)

Wolfeboro

POP 6500

Wolfeboro is an idyllic town where children still gather around the ice cream stand on warm summer nights and a grassy lakeside park draws young and old to weekly con-certs. Named for General Wolfe, who died vanquishing Montcalm on the Plains of Abraham in Quebec, Wolfeboro (founded in 1770) claims to be 'the oldest summer resort in America.' Whether that's true or not, it's certainly the most charming, with pretty lake beaches, intriguing museums, cozy B&Bs and a worthwhile walking trail that runs along several lakes as it leads out of town.

Wolfeboro is on the eastern shore of Lake Winnipesaukee, at the intersection of NH 28 with the lakeside NH 109.

◎ Sights & Activities

Wentworth State Beach   BEACH
(☑ 603-569-3699; NH 109; adult/child $4/2; ☺ dawn-dusk daily mid-Jun–early Sep, dawn-dusk Sat & Sun late May–mid-Jun) If your lodging or campsite does not have access to the lake, head to this small beach on the serene Wentworth Lake. Much smaller but much less developed than Winnipesaukee, Wentworth Lake offers all the same opportunities for swimming, picnicking, hiking and fishing.

Clark House Museum Complex   MUSEUM
(☑ 603-569-4997; 233 S Main St; ☺ 10am-4pm Wed-Fri, to 2pm Sat Jul & Aug) FREE Wolfeboro's eclectic historical museum comprises three historic buildings: the 1778 Clark family farmhouse, an 1805 one-room schoolhouse and a replica of an old firehouse. The buildings contain relevant artifacts (such as fire engines!), furniture and the like. Admission was free when we were there, but a fee was being considered.

Wright Museum   MUSEUM
(☑ 603-569-1212; www.wrightmuseum.org; 77 Center St; adult/child $10/free; ☺ 10am-4pm Mon-Sat, noon-4pm Sun May-Oct, Sun only Feb-Apr, closed Nov-Jan) For a Rosie-the-riveter and baked-apple-pie look at WWII, visit this museum's interactive exhibitions that feature music, documentary clips, posters and other American paraphernalia. There are also uniforms, equipment and military hardware (including a 42-ton Pershing tank), meticulously restored by the museum. The Tuesday-evening summer lecture series (June to mid-September) is a huge draw – speakers range from authors to war refugees.

New Hampshire Boat Museum   MUSEUM
(☑ 603-569-4554; www.nhbm.org; 397 Center St; adult/student $6/4; ☺ 10am-4pm Mon-Sat, noon-4pm Sun late May-early Oct) Wolfeboro is an appropriate place for this boat museum. Nautical types will appreciate the collection of vintage watercraft, motors, photographs and other memorabilia.

Cotton Valley Trail   WALK
Wolfeboro is a pretty town with some good examples of New England's architectural styles, from Georgian through Federal, Greek Revival and Second Empire. It also has this excellent multi-use trail starting near the information office and running for 12 miles along a former railroad. It links the towns of Wolfeboro, Brookfield and Wakefield and passes by two lakes, climbs through Cotton Valley and winds through forests and fields around Brookfield. The Wolfeboro chamber of commerce carries a fantastic map detailing the walk.

🛏 Sleeping

Wolfeboro Campground   CAMPGROUND $
(☑ 603-569-9881; www.wolfeborocampground. com; 61 Haines Hill Rd; tent & RV sites $32; ☺ mid-May–mid-Oct) Off NH 28, and about 4.5 miles north of Wolfeboro's town center, this campground has 50 private, wooded sites.

Tuc' Me Inn B&B   B&B $$
(☑ 603-569-5702; www.tucmeinn.com; 118 N Main St; r incl breakfast $140-170; @ 🛜) This cheery B&B has seven pretty rooms with various charms that include handmade quilts, four-poster beds, cathedral ceilings and private porches. Breakfast at the chef-owned inn is particularly delightful, featuring options like rum-raisin French toast, blueberry pancakes and orange-glazed waffles.

Topsides B&B   B&B $$
(☑ 603-569-3834; www.topsidesbb.com; 209 S Main St; r incl breakfast $120-230; 🛜) Just a

---

CRUISES, DIVING & KAYAKING

The MS *Mount Washington* (p342) stops in Wolfeboro as part of its 2½-hour cruise around Lake Winnipesaukee.

For bigger adventures across and into the deep blue, stop in at Dive Winnipesaukee (☑ 603-569-8080; www.divewinnipesaukee.com; 4 N Main St, Wolfeboro; Kayak $38 per day; ☺ 9am-7pm Mon-Sat, 8am-6pm Sun Jun-Aug, reduced hours Sep-May), which rents kayaks and offers a range of diving courses in the frigid lake.

short walk to the center of town, this handsome B&B has five elegant, classically furnished rooms with wood floors. Several have lake views.

Wolfeboro Inn INN $$$
(✆603-569-3016; www.wolfeboroinn.com; 90 N Main St; r incl breakfast $189-290; 🕸) The town's best-known lodging is right on the lake with a private beach. One of the region's most prestigious resorts since 1812, it has 44 rooms across a main inn and a modern annex. Rooms have modern touches like flat-screen TVs, new beds and contemporary furnishings: it feels less historic but oh-so-luxurious. Facilities include a restaurant and pub, Wolfe's Tavern.

✖ Eating

Wolfboro Diner DINER $
(5 N Main St; mains $5-12; ⊙7am-2pm) One of the best old-school greasy spoons in New Hampshire serves up uncomplicated eggs, pancakes, salads, soups and sandwiches. It's all delivered with love and a smile straight to your vinyl booth, or at the Formica bar (as you perch on swivel stools, of course).

Bailey's Bubble ICE CREAM $
(✆603-569-3612; Railroad Ave; ice cream $2-4) This old-time fave has scooped ice cream for generations of families, and is still the most popular gathering spot in the summer. There are more than 20 different flavors; feel free to mix and match, but the servings are huge!

★Wolfetrap Grill & Rawbar SEAFOOD $$
(www.wolfetrap.com; 19 Bay St; mains $13-34; ⊙11:30am-late) Nantucket meets new Hampshire at this airy raw bar and grill tucked away on Back Bay, an inlet from Lake Winnipesaukee. Inside tables are covered with parchment paper – ready for you to attack and get messy with that shellfish (oysters, clams, shrimp, lobster) – while the deck has loungey chairs overlooking the water. The bar hops until late or, as the bartenders say, 'till the wolf howls'.

On the same property is the summer-only ice cream bar, Wolfetreat, and Wolfecatch, which sells fresh seafood and gourmet takeout like fish fry and pizza.

Wolfe's Tavern AMERICAN $$
(Wolfeboro Inn, 90 N Main St; mains $10-26; ⊙8am-10pm) The bar menu at the rustically colonial Wolfeboro Inn ranges from burgers and grilled meats to pasta and seafood. Terrace tables are set outside in good weather.

Mise En Place FRENCH, AMERICAN $$
(✆603-569-5788; http://miseenplacenh.com; 96 Lehner St; mains $16-29; ⊙5-9pm Tue-Sat) With its minimalist decoration and pleasant patio, this is a wonderful place for dinner. Think buttery steaks and a wide selection of seafood dishes, from citrus-and-lime scallops to risotto with lobster and crab. Reservations advisable.

☆ Entertainment

Wolfeboro Folk LIVE MUSIC
(✆603-522-8697; tickets $15-25) The local organization Wolfeboro Folk attracts some of the country's top folk musicians. In the summer, concerts take place north of Wolfeboro at Moody Mountain Farm (100 Pork Hill Rd, off NH 28). Concerts in spring and fall are held at Tumbledown Farm (295 Governor Wentworth Rd, off NH 109, Brookfield). You can also reserve a pre-concert dinner (from US$15 per person), which features locally sourced, often organic products.

ℹ Information

Wolfeboro Chamber of Commerce Information Booth (✆603-569-2200; www.wolfeboro chamber.com; 32 Central Ave; ⊙10am-5pm Mon-Sat, 11am-2pm Sun) Located inside the old train station.

ℹ Getting There & Away

Wolfeboro is on the east side of Lake Winnipesaukee. From I-93, take US 3 to its intersection with NH 11. Follow this road south as it skirts the lake. Pick up NH 28 in Alton and head north.

Squam Lake

Northwest of Lake Winnipesaukee, Squam Lake is more tranquil, more tasteful and more pristine than its big sister. It is also less accessible, lacking any public beaches. Nonetheless, if you choose your lodging carefully, you can enjoy Squam Lake's natural wonders, just like Katherine Hepburn and Henry Fonda did in the 1981 film *On Golden Pond*. With 67 miles of shoreline and 67 islands, there are plenty of opportunities for fishing, kayaking and swimming.

Holderness is the area's main town, at the southwest corner of Squam Lake. Little Squam Lake is a much smaller branch further southwest.

⊙ Sights & Activities

Squam Lakes Natural Science Center
SCIENCE CENTER

(☑603-968-7194; www.nhnature.org; NH 113, Holderness; adult/child $15/10, boat tours adult/child $21/17; ⊙9:30am-4:30pm May-Oct) To get up close and personal with the wildlife in the Lakes Region, visit the Squam Lakes Natural Science Center. Four nature paths weave through the woods and around the marsh. The highlight is the Gephart Trail, leading past trailside enclosures that are home to various creatures including bobcat, fisher (a kind of marten), mountain lion and a bald eagle.

The best boat tours of Squam Lake are run by the center; among other tours, it offers pontoon-boat cruises that observe the loons and eagles, visit sites from *On Golden Pond* or watch the sun set over the lake. Combination tickets for the center and tour are available.

The nearby Kirkwood Gardens, featuring many species of New England native shrubs and flowers, are specially designed to attract birds and butterflies.

Squam Lakes Camp Resort
BOATING

(☑603-968-7227; www.squamlakesresort.com; 1002 US 3, Holderness; canoes per day $58, pontoon boats per day $130-300) Rents out 16ft canoes and pontoon boats of varying sizes.

⊨ Sleeping & Eating

Squam Lake Inn
INN $$

(☑603-968-4417; www.squamlakeinn.com; cnr Shepard Hill Rd & US 3, Holderness; r incl breakfast $170-210; ℗@🐾) This century-old Victorian farmhouse has eight rooms, all decorated in vintage New England style – quilts on the beds, antique furnishings and a local 'Lakes' theme – with modern touches like iPod docking stations. Higher-priced rooms include gas fireplaces and/or stoves. A mahogany deck and wraparound porch overlook woodsy grounds.

Cottage Place on Squam Lake
COTTAGES $$

(☑603-968-7116; www.cottageplaceonsquam.com; US 3, Holderness; r $110, cottages $95-225; 🐾) The cozy, comfortable Cottage Place fronts Squam Lake, offering a private beach, a swimming raft and docking space for boats. There is a wide variety of accommodations, including standard rooms and lakefront cottages; all come with a kitchen, many with wood-burning fireplaces. Weekly rentals are encouraged in summer.

★ Manor on Golden Pond
B&B $$$

(☑603-968-3348; www.manorongoldenpond.com; US 3, Holderness; r incl breakfast $285-490, cottages $380; ⊙mid-May–mid-Oct; 🐾🐾) This luxurious B&B is perched on Shepard Hill, overlooking serene Squam Lake. Elegant rooms (some with fireplaces and Jacuzzis), gourmet breakfasts and a lovely private beach make this one of the lake region's finest retreats. Extra perks include clay tennis courts, a full-service spa and an excellent dining room. Children under 12 are not welcome here.

Holderness General Store
SANDWICHES $

(☑603-968-3446; US 3, Holderness; meals $7-11; ⊙7am-9pm Mon-Fri, to 10pm Sat & Sun) This gourmet grocery store and bakery serves excellent breakfast and lunch sandwiches, local homemade fudge, and other goodies. You'll also find wines, sake, marinated meats and veggies (ready for grilling), pasta salads and marvelous scones.

Walter's Basin
AMERICAN $$$

(☑603-968-4412; US 3, Holderness; mains $15-35; ⊙11:30am-11pm) Lake trippers are encouraged to dock their boats and come on in for a meal at this casual waterfront spot. Located on Little Squam Lake near the bridge, the friendly restaurant features stuffed haddock, turkey dinner, lobster macaroni and cheese and other comfort fare.

ⓘ Information

There is no tourist information office per se, but the Squam Lakes Area **Chamber of Commerce** (www.squamlakeschamber.com) has basic information and a regional information leaflet available for download.

ⓘ Getting There & Away

US 3 follows the south shore of Squam Lake to Holderness. The road then turns west, skirting the north shore of Little Squam Lake before rejoining I-93 at Ashland.

Concord Coach Lines (Concord Trailways; www.concordcoachlines.com) stops in Center Harbor, on the east side of Squam Lake, en route from Boston to Berlin. The bus stop is at Village Car Wash & Laundromat, on US 25 in Center Harbor. Useful routes:

Concord (one way $13, one hour)

Boston South Station (one way $26, 2½ hours)

Logan International Airport (one way $30, 2½ hours)

I PICKED THAT BERRY

Sun-warmed raspberries, plump blueberries, oversize pumpkins – if you want to pick it, New Hampshire probably has it. Pick-your-own farms dot the state, and it's fun and delicious for all ages. Some of our favorites include Monadnock Berries (www.monadnockberries.com; Troy), a pretty farm with blueberries, raspberries, blackberries, gooseberries and currants to pick, and Butternut Farm (www.butternutfarm.net; Farmington), where you can pick apples, peaches, plums, nectarines, pumpkins and – of course – blueberries.

The sheer number of pick-your-own farms in New Hampshire is mind-boggling: chances are, there's a location near you. Pick Your Own (www.pickyourown.org/NH.htm) lists farms throughout the country and includes a section on New Hampshire; the website is unwieldy but generally up to date. Better yet, ask a local or your innkeeper for the closest and best in your area. Offerings vary by the season and many are only open May to October, so be sure to call ahead.

WHITE MOUNTAIN REGION

Covering one quarter of New Hampshire (and part of Maine), the vast White Mountains area is a spectacular region of soaring peaks and lush valleys, and contains New England's most rugged mountains. There are numerous activities on offer, including hiking, camping, skiing and canoeing. Much of the area – 780,000 acres – is designated as the White Mountain National Forest (WMNF), thus protecting it from overdevelopment and guaranteeing its wondrous natural beauty for years to come. Keep in mind, however, that this place is popular: six million visitors flock here every year, making it the nation's second-most-visited park after the Great Smoky Mountains.

Parking at National Forest trailheads costs $3/5/20 per day/week/season. Purchase parking permits at any of the visitors centers in the area.

North Woodstock & Around

POP 1100

North Woodstock and its neighboring settlement Lincoln gather a mix of adventure seekers and drive-by sightseers en route to the Kancamagus Hwy (NH 112). North Woodstock has a busy but small-town feel with battered motels and diners lining the main street and a gurgling river running parallel to it. Nearby Lincoln has less charm, but serves as the starting point for the entertaining Hobo Railroad and two family-friendly favorites – a zip line across the Barron Mountain and an aerial park.

Unless otherwise indicated, listings are in North Woodstock.

◉ Sights & Activities

Lost River Gorge & Boulder Caves CAVES, GORGE
(☑603-745-8031; www.findlostriver.com; NH 112, Kinsman Notch; adult/child $16/12, lantern tours per person $22; ⊙9am-5pm mid-May–late Oct) Adventurous kids will enjoy exploring the lost river gorge and boulder caves, a network of caverns and crevices formed by glaciers millions of years ago. Each cave has its own title and story, from the Bear Crawl to the Dungeon. Climbing, crawling and squeezing is required. From mid-June to early September, Saturday evenings also feature guided 1½-hour lantern tours, which culminate with a marshmallow and s'mores treat around a fire pit. This place is west of North Woodstock on NH 112.

Clark's Trading Post & The Whale's Tale AMUSEMENT PARK
(☑603-745-8913; www.clarkstradingpost.com; US 3, Lincoln; adult/3-5yr $19/8; ⊙9:30am-6pm Jun–mid-Oct, reduced hours May & Mon-Fri Sep & Oct) Just north of North Woodstock on US 3, Clark's has been a traditional family stop since 1928. If the children are bored from too much time in the car, Clark's has an old-fashioned photo parlor, water-bumper boats, a magic house and a Segway park (yup, you hop on a Segway and tool through the woods). Or take an excursion on a narrow-gauge steam locomotive. The featured attraction is the bear show, where a team of North American black bears does various tricks.

10 km
6 miles

MAINE

VERMONT

White Mountain National Forest

Bethel
Gilead
Shelburne
Berlin (5mi);
Dixville Notch (46mi)
Gorham
Jefferson
Whitefield
Littleton
Lisbon
St Johnsbury
Woodsville
North Haverhill
Bradford
Lyme
Hanover (10mi)
Warren
Campton
North Sandwich
Center Sandwich
West Ossipee
Albany
Conway
Center Conway
North Conway
Fryeburg
Kearsarge North (3268ft)
Mt Cranmore
Covered Bridge Campground
Intervale
Jackson
Glen
Bartlett
Black Mtn Ski Area
Black Mtn (3203ft)
Wildcat Mtn (4422ft)
Wildcat Mtn Ski Area
Pinkham Notch Camp
Pinkham Notch
Mt Moriah (4047ft)
Mt Washington (6288ft)
Mt Washington Auto Rd (toll)
Tuckerman Ravine
Cog Railway
Mt Jefferson (5711ft)
Fabyan
Bretton Woods
Twin Mountain
Bethlehem
Franconia
Sugar Hill Village
Bishop Farm
Fransted Family Campground
Franconia Notch State Park
Lost River Valley
Cannon Mtn
Lafayette Place Campground
Mt Lincoln (5089ft)
Mt Flume (4326ft)
Loon Mtn (3050ft)
Lincoln
North Woodstock
White Mountains
Moosilauke Ravine Lodge
Stinson Lake
White Mountain National Forest
Crawford Notch State Park
Saco Rv
Mt Carrigain (4678ft)
Kancamagus Hwy
Hancock Campground
Mt Kancamagus (3726ft)
Mt Tecumseh (4004ft)
Tripoli Rd
Waterville Valley
Passaconaway
Passaconaway Campground
Jigger Johnson Campground
Mt Tripyramid (4140ft)
Mt Chocorua (3475ft)
Sandwich Mtn (3993ft)
Echo Lake State Park
Conway Lake
Silver Lake
Saco Ry
Connecticut River
Forest Lake
Lake Tarleton
Pemigewasset River
Appalachian Trail
Concord (48mi); Boston (114mi)

Hobo Railroad
TRAIN

(☑603-745-2135; www.hoborr.com; Kancamagus Hwy, Lincoln; adult/child $15/10; ⊗mid-Jun–Oct, reduced service Nov-early Jun) The Hobo is a scenic 1½-hour train ride from Lincoln south to Woodstock. Seasonal themes include foliage trains and Santa trains that follow the same route, and summers feature Sunday storybook trips, where characters like Winnie-the-Pooh and Curious George hop aboard and entertain during the ride.

Café Lafayette
TRAIN

(☑603-745-3500; www.nhdinnertrain.com; NH 112; adult/child from $79/59; ⊗late May–late Oct) Travel in the 1st-class dining car of the 1924 Pullman-Standard Victorian Coach while enjoying a five-course meal. The dining car has been completely and beautifully restored and decorated with dark wood, stained glass and brass fixtures. The train rides along a spur of the Boston and Maine railroad for two hours.

Alpine Adventure
ADVENTURE PARK

(☑603-745-9911; www.alpinezipline.com; 41 Main St, Lincoln; zips $92; ⊗9am-4pm) Alpine Adventures offers two types of zip-line fun: Thrillsville is an aerial park where you can clamber and fly (you're attached by a harness) over a hodgepodge of specially constructed bridges, cargo nets, rope ladders, zip lines, giant swings, treehouses and a freefall device. More high-speed thrills await at the Barron Mountain zip-line course (10 minutes from Lincoln), a 2000ft course with seven platforms ranging between 15ft and 65ft high. The whole trip lasts two hours including transportation there and back.

👉 Tours

Pemi Valley Excursions
WILDLIFE-WATCHING

(☑603-745-2744; www.moosetoursnh.com; NH 112, Lincoln; tours adult/child $25/18) Trips include a 'twilight tour,' which tracks moose and other wildlife (with a 95% success rate) in a 33-passenger bus from June to October.

🛏 Sleeping

There are USFS campgrounds along the Kancamagus Hwy east of Lincoln.

Franconia Notch Motel
MOTEL $

(☑603-745-2229, 800-323-7829; www.franconia notch.com; 572 US 3, Lincoln; r $55-85, cottages $65-90) This tidy place has 18 simple rooms and cottages facing the Pemigewasset River. It's friendly, family-run and convenient to area hikes, and the grounds include picnic tables and grills for guest use.

EXPLORING THE WHITE MOUNTAINS

With 1200 miles of hiking trails (including 100 miles of the Appalachian Trail) and 48 peaks over 4000ft across 786,000 acres, the White Mountains' inspiring landscape wows all the senses. It's brimming with scintillating hikes, scenic drives and miles of ski slopes and cross-country trails.

Hiking

Franconia Notch State Park (p354) has many trailheads as well as spectacular sights such as the Flume Gorge and an aerial tramway from the park that goes up Cannon Mountain. Additionally, check out Moosilauke Ravine, Crawford Notch State Park (p363), Mt Washington (www.mountwashington.com) and Pinkham Notch (p364) for additional hiking highlights.

The Kancamagus Hwy (p353), a scenic road set along a wandering river, is another popular place for hiking. For more info on hikes, pick up the excellent *White Mountain Guide* ($25.95) published by the Appalachian Mountain Club (www.outdoors.org). It's available online and in some New Hampshire bookstores.

Hit the Slopes

Winter sports enthusiasts can hit the slopes at a number of resorts, including the downhill runs at Cannon Mountain (p355), near Franconia Notch State Park, or Loon Mountain (p353), just off the Kancamagus Hwy. Additional options include Black Mountain (p362), Attitash (p362), Mt Washington Resort (p364), Wildcat Mountain (p365) and Mt Cranmore (p359). Wherever you go, be prepared for fierce winds and strong storms that can appear out of nowhere.

DON'T MISS

A SUMMER RETREAT

Educational nonprofit **World Fellowship Center** (☑603-447-2280; www.worldfellowship. org; 368 Drake Hill Rd, Albany; tent sites incl meals from $46, s/d with shared bathroom incl meals from $51/55; ⊙ Jun-Sep)✦ labels itself a 'camp with a social conscience.' We agree. Home to campsites, five simple lodges, communal buildings and a tiny farm, it's both an affordable lodging choice and a place to learn, take a workshop, exercise, relax and commune with nature.

Daily offerings like yoga, nature walks, lectures and workshops (on topics like operating a sustainable business, writing or storytelling) give you the option to meet fellow guests, but it's perfectly fine to take part in none and just enjoy the grounds, which include the tranquil Whitton Pond (rowboats and canoes available), nature trails, a basketball and volleyball court, and a Ping Pong table. Summer evenings often feature live music, and the center offers volunteer working-holiday options. Meals, served at long, communal tables, are mainly organic and vegetarian (much of the produce comes from the on-site farm, and they grind their own organic wheat for the homemade bread); lunch and dinner is often themed, like Sunday's midday New England turkey and the Thursday-night cookout. Weekly rates are available.

Riverbank Motel & Cottages MOTEL $

(☑603-745-3374, 800-633-5624; www.riverbank motel.com; NH 3A; r/cottages from $62/68; 🛜 ⊠) In a peaceful riverside setting just outside of North Woodstock, this inexpensive option has 11 motel rooms and four cottages. Accommodations are basic, though all but the cheapest rooms have small kitchen units. The cabins also have fireplaces.

Lost River Valley Campground CAMPGROUND $

(☑603-745-8321, 800-370-5678; www.lostriver. com; NH 112; tent/RV sites from $27/37, cabins $58-69; ⊙mid-May–mid-Oct) This excellent 200-acre campground (which also contains rustic honest-to-goodness log cabins with electricity, beds and ceiling fans) is on the site of a turn-of-the-century lumber mill, and the water wheel still churns. Many of the 125 sites are on the river, which also offers fishing and hiking possibilities. There's a two-night minimum stay May to late June and a three-night minimum stay late June to early September. To get there, take exit 32 off I-93 and turn right onto NH 112.

Wilderness Inn B&B $$

(☑603-745-3890; www.thewildernessinn.com; cnr US 3 & NH 112; r incl breakfast $95-185, cottage from $140; 🛜) This former lumber mill owner's house has seven lovely guest rooms, ranging from small to suite-size, as well as a family-size cottage overlooking Lost River. Each is individually decorated with stenciled walls and cozy furnishings, and all but one has wood floors. Breakfasts are marvelous and served on the sun porch when it's warm.

Woodstock Inn INN $$

(☑603-745-3951; www.woodstockinnnh.com; US 3; r incl breakfast with shared/private bath from $78/120; 🛜) This Victorian country inn is North Woodstock's centerpiece. It has 33 individually appointed rooms across five separate buildings (three in a cluster, two across the street), each with modern amenities but old-fashioned style. The on-site upscale restaurant, Woodstock Station & Microbrewery, has outdoor seating on the lovely flower-filled patio.

Woodward's Resort HOTEL $$

(☑603-745-8141, 800-635-8968; www.woodward sresort.com; US 3; r $99-139, cottages $189-259; 🛜 ⊠) Woodward's has lovely landscaped grounds (with a duck and trout pond) and lots of facilities, including a cocktail bar, a cozy lounge with a fireplace, a sauna, a hot tub and a tennis court. Rooms are spacious, modern and attractive.

✗ Eating & Drinking

Peg's Restaurant AMERICAN $

(☑603-745-2740; Main St; mains $8-13; ⊙5:30am-4pm Jul-Oct, to 2pm Nov-Jun) Locals flock to this no-frills eatery for hearty early breakfasts and late-lunch sandwiches, such as roast turkey and meat loaf with gravy. Lunch specials, kids specials and the infamous 'Hungry Man's Special' make everyone feel pretty special.

Woodstock Inn Station & Brewery PUB $$

(☑603-745-3951; US 3; mains $12-28; ⊙11:30am-10pm) Formerly a railroad station, this eatery tries to be everything to everyone. In the end, with more than 150 items, it can probably satisfy just about any food craving, but the pasta, sandwiches and burgers are the most interesting. The beer-sodden rear tavern here is one of the most happening places in this neck of the woods.

Truant's Tavern PUB **$$**
(96 Main St; mains $12-25; ⊙ 11.30am-10pm) This popular place has live music, pool tables and darts, and serves hearty pub fare like sandwiches, burgers, and fish-and-chips.

☆ Entertainment

Papermill Theatre THEATER
(☑ 603-745-2141; www.papermilltheatre.org; NH 112, Inn Season Resorts, Lincoln; tickets adult/child $29/20) This local theater stages musicals and plays, as well as regular performances of children's theater throughout the summer.

❶ Information

Lincoln/Woodstock Chamber of Commerce
(☑ 603-745-6621; www.lincolnwoodstock .com; Main St/NH 112, Lincoln; ⊙ 9am-5pm Mon-Fri) Located above the Laconia Savings Bank.

❶ Getting There & Away

It's about 3¼ hours (140 miles) from Boston to Lincoln via I-93.

Concord Coach Lines (Concord Trailways; www.concordcoachlines.com) runs buses between Boston and Littleton; the local stop is **Munce's Konvenience/Shell gas station** (☑ 603-745-3195; 36 Main St, Lincoln). Destinations include **Concord** (one way $16, 1½ hours), **Boston South Station** (one way $28, three hours) and **Logan International Airport** (one way $34, three hours)

Kancamagus Highway

The winding Kancamagus Hwy (NH 112) between Lincoln and Conway runs right through the WMNF and over Kancamagus Pass (2868ft). Unspoiled by commercial development, the paved road offers easy access to USFS campgrounds, hiking trails and fantastic scenery.

Though the Kancamagus Hwy was paved only in 1964, its name dates to the 17th century. The route is named for Chief Kancamagus ('The Fearless One'). In about 1684 Kancamagus assumed the powers of *sagamon* (leader) of the Penacook Native

American tribe. He was the final *sagamon*, succeeding his grandfather, the great Passaconaway, and his uncle Wonalancet. Kancamagus tried to maintain peace between the indigenous peoples and European explorers and settlers, but the newcomers pushed his patience past breaking point. He finally resorted to battle to rid the region of Europeans, but in 1691 he and his followers were forced to escape northward.

The Kancamagus Hwy (NH 112) runs for 35 miles from Lincoln to Conway. Since there are no services along the highway, the towns are convenient for picking up picnic supplies before hitting the trails.

🏃 Activities

The WMNF is laced with excellent hiking trails of varying difficulty. For detailed trail-by-trail information, stop at any of the WMNF ranger stations or the White Mountains Attractions Association.

Lincoln Woods Trail HIKING
The trailhead for this 2.9-mile, 1157ft-elevation trail is on the Kancamagus Hwy, 5 miles east of I-93. Among the easiest and most popular in the forest, the trail ends at the Pemigewasset Wilderness Boundary (elevation 1450ft).

Wilderness Trail HIKING
The easy Wilderness Trail begins where the Lincoln Woods Trail ends, at Pemigewasset

DON'T MISS

LOON MOUNTAIN

For winter fun **Loon Mountain** (☑ 603-745-8111; www.loonmtn.com; Kancamagus Hwy, Lincoln; tubing walk-up/lift $10/16, gondola adult/child $17/11, lift ticket adult/child 13-18/child 6-12 & seniors $79/69/59; ⊙ tubing 6-9:40pm Wed-Sun, gondola 9:30am-5:30pm late Jun–mid-Oct) offers 20 miles of trails crisscrossing the 3050ft peak, which has a 2100ft vertical drop. Skis and snowboards are available for rental. At night the trails open up for **tubing**.

The mountain offers its fair share of summer activities as well. A **gondola** rides to the summit, and the facility also offers mountain-bike rentals (adult/child $32/30 per day), a climbing wall ($8), a zip line ($25) and horseback riding (from $50).

Wilderness Boundary, and it continues for 6 miles to Stillwater Junction (elevation 2060ft). From there you can follow the Cedar Brook and Hancock Notch Trails to return to the Kancamagus Hwy at a point on the road that is some miles east of the Lincoln Woods trailhead parking lot.

🛏 Sleeping

Village of Loon Mountain   RESORT **$$**
(☎ 800-228-2968, 603-745-3401; www.villageof loon.com; Kancamagus Hwy, Lincoln; ste $99-219, apt $125-335; 🕱🖳) This lodge has basic, modern suites that sleep at least four people, as well as condos right on the mountainside, so you can ski out the door to the chair lift. Recreational facilities are unlimited here, with several pools and hot tubs, tennis courts, horseback riding, hiking and biking on offer.

Econo Lodge at Loon   MOTEL **$$**
(☎ 603-745-3661, 800-762-7275; www.econo lodgeloon.com; US 3, Loon Mountain; r incl breakfast $85-160, cottages $130-260; 🕱🖳) This large, nicely outfitted lodge caters to skiers and snowmobilers, who appreciate the sauna, Jacuzzi and spa. Fifty-three rooms – many with kitchenettes – offer decent value, while cottages add space and coziness to the equation.

ⓘ Information

Conway Village Chamber of Commerce Info Booth (☎ 603-447-2639; www.conway chamber.com; 250 Main St/NH 16, Conway; ⊙ 9am-5pm Apr-Oct) The eastern gateway to the scenic highway.

White Mountains Attractions Association (☎ 603-745-8720; www.visitwhitemountains. com; 200 Kancamagus Hwy; ⊙ 8:30am-5pm Apr-Oct) You can pick up detailed hiking brochures for area trails here. It's about a mile west of Conway.

Franconia Notch State Park

Franconia Notch, a narrow gorge shaped over the eons by a wild stream cutting through craggy granite, is a dramatic mountain pass. This was long the residence of the infamous Old Man of the Mountain, a natural rock formation that became the symbol of the Granite State. Sadly, the Old Man collapsed in 2003, which does not stop tourists from coming to see the featureless cliff that remains.

Despite the Old Man's absence, the attractions of Franconia Notch are many, from the dramatic hike down the Flume Gorge to the fantastic views of the Presidentials.

The most scenic parts of the notch are protected by the narrow Franconia Notch State Park. Reduced to two lanes, I-93 (renamed the Franconia Notch Parkway) squeezes through the gorge.

DON'T MISS

CAMPING ON THE KANCAMAGUS

The heavily wooded US Foresty Service (USFS) campgrounds east of Lincoln along the Kancamagus Hwy are primitive sites (mostly with pit toilets only) but are in high demand in the warm months: if you're up for camping, this is one of the best ways to experience the Kanc. It is not possible at every campground, but **advance reservations** (☎ 877-444-6777; www.reserveusa.com) are highly recommended. Otherwise, arrive early, especially on weekends.

Hancock Campground (☎ 603-744-9165; campsites $22) Lies 4 miles east of Lincoln; 56 sites near the Pemigewasset River and the Wilderness Trail.

Passaconaway Campground (☎ 603-477-5448; campsites $20; ⊙ mid-May–Oct) Situated 12 miles west of Conway; 33 sites on the Swift River, which is good for fishing.

Jigger Johnson Campground (☎ 603-477-5448; campsites $22; ⊙ late May-Oct) Located 10 miles west of Conway; 74 sites, flush toilets and pay hot showers. Nature lectures on summer weekends.

Covered Bridge Campground (☎ 845-439-5093; www.coveredbridgecampsite.com; tent/RV sites from $29/39; ⊙ mid-May–Oct) Set 6 miles west of Conway; 49 sites, some of which can be reserved. The site is vast and includes a small farm with donkeys, turkeys and goats. And yes, you do cross the Albany Covered Bridge to reach the campground.

THE SOUL OF AN OLD MAN

Geologists estimate that the Old Man of the Mountain had gazed out over Profile Lake for more than 12,000 years. That's why it was such a shock when, on May 3, 2003, he crumbled down the mountainside.

The collapse of the Old Man of the Mountain was no surprise to those in the know. In fact, the Appalachian Mountain Club had reported on his precarious state as early as 1872. Everybody recognized that it wouldn't do to have the stoic symbol of New Hampshire drop off the side of the mountain, so attempts to anchor the top-heavy face began in 1916 and continued for the next four generations. But Mother Nature could not be thwarted. Every year snow and rain were driven into the cracks and caverns. As temperatures dropped the water expanded, exacerbating the cracks. The gradual process of wear and tear finally upset the balance and the Old Man crumbled.

Following his destruction, some have claimed the state will soon find a 'new' Old Man to replace him, and contenders sprout up every few months, but for purists this is out of the question. New Hampshire residents seem determined not to forget the iconic old sourpuss. His visage still adorns their license plates – and may long remain in their hearts. The first phase of the Old Man Memorial opened in 2013.

⊙ Sights

Cannon Mountain

Aerial Tramway CABLE CAR
(☏603-823-8800; www.cannonmt.com; I-93, exit 34B; round-trip adult/child $15/12; ⊙9am-5pm late May–mid-Oct; ⛄) This tram shoots up the side of Cannon Mountain, offering a breathtaking view of Franconia Notch. In 1938 the first passenger aerial tramway in North America was installed on this slope. It was replaced in 1980 by the current, larger cable car, capable of carrying 80 passengers up to the summit of Cannon Mountain in five minutes – a 2022ft, 1-mile ride. You can also hike up the mountain and take the tramway down.

Old Man Historic Site HISTORIC SITE
(I-93 exit 34B) In the wake of the Old Man's collapse in 2003, New Hampshire struggled over the future of this historic site that once held the symbol of the state. Proposals were debated until 2007, when The Old Man of the Mountain memorial design was finally unveiled. The first phase of memorial, granite benches and stones engraved with people's memories of the Old Man, opened in 2013. Future updates will include interpretive signs detailing the Old Man's history and importance in the area.

Echo Lake BEACH
(☏603-823-8800; I-93, exit 34C; adult/child $4/2; ⊙10am-5:30pm) Despite its proximity to the highway, this little lake at the foot of Cannon Mountain is a pleasant place to pass an afternoon swimming, kayaking or canoeing (rentals from $11 per hour) in the crystal-clear waters. And many people do: the small beach gets packed, especially on weekends.

🏃 Activities

The park has good hiking trails; most are relatively short, but some may be steep.

Cannon Mountain Ski Area SKIING
(☏603-823-7771; www.cannonmt.com; I-93 exit 2; adult/child & senior Mon-Fri $47/26, Sat & Sun $56/32) The slopes at Cannon Mountain enjoy a prime geographic position to receive and retain the 150in of snow that falls annually. It has 55 runs (nine novice, 26 intermediate and 20 expert) making up 22 miles of trails (its longest run is 2.3 miles), with a vertical drop of 2146ft. The slopes are equipped with an aerial tramway, three triple and two quad chairlifts, two rope tows and a wonder carpet (a moving walkway for beginners). Other facilities include three cafeterias, a nursery, a ski school and a ski shop with rental equipment.

Recreation Trail CYCLING
For a casual walk or bike ride, you can't do better than head out to this 8-mile paved trail that wends its way along the Pemigewasset River and through the notch. Bikes are available for rental at the Franconia Sports Shop (p357). Pick up the trail in front of the Flume Gorge Visitor Center.

Bald Mountain & Artists Bluff Trail HIKING
Just north of Echo Lake, off NH 18, this 1.5-mile loop skirts the summit of Bald Mountain

DON'T MISS

FLUME GORGE & THE BASIN

To see this natural wonder, take the 2-mile self-guided nature walk that includes the 800ft boardwalk through the **Flume** (www.flumegorge.com; adult/child $14/11; ⊙9am-5pm May-Oct), a natural 12ft- to 20ft-wide cleft in the granite bedrock. The granite walls tower 70ft to 90ft above you, with moss and plants growing from precarious niches and crevices. Signs along the way explain how nature formed this natural phenomenon. A nearby covered bridge is thought to be one of the oldest in the state, erected perhaps as early as the 1820s.

The **Basin** is a huge glacial pothole, 20ft in diameter, that was carved deep into the granite 15,000 years ago by the action of falling water and swirling stones. It offers a nice (short) walk and a cool spot to ponder one of nature's minor wonders.

(2320ft) and Artists Bluff (2368ft), with short spur trails to the summits.

Kinsman Falls   HIKING
On the Cascade Brook, these falls are a short half-mile hike from the Basin via the Basin Cascade Trail.

Lonesome Lake Trail   HIKING
Departing from Lafayette Place and its campground, this trail climbs 1000ft in 1½ miles to Lonesome Lake. Various spur trails lead further up to several summits on the Cannon Balls and Cannon Mountain (3700ft to 4180ft) and south to the Basin.

Mt Pemigewasset Trail   HIKING
This trail begins at the Flume Visitor Center and climbs for 1.4 miles to the 2557ft summit of Mt Pemigewasset (Indian Head), offering excellent views. Return by the same trail or the Indian Head Trail, which joins US 3 after 1 mile. From there, it's a 1-mile walk north to the Flume Visitor Center.

🛏 Sleeping

Lafayette Place Campground   CAMPGROUND **$**
(☑603-271-3628; www.reserveamerica.com; campsites $21; ⊙mid-May–early Oct) This popular campground has 97 wooded tent sites that are in heavy demand in summer. Reservations are accepted for 88 of the sites. For

the others, arrive early in the day and hope for the best. Many of the state park's hiking trails start here.

❶ Information

Services are available in Lincoln and North Woodstock to the south and in Franconia and Littleton further north.

There are two branches of the **Franconia Notch Visitor Center** (☑603-745-8391; www.franconianotchstatepark.com; I-93, exit 34A).

Franconia Town & Around
POP 3500

A few miles north of the notch via I-93, Franconia is a tranquil town with splendid mountain views and a poetic attraction: Robert Frost's farm. As a rule, the further the distance from the highway, the more picturesque and pristine the destination. Accordingly, the little town of **Bethlehem** (north along NH 142) and the tiny village of **Sugar Hill** (a few miles west along tranquil NH 117) are delightful. All are perfect for whiling away an afternoon driving down country roads, poking into antique shops, browsing farm stands and chatting up the locals at divey diners.

◎ Sights & Activities

★**Frost Place**   HISTORIC SITE
(☑603-823-5510; www.frostplace.org; 158 Ridge Rd, Franconia; adult/child $5/3; ⊙1-5pm Sat & Sun late May-Jun, 1-5pm Wed-Mon Jul–mid-Oct) Robert Frost (1874–1963) was America's most renowned and best-loved poet in the mid-20th century. For several years he lived with his wife and children on a farm near Franconia, now known as the Frost Place. Many of his best and most famous poems describe life on this farm and the scenery surrounding it, including 'The Road Not Taken' and 'Stopping by Woods on a Snowy Evening,' and the years spent here were some of the most productive and inspired of his life. The farmhouse has been kept as faithful to the period as possible, with numerous exhibits of Frost memorabilia.

In the forest behind the house there is a half-mile nature trail. Frost's poems are mounted on plaques in sites appropriate to the things the poems describe, and in several places the plaques have been erected at the exact spots where Frost was inspired to compose the poems. To find Frost's farm, follow NH 116 south from Franconia. After exactly a mile, turn right onto Bickford Hill Rd, then left onto unpaved Ridge Rd. It's a short distance along on the right.

Sugar Hill Sampler   MUSEUM
(☏ 603-823-8478; www.sugarhillsampler.com; NH 117, Sugar Hill Village; ⊙ 9:30am-5pm Sat & Sun mid-Apr–mid-May, 9:30am-5pm mid-May–Oct, 10am-4pm Nov-Dec, closed Jan–mid-Apr) `FREE` It all started with a collection of heirlooms amassed by the Aldrich family over the many years they have lived in Sugar Hill Village. These days, this collection has expanded to include all sorts of local memorabilia dating from 1780, all housed in an old barn built by the Aldrich ancestors themselves. There's also a store selling homemade arts and crafts and edibles.

Franconia Sports Shop   BICYCLE RENTAL
(☏ 603-823-5241; www.franconiasports.com; Main St, Franconia; road/mountain bikes per day $20/28) Offers bike rental.

🛏 Sleeping

Pinestead Farm Lodge   LODGE $
(☏ 603-823-8121; www.pinesteadfarmlodge.com; 2059 Easton Rd/NH 116, Franconia; r/apt from $65/145) This is a rarity in Franconia: a working farm. The family here rents clean, simple rooms in several apartments with shared bathroom and communal kitchen/ sitting rooms. You can also rent entire apartments. Hosts Bob and Kathleen Sherburn, whose family has owned the property since 1899, have an assortment of cattle, chickens, ducks and horses. If you come in March or April, you can watch maple sugaring.

Fransted Family Campground   CAMPGROUND $
(☏ 603-823-5675; www.franstedcampground. com; NH 18, Franconia; tent/RV sites from $36/43; ⊙ May–mid-Oct) Two miles northwest of Franconia Notch State Park, this wooded campground caters more to tenters (70 sites) than RVers (40 sites). Many sites are along a stream.

★ Sugar Hill Inn   INN $$
(☏ 800-548-4748, 603-823-5621; www.sugar hillinn.com; NH 117, Sugar Hill Village; r/ste incl breakfast from $135/215; ☎) This restored 1789 farmhouse sits atop a hill that has stunning panoramic views, especially in the fall, when the sugar maples lining the hill are ablaze. Sixteen acres of lawns and gardens and 14 romantic guest rooms (many with gas fireplaces and Jacuzzis), not to mention the de-

lectable country breakfast, make this a top choice.

Kinsman Lodge   B&B $$
(☏ 603-823-5686; www.kinsmanlodge.com; 2165 Easton Rd/NH 116, Franconia; s/d with shared bathroom incl breakfast from $65/105; ☎) This lodge built in the 1860s has nine comfortable, unpretentious rooms on the 2nd floor. The 1st floor consists of cozy common areas and an inviting porch. The homemade breakfasts, with offerings such as buttermilk pancakes and luscious omelets, are superb.

Horse & Hound Inn   INN $$
(☏ 603-823-5501; www.horseandhoundnh.com; 205 Wells Rd, Franconia; r/ste incl breakfast from $95/125; ☎) This pleasant country inn offers eight frilly rooms set in a cozy 1830 farmhouse. Some rooms feature antiques, while others – those with rosy curtains and floral bedspread – can be a bit over the top, but it's good value for the area. The property also has a restaurant, the Hunt Room, which serves American fare in a cozy setting (mains $12 to $24).

Bishop Farm   B&B $$
(☏ 603-838-2474; www.bishopfarm.com; 33 Bishop Cutoff, Lisbon; r/ste incl breakfast from $160/199, cottages from $149; ☎) This family-run farmhouse has seven attractively designed rooms done in a trim, contemporary look (but with old-fashioned touches such as claw-foot tubs) and six cottages with full kitchens. The house is set on 19 forested acres, which means snowshoeing and cross-country skiing in the winter and mountain biking or hiking in the summer. The front porch is an idyllic spot for enjoying the scenery. It's 9 miles west of Franconia, just off US 302.

Franconia Inn   INN $$
(☏ 800-473-5299, 603-823-5542; www.franconia inn.com; NH 116, Franconia; r/ste incl breakfast from $135/180; ⊙ closed Apr–mid-May; ☎🏊) This excellent 29-room inn, just 2 miles south of Franconia, is set on a broad, fertile, pine-fringed river valley. You'll find plenty of common space and well-maintained, traditional guest rooms. The 107-acre estate has prime cross-country skiing possibilities and summertime hiking and horseback riding.

Sunset Hill House   B&B $$$
(☏ 603-823-5522; www.sunsethillhouse.com; 231 Sunset Hill Rd, Sugar Hill Village; r incl breakfast

from $210; ☎) This 'Grand Inn,' as it is called, lives up to its moniker. All 30 rooms, spread across two buildings, have lovely views of either the mountains or the golf course next door. The pricier rooms have Jacuzzis, fireplaces and private decks, but all the rooms are lovely. The dining room is a formal affair, but there is also a more casual tavern.

Eating

Many of Franconia's inns offer fine dining, including the Horse & Hound, Sugar Hill Inn, Franconia Inn and Sunset Hill House.

Polly's Pancake Parlor   AMERICAN $$
(☑603-823-5575; NH 117, Sugar Hill Village; mains $10-18; ☺7am-2pm) Attached to a 19th-century farmhouse 2 miles west of Franconia, this local institution offers pancakes, pancakes and more pancakes. They're excellent, made with home-ground flour and topped with the farm's own maple syrup, eggs and sausages. Polly's cob-smoked bacon is excellent, and sandwiches (made with homemade bread) and quiches are also available.

★Cold Mountain Cafe & Gallery   INTERNATIONAL $$
(☑603-869-2500; www.coldmountaincafe.com; 2015 Main St, Bethlehem; sandwiches $8-13,

WILD AT HEART

One of the great unsung festivals of this corner of New Hampshire is the summertime **Fields of Lupine Festival**. You've probably heard about the spectacular (and crowded) fall foliage season. Well, in June the hillsides and valleys of the Franconia region are carpeted with purples, blues and pinks, as this spring-blooming wildflower blossoms. Framed against the mountains and dotted with butterflies, the vast carpets of flowers are a spectacular sight.

The lupine festival celebrates the annual bloom with garden tours, art exhibitions and concerts throughout the month. It's a big event but with a fraction of the leaf-peeping crowds. Other festival events include horse-drawn wagon rides through the lupine fields, tours of local inns, open-air markets, nighttime astronomy tours and craft shows. For more on the fest, visit www.franconianotch.org.

mains $13-22; ☺9am-9pm Mon-Sat) Hands down the best restaurant in the region, this casual cafe and gallery has an eclectic, changing menu, featuring gourmet sandwiches and salads at lunch and rich bouillabaisse, seafood curry and rack of lamb at dinner. Everything is prepared with the utmost care and nicely presented, but the atmosphere is very relaxed. Be prepared to wait for your table (outside, since the place is cozy). There's regular live music, from jazz to folk.

☆ Entertainment

Colonial Theater   THEATER, CINEMA
(☑603-869-3422; www.bethlehemcolonial.org; Main St, Bethlehem; live shows from $18) This classic theater in downtown Bethlehem is a historic place to hear the jazz, blues and folk musicians that pass through this little town. The venue also serves as a cinema, showing independent and foreign films.

🛍 Shopping

Harman's Cheese & Country Store   FOOD
(☑603-823-8000; 1400 NH 117, Sugar Hill Village; ☺9:30am-5pm daily May-Oct, to 4:30 Mon-Sat Nov-Apr) If you need to pack a picnic for your hike – or if you simply wish to stock up on New England goodies before heading home – don't miss this country store, which stocks delicious cheddar cheese (aged for at least two years), maple syrup, apple cider (in season) and addictive spicy dill pickles.

ℹ Information

Bethlehem Chamber of Commerce (☑888-845-1957; www.bethlehemwhitemtns.com; 2182 Main St/NH 302, Bethlehem; ☺10am-4pm Jun-Oct, hours vary Nov-Feb, closed Mar-May)

Franconia Notch Chamber of Commerce (☑800-237-9007, 603-823-5661; www.franconianotch.org; Main St, Franconia; ☺11am-5pm Tue-Sun mid-May–mid-Oct; ☎) Southeast of the town center.

ℹ Getting There & Away

Concord Coach Lines buses (Concord Trailways; www.concordcoachlines.com) stop at **Macs Market** (347 Main St, Franconia). Useful routes:
Boston South Station (one way $34, 3½ hours)
Logan International Airport (one way $38, 3½ hours)

MT WASHINGTON VALLEY

Dramatic mountain scenery surrounds the tiny villages of this popular alpine destination, providing an abundance of outdoor adventures. There's great hiking, skiing, kayaking and rafting, along with idyllic activities like swimming in local creeks, overnighting in country farmhouses and simply exploring the countryside.

Mt Washington Valley stretches north from Conway, at the eastern end of the Kancamagus Hwy, and forms the eastern edge of the White Mountain range. The valley's hub is North Conway, though any of the towns along NH 16/US 302 (also called the White Mountain Hwy) can serve as a White Mountain gateway. The valley's namesake is – of course – Mt Washington, New England's highest peak (6288ft), which towers over the valley in the northwest.

North Conway & Around

POP 2300

Gateway to mountain adventure, North Conway is a bustling one-street town lined with motor inns, camping supply stores, restaurants and other outfits designed with the traveler in mind. Although most people are just passing through, North Conway does have its charm, with a pleasant selection of restaurants, cozy cafes and nearby inns with historic allure.

◉ Sights & Activities

★ **Conway Scenic Railroad** TRAIN
(☑ 603-356-5251; www.conwayscenic.com; NH 16, North Conway; Notch Train adult/child from $27/16, Valley Train from $14/10; ⊙ daily May-Oct, Sat & Sun Apr & Nov; ☑) The Notch Train, built in 1874 and restored in 1974, offers New England's most scenic journey. The spectacular 5½-hour trip passes through Crawford Notch. Accompanying live commentary recounts the railroad's history and folklore. Reservations are required.

Alternatively, the same company operates the antique steam Valley Train, which makes a shorter journey south through the Mt Washington Valley, stopping in Conway and Bartlett. Sunset trains, dining trains and other special events are all available.

Both offer the option of 1st-class or dome car seats for an extra $10 to $30. It's only worth the extra on the Valley train: 1st-class

seats are in a perfectly restored Pullman observation car, which features wicker chairs, mahogany woodwork and an open observation platform.

Echo Lake State Park PARK
(www.nhstateparks.org; River Rd; adult/child $4/2) Two miles west of North Conway via River Rd, this placid mountain lake lies at the foot of White Horse Ledge, a sheer rock wall. A scenic trail circles the lake. There is also a mile-long auto road and hiking trail leading to the 700ft-high Cathedral Ledge, with panoramic White Mountains views. Both Cathedral Ledge and nearby White Horse Ledge are excellent for rock climbing. This is also a fine spot for swimming and picnicking.

Mt Cranmore Resort SKIING
(☑ lodging 603-356-5543, snow report 800-786-6754; www.cranmore.com; lift ticket adult/child & senior $49/27; ⊙ 9am-4pm Sun-Fri, 8:30am-9pm Sat) This ski resort on the outskirts of North Conway has a vertical drop of 1200ft, 40 trails (36% beginner, 44% intermediate and 20% expert), nine lifts and 100% snowmaking ability. There's also a terrain park, tubing and abundant facilities for nonskiers (including Jacuzzi, swimming pool, climbing wall and indoor and outdoor tennis courts).

Eastern Mountain Sports Climbing School ROCK CLIMBING
(☑ 603-356-5433, 800-310-4504; www.emsclimb. com; 1498 White Mountain Hwy; lessons per day $150-220; ⊙ 10am-7pm Mon-Sat, to 5pm Sun) This shop and climbing school sells maps and guides to the WMNF and rents camping

equipment, cross-country skis and snow-shoes. Year-round, the school offers classes and tours, including one-day ascents of Mt Washington, and the grueling Presidential Range traverse. Class rates depend on how many are in a group (three maximum).

Saco Bound CANOEING
(☎603-447-2177; www.sacobound.com; 2561 E Main/US 302, Conway; rentals per day $28) Rents out canoes and kayaks and organizes guided canoe trips – including the introductory trip to Weston's Bridge ($22) – and overnight camping trips.

Eastern Slope Campground CANOEING
(584 White Mountain Hwy, Conway; kayaks/canoes per day $35/50) This campground rents kayaks and canoes and can provide transportation up the Saco River ($10 to $20 per person) so you can have a leisurely paddle downriver (either 5.5 miles or 7.5 miles).

✦ Festivals & Events

Fryeburg Fair AGRICULTURAL
(www.fryeburgfair.com; adult/child $10/free) Just over the state border in Maine, this annual county fair is one of New England's – if not the country's – largest and best-known agricultural events. Held every year in early October, the weeklong fair features harness-racing, ox-pulling, wreath-making and judging of just about every kind of farm animal you can imagine. There is also plenty of music, food and other fun. Parking is $5.

Cranmore Resort MUSIC
(www.cranmore.com; FREE) Throughout the summer the resort hosts free outdoor concerts showcasing blues, classical, jazz and show tunes. It's a fun family affair (bring your own picnic or buy food on the grounds) that sometimes ends with fireworks over the mountain.

🛏 Sleeping

Saco River Camping Area CAMPGROUND $
(☎603-356-3360; www.sacorivercampingarea.com; 1550 NH 16; tent/RV sites $33/39; ☺May–mid-Oct; ⬚⬚) This riverside campground away from the highway has 140 wooded and open sites and rustic lean-tos. Canoe and kayak rental is available.

White Mountains Hostel HOSTEL $
(☎603-447-1001; www.whitemountainshostel.com; 36 Washington St, Conway; dm/r $24/60; ⬚⬚) ⬚ Set in an early-1900s farmhouse, New Hampshire's only youth hostel is this cheery place off Main St (NH 16) in Conway. The environmentally conscientious hostel has five bedrooms with bunk beds and four family-size rooms, and a communal lounge and kitchen. Excellent hiking and bicycling opportunities are just outside the door, and canoeists can easily portage to two nearby rivers. Our only gripe is the location, which puts you 5 miles south of the action in North Conway. This place is smoke- and alcohol-free.

Cabernet Inn INN $$
(☎603-356-4704, 800-866-4704; www.cabernetinn.com; NH 16; r incl breakfast $120-285; ⬚) This 1842 Victorian cottage is north of North Conway center, near Intervale. Each of the 11 guest rooms has antiques and queen beds, while pricier rooms also have fireplaces or Jacuzzis. Two living rooms with fireplaces and a shady deck are open for guests to enjoy and relax in. The large gourmet kitchen is the source of a decadent country breakfast. While many inns and B&Bs put out afternoon treats for guests, Cabernet goes one notch higher and offers sweet delights like seasonal parfaits and warm gingerbread.

Cranmore Inn B&B $$
(☎603-356-5502; www.cranmoreinn.com; 80 Kearsarge St; r incl breakfast $99-169; ⬚⬚) The Cranmore has been operating as a country inn since 1863, and it has been known as reliably good value for much of that time. Traditional country decor predominates, meaning lots of floral and frills. In addition to standard rooms, there is a two-room suite and an apartment, and there's a hot tub on site – perfect for post-hike sore muscles.

Spruce Moose Lodge LODGE $$
(☎603-356-6239, 800-600-6239; www.sprucemooselodge.com; 207 Seavey St; r $120-220, cottages $220-350; ⬚) Located a five-minute walk from town, Spruce Moose has charming rooms set inside a spruce-green 1850s home. Styles vary from classic, pine-floored rooms with dark-wood furnishings to cheery, modern, carpeted quarters. There are also attractive wood-floored cottages with country charm, cozy bungalows with Jacuzzis and two entire houses for rent (rates are highly variable; inquire for details).

Kearsarge Inn INN $$
(☎603-356-8700; www.kearsargeinn.com; 42 Seavey St; r/ste from $120/230; ⬚) Just off Main St in the heart of North Conway, this lovely inn is the perfect setting for an intimate ex-

perience near the center of town. The inn is a 'modern rendition' of the historic Kearsarge House, one of the region's first and grandest hotels. Each of the 15 rooms and one suite are spread across the main building. Cottages offers a choice of king- or queen-size beds, gas fireplaces, period furnishings and Jacuzzis. The innkeepers also operate the lively steakhouse next door, Decades.

✖ Eating & Drinking

Many inns – especially those north of the town center and in Jackson – have elegant dining rooms with excellent, traditional menus.

Met CAFE $
(☑603-356-2332; Main St; pastries $2-4; ⊘7am-9pm Mon-Sat, to 10pm Sun; 🛜) Just north of Schouler Park, this small coffeehouse is the best place in town for a cup of coffee or a pastry. You can sink into a plush sofa, or grab a table out front in the summer and enjoy the passing people parade. Artwork (all for sale, mainly by local artists) decorates the walls, and baristas play an eclectic mix of world tunes and jazz.

Peach's CAFE $
(www.peachesnorthconway.com; 2506 White Mountain Hwy; mains $6-11; ⊘7am-2:30pm) Away from the in-town bustle, this perennially popular little house is an excellent option for soups, sandwiches and breakfast. Who can resist fruit-smothered waffles and pancakes and fresh-brewed coffee, served in somebody's cozy living room?

**★ Moat Mountain
Smoke House & Brewing Co** PUB $$
(☑603-356-6381; www.moatmountain.com; 3378 White Mountain Hwy; mains $10-24; ⊘11:30am-11pm) Come here for a variety of American food with a nod to southern fare: BBQ Reuben sandwiches, bowls of beefy chili, juicy burgers, luscious salads, wood-grilled pizzas and cornmeal-crusted catfish. Wash it down with one of the eight brews made on site. The friendly bar is also a popular local hang-out.

May Kelly's Cottage AMERICAN, IRISH $$
(www.maykellys.com; 3002 White Mountain Hwy; mains $12-24; ⊘from 4pm Tue-Thu, from noon Fri-Sun) Irish conviviality and friendliness? May Kelly's is the real deal. Local-attic decor, helpful servers, mountain views and hearty mains make it a top choice.

Horsefeathers AMERICAN $$
(☑603-356-2687; Main St; mains $15-28; ⊘11:30am-10:30pm) The most popular gathering place in town has an encyclopedic menu featuring pasta, salads, sandwiches (including lobster rolls), burgers, bar snacks and main-course platters, plus house-made soups like clam chowder. Many simply come to grab a beer, chew the fat and watch the game on the slew of TVs scattered around the bar.

ℹ Information

Mt Washington Valley Chamber of Commerce (☑603-356-5701; www.mtwashingtonvalley.org; 2617 White Mountain Hwy; ⊘9am-5pm) Tourist information just south of the town center. Hours are notoriously unreliable.

ℹ Getting There & Around

Concord Coach Lines (Concord Trailways; www.concordcoachlines.com) runs a daily route between Boston and Berlin, which stops in North Conway at the Eastern Slope Inn. Other stops:
Concord (one way $18.50, 2½ hours)
Boston South Station (one way $30, four hours)
Logan International Airport (one way $35, 4¼ hours)

Jackson & Around

POP 850

The quintessential New England village, Jackson is home to Mt Washington Valley's premier cross-country ski center. Glen, a hamlet 3 miles south of Jackson, is a magnet for families as it's home to one of New Hampshire's most popular amusement parks, Story Land.

◉ Sights & Activities

Jackson Falls WATERFALL
One of the best ways to spend a sun-drenched afternoon in Jackson is to take a swim in these falls on the Wildcat River just outside of town. You'll have marvelous mountain views as you splash about. To get there, take the Carter Notch Rd (NH 16B) half a mile north of town.

Story Land AMUSEMENT PARK
(☑603-383-4186; www.storylandnh.com; NH 16, Glen; adult/under 3yr $30/free; ⊘9am-6pm Jul & Aug, 9am-5pm Sat & Sun late May-Jun & early Sep–mid-Oct) This delightful 30-acre theme

and amusement park is aimed at the three- to nine-year-old crowd. The rides, activities and shows are small-scale and well done – a refreshing break from the mega amusements in other places.

Jackson Ski Touring Foundation Center   SKIING
(☑ 603-383-9355; www.jacksonxc.org; 153 Main St; day passes adult/child $21/10) Jackson is famous for its 93 miles of cross-country trails. Stop here for passes and to inquire about lessons and groomed trails. You can rent skis (from $16 per day) or snowshoes (from $12 per day).

Black Mountain Ski Area   SKIING
(☑ 603-383-4490; www.blackmt.com; NH 16B; weekends & holidays lift ticket adult/child $49/32, weekday lift ticket adult/child $35/25; ⚑) This smaller ski area has a vertical drop of 1100ft. Forty trails – about equally divided between beginner, intermediate and expert slopes – are served by four lifts. This a good place for beginners and families with small children. In summer, the resort also offers horseback ($45 per hour) and pony rides ($10 per half hour).

Attitash   SKIING
(☑ 603-374-2368; www.attitash.com; US 302, Bartlett; lift ticket adult/13-18yr/6-12yr & seniors weekends & holidays $70/55/50, weekday $63/48/39) West of Glen, you can play and stay at Attitash. The ski resort includes two mountains, Attitash and Bear Peak, which offer a vertical drop of 1750ft, 12 lifts and 70 ski trails. Half the trails are intermediate level, while the other half are equally divided between expert and beginner levels. From mid-June to mid-October the resort offers a slew of activities, including an alpine slide, horseback riding, mountain biking, bungee trampolines, a chair-lift ride, a water slide, a climbing wall and a mountain coaster (a roller coaster that barrels down the mountain). You can choose various half- and full-day combo tickets ($30 to $45) including all of the above or opt for single-ride tickets (from $15).

🛏 Sleeping

★ Snowflake Inn   INN $$
(☑ 603-383-8259; www.thesnowflakeinn.com; 95 Main St; ste incl breakfast from $175; 🕿🛋) All of the suites at this elegant inn are spacious and have fireplaces and two-person Jacuzzis. There are plenty of modern creature com-

forts, including 400-count triple sheeting, flat-screen TVs and lavish sitting areas. An on-site spa adds to the charm.

Wildcat Inn & Tavern   INN $$
(☑ 800-228-4245, 603-383-4245; www.wild cattavern.com; 3 Main St; r/ste/cottages from $89/139/285) This centrally located village lodge has a dozen cozy rooms with antique furnishings. The cottage – known as the 'Igloo' – sleeps up to six. One of Jackson's best restaurants, Wildcat Tavern, is on site and offers New England–leaning American food, as well as fun themed evenings like ladies' nights and a Friday-night fish fry.

Wentworth   INN $$$
(☑ 603-383-9700; www.thewentworth.com; NH 16B; r $150-260, apt $300-375; 🕿) This grand country inn is on the edge of Jackson Village, beside a gorgeous public golf course. It's an elegant affair, with 51 spacious rooms, a gracious lobby and dining room and outdoor facilities such as tennis courts. The best rooms have fireplaces, outdoor hot tubs·and gorgeous antique furnishings.

🍴 Eating & Drinking

Many of Jackson's inns have excellent (and expensive) dining rooms.

★ White Mountain Cider Co   CAFE, AMERICAN $
(☑ 603-383-9061; US 302, Glen; snacks $2-8; ⊙ noon-6pm, reduced hours in winter) If you are packing a picnic for your day hike, stop at this country store and cafe. Besides jugs of cider, you'll find gourmet coffee, cider doughnuts, apple pie and a whole range of specialty New England products. In winter, it serves single cups of piping-hot cider; in summer, cider slushies cool you right down. Next door is a formal restaurant that's open for dinner (mains $20 to $28, open noon to 3pm and 5pm to 9pm), when it serves expertly prepared cuisine (bacon-crusted sea scallops; fontina, spinach, tomato chutney and polenta torte; grilled hanger steak) in an elegant 1890s farmhouse.

Shannon Door   PUB $$
(☑ 603-383-4211; NH 16; mains $11-18; ⊙ 4-9pm Sun-Thu, to 11pm Fri & Sat) This long-running Irish pub (around since the 1950s) serves shepherd's pie, but most of its menu is non-Gaelic in flavor: delicious thin-crust pizzas, steak au poivre, and baked manicotti, to name a few options. It also has 14 beers on tap, a welcoming crowd and live enter-

tainment (folk bands and such) Thursday through Sunday.

Thompson House Eatery   NEW AMERICAN $$$
(✆603-383-9341; www.thompsonhouseeatery.com; 193 Main St/NH 16B; mains $15-35; ☺noon-2pm Thu-Mon, 5-10pm daily) Casual but cool, this restaurant and bar is a local favorite for its creative seasonal menu. It's big on organic, locally grown produce, which is also for sale at the farm stand outside. Eat on the porch, with light filtering through the stained-glass windows, or at the friendly bar.

❶ Information

Jackson Area Chamber of Commerce
(✆603-383-9356; www.jacksonnh.com; Jackson Falls Marketplace; ☺9am-4pm Mon-Fri year-round, 9am-1pm Sat Jul-Feb) The most helpful and knowledgeable chamber of commerce we came across in the entire state. Has loads of local insight; ask here about scenic walks in the area.

❶ Getting There & Away

Jackson is 7 miles north of North Conway. Take NH 16 and then cross the Ellis River via the historic red covered bridge.

Concord Coach Lines (Concord Trailways; www.concordcoachlines.com) runs a daily bus between Boston ($31, four hours) and Berlin, making a stop in Jackson at the Chamber of Commerce.

Crawford Notch & Bretton Woods

Before 1944 this area was known only to locals and wealthy summer visitors who patronized the grand Mt Washington Hotel (now renamed the Omni Mt Washington Hotel & Resort). When President Roosevelt chose the hotel as the site of the conference to establish a new global economic order after WWII, the whole world learned about Bretton Woods.

The mountainous countryside is as stunning now as it was during those historic times. The hotel is almost as grand and the name still rings with history. At the very least, stop to admire the view of the great hotel set against the mountains. Ascending Mt Washington on a cog railway powered by a steam locomotive is dramatic fun for all, and a must for railroad buffs.

US 302 travels west from Glen, then north to Crawford Notch (1773ft), continuing on to Bretton Woods.

◉ Sights & Activities

★**Mount Washington Cog Railway**   TRAIN
(✆603-278-5404; www.thecog.com; adult/child $62/39; ☺May-Oct) Purists walk and the lazy drive, but certainly the quaintest way to reach the summit of Mt Washington is to take this cog railway. Since 1869 coal-fired, steam-powered locomotives have followed a 3.5-mile track up a steep mountainside trestle for a three-hour round-trip scenic ride, with two daily departures (weekend departures only from late April to late May). Reservations are highly recommended.

Instead of having drive wheels, a cog locomotive applies power to a cogwheel (gear wheel) on its undercarriage. The gears engage pins mounted between the rails to pull the locomotive and a single passenger car up the mountainside, burning a ton of coal and blowing a thousand gallons of water into steam along the way. Up to seven locomotives may be huffing and puffing at one time here, all with boilers tilted to accommodate the grade, which at the Jacob's ladder trestle is 37% – the second-steepest railway track in the world (the steepest is at Mt Pilatus, Switzerland).

The base station is 6 miles east of US 302. Turn east in Fabyan, just northwest of the Mt Washington Hotel (between Bretton Woods and Twin Mountain). Also, remember that the average temperature at the summit is 40°F in summer and the wind is always blowing, so bring a sweater and windbreaker.

Crawford Notch State Park   PARK
(✆603-374-2272; www.nhstateparks.org; adult/child $4/2) In 1826 torrential rains in this steep valley caused massive mud slides that descended on the home of the Willey family. The house was spared, but the family was not – they were outside at the fatal moment and were swept away by the mud. The dramatic incident made the newspapers and fired the imaginations of painter Thomas Cole and author Nathaniel Hawthorne. Both men used the incident for inspiration, thus unwittingly putting Crawford Notch on the tourist maps. Soon visitors arrived to visit the tragic spot – and they stayed for the bracing mountain air and healthy exercise.

From the Willey House site, now used as a **state park visitors center** (✆603-374-2272; www.nhstateparks.org; ☺9am-5pm Mon-Fri, 8:30am-6pm Sat & Sun late May-late Oct), you can walk the easy half-mile Pond Loop Trail, the 1-mile Sam Willey Trail and the Ripley

Falls Trail, a 1-mile hike from US 302 via the Ethan Pond Trail. The trailhead for Arethusa Falls, a 1.3-mile hike, is half a mile south of the Dry River Campground on US 302.

Mt Washington Resort
SKIING

(Bretton Woods; day passes adult/child & senior $21/12) Mt Washington Resort at Bretton Woods includes a **ski station** (603-278-3320; www.brettonwoods.com; US 302; weekends & holidays lift ticket adult/child 13-17/child 6-12 & seniors $79/64/49, weekdays $54/43/33) with a vertical drop of 1500ft. Seven chair lifts serve 88 trails, most of which are intermediate. The ski and snowboard school offers childcare and ski lessons for kids. All equipment is available for rental.

The resort also maintains a 62-mile network of trails for **cross-country skiing**. The trails traverse the resort grounds, crossing open fields, wooded paths and mountain streams. Ski rental and lessons are also available.

🛏 Sleeping & Eating

In addition to offering lavish accommodations, the Mt Washington Hotel has an extensive breakfast buffet and dress-up dinners, and there are restaurants at both the Bretton Arms Inn and the Lodge.

Crawford Notch General Store & Campground
CAMPGROUND $

(603-374-2779; www.crawfordnotchcamping.com; US 302, Bretton Woods; tent sites $29-35, cabins $69-107, yurts $69; ☉May–mid-Oct) This handy all-purpose place sells camping supplies and groceries to use at its lovely wooded sites. You'll also find small, rustic, but rather handsome wooden cabins and yurts. Some of the sites are on the Saco River, and there's good swimming right in front.

Above the Notch
MOTEL $

(603-846-5156; www.abovethenotch.com; NH 302, Crawford Notch; r $80-95; 🔊) For lower-priced lodging, you'll have to drive a fair bit away from the Omni Mt Washington Hotel & Resort. This classic drive-up motel is a simple, friendly place, with clean, basic rooms. It's conveniently located next to Bretton Woods ski resort and the cog railway.

Lodge at Bretton Woods
LODGE $$

(800-314-1752, 603-278-1000; www.mtwashington.com; US 302, Bretton Woods; r $130-195, mains $12-26; 🔊🎿) This modern place with 50 spacious rooms actually enjoys the best view of the Omni Mt Washington Hotel & Resort

and its mountain backdrop. It has a motor-inn layout and a hot tub on site.

AMC Highland Center
LODGE $$

(603-466-2727; www.outdoors.org/lodging/whitemountains/highland; NH 302, Bretton Woods; dm adult/child $92/55, s/d incl breakfast & dinner $155/210) This cozy Appalachian Mountain Club (AMC) lodge is set amid the splendor of Crawford Notch, an ideal base for hiking Mt Washington and many other trails in the area. The grounds are beautiful, rooms are basic but comfortable, meals are hearty and guests are all outdoor enthusiasts. Discounts are available for AMC members. The center also has loads of information about hiking in the region.

Bretton Arms Inn
INN $$

(800-258-0330, 603-278-1000; www.mtwashington.com; US 302, Bretton Woods; r $110-260) People have been staying here for almost a century. On the same estate as the Mt Washington Hotel, this manse was built as a grand 'summer cottage' in 1896, but it has been an inn since 1907. It offers an intimate and folksy atmosphere.

⭐Omni Mt Washington Hotel & Resort
HOTEL $$$

(603-278-1000; www.brettonwoods.com; 310 Mt Washington Hotel Rd, Bretton Woods; r $299-480, ste $560, mains $15-32; ✳@🔊🎿) Open since 1902, this grand hotel maintains a sense of fun – note the moose's head overlooking the lobby and the framed local wildflowers in many of the guest rooms. Also offers 27 holes of golf, red-clay tennis courts, an equestrian center and a spa. There's a $25 daily resort fee.

❶ Information

Complete information about hiking, biking and camping in the area is available from AMC Highland Center (p364), including maps and trail guides. Daily activities and guided hikes are offered.

Pinkham Notch

Pinkham Notch (2032ft) is a mountain pass area known for its wild beauty, and its useful facilities for campers and hikers make it one of the most popular and crowded activity centers in the White Mountains. Wildcat Mountain and Tuckerman Ravine offer good skiing, and an excellent system of trails provides access to the natural beauties of the Presidential Range, especially Mt Washington. For the less athletically inclined, the Mt Washington Auto Rd provides easy access to the summit.

NH 16 goes north 11 miles from North Conway and Jackson to Pinkham Notch, then past the Wildcat Mountain ski area and Tuckerman Ravine, through the small settlement of Glen House and past the Dolly Copp Campground to Gorham and Berlin.

🏃 Activities

Mt Washington Auto Road   SCENIC DRIVE
(☑603-466-3988;   www.mountwashingtonautoroad.com; off NH 16; car & driver $26, extra adult/child $8/6; ☺mid-May–mid-Oct) The Mt Washington Summit Rd Company operates an 8-mile-long alpine toll road from Pinkham Notch to the summit of Mt Washington. If you'd rather not drive, you can take a 1½-hour **guided tour**, which allows you 30 minutes on the summit. In severe weather the road may be closed (even in summer).

Pinkham Notch Visitor Center   OUTDOORS
(☑603-466-2727;   www.outdoors.org;   NH 16; ☺6:30am-10pm) Guided nature walks, canoe trips, cross-country ski and snowshoe treks and other outdoor adventures are organized by the AMC out of Pinkham Notch Camp, which also operates a summer hikers' shuttle that stops at many trailheads along US 302 in Pinkham Notch.

The *AMC White Mountain Guide,* on sale here or online from the AMC website, includes detailed maps and statistics for each trail.

The AMC maintains hikers' 'high huts' providing meals and lodging. Carter Notch Hut is located on Nineteen-Mile Brook Trail, and Lakes of the Clouds Hut is on Crawford Path. For those hiking the Appalachian Trail, the Zealand and Carter huts are open year-round.

Wildcat Mountain   SKIING
(☑800-255-6439,   603-466-3326,   snow report 800-754-9453;   www.skiwildcat.com;   NH 16; Pinkham Notch; adult/child & senior $62/32) With a vertical drop of 2112ft, Wildcat Mountain tops out at 4415ft. Just north of Jackson, Wildcat's 225 acres include 47 downhill ski trails (25% beginner, 45% intermediate, 30% expert), four lifts and 90% snowmaking capacity. The longest run is 2.75 miles.

Tuckerman Ravine   SKIING
The cirque at this ravine has several ski trails for purists. What's pure about it? No lifts. You climb up the mountain then ski down. Purists posit that, if you climb up, you will have strong legs that won't break easily in a fall on the way down. Tuckerman is perhaps best in spring, when most ski resorts are struggling to keep their snow cover, since nature conspires to keep the ravine in shadow much of the time. Park in the Wildcat Mountain lot for the climb up the ravine.

Wildcat Ziprider & Skyride   RIDE
(Ziprider $20, Skyride adult/child $13/7; ☺Ziprider 10am-5pm Sat & Sun mid-May–mid-Jun, daily mid-Jun–Oct, Skyride 10am-5pm mid-May–mid-Oct) Wildcat Mountain's summertime Ziprider (like a zip line, but you are suspended from the steel cables) is the only one of its kind in New Hampshire. It operates in summer just for the fun of the ride and the view, though while you fly by at 45 miles per hour, the view is secondary to the adrenaline rush. The mountain's summertime Gondola Skyride is a more tranquil experience, but still fun.

🛏 Sleeping

Joe Dodge Lodge   LODGE $
(☑603-466-2727; 361 NH 16; r incl breakfast & dinner $78) The AMC camp at Pinkham Notch incorporates this lodge, with dorms housing more than 100 beds. Reserve bunks in advance. Discounts are available for AMC members.

Dolly Copp Campground   CAMPGROUND $
(☑603-466-2713; www.campsnh.com; NH 16; tent/RV sites $22/26; ☺mid-May–mid-Oct) This USFS campground has 176 primitive sites. Reservations are accepted at a few sites, but most are first come, first served.

ℹ Information

The nerve center for hiking in the Whites is the AMC Pinkham Notch Camp Visitor Center (p365).

ℹ Getting There & Away

Concord Coach Lines (Concord Trailways; www.concordcoachlines.com) provides daily bus service to Boston ($35, four hours) and Berlin. The bus stop is at the Pinkham Notch Camp Visitor Center.

Great North Woods

Not too many people make it all the way up here, north of Berlin, but there are two scenic routes north of the Notches and Bretton

Woods. If you've been feeling like you can't see the forest for the trees, nothing beats US 2 from the Vermont–New Hampshire state line to the Maine–New Hampshire state line: the expansive but looming mountain views are unparalleled. Alternatively, if you really want to get remote, or are heading to the outposts of Maine, take NH 16 north from Gorham to Errol. This route runs parallel to the birch-lined Androscoggin River.

Assuming you're out at dawn or dusk, you should be able to catch a glimpse of a moose in the **Northern Forest Heritage Park** (☑ 603-752-7202; www.northernforestheritage.org; 961 Main St/NH 16, Berlin). The park currently offers 90-minute **boat tours** (adult/child $15/8) along the Androscoggin River, departing at 2pm Saturday from late May to mid-October.

You'll have an even better chance of spotting a moose on one of the **moose tours** (☑ 603-466-3103; www.gorhammoosetours.org; 20 Park St, Gorham; adult/child $26/16; ☺ Mon & Wed-Sat May, Jun, Sep & Oct, Mon-Sat Jul & Aug) sponsored by the town of Gorham. These three-hour passenger-van tours are led by naturalist guides, who claim a 95% success rate at spotting moose. Tours depart at roughly 6pm; call for exact times.

Maine

📞 207 / POP 1.3 MILLION

Best Places to Eat

➡ Fore Street (p382)

➡ Shepherd's Pie (p397)

➡ Red's Eats (p391)

➡ Primo (p395)

➡ Five Islands Lobster Company (p390)

➡ Mâche Bistro (p403)

Best Places to Stay

➡ LimeRock Inn (p395)

➡ Norumbega (p397)

➡ Danforth (p381)

➡ Cabot Cove Cottages (p375)

Why Go?

With more lobsters, lighthouses and charming resort villages than you can shake a stick at, Maine is New England at its most iconic. The sea looms large here, with mile upon mile of jagged sea cliffs, peaceful harbors and pebbly beaches. Eat your way through food- and art-crazed Portland, one of America's coolest small cities. Explore the historic shipbuilding villages of the Midcoast. Hike through Acadia National Park, a spectacular island of mountains and fjord-like estuaries. Let the coastal wind whip through those cobwebs and inhale the salty air. Venture into the state's inland region, a vast wilderness of pine forest and snowy peaks.

Outdoor adventurers can race white-water rapids, cycle the winding shore roads, or kayak beside playful harbor seals. For slower-paced fun, there are plenty of antique shops, cozy lobster shacks, charming B&Bs and locally brewed beer on hand.

And, oh, did we mention the lobster?

When to Go
Portland

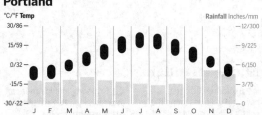

Jun–Sep Coastal towns fill up with lobster-hungry travelers.

Oct Leaf peepers descend upon villages with cameras at the ready.

Nov–Mar Skiers and snowmobile riders attack the mountain trails.

Maine Highlights

❶ Exploring the cafes, bars and galleries lining the cobblestone backstreets of Portland's 19th-century **Old Port district** (p377)

❷ Bagging the peak of Baxter State Park's **Mt Katahdin** (p408), the end point of the 2179-mile-long Appalachian Trail

❸ Exploring iconic American art in Rockland's **Farnsworth Art Museum** (p395)

❹ Picking up a cozy new fleece and preppy-chic wellies at the original **LL Bean** (p386) in Freeport

❺ Painting or photographing the windswept rocks of **Monhegan Island** (p393)

❻ Hiking up Cadillac Mountain, then taking a (chilly) dip in Echo Lake at **Acadia National Park** (p403)

❼ Tying on your bib and cracking a freshly steamed crustacean at one of Maine's many **lobster pounds** (p372)

National & State Parks

Maine has an excellent assortment of state parks, with areas suitable for every conceivable outdoor activity. It also boasts New England's only national park, Acadia National Park, an extremely popular getaway in the summer.

The state's 35 parks are overseen by the Bureau of Parks & Lands (☑207-287-3821; www.maine.gov/doc/parks). Upon request, staff will send you an information pack that describes each park in detail. For camping at these parks, call the central reservation hotline.

About 275 miles of the 2179-mile Appalachian Trail runs through Maine, and its northern terminus is Baxter State Park and the summit of Mt Katahdin. The White Mountain National Forest also has dramatic sections of protected land in northern Maine, although most people tend to think that the forest stops at the New Hampshire border.

Maine has abundant wildlife in its thick forests. Foremost is the moose, a magnificent animal standing 6ft to 7ft tall at the shoulder and weighing up to 1200lb; there are an estimated 30,000 of them in the state. Other animals present include harbor seals, black bear, beaver, eastern coyotes, skunks, otter, snowshoe hares, white-tailed deer and over 400 species of bird.

ⓘ Information

Maine Office of Tourism (☑888-624-6345; www.visitmaine.com; 59 State House Station, Augusta) These folks maintain information centers on the principal routes into the state – Calais, Fryeburg, Hampden, Houlton, Kittery and Yarmouth. Each facility is open 9am to 5pm, with extended hours in summer.

Maine Tourism Association (☑207-623-0363; www.mainetourism.com) Links all chamber-of-commerce offices in Maine.

Maine.gov (www.maine.gov) The state's official website, with info on state parks.

ⓘ Getting There & Around

AIR

Portland International Jetport (PWM; ☑207-874-8877; www.portlandjetport.org) is the state's main airport, but a number of airlines serve Bangor International Airport (p438).

BOAT

Maine State Ferry Service (☑207-596-2202; www.maine.gov/mdot/msfs/) operates boats to several larger islands, mostly in the Penobscot Bay region.

BUS

Concord Coach Lines (☑800-639-3317; www.concordcoachlines.com) operates daily buses between Boston and many Maine towns (including Bangor, Bar Harbor, Bath, Belfast, Brunswick, Camden, Rockport, Damariscotta, Ellsworth, Lincolnville, Portland, Rockland, Searsport, Waldoboro and Wiscasset). Some of these connect with the Maine State Ferry Service to islands off the coast. **Greyhound** (☑800-231-2222; www.greyhound.com) stops in Bangor, Portland, Bath, Rockland and various other towns. From Bangor, **Maritime Bus** (☑800-575-1807) connects Maine with New Brunswick and Nova Scotia.

CAR & MOTORCYCLE

Except for the Maine Turnpike (I-95 and I-495) and part of I-295, Maine has no fast, limited-access highways. Roads along the coast flood with traffic during the summer tourist season. As a result, you must plan for more driving time when traveling in Maine.

Note: moose are a particular danger to drivers in Maine, even as far south as Portland. They've been known to cripple a bus and walk away. Be especially watchful in spring and fall and around dusk and dawn, when the moose are most active.

TRAIN

The *Downeaster*, run by **Amtrak** (☑800-872-7245; www.amtrak.com), makes four or five trips daily between Boston, MA, and Portland, ME.

SOUTHERN MAINE COAST

Maine's southern coast embodies the state slogan 'Vacationland,' with busy commercial strips, sandy beaches and resort towns that get packed in the summer months. Despite the crowds, there are some charming

ⓘ SEASONAL PRICE FLUX

Maine travel is highly seasonal. Most coastal towns slumber from fall to spring, then explode with action in summer. As a result, off-season hotel rooms can be as little as half their summer prices. The same principle holds for the mountain towns, only in reverse – fall and winter are high season. Portland, being less of a tourist destination, doesn't have nearly as much price flux.

DON'T MISS

MAINE LEEF PEEPS

Maine is better known for its coast than its mountains, but inland Maine still offers its own array of superb colors. The best leaf-peeping route follows US2 between Bethel and Rangeley Lake (see p406).

➡ The town of **Bethel** is a destination in and of itself and serves as a great base for hiking through the rainbow of colors in nearby Grafton Notch State Park.

➡ Primarily known as a winter ski resort, **Sunday River Ski Resort** also offers non-ski activities in the autumn like chair-lift rides, ATV tours, canoeing and mountain biking. All boast fine views of the Fall foliage.

➡ **Shelburne birches** (between Gilead and Shelburne) is also excellent for viewing the vibrant colors.

features to this coast. While Kittery is a long, commercial strip mall, Ogunquit has a lovely beach and is Maine's gay mecca. Between the two lies quaint York Village, and busy, populist York Beach. Beyond, the Kennebunks are small historic settlements with lavish mansions (some of which are B&Bs) near pretty beaches and rugged coastline. Although you'll have to use your imagination, the southern coast is deeply associated with the works of American artist Winslow Homer, who spent his summers in Prout's Neck (just south of Portland), which still has some magnificent scenery.

Kittery

POP 10,600

The only reason most travelers visit Kittery is to shop. The busy roads leading from New Hampshire are lined with shopping malls and vast parking lots. While there's no natural beauty among the concrete, there are some great deals if you feel like browsing the many outlet malls.

To escape the mayhem, head south to the pretty back roads along the coast. Founded in 1623, Kittery is one of Maine's oldest settlements and you'll find historic homes, manicured parks and some enticing lobster restaurants if you follow ME 103 a few miles out of town to Kittery Point.

◉ Sights & Activities

Cap & Patty   CRUISE
(☑877-439-8976; www.capandpatty.com; Town Dock, Pepperell Rd; adult/child $12/8; ⊙Tue-Sun Jun–mid-Oct) Cruise along the Piscataqua River, taking in the lighthouses, forts and the navy yard around the basin. Tours last

approximately 80 minutes and are offered six times per day in summer.

🛏 Sleeping & Eating

Kittery has several chain hotels and motor lodges, but if you're looking for character, cross the bridge to find a wealth of charming B&Bs in downtown Portsmouth in New Hampshire.

Bob's Clam Hut   SEAFOOD $
(www.bobsclamhut.com; 315 US 1; ⊙11am-9pm) Touristy? Yeah. Awesome? Completely. Order a basket of fried whole-belly clams at the walk-up window and sit at a picnic table watching the bumper-to-bumper traffic on US 1. Expect crowds in summer.

🛍 Shopping

Outlet Malls   MALL
(☑888-548-8379, 207-439-4367; www.thekittery outlets.com; ⊙9am-8pm Mon-Sat, 9am-7pm Sun, extended hours in summer) Kittery's mile-long stretch of US 1 is lined with several outlet malls containing hundreds of name-brand shops. For some local flavor, try the **Kittery Trading Post** (☑888 587 6246; www.kitterytrad ingpost.com; 301 US 1; ⊙Mon-Sat 9am-7pm, Sun 9am-6pm, extended hours in summer). Opened as a one-room store in 1938, it now sells everything from kids' pajamas to second-hand guns.

❶ Getting There & Away

From Portsmouth, NH, it's a mere 3 miles to Kittery via US 1 or I-95 across the Piscataqua River. Buses depart from Portsmouth for Boston, New York, and the further north parts of Maine, but don't stop in Kittery itself.

The Yorks

POP 16,300

York Village, York Harbor, York Beach and Cape Neddick collectively make up the Yorks. York Village, the first city chartered in English North America, feels like a living history museum, with a small downtown filled with impeccably maintained historic buildings. York Harbor was developed more than a century ago as a posh summer resort and many of its grand Victorian mansions and hotels remain. York Beach has a more populist vibe, with RV parks, candy shops and arcades galore. Cape Neddick, a small, mostly residential peninsula jutting out into the sea, is home to the famous Nubble Light.

👁 Sights & Activities

Museums of Old York   HISTORICAL BUILDINGS
(www.oldyork.org; adult 1 bldg/all bldgs $6/12, child $3/5; ☺10am-5pm Mon-Sat Jun-Oct) York, called Agamenticus by its original Native American inhabitants, was settled by the British in 1624 and granted a charter by King Charles I in 1641. Nine of its best-preserved buildings are now cared for by the Old York Historical Society, which has turned them into individual museums. Highlights include the prisoner's cells and stockades of the Old Gaol; the Emerson-Wilcox House, now a museum of New England decorative arts; and John Hancock Wharf, a warehouse with displays commemorating the area's maritime history. Pick up tickets and maps at the **visitor center** (3 Lindsay Rd, York Village) next to the 19th-century Remick Barn, which hosts seasonal exhibits and special educational programs.

Harbor Adventures   KAYAKING, CYCLING
(📞207-363-8466;   www.harboradventures.com; Town Dock No 2, York Harbor) This York Harbor–based tour company offers a chance to explore the scenic coastline by sea kayak or mountain bike. Popular kayaking options include the two-hour harbor tour ($45), the sunset tour ($45) and the lobster luncheon ($65), which consists of paddling along Chauncey Creek and around Kittery Point peninsula before docking for a meal of lobster.

Nubble Light   LIGHTHOUSE
(Nubble Rd, Cape Neddick) Perched on Nubble Island, just off the tip of Cape Neddick, this white lighthouse and Victorian lighthouse keeper's cottage provide one of Maine's best photo ops.

York's Wild Kingdom   ZOO
(📞207-363-4911,   800-456-4911;   www.yorkzoo.com; US 1, York Beach; adult/child $19.75/14.75; ☺10am-6pm late May–mid-Sep; 🚻) This zoo and amusement park makes for a diverting afternoon for families with children.

🛏 Sleeping & Eating

Dockside Guest Quarters   INN $$
(📞207-363-2868, 888-860-7428; www.docksidegq.com; 22 Harris Island Rd, York; r incl breakfast $152-320; ☺daily Jun-Oct, Fri & Sat Apr-May & Nov-Dec) On a hill overlooking the harbor, this friendly guesthouse has been a York tradition since the 1950s. The 26 rooms have a classic New England cottage feel, with white-painted furniture and crisp nautical prints. Try to snag one in the 19th-century Maine House, which has more charm than the adjacent contemporary outbuildings.

Inn at Tanglewood Hall   B&B $$
(📞207-351-1075;   www.tanglewoodhall.com;   611 York St, York Harbor; r incl breakfast Jul & Aug $165-235; ☺Apr-Nov) This lovely B&B has six sweetly furnished rooms with feather beds and abundant country charm. Several rooms have gas fireplaces and private porches. The wraparound verandah provides a peaceful vantage point overlooking the gardens.

**Stonewall Kitchen
Company Store & Cafe**   CAFE $
(www.stonewallkitchen.com; 2 Stonewall Lane, York; mains $8-13; ☺5am-6pm) Fill up on dozens of free samples (wild blueberry jam, tapenade, raspberry fudge sauce...yum-yum) at the flagship store of the Stonewall Kitchen specialty foods empire. Or just buy a bowl of homemade granola or a salad at the on-site cafe. Great for buying gifts.

**Brown's Old-Fashioned
Ice Cream**   ICE CREAM $
(232 Nubble Rd, Cape Neddick; cones $3-5; ☺noon to 8pm, later in summer) Grabbing a cone at Brown's on the way to see the Nubble Light is a well-loved summer tradition. Try the Grape-Nuts flavor, a quirky New England favorite.

Cape Neddick Lobster Pound   SEAFOOD $$
(www.capeneddick.com; 60 Shore Rd, Cape Neddick; mains $18-38; ☺lunch & dinner) In a tranquil spot overlooking the Cape Neddick River, this sunny, open dining room is popular with locals and in-the-know summer regulars. Ignore the fancy-sounding appetizers and stick with the classics – fresh-steamed lobster dripping with

MAINE THE YORKS

MAINE'S BEST LOBSTER POUNDS

Once considered a food fit only for prisoners and indentured servants, the American lobster has come a long way in the last 200 years. The tasty crustacean has come to be the most iconic of Maine foods and many Mainers still make their living hauling lobster traps out of the sea. The coast is lined with 'lobster pounds,' informal restaurants serving fresh lobster by weight. For step-by-step instructions on how to crack and eat the spiny little beasts, check out the Gulf of Maine Research Institute's useful website (www.gma.org/lobsters).

From south to north, here is a sampling of our favorite places to tie on a bib and dig in. Note: for lobster rolls, another divine Maine delicacy, head to your nearest 'lobster shack,' an even more informal type of eating establishment, often lacking indoor seating.

Cape Neddick Lobster Pound (p371) In Cape Neddick, near York.

Nunan's Lobster Hut (p376) In Cape Porpoise, near Kennebunkport.

Harraseeket Lunch & Lobster (p386) In Freeport.

Five Islands Lobster Company (p390) In Georgetown, near Bath.

Thurston's Lobster Pound (p405) In Bass Harbor on Mount Desert Island.

MAINE OGUNQUIT & WELLS

melted butter, washed down with an icy gin and tonic.

ⓘ Information

For visitor information, stop by the helpful **Greater York Chamber of Commerce** (☎ 207-363-4422; www.gatewaytomaine.org; Stonewall Lane, York; ◷ 9am-5pm Mon-Sat, 10am-4pm Sun), just off US 1.

ⓘ Getting There & Away

From Kittery, it's another 6 miles up US 1 or I-95 to York. York Harbor is about 1 mile east of York via US 1A; York Beach is 3 miles north of York via US 1A. Cape Neddick is just north of York Beach. The nearest major bus station is 10 miles away in Portsmouth, NH.

Ogunquit & Wells

POP OGUNQUIT 1300, WELLS 9900

Known to the Abenaki tribe as the 'beautiful place by the sea,' Ogunquit is justly famous for its 3-mile sandy beach. Wide stretches of pounding surf front the Atlantic, while warm back-cove waters make an idyllic setting for a swim. In summer, the beach draws hordes of visitors from near and far, increasing the town's population exponentially.

Prior to its resort status, Ogunquit was a shipbuilding center in the 17th century. Later it became an important arts center, when the Ogunquit art colony was founded in 1898. Today, Ogunquit is the northeastern-most gay and lesbian mecca in the US, add-

ing a touch of open San Francisco culture to the more conservative Maine one. For more information, visit www.gayogunquit.com.

Neighboring Wells to the northeast is little more than an eastward continuation of Ogunquit Beach, with a long stretch of busy commercial development. Wells has good beaches, though, and many relatively inexpensive motels and campgrounds.

◉ Sights & Activities

Marginal Way & Perkins Cove　　　WALK
Tracing the 'margin' of the sea, Ogunquit's famed mile-long footpath winds high above the crashing gray waves. The neatly paved path, fine for children and slow walkers, starts southeast of Beach St at Shore Rd. It ends near Perkins Cove, a picturesque inlet dotted with sailboats. A narrow pedestrian bridge spans the harbor and leads to a handful of attractive restaurants, art galleries and boutiques. If you don't want to walk back, you can hop on the summertime **trolley** (adults/kids 12 and under $1.50/free).

Ogunquit Beaches　　　BEACHES
A sublime stretch of family-friendly coastline, **Ogunquit Beach** is only a five-minute walk along Beach St, east of US 1. Walking to the beach is a good idea in summer, because the parking lot fills up early (and it costs $4 per hour to park). The 3-mile beach fronts Ogunquit Bay to the south; on the west side of the beach are the warmer waters of the tidal Ogunquit River. **Footbridge Beach**, 2 miles to the north near Wells, is actually the

northern extension of Ogunquit Beach. **Little Beach**, near the lighthouse on Marginal Way, is best reached on foot.

Ogunquit Museum of American Art
MUSEUM

(⏎207-646-4909; www.ogunquitmuseum.org; 543 Shore Rd, Ogunquit; adult/child/student & senior $10/free/9; ⏰10am-5pm Mon-Sat, 1-5pm Sun early May-late Oct) Dramatically situated overlooking the Atlantic, this midsize museum houses an exquisite collection of American paintings, sculptures and photographs. Standouts include paintings by Reginald Marsh, Marsden Hartley and Robert Henri, as well as the large collection of works by Maine artists.

Wells National Estuarine Research Reserve
NATURE RESERVE

(⏎207-646-1555; www.wellsreserve.org; 342 Laudholm Farm Rd, Wells; adult/child $3/1; ⏰7am-sunset) 🏃 Wildlife lovers adore wandering these 1600 acres of protected coastal ecosystems, with 7 miles of hiking and cross-country ski trails past woodlands, fields, wetlands, beaches and dunes. Its diverse habitats make it a particularly intriguing place for bird-watchers.

Rachel Carson National Wildlife Reserve
NATURE RESERVE

(⏎207-646-9226; www.fws.gov/northeast/rachel carson; 321 Port Rd; ⏰dawn-dusk) 🏃 Named for the famous environmentalist, this reserve consists of more than 9000 acres of protected coastal areas and four trails scattered along 50 miles of shoreline. The 1-mile Carson Trail, found here at the refuge's Wells headquarters, is by far the most popular, meandering along tidal creeks and salt marshes.

🧭 Tours

Excursions
KAYAKING

(⏎207-363-0181; www.excursionsinmaine.com; 1740 US 1, Cape Neddick; ⏰mid-Jun–Sep) This outfitter offers leisurely half-day kayak tours ($62) and two-day overnight adventures with camping on a remote island ($255). Proficient kayakers can rent their own boat for $58 a day.

Finestkind Scenic Cruises
CRUISES

(⏎207-646-5227; www.finestkindcruises.com; Perkins Cove; adult/child from $17/9) Offers many popular trips, including a 50-minute lobstering trip, a sunset cocktail cruise and a two-hour cruise aboard the twin-sailed *Cricket*.

Silverlining
SAILING

(⏎207-646-9800; www.silverliningsailing.com; Perkins Cove, Ogunquit; adult $35-40; ⏰late May-Sep) Has five two-hour trips daily on a 42ft Hinckley sloop (single-masted sailboat), cruising the tranquil and rocky shoreline near Ogunquit.

🛏 Sleeping

Pinederosa Camping
CAMPGROUND $

(⏎207-646-2492; www.pinederosa.com; 128 North Village Rd, Wells; campsites $30; ☀🅿) This wholesome, wooded campground has 162 well-tended sites, some of which overlook the Ogunquit River. Amenities include a lovely in-ground pool, camp store and summer shuttle to Ogunquit Beach, about 3 miles away.

Gazebo Inn
B&B $$

(⏎207-646-3733; www.gazeboinnogt.com; 572 Main St; r incl breakfast $109-245; 🛜☀) This stately 1847 farmhouse features 14 rooms and feels more like a private boutique hotel. Rustic-chic touches include heated wood floors, stone fireplaces in the bathrooms, and a media room with beamed ceilings and a wall-sized TV.

Ogunquit Beach Inn
B&B $$

(⏎207-646-1112; www.ogunquitbeachinn.com; 67 School St; r incl breakfast $139-179; @🛜) In a tidy little Craftsman-style bungalow, this gay-and-lesbian-friendly B&B has colorful, homey rooms and chatty owners who know all about the best new bistros and bars in town. The central location makes walking to dinner a breeze.

Rockmere Lodge
B&B $$

(⏎207-646-2985; www.rockmere.com; 150 Stearns Rd, Ogunquit; r incl breakfast $175-235) In a shingled Victorian mansion perched high above the ocean, the Rockmere has the quirky charm of your slightly batty Great Aunt Alice's house. The parlors and eight guest rooms are decorated in a style that might be called 'flea-market maximalism,' with faux flowers, chipped vases and gilt-framed amateur oil paintings.

Norseman
HOTEL $$$

(⏎207-646-2823, 207-646-9093; www.ogunquit-beach.com; 135 Beach St, Ogunquit; d $190-340; 🛜☀) In an impossible-to-miss spot at the tip of the Ogunquit Beach peninsula, the sprawling Norseman has a retro family-resort charm. Kitschy faux-Nordic touches, such as beamed ceilings, add ambience to otherwise motel-style rooms.

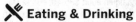 Eating & Drinking

Bread & Roses
BAKERY $

(www.breadandrosesbakery.com; 246 Main St; snacks $3-9; ☺7am-7pm; 🖉) 🍴 Get your fix of coffee and blueberry scone at this teeny slip of a bakery, in the heart of downtown Ogunquit. The cafe fare is good for a quick lunch, with dishes such as veggie burritos and organic egg salad sandwiches. No seating.

Caffe Prego
ITALIAN $$

(🖉207-646-7734; 44 Shore Rd, Ogunquit; mains $9-18; ☺lunch & dinner late Apr–mid-Oct) In a sleek downtown bungalow, Prego has good pizza, panini, gelato and cappuccinos, and even better people-watching. Summer means live music on the porch.

Arrows
NEW AMERICAN $$$

(🖉207-361-1100; www.arrowsrestaurant.com; Berwick Rd, Ogunquit; mains $42, 10-course tasting menu $135; ☺dinner Tue-Sun in summer, fewer days May-Dec) Eating at Arrows, considered by some to be one of the best restaurants in America, is an Event with a capital 'E.' The actual restaurant, in a gray farmhouse on the outskirts of Ogunquit, is difficult to find without a GPS. Reservations are crucial; dressing up is strenuously recommended. Descriptions of dishes take up whole paragraphs. Things like 'foie gras croutons' are served without irony. If you dig pomp and circumstance, you'll have a blast. If not, come for one of the lower-key Friday 'bistro nights' – $40 for a three-course meal.

Barnacle Billy's
SEAFOOD $$$

(🖉207-646-5575; www.barnbilly.com; 183 Shore Rd; mains $12-35; ☺11am-9pm) This big, noisy barn of a restaurant overlooking Perkins Cove is a longtime favorite for casual seafood – steamers, crab rolls, clam chowder and, of course, whole lobsters.

MC Perkins Cove
NEW AMERICAN $$$

(🖉207-646-6263; www.mcperkinscove.com; 111 Perkins Cove Rd, Ogunquit; mains $19-31; ☺lunch & dinner) Owned by chefs Mark Gaier and Clark Frasier ('M' and 'C,' respectively) of Arrows fame, MC Perkins Cove has won raves for its casual but exquisite way with local seafood. Start with house-cured gravlax and move on to Moroccan-style calamari or sesame-encrusted rainbow trout. The handsome interior, all glass and burnished wood, looks right

out over the Atlantic. The bar is nice for quick lunches or solo dining.

Front Porch
BAR

(🖉207-646-4005; www.thefrontporch.net; Ogunquit Sq, Ogunquit; ☺from 5pm) This kitschy, fun piano bar attracts a mixed crowd to its many off-key sing-alongs, and is a dapper setting for a cocktail. There's tasty seafood served in the adjoining restaurant.

☆ Entertainment

Ogunquit Playhouse
THEATER

(🖉207-646-5511; www.ogunquitplayhouse.org; 10 Main St, Ogunquit; tickets $35-50; ☺performances May-Sep) This 1933 theater hosts four or five musicals annually in the 750-seat theater. Well-known performers occasionally perform in the cast, although the productions are high quality even without them.

ℹ Information

Ogunquit Chamber of Commerce (🖉207-646-2939; www.ogunquit.org; 36 Main St; ☺9am-5pm Mon-Fri, 10am-3pm Sat & Sun) Located on US 1, near the Ogunquit Playhouse and just south of the town's center.

ℹ Getting There & Around

There's no direct bus service to Ogunquit; the nearest **Greyhound** (www.greyhound.com) stop is in Portsmouth, NH, 16 miles south. Amtrak's **Downeaster** (www.amtrakdowneaster.com) stops in Wells on its Portland–Boston loop. The nearest major airport is in Portland.

In summer, red trolleys ($1.50 per trip) circulate through Ogunquit every 10 minutes from 8am to 11pm. Leave the driving to them in this horribly congested town; they'll take you from the center to the beach or Perkins Cove.

The Kennebunks

POP 15,300

A longtime destination of moneyed East Coasters, the towns of Kennebunk and Kennebunkport make up the Kennebunks. Kennebunk is a modest working-class town with few tourist attractions aside from its marvelous white sand beaches. Just across the river, proudly waspy Kennebunkport crawls with tourists year-round. The epicenter of activity is Dock Sq, lined with cafes, art galleries and upscale boutiques selling preppy essentials (whale-print shirts, anyone?). Drive down Ocean Ave to gawk at the grand mansions and hotels overlooking the surf, including the massive George Bush Sr compound on a protected spit of land called Walker's Point. At the eastern terminus of School St is the charming hamlet of Cape Porpoise, home to some of the area's more affordable hotels and restaurants.

◉ Sights

Beaches   BEACHES

Kennebunkport proper has only one beach, **Colony Beach**, which is dominated by the Colony Hotel. But Beach Ave and Sea Rd (west of Kennebunk River and then south of Kennebunk Lower Village) lead to three good public beaches: Gooch's Beach, Middle Beach and Mother's Beach, known collectively as **Kennebunk Beach**. Beach parking permits cost $15 daily, $25 weekly and $50 seasonally.

Seashore Trolley Museum   MUSEUM

(www.trolleymuseum.org; 195 Log Cabin Rd, Kennebunkport; adult/child $10/7.50; ⊙10am-5pm May-Oct; ☑) On the outskirts of town, this family-friendly museum has some 250 streetcars (including one named Desire), as well as antique buses and public-transit paraphernalia.

🏃 Activities

First Chance   SAILING

(☑207-967-5507; www.firstchancewhalewatch.com; 4 Western Ave, Kennebunk; lobster tour adult/child $20/15; whale watch adult/child $49/29; ⊙May-Oct) Offers a 1½-hour lobster boat cruise and a four-hour whale-watching voyage departing from Kennebunk's Lower Village.

Schooner Eleanor   SAILING

(☑207-967-8809; schoonersails@gwi.net; Arundel Wharf, Kennebunkport; cruises $43) A splendid 55ft schooner offering two-hour sails off Kennebunkport (season and weather dependent).

Southern Maine Kayaks   SAILING, KAYAKING

(☑888-925-7496; www.southernmainekayaks. com; 4 Western Avenue, Kennebunk; tours $50, half/ full day rentals $35/55) An operator offering guided tours, sunset and moonlight trips, and kayak rental.

🛌 Sleeping

Salty Acres Campground   CAMPGROUND $

(☑207-967-2483; www.saltyacrescampground. com; ME 9, Kennebunkport; tent sites $28; ⊙mid-May–mid-Oct; ☑) This huge, well-tended campground, a mile from Goose Rocks Beach, has

several hundred tent and RV sites. Family-friendly amenities include a pool, laundromat and camp store.

Colony Hotel   HOTEL $$

(☑207-967-3331; www.thecolonyhotel.com; 140 Ocean Ave; r incl breakfast $129-299; 🛜🏊) Built in 1914, this grand dame of a summer resort evokes the splendor of bygone days. Inside, the 124 old-fashioned rooms have vintage cabbage-rose wallpaper and authentically creaky floors. Outside, ladies recline on Adirondack chairs on the manicured lawn, while young men in polo shirts play badminton nearby and children splash around at the private beach across the street.

Franciscan Guest House   GUESTHOUSE $$

(☑207-967-4865; www.franciscanguesthouse. com; 26 Beach Ave; r incl breakfast $89-159; 🛜🏊) You can almost smell the blackboard chalk inside this high school–turned-guesthouse, on the peaceful grounds of the St Anthony Monastery. Guest rooms, once classrooms, are basic and unstylish – acoustic tile, faux wood paneling, motel beds. If you don't mind getting your own sheets out of the supply closet (there's no daily maid service), staying here is great value and a unique experience.

Cove House B&B   B&B $$

(☑207-967-3704; www.covehouse.com; 11 S Maine St; r incl breakfast $165, 2-night min weekends Jul & Aug; cabin $1000 per week Jul & Aug, $165 per night with 3-night min Sep-Jun) A small but comfortable inn overlooking Chick's Cove on the Kennebunk River, this B&B has spacious rooms and a one-bedroom cabin (full kitchen) with wood floors, Oriental carpets and antique furnishings.

1802 House   B&B $$

(☑207-967-5632; www.1802inn.com; 15 Locke St, Kennebunkport; r incl breakfast $188-261; 🛜) In a restored 19th-century farmhouse in a quiet residential neighborhood, this B&B has six sweet, country-style rooms. All but one have their own fireplaces, making this a particularly cozy place to stay in winter.

★ Cabot Cove Cottages   COTTAGES $$$

(☑800-962-5424, 207-967-5424; www.cabotcove cottages.com; 7 S Maine St, Kennebunkport; cottage incl breakfast $325-695; ⊙early May–mid-Oct; 🛜) Set in a semicircle in a forest glade, these 14 miniature cottages look almost like fairy houses. Decor is airy and peaceful, all white-washed walls and vintage botanical prints.

Cottages range in size; all have full kitchens. Breakfast is dropped off on your doorstep each morning.

Cape Arundel Inn   INN $$$

(☑207-967-2125; www.capearundelinn.com; 208 Ocean Ave, Kennebunkport; r incl breakfast $295-375; ⊙Mar-Jan; 🛜) Perched high above the sea on Kennebunkport's famed Ocean Ave, this shingled 19th-century beach mansion has some of the most dramatic views in town. The 13 sunny guest rooms are done up in pale blues, whites and pinks for a summery feel. The hotel's fine-dining restaurant is well regarded.

✖ Eating

Dock Square Coffee House   COFFEE SHOP $

(☑207-967-4422; www.docksquarecoffeehouse.com; 18 Dock Sq, Kennebunkport; pastries $2-5; ⊙7:30am-5pm mid-Apr–Dec) This tiny downtown cafe is a cozy spot for coffee, tea and pastries. Open to 10pm in summer.

★Nunan's Lobster Hut   SEAFOOD $$

(☑207-967-4362; www.nunanslobsterhut.com; 9 Mills Rd, Cape Porpoise; mains $11-23; ⊙5-10pm; 🐾) Four miles east of Kennebunkport, Nunan's is *the* place to roll up your sleeves and flex your lobster-cracking muscles. Owners Richard and Keith Nunan still trap and cook the lobsters just like their grandfather did when he opened the restaurant in 1953. Decor is 'haute Maine fishing shack,' with wooden walls hung with ancient nets and buoys.

Lobster haters can order the Delmonico steak dinner, though you'll probably get some mighty strange looks.

Clam Shack   SEAFOOD $$

(2 Western Ave; mains $7-22; ⊙11am-9:30pm) Standing in line at this teeny gray hut, perched on stilts above the river, is a time-honored Kennebunkport summer tradition. Order a box of fat, succulent fried whole-belly clams or a one-pound lobster roll, which is served with your choice of mayo or melted butter. Outdoor seating only.

Federal Jack's
Restaurant & Brew Pub   AMERICAN $$

(☑207-967-4322; www.federaljacks.com; 8 Western Ave, Kennebunkport; mains $10-23; ⊙11:30am-12:30am) Above the Kennebunkport Brewing Co, crowds dine on international pub fare, such as nachos, steamed mussels and Cajun-style blackened fish. The real draws, though, are the microbrews and the harbor views.

Free brewery tours are offered by appointment through the coffee shop downstairs.

Hurricane   AMERICAN $$$

(☑207-967-9111; www.hurricanerestaurant.com; 29 Dock Sq; mains $12-45; ⊙11:30am-9:30pm) On Dock Sq, this popular fine-dining bistro specializes in the classics: crab-stuffed baked lobster, rack of lamb in a red wine reduction, bread pudding. Small plates are more modern and creative: tempura-fried spicy tuna rolls, duck-liver mousse with fig jam. Crowds tend to be middle-aged, well heeled and high on wine.

White Barn Inn   NEW AMERICAN $$$

(☑207-967-2321; www.whitebarninn.com; 37 Beach Ave, Kennebunkport; 3-course dinner $98, 10-course tasting menu $140; ⊙5-10pm) One of Maine's most renowned restaurants, the White Barn boasts country-elegant decor and a menu that changes weekly. Expect local seafood, meat and produce such as New England quail breast served with morels, white asparagus and poached rhubarb; and Atlantic halibut perched atop a bed of braised fennel 'risotto.' Reservations are crucial, as is proper attire (no cut-off jean shorts/beach wear).

Guests cleanse their palates between courses with sorbets in creative flavors like orange-carrot or pineapple-sage.

❶ Information

Kennebunkport Information & Hospitality Center (☑207-967-8600; www.visitthekennebunks.com; Union Sq, Kennebunkport; ⊙10am-9pm Mon-Fri, 9am-9pm Sat & Sun) This center has helpful staff who might be able to find you accommodations. Shorter hours outside of summer.

Kennebunk-Kennebunkport Chamber of Commerce Information Center (☑207-967-0857; 17 Western Ave; ⊙10am-5pm Mon-Fri year-round, plus 10am-3pm Sat & Sun Jun-Sep) Shorter hours outside of summer.

❶ Getting There & Around

The Kennebunks lie halfway (28 miles from each city) between Portsmouth, NH, and Portland, ME, just off I-95 on ME 9. There's no direct bus service to Kennebunkport; **Greyhound** (www.greyhound.com) stops in both Portland and Portsmouth. Amtrak's **Downeaster** (www.amtrakdowneaster.com) stops in Wells, about 9 miles to the south, on its Boston–Portland loop.

The **Intown Trolley** (www.intowntrolley.com; day pass adult/child $15/5; ⊙hourly 10am-4pm) circulates through Kennebunkport, with stops at the beaches, the Bush compound, the

Franciscan monastery and other points of interest. You can ride the entire route on a 45-minute narrated tour, or hop on and off at designated stops, including along Ocean Ave. Runs shorter hours outside summer.

Old Orchard Beach

POP 9400

This quintessential New England beach playground is saturated with lights, music and noise. Skimpily clad crowds of fun-loving sun worshippers make the rounds of candy shops, mechanical amusements and neon-lit trinket emporiums. Many of them will be speaking French, as Old Orchard Beach has long been the preferred summer destination for *québécois* families.

The Palace Playland (www.palaceplayland. com; 1 Old Orchard St; day pass incl unlimited rides adult/child $31.50/23.50), a vintage beachfront amusement park, is the town's fitting symbol. Its carousel, Ferris wheel, children's rides, fried clam stands and souvenir shops have been a source of summer fun for more than 60 years. It's open weekends only in spring and fall, and closed in winter.

Dozens of little motels and guesthouses line the beaches to the north and south of the town center, and all are full from late June to early September. Before and after that, Old Orchard Beach slumbers.

PORTLAND

POP 66,400

Maine's largest city has capitalized on the gifts of its port history – the redbrick warehouse buildings, the Victorian shipbuilders' mansions, the narrow cobblestone streets – to become one of the hippest, most vibrant small cities in America. With a lively waterfront, excellent museums and art galleries, abundant green space, and a food scene worthy of a town many times its size, it's worth much more than a quick stopover.

On a peninsula jutting into the grey waters of Casco Bay, Portland's always been a city of the sea. Established in 1633 as a fishing village, it grew to become New England's largest port. Today, the Old Port district is the town's historic heart, with handsomely restored brick buildings filled with cafes, shops and bars. The working wharves keep things from getting too precious or museum-like, as fishmongers in rubber boots mingle with well-heeled Yankee matrons.

BLUE BLOOD

Forget those supermarket fakes – fresh Maine blueberries can't be imitated. Maine farmers grow more than 25% of the world's blueberries (and more than 90% of its wild blueberries), and do-it-yourself berry picking is one of Maine's best-loved summer traditions. The pea-size fruits grow best in July and August, when many roadside fruit farms open their doors to DIY pickers. Or just drive up US 1 and look out for handmade cardboard signs. If you've got kids in tow, buy them a copy of Robert McCloskey's classic children's book, *Blueberries for Sal*.

Congress St is the main thoroughfare through downtown, passing Portland's most imposing buildings: city hall, banks, churches and hotels. Commercial St, where many businesses are located, runs the length of the harbor. Two promenades (upscale Western and more workaday Eastern) frame downtown Portland at opposite ends of the peninsula. The West End neighborhood is home to an impressive collection of 19th-century mansions and the bulk of the city's charming B&Bs. In the east, Munjoy Hill is Portland's up-and-coming hipster enclave.

◉ Sights

Old Port NEIGHBORHOOD
Handsome 19th-century brick buildings line the streets of the Old Port, with Portland's most enticing shops, pubs and restaurants located within this five-square-block district. By night, flickering gas lanterns add to the atmosphere. What to do here? Eat some wicked fresh seafood, down a local microbrew, buy a nautical-themed T-shirt from an up-and-coming designer or peruse the many tiny local art galleries. Don't forget to wander the authentically stinky wharfs, ducking into a fishmongers to order some lobsters to ship home.

Portland Museum of Art MUSEUM
(☑207-775-6148; www.portlandmuseum.org; 7 Congress Sq; adult/child $12/6, 5-9pm Fri free; ◐10am-5pm Sat-Thu, to 9pm Fri, closed Mon mid-Oct–May) This well-respected museum (founded in 1882) houses an outstanding collection of American artists. Maine artists,

Central Portland

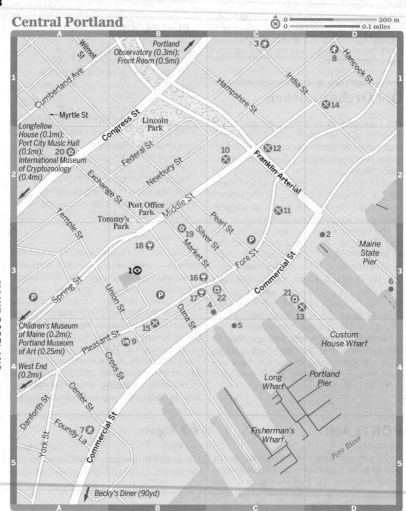

including Winslow Homer, Edward Hopper, Louise Nevelson and Andrew Wyeth, are particularly well represented. You'll also find a few works by European masters, including Degas, Picasso and Renoir. The collections are spread across three separate buildings. The majority of works are found in the postmodern Charles Shipman Payson building, designed by the firm of famed architect IM Pei. The 1911 beaux-arts-style LDM Sweat Memorial Gallery and the 1801 Federal-style McLellan House hold the 19th-century American art collection.

West End NEIGHBORHOOD

Portland's loveliest neighborhood is a hillside enclave of brick town houses, elegant gardens and stately mansions, some of which date from the neighborhood's founding in 1836. This is a fairly mixed community along the gay-straight, young-elderly divide, with smaller pockets of working-class families living amid their higher-mortgage-paying neighbors. There's cultural diversity, some of Portland's best B&Bs and the scenic **Western Promenade**, a grassy pathway with fine views over the harbor.

Central Portland

Portland Observatory　　OBSERVATORY
(www.portlandlandmarks.org/observatory; 138 Congress St; adult/child $9/5; ⊘10am-5pm late May-early Oct) Built in 1807 atop Munjoy Hill, this seven-story brick tower was originally used to warn Portlanders of incoming fishing, military and merchant vessels. Now restored, the observatory has stunning panoramic views of Portland and its harbor. Admission includes a 45-minute guided tour of the observatory. From late July to late August, special Thursday night sunset tours offer views of the sun setting behind the White Mountains.

Fort Williams Park　　LIGHTHOUSE
(⊘sunrise-sunset) 🅟 FREE Four miles southeast of Portland on Cape Elizabeth, 90-acre Fort Williams Parkis worth visiting simply for the panoramas and picnic possibilities. Stroll around the ruins of the fort, a late-19th-century artillery base, checking out the WWII bunkers and gun emplacements (a

German U-boat was spotted in Casco Bay in 1942) that still dot the rolling lawns. Strange as it may seem, the fort actively guarded the entrance to Casco Bay until 1964.

Adjacent to the fort stands the Portland Head Light, the oldest of Maine's 52 functioning lighthouses. It was commissioned by George Washington in 1791 and staffed until 1989, when machines took over. The keeper's house has been passed into service as a **museum** (✆207-799-2661; www.portlandheadlight.com; 1000 Shore Rd; lighthouse museum adult/child $2/1; ⊘10am-4pm Jun-Oct) which traces the maritime and military history of the region.

International Museum of Cryptozoology　　MUSEUM
(www.cryptozoologymuseum.com; 661 Congress St; admission $5; ⊘11am-6pm Wed-Sat, noon-6pm Sun; 🅟) In the back of a used bookstore, Loren Coleman displays his extensive collection of model 'cryptids' – animals thought by mainstream science to, er, not really exist. But after a few minutes of listening to Coleman talk about the Casco Bay Monster (Portland's answer to Scotland's Nessie), you'll be reconsidering your thoughts on yetis and the Mothman. Coleman, who's been a consultant on dozens of monster-related TV shows, is happy to answer even the weirdest questions. Get a picture with the 9ft-tall Bigfoot on the way out.

Children's Museum of Maine　　MUSEUM
(✆207-828-1234; www.childrensmuseumofme.org; 142 Free St; admission $9; ⊘10am-5pm Mon-Sat, noon-5pm Sun, closed Mon Sep-May; 🅟) Kids aged zero to 10 shriek and squeal as they haul traps aboard a replica lobster boat, milk a fake cow on a model farm, or monkey around on an indoor rock-climbing wall. The highlight of this ultra-interactive museum might be the 3rd-floor camera obscura, where a single pinhole projects a panoramic view of downtown Portland.

Victoria Mansion　　HISTORIC HOME
(✆207-772-4841; www.victoriamansion.org; 109 Danforth St; adult/child $15/5; ⊘10am-4pm Mon-Sat, 1-5pm Sun late May-early Oct) Just a few blocks southeast of the art museum, this outstanding Italianate palace dates back to 1860. Inside, it's decorated sumptuously with rich furniture, frescoes, paintings, carpets, gilt and exotic woods and stone. The admission price includes a 45-minute guided tour.

MAINE PORTLAND

Longfellow House
HISTORIC BUILDING

(☑207-879-0427; www.mainehistory.org; 489 Congress St; adult/child $12/3; ☺10am-5pm Mon-Sat, noon-5pm Sun May-Oct) The revered American poet Henry Wadsworth Longfellow grew up in this Federal-style house, built in 1788 by his Revolutionary War–hero grandfather. The house has been impeccably restored to look like it did in the 1800s, complete with original furniture and artifacts.

Museum of African Culture
MUSEUM

(☑207-871-7188; www.museumafricanculture.org; 13 Brown St; admission $5; ☺10:30am-4pm Tue-Fri, noon-4pm Sat) New England's only African culture museum houses over 1500 pieces of art and craftwork from the continent's sub-Saharan region, with a particularly impressive collection of ceremonial masks. Pottery, ivory flutes and nicely executed changing exhibitions add to the portfolio.

Activities

Portland Trails
HIKING

(www.portlandtrails.org) Thanks to the efforts of the Portland Trails conservation organization, there are some 50 miles of multi-use trails sprinkled about the Greater Portland area. One of the most popular paths is the 3.5-mile Back Cove Loop, which provides excellent water and city views northwest of the city center. This trail connects to the Eastern Promenade, a 2.1-mile paved waterfront path that follows a former railway, just east of East End.

For a complete rundown of trails (26 in all), with maps, visit the website.

Maine Island Kayak Company
KAYAKING

(☑207-766-2373; www.maineislandkayak.com; 70 Luther St, Peaks Island; tour $70; ☺May-Nov) On Peak Island, a 15-minute cruise from downtown on the Casco Bay Lines, this well-run outfitter offers fun day and overnight trips exploring the islands of Casco Bay.

Cycle Mania
CYCLING

(☑207-774-2933; www.cyclemania1.com; 59 Federal St; bike rental day/week $36/150) Rent a road bike or a hybrid cruiser, perfect for exploring the Portland Trails.

Tours

Casco Bay Lines
CRUISE

(☑207-774-7871; www.cascobaylines.com; 56 Commercial St; adult $13-24, child $7-11) This outfit cruises the Casco Bay islands delivering mail, freight and visitors. It also offers cruises to Bailey Island (adult/child $25/12).

Eagle Island Tours
CRUISE

(☑207-774-6498; www.eagleislandtours.com; Long Wharf, 170 Commercial St; adult/child $35/22; ☺Jun-Sep) Runs sightseeing trips out to the Portland Head Light and Eagle Island, where you can tour the summer home of explorer Robert Peary, the first man to visit the North Pole.

Portland Schooner Company
CRUISE

(☑207-776-2500; www.portlandschooner.com; 56 Commercial St; adult/child $35/10; ☺May-Oct) Offers tours aboard an elegant, early-20th-century schooner. In addition to two-hour sails, you can book overnight tours ($240 per person, including dinner and breakfast).

Greater Portland Landmarks
WALKING TOUR

(☑207-774-5561; www.greaterportlandlandmarks. org; adult/child $10/free; ☺Mon-Sat Jun–mid-Oct) This place offers fun, historical architectural walking tours of the Old Port, the city's grand 19th-century homes and the 350-year-old Eastern Cemetery. Call ahead for details of where to buy tickets.

Downeast Duck Tours
CRUISE

(☑207-774-3825; www.downeastducktours.com; 177 Commercial St; adult/child $25/18; ☺mid-May–mid-Oct; ⬤) This 65-minute amphibious bus tour putters through the Old Port, before plunging into the bay for a waterside look at the wharves.

Sleeping

Portland has a healthy selection of midrange and upscale B&Bs, though very little at the budget end. The most idyllic accommodations are in the old town houses and grand Victorians in the West End.

Inn at St John
INN $

(☑207-773-6481; www.innatstjohn.com; 939 Congress St; r incl breakfast $79-169; P☜) This turn-of-the-century hotel has a stuck-in-time feel, from the old-fashioned pigeonhole mailboxes behind the lobby desk to the narrow, sweetly floral rooms. Ask for a room away from noisy Congress St.

West End Inn
B&B $$

(☑800-338-1377; www.westendbb.com; 146 Pine St; r incl breakfast $180-225; P☜) In a red-brick town house in Portland's tony Western Promenade district, this six-room B&B is arty and elegant. Rooms are sunny and unfussy, with decor ranging from sweet florals to crisp nautical prints. The pale-aqua Under the Sea Room is a favorite.

★ **Danforth**   HOTEL **$$$**

(☎ 207-879-8755; www.danforthmaine.com; 163
Danforth St; r incl breakfast $185-295; P 🛜) Stay-
ing at this ivy-shrouded West End boutique
hotel feels like being a guest at an eccentric
millionaire's mansion. Shoot pool in the
wood-paneled game room (a former speak-
easy) or climb into the rooftop cupola for
views across Portland Harbor. The nine
rooms are decorated in a breezy, eclectic mix
of antiques and modern prints. Breakfast
is served in the sunlight-flooded enclosed
porch.

Pomegranate Inn   B&B **$$$**

(☎ 800-356-0408, 207-772-1006; www.pomegran
ateinn.com; 49 Neal St; r incl breakfast $185-295;
P 🛜) Whimsy prevails at this eight-room
inn, a historic home transformed into a
showcase for antiques and contemporary
art: life-size classical statutes, leopard rugs,
Corinthian columns and abstract sketches.
The common spaces are a riot of colors and
patterns. Guest rooms are hand-painted
with oversized flower patterns and outfitted
with a wild mix of antique and contemporary furniture. Somehow everything seems
to fit together.

Inn on Carleton   B&B **$$$**

(☎ 207-775-1910; www.innoncarleton.com; 46
Carleton St; r with breakfast $195-210; P) Inside
a restored 1869 Victorian, this inn has six
grandiose rooms, all with high ceilings and
large windows, allowing ample light into the
antique-filled rooms (the carved wooden
headboards in several rooms are astound-
ing). The English garden in back is a partic-
ularly peaceful setting in which to unwind.

Portland Harbor Hotel   HOTEL **$$$**

(☎ 207-775-9090; www.portlandharborhotel.com;
468 Fore St; r from $269; P 🛜) This independ-
ent hotel has a classically coiffed lobby,
where guests relax on upholstered leather
chairs surrounding the glowing fireplace.
The rooms carry on the classicism, with sunny gold walls and pert blue toile bedspreads.
The windows face Casco Bay, the interior
garden or the street; garden rooms are quieter. Parking is $16.

✗ **Eating**

Portland's food scene is hot, hot, hot right
now. Young chefs fleeing the higher rents in
East Coast cities like New York and Boston
have set up shop here, turning out creative
cuisine using the best of Maine's local ingredients. Seafood is big, naturally – look out
for New England specialties like periwin-
kles, quahog clams and, of course, lobster.
Cafe and bakery culture is strong too, so
you're never more than a few blocks from
an excellent cup of joe. The bulk of the best
restaurants are in the Old Port, but Munjoy
Hill and the West End also have some culinary gems.

Micucci Grocery   PIZZA **$**

(45 India St; pizza slice $4-6; ⊗ 11am-2pm) In-
the-know local foodies line up for the thick,
chewy 'Sicilian slab' at this old-school Italian
market, which sells pizza from a tiny bakery
in the back.

Becky's Diner   DINER **$**

(☎ 207-773-7070; www.beckysdiner.com; 390 Commercial St; mains $7-20; ⊗ 4am-9pm; 🍴) Once a
favorite of working fishermen, the booths at
this wharf-side diner are now packed with
Portland professionals and families with
young children. Try the haddock chowder,
the all-day breakfast or the unholy whoopie-
pie cake.

★ **Green Elephant**   VEGETARIAN **$$**

(☎ 207-347-3111; www.greenelephantmaine.com;
608 Congress St; mains $9-13; ⊗ 11:30am-2:30pm
Tue-Sat & 5-9:30pm Tue-Sun; 🍴) Even carni-
vores shouldn't miss the brilliant vegetar-
ian fare at this Zen-chic, Thai-inspired cafe.
Start with the crispy spinach wontons, then
move on to one of the exotic soy creations
such as gingered 'duck' with shiitake mush-
rooms. Save room for the incredible choco-
late orange mousse pie.

Front Room   NEW AMERICAN **$$**

(☎ 207-773-3366; www.frontroomrestaurant.
com; 73 Congress St; mains $11-21; ⊗ 8am-10pm)
Crowded, noisy and perfumed with smoke
from the open kitchen, this Munjoy Hill hot
spot is a jolly refuge from chilly Portland
evenings. Specializing in modern twists on
rib-sticking Yankee classics, it serves hearty
bowls of garlicky mussels, sandwiches with
house-smoked salmon pastrami, and a killer
baked-bean dinner (with local hot dogs, of
course). Order a pan of skillet corn bread for
the table.

Miyake   JAPANESE **$$**

(www.restaurantmiyake.com; 129 Spring St; sushi
$8-15, omakase menu from $38; ⊗ 11:30am-2pm
Mon-Fri, 5-10pm Mon-Sat; 🍴) Near the Museum
of Art, this tiny cult favorite sushi bar offers
some of the freshest fish in Portland – and

MAINE PORTLAND

that's saying a lot. Order à la carte or choose one of chef Masa Miyake's *omakase* (chef's choice) menus, which often include local ingredients like quahog clams or lobster sashimi. Miyake will even do an all-vegetarian meal. BYOB; the nearby West End Deli has a decent sake selection.

Schulte & Herr
GERMAN $$

(www.schulteundherr.wordpress.com; 349 Cumberland Ave; ⊙ 5-9pm Wed-Sun, 11:30am-2pm Fri, 10am-2pm Sat, 8am-2pm Sun) Bring along your favorite vino or New England microbrew (it's BYOB only) to match with the southern German food – think spaetzle with caramelized onions, emmentaler cheese, red onions, chives and cucumber salad, or split pea soup with smoked ham. But whatever you choose, you'll be treated to hearty German rye sourdough bread in an unassuming space that has a comfy farmhouse feel.

Susan's Fish & Chips
SEAFOOD $$

(www.susansfishnchips.com; 1135 Forest Ave/US 302; mains $7-19; ⊙ 11am-8pm) Pop in for fish and chips at this no-fuss eatery on US 302, where the tartar sauce comes in mason jars. Located in a former garage.

J's Oyster
SEAFOOD $$

(www.jsoyster.com; 5 Portland Pier; mains $6-24; ⊙ 11:30am-11:30pm Mon-Sat, noon-10:30pm Sun) This well-loved dive has the cheapest raw oysters in town. Eat 'em on the deck overlooking the pier. The oyster-averse have plenty of sandwiches and seafood mains to choose from.

Lobster Shack at Two Lights
SEAFOOD $$

(www.lobstershacktwolights.com; 225 Two Lights Rd, Cape Elizabeth; mains $12-25; ⊙ 11:30am-9pm Mar-Oct) Crack into a lobster at this well-loved Cape Elizabeth seafood shack, with killer views of the crashing Atlantic from both indoor and outdoor seating areas.

★ Fore Street
NEW AMERICAN $$$

(☑ 207-775-2717; www.forestreet.biz; 288 Fore St; mains $20-31; ⊙ 5:30-11pm) Chef-owner Sam Hayward has turned roasting into high art at Fore Street, one of Maine's most lauded restaurants. Chickens turn on spits in the open kitchen as chefs slide iron kettles of mussels into the wood-burning oven. Local, seasonal eating is taken very seriously here and the menu changes daily to offer the freshest ingredients. Dinner might consist of a fresh pea salad, periwinkles (a local shellfish) in herbed cream, and roast blue-

fish with pancetta. The large, noisy dining room nods towards its warehouse past with exposed brick and pine paneling. It's also ecofriendly.

Hugo's
FUSION $$$

(☑ 207-774-8538; www.hugos.net; 88 Middle St; mains $24-30; ⊙ 5:30-9pm Tue-Sat) James Beard Award–winning chef Rob Evans presides over this temple of molecular gastronomy. The menu, which changes regularly, might include such palate-challenging dishes as oxtail and monkfish dumplings, crispy fried pig ears, and bacon crème brûlée. The 'blind' tasting menu – diners only find out what they've eaten after they've eaten it – is the culinary equivalent of an avant-garde opera.

Bresca
ITALIAN $$$

(☑ 207-772-1004; www.bresca.org; 111 Middle St; mains $22-26; ⊙ 5-10pm Tue-Sat) This tiny jewel box of a restaurant serves wonderfully innovative Italian-influenced dishes – sea-urchin linguini with basil and lemon, braised Tuscan kale with seaweed butter, olive-oil gelato. Reservations are essential.

Five Fifty-Five
AMERICAN $$$

(☑ 207-761-0555; www.fivefifty-five.com; 555 Congress St; mains $16-31; ⊙ 5:30-10pm, brunch 8am-3pm Sun) This sleek, modern restaurant is perpetually crowded with hip Portlanders munching of-the-moment dishes like house-smoked pork belly with heirloom baked beans or homemade s'mores. Upstairs seats are best.

Evangeline
FRENCH $$$

(☑ 207-791-2800; www.restaurantevangeline.com; 190 State St; mains $14-28; ⊙ 5-10pm Mon-Sat) Impeccable French bistro standards, like mussels and *frites,* in a straight-out-of-Montmartre atmosphere, all vintage mirrors and black-and-white tiles. Monday is three-course prix fixe night ($30).

Street & Co
SEAFOOD $$$

(☑ 207-775-0887; www.streetandcompany.net; 33 Wharf St; meals $20-32; ⊙ 5-10:30pm) A longtime Old Port favorite for fresh seafood – grilled, blackened, broiled, tossed with pasta. Lobster *diavolo* for two is the house specialty. Reservations essential.

❂ Drinking & Nightlife

After dinner, Wharf St transforms into one long bar, with a young, easily intoxicated crowd spilling onto the streets. Other places to browse for a drink are along Fore St, between Union and Exchange Sts. If you're

PORTLAND BREWERY TOURS

Portland's foodie culture and its love of a nice cold beer combine to make the city a hot spot for microbreweries. Several of these are open for tours, making for a fun day of self-guided brewery hopping – just bring a designated driver! Here are a few of the top places to knock back a brew or two:

Shipyard Brewing Company (☑207-761-0807; www.shipyard.com; 86 Newbury St; ⊙tours 5:30pm Tue) Offers weekly Tuesday night tours of its waterfront facility, where brews, such as the full-bodied Export Ale and the malty Blue Fin Stout, are born. Call *far* ahead for a spot.

Allagash Brewing Company (☑800-330-5385; www.allagash.com; 50 Industrial Way; ⊙tours 11am, 1pm & 3pm Mon-Fri) Nationally known for its Belgian-style beers, Allagash opens its doors for three tours and tastings every weekday. The brewery is located 3.5 miles northwest of Portland's Old Port, off Forest Road.

DL Geary (☑207-878-2337; www.gearybrewing.com; 38 Evergreen Dr) Call ahead for tours of Maine's first microbrewery, which specializes in classic British ales. Located a few streets away from Allagash Brewing Company.

looking for something more low-key, try the West End or Munjoy Hill. Last call for alcohol is 1am, so things wind down relatively early. Beer geeks will be in heaven here, as Portland is a center of microbrew culture.

Great Lost Bear　　　　　PUB
(www.greatlostbear.com; 540 Forest Ave; ⊙noon-11pm; @🐾) Decked out in Christmas lights and flea-market kitsch, this sprawling cave of a bar and restaurant is a Portland institution. Sixty-nine taps serve 50 different Northeastern brews, including 15 from Maine, making the GLB one of America's best regional beer bars. Atmosphere is high energy and family friendly (at least early in the evening), with a massive menu of burgers, quesadillas and other bar nibbles.

Novare Res Bier Cafe　　　　PUB
(www.novareresbiercafe.com; Lower Exchange St alley; ⊙4pm-midnight Mon-Thu, 3pm-midnight Fri, noon-1am Sat & Sun) Tucked away off the Lower Exchange St alley, this European-style beer garden attracts a mixed-age crowd, who sit at communal tables quaffing from a 13-page menu of international brews and nibbling from meat and cheese plates.

Bull Feeney's　　　　　　PUB
(☑207-773-7210; 375 Fore St; ⊙11:30am-1am) Despite the mediocre food, Bull Feeney's remains a local favorite for its central location, warm ambience (it spills over two floors, with a crackling fire in one room) and garrulous crowd. Live bands play Thursday through Saturday.

Gritty McDuff's Brew Pub　　BREWPUB
(www.grittys.com; 396 Fore St; ⊙11am-1am) Gritty is an apt description for this party-happy Old Port pub. You'll find a generally raucous crowd drinking excellent beers – Gritty brews their own award-winning ales downstairs.

Back Bay Grill　　　　　　BAR
(www.backbaygrill.com; 65 Portland St; ⊙5:30-9pm Mon-Thu, 5pm-late Fri & Sat) The lounge area at this swank Old Port restaurant is the place to go for 25-year-old scotch or fancy gin cocktails.

Big Easy Blues Club　　　　CLUB
(www.bigeasyportland.com; 55 Market St; ⊙9pm-1am Tue-Sat, 4-9pm Sun, 6-10pm Mon) This small music club features a mostly local lineup of rock, jazz and blues bands, as well as open-mike hip-hop nights.

☆ Entertainment

Port City Music Hall　　CONCERT HALL
(www.portcitymusichall.com; 504 Congress St) This three-storey performance space hosts big-name bands and comedy tours.

Portland Symphony　　CLASSICAL MUSIC
(☑207-842-0800; www.portlandsymphony.com; Merrill Auditorium, 20 Myrtle St; admission $26-71; ⊙from 7pm Thu-Mon) The Portland Symphony has a solid reputation in these parts; it has been around since 1924 and continues to perform popular classical and pop concerts.

MAINE PORTLAND

🛍 Shopping

Going 'antiquing' in Portland largely means trolling Congress (west of Monument Sq) and Fore Sts, both of which have their gems.

Portland Farmers Market   FARMERS MARKET
(http://portlandmainefarmersmarket.org; ⊘ 7am-noon Sat, to 2pm Mon & Wed) On Saturdays in Deering Oak Park, vendors hawk everything from Maine blueberries to homemade pickles. On Monday and Wednesday the market is in Monument Sq.

Harbor Fish Market   FISHMONGER
(www.harborfish.com; 9 Custom House Wharf; ⊘ 7am-noon Mon-Sat) On Custom House Wharf, this iconic fishmonger packs lobsters to ship anywhere in the US.

Maine Potters Market   POTTERY
(www.mainepottersmarket.com; 376 Fore St; ⊘ 10am-8pm Mon-Fri, to 6pm Sat & Sun) A co-operatively owned gallery featuring the work of a dozen or so Maine ceramists.

ℹ Information

Greater Portland Convention & Visitors Bureau (www.visitportland.com; Ocean Gateway Bldg, 239 Park Ave; ⊘ 8am-5pm Mon-Fri, 10am-5pm Sat)

Maine Medical Center (☏ 207-662-0111; 22 Bramhall St; ⊘ 24hr) Emergency room open 24 hours.

Maine State Police (☏ 207- 624-7076)

Mercy Hospital (☏ 207-879-3265; 144 State St) Emergency room open 24 hours.

Portland Police (☏ 207-874-8479)

ℹ Getting There & Away

AIR

Portland International Jetport (p369) is Maine's largest and most chaotic air terminal. The lines here are dreadful: arrive at least 90 minutes before a flight or risk missing it.

BOAT

There are passenger ferry cruises between Portland and the islands of Casco Bay. The once-popular CAT ferry from Portland to Nova Scotia was discontinued in 2009, though some are campaigning to bring it back.

BUS

Greyhound (www.greyhound.com) offers multiple direct daily trips to Bangor ($28) and Boston ($24), with connections on to the rest of the US.

CAR & MOTORCYCLE

Coming from the south, take I-95 to I-295, then exit 7 onto Franklin St, which leads down to the Old Port. To bypass Portland, simply stay on I-95.

TRAIN

Amtrak's **Downeaster** (☏ 800-872-7245; www. amtrakdowneaster.com; 100 Thompson's Point Rd) runs five loops daily between Portland and Boston ($24), with brief stops in southern Maine and Dover, Durham and Exeter, New Hampshire.

ℹ Getting Around

TO/FROM THE AIRPORT

Metro bus 5 takes you to the center of town for $1.50. Taxis are about $17 to downtown.

BUS

Portland's city bus company is the **Metro** (www. gpmetrobus.com; fares $1.50). The main terminal is the 'Metro Pulse,' near Monument Sq. Routes serve Old Port, the Jetport, the Maine Mall, Cape Elizabeth and Falmouth, among other locations.

CAR & MOTORCYCLE

Parking is a challenge downtown; for quick visits, you can usually find a metered space (two hours maximum) in the Old Port, but rarely on Commercial St. A parking garage is an easier bet.

TAXI

Citywide rates are $1.90 for the first 0.1 miles, and $0.30 for every additional 0.1 miles. While you may get lucky and snag a taxi in the Old Port, you'll usually need to call ahead. Try **ASAP Taxi** (☏ 207-791-2727; www.asaptaxi.net) or **American Taxi** (☏ 207-749-1600; www.americantaxi maine.com).

Around Portland

Freeport

POP 8400

Nestled amid the natural beauty of Maine's rockbound coast is a town devoted almost entirely to shopping. Nearly 200 stores line the town's mile-long stretch of US 1, leading to long traffic jams during the summer. Strict zoning codes forbid the destruction of historic buildings, which is why you'll find a McDonald's housed in an 1850s Greek Revival home and an Abercrombie & Fitch outlet in a turn-of-the-century library. It all adds up to a slightly eerie 'Main St, USA' vibe.

Freeport's fame and fortune began a century ago when Leon Leonwood Bean opened a shop to sell equipment and provisions to hunters and fishermen heading north into the Maine woods. His success later brought other retailers to the area, making Freeport what it is today.

During the summer, LL Bean sponsors free Saturday evening concerts (www. llbean.com/events) in Freeport at Discovery Park.

◉ Sights & Activities

LL Bean Outdoor
Discovery School · OUTDOORS
(📞 888-552-3261; www.llbean.com/ods) Is 'learning to fly fish' on your bucket list? LL Bean offers intro and intermediate courses in casting techniques ($99), as well as private lessons. It also runs half-day kayaking trips on Casco Bay ($59), multiday canoe and kayak tours (from $250) and very short 'walk-on adventures' ($20) in fishing, kayaking, archery and clay-pigeon shooting.

Desert of Maine · MUSEUM
(📞 207-865-6962; www.desertofmaine.com; 95 Desert Rd; adult/child/teen $10.25/6.25/7.25; ⊘ 9am-4:30pm May-Oct; ♿) William Tuttle came to Freeport in 1797 to farm potatoes, but his deadly combination of clear-cutting and overgrazing caused enough erosion to expose the glacial desert hidden beneath the topsoil. The shifting dunes, which are 90ft deep in some areas, cover entire trees and the old farm's buildings. Admission includes a 30-minute tram tour and lots of kiddie attractions, such as gemstone hunting and a butterfly room.

Atlantic Seal Cruises · NATURE CRUISE
(📞 207-865-6112; www.atlanticsealcruises.com; Freeport Town Wharf; adult/child $55/40; ⊘ May-Oct) You'll risk a serious cuteness overdose as you watch baby seals frolic in the waters on the way to Seguin Island, the destination of this four-hour cruise. Once there, tour the lighthouse and enjoy your own picnic. An evening seal- and osprey-watching trip is also available.

DeLorme Mapping Company · BUILDING
(📞 207 846 7100; www.delorme.com; 2 DeLorme Dr; ⊘ 9:30am-6pm) Don't miss a visit to this office, with its giant 5300 sq ft rotating globe, Eartha, in nearby Yarmouth at exit 17 off I-95. Maker of the essential *Maine Atlas and Gazetteer,* DeLorme also creates maps and software for every destination in the United States.

Bradbury Mountain State Park · PARK
(📞 207-688-4712; 528 Hallowell Rd/ME 9, Pownal; adult/child $3/1) There are several miles of forested hiking trails here, including an easy 10-minute hike to a 485ft summit. It yields a spectacular view all the way to the ocean. There's camping as well.

Wolf Neck Woods State Park · PARK
(📞 207-865-4465; Wolf Neck Rd; admission $1.50) Just outside Freeport, this park has 5 miles of easy hiking trails, including a scenic shoreline walk that skirts Casco Bay. To reach the park, take Bow St and turn right on Wolf Neck Rd.

🛏 Sleeping

Recompense Shore
Campsites · CAMPGROUND $
(📞 207-865-9307; www.freeportcamping.com; 134 Burnett Rd; campsites $26-44; ⊘ May-Oct; 🛜) On the other side of the bay from South Freeport, this attractive campground has 115 shaded sites and a handful of cabins, some right along the water.

White Cedar Inn · B&B $$
(📞 207-865-9099; www.whitecedarinn.com; 178 Main St; r incl breakfast $150-185; 🛜) The former home of Arctic explorer Donald MacMillan, this Victorian-era B&B is conveniently located within walking distance of the shops. It has seven homey rooms, with brass beds and working fireplaces.

Royalsborough Inn · B&B $$
(📞 207-865-6566; www.royalsboroughinn.com; 1290 Royalsborough Rd, Durham; r incl breakfast $135-175; 🛜) A 10-minute drive from Freeport in rural Durham, this restored 18th-century farmhouse has seven handsome rooms, with burnished wood floors, beamed ceilings and handmade quilts. Yes, those are llamas you see out back – the Royalsborough's owners run a yarn business on the side.

Harraseeket Inn · INN $$
(📞 207-865-9377; www.harraseeketinn.com; 162 Main St; r incl breakfast $110-305; 🛜🐾) This big, white clapboard inn is a Freeport tradition, with a lodge-style lobby complete with crackling fireplace. While most of the 93 rooms have traditional florals and wall-to-wall carpet, the Thomas Moser Room is decked out in sleek slate and wood – stylish. The inn is just steps away from the LL Bean outlet, so you won't have to carry your shopping bags far.

🍴 Eating & Drinking

Eating in Freeport is a pretty middlebrow affair, with lots of chain restaurants and mediocre fast-food-style joints. But there are a few notable exceptions, especially if you like lobster.

MAINE AROUND PORTLAND

WHOOPIE!

Looking like steroid-pumped Oreos, these marshmallow-cream-filled chocolate snack cakes are a staple of bakeries and seafood shack dessert menus across the state. Popular both in Maine and in Pennsylvania's Amish country, whoopie pies are said to be so named because Amish farmers would shout 'whoopie!' when they discovered one in their lunch pail. Don't leave the state without trying at least one. For our money, Portland's Two Fat Cats bakery has the best, but Friars Bakehouse in Bangor is a close second.

Gritty McDuff's PUB $
(187 Lower Main St; meals $8-13; ⊙ lunch & dinner) Two miles south of LL Bean, this offshoot of the popular Portland tavern of the same name is a solid choice for pub grub and tasty microbrews.

Wicked Whoopies BAKERY $
(www.wickedwhoopies.com; 32 Main St; whoopie pies $1-3; ⊙ 7am-5pm; P) Head to the Isamax Snacks outlet to pick up a few ginormous whoopie pies in flavors like red velvet, maple, peanut butter and pumpkin. Perfect for gifts.

★ **Harraseeket**
Lunch & Lobster Co SEAFOOD $$
(📞 207-865-4888; www.harraseeketlunchandlobster.com; 36 Main St, South Freeport; mains $10-26; ⊙ 11am-7:45pm, to 8:45pm Jul & Aug; 🚹) Head down to the marina to feast on lobster at this iconic red-painted seafood shack. If it's nice out, grab a picnic table – or just do like the locals and sit on the roof of your car. Come early to beat the crowds. Finish with a slice of blueberry pie. BYOB.

Broad Arrow Tavern AMERICAN $$
(www.harraseeketinn.com; 162 Maine St; mains $12-28; ⊙ 11:30am-10pm Sun-Thu, to 11pm Sat-Sun) In the Harraseeket Inn, this wood-floored charmer has a good selection of microbrews and high-end bistro fare, including steamed clams, prime rib au jus, and wood-fired pizzas.

🛍 Shopping

LL Bean Flagship Store OUTDOOR EQUIPMENT
(www.llbean.com; Main St; ⊙ 24hr) The LL Bean store has expanded to add sportswear to its outdoor gear. Although a hundred other stores have joined the pack, the wildly popular LL Bean is still the epicenter of town and one of the most popular tourist attractions in Maine. It's part store, part outdoor-themed amusement park, with an archery range, an indoor trout pond and a 10ft-tall model of the Bean Boot.

ⓘ Information

Freeport Merchants Marketing Association
(📞 207-865-1212; www.freeportusa.com; 23 Depot St; ⊙ 9am-5pm Mon-Fri) Maintains an information kiosk one block south of Main St and another on Mallet St, near Main St.
State of Maine Information Center (📞 207-846-0833; www.visitmaine.com) Maintains an information kiosk one block south of Main St and another on Mallet St, near Main St.

ⓘ Getting There & Away

Freeport, 15 miles north of Portland via I-295, is a mile off the interstate on US 1. Buses do not stop in Freeport. A taxi from the Portland Jetport costs about $53.

Sabbathday Lake & Poland Spring

The Shakers, a Protestant religious sect named for their habit of ecstatic spiritual dancing, once inhabited communities up and down the East Coast. They believed in simple living, prayer, egalitarianism and hard work. They also believed in celibacy, which is likely why their numbers have dwindled over the centuries to precisely three remaining members. These three, now elderly, live 45 minutes from Portland at Sabbathday Lake (📞 207-926-4597; www.shaker.lib.me.us; adult/child $6.50/2; ⊙ tours 10:30am-3:15pm Mon-Sat late May–mid-Oct), the last active Shaker community in the world. New members are very much welcome but, if you didn't come to sign up, you can still take an interesting 1½-hour guided tour of the lovely 19th-century farm village. Among the plain white, well-kept buildings of the community are the meeting house, a museum and a shop selling the community's famed crafts. Most other buildings, including the impressive Brick Dwelling House, are not open to visitors.

A few miles to the north is the village of Poland Spring, famous for its mineral water, which is now sold throughout the US. In the early 19th century, a visitor was miraculously cured by drinking water from Poland

MAINE AROUND PORTLAND

Spring. Not known to miss a good thing, the locals opened hotels to cater to those wanting to take the waters.

To reach the Sabbathday Lake village, take I-95 to exit 63, then continue along ME 26 (Shaker Rd) for another 12 miles. Poland Spring is 3 miles north of there, also along ME 26.

MIDCOAST MAINE

Carved by ancient glaciers, the coastline of Midcoast Maine is jagged and dramatic. With its wild natural beauty and down-to-earth residents, the region is what many people imagine when they think of Maine. Ride bikes and shop for antiques in postcard-pretty seaside villages, take ambling scenic drives down the rural peninsulas, and ride the deep blue seas aboard one of the Midcoast's famous windjammers (multi-masted sailing ships). It's a landscape that bears

slow, aimless exploration – you never know when you're going to stumble upon the next great lobster shack, lost-in-time fishing village, or you-pick blueberry patch.

The English first settled this region in 1607, which coincided with the Jamestown settlement in Virginia. Unlike their southerly compatriots, though, these early settlers returned to England within a year. British colonization resumed in 1620. After suffering through the long years of the French and Indian War, the area became home to a thriving shipbuilding industry, which continues today.

Brunswick

POP 22,000

On the banks of the powerful Androscoggin River, Brunswick (first settled in 1628) is a handsome, well-kept town with a pretty village green and historic homes tucked along its tree-lined streets. It's home to the highly

Midcoast Maine

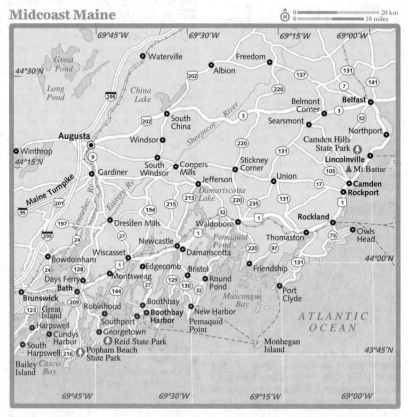

ALL ABOARD! A SCENIC TRAIN RIDE

For scenic views of the Midcoast, hop aboard the **Maine Eastern Railroad** (☏866-637-2457; www.maineeasternrail road.com; adult/child one-way $30/18; ⊙Sat & Sun late May-late Jun, Wed-Sun late Jun-Oct), with round-trip service between Brunswick and Rockland, with stops at Bath and Wiscasset. The two-hour, 57-mile journey, aboard restored mid-20th-century rail cars, passes along lovely stretches of coast. There's a dining car where you can enjoy wine and a light meal while watching seaside villages and rugged coastline drift slowly past.

respected Bowdoin College (founded in 1794), which infuses the town with a lively intellectual and artistic culture.

A short drive through the city center reveals stately Federal and Greek mansions built by wealthy sea captains. Harriet Beecher Stowe wrote *Uncle Tom's Cabin* at 63 Federal St. This poignant story of a runaway slave, published in 1852, was hugely popular and fired the imagination of people in the northern states, who saw the book as a powerful indictment against slavery.

Brunswick's green, called the Town Mall, is along Maine St. Farmers markets are set up Tuesday and Friday and there are concerts Wednesday evening in summer. Also worth seeing are the Androscoggin Falls, once a source of hydroelectric power for 18th-century sawmills.

⊙ Sights

The town's main sights are all on or near the campus of Bowdoin College, one of the oldest colleges in the US and the alma mater of Henry Wadsworth Longfellow, Nathaniel Hawthorne and US president Franklin Pierce. For a campus tour, follow the signs from Maine St to Moulton Union. Smith Union is the student center, with an information desk on the mezzanine level, as well as a cafe, pub, lounge and small art gallery.

Bowdoin College Museum of Art MUSEUM (www.artmuseum.bowdoin.edu; Bowdoin quadrangle; ⊙10am-5pm Tue-Sat, 1-5pm Sun) FREE In a 19th-century building with a dramatic modern glass entrance pavilion, this campus art museum is small but impressive. The 14,500-piece collection is particularly strong in the works of 19th- and 20th-century European and American painters, including Mary Cassatt, Andrew Wyeth, Winslow Homer and Rockwell Kent.

Peary-MacMillan Arctic Museum MUSEUM (☏207-725-3416; www.bowdoin.edu/arctic-mu seum; Hubbard Hall; ⊙10am-5pm Tue-Sat, 2-5pm Sun) FREE This small campus museum holds memorabilia from the expeditions of Robert Peary and Donald MacMillan, Bowdoin alumni who were among the first explorers to reach the North Pole. Particularly notable are MacMillan's massive collection of black-and-white Arctic photos.

Pejepscot Museums MUSEUMS The Pejepscot Historical Society preserves several house museums, which provide a fascinating glimpse into the past. You can visit them all for an $8 combination ticket.

The **Pejepscot Museum** (☏207-729-6606; 159 Park Row; ⊙9am-5pm Tue-Fri, noon-4pm Sat) FREE displays changing exhibits relating to Brunswick history, with photographs and artifacts pulled from its 50,000-piece inventory. **Skolfield-Whittier House** (☏207-729-6606; 161 Park Row; adult/child $5/2.50; ⊙tours 11am & 2pm Thu, Fri & Sat mid-May–mid-Oct), an adjacent 17-room brick mansion, is a virtual time capsule, closed as it was from 1925 to 1982. Victorian furnishings and decor are handsomely preserved – even the spices in the kitchen racks are authentic. The **Joshua L Chamberlain Museum** (☏207-725-6958; 226 Maine St; adult/child $5/2.50; ⊙10am-4pm Tue-Sat mid-May–mid-Oct) exhibits artifacts from the late owner's eventful life as college professor, Civil War hero, president of Bowdoin College and four-term governor of Maine. Tours of this museum are included with the admission fee.

✷ Festivals & Events

Bowdoin's Pickard Theater THEATER (☏207-725-8769; www.msmt.org; cnr Park Row & Bath Rd, Bowdoin campus) During summer, this theater hosts the Maine State Music Theater series, a run of Broadway musicals with performances from June through August.

Bowdoin International Music Festival CLASSICAL MUSIC (www.bowdoinfestival.org; ⊙late Jun-early Aug) In summer, this festival features classical concerts at venues throughout town.

🛏 Sleeping & Eating

Brunswick Inn B&B $$
(☑207-729-4914; www.brunswickinnparkrow.com; 165 Park Row; r incl breakfast $148-270; ☎) Overlooking Brunswick's town green, this elegant guesthouse has 15 rooms ranging from small to spacious. Each is uniquely designed in an airy farmhouse-chic style, a mix of worn woods and modern prints. The guest bar on the 1st floor is an excellent place to enjoy a glass, particularly on the patio overlooking the park.

★Frontier Cafe CAFE $$
(www.explorefrontier.com; 14 Main St; mains $9-15; ⊘8am-9pm) On the 2nd floor of the colossal Fort Andross mill complex overlooking the Androscoggin, this raw, loft-like space is part cafe, part bar, part cinema, part gallery. Arty student and professor types recline on vintage couches, sipping coffee or wine and nibbling hummus platters or gourmet panini. The theater features an ever-changing schedule of art-house flicks and live theater and music performances.

ⓘ Getting There & Away

Brunswick, off I-295 exit 31, is the point at which I-295 heads north and inland toward Augusta, Waterville and Bangor, and US 1 heads northeast along the coast. It's about 9 miles from Freeport and 8 miles from Bath. **Concord Coach Lines** (www.concordcoachlines.com; 101 Bath Rd) offers bus services to Bangor ($24), Portland ($13), Boston ($31) and a handful of Midcoast towns, departing from the Puffin Stop gas station.

Bath & Around

POP 8900

Known as the 'City of Ships,' this quaint Kennebec River town was once home to more than 20 shipyards producing more than a quarter of early America's wooden sailing vessels. In Bath's 19th-century heyday, it was one of Maine's largest cities, with a bustling downtown lined with banks and grand municipal buildings. Bath-built schooners and clipper ships sailed the seven seas and the city's name was known far and wide.

The shipbuilding tradition is still very much alive here in Bath. Across US 1 from downtown, Bath Iron Works (founded in 1884) is still one of the largest and most active shipyards in the US, producing steel frigates, cruisers and other naval craft. Locals know to avoid driving in or out of town around 3:30pm on weekdays, when the work shift changes and the roads choke with cars. South of the shipyard, the Maine Maritime

MAINE BATH & AROUND

WORTH A TRIP

BELFAST & SEARSPORT

Just north of Camden on US 1 lies Belfast, a lively working-class town with a handsome 19th-century Main St. A pleasant seaside park and a welcome shortage of tourists make Belfast a worthwhile stop. Five miles northeast, Searsport has a fine historic district with its share of 19th-century mansions. Searsport is also home to the superb **Penobscot Marine Museum** (☑207-548-2529; www.penobscotmarinemuseum.org; 5 Church St/US 1; adult/child $8/3; ⊘10am-5pm Mon-Sat, noon-5pm Sun late May-early Oct), housing Maine's biggest collection of mariner art and artifacts, which are spread throughout a number of historic buildings.

You can also explore Sears Island, an uninhabited 940-acre conservation area connected to the mainland by a causeway. Paddle here by kayak from **Searsport Shores Camping Resort** (☑207-548-6059; www.campocean.com; 216 W Main St; kayak per half/full day $30/50), a mile south of Searsport, or walk the pedestrian causeway (you can drive to the end of the causeway, but you'll have to walk from there). The resort also offers tent sites from $39. Then hike around the island and appreciate ospreys, bald eagles and bears (be careful!) in their natural habitat.

In downtown Belfast, the new **Belfast Bay Inn** (☑207-338-5600; www.belfastbayinn. com; 72 Main St, Belfast; r incl breakfast $275-410; ☎) has eight luxe suites with exposed brick walls and preppy New England prints. Breakfast is delivered to your door.

Open since 1865, **Darby's** (☑207-338-2339; www.darbysrestaurant.com; 155 High St, Belfast; mains $13-21; ⊘8am-9pm; ☑) is a picture-book bistro with tin ceilings, an original antique bar, and paintings by local artists adorning the walls. Eclectic fare includes crab melts, pecan-encrusted haddock and pad Thai.

Museum is an excellent place to learn about Bath's 400-year-old shipbuilding history.

Downtown, redbrick sidewalks and solid 19th-century buildings line quaint Main St, while just downhill lies a small grassy park overlooking the water.

◉ Sights & Activities

Maine Maritime Museum MUSEUM
(☏ 207-443-1316; www.mainemaritimemuseum.org; 243 Washington St; adult/child $15/10; ◷9:30am-5pm) On the western bank of the Kennebec River, this wonderful museum preserves the Kennebec's long shipbuilding tradition. The Maritime History Building contains paintings, models and hands-on exhibits that tell the tale of the last 400 years of seafaring. One highlight is the remains of the *Snow Squall,* a three-mast 1851 clipper ship. The on-site 19th-century Percy & Small Shipyard, preserved by the museum, is America's only remaining wooden-boat shipyard. Here you'll find a life-size sculpture of the *Wyoming,* the largest wooden sailing vessel ever built.

In summer, the museum offers a variety of boat trips and tours ($20-$40), ranging from 50-minute tours along the Kennebec River and 3½-hour afternoon lighthouse cruises to trolley tours through the Bath Iron Works.

Popham Beach State Park BEACH
(☏ 207-389-1335; 10 Perkins Farm Lane; admission $1.50; ◷9am-sunset) This 6-mile-long sandy stretch is one of the prettiest in the state, with views of offshore islands and the Kennebec and Morse Rivers framing either end. Lifeguards are on hand, but the surf is strong, with undertows and riptides. It's located off ME 209, about 14 miles south of Bath.

🛏 Sleeping

Meadowbrook Campground CAMPGROUND $
(☏ 207-443-4967; www.meadowbrookme.com; 33 Meadowbrook Rd, Phippsburg; sites $29; ◷May-Sep; ⛺) In Phippsburg, this friendly campground is well located to take advantage of pretty Popham Beach a few miles away, though you'll be sharing the grounds with many RVs.

Inn at Bath B&B $$
(☏ 207-443-4294; www.innatbath.com; 969 Washington St; r incl breakfast $180-220; 🛜🐾) Once a shipbuilder's mansion, this stately Greek Revival home in Bath's manicured historic

district has eight guest rooms done up in an appealing country style – lots of pale woods, soothing sage and green tones, and vintage botanical prints.

✖ Eating & Drinking

Five Islands Lobster Company SEAFOOD $$
(www.fiveislandslobster.com; 1447 Five Islands Rd, Georgetown; mains $6-25; ◷11:30am-9pm late May–mid-Oct) Crab cakes with fresh dill tartar sauce, golden fried clams, and lobsters dripping with melted butter. This wharf-side lobster shack, 14 miles south of Bath in the fishing hamlet of Georgetown, is a cut above average.

Solo Bistro NEW AMERICAN $$$
(☏ 207-443-3373; www.solobistro.com; 128 Front St; mains $16-25; ◷5-10pm) In a downtown storefront, Bath's most praised fine-dining restaurant has a small, seasonal menu of creative New American dishes, such as five-spice scallops and lobster risotto with truffle salt. The sleek, minimalist dining room could double as an IKEA showroom.

Kennebec Tavern AMERICAN $$$
(☏ 207-442-9636; www.kennebectavern.com; 119 Commercial St; mains $18-42; ◷11:30am-10pm, brunch 8am-2pm Sun) On downtown Bath's riverfront, this upscale-casual restaurant is a favorite for its huge selection of sandwiches, pastas and seafood. The outdoor seating's a big draw.

❶ Getting There & Away

Bath is 8 miles east of Brunswick and 10 miles southwest of Wiscasset on US 1. **Concord Coach Lines** (www.concordcoachlines.com; 10 State Rd) offers bus service to Bangor ($24), Portland ($14), Boston ($32) and a number of other Midcoast towns, leaving from in front of the Mail It 4 U shipping store.

Wiscasset

POP 3800

As the sign says, 'Welcome to Wiscasset, the Prettiest Village in Maine.' Other villages may dispute this claim, but Wiscasset's history as a major shipbuilding port in the 19th century has left it with a legacy of exceptionally beautiful houses. Set near the Sheepscot River, Wiscasset has some fine vantage points and its tidy streets are dotted with antique shops, galleries, restaurants and a few old-fashioned inns.

Like Bath, Wiscasset was a shipbuilding and maritime trading center. Great four-masted schooners carrying timber, molasses, salt, rum and cod sailed down the Sheepscot bound for England and the West Indies, a route known as the 'triangle trade.'

One caveat: as with other pretty towns astride US 1, Wiscasset has bad traffic jams in the summer.

⊙ Sights

Musical Wonder House   MUSEUM
(📞207-882-7163; www.musicalwonderhouse.com; 18 High St; half/full/grand tour $11/21/41; ⊙10am-5pm late May–mid-Oct) This 32-room Victorian sea captain's mansion tinkles with the sound of more than 5000 music boxes, player pianos, singing teapots, musical birds and other whimsical delights. Half and full tours let you explore downstairs; only the 'grand tour' allows entrance to the rarest music boxes in the Bird of Paradise Room upstairs.

Lincoln County Jail Museum   MUSEUM
(📞207-882-6817; 133 Federal St/ME 218; admission $4.50; ⊙10am-4pm Tue-Sat & noon-4pm Sun Jul & Aug, 10am-4pm Sat, noon-4pm Sun Jun & Sep) The first prison in the district of Maine opened in 1811 and, surprisingly, remained in operation until 1953. The hilltop structure of granite, brick and wood holds 12 tiny cells, complete with graffiti and other mementos from its earliest days. These days, the jail is a museum, with changing exhibitions covering episodes from Wiscasset's history.

Castle Tucker   HISTORIC HOME
(📞207-882-7364; cnr High & Lee Sts; adult/child/senior $5/2.50/4; ⊙11am-5pm Wed-Sun Jun–mid-Oct) OK, so it's not really a castle. Still, Wiscasset's grandest and best-situated mansion has a certain regal air about it. Judge Silas Lee had the Federal-style house built in 1807 to resemble a Scottish manor. It was later sold to a sea captain and today it remains a marvelous refuge of Victoriana, with 19th-century furnishings and wallpaper, and a commanding view over the countryside.

🛏 Sleeping

Highnote B&B   B&B $
(📞207-882-9628; www.wiscasset.net/highnote; 26 Lee St; r incl breakfast from $85) If Wiscasset were a movie set, the Highnote would be the haunted house on the hill. The spindly, Gothic-style Victorian has three atmospherically dim rooms with period furnishings and a shared bathroom. No ghosts, sadly.

★**Squire Tarbox Inn**   B&B $$
(📞207-882-7693; www.squiretarboxinn.com; 1181 Main Rd, Westport Island; r incl breakfast $118-210; ⊙Apr-Dec; 🐾) Ten miles southwest of Wiscasset on tranquil Westport Island, this 1763 farmhouse has been converted into a charmingly rustic country inn. The 11 guest rooms are sunny and old-fashioned, some with wood-burning fireplaces and beamed ceilings. The Swiss owner serves hearty, European-style dinners Wednesday through Sunday, using his own farm-fresh eggs and vegetables. Borrow a rowboat and explore the salt marsh, or wander out to the barn to visit with the goats.

✗ Eating

Treat's   MARKET $
(📞207-882-6192; www.treatsofmaine.com; 80 Main St; mains $3-15; ⊙10am-6pm Mon-Sat, 10am-3pm Sun) With a well-edited selection of fancy cheeses and a bakery overflowing with gorgeously browned baguettes and homemade fruit tarts, this little food store is a picnicker's heaven.

★**Red's Eats**   SEAFOOD $$
(Main St/US 1; mains $6-16; ⊙11:30am-9pm Apr-Sep) The lines for this iconic US 1 seafood shack, just before the downtown bridge, slow traffic so much in summer that the local government is considering building a $100 million bypass around downtown. No joke. Incredible lobster rolls, overflowing with chunks of fresh knuckle meat and slicked with your choice of drawn butter or creamy mayo, are what draws 'em in. Order at the counter and take a seat at one of the plastic tables overlooking the river.

Le Garage   AMERICAN $$
(📞207-882-5409; www.legaragerestaurant.com; 15 Water St; mains $9-26; ⊙11:30am-2:30pm & 5-9pm Tue-Sun) In an old stone garage overlooking Wiscasset Harbor, this longtime bistro serves upscale European and American standards – Caesar salad, seafood Alfredo, stuffed fillet of sole – in a French country atmosphere. Creamed finnan haddie (smoked haddock, a Maine classic) is the house specialty. The bar is a lovely spot for a glass of red and a bit of people-watching.

❶ Getting There & Away

Wiscasset is 10 miles northeast of Bath, 13 miles north of Boothbay Harbor and 23 miles south of Augusta. **Concord Coach Lines** (📞800-639-3317; www.concordcoachlines.com; 279 US 1) stops at Huber's Market on US 1, with services to Bangor ($23), Portland ($15), Boston ($33) and a number of other Midcoast towns.

Boothbay Harbor

POP 2200

Once a beautiful little seafarers village on a wide blue harbor, Boothbay Harbor is now an extremely popular tourist resort in the summer, when its narrow and winding streets are packed with visitors. Still, there's good reason to join the holiday masses in this picturesque place. Overlooking a pretty waterfront, large, well-kept Victorian houses crown the town's many knolls, and a wooden footbridge ambles across the harbor. From May to October, whale watching is a major draw.

After you've strolled the waterfront along Commercial St and the business district along Todd and Townsend Aves, walk along McKown St to the top of McKown Hill for a fine view. Then, take the footbridge across the harbor to the town's East Side, where there are several huge, dockside seafood restaurants.

Boothbay and East Boothbay are separate from Boothbay Harbor, the largest, busiest and prettiest of the three towns. Dealing with Boothbay Harbor's narrow, often one-way roads and scarce parking isn't any fun. Avoid it by parking at the small mall on Townsend Ave and catching the free Rocktide Inn shuttle into town. Once in town, hop aboard the trolley ($1) that tools around.

⊙ Sights & Activities

★ Coastal Maine Botanical Gardens
GARDENS

(☑207-633-4333; www.mainegardens.org; Barters Island Rd; adult/child $14/6; ⊙9am-5pm daily; 🅿) These magnificent gardens are one of the state's most popular attractions. The verdant waterfront kingdom has 248 acres, with groomed trails winding through forest, meadows and ornamental gardens blooming with both native and exotic plant species. The storybook-themed children's garden, opened in 2010, offers interactive fun, with water-spraying whale sculptures, a pond with rowboats and a winding grass maze. Don't miss a reading from a costumed Miss Rumphius, the lupine-planting heroine of the classic Maine children's book of the same name.

Boothbay Railway Village
MUSEUM

(☑207-633-4727; www.railwayvillage.org; 586 ME 27; adult/child $10/5; ⊙9:30am-5pm late May–mid-Oct; 🅿) Ride the narrow-gauge steam train through this endearing village, a historic replica of an old-fashioned New England town. The 28 buildings house more than 60 antique steam- and gas-powered vehicles, as well as exhibits on turn-of-the-century Maine culture. Frequent special events include craft fairs, auto shows and Thomas the Tank Engine visits.

Boothbay Region Land Trust
HIKING

(www.bbrlt.org; 2nd fl, 137 Townsend Ave) This land trust manages over 30 miles of hiking trails traversing tidal coves, shoreline forest, flower meadows and salt marshes. Birdwatchers should keep their eyes peeled for great blue herons, eider ducks, herring gulls and migratory birds. Stop by the office or go online for maps and schedules of guided hikes and bird-watching tours.

⟳ Tours

Boothbay Whale Watch
WHALE WATCHING

(☑207-633-3500; www.whaleme.com; Pier 6; adult/child $40/27; ⊙May-Oct) Ride the 100ft-long *Harbor Princess* in search of humpbacks and minkes. If you don't see one, your next cruise is free.

Balmy Days Cruises
CRUISE

(☑207-633-2284; www.balmydayscruises.com; Pier 8; harbor tour adult/child $15/8, daytrip cruise to Monhegan adult/child $32/18, sailing tour $24/18) This outfit takes day-tripping passengers to Monhegan Island (90 minutes) or on sailing tours of the harbor's many scenic island lighthouses.

✹ Festivals & Events

Boothbay Fisherman's Festival
FESTIVAL

(⊙late Apr) Yep, it's all about fishing and fun: think lobster crate races to cod fish relays to a classic boat parade. And of course, everyone is serving up seafood (mainly fish fries) all around town.

⨰ Sleeping

Budget accommodations are few and far between in this neck of the woods. Cheap motel seekers may have to backtrack as far as US 1.

Gray Homestead
CAMPGROUND $

(☑207-633-4612; www.graysoceancamping.com; 21 Homestead Rd, Southport; campsites $39) South of Boothbay Harbor on Southport

PEMAQUID POINT

Along a 3500-mile coastline famed for its natural beauty, Pemaquid Point stands out for its twisted rock formations pounded by the restless seas.

Perched on top of the rocks in Lighthouse Park (☏207-677-2494; www.bristolparks. org; Pemaquid Point; adult/child $2/free; ☺sunrise-sunset) is the 11,000-candlepower Pemaquid Light, built in 1827. It's one of the 61 surviving lighthouses along the Maine coast, 52 of which are still in operation. The keeper's house now serves as the Fishermen's Museum (☺9am-5:15pm mid-May-mid-Oct), displaying fishing paraphernalia and photos, as well as a nautical chart of the entire Maine coast with all the lighthouses marked.

ME 130 goes from Damariscotta (just north of Wiscasset) through the heart of the Pemaquid Peninsula (the longest on the coast of Maine) to Pemaquid Point, a major destination for its natural beauty. Artists and dilettantes from across the globe come here to record the memorable seascape in drawings, paintings and photographs.

Island, Gray Homestead has 40 wooded, oceanfront sites. There's swimming at the beach and kayak rental.

Topside Inn
B&B $$

(☏207-633-5404; www.topsideinn.com; 60 McKown St; r incl breakfast $165-275; ☏) Atop McKown Hill, this grand gray mansion has Boothbay's best harbor views. Rooms are elegantly turned out in crisp nautical prints and beachy shades of sage, sea glass and khaki. Main-house rooms have more historic charm, but rooms in the two adjacent modern guesthouses are sunny and lovely, too. Enjoy the sunset from an Adirondack chair on the inn's sloping, manicured lawn.

Newagen Seaside Inn
RESORT $$$

(☏207-633-5242; www.newagenseasideinn.com; 60 Newagen Colony Rd, Southport Island; r $185-295; ☺late-May-mid-Oct; ☏) A relic of the days when wealthy Northeastern families would descend on the summer colonies of Maine for weeks at a time, the Newagen is a world apart. On a secluded stretch of Southport Island coast, its grand white inn and cottages are hidden beneath the pines. Don your 1920s tennis whites and spend your days on the courts, relax in an Adirondack chair by the water, or retreat to the retro candlepin bowling alley.

✗ Eating & Drinking

In summer, the restaurants of Boothbay Harbor are Crowded with a capital 'C.'

Lobster Dock
SEAFOOD $$

(www.thelobsterdock.com; 49 Atlantic Ave; mains $10-26; ☺11:30am-8:30pm) Of all the lobster joints in Boothbay Harbor, this sprawling wooden waterfront shack is one of the best

and cheapest. It serves traditional fried seafood platters, sandwiches and steamers, but whole, butter-dripping lobster is definitely the main event.

Ports of Italy
ITALIAN $$

(☏207-633-1011; 47 Commercial St; meals $17-20; ☺5-10pm) This upscale Northern Italian spot has been winning raves for dishes like tagliatelle with mussels, lobster risotto and classic tiramisu. The wine list also gets two thumbs up. If the weather's nice, grab a balcony table – the dining room's a bit dark.

Boat Bar
BAR

(☏207-633-5761; www.chowderhouseinc.com; Granary Way; ☺mid-Jun–early Sep) Behind the Chowder House, this unpretentious waterfront spot features a bar made from an actual sailboat. Fun.

ⓘ Information

Boothbay Harbor Region Chamber of Commerce (☏207-633-2353; www.boothbayharbor. com; 192 Townsend Ave; ☺8am-5pm Mon-Fri) has useful downloadable maps.

ⓘ Getting There & Away

From Wiscasset, continue on US 1 for 2 miles and then head south on ME 27 for 12 miles through Boothbay to Boothbay Harbor. Unfortunately, there's no direct bus service to Boothbay Harbor. **Concord Coach Lines** (www.concordcoachlines.com) stops in Wiscasset.

Monhegan Island

POP 65

Monhegan Island is not for the faint-hearted or easily bored. There are no TVs, no bars and no shopping, save for a few small convenience stores. The weather is unpredictable and often foggy. The 1½-hour mailboat ride from the mainland can be bumpy.

But for a world that's almost completely removed from the bustle of the 21st century, this tiny chunk of rock is a refuge. With dramatic granite cliffs, gnarled maritime forest and lush flower meadows, the island's isolated vistas have been attracting artists since the 19th century. To this day, Monhegan residents and visitors are drawn to plain living, traditional village life and peaceful contemplation. The sole village remains small and very limited in its services, with almost no cars. The few unpaved roads are lined with stacks of lobster traps.

What to do on Monhegan? Paint, read, hike, bird-watch, think. The island is laid out for walking, with 17 miles of forest and cliff-top trails, some quite overgrown. Pick up a trail map at the ferry office or at any hotel. Children, in particular, enjoy the Lobster Cove trail, with lots of rocks to climb and the wreck of a metal ship lying like a beached whale. Wander through Cathedral Woods to search for fairy houses (stones and twigs stacked to resemble tiny forest dwellings). Climb the hill for sweeping views from the base of the 19th-century granite lighthouse. In the village, check out the working one-room schoolhouse. A number of artists open their studios to visitors during the summer months – check out the notices posted on the village Rope Shed, the unofficial community notice board.

Browse Monhegan Welcome (www.monheganwelcome.com) for more information.

🛏 Sleeping & Eating

Island accommodations are simple and old-fashioned; few rooms have private bathrooms and none have televisions. Reserve well in advance. There are a handful of hotel restaurants open to the public and a handful of small convenience stores with predictably high prices on basics such as milk and pasta. If you're planning a long stay, stock up on the mainland.

★Shining Sails   B&B $$
(☑207-596-0041; www.shiningsails.com; r incl breakfast $140-225; 🛜) Run by a friendly lobsterman and his wife, this year-round B&B has six comfy, basic rooms, some with kitchenettes. Stay upstairs for the best ocean views. The fresh blueberry muffins at breakfast are a treat. The owners also rent out various rooms and cottages throughout the island. The B&B is easy walking distance from the ferry dock.

Island Inn   INN $$$
(☑207-596-0371; www.islandinnmonhegan.com; r incl breakfast $165-410; ☺May-Oct; 🛜) The island's most elegant digs, this Victorian mansard-roofed summer hotel has 32 simple but plush rooms with crisp white linens and Oriental rugs. The wide front porch has killer views of the roiling Atlantic. The dining rooms serve three meals a day for both guests and visitors.

The Novelty   DELI $
(www.monheganhouse.com; ☺May–mid-Oct) Behind Monhegan House, this general store sells sandwiches, beer and wine, and freshly baked goods, like whoopie pies. It's also got Monhegan's only ATM and its only public wi-fi hot spot.

Fish House Market   SEAFOOD $
(☺11:30am-9pm in summer) On Fish Beach, this fresh seafood market also sells lobster rolls and chowder, to eat at the nearby picnic tables.

ℹ Getting There & Away

During high season, **Monhegan Boat Line** (☑207-372-8848; www.monheganboat.com; round-trip adult/child $32/18) runs several daily trips to Monhegan Island from Port Clyde. Schedules and fares vary according to the season; advance reservations are always a must.

Hardy Boat Cruise (☑207-677-2026; www.hardyboat.com; 132 ME 32, New Harbor; round-trip adult/child $34/20; ☺mid-May–mid-Oct) departs for Monhegan from New Harbor twice daily in summer, and less frequently in spring and fall.

You can also visit Monhegan on a day excursion from Boothbay Harbor.

Rockland

POP 7600

This thriving commercial port boasts a large fishing fleet and a proud year-round population that gives Rockland a vibrancy lacking in some other Midcoast towns. Main St is a window into the city's sociocultural diversity, with a jumble of working-class diners, Bohemian cafes and high-end bistros alongside galleries, old-fashioned storefronts and one of the state's best art museums and most renowned restaurants.

Settled in 1769, Rockland was once an important shipbuilding center and a transportation hub for goods moving up and down the coast. Today, tall-masted sailing ships still fill the harbor, as Rockland is a center for Maine's busy windjammer cruises (as is Camden). Rockland is also the birthplace of poet Edna St Vincent Millay (1892–1950), who grew up in neighboring Camden.

⊙ Sights

★Rockland
Breakwater Lighthouse LIGHTHOUSE
(www.rocklandharborlights.org) Stroll down the 4300ft granite breakwater to gape at the sweet white light sitting atop the brick-and-white house with a sweeping view of town.

Farnsworth Art Museum MUSEUM
(www.farnsworthmuseum.org; 16 Museum St; adult/child/student & senior $12/free/10; ⊙10am-5pm daily May 15-Oct 31, 10am-5pm Wed-Sun Nov 1-May 14, closed Mon & Tue in winter) One of the country's best small regional museums, the Farnsworth collection spans 200 years of American art. Artists who have lived or worked in Maine are the museum's definite strength – look for works by Edward Hopper, Louise Nevelson, Rockwell Kent and Robert Indiana. Exhibits on the Wyeth family – Andrew, NC and Jamie – are housed in a renovated church across the garden.

Olson House MUSEUM
(www.farnsworthmuseum.org/olson-house; 427 Hathorne Point Rd; admission $5; ⊙11am-4pm late May–mid-Oct) This rawboned Maine farmhouse was made iconic when Andrew Wyeth painted it as the backdrop of his most famous painting, *Christina's World*. Wyeth viewed Christina Olson, the paralyzed daughter of the home's owner, as a symbol of Yankee forbearance. The house, part of the Farnsworth Art Museum, is now a small museum with text exhibits on Wyeth's life. It's located a pleasant half-hour drive from downtown Rockland.

Maine Lighthouse Museum MUSEUM
(☎207-594-3301; www.mainelighthousemuseum.com; 1 Park Dr; adult/child $5/free; ⊙9am-5pm Mon-Fri, 10am-4pm Sat & Sun; ⊕) Perched over Rockland harbor, this nifty little museum features vintage Fresnel lenses, foghorns, marine instruments and ship models, with hands-on exhibits for children.

Owls Head Lighthouse LIGHTHOUSE
(Owls Head State Park, off ME 73, Owls Head) This photogenic mid-19th-century lighthouse and keeper's cottage are not open to visitors,

but you can stroll the surrounding walking paths and pebbly beach.

🎊 Festivals & Events

The big events in Rockland are the **Maine Lobster Festival** (www.mainelobsterfestival.com; ⊙early Aug) and the **North Atlantic Blues Festival** (www.northatlanticbluesfestival.com; ⊙mid-Jul). Both of these are huge events, with accommodation booked up for many miles surrounding Rockland.

🛏 Sleeping & Eating

LimeRock Inn B&B $$
(☎207-594-2257; www.limerockinn.com; 96 Limerock St; r incl breakfast $119-245; ☎) This eight-bedroom mansion, built in 1890 for a local congressman, has been lovingly furnished in a tasteful mix of antique and modern furniture. The sunny Island Cottage room, with views of the backyard gazebo, is our favorite.

Captain Lindsey House BOUTIQUE HOTEL $$$
(☎207-596-7950; www.lindseyhouse.com; 5 Lindsey St; r incl breakfast $178-225; ☎) On a downtown side street, this small boutique hotel has been polished to its original Federal-style grandeur. The lobby evokes a 19th-century sea captain's parlor: Oriental carpets, dark wood, carved angels above the mantle. Rooms are classically furnished, some with fireplaces. Full English breakfasts are served in the oak-paneled, plaid-upholstered Scottish dining room.

Contes 1894 SEAFOOD $$
(148 S Main St; mains $15-28; ⊙dinner) After celebrity chef and TV personality Anthony Bourdain paid a visit this local secret was out. Contes 1894 has a quirky owner and massive portions served in a ramshackle old house, with tables covered in newspaper and flickering candles.

In Good Company INTERNATIONAL $$
(http://ingoodcompanymaine.com; 415 Main St; mains $10-19; ⊙4:30-11pm or midnight) This inviting wine bar–ish haven looks more like a tasteful friend's living room scattered with multiple tables and sofas. Here you can kick back, enjoy a glass of something special and nibble on bites like goat-cheese-stuffed sweet 'n' spicy pepperdews or feast on a full plate of curried shrimp and haddock chowder.

★Primo AMERICAN $$$
(☎207-596-0770; www.primorestaurant.com; 2 S Main St/ME 73; mains $25-48; ⊙dinner Wed-Mon

mid-May–Oct) In a sprawling Victorian house a mile from downtown, Primo is widely considered one of the best restaurants in Maine. Chef Melissa Kelly has reached celebrity status for her creative ways with New England ingredients – think local swordfish atop a bed of foraged dandelion greens, or grilled duck breast with buttered fiddlehead ferns. The menu changes daily. The atmosphere is unpretentious farmhouse chic, with warm yellow walls and burnished wooden floorboards. Reservations are critical. It's eco-friendly.

ℹ️ Information

For area information, stop in at the **Penobscot Bay Chamber of Commerce** (☑ 207-596-0376; www.therealmaine.com; 1 Park Dr; ☺ 9am-5pm Mon-Fri), just off Main St. It's in the same building as the Maine Lighthouse Museum. Also open weekends in summer.

ℹ️ Getting There & Away

Cape Air (www.flycapeair.net) connects Rockland's Knox County Regional Airport and Boston's Logan Airport.

Concord Coach Lines (www.concordcoachlines.com; 517A Main St) runs buses to and from Boston ($36), Portland ($21) and various other Midcoast towns, departing from the Maine State Ferry Terminal.

Camden & Rockport

POP 5400

Camden and its picture-perfect harbor, framed against the mountains of Camden Hills State Park, is one of the prettiest sites in the state. Home to Maine's large and justly famed fleet of windjammers, Camden continues its historic intimacy with the sea. Most vacationers come to sail, but Camden also has galleries, fine seafood restaurants and back streets ideal for exploring. Pick up a walking tour guide to the town's historic buildings at the chamber of commerce. The adjoining state park offers hiking, picnicking and camping.

Like many communities along the Maine coast, Camden has a long history of shipbuilding. The mammoth six-masted schooner *George W Wells* was built here, setting the world record for the most masts on a sailing ship.

Two miles south of Camden, the sleepy harborside town of Rockport is a much smaller and more peaceful settlement that's known for the world-renowned Maine Media Workshops.

◉ Sights & Activities

Camden Hills State Park   PARK
(☑ 207-236-3109; 280 Belfast Rd/US 1; adult/child $4.50/1; ☺ 7am-sunset) With more than 30 miles of trails, this densely forested park is a choice place to take in the exquisite Midcoast. A favorite hike is the 45-minute (half mile) climb up Mt Battie, which offers exquisite views of Penobscot Bay. Simple trail maps are available at the park entrance, just over 1.5 miles northeast of Camden center on US 1. The picnic area has short trails down to the shore.

Isleboro   ISLAND
(☑ 207-789-5611) From Lincolnville, hop the ferry to this small resort island, one of the finest places to ride a bike in Maine. A popular 28-mile bike loop offers majestic vistas of Penobscot Bay. Picnic at Pendleton Point, where harbor seals and loons often lounge on the long, striated rocks.

To get here, grab one of the multiple daily state-run **ferries** (☑ 207-789-5611; www.maine.gov/mdot; round trip passenger/bike/car $10/8.50/27.50).

Maine Sport   CYCLING, KAYAKING
(☑ 207-236-7120; www.mainesport.com; Main St & US 1, Camden; bike/kayak rental per day from $20/38) Explore Isleboro on a rental bike or take one of the Camden Harbor kayak tours offered by this Camden outfitter.

ℹ️ Tours

Like nearby Rockland, Camden offers many windjammer cruises, from two-hour trips to multiday journeys up the coast.

The following boats depart from Camden's Town Landing or adjoining Bayview Landing: **Appledore II** (☑ 207-236-8353; www.appledore2.com), **Olad** (☑ 207-236-2323; www.maineschooners.com) and **Surprise** (☑ 20 7-236-4687; www.camdenmainesailing.com; 2hr sail $35; ☺ May–mid-Oct).

🛏️ Sleeping

For budget accommodation options, troll the motels along US 1, just north or south of Camden.

Camden Hills State Park   CAMPGROUND $
(☑ 207-624-9950; www.campwithme.com; 280 Belfast Rd/US 1; campsites $29; ☺ mid-May–mid-Oct; 🛜) The park's campground has hot show-

ers and wooded sites, some with electric hookups. Reserve online at Maine's government reservations portal.

Whitehall Inn   INN $$

(☑207-236-3391; www.whitehall-inn.com; 52 High St, Camden; r incl breakfast $119-230; ⊗May-Oct; 🕾) Camden-raised poet Edna St Vincent Millay got her start reciting poetry to guests at this old-fashioned summer hotel. Read about her wild, often tragic life in the inn's Millay Room parlor, which still has the Steinway piano she once played. The 45 rooms have a vintage boarding-house character, some with Victorian striped wallpaper, in-room pedestal sinks and claw-foot tubs. Rocking chairs on the wide front porch are a nice place for evening socializing.

Camden Maine Stay Inn   B&B $$

(☑207-236-9636; www.camdenmainestay.com; 22 High St; r incl breakfast $135-270; 🕾) Built by a *Mayflower* descendent, this fine Greek Revival home has eight simple, country-chic rooms and friendly Italian owners.

★Norumbega   B&B $$$

(☑207-236-4646; www.norumbegainn.com; 63 High St, Camden; r incl breakfast $275-525; 🕾) Looking like something out of a slightly creepy fairy tale, this 1886 turreted stone mansion was built to incorporate elements of the owner's favorite European castles. Today, it's Camden's poshest and most dramatically situated B&B, perched on a hill above the bay. Of the 12 rooms, the coolest are the two-story Library Suite, with a book-lined upper balcony, and the Penthouse, with a private deck and panoramic water views.

✗ Eating

★Shepherd's Pie   AMERICAN $$

(www.shepherdspierockport.com; 18 Central St, Rockport; mains $12-22; ⊗5pm-late) Brian Hill, who runs successful restaurant Francine in neighboring Camden, opened this more laidback temple of food in a dark-wood pubby space with a tin ceiling. With a menu boasting four main sections (Bar snacks, From the Grill, Plates and Sides), you can swing by for a bite or a full meal. Choose from usual suspects with a twist such as seasonal pickles, smoked alewife (a fish) caesar, grilled pork chop with apple sauce and salted caramel or buttermilk potatoes.

Lobster Pound Restaurant   SEAFOOD $$

(☑207-789-5550; www.lobsterpoundmaine.com; US 1, Lincolnville; mains $18-29; ⊗noon-8pm daily

May-Oct; 🖼) Fresh lobster is the name of the game at this highly recommended pound on Lincolnville's beach, though there are plenty of other seafood and non-seafood options. The massive restaurant is especially family friendly, with a kid's menu and a gift shop hawking stuffed lobsters and the like.

Cappy's   SEAFOOD $$

(www.cappyschowder.com; 1 Main St, Camden; mains $8-17; ⊗11am-11pm; 🕾) This friendly longtime favorite is better known for its bar and its convivial atmosphere than its food, though it does serve a decent bowl of chowder and other casual New England fare.

Francine Bistro   NEW AMERICAN $$$

(☑207-230-0083; 55 Chestnut St, Camden; mains $26-34; ⊗5:30-10pm Tue-Sat) 🍴 In a cozy house on a residential downtown side street, this New American bistro is one of the Midcoast's choicest picks for a creative meal. The ever-changing menu showcases chef Brian Hill's deft ways with local ingredients – lobster-stuffed squash blossoms, sorrel soup, halibut with beet greens and mussel vinaigrette. Everyone raves about the steak frites. Reservations essential.

ℹ Information

Camden-Rockport-Lincolnville Chamber of Commerce (☑207-236-4404; www.camdenme. org; 2 Public Landing; ⊗9am-5pm) has an information office on the waterfront at the public landing in Camden, behind Cappy's. Also open weekends in summer.

ℹ Getting There & Away

South of Bangor (53 miles) on US 1, Camden is 85 miles north of Portland and 77 miles southwest of Bar Harbor.

Concord Coach Lines (Concord Trailways; www.concordcoachlines.com) leaves from in front of the Maritime Farms in Rockport for Boston ($38), Portland ($24), Bangor ($18) and multiple Midcoast towns.

DOWN EAST

Without question, this is quintessential Maine: as you head further and further up the coast toward Canada, the peninsulas seem to become more and more narrow, jutting further into the sea. The fishing villages seem to get smaller; the lobster pounds, closer and closer to the water.

Down East

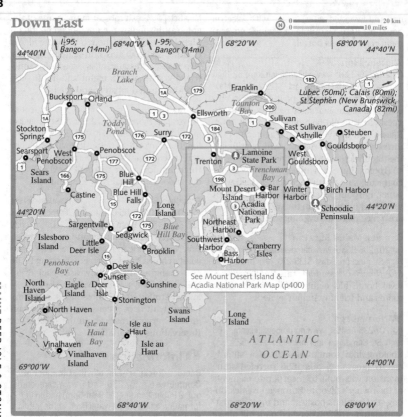

MAINE DEER ISLE & STONINGTON

'Down East' starts around Penobscot Bay. If you make time to drive to the edge of the shore, south off US 1, let it be here.

The region continues 'further down east,' from Acadia all the way to the border with New Brunswick, Canada.

Deer Isle & Stonington

POP 1900

Traveling south along ME 15, the forest opens up to reveal tranquil harbors framed against hilly islands off in the distance. This is Deer Isle, actually a collection of islands joined by causeways and connected to the mainland by a picturesque suspension bridge near Sargentville. Sights are few but the area is worth it for the gorgeous views.

Stonington is a quaint settlement where lobstermen and artists live side by side. A few galleries and restaurants draw the odd traveler or two.

Boats depart from Stonington for Isle au Haut.

🛏 Sleeping & Eating

Boyce's Motel MOTEL $
(📞207-367-2421; www.boycesmotel.com; 44 Main St, Stonington; r $69-145; 🖥) Quiet, cheap and friendly, this year-round cedar-shingle motel is a solid pick for simple, clean rooms and cottages in the heart of Stonington village.

★ **Pilgrim's Inn** INN $$
(📞207-348-6615; www.pilgrimsinn.com; 20 Main St, Deer Isle village; r incl breakfast $105-220; ⊙mid-May–mid-Oct; 🖥) Overlooking the Northwest Harbor, this handsome post-and-beam inn was built in 1793 and offers refined country charm in its 12 rooms and three cottages. Pine floors and solid wood furnishings are common throughout, while some rooms have gas fireplaces and pretty views over the millpond. Inside the inn's converted barn,

the **Whale's Rib Tavern** (☑207-348-6615; meals $14-27; ☺dinner) serves upscale Maine comfort food, such as steamed local clams, smoked Maine salmon with goat cheese, and blueberry bread pudding. Reservations are recommended.

Cockatoo PORTUGUESE $$$
(☑207-367-0900; www.thecockatoorestaurant. com; Oceanville Rd; meals $20-35; ☺dinner) At Goose Cove Resort, this secluded waterfront dining room is an unexpected delight for Portuguese-inspired seafood dishes. Start with crisp codfish balls, followed by mussels over linguine or paella and wash it down with crisp *vinho verde* (semi-sparkling white wine). To reach Cockatoo, take ME 15 a few miles north from Stonington and drive east on Oceanville Rd, following the signs.

❶ Information

The **Deer Isle–Stonington Chamber of Commerce** (☑207-348-6124; www.deerislemaine. com; ☺10am-4pm mid-Jun–early Sep) maintains an information booth a quarter-mile south of the suspension bridge.

❶ Getting There & Away

From Blue Hill, take ME 176 west for 4 miles and then head south on ME 175/15 for 9 miles to Little Deer Isle.

Isle au Haut

POP 60

Much of Isle au Haut, a rocky island 6 miles long, is under the auspices of Acadia National Park. More remote than the parklands near Bar Harbor, it is not flooded with visitors in summer. Serious hikers can tramp the island's miles of trails and camp for the night in the **Duck Harbor Campground** (www.nps.gov/acad; tent sites $27; ☺mid-May–mid-Oct), which has five shelters maintained by the National Park Service (NPS).

For information on hiking and camping on Isle au Haut, contact **Acadia National Park** (☑207-288-3338; www.nps.gov/acad). Reservations for shelters must be accompanied by payment (made after April 1).

For a less rustic experience, the **Inn at Isle au Haut** (☑207-335-5141; www.innatisleauhaut.com; r incl breakfast, lunch & dinner $300-390; ☺Jun-Sep) offers four bright, cheerfully decorated rooms with antique furniture and quilted bedspreads; two rooms have ocean views. Meals are included in the rate and are generally excellent. There is a two-night minimum stay. Bicycles are available for exploring the island.

The **Isle au Haut Boat Company** (☑207-367-5193; www.isleauhaut.com; adult/child $18/9.50) operates daily, year-round mailboat trips from Stonington's Atlantic Ave Hardware Dock to the village of Isle au Haut. In summer, five boats a day make the 45-minute crossing from Monday through Saturday. There are fewer or no boats on Sundays, holidays and during the off-season. Bicycles, boats and canoes (no cars) can be carried to the village of Isle au Haut for a fee. To park your car in Stonington while visiting Isle au Haut costs around $10 per day.

MOUNT DESERT ISLAND & ACADIA NATIONAL PARK

Formed by glaciers some 18,000 years ago, Mount Desert Island is the jewel of the 'down east' region. It offers vast geographical variety, from freshwater lakes to dense forests to stark granite cliffs to voluptuous river valleys. There are many ways to experience the 108-sq-mile island's natural beauty, whether hiking the forested mountains, swimming in the secluded lakes or kayaking the rocky coast. About two-thirds of Mount Desert Island belong to Acadia National Park, one of New England's biggest draws.

Samuel de Champlain, the intrepid French explorer, sailed along this coast in the early 17th century. Seeing the bare, windswept granite summit of Cadillac Mountain, he called the island on which it stood L'Île des Monts Déserts. The name is still technically pronounced 'day-zehr' almost 400 years later, though most people just say 'dessert' (as in ice cream!).

The island has four townships, each containing multiple villages. **Bar Harbor**, on the northeast side, is by far the largest, and functions as the gateway to the park for most travelers. Further south, the towns of **Southwest Harbor** and **Northeast Harbor** sit on opposite sides of the Somes Sound, which nearly cleaves the island in two. Northeast Harbor is a posh resort community, while Southwest Harbor is more populist in nature. On the southwest coast, **Tremont** is a quiet fishing village.

While the coastal vistas and spruce forests are impressive, Acadia draws enormous

Mount Desert Island & Acadia National Park

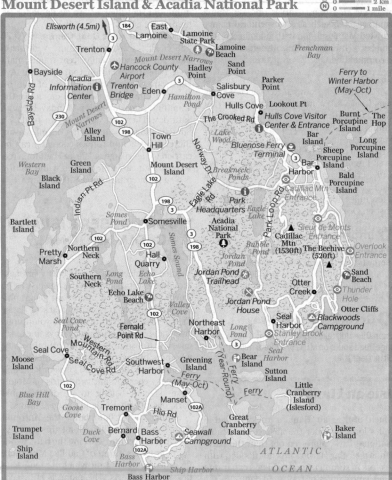

crowds, particularly in July and August. Be prepared for long lines and heavily congested roads, or plan your visit for the off-season.

ℹ Information

The park's main Hulls Cove entrance, which is 3 miles northwest of Bar Harbor via ME 3, has the **Hulls Cove Visitor Center** (☏207-288-3338; ME 3; 7-day park admission per vehicle $22, walkers & cyclists $12; ⏰8am-4:30pm mid-Apr–mid-Jun & Oct, to 6pm mid-Jun–Aug, to 5pm Sep), from where the 20-mile-long Park Loop Rd circumnavigates the northeastern sec-

tion of Mount Desert Island. It is a one-way road for much of its length. Off-season, head to Park Headquarters for information, which is 3 miles west of Bar Harbor on ME 233.

Bar Harbor

POP 5300

In 1844 landscape painters Thomas Cole and Frederick Church came to Mount Desert and liked what they saw. They sketched the rugged landscape and later returned with their art students. Naturally enough, the wealthy families who purchased their paintings asked Cole and Church about the beautiful land depicted in their paintings, and soon the families began to spend summers on Mount Desert. By the end of the 19th century, Bar Harbor rivaled Newport, RI, as the eastern seaboard's most desirable summer resort.

WWII damaged the tourist trade, but worse damage was to come. In 1947 a forest fire torched 17,000 acres of parkland, along with 60 palatial summer cottages, putting an end to Bar Harbor's Gilded Age. But the town recovered as a destination for the new mobile middle class of the postwar years.

Today, Bar Harbor is crowded for most of the year with vacationers and cruise-ship passengers on shore visits. The busy downtown is packed with souvenir stores, ice-cream shops, cafes and bars, each advertising bigger and better happy hours, early-bird specials or two-for-one deals. On the quieter residential backstreets, most blocks seem to have almost as many B&Bs as private homes.

Although the hustle and bustle of Bar Harbor is not for everybody, it has by far the most amenities of any town in the region. Even if you stay somewhere else, you'll probably wind up here to eat dinner, grab a drink, or schedule a kayaking, sailing or rock-climbing tour.

Bar Harbor's busiest season is late June through August. There's a short lull just after Labor Day (early September), but then it gets busy again for foliage season which lasts through mid-October.

⊙ Sights & Activities

Bar Harbor has its share of attractions, but it's also the base for many activities in other parts of Mount Desert Island.

Downtown   NEIGHBORHOOD
Despite the gorgeous scenery just outside of town, there's plenty of human-made distractions in Bar Harbor. Restaurants, taverns and boutiques are scattered along Main St and the intersecting roads of Mount Desert and Cottage Sts. You'll find shops selling everything from wool sweaters and fudge to camping gear, books, handicrafts and musical instruments. Dozens of art galleries of varying quality jockey for business here. The best of the bunch include **Argosy** (110 Main St), with landscapes and still life paintings by local artists; and **Island Artisans** (✐ 207-288-4214; 99 Main St), featuring more than 100 Maine glassblowers, jewelers, ceramists and more.

Shore Path   WALK
For a picturesque view of the harbor, take a stroll along the Shore Path. This half-mile walkway, first laid down in 1880, begins near Agamont Park and continues past birch-tree-lined Grant Park, with views of the Porcupine Islands offshore and the historic mansions set back from the path. Complete the loop by returning along Wayman Lane.

☞ Tours

Numerous outfits offer adventures out on the water. Keep in mind that it is often 20°F (11°C) cooler on the water than on land, so bring a jacket.

Bar Harbor Whale Watch Co   CRUISE
(✐ 207-288-2386; www.barharborwhales.com; 1 West St; adult $34-64, child $22-34; ⊗ mid-May–Oct) Operates four-hour whale-watching and puffin-watching cruises, among other options.

Downeast Windjammer Cruises   CRUISE
(✐ 207-288-4585; www.downeastwindjammer.com; 27 Main St; adult/child $40/30) Offers two-hour cruises on the majestic 151ft, four-masted schooner *Margaret Todd*.

Acadian Nature Cruises   CRUISE
(✐ 207-288-2386; www.acadiannaturecruises.com; 1 West St; adult/child $28/17; ⊗ mid-May–Oct) See whales, porpoises, bald eagles, seals and more on these narrated two-hour nature cruises.

National Park Sea Kayak Tours   KAYAKING
(✐ 800-347-0940; www.acadiakayak.com; 39 Cottage St, Bar Harbor; half-day tour $50; ⊗ May-Oct) Tours and day rental of kayaks.

Bar Harbor Bicycle Shop   CYCLING
(✐ 207-288-3886; www.barharborbike.com; 141 Cottage St, Bar Harbor; per day $23-38) Rent bikes here for the day. Acadia National Park's 45 miles of carriage roads are excellent settings for cycling.

🛏 Sleeping

Bar Harbor has thousands of guest rooms found in both cookie-cutter motels and Victorian charmers. Reservations are essential in summer.

There is camping in the park and there are commercial campgrounds along ME 3 near Ellsworth and clustered around the entrances to the park. Numerous inexpensive motels line ME 3 from Ellsworth to Bar Harbor.

Bar Harbor Youth Hostel HOSTEL $
(☑207-288-5587; www.barharborhostel.com; 321 Main St; dm/r $27/82; 🗺) In a converted home a few blocks south of the village green, this pleasant, friendly and very clean hostel has simple male and female dorm rooms, each sleeping 10, and a private room that sleeps four.

Anne's White Columns Inn B&B $$
(☑207-288-5357; www.anneswhitecolumns.com; 57 Mount Desert St; r incl breakfast $85-175; ❄) Once a Christian Scientist church, this B&B's name refers to its dramatic columned entrance. Rooms have a quirky Victorian charm, with plenty of florals and bric-a-brac. Get here in time for the afternoon wine and cheese reception.

2 Cats B&B $$
(☑207-288-2808; www.2catsbarharbor.com; 130 Cottage St; r incl breakfast $130-210) This cozy guesthouse has three bright, sunny rooms, each with wood floors, four-poster beds, a sitting area and a private entrance. It's adjacent to the popular cafe of the same name, so breakfasts are excellent (muffins with strawberry butter, big cappuccinos…yum-yum).

Holland Inn B&B $$
(☑207-288-4804; www.hollandinn.com; 35 Holland Ave; r incl breakfast $95-185; 🗺) In a quiet residential neighborhood walking distance from downtown, this restored 1895 house and adjacent cottage has nine homey, unfrilly rooms. Ambience is so low-key you'll feel like you're staying in a friend's private home.

Aurora Inn MOTEL $$
(☑207-288-3771; www.aurorainn.com; 51 Holland Ave; r $89-169; 🗺) This retro motor lodge has 10 clean rooms and a good location within walking distance of everything. Guests can use the heated pool and Jacuzzi of the nearby Quality Inn.

Aysgarth Station Inn B&B $$
(☑207-288-9655; www.aysgarth.com; 20 Roberts Ave; r incl breakfast $115-165; ❄) On a quiet side street, this 1895 B&B has six cozy rooms with homey touches. Request the Tan Hill room, which is on the 3rd floor, for a view of Cadillac Mountain.

★ Bass Cottage INN $$$
(☑207-288-3705, 866-782-9224; www.basscottage.com; 14 The Field; r incl breakfast $185-380; ☺May-Oct) If most Bar Harbor B&Bs rate about a '5' in terms of stylishness, this Gilded Age mansion deserves an '11.' The 10 light-drenched guest rooms have an elegant summer-cottage chic, all crisp white linens and understated botanical prints.

Tickle the ivories at the parlor's grand piano or read a novel beneath the Tiffany stained-glass ceiling of the wood-paneled sitting room. The location, tucked away in a hidden meadow just across the street from downtown, is Bar Harbor's best.

🍴 Eating

Bar Harbor is home to countless restaurants. Stroll along Rodick, Kennebec and Cottage Sts for more options.

Mount Desert Island Ice Cream ICE CREAM $
(www.mdiic.com; 7 Firefly Lane; ice cream $3-5; ☺10am-10pm daily) A cult hit for edgy flavors like salted caramel, boozy White Russian and blueberry-basil sorbet, this postage-stamp-sized ice-cream counter is a post-dinner must.

Rosalie's Pizza PIZZA $
(www.rosaliespizza.com; 46 Cottage St; mains $5-10; ☺11am-10pm; 🚼) Dinner at Rosalie's is a tradition among Bar Harbor's summer families. The two-story pizza joint, decked out in retro Americana (jukebox, B&W Rat Pack photos), is a favorite for calzone, hot Italian subs and, of course, classic thin-crust pizza.

Cafe This Way AMERICAN $$
(☑207-288-4483; www.cafethisway.com; 14½ Mount Desert St; mains breakfast $6-9, dinner $15-25; ☺7-11:30am Mon-Sat, 8am-1pm Sun, 5:30-9pm nightly) In a sprawling white cottage, this quirky eatery is *the* place for breakfast, with plump Maine blueberry pancakes and eggs Benedict with smoked salmon. It also serves eclectic, sophisticated dinners, such as roasted duck with blueberries, Moroccan-style squash and tuna tempura. Sit in the garden.

2 Cats CAFE $$
(☑207-288-2808; www.2catsbarharbor.com; 130 Cottage St; mains $8-19; ☺7am-1pm) On weekends crowds line up for smoked-trout omelets and homemade muffins at this sunny, arty little cafe. Lunch offerings include slightly heartier fare, such as burritos and

seafood dishes. Pick up a kitty-themed gift in the gift shop.

Poor Boy's
INTERNATIONAL $$

(☎207-288-4148; www.poorboysgourmet.com; 300 Main St; ⏰5-10pm) This locally owned favorite has an enormous menu of lobster, grilled fish and chicken dishes, roast meats, pastas, salads and a dozen desserts. It's good value, and the quality is generally high.

Galyn's
AMERICAN $$

(www.galynsbarharbor.com; 17 Main St; mains $14-27; ⏰11:30am-2pm & 5-10pm) One of the better restaurants on the harbor end of downtown, Galyn's does tasty upscale comfort food, like baked Brie, tarragon chicken and lobster linguine. We recommend the crab cakes.

The narrow space has multiple small dining areas, all cozy and unpretentious.

Mâche Bistro
FRENCH $$$

(☎207-288-0447; www.machebistro.com; 135 Cottage St; mains $18-28; ⏰5-10:30pm Mon-Sat) Almost certainly Bar Harbor's best midrange restaurant, Mâche serves contemporary French-inflected fare in a stylishly renovated cottage. The changing menu highlights the local riches – think pumpkin-seed-dusted scallops, lobster and Brie flat bread, and wild blueberry trifle. Specialty cocktails add to the appeal. Reservations are essential.

Cafe Bluefish
NEW AMERICAN $$$

(☎207-288-3696; www.cafebluefishbarharbor. com; 122 Cottage St; mains $16-29; ⏰11:30am-2:30pm & 5-10pm May-Oct) This intimate storefront bistro serves creative, internationally influenced dishes, such as scallops with Thai chili butter, Creole-spiced lobster and green-tea shaved ice. Try the lobster strudel, as seen on the Food Network. Crowds are well heeled and wine loving.

🍸 Drinking

Dog & Pony Tavern
PUB

(www.dogandponytavern.com; 4 Rodick Pl; ⏰11:30am-about 1am) On a quiet back street, this locals' favorite has a laid-back neighborhood pub vibe, with lots of regional microbrews and a leafy garden to drink them in.

Lompoc Café
CAFE

(☎207-288-9392; www.lompoccafe.com; 36 Rodick St; cover charge $3-10; ⏰4:30-10pm) Order a glass of blueberry ale and watch bluegrass, indie rock, jazz or folk musicians play on the patio of this arty cafe and bar.

Thirsty Whale
BAR

(☎207-288-9335; 40 Cottage St; ⏰4pm-late) Head here to mingle with locals and lobstermen over a pint and some hearty, inexpensive seafood. There's often live music Wednesday through Saturday nights.

☆ Entertainment

Reel Pizza Cinerama
MOVIE THEATER

(www.reelpizza.net; 33B Kennebec Pl; pizza $15-22; ⏰open daily) Sip a local microbrew and munch on pizzas with cinematic names, like The Manchurian Candidate (chicken, scallions and peanut sauce) and Hawaii 5-0 (ham and pineapple), while watching a flick on the big screen.

ℹ Getting There & Away

US Airways Express, operated by **Colgan Air** (☎800-428-4322; www.colganair.com), connects Bar Harbor and Boston with daily flights year-round. The Hancock County Airport is in Trenton, off ME 3, just north of the Trenton Bridge.

Getting to Bar Harbor by public transport has become increasingly difficult in recent years. The famous CAT ferry to and from Nova Scotia was discontinued, though many hope it will be back soon. The only bus route to Bar Harbor is from Bangor or Ellsworth, via **Downeast Transportation's shuttle** (☎207-667-5796; www. downeasttrans.org).

Acadia National Park

The only national park in all of New England, Acadia National Park offers unrivaled coastal beauty and activities for both leisurely hikers and adrenaline junkies.

◎ Sights & Activities

Acadia has more than 125 miles of trails. Some are easy enough to stroll with a small child, while others require sturdy boots, full water bottles and plenty of lung power. For an easy start, drive up Cadillac Mountain and walk the paved half-mile Cadillac Mountain Summit Loop, with panoramic views of Frenchman Bay. It's popular with early birds at sunrise, though we think it's just as nice at the more-civilized sunset hour. A good moderate pick is the forested 2.2-mile trail to the summit of Champlain Mountain. The Beehive Trail, at less than a mile, involves clinging to iron rings bolted to the cliff face.

WORTH A TRIP

SCHOODIC PENINSULA

Jutting into the Atlantic Ocean, the southern tip of this peninsula contains a quiet portion of Acadia National Park. It includes a 7.2-mile shore drive called Schoodic Point Loop Rd, which offers splendid views of Mount Desert Island and Cadillac Mountain. The one-way loop road is excellent for cycling since it has a smooth surface and relatively gentle hills. The Fraser's Point park entrance also has a nice little picnic area. Further along the loop, reached by a short walk from the road, you'll find Schoodic Head, a 400ft-high promontory with fine ocean views. This is definitely the quieter part of Acadia, with fewer crowds – but also fewer activities.

For information on local businesses, check out the website for the **Schoodic Peninsula Chamber of Commerce** (207-963-7658; www.acadia-schoodic.org). From Bar Harbor, follow US 1 east before turning south onto State Route 186.

Swimmers can brave the icy (55°F, even in midsummer!) waters of lifeguard-patrolled Sand Beach or take a dip in the marginally warmer Echo Lake.

Park Loop Road
DRIVE

For some visitors, driving the 20-mile Park Loop Rd is the extent of their trip to Acadia National Park. While we recommend getting beyond the pavement, it is nice to start your tour with a relaxed orienteering drive. You can also cover this trip on the park's free Island Explorer bus system. On the portion called Ocean Dr, stop at **Thunder Hole**, south of the Overlook entrance, for a look at the surf crashing into a cleft in the granite. The effect is most dramatic with a strong incoming tide. **Otter Cliffs**, not far south of Thunder Hole, is basically a wall of pink granite rising right out from the sea. This area is popular with rock climbers.

Jordan Pond
WALK

On clear days, the glassy waters of this 176-acre pond reflect the image of Penobscot Mountain like a mirror. A stroll around the pond and its surrounding forests and flower meadows is one of Acadia's most popular and family-friendly activities. Sorry, no swimming. Follow the 3-mile self-guided nature trail around the pond before stopping for a cup of Earl Grey at the Jordan Pond House tearoom.

Carriage Roads
CYCLING, RIDING

John D Rockefeller Jr, a lover of old-fashioned horse carriages, gifted Acadia with some 45 miles of carriage roads. Made from crushed stone, the roads are free from cars and are popular with cyclists and equestrians.

Wild Gardens of Acadia
GARDENS

(Park Loop Rd & Route 3) FREE These 1-acre botanic gardens show 12 of Acadia's biospheres in miniature, from bog to coniferous woods to meadow. Botany nerds will appreciate the plant labels.

🛏 Sleeping & Eating

Most of the hotels, B&Bs and private campgrounds are in Bar Harbor.

Acadia National Park Campgrounds
CAMPGROUND $

(877-444-6777; www.nps.gov/acad; tent sites $14-24;) There are two great rustic campgrounds in the Mount Desert Island section of the park, with more than 500 tent sites between them. Four miles south of Southwest Harbor, **Seawall** has both reservation and walk-up sites. Five miles south of Bar Harbor on ME 3, year-round **Blackwoods** requires reservations in summer. Both have restrooms and pay showers. Both are densely wooded but only a few minutes' walk to the ocean.

Jordan Pond House
AMERICAN $$

(207-276-3316; www.thejordanpondhouse.com; afternoon tea $9.50, mains $10-28; ⏰ 11:30am-9pm mid-May–Oct) Afternoon tea at this lodge-like teahouse has been an Acadia tradition since the late 1800s. Steaming pots of Earl Gray come with hot popovers (hollow rolls made with egg batter) and strawberry jam. Eat outside on the broad lawn overlooking the lake. The park's only restaurant, Jordan Pond also does fancy but often mediocre lunches and dinners.

ℹ Getting There & Around

The free shuttle system, the **Island Explorer** (www.exploreacadia.com; ⏰ late Jun-early Oct), features eight routes that link hotels, inns and campgrounds to destinations within Acadia National Park. Route maps are available at local establishments and online.

Northeast Harbor

Simply called 'Northeast' by locals, this fishing village is a popular getaway for the preppy East Coast yachtie set. The tiny Main St is dotted with art galleries and cafes, and the hillsides are lined with Gilded Age mansions hidden behind the trees.

◉ Sights & Activities

Asticou Azalea Garden   GARDEN
(suggested donation $3; ☺ dawn-dusk May 1-Oct 31, Thuya Lodge 10am-5pm late Jun-early Sep) Designed in 1900, this simply lovely 200-acre garden is laced with paths, little shelters and ornamental Japanese-style bridges. Azaleas and rhododendrons bloom profusely from mid-May to mid-June.

🛏 Sleeping & Eating

Harbourside Inn   INN $$
(☑ 207-276-3272; www.harboursideinn.com; 48 Harborside Rd; r $135-295; ☺ mid-Jun–mid-Sep) On a wooded hillside above the village, this shingled 1880s summer cottage has 22 homey, antique-furnished rooms and three suites.

Asticou Inn   INN $$$
(☑ 207-276-3344; www.asticou.com; 15 Peabody Dr; r incl breakfast Jul-Aug $190-380; ☺ late-May–mid-Oct; 🛜 ⛱) Guests have been arriving at this classic Maine summer hotel since the days of steamer trunks and whalebone corsets. Overlooking Northeast Harbor, the grand gray shingled building has 31 sunny rooms with hardwood floors and Victorian furnishings.

Burning Tree   NEW AMERICAN $$$
(☑ 207-288-9331; 69 Otter Creek Dr/ME 3; mains $23-32; ☺ 5-9pm; 🖋) Dine on sun-warmed greens from the backyard gardens or locally caught halibut with green peppercorns at this intimate cottage restaurant, one of the best in the region. The menu is seafood heavy and has plenty of interesting veggie options (try the herby edamame wontons). Reserve ahead. It's midway between Northeast Harbor and Bar Harbor.

Southwest Harbor & Bass Harbor

POP 2000

More laid-back and less affluent than Northeast Harbor, 'Southwest' is also quite tranquil. But that's a bit deceiving: it's also a major boat-building center and a commercial fishing harbor.

From the Upper Town Dock – a quarter-mile along Clark Point Rd from the flashing light in the center of town – boats venture out into Frenchman Bay to the Cranberry Isles.

A few miles south of Southwest Harbor lies the somnolent fishing village of Bass Harbor, home to the Bass Harbor Head Light. Built in 1858, the 26ft lighthouse still has a Fresnel lens from 1902.

🛏 Sleeping & Eating

Penury Hall   B&B $$
(☑ 207-244-7102; www.penuryhall.com; 374 Main St, Southwest Harbor; r incl breakfast $105-130) Mount Desert Island's first B&B, this 1865 schoolhouse has three snug rooms outfitted in a funky mix of bold modern colors and antique furniture. The friendly owners keep their homey common spaces full of games and puzzles for rainy days.

Claremont   HOTEL $$$
(☑ 207-244-5036; www.theclaremonthotel.com; Claremont Rd, Southwest Harbor; r $220-345; ☺ late May–mid-Oct) The island's oldest and most graceful hotel, the Claremont has some of the most stunning views from any guesthouse in the area, with a wraparound porch and sloping broad lawns giving way to boats bobbing in the ocean. Its 24 guest rooms are decorated in period cottage-style furnishings. There's a fantastic restaurant and an elegant bar on site.

★ Thurston's Lobster Pound   SEAFOOD $$
(☑ 207-244-7600; www.thurstonslobster.com; Steamboat Wharf, Bernard; mains $14-25; ☺ 11:30am-9pm, later May-Sep) Tie on your bib and crack into a steamy, butter-dripping lobster fresh from the sea at Thurston's, overlooking Bass Harbor in Bernard. This casual spot is rumored to be the island's best seafood shack.

Red Sky   NEW AMERICAN $$$
(☑ 207-244-0476; www.redskyrestaurant.com; 14 Clark Point Rd, Southwest Harbor; mains $19-29; ☺ 5-9:30pm) 🖋 This year-round spot is a neighborhood bistro for the 21st century. Guests dine on local roast chicken, Maine crab cakes with caper aioli, steamed Blue Hill mussels and other local, seasonal, sustainably raised comfort foods. Yellow-painted walls and a low wood ceiling give a French country ambience.

ISLANDS OFF THE ISLAND

East of Mount Desert Island and accessible only by ferry, the Cranberry Isles (www.cranberryisles.com) are an off-the-beaten-path delight. The 400-acre Little Cranberry, home to the village of Islesford, is about 20 minutes offshore from Southwest Harbor. Diversions include a few galleries, a couple of B&Bs and the Islesford Market (☑207-244-7667; ☺Mon-Sat mid-Jun–early Sep), where the 80-odd year-rounders and 400-odd summer folk gather around like it's their own kitchen. Great Cranberry Island is even more low-key. Stop in at the Seawich Café & Cranberry Store (☑207-244-5336; ☺8am-4pm Mon-Thu, 8am-11:30pm Fri, longer hours in summer) by the dock to see who's around and what's up.

Cranberry Cove Boating Co (☑207-244-5882; round-trip adult/child $24/16; ☺May-Oct) carries passengers to and from the Cranberry Isles, departing from Southwest Harbor, aboard the 47-passenger *Island Queen*, which cruises six times daily in summer.

The Beal & Bunker Mailboat (☑207-244-3575; round-trip adult/child $24/12) offers frequent year-round service between Northeast Harbor and the Cranberry Isles.

WESTERN LAKES & MOUNTAINS

Western Maine receives far fewer visitors than the coast, which thrills the outdoorsy types who love its dense forests and solitary peaks just the way they are. While much of the land is still wilderness, there are some notable settlements. The fine old town of Bethel and the mountain setting of Rangeley Lakes are relatively accessible to city dwellers in the northeast.

In the fall, leaf peepers stream inland with their cameras and picnic baskets. In winter, skiers and snowmobile riders turn the mountains into their playground.

This is rural America at its most rustic. So bring a map and don't expect to rely on your cell phone – signals can be few and far between in these parts.

Bethel

POP 2600

An hour and a half northwest of Portland, Bethel is surprisingly lively and refined for a town surrounded on all sides by deep dark woods. Summer visitors have been coming here to escape the coastal humidity since the 1800s, and many of its fine old cottages and lodges are still operating. It's a prime spot to be during Maine's colorful fall foliage months and during the winter ski season. If you head west on US 2 toward New Hampshire, be sure to admire the Shelburne birches, a high concentration of the white-barked trees that grow between Gilead and Shelburne.

◉ Sights & Activities

Roughly 50,000 acres of the White Mountain National Forest lie inside Maine. The mountains near Bethel are home to several major ski resorts and winter is definitely the town's high season. For a dose of alpine scenery, consider a scenic drive along NH 113 from Gilead south to Stow.

Hiking   HIKING

Surrounded by mountains and deep forest cut through with silvery streams, Bethel has terrific hiking opportunities. The 3-mile Mt Will Trail starts from US 2, east of Bethel, and ascends to mountain ledges with fine views of the Androscoggin Valley. Grafton Notch State Park, north of Bethel via ME 26, offers hiking trails and pretty waterfalls, but no camping. Try the park's 1.5-mile trail up to Table Rock Overlook, or the walk to Eyebrow Loop and Cascade Falls, with excellent picnicking possibilities right by the falls.

Sunday River Ski Resort   SKIING

(☑800-543-2754; www.sundayriver.com; ME 26; full-day lift ticket adults/child 13-18/child under 12 & seniors $87/69/56, half-day $63/55/45; ⊕) Six miles north of Bethel along ME 5/26, Sunday River has eight mountain peaks and 132 trails, with 16 lifts. It's regarded as one of the region's best family ski destinations. They've also got summer activities, including chairlift rides, canoeing, ATV tours and a mountain-bike park. Two huge lodges have more than 400 rooms.

Bethel Outdoor Adventure   KAYAKING

(☑207-824-4224; www.betheloutdooradventure.com; 121 Mayville Rd/US 2; per day kayak/canoe $46/67; ☺8am-6pm) This downtown outfitter rents out canoes, kayaks and bicycles, and it arranges lessons, guided trips and shuttles to and from the Androscoggin River.

🛏 Sleeping

**White Mountain
National Forest** CAMPGROUND $

(☑877-444-6777; www.recreation.gov; campsites $18) There are five simple public campgrounds, with well water and toilets, in the Maine portion of the White Mountain National Forest: Basin, Cold River, Crocker Pond, Hastings and Wild River. For more information, contact the **Evans Notch Visitor Center** (☑207-824-2134; www.fs.fed.us/r9/white; 18 Mayville Rd/US 2; ☺8am-4:30pm Tue-Sat May-Oct, 8am-4:30pm Fri & Sat Nov-Apr).

★**Austin's Holidae House B&B** B&B $$

(☑207-824-3400; www.holidae-house.com; 85 Main St; r incl breakfast $100-135; 🛜) This 1902 Victorian has seven rooms done up in high Victorian kitsch, all florals, doilies, pedestal sinks and painted ceiling murals. Some have shared bathrooms. The English owner cooks up a mean breakfast.

✖ Eating & Drinking

Bethel has a growing number of decent restaurants, with enticing and appetising options for vegetarians.

SS Milton AMERICAN $$

(☑207-824-2589; 43 Main St; mains $17-25; ☺5-9:30pm) For slightly retro 'fancy' seafood dishes such as Ritz-cracker-topped scallops or buttery lobster casserole, this downtown establishment is a solid pick. Snag a porch table if you can.

Sunday River Brewing Company PUB

(☑207-824-4253; www.sundayriverbrewpub.com; cnr US 2 & Sunday River Rd; ☺noon-10pm) Bethel's brewpub pours a half-dozen of its own brews (from a light golden lager to a black porter) and offers mediocre bar food. Live bands fire things up on weekends.

❶ Information

The helpful **Bethel Area Chamber of Commerce** (☑207-824-2282; www.bethelmaine.com; 8 Station Pl; ☺9am-5pm Mon-Fri) maintains an information office in the Bethel Station building.

❶ Getting There & Away

Bethel lies 70 miles north of Portland, via ME 26 . If you're heading into the White Mountains of New Hampshire, take US 2 east from Bethel toward Gorham (22 miles) and head south to North Conway.

Rangeley Lake & Around

POP 1100

Surrounded by mountains and thick hardwood forests, the Rangeley Lake region is a marvelous year-round destination for adventurers. The gateway to the alpine scenery is the laid-back town of **Rangeley**, whose tidy inns and down-home restaurants make a useful base for skiing, hiking, white-water rafting and mountain biking in the nearby hills.

During the early 20th century, the lakes in this region were dotted with vast frame hotels and peopled with vacationers from Boston, New York and Philadelphia. Though most of the great hotels are gone, the reasons for coming here remain.

🏃 Activities

The mountains around Rangeley offer good skiing and snowboarding options.

Sugarloaf SKIING

(☑800-843-5623, 207-237-2000; www.sugarloaf.com; ME 16, Kingfield; full-day lift tickets adults/child 13-18/child under 12 & seniors $81/67/56, half-day $61/54/46) Rangeley's most popular ski resort has a vertical drop of 2820ft, with 138 trails and 15 lifts. This is Maine's second-highest peak (4237ft). Summer activities include lift rides, zip lines and golf. The resort

MAINE RANGELEY LAKE & AROUND

DON'T MISS

QUODDY HEAD STATE PARK

When the fog's not obscuring the view, the 541-acre **Quoddy Head State Park** (☑207-733-0911; 973 S Lubec Rd, Lubec; adult/child $3/1) has darn dramatic scenery. From the parking lot, catch the Coastal Trail, which leads along the edge of towering, jagged cliffs. Keep an eye to the sea for migrating whales (finback, minke, humpback and right whales) which migrate along the coast in the summer. The much-photographed red-and-white-banded West Quoddy Light (1858) is the easternmost point in the United States.

From Bar Harbor, head 76 miles northeast on US 1, then take ME 189 northeast for 11 miles to reach Lubec.

village complex also has an enormous mountain lodge, an inn and rental condos.

Sugarloaf Outdoor Center SKIING
(📞207-237-6830; www.sugarloaf.com; ME 27/ME 16, Carrabassett Valley; adult/child under 12 & seniors $22/13) Near Sugarloaf's slopes, the center has 56 miles of groomed cross-country trails and an NHL-size skating rink.

🛏 Sleeping & Eating

Rangeley Inn INN $
(📞207-864-3341; www.rangeleyinn.com; 2443 Main St; r $84-120) Relax by the fire and admire the mounted bear in the lobby of this big creaky turn-of-the-century lodge. Rooms are simple and old-fashioned, with Victorian floral wallpaper and brass beds.

Loon Lodge LODGE $$
(📞207-864-5666; www.loonlodgeme.com; 16 Pickford Rd; r incl breakfast $125-172; 🖥) Hidden in the woods by the lake, this log-cabin lodge has nine rooms, most with a backwoods-chic look, with wood-plank walls and handmade quilts.

Red Onion LODGE $$
(www.rangeleyredonion.com; 2511 Main St; mains $10-17; 🍴) A big plate of chicken parmesan after a day on the slopes has been a Rangeley tradition for four decades. This boisterous Italian-American joint is also known for its pizzas and its 1970s wood-paneled bar.

ℹ Information

The **Rangeley Lakes Chamber of Commerce** (📞207-864-5364; www.rangeleymaine.com; 6 Park Rd; ⊙9am-5pm Mon-Sat), just off Main St, can answer questions.

ℹ Getting There & Away

Rangeley is about 2½ hours north of Portland by car, on the northeast side of Rangeley Lake. From I-95, take ME 4 N to ME 108 W, then take ME 17 W to 4 S.

BAXTER STATE PARK

Baxter State Park (📞207-723-5140; www.baxterstateparkauthority.com; per car $14) is Maine at its most primeval: the wind whips around 47 mountain peaks, black bears root through the underbrush, and hikers go for miles without seeing another soul. Visitors can hike the park's 200 miles of trails, climb the sheer cliffs (this is a true rock climber's paradise), fly-fish the ponds and rivers, and spot wild animals, like bald eagles, moose and fox-like martens. The park is most popular in the warmer months, but it's also open for winter sports like snowmobiling.

Baxter's 5267ft Mt Katahdin – the park's crowning glory – is Maine's tallest mountain and the northern end of the over-2000-mile-long Appalachian Trail.

Limited visitors are allowed in the park each day, so arrive at the entrance early – very early. There are no treated water sources in the park, so bring your own or carry purifying tablets. Baxter's two main gates are Matagamon, in the north, and Togue Pond, in the south. Togue Pond has the park's main visitors' center, where you can pick up maps and other info. It's about 22 miles from the town of Millinocket (population 4800). The less-popular Matagamon gate can be accessed via the town of Patten (pop 1100).

Baxter State Park's 200 miles of hiking trails (📞parking reservation line 207-723-3877; www.baxterstateparkauthority.com) range from simple strolls to the arduous climb up Mt Katahdin. For an easy day hike from the Togue Pond gate, try the mile-long walk to Katahdin Stream Falls, or the pleasant 2-mile nature path around Daicey Pond. Those looking to bag Mt Katahdin itself, whose summit is known as Baxter Peak, should check the weather reports, start out early, and plan on eight to 10 hours of solid uphill climbing. Katahdin hikers can reserve parking spots using Baxter's reservations line.

For more info including area accommodations, check with **Katahdin Area Chamber of Commerce** (📞207-723-4443; www.katahdinmaine.com; 1029 Central St, Millinocket).

Understand New England

New England Today

Recalling its revolutionary roots, New England continues to claim its place as one of the nation's most forward-looking and barrier-breaking regions. This is most evident in the political sphere, as controversial topics like same-sex marriage and universal healthcare are already old news here. A diverse economic base means that New England has fared well during the slow economy, as evidenced by the region's revitalized cities and increasing number of farms.

Best in Film

Good Will Hunting (1998) About a blue-collar boy from South Boston who becomes a math savant at the Massachusetts Institute of Technology.
The Cider House Rules (2000) Won Michael Caine an Academy Award for his role as a doctor in an orphanage in rural Maine.
Mystic River (2006) The story of three friends who are thrown together in adulthood when one of their daughters is murdered in Boston.

Best in Print

Walden; Or, Life in the Woods (Henry David Thoreau, 1854) A story of the author's 26 months in a cabin on Walden Pond.
The Hungry Ocean (Linda Greenlaw, 1999) Greenlaw recounts her adventures as the captain of a swordfish boat near Mohegan Island.
Land's End (Michael Cunningham, 2002) Explores the artistic history and alternative lifestyle of Provincetown (which in Provincetown is not the alternative but the norm).

East Coast Liberals

New England is politically liberal. That said, a lasting strain of independent politics is evident in New England's northern states, sustained by fiscal conservatism, social libertarianism and a healthy suspicion of politics.

One of the most definitive features is the region's supportive political climate for social reformers, carrying on a legacy that includes 19th-century abolitionists, 20th-century suffragettes and 21st-century gay-rights advocates. The region has recently been at the forefront of countless 'progressive' issues, such as healthcare and marriage equality. The national healthcare legislation enacted in 2010 was modeled after a pre-existing system of universal healthcare in Massachusetts. All six New England states had legalized some form of same-sex union before it was legitimized at the federal level in 2013.

Cultural Diversity

New England is increasingly international. Irish, Italian and Portuguese communities have been well established in the urban areas since the 19th century. In more recent years, New England cities have continued to attract immigrants from non-European origins: you can hear Caribbean rhythms in Hartford and Springfield, smell Vietnamese and Cambodian cooking in Cambridge and Lowell, and see Brazilian flags waving in Somerville.

Much of the region is dependent on immigrant labor to keep the economy running. Unfortunately, immigrants continue to confront obstacles of adaptation, including language barriers, financial limitations and legal hazards. Many New Englanders anxiously await immigration reform at the federal level.

The challenges of multiculturalism were on full display in 2013, when two bombs exploded at the finish line of the Boston Marathon, killing three and injuring hundreds. Boston endured several days of confusion (including a citywide lockdown) before one alleged perpetrator was caught and another killed. They were two brothers – Chechen immigrants and Muslim extremists – who claimed to seek retribution for US killings of innocent Muslims. Recovered from the shock of the tragedy, the city has gone back to business – hearts are saddened but spirits never dampened.

Economic Diversity

New England has one of the healthier regional economies in the US. Tourism, education and medicine are all major players. The largely recession-resistant technology and biotechnology industries were spawned from local university research labs.

That said, the region was not immune to the recent recession, as evidenced by the regional unemployment rate that still hovers around 6.8% in 2013 (lower than the national average, but still up about two points from 2007). Boston is a major center for financial services, while Hartford is the country's insurance capital, and both industries were hard hit. Still, the region's economic diversity means that it is recovering better than others, and economists predict modest growth for the coming years.

Rural Renewal

New England is a patchwork of farmland, yielding Massachusetts cranberries, Maine potatoes and Vermont cheeses. Some 28,000 farms blanket the region. The farmer's life is not easy, and this is highlighted by the decreasing number of family farms. But environmental awareness and changing eating habits have created new opportunities, as diners are willing to pay for food that is grown organically and locally.

Urban Renewal

Industrial and port cities around New England were built on the backs of factory workers, mill girls and sailors. Today towns like Salem, Mystic, Lowell, Providence and Portland have remade themselves as tourist destinations, building museums out of former factories, opening restaurants in old warehouses, and offering cruises on canals and walks around harbors.

Populations are turning over in these cities. Expensive real estate means that property is sold to the highest bidder, no matter where they come from. Many people in the old enclaves welcome newcomers, recognizing the advantages of diversity and development. But others resent being invaded by outsiders, whether they're immigrants or yuppies.

HIGHEST POINT: **MT WASHINGTON (6288FT)**

MILES OF COASTLINE: **4965**

AREA: **71,992 SQUARE MILES**

POPULATION: **14,444,900**

if New England were 100 people

80 would be European American
8 would be Latino
6 would be African-American
6 would be other

belief systems
(% of population)

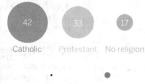

42 Catholic 33 Protestant 17 No religion

2 Jewish   6 Other

population per sq mile

NEW ENGLAND   USA   NEW JERSEY

👤 ≈ 80 people

History

When the Pilgrims landed in Plymouth back in 1620, they started something big. In the four centuries since, New England has been at the forefront of American history, instigating the War for Independence, inspiring the transcendentalist thinkers and writers, embracing technological innovation and spurring on social change.

When New Worlds Collide

James Mayer and Byron Dix provide detailed, illustrated descriptions of Native American archaeological sites around New England in *Manitou: The Sacred Landscape of New England's Native Civilization.*

When the first European settlers arrived in the New World, they found about 100,000 Native American inhabitants, mostly Algonquians, organized into small regional tribes. The northern tribes were solely hunter-gatherers, while the southern tribes hunted and practiced slash-and-burn agriculture, growing corn, squash and beans.

Before the English Pilgrims, the Native Americans were already acquainted with Portuguese fishermen, French fur traders, English explorers, Dutch merchants and Jesuit missionaries. The Europeans were welcomed as a source of valued manufactured goods, but they were also feared, and for good reason – in the Great Sadness of 1617, a smallpox epidemic had devastated the Native American population in the southeast. The Pilgrims were notable as the first Europeans to make a successful settlement in New England. Chief Massasoit of the Wampanoag tribe did not view this scrawny band of settlers as a threat and even hoped that they might be useful allies against his tribal rivals.

But the clash of cultures soon proved fatal to the Native American way of life. English coastal encampments spread as seemingly unoccupied lands were claimed – John Winthrop, the first governor of the Massachusetts Bay Colony, declared 'God hath hereby cleared our title to this place.' In less than a hundred years, the indigenous population was reduced by 90% due to disease, war and forced migration.

A Shining City on a Hill

Seventeenth-century England was torn by religious strife. The Protestant Pilgrims were assailed by the Catholic-leaning King James I, who vowed to 'harry them out of the country.' In 1620, the Pilgrims – led by

TIMELINE	1497	1606–07	1614
	The Italian explorer John Cabot lands in Newfoundland and explores the coast of New England, claiming the territory for his patron, King Henry VII of England.	King James I issues a charter for the Plymouth Company to establish a settlement in the New World. The resulting Popham Colony (in present-day Maine) was abandoned after one year.	At the behest of future King Charles, Captain John Smith braves the frigid North Atlantic, makes his way from Maine to Cape Cod, maps the coastline and dubs the region 'New England.'

Separatist devotee William Bradford – crossed the Atlantic to establish a community dedicated to religious austerity.

Trouble arose when the badly off-course *Mayflower* weighed anchor in Cape Cod Bay. A group of nonreligious passengers had booked their fares expecting to strike out on their own in Virginia; they threatened a mutiny when they realized they would have to spend the winter with the Separatists. The resulting Mayflower Compact brokered a deal in which both parties would have an equal say in matters of governance. Under Bradford's capable leadership, Plymouth Colony maintained a religious focus and grew modestly over the next decade. Today, you can visit a historically accurate re-creation of this first settlement at Plimoth Plantation.

In 1630 the merchant vessel *Arbella* delivered another group of Protestant Separatists, the Puritans, 50 miles north of Plymouth. The Puritans were better prepared: they were well financed, well equipped and 1000 strong, and included those of high social rank. At the head of their party, John Winthrop stood atop the Shawmut peninsula of present-day Boston and proclaimed the founding of 'a shining city on a hill.'

The Massachusetts Bay Colony was a product of the Puritan gentry's ambition to build a Christian community of personal virtue and industriousness – a community purified of pompous ceremony and official corruption, and disdainful of tyranny. Theirs was a kind of legalistic Calvinism, enforced Old Testament style. Anyone who missed church without good cause was apt to catch a whipping. Governor Winthrop constructed centralized institutions to maintain unity among the settlers, who dispersed to choice locations around the harbor and along the rivers. The General Court, an assembly of propertied men, became the principal mechanism of government. Church membership was a prerequisite for political and property rights.

The Puritan theocracy did not go unchallenged. In Boston, Anne Hutchinson started a women's Bible circle, promoting the idea of salvation through personal revelation. The popularity of this individualist-inspired view was threatening to the colony's patriarchal elders, who arrested the heretic Hutchinson and banished her to an island. One of Hutchinson's defenders was her brother-in-law, the Reverend John Wheelwright, who led a group to resettle in New Hampshire. This was the beginning of a trend in which independent folk, exasperated by encroachments on individual liberty by the Massachusetts state, would found their own settlements.

From his pulpit in Salem, Roger Williams sermonized for religious tolerance, separation of church and state, and respect for Native American rights. In 1636, Williams and a small group of backers founded a new settlement, Providence, along Narragansett Bay. The Rhode Island Colony

Colonial History

Pilgrim Monument, Provincetown

Plimoth Plantation, Plymouth

Mayflower II, Plymouth

Witch House, Salem

College Hill, Providence

HISTORY A SHINING CITY ON A HILL

Governor John Winthrop sermonized from the *Arabella*, en route to Massachusetts: 'we shall be as a city upon a hill. The eyes of all people are upon us. So that if we shall deal falsely with our God in this work…we shall be made a story and a byword throughout the world.'

1614–17	**1620**	**1630**	**1636**
In his records, Captain John Smith mentions the Massachusett Indians living around Boston Bay. Over the course of three years, three different epidemics wipe out 75% of the native population.	A group of English religious dissidents known as Pilgrims sail from their self-imposed exile in Holland and establish Plymouth Colony, the second successful European settlement in the New World.	Led by Governor John Winthrop, Puritan settlers flee the repressive Church of England and establish the theocratic Massachusetts Bay Colony.	Freethinking theologian Roger Williams founds the colony of Rhode Island and Providence Plantations. His radical ideas include freedom of religion and separation of church and state.

welcomed Anne Hutchinson, declared religious freedom and made peace with the Native Americans.

Meanwhile, Bay Colony officials exiled yet another 'heretic' parson, Thomas Hooker, who suggested that nonpropertied men should not be excluded from political affairs. Hooker relocated to Hartford, amid the growing farm communities of the Connecticut River Valley.

Over time, the Puritan gentry were less effective in compelling others to embrace their vision of an ideal Christian community. The incessant pull of individual interests and the rise of a secular commercial culture proved to be the undoing of Winthrop's vision.

Cradle of Liberty

In the late 18th century, New England and the British throne clashed over the issue of taxation, exposing the conflicting strains of royal subject and personal liberty.

In 1765 the British Parliament passed the Stamp Act to finance colonial defense. Massachusetts colonists were the first to object. To safeguard colonial autonomy, local businessman Sam Adams formed the Sons of Liberty, which incited a mob to ransack the royal stamp office. The actions were defended in a treatise written by a local lawyer, Sam's cousin John Adams, who cited the Magna Carta's principal of no taxation without representation. Eastern Connecticut and Rhode Island joined the protest. When New England merchants threatened a boycott of British imports, the measure was repealed.

The British government devised new revenue-raising schemes. Again, they were met with hostile noncompliance, and Boston emerged as the center of conflict. Parliament closed the Massachusetts General Assembly and dispatched two armed regiments to the city, which only inflamed local passions.

Forced underground, the Sons of Liberty set up a covert correspondence system to agitate public sentiment and coordinate strategy with sympathizers. In December 1773, the Sons of Liberty disguised themselves as Mohawks and dumped a cargo of taxable tea into the harbor. The Boston Tea Party enraged King George, whose retribution was swift and vengeful. The port was blockaded and the city placed under direct military rule.

The conflict tested the region's political loyalties. Tory sympathizers included influential merchants, manufacturers and financiers, while the rebels tended to be drawn from lesser merchants, artisans and yeoman farmers. The colonial cause was strongly supported in Rhode Island, Hartford and New Hampshire, where local assemblies voted to provide economic assistance to Boston. Aroused Providence residents even set fire to the British warship *Gaspee* when it ran aground in Narragansett

Everyone knows that March 17 is St Patrick's Day, but it is also Evacuation Day in the greater Boston area, commemorating the day in 1776 that British troops relinquished the city of Boston after 11 months of occupation.

The first naval skirmish of the Revolutionary War took place in Machiasport, Maine, when drunken colonists killed an English sea captain and ransacked the royal ship that was supposed to be monitoring the lumber trade. The crown's swift response was to burn the town of Portland to the ground.

1675–78	1686–89	1692–93	1754–63
Wampanoag chief King Philip terrorizes the colonists. Twenty-five towns are destroyed and thousands are killed before he is shot, ending King Philip's War.	After the colonies openly flout trade restrictions such as the Navigation Acts, King James II establishes the Dominion of New England, instituting more rigorous controls over the colonies.	Witch hysteria in Salem sends 14 women and five men to the gallows. One man is crushed to death when he refuses to confess his guilt.	New Englanders are drawn into the French and Indian War, in which the British fought the French in the New World. The king levies taxes on the colonies to pay for war efforts.

Bay while chasing suspected smugglers. New Hampshire instigators seized Fort William and Mary when the panicky loyalist governor attempted to enlist more British reinforcements.

In April 1775 the British again attempted to break colonial resistance, this time arresting rebel ringleaders Sam Adams and John Hancock and seizing a secret store of gunpowder and arms. As the troops assembled, Paul Revere slipped across the river into Charlestown, where he mounted his famous steed Brown Beauty and galloped off into the night to spread the alarm. By next morning, armed local militias began converging on the area. The incident sparked a skirmish between British troops and local farmers on the Old North Bridge in Concord and the Lexington Green, leaving over a hundred dead. The inevitable had arrived: war for independence.

Other colonies soon joined ranks, heeding the advice of Boston-born Benjamin Franklin, who said 'if we do not hang together, we will surely hang separately.' New Hampshire, Connecticut and Maine (then part of Massachusetts) wholeheartedly supported the revolutionary cause. The Green Mountain Boys, led by Ethan Allen, was a bandit gang that resisted the advances of the New York colony into northwest New England.

The war did not go well at first for the feisty but ill-prepared colonists, but the tide turned when the French were finally persuaded to ally with the rebellion. In 1781, the American army and French navy cornered the main British army on the Yorktown peninsula in Virginia and forced their surrender. British rule had come to an end in the American colonies.

Of Sails & Whales

New England port cities flourished during the Age of Sail. In the 17th century, the infamous 'triangular trade route' was developed, involving West Indian sugar, New England rum and West African slaves. Merchants who chose not to traffic in human cargo could still make large profits by illicitly undercutting European trade monopolies. In the late 17th century, Rhode Island provided a safe haven for pirates; indeed, Captain Kidd and Blackbeard were on a first-name basis with most Newport proprietors.

In the 18th century, Britain's stricter enforcement of trade monopolies and imposition of higher tariffs squeezed the merchants' profits. But after the American Revolution, New England merchants amassed fortunes by opening up trade routes to the Far East. Shipbuilding thrived in Massachusetts, Maine and Connecticut, and cities such as Salem, Newburyport and Portsmouth were among the richest trading cities in the world.

The whaling industry also thrived. Even today, the rich feeding grounds of Stellwagen Bank off Cape Cod attract whales to the region.

HISTORY OF SAILS & WHALES

Revolutionary History

Freedom Trail, Boston

Minute Man National Historic Park, Lexington

Old North Bridge, Concord

Old Lighthouse Museum, Stonington

Fort Griswold Battlefield State Park, Groton

Bennington Battlefield Historic Site, Bennington

1765	1770	1775
The Stamp Act incites protests among colonists, who argue against taxation without representation. Opponents form the Sons of Liberty to protest British policies in the colonies.	Provoked by a local gang throwing snowballs, British troops fire into a crowd in Boston and kill five people, an incident dubbed the Boston Massacre.	British troops respond to reports that colonists are stockpiling weapons. Warned by Paul Revere and William Dawes, the Minutemen confront the Redcoats in Lexington and Concord, starting the War for Independence.

AGNIESZKA GAUL

➡ Paul Revere statue, Boston

In the preindustrial period, whales provided commodities, such as oil for lamps, teeth and bone for decorative scrimshaw, and other material for hoop skirts, umbrellas and perfume.

The whalers in New England were strategically placed to pursue the highly sought-after sperm whales along Atlantic migratory routes. Buzzards Bay, Nantucket Island and New Bedford were all prominent whaling centers. In the mid-19th century, New Bedford hosted a whaling fleet of over 300 ships, employing over 10,000 people directly and indirectly, and cashing in over $12 million in profits.

Industrial Revolution

New England's industrial revolution began in Rhode Island when Quaker merchant Moses Brown contracted English mechanic Samuel Slater to construct a water-powered cotton-spinning factory. The Brown-Slater partnership was a brilliant success. Their mills sprouted up along the Blackstone River, driving a vibrant Rhode Island textile industry.

Thirty miles northwest of Boston, along the Merrimack River, a group of wealthy merchants built one of the wonders of the industrial age: a planned city of five-story red-brick factories, lining the river for nearly a mile, driven by a network of power canals. Named for the project's

WHO WAS FIRST?

Everyone wants to be first. Both Rhode Island and New Hampshire make claims about being the first colony to declare independence from Great Britain. But there is only one 'first.' So whose claim is legit?

The New Hampshire Provincial Government was kicked out of Portsmouth in 1774, so it moved up the road to Exeter, thus establishing the *first* independent government in the colonies. In January 1776, this local body ratified a constitution, the *first* colony to do so. But the document was explicit in 'declaring that we never sought to throw off our dependence upon Great Britain, but felt ourselves happy under Her protection while we could enjoy our constitutional rights and privileges, and that we shall rejoice if such a reconciliation between us and our parent state can be affected.' The local governance was a temporary provision, put in place until the dispute with Britain could be resolved. Not exactly a declaration of independence.

In May of that same year, still two months before the unveiling of *the* Declaration of Independence, Rhode Island issued its formal statement. With none of the stipulations and explanations of New Hampshire's constitution, Rhode Island was the first to declare outright independence.

Several colonies followed suit. New Hampshire finally came around six weeks later, resolving that 'the Thirteen United Colonies should be declared a free and independent state.'

1776	1777	1787	1789–1801
Colonial leaders from 13 colonies (including Connecticut, Massachusetts, New Hampshire and Rhode Island) sign the Declaration of Independence, asserting that they are no longer a part of the British Empire.	The Republic of Vermont declares its independence, not only from Britain but also from New York. The state constitution is the first to abolish slavery and advocate universal male suffrage.	The Beverly Cotton Manufactory – the country's first cotton mill – is constructed in Beverly, Massachusetts, kicking off the industrial revolution. The era's largest mill operates for more than 40 years.	John Adams of Quincy, Massachusetts, serves two terms as the vice president and one term as the president of the newly independent United States of America.

deceased visionary, Francis Cabot Lowell, the city counted over 40 mills and employed over 10,000 workers; machines hummed 12 hours a day, six days a week.

This was not the grimy squalor of Manchester. Lowell was an orderly city. The workforce at first was drawn from the region's young farm women, who lived in dormitories under paternalistic supervision. The 'mill girls' were gradually replaced by cheaper Irish immigrant labor.

By the mid-19th century, steam power and metal machines had transformed New England. Railroads crisscrossed the region, hastening industrialization and urbanization. Textile mills arose along rivers in Lawrence, Nashua, Concord and Fall River. Leather works and shoemaking factories appeared near Boston. Springfield and Worcester became centers for tool and dye making, southern Connecticut manufactured machinery, and the Maine woods furnished paper mills. Even Paul Revere abandoned his silversmith shop in the North End and set up a rolling copper mill and foundry 15 miles southwest along the Neponset River.

New England Melting Pot

The rapid rise of industry led to social as well as economic changes. The second half of the 19th century brought a wave of immigrant laborers to New England, throwing the world of English-descended Whig Protestants into turmoil.

The first Irish immigrants arrived to work in the mills in the 1820s. Disparaged by native New Englanders, the Irish were considered an inferior race of delinquents, whose spoken brogue suggested that one had a 'shoe in one's mouth.' They undercut local workers in the job market and, worse yet, brought the dreaded papist religion from which the Puritans had fled. Tensions ran high, occasionally erupting in violence. In 1834, rumors of licentiousness and kidnapping led a Boston mob to torch the Ursuline Convent in present-day Somerville, Massachusetts.

A potato famine back home spurred an upsurge in Irish immigration to Boston. Between 1846 and 1856, more than 1000 new immigrants stepped off the boat per month, a human flood tide that the city was not prepared to absorb. Anti-immigrant and anti-Catholic sentiments were shrill. As a political expression of this rabid reaction, the Know Nothing Party swept into office in Massachusetts, Rhode Island and Connecticut, promising to reverse the flow of immigration, deny the newcomers political rights and mandate readings from the Protestant Bible in public school.

Subsequent groups of Italian, Portuguese, French Canadian and East European Jewish immigrants suffered similar prejudices and indignities. By the end of the 19th century, the urban landscape of New England resembled a mosaic of clannish ethnic enclaves. Sticking together became

Maritime History

Salem Maritime National Historic Site

Peabody Essex Museum, Salem

Custom House, Newburyport

Albacore Park, Portsmouth

New Bedford Whaling National Historic Park

Nantucket Whaling Museum

Mystic Seaport Museum

Industrial Revolution History

Slater Mill, Pawtucket, Rhode Island

Lowell National Historical Park, Massachusetts

1820 Maine gains independence from Massachusetts, becoming the 23rd state to enter the Union.

1836 With the publication of his essay *Nature*, Ralph Waldo Emerson introduces the philosophy of transcendentalism, which elevates intuition over doctrine and spirituality over empiricism.

1863 Massachusetts native Robert Gould Shaw leads the 54th Regiment of black troops into battle in the Civil War. Colonel Shaw is killed in action and buried in a common grave next to the fallen black soldiers.

1895 Massachusetts native WEB Du Bois becomes the first African American to earn a PhD from Harvard University. The historian becomes a tireless advocate for civil rights for blacks.

an immigrant survival strategy for finding work, housing and companionship. Neighborhoods took on the feel of the old country with familiar language, cuisine and customs. The New England melting pot was more like a stew than a puree.

In the early 20th century, when new southern and Eastern European immigrants began preaching class solidarity, they were met with renewed fury from New England's ruling elite. Labor unrest in the factories mobilized a harsh political reaction against foreigners and socialism.

Reform & Racism

Local history professor Thomas O'Connor recounts the history of an Irish enclave in *South Boston: My Home Town*.

The legacy of race relations in New England is marred by contradictions. Abolitionists and segregationists, reformers and racists have all left their mark.

The first slaves were delivered to Massachusetts Bay Colony from the West Indies in 1638. By 1700, roughly 400 slaves lived in Boston. In the 18th century, Rhode Island merchants played a leading role in the Atlantic slave trade, financing over 1000 slave ventures and transporting more than 100,000 Africans.

A number of New England's black slaves earned their freedom by fighting against the British in the Revolution. Crispus Attucks, a runaway slave of African and Native American descent, became a martyr by falling victim in the Boston Massacre. Salem Poor, an ex-slave who bought his freedom, was distinguished for heroism in the Battle of Bunker Hill.

In the early 19th century, New England became a center of the abolition movement. In Boston, newspaper publisher William Lloyd Garrison, Unitarian minister Theodore Parker and aristocratic lawyer Wendell

NOT SO SLOW

For years Boston was a leader in the production and export of rum, made from West Indian sugar cane. Near the water's edge in the North End stood a storage tank for the Purity Distilling Company. On a January morning in 1919, the large tank, filled to the brim with brown molasses, suddenly began shuddering and rumbling as its bindings came undone.

The pressure caused the tank to explode, spewing two million gallons of molasses into the city like a volcano. The sweet explosion leveled surrounding tenements, knocked buildings off their foundations and wiped out a loaded freight train. Panic-stricken, man and beast fled the deadly ooze. A molasses wave surged down the streets drowning all in its sticky path. The Great Molasses Flood killed a dozen horses and 21 people, and injured more than 100. The cleanup lasted nearly six months. *Dark Tide*, by journalist Stephen Puleo, provides a fascinating account of the causes and controversy surrounding this devastating explosion.

1919	1927	1960	1966
Boston police strike for the right to form a trade union; chaos reigns until the military reserve arrives. The failed strike is portrayed as a socialist scheme to destroy society.	Two Italian anarchists, Nicola Sacco and Bartolomeo Vanzetti, are executed on trumped-up murder charges, revealing the persistence of class and ethnic animosities in Boston.	Massachusetts native John F Kennedy is elected president, ushering in the era of Camelot. As the first Irish American president and the first Catholic president, JFK makes his home state proud.	Republican Edward Brooke of Massachusetts is the first African American popularly elected to the US Senate. During two terms, Brooke is an relentless advocate for affordable housing.

Phillips launched the Anti-Slavery Society to agitate public sentiment. New England provided numerous stops along the Underground Railroad, a network of safe houses that helped runaway slaves reach freedom in Canada.

The New England states still maintained their own informal patterns of racial segregation, however, with African Americans as an underclass. Although Massachusetts was the first state to elect an African American to the US Senate by popular vote in 1966, race relations were fraught. In the 1970s Boston was inflamed by racial conflict when a judge ordered the city to desegregate the schools through forced busing. The school year was marked by a series of violent incidents involving students and parents.

20th-Century Trends

The fears of the Yankee old guard were finally realized in the early 20th century when ethnic-based political machines gained control of city governments in Massachusetts, Rhode Island and Connecticut.

While the Democratic Party was originally associated with rural and radical interests, it became the political instrument of the recently arrived working poor in urban areas. Flamboyant city bosses pursued a populist and activist approach to city politics. Their administrations were steeped in public works and patronage. According to Providence boss Charlie Brayton, 'an honest voter is one who stays bought.'

The Republican Party in New England was cobbled together in the mid-19th century from the Whigs, the Know Nothings and the antislavery movement. In the 20th century, it became the political vehicle for the old English-descended elite, who envisioned a paternalistic and frugal government and preached self-help and sobriety.

Economically, New England has experienced its share of booms and busts over the past century. The good times of the early 20th century crashed down in the Great Depression. After a brief recovery, the region began to lose its textile industry and manufacturing base to the south. With the mills shut down and the seaports quieted, the regional economy languished and its cities fell into disrepair.

But entrepreneurial spirit and technological imagination combined to revive the region, sustained by science, medicine and higher education. Boston, Providence and Hartford were buoyed by banking, finance and insurance. The biggest boost came from the technological revolution, which enabled local high-tech companies to make the Massachusetts Miracle, an economic boom in the 1980s. Even with stock-market corrections and bubble bursts, technological developments continue to reinvigorate New England.

African American History

Black Heritage Trail, Boston

African Meeting House, Nantucket

Oak Bluffs, Martha's Vineyard

Harriet Beecher Stowe House, Hartford

Sarah Messer's youth in the historic Hatch house in Marshfield, Massachusetts, inspired her to write *Red House: Being a Mostly Accurate Account of New England's Oldest Continuously Lived-in House* (2004).

1980s
Massachusetts experiences a period of economic growth. Known as the Massachusetts Miracle, the economic turnaround is fueled by the technology industry.

2000
Vermont becomes the second state in the US (after Hawaii) to legalize same-sex civil unions, allowing many of the same benefits afforded to married couples.

2013
Two bombs explode at the Boston Marathon, killing three and injuring hundreds. In response to the terrorist attack, the city embraces the motto 'Boston Strong.'

STEVE DUNWELL

→ Downtown Boston

New England Literature

New England's reverence for the written word arrived with the Puritans and was nurtured over the centuries by the area's universities and literary societies. Indeed, the region was the nucleus of the Golden Age of American Literature, with the nation's formative writers coming out of Boston, Concord and Hartford. This literary tradition thrives today, as writers and scholars continue to congregate in university classrooms and crowded cafes around New England.

Concord Literary Sites

Ralph Waldo Emerson Memorial House

....

Orchard House

....

Walden Pond

....

Old Manse

Colonial Literature

The literary tradition in New England dates to the days of Puritan settlement. As early as 1631, Anne Bradstreet was writing poetry and meditations. Shortly thereafter, Harvard College was founded (1636) and the first printing press was set up (1638), thus establishing Boston/Cambridge as an important literary center that would attract writers and scholars for generations to come.

Early colonial writings were either spiritual or historical in nature. Governor John Winthrop chronicled the foundation of Boston in his journals. Governor William Bradford, the second governor of Plymouth Colony, was the author of the primary historical reference about the Pilgrims, *Of Plimouth Plantation*. The most prolific writer was Reverend Cotton Mather (1663–1728), who wrote more than 400 books on issues of spirituality – most notably the Salem witch trials.

The Golden Age

During the 19th century New England became a region renowned for its intellect. The universities had become a magnet for writers, poets and

LOWELL: THE TOWN & THE CITY

'Follow along to the center of town, the Square, where at noon everybody knows everybody else.' So Beat Generation author Jack Kerouac described his hometown of Lowell, Massachusetts, in his novel *The Town & The City*.

One of the most influential American authors of the 20th century, Jack Kerouac (1922–69) was born in Lowell at the mill town's industrial peak. He inhabited its neighborhoods, he graduated from Lowell High School and he wrote for the *Lowell Sun*. It is not surprising that the author used Lowell as the setting for five of his novels that draw on his youth.

Kerouac is remembered annually during the Lowell Celebrates Kerouac (LCK) festival (p99). Aside from the festival, there are walking tours and films based on places that Kerouac wrote about and experienced.

Of course Kerouac is most famous for his classic novel *On the Road*. With it, he became a symbol of the spirit of the open road. He eventually went to New York, where he, Allen Ginsberg and William Burroughs formed the core of the Beat Generation of writers. Nonetheless, Kerouac always maintained ties to Lowell, and he is buried in Edson Cemetery, a pilgrimage site for devotees who were inspired by his free spirit.

philosophers, as well as publishers and bookstores. Local literati were expounding on social issues such as slavery, women's rights and religious reawakening. Boston, Cambridge and Concord were breeding grounds for ideas, nurturing the seeds of America's literary and philosophical flowering. This was the Golden Age of American literature, and New England was its nucleus.

Ralph Waldo Emerson (1803–82) promulgated his teachings from his home in Concord. He and Henry David Thoreau (1817–62) wrote compelling essays about their beliefs and their attempts to live in accordance with the mystical unity of all creation. Thoreau's notable writings included *Walden; or, Life in the Woods* (1854), which advocated a life of simplicity and living in harmony with nature, and *Civil Disobedience* (1849), a treatise well before its time.

Nathaniel Hawthorne (1804–64) traveled in this Concordian literary circle. America's first great short-story writer, Hawthorne was the author of *The Scarlet Letter* (1850) and *The House of the Seven Gables* (1851), both offering insightful commentary on colonial culture. Louisa May Alcott (1832–88) grew up at Orchard House, also in Concord, where she wrote her largely autobiographical novel *Little Women* (1868). This classic is beloved by generations of young women.

Around this time, poet Henry Wadsworth Longfellow (1807–82) was the most illustrious resident of Cambridge, where he taught at Harvard. Longfellow often hosted his contemporaries from Concord for philosophical discussions at his home on Brattle St (now the Longfellow National Historic Site). Here he wrote poems such as 'Song of Hiawatha' and 'Paul Revere's Ride,' both cherished accounts of American lore.

Meanwhile, some of these luminaries would travel one Saturday a month to Boston to congregate with their contemporaries at the old Parker House (now the Omni Parker House hotel). Presided over by Oliver Wendell Holmes, the Saturday Club was known for its jovial atmosphere and stimulating discourse, attracting such renowned visitors as Charles Dickens. Out of these meetings was born the *Atlantic Monthly*, a literary institution that continues to showcase innovative authors and ideas.

Down the street, the Old Corner Bookstore (now a stop on the Freedom Trail) was the site of Ticknor & Fields, the first publishing house to offer author royalties. Apparently Mr Fields had a special gift for discovering new local talent; by all accounts, his bookstore was a lively meeting place for writers and readers.

Around the region, writers fueled the abolitionist movement with fiery writings. William Lloyd Garrison founded the radical newspaper *The Abolitionist* on Beacon Hill. Activist Lydia Maria Child had her privileges at the Boston Athenaeum revoked for her antislavery pamphlets. Harriet Beecher Stowe (1811–96), whose *Uncle Tom's Cabin* recruited thousands to the antislavery cause, was born in Litchfield, Connecticut, and lived in Brunswick, Maine, before she moved to Hartford.

LITERARY NEW ENGLAND

1638 First Printing Press
Operation of the first printing press in the New World in Cambridge, Massachusetts.

1647 Anne Bradstreet
Publication of the book of poetry, *The 10th Muse Sprung up Lately in America*, by Anne Bradstreet, the first woman published in the New World.

17th–18th Century Early Colonial Literature
Early colonial literature is dominated by writing about spirituality and governance, which were often inseparable.

19th Century Golden Age
The Golden Age of New England literature features writings by transcendentalist thinkers, abolitionist activists and other celebrated poets and philosophers.

1852 Uncle Tom's Cabin
Publication of *Uncle Tom's Cabin*, by Harriet Beecher Stowe, fueling support for the abolitionist movement.

1868 Little Women
Publication of *Little Women*, by Louisa May Alcott, beloved by generations of young women.

1916 Provincetown Players
A group of writers found the Provincetown Players on Cape Cod.

NEW ENGLAND LITERATURE THE GOLDEN AGE

In 1895 WEB Du Bois (1868–1963) became the first black man to receive a PhD from Harvard University. A few years later, he wrote his seminal tract *The Souls of Black Folk,* in which he sought to influence the way blacks dealt with segregation, urging pride in African heritage.

New England Bookstores

....

Montague Book-mill, Montague

....

Harvard Book Store, Cambridge

....

Concord Bookshop, Concord

Banned in Boston

In the 20th century, New England continued to attract authors, but the Golden Age was over. The region was no longer the center of progressive thought and social activism that had so inspired American literature.

This shift in cultural geography was due in part to a shift in consciousness in the late 19th century. Moral crusaders and city officials promoted stringent censorship of books, films and plays that they deemed offensive or obscene. Many writers were 'banned in Boston' – a trend that contributed to the city's image as a provincial outpost instead of a cultural capital. Eugene O'Neill (1888–1953) is the most celebrated example. He attended Harvard, he was a key participant in the Provincetown Players on Cape Cod and he spent the last two years of his life in Back Bay; but his experimental play *Strange Interlude* was prohibited from showing on Boston stages.

Henry James (1843–1916) grew up in Cambridge. Although he was undoubtedly influenced by his New World upbringing, he eventually emigrated to England. A prolific writer, he often commented on American society in his novels, which included *Daisy Miller* and *The Bostonians.*

Robert Frost Sites

....

Robert Frost Stone House Museum, Shaftsbury

....

Frost Place, Franconia

Revolutionary poet ee cummings (1894–1962) was born in Cambridge, although his experiences in Europe inspired his most famous novel, *The Enormous Room.* Descended from a New England family, TS Eliot (1888–1965) taught at Harvard for a spell, but wrote his best work in England.

Robert Lowell (1917–77) was another Boston native who was restless in his hometown. He spent many years living in Back Bay and teaching at Boston University, where he wrote *Life Studies* and *For the Union Dead.* Encouraged by his interactions with Beat Generation poet Allen Ginsberg, Lowell became the seminal 'confessional poet.' At BU, he counted Sylvia Plath (1932–63) and Anne Sexton (1928–74) among the students he inspired before he finally moved to Manhattan.

LITERARY LIGHTS

Ralph Waldo Emerson (1803–82) Essayist with a worldwide following and believer in the mystical beauty of all creation; founder of transcendentalism.

Henry David Thoreau (1817–62) Best remembered for *Walden; or, Life in the Woods,* his journal of observations written during his solitary sojourn from 1845 to 1847 in a log cabin at Walden Pond.

Emily Dickinson (1830–86) This reclusive 'Belle of Amherst' crafted beautiful poems, mostly published after her death.

Mark Twain (Samuel Clemens; 1835–1910) Born in Missouri, Twain settled in Hartford, Connecticut, and wrote *The Adventures of Tom Sawyer* and *The Adventures of Huckleberry Finn.*

Edith Wharton (1862–1937) This Pulitzer Prize–winning novelist's best-known work, *Ethan Frome,* paints a grim portrait of emotional attachments on a New England farm.

Robert Frost (1874–1963) New England's signature poet, whose many books of poetry use New England themes to explore the depths of human emotions and experience.

Eugene O'Neill (1888–1953) From New London, Connecticut, O'Neill wrote the play *A Long Day's Journey into Night.*

John Irving (b 1942) New Hampshire native writes novels set in New England, including *The World According to Garp, The Hotel New Hampshire* and *A Prayer for Owen Meany.*

Stephen King (b 1947) Maine horror novelist; wrote *Carrie* and *The Shining.*

One of the Beat Generation's defining authors, Jack Kerouac was born in Lowell, Massachusetts. His hometown features prominently in many of his novels, but he too eventually decamped to the south.

America's favorite poet, Robert Frost (1874–1963), was an exception to this trend. He moved from California and lived on farms in Shaftsbury, Vermont, and Franconia, New Hampshire, where he wrote poems including 'Nothing Gold Can Stay' and 'The Road Not Taken.'

Contemporary Literature

Boston never regained its status as the hub of the literary solar system. But its rich legacy and ever-influential universities ensure that the region continues to contribute to American literature. Many of New England's most prominent writers are transplants from other cities or countries, drawn to its academic and creative institutions. John Updike (1932–2009), author of the Pulitzer Prize–winning Rabbit series, moved to Massachusetts to attend Harvard (where he was president of *Harvard Lampoon*), before settling in Ipswich, where he died in 2009.

Born in Ithaca, New York, David Foster Wallace (1962–2008) studied philosophy at Harvard. Although he abandoned the course and moved out of the city, his Boston-based novel, *Infinite Jest,* earned him a MacArthur Genius Award. Jhumpa Lahiri (b 1967) is a Bengali American writer who studied creative writing at Boston University. Her debut collection of short stories, *Interpreter of Maladies,* won a Pulitzer Prize for Fiction in 2000. Set in Boston and surrounding neighborhoods, her works address the challenges and triumphs in the lives of her Indian American characters. Geraldine Brooks is an Australian-born writer who resides part-time on Martha's Vineyard. Several of her novels are set in New England, including *March,* which earned her a Pulitzer Prize.

Of course, New England has also fostered some homegrown contemporary talent. John Cheever (1912–82) was born in Quincy and lived in Boston. His novel *The Wapshot Chronicle* takes place in a Massachusetts fishing village. Born and raised in Dorchester, Dennis Lehane (b 1966) wrote *Mystic River* and *Gone, Baby Gone,* both compelling tales set in a working-class Boston 'hoods; both were made into excellent films.

Stephen King (b 1947), author of horror novels such as *Carrie* and *The Shining,* lives and sets his novels in Maine. King is a well-known Red Sox fan, who is often sighted at home games. Also from Maine, Elizabeth Strout (b 1956) used a small coastal town as the setting for her wonderful quirky novel, *Olive Kitteridge,* which won the Pulitzer Prize for Fiction in 2009.

John Irving (b 1942) was born and raised in Exeter, New Hampshire, which serves as the setting for many of his stories, including *The World According to Garp, A Prayer for Owen Meany* and *A Widow for a Year.* In 1999 Irving won an Academy Award for his adapted screenplay of *The Cider House Rules,* which takes place in rural Maine.

Novelist Annie Proulx (b 1935), the author of *The Shipping News* and *Brokeback Mountain,* was born in Connecticut and grew up in Maine. Although she lived for more than 30 years in Vermont, most of her stories are not set in New England.

20th Century Banned in Boston

New England is a breeding ground for innovative writing styles and ideas, but the region's conservative social atmosphere drives away the most talented authors.

1984 The Witches of Eastwick

Publication of *The Witches of Eastwick,* John Updike's whimsical novel about a coven of witches in Rhode Island.

2000 Interpreter of Maladies

Bengali American writer Jhumpa Lahiri wins the Pulitzer Prize for Fiction for her collection of short stories, *Interpreter of Maladies.*

21st Century Today

Local universities continue to attract prominent writers, many of whom settle in the region (and set their stories there).

Back to School

No single element has influenced the region as profoundly as its educational institutions. New England's colleges and universities attract scholars, scientists, philosophers and writers who thrive off and contribute to the region's evolving culture. This renewable source of cultural energy supports sporting events, film festivals, music scenes, art galleries, coffee shops, hip clubs and Irish pubs. Take your pick from the eminent Ivies, the urban campuses, the liberal arts colleges or the edgier art and music schools.

Ivy League

In the 1980s Yale University became known as the 'gay ivy,' after the *Wall Street Journal* published an article about homosexuality on campus. The active community at Yale originated the LGBT rallying cry 'One in Four, Maybe More.'

New England is home to four of the eight Ivy League universities, all of which were founded before the American Revolution. They are known for academic excellence, selective admissions and Yankee elitism.

Yale University

Yale University is the centerpiece of the gritty city of New Haven, Connecticut. Founded in 1701 as the Collegiate School, the university was renamed in 1718 to honor a gift from rich merchant Elihu Yale. In the 1930s Yale instituted a system of residential colleges, whereby students eat, sleep, study and play in a smaller community within the larger university. There are now 12 residential, Oxford-style colleges, each with its own distinctive style of architecture. The school is also home to the enigmatic 'Skull and Bones,' an elitist secret society of aspiring kleptomaniacs. So-called 'Bonesmen' try to outdo each other by 'crooking' valuable artifacts and *objets d'art* from around the university. Its alumni include presidents, senators, Supreme Court justices and other upstanding citizens.

Brown University

Brown University's most esteemed faculty member is Josiah Carberry, professor of psychoceramics (the study of cracked pots). Every Friday the 13th is known as Carberry Day, when students donate their loose change to a fund for books.

Brown University has lent its progressive viewpoints to Providence, Rhode Island, since 1764 (though prior to American independence, it was known as the College in the English Colony of Rhode Island and Providence Plantations). The university charter specified that religion would not be a criterion for admission – the first institution in the New World to do so.

Brown has earned a reputation for refined radical-chic academics. In 1969 the university adopted the New Curriculum, which eliminated distribution requirements and allowed students to take courses without grades. In 1981 the university opened a research center devoted to sexuality and gender. The previous university president, Ruth J Simmons, was the first African American president of an Ivy League institution.

Today, the Georgian-era campus on College Hill enrolls about 6000 undergraduate students and 2000 graduate students. Although the *US News & World Report* ranks Brown 15th among national universities, a *Princeton Review* poll has ranked the school first on its list of America's happiest college students.

Dartmouth College

Dartmouth College dominates Hanover, New Hampshire, making it the quintessential New England college town. Dartmouth is unique among the Ivies for its small size, its rural setting and its emphasis on undergraduate education. Dartmouth also employs a year-round quarter system, known as the D-Plan. The school is famed for its spirited student body and the cult-like loyalty of its alumni. To get a sense of campus culture, think William F Buckley in Birkenstocks.

Dartmouth's 270-acre Georgian-era campus is centered on a picturesque green. The university also owns huge tracts of land in the White Mountains region and in Northern New Hampshire. No surprise, then, that the university has an active outing club (which incidentally maintains portions of the Appalachian Trail).

In 2005 a group of Dartmouth Frisbee players converted a school bus to run on waste vegetable oil. Since then, the so-called Big Green Bus spends its summers traveling the country and hosting events to promote sustainability and environmental awareness.

Dartmouth alum Chris Miller wrote the film *National Lampoon's Animal House* based on his fraternity days.

Harvard University

A slew of superlatives accompany the name of this venerable institution in Cambridge, Massachusetts. It is America's oldest university, founded in 1636. It still has the largest endowment, measuring $32 billion in 2013, having nearly recovered from the hit it took during the recession. It is often first in the list of national universities, according to *US News & World Report*. Harvard is actually comprised of 10 independent schools dedicated to the study of medicine, dentistry, law, business, divinity, design, education, public health, arts and science, and public policy, in addition to the traditional Faculty of Arts and Sciences.

Harvard Yard is the heart and soul of the university campus, with buildings dating back to its founding. But the university continues to expand in all directions. Most recently, Harvard has acquired extensive land across the river in Allston, with intention of converting this working-class residential area into a satellite campus with parkland and community services.

In 2003 a couple of Harvard computer-science students hacked into university computers to copy students' photographs and publish them online. Although their site was shut down by Harvard officials, the students were inspired to found Facebook. See how the story unfolds in the film *The Social Network*.

Boston & Cambridge Institutions

More than 50 institutions of higher education (too many to mention here) are located in Boston. About a dozen smaller schools are located in the Fenway, while the residential areas west of the center (Brighton and Allston) have been dubbed the 'student ghetto.'

Massachusetts Institute of Technology

On the opposite bank of the Charles River, the Massachusetts Institute of Technology (MIT) offers a completely novel perspective on Cambridge academia: proudly nerdy and not so tweedy as Harvard. It excels in science, design and engineering. MIT seems to pride itself on being offbeat. Wander into a courtyard and you might find it is graced with a sculpture by Henry Moore or Alexander Calder; or you might just as well find a Ping-Pong table or a trampoline. In recent years, it seems the university has taken this irreverence to a new level, as a recent frenzy of building has resulted in some of the most architecturally unusual and intriguing structures you'll find on either side of the river.

Boston University

Boston University (BU) is a massive urban campus sprawling west of Kenmore Sq. BU enrolls about 30,000 undergraduate and graduate students in all fields of study. The special collections of BU's Mugar Memorial Library include 20th-century archives that balance pop-culture and scholarly appeal. Peruse the rotating exhibits and you might find papers from Arthur Fiedler's collection, the archives of Douglas Fairbanks, Jr, or the correspondence of BU alumnus Dr Martin Luther King, Jr.

A WALK ACROSS THE HARVARD BRIDGE

The Harvard Bridge – from Back Bay in Boston to Massachusetts Institute of Technology (MIT) in Cambridge – is the longest bridge across the Charles River. It is not too long to walk, but it is long enough to do some wondering while you walk. You might wonder, for example, why the bridge that leads into the heart of MIT is named the Harvard Bridge.

According to legend, the state offered to name the bridge after Cambridge's second university. But the brainiac engineers at MIT analyzed the plans for construction and found the bridge was structurally unsound. Not wanting the MIT moniker associated with a faulty feat of engineering, it was suggested that the bridge better be named for the neighboring university up the river. That the bridge was subsequently rebuilt validated the superior brainpower of MIT.

That is only a legend, however (one invented by an MIT student, no doubt). The fact is that the Harvard Bridge was first constructed in 1891 and MIT only moved to its current location in 1916. The bridge was rebuilt in the 1980s to modernize and expand it, but the original name has stuck, at least officially. Most Bostonians actually refer to this bridge as the 'Mass Ave bridge' because, frankly, it makes more sense.

By now, walking across the bridge, perhaps you have reached the halfway point: 'Halfway to Hell' reads the scrawled graffiti. What is this graffiti anyway? And what is a 'smoot'?

A smoot is an obscure unit of measurement that was used to measure the distance of the Harvard Bridge, first in 1958 and every year since. One smoot is approximately five feet, seven inches, the height of Oliver R Smoot, who was a pledge of the MIT fraternity Lambda Chi Alpha in '58. He was the shortest pledge that year. And, yes, his physical person was actually used for all the measurements that year.

And now that you have reached the other side of the river, surely you are wondering exactly how long this bridge is. We can't speak for Harvard students, but certainly every MIT student knows that the Harvard Bridge is 364.4 smoots plus one ear.

Boston College

Not to be confused with BU, Boston College (BC) could not be more different. BC is situated between Brighton in Boston and Chestnut Hill in the tony suburb of Newton; the attractive campus is recognizable by its neo-Gothic towers. It is home to the nation's largest Jesuit community. Its Catholic influence makes it more socially conservative and more social-service oriented than other universities. Visitors to the campus will find a good art museum and excellent Irish and Catholic ephemera collections in the library. Aside from the vibrant undergraduate population, it has a strong education program and an excellent law school. Its basketball and football teams are usually high in national rankings.

University Art Collections

Hood Museum of Art, Dartmouth College

Museum of Art, RISD

Yale Center for British Art

Harvard Art Museum

List Visual Arts Center, MIT

Liberal Arts Colleges

The small, private liberal-arts college is a New England social institution. Dedicated to a well-rounded traditional curriculum, these schools are known for first-rate instruction, high-income tuition and upper-class pretension. The schools place an emphasis on the undergraduate classroom, where corduroy-clad professors are more likely to be inspiring teachers than prolific researchers. Their cozy campuses are nestled amid white steeples and red barns in the rolling New England countryside. Mandatory for all first-year students: *Plato's Republic,* rugby shirt and lacrosse stick.

Little Ivies

The 'Little Ivies' are a self-anointed collection of a dozen elite liberal-arts colleges, 10 of which are found in New England: Amherst, Williams and Tufts in Massachusetts; Connecticut College, Trinity and Wesleyan in Connecticut; Middlebury in Vermont; Bowdoin, Bates and Colby in Maine. From this select cohort, Amherst and Williams annually battle it out for top spot on the *US News & World Report* ranking of Best Liberal Arts Colleges. Williams in the Berkshires has received the honor 13 times, while Amherst in the Pioneer Valley has taken the prize 10 times.

Seven Sisters

Massachusetts is also home to four of the Seven Sisters, elite undergraduate women's colleges, founded in the days when the Ivy League was still a boys-only club. Mount Holyoke and Smith College are situated in the state's hippie-chic central Pioneer Valley; Wellesley is found in a posh Boston suburb of the same name; and Radcliffe is in Cambridge next to Harvard, to which it now officially belongs.

Art & Music Schools

Rhode Island School of Design

In a league of its own, the Rhode Island School of Design (RISD) boasts many famous graduates who have become pop-culture path cutters, such as musician David Byrne and his fellow members of the Talking Heads, graffiti artist and designer Shepard Fairey, and animation expert Seth MacFarlane. The concentration of creativity at RISD makes this Providence neighborhood among the edgiest and artiest in all New England.

MassArt

More formally known as the Massachusetts College of Art, this is the country's first and only four-year independent public art college. In 1873 state leaders decided the new textile mills in Lowell and Lawrence needed a steady stream of designers, so they established MassArt in Boston to educate some. With thousands of square feet of exhibition space on campus, there's always some thought-provoking or sense-stimulating exhibits to see.

Berklee College of Music

Housed in and around the Back Bay in Boston, Berklee is an internationally renowned school for contemporary music, especially jazz. The school was founded in 1945 by Lawrence Berk (the Lee came from his son's first name). Created as an alternative to the classical agenda and stuffy attitude of traditional music schools, Berk taught courses in composition and arrangement for popular music. Not big on musical theory, Berk emphasized learning by playing. His system was a big success and the school flourished. Among Berklee's Grammy-laden alumni are jazz musicians Gary Burton, Al Di Meola, Keith Jarrett and Diana Krall; pop and rock artists Quincy Jones, Donald Fagen and John Mayer; and film composer Howard Shore.

Emerson College

Founded in 1880, Emerson is a liberal-arts college that specializes in communications and the performing arts. Located in Boston's theater district, the college operates the Cutler Majestic Theater and the Paramount Theater, and its students run Boston's coolest radio station, WERS. Emerson celebs include Norman Lear, Jay Leno and 'the Fonz,' Henry Winkler.

The Williams College class of 1887 were the first students in America to wear caps and gowns at their graduation. The college copied the tradition from Oxford University in order to avoid an embarrassing discrepancy in the dress of rich and poor students.

RISD was founded when a local women's group had $1675 left over in their fund for Rhode Island's exhibit at the 1876 Centennial Exhibition. Some sources claim the competing proposal for the funds was for a drinking fountain in the local park.

Outdoor Activities

New England offers unlimited opportunities to get out and enjoy the Great Outdoors. The White Mountains of New Hampshire and Maine, the Green Mountains in Vermont and the Berkshires in Western Massachusetts are high points for skiing and hiking. Thousands of miles of coastline entice travelers with sailing, sea kayaking and whale-watching. Hundreds of glacial lakes and pretty ponds provide places for swimming, canoeing and fishing.

The *AMC White Mountain Guide* (2012) features the most complete trail information for hiking in New Hampshire; *Hiking Maine* (2002) offers maps and trail information for 72 hikes in the northernmost New England state.

Mountain Hiking

You can't go wrong when deciding which rearing peaks deserve the effort of lugging your knapsack, backpack or climbing gear.

The White Mountains in New Hampshire experience some of the foulest weather on record, but still draw everyone from day-hikers to multiday technical mountaineers. Pick a trail along the Kancamagus Hwy or around Crawford or Pinkham Notch.

New Hampshire's utterly accessible Mt Monadnock is a 'beginners mountain,' a relatively easy climb up a bald granite batholith. Much less traveled, Moosilauke Ravine Lodge offers great views, few crowds and miles of trails.

Maine's sublime Mt Katahdin remains practically untouched by tourism. Those who make it across the infamous Knife Edge will remember the experience for life. Acadia National Park and Grafton Notch State Park have miles of groomed trails for all skill levels.

Vermont's Green Mountains are seamed with hiking trails, particularly Vermont's own end-to-ender, the Long Trail, with both easy and challenging hikes. Many excellent trails radiate out of the Stowe area, which also has world-class ice climbing.

Mt Greylock in the Berkshires of Western Massachusetts makes an excellent goal for a day's walk from Williamstown.

Cycling

Bicycle Touring

See Boston by bike from the Charles River Bike Path, or follow part of Paul Revere's midnight ride from Boston to Lexington on the Minuteman Commuter Bikeway.

On Cape Cod in Massachusetts, tool around the Cape Cod Canal, the Shining Sea Bikeway, the Cape Cod Rail Trail or the Cape Cod National Seashore bike paths. In Rhode Island, take a spin on the beautiful 14.5-mile East Bay Bicycle Path, which follows the waterfront out of Providence and weaves past picnic-worthy state parks.

The Burlington Recreation Path follows the shore of Lake Champlain for 7.5 miles of smooth riding. It links up with the 12-mile Island Line Trail that takes cyclists out to the Colchester causeway.

Islands are particularly well-suited for great biking. Rent wheels for the quaint roads of Block Island, Rhode Island; the carriage roads of Mt Desert Island, Maine; the beachy trails of Nantucket and Martha's Vineyard, Massachusetts; and the long loop around Isleboro, Maine.

Mountain Biking

Fire roads, snowmobile trails and hairy drops at ski areas are fair game for mountain bikers. New England embraces the sport more each year as resorts add miles of singletrack to their offerings. Foliage season is prime time for gallivanting through psychedelic forests. Springtime thaws in April and early May are recuperative times for the trails, freshly exposed after a long winter's snow. Local bike shops will gladly reveal their favorite haunts.

In Stowe, Vermont, the hills are alive with whoops and hollers as riders roam the slopes on some of the most challenging terrain around. The Loon Mountain ski area of New Hampshire zooms daredevils up the mountain in a handy gondola for a white-knuckle, tooth-rattling trip back down. As usual, ask bike-shop dudes for the lowdown on cool local rides.

Western Maine's Bethel Outdoor Adventure (p406) will set your wheels in motion in that stunning countryside, home of the Sunday River ski area.

Swimming

The ocean never really heats up in New England, but that doesn't stop hoards of hardy Yankees from spilling onto the beaches and into the sea on hot summer days. Protected from the arctic currents, Rhode Island's beaches tend to be the warmest, particularly at Block Island and Newport.

Plum Island, just barely off the coast of Massachusetts, offers a nice combination of dunes, a wide beach and a wildlife sanctuary harboring more than 800 species of plants and wildlife. In Ipswich, Crane Beach is a wonderful, pristine stretch of sand in the heart of a wildlife refuge, with trails traversing its dunes. Beaches on Cape Cod, Nantucket and Martha's Vineyard are legendary. Bring your surfboard and hang ten at Good Harbor and Long Beach in Gloucester.

New Hampshire's short coastline is hemmed in with condos, but Rye Beach is an old favorite. Maine has a scattering of coastal beaches with icy water, including Ogunquit, Kennebunkport and Bar Harbor.

Rangeley Lake in Maine and Lake Winnipesaukee in New Hampshire are two of New England's largest inland lakes that are ideal for a dip: the former is quite isolated, but the latter is bursting with resorts, shops and services.

Rails-to-Trails (www.railtrails. org) details railroad beds that have been converted to hiking and biking trails. The New England Mountain Bike Association (www.nemba. org) is a wealth of information about places to ride, trail conditions and ways to connect with other riders.

APPALACHIAN TRAIL

Every year, thousands of ambitious souls endeavor to hike the complete 2179 miles of the Appalachian Trail (AT). Everyone has their own reasons for taking on this challenge, but almost all hikers share at least one goal: a life-changing experience. How could it not be that? Half a year carrying your life on your back – facing the harshest weather conditions and the most grueling physical challenges – is bound to affect you somewhere deep inside.

Such extreme challenges are not for everybody. Indeed, when the AT was dreamed up, it was never intended to be hiked all in one go. Rather, it was meant to connect various mountain communities where people could go to refresh and rejuvenate. As far as refreshing and rejuvenating, the trail has been a smashing success: it's estimated that two to three million visitors hike a portion of the trail every year, inhaling the fresh air, admiring the spectacular scenery and partaking of the great outdoors.

New England offers myriad opportunities to do just that. Even if you don't have five to seven months to spare for a thru-hike, you can still challenge yourself: every New England state except Rhode Island offers access to the AT; New Hampshire and Maine contain portions that are considered among the most difficult of the entire trail. New England also offers some of the most amazing vistas and remote wilderness along the trail. So load up your backpack and take a hike – even if it's just for the day.

SAILING, TAKE ME AWAY

For maritime sails, options are wonderfully varied. Pluck lobster from their traps on a boat out of Ogunquit, Maine. Hop aboard a research vessel out of Norwalk, Connecticut, and learn about the inhabitants of the sea. Inherit the wind aboard a windjammer out of Camden, Maine, or a 19th century–style schooner in Mystic, Connecticut. Holler 'thar she blows' from whale-watching boats that depart from Gloucester, Provincetown, Boston and Plymouth, all in Massachusetts.

Canoeing & Kayaking

You'll see more kayaks and canoes atop cars speeding down the byways of New England than you can shake a paddle at. The coast and inland areas are thick with kayaking opportunities for serious sea-kayakers and Sunday-afternoon duffers.

The region's enormous inland lakes – such as Vermont's Champlain, New Hampshire's Winnipesauke, and Maine's Moosehead – create their own, swift-moving weather patterns, wild currents and swells that challenge the technique, navigational skills and adrenaline demands of expert kayakers. The key is getting the lowdown on local tides, currents and weather prognostications from the locals themselves. Local boat purveyors always have tide charts and advice you would do well to heed.

The Maine islands are great fun to thread through; when the water is frisky, sea kayakers love playing in the rolling chop. LL Bean (p386) in Freeport will set you up with a boat, tours, lessons and a list of locations for beginners and experts. Ferry out from Casco Bay to Peaks Island for a frolic, paddle past ospreys, eagles and bear at Sears Island, or wiggle through cranberry bogs or swing with the swells just off Acadia National Park.

The Sakonnet River in Rhode Island feeds into the sea, with estuaries for recreational kayakers and big swells with big fish for experts. Meanwhile, you can serenely paddle between interconnected salt ponds on Block Island, communing with the land, sea and sky.

Plum Island is a sweet spot for all levels, rife with seals and birds galore. Watch the tides, though, or you'll be dragging your yak through sneaker-sucking mud and scootching across sandbars at low tide. The Norwalk Islands off the coast of Connecticut are a half-mile out and make for a nice, watery ramble.

The Deerfield River in the Berkshires of Massachusetts gives a thrilling ride. For one of the best floats, with a slow but steady current and some slight riffles, paddle down Vermont's Battenkill from Bennington.

When Henry David Thoreau was 40 years old, he took a canoe trip in the remote Maine woods. He recorded his observations and meditations in a volume called *Canoeing in the Wilderness*.

Skiing & Snowboarding

New England has no shortage of snow, and there's no better way to enjoy it than to strap on the skis. These days, the downhill variety takes all forms, including free-heeling, telemarking and snowboarding. Vermont is arguably ski central in New England. Killington ski area is known for its extensive snowmaking apparatuses and its steep mogul field. Mad River Glen is a rough-and-ready spot that refuses admittance to boarders. For intermediate skiers, Gunstock ski area in New Hampshire is one of the best family-style resorts in the region. Maine is home to the massive Sunday River Ski Resort, with slopes on eight peaks, as well as Sugarloaf resort, sitting on the slopes of the state's second-highest mountain (4237ft).

If the gravity of the situation makes you nervous, you might prefer Nordic skiing. Stowe, Vermont hosts the largest connected cross-country ski trail network in the east. Located in the wooded hills of the Northeast Kingdom, Craftsbury Outdoor Center (p322) sports 80 miles of groomed and ungroomed trails for your exploration.

Survival Guide

Directory A–Z

Accommodations

New England provides an array of accommodations, but truly inexpensive options are rare. The most comfortable accommodations for the lowest price are usually found in that great American invention, the roadside motel.

If you're traveling with children, be sure to ask about child-related policies before making reservations.

Our reviews indicate rates for single (s) or double occupancy (d), or simply the room (r) or suite (ste) when there's no appreciable difference in the rate for one or two people.

A reservation guarantees your room. Some reservations require a deposit, which might be only partially refundable. Note the cancellation policies and other restrictions before making a deposit.

In general, the peak travel season to New England is summer and fall. High season varies slightly depending on the region within New England. For example, high season on Cape Cod and the Maine coast is late June to early September, but in the mountains of New Hampshire, it's mid-September to mid-October. In some Vermont regions, high season means ski season (late December to late March). High-season prices are provided in our reviews, so if you are traveling off season you can generally expect significantly reduced rates.

Public holidays and school vacations always command premium prices. If traveling when demand peaks, book lodgings well in advance.

B&Bs, Inns & Guesthouses

Accommodations in New England vary from small B&Bs to rambling old inns that have sheltered travelers for several centuries. Accommodations and amenities can vary widely, from the very simple to the luxurious (and prices vary accordingly). Many inns require a minimum stay of two or three nights on weekends, advance reservations and bills paid by check or in cash (not by credit card). Some inns do not welcome children under a certain age.

Many B&Bs are booked through agencies, including **Bed & Breakfast Reservations** (☏617-964-1606, 800-832-2632; www.bbreserve. com; 11A Beach Rd, Gloucester, MA), which books B&Bs, inns and apartments in Massachusetts and northern New England.

Camping

With few exceptions, you'll have to camp in established campgrounds (there's no bivouacking on the side of the road). Make reservations well in advance (especially in July and August) for the best chance of getting a site. Most campgrounds are open from mid-May to mid-October.

Rough camping is occasionally permitted in the Green Mountain National Forest or the White Mountain National Forest, but it must be at established sites. State park sites usually offer a few more services (like flush toilets, hot showers and dump stations for RVs). Campsites at these places cost between $15 and $25. Private campgrounds are usually more expensive ($20 to $40) and less spacious than state parks, but they often boast recreational facilities like playgrounds, swimming pools, game rooms and miniature golf.

BOOK YOUR STAY ONLINE

For more accommodations reviews by Lonely Planet authors, check out http://lonelyplanet.com/hotels/. You'll find independent reviews, as well as recommendations on the best places to stay. Best of all, you can book online.

The following resources provide camping information:

Connecticut Department of Environmental Protection (☏860-424-3000; www.ct.gov/dep) Has a large section about outdoor recreation in Connecticut.

Maine Bureau of Parks and Land (☏800-332-1501; www.campwithme.com) Offers camping in 12 state parks.

Massachusetts Department of Conservation and Recreation (☏617-626-1250; www.mass.gov/eea) Offers camping in 29 state parks.

Rhode Island Division of Parks & Recreation (☏401-222-2632; www.riparks.com) For a listing of all of Rhode Island's state beaches.

Vermont State Parks (☏888-409-7579; www.vtstateparks.com) Complete camping and parks information.

Cottages, Cabins & Condos

Cottages and cabins are generally found on Cape Cod, Nantucket, Martha's Vineyard and in New England's woods. They are two- or three-room vacation bungalows with basic furnishings, bathroom and kitchen. Condos are usually capable of accommodating more people than an efficiency unit. Rates vary greatly, from $80 to $700 per night, depending upon the location, season and size.

Efficiencies

An 'efficiency,' in New England parlance, is a room in a hotel, motel or inn with cooking and dining facilities: stove, sink, refrigerator, dining table and chairs, cooking utensils and tableware. Efficiency units are located throughout New England. They cost slightly more than standard rooms.

Hotels & Resorts

New England hotels, mostly found in cities, are generally large and lavish, except for a few 'boutique' hotels (which are small and understatedly lavish). Resorts often offer a wide variety of guest activities, such as golf, horseback riding, skiing and water sports. Prices range from $100 and up per night.

Hostels

Hosteling isn't as well developed in New England as it is in other parts of the world. But some prime destinations, including Boston, Cape Cod, Bar Harbor, Martha's Vineyard and Nantucket, have hostels that allow you to stay in $150-per-night destinations for $30 to $60 per night.

US citizens/residents can join **Hostelling International USA** (HI-USA; ☏240-650-2100; www.hiusa.org). Non-US residents should buy HI membership in their home countries. If you are not a member, you can still stay in US hostels for a slightly higher rate.

Motels

Motels, located on the highway or on the outskirts of most cities, range from 10-room places in need of a fresh coat of paint to resort-style facilities. Prices range from $65 to $150. Motels offer standard accommodations: a room entered from the outside, with private bathroom, color cable TV, heat and air-con. Some have small refrigerators, and many provide a simple breakfast, often at no extra charge.

Children

Traveling within New England with children presents no destination-specific problems. In fact, parents will probably find that New England offers a great variety of educational and entertaining ways to keep their kiddies busy. They will also find that most facilities – including hotels and restaurants – welcome families with children. Look for the family-friendly icon 🖈 in the listings for particularly welcoming spots.

Sleeping

Children are not welcome at many smaller B&Bs and inns (even if they do not say so outright); make sure you inquire before booking. In motels and hotels, children under 17 or 18 are usually free when sharing a room with their parents. Cots and roll-away beds are usually available (sometimes for an additional fee) in hotels and resorts. Campsites are fantastic choices for families with kids – many are situated on waterways or lakes and offer family activities (tube rental, swimming, kayaking etc). For those who don't want to rough it, many campsites also offer simple cabins to rent.

Eating

Many restaurants have children's menus with significantly lower prices. High chairs are usually available, but it pays to inquire ahead of time. Roadside stands pepper rural New England, offering kid-friendly fare like fried fish or fish sticks, burgers, fries, chicken fingers and other small plates – most also include a kids' plate.

Transportation

Most car-rental companies lease child safety seats, but they don't always have them on hand; reserve in advance if you can. Rest stops generally have changing stations for parents' convenience. Most public transportation (bus, train etc) offers half-price tickets or reduced fare for children.

Customs Regulations

Each visitor is allowed to bring 1L of liquor and 200 cigarettes duty free into the US, but you must be at least 21 years old to possess the former and 18 years old to possess the latter. In addition, each traveler is permitted to bring gift merchandise up to the value of $100 into the US without incurring any duty.

Discount Cards

Many museums and other attractions offer discounts to college students with a valid university ID. Travelers aged 50 years and older can also receive rate cuts and benefits, especially members of the **American Association of Retired Persons** (AARP; www.aarp.org). There are several programs that offer discounts to Boston-area attractions:

Smart Destinations (www.smartdestinations.com; adult/child 1 day $48/32, 3 days $88/72, 7 days $148/112)

City Pass (www.citypass.com; adult/child $46/29)

Electricity

120V/60Hz

Food

New England is America's seafood capital, home of the mighty cod and the boiled lobster. Here are some of the region's seafood staples:

Chowder A thick, cream-based soup that is chock-full of clams or fish.

Oysters These are normally served raw on the half-shell. Sweetest are Wellfleet oysters from Cape Cod.

Steamers Steamed clams served in a bucket of briny broth.

Lobster roll Eliminate the work of eating a lobster. Lobster meat, usually with a touch of mayo, is served on a lightly toasted roll.

Clam bake Steamed lobster, clams and corn on the cob.

Scrod Could be any white-fleshed fish. Often broiled or fried and served with fries in the classic fish-and-chips combo.

Gay & Lesbian Travelers

Out and active gay communities are visible across New England, especially in cities such as Boston, Portland, New Haven and Burlington, which have substantial GLBT populations. Provincetown, MA, and Ogunquit, ME, are gay meccas, especially in summer. Northampton, MA, and Burlington, VT, also have lively queer communities. See p73 for GLBT venues in Boston and p157 for Provincetown.

Insurance

Travelers should protect themselves in case of theft, illness or car accidents. Your regular home owners insurance, auto insurance and health insurance may offer certain coverage while traveling but be sure to check your policies. Worldwide travel insurance is available at www.lonelyplanet.com/travel_ services. You can buy, extend and claim online anytime – even if you're already on the road.

Internet Access

Many hotels, restaurants and public spaces offer wireless access for free or for a small fee. Cybercafes and libraries offer inexpensive online computer access. If you bring a laptop with you from outside the US, it's worth investing in a universal AC and plug adapter.

EATING PRICE RANGES

The following price ranges refer to a standard main course. Unless otherwise stated, a service charge and taxes are not included.

$ Less than $10

$$ $10–20

$$$ More than $20

TAXES

STATE	MEAL	LODGING	SALES
Connecticut	6%	12%	6%
Maine	7%	7%	5%
Massachusetts	6.25%	5.7%	6.25%
New Hampshire	9%	9%	n/a
Rhode Island	8%	13%	7%
Vermont	9%	9%	6%

Legal Matters

The minimum age for drinking alcoholic beverages is 21. You'll need a government-issued photo ID (such as a passport or US driver's license). Stiff fines, jail time and penalties can be incurred if you are caught driving under the influence of alcohol or providing alcohol to minors.

Money

The dollar ($; commonly called a buck) is divided into 100 cents (¢). Coins come in denominations of one cent (penny), five cents (nickel), 10 cents (dime), 25 cents (quarter) and the rare 50-cent piece (half dollar). Notes come in denominations of one, five, 10, 20, 50 and 100 dollars.

ATMs & Cash

Automatic teller machines (ATMs) are ubiquitous in towns throughout New England. Most banks in New England charge at least $2 per withdrawal. The Cirrus and Plus systems both have extensive ATM networks that will give cash advances on major credit cards and allow cash withdrawals with affiliated ATM cards.

If you're carrying foreign currency, it can be exchanged for US dollars at Logan International Airport in Boston. Many banks do not change currency, so stock up on dollars when there's an opportunity to do so.

Credit Cards

Major credit cards are widely accepted throughout New England, including at car-rental agencies and most hotels, restaurants, gas stations, grocery stores and tour operators. However, many B&Bs and some condominiums, particularly those handled through rental agencies, do not accept credit cards. We have noted in our reviews when this is the case.

Tipping

Many service providers depend on tips for their livelihoods, so tip generously for good service.

Baggage carriers $1 per bag

Housekeeping $2-5 per day, $5-10 per week

Servers and bartenders 15-20%

Taxi drivers 15%

Tour guides $5-10 for a one-hour tour

Opening Hours

The following is a general guideline for business operating hours. Shorter hours may apply during low seasons, when some venues close completely. Seasonal variations are noted in the listings.

Banks & offices 9am or 10am to 5pm or 6pm Monday to Friday

Restaurants Breakfast 6am to 10am, lunch 11:30am to 2:30pm, dinner 5pm to 10pm

Bars & pubs 5pm to midnight, some until 2am

Shops 9am to 5pm Monday to Saturday; some open noon to 5pm Sunday, or until evening in tourist areas

Post

No matter how much people like to complain about it, the **US postal service** (USPS; ☎800-275-8777; www.usps.com) provides great service for the price. If you have the correct postage, drop your mail into any blue mailbox. However, to send a package that weighs 16oz or more, you must bring it to a post office.

Post offices are generally open from 8am to 5pm weekdays and 9am to 3pm on Saturday, but it depends on the branch.

Public Holidays

New Year's Day January 1

Martin Luther King Jr Day Third Monday of January

Presidents' Day Third Monday of February

Easter In March or April

Memorial Day Last Monday of May

Independence Day July 4

Labor Day First Monday of September

Columbus Day Second Monday of October

Veterans Day November 11

Thanksgiving Fourth Thursday of November

Christmas Day December 25

Telephone

Always dial '1' before toll-free (800, 888 etc) and domestic long-distance numbers. Remember that some toll-free numbers may only work within the region or from the US mainland.

All phone numbers in the US consist of a three-digit area code followed by a seven-digit local number. You now must dial 1 plus the area code plus the seven-digit number for local and long-distance calls in most areas, particularly in Eastern Massachusetts.

Pay phones aren't as readily found at shopping centers, gas stations and other public places now that cell phones are more prevalent, but keep your eyes peeled and you'll find them. Calls made within town are local and cost 50¢.

To make direct international calls, dial 011 plus the country code plus the area code plus the number. (An exception is calls made to Canada, where you dial 1 plus the area code plus the number. International rates apply to Canada.) For international operator assistance, dial 0.

If you're calling New England from abroad, the international country code for the US is 1. All calls to New England are then followed by the area code and the seven-digit local number.

Cell Phones

The US uses a variety of cell-phone systems, and most are incompatible with the GSM 900/1800 standard used throughout Europe and Asia. Check with your cellular service provider before departure about using your phone in New England. Verizon has the most extensive cellular network in New England, but Cingular and Sprint also have decent coverage. Once you get up into the mountains and off the main interstates in Vermont, New Hampshire and Maine, cell-phone reception is often downright nonexistent. Forget about using it on hiking trails.

Phonecards

These private prepaid cards are available from convenience stores, supermarkets and pharmacies. Cards sold by major telecommunications companies like AT&T may offer better deals than upstart companies.

Time

New England is on US Eastern Standard Time (GMT+5). New England observes daylight saving time, which involves setting clocks ahead one hour on the second Sunday in March and back one hour on the first Sunday in November.

Toilets

Most parks, beaches and other public places offer public toilets, although they are not common in big cities. There is no public mandate stating that restaurants, hotels or public sites must open their doors to those in need, but you can usually find relief at information centers, libraries, museums and larger hotels.

Americans have many names for public toilet facilities, but the most common names are 'restroom,' 'bathroom,' or 'ladies'/men's room.' Of course, you can just ask for the 'toilet.'

Tourist Information

Chambers of Commerce

Often associated with convention and visitors bureaus (CVBs), these are organizations for local businesses including hotels, restaurants and shops. Although they often provide maps and other useful information, they focus on establishments that are members of the chamber.

A local chamber of commerce often maintains an information booth at the entrance to town or in the town center, often open only during tourist seasons.

TOURIST OFFICES

TOURIST OFFICE	PHONE NUMBER	WEBSITE
Connecticut Office of Tourism	☑888-288-4748	www.ctvisit.org
Greater Boston Convention & Visitors Bureau (GBCVB)	☑617-536-4100, 800-888-5515	www.bostonusa.com
Maine Office of Tourism	☑207-287-5711, 888-624-6345	www.visitmaine.com
Massachusetts Office of Travel & Tourism	☑617-973-8500, 800-227-6277	www.massvacation.com
New Hampshire Division of Travel & Tourism	☑603-271-2665	www.visitnh.gov
Rhode Island Tourism Division	☑800-556-2484	www.visitrhodeisland.com
Vermont Division of Tourism & Marketing	☑802-828-3236	www.vermontvacation.com

Travelers with Disabilities

Travel within New England is becoming less difficult for people with disabilities, but it's still not easy. Public buildings are now required by law to be wheelchair accessible and also to have appropriate restroom facilities. Public transportation services must be made accessible to all, and telephone companies are required to provide relay operators for the hearing impaired. Many banks provide ATM instructions in braille, curb ramps are common, many busy intersections have audible crossing signals, and most chain hotels have suites for disabled guests.

A number of organizations specialize in the needs of travelers with disabilities:

Mobility International USA (☏541-343-1284; www.miusa.org) Advises disabled travelers on mobility issues and runs educational international exchange programs.

Society for the Advancement of Travel for the Handicapped (☏212-447-7284; www.sath.org) Publishes a quarterly magazine; has various information sheets on travel for the disabled.

Visas

Since the establishment of the Department of Homeland Security following the events of September 11, 2001, immigration now falls under the purview of the **Immigration & Customs Enforcement** (www.ice.gov).

For up-to-date information about visas and immigration, check with the **US State Department** (www.travel.state.gov).

Visa Waiver Program

The US has a Visa Waiver Program in which citizens of certain countries may enter the US for stays of 90 days or less without first obtaining a US visa. This list is subject to continual re-examination and bureaucratic rejigging. For an up-to-date list of countries included in the program, see the US Department of State website (http://travel.state.gov/visa). Under the program you must have a round-trip ticket (or onward ticket to any foreign destination) that is nonrefundable in the US and you will not be allowed to extend your stay beyond 90 days.

To participate in the Visa Waiver Program, travelers are required to have a passport that is machine-readable. Also, your passport should be valid for at least six months longer than your intended stay.

Electronic System for Travel Authorization

Since January 2009 the US has had the Electronic System for Travel Authorization (ESTA), a system that has been implemented to mitigate security risks concerning those who travel to the US by air or sea (this does not apply to those entering by land, such as via Canada). This pre-authorization system applies to citizens of all countries that fall under the Visa Waiver Program. This process requires that you register specific information online, prior to entering the US. Information required includes details like your name, current address and passport information (including the number and expiration date) and details about any communicable diseases you may carry (including HIV). It is recommended that you fill out the online form as early as possible, and at least 72 hours prior to departure. You will receive one of three responses:

➡ 'Authorization Approved' usually comes within minutes; most applicants can expect to receive this response.

➡ 'Authorization Pending' means you should go back online to check the status within roughly 72 hours.

➡ 'Travel not Authorized' indicates that your application is not approved and you will need to apply for a visa.

Once approved, registration is valid for two years, but note that if you renew your passport or change your name, you will need to re-register. The cost is $14. The entire process is stored electronically and linked to your passport, but it is recommended that you bring a printout of the ESTA approval just to be safe. If you don't have access to the internet, ask your travel agent, who can apply on your behalf.

Visa Applications

For visa applications, the paperwork will need to include a recent photo (2in by 2in). Documents of financial stability and/or guarantees from a US resident are sometimes required, particularly for those from developing countries. Visa applicants may be required to 'demonstrate binding obligations' that will ensure their return home. Because of this requirement, those planning to travel through other countries before arriving in the US are generally better off applying for their US visa while they are still in their home country rather than while on the road.

The validity period for a US visitor visa depends on your home country. The actual length of time you'll be allowed to stay in the US is determined by the Bureau of Citizenship and Immigration Services at the port of entry.

As with the Visa Waiver Program, your passport should be valid for at least six months longer than your intended stay.

Transportation

GETTING THERE & AWAY

While the two most common ways to reach New England are by air and car, you can also get here easily by train and bus. Boston is the region's hub for air travel, but some international travelers fly into New York City to do some sightseeing before heading up to New England. Flights, tours and rail tickets can be booked online at lonelyplanet.com/bookings.

Entering the Region

Entering New England is no different than any other major port of entry. Driving across the border from Canada, the worst problems you will encounter are long lines waiting in your car.

Air

Because of New England's location on the densely populated US Atlantic seaboard between New York and eastern Canada, air travelers have a number of ways to approach the region.

Airports & Airlines

The major gateway to the region is Boston's **Logan International Airport** (☑800-235-6426; www.massport.com/logan), which offers many direct, nonstop flights from major airports in the US and abroad.

Depending on where you will be doing the bulk of your exploring, several other airports in the region receive national and international flights. It's also feasible to fly into one of New York's major airports.

Bangor International Airport (☑866-359-2264; www.flybangor.com; 287 Godfrey Blvd) The Bangor International Airport is served by regional carriers associated with Continental, Delta and US Airways.

Bradley International Airport (BDL;☑860-292-2000; www.bradleyairport.com) Equidistant between Springfield, MA, and Hartford, CT, Bradley International Airport is the region's second-busiest airport.

Burlington International Airport (BTV;☑802-863-2874; www.burlingtonintlairport.com) Vermont's major airport.

Green Airport (PVD;☑888-268-7222; www.pvdairport.com) Serves Providence, RI.

Manchester Airport (☑603-624-6556; www.flymanchester.com) A quiet alternative to Logan, Manchester Airport is just 55 miles north of Boston in New Hampshire.

Portland Jetport (PWM; ☑207-774-7301; www.portlandjetport.org) Serves coastal Maine.

Land

Border Crossings

Generally, crossing the United State/Canada border is pretty straightforward. The biggest hassle is usually the length of the lines. All travelers entering the United States are required to carry their passports, including citizens of Canada and the United States.

Bus

You can get to New England by bus from all parts of the United States and Canada, but the trip will be long and may not be much less expensive than a discounted flight. Bus companies usually offer special promotional fares.

Greyhound (www.greyhound.com) is the national bus line, serving all major cities in the United States.

Peter Pan Buslines (☑800-343-9999; www.peterpanbus.com) is a regional bus company, serving 54 destinations in the northeast, as far north as Concord, NH, and as far south as Washington, DC, as well as into western Massachusetts.

Go Buses (www.gobuses.com; one way from $15; ☎; ⓣAlewife) and **Yo! Bus** (www.yobus.com; one way $12-28; ☎; ⓣSouth Station) offer inexpensive bus fares between New York City and Boston. Also see p85.

Car & Motorcycle

Interstate highways criss-cross New England and offer forest, farm and mountain scenery, once you are clear of urban areas and the I-95 corridor between Boston and New York. These interstate highways connect the region to New York, Washington, DC, Montreal and points west.

Train

Amtrak (☑800-872-7245; www.amtrak.com) is the main rail passenger service in the US.

Services along the Northeast Corridor (connecting Boston, Providence, Hartford and New Haven with New York and Washington, DC) are some of the most frequent in Amtrak's system. Amtrak's high-speed *Acela Express* makes the trip from New York City to Boston in three hours.

Other Amtrak services to New England:

➡ The *Vermonter* runs through New Haven and Hartford in Connecticut, Springfield and Amherst in Massachusetts, and then on to St Albans in Vermont.

➡ The *Montrealer* runs through northern Vermont to Montreal along the Connecticut River Valley, with stops in New Haven in Connecticut; Amherst in Massachusetts; and Essex Junction (for Burlington), White River Junction and Brattleboro in Vermont.

➡ The *Lake Shore Limited* departs from Boston, stopping at Worcester, Springfield and Pittsfield before crossing into New York and continuing west.

Sea

Bridgeport & Port Jefferson Steamboat Company (☑in Connecticut 888-443-3779, in Long Island 631-473-0286; www.bpjferry.com) Daily ferry between Long Island and Connecticut.

Cross Sound Ferry (☑516-323-2525, 860-443-5281; www.longislandferry.com) Year-round ferry from Orient Point on Long Island to New London.

Fishers Island Ferry (☑860-442-0165; www.fiferry.com; adult/senior & child mid-May–mid-Sep $25/18, mid-Sep–mid-May $19/14, cars $51/35) Year-round ferry between New London and Fishers Island in New York.

Lake Champlain Ferries (Map p304; ☑802-864-9804; www.ferries.com; adult/child/car $8/3.10/30) Ferries run from Burlington to New York State, traversing the lake.

Seastreak (☑800-262-8743; www.seastreak.com) High-speed ferry service connecting Martha's Vineyard to Highlands, NJ, and New York City (six hours) on weekends in season.

As early as 2014, travelers may be able to reach Portland, ME, by ferry from Yarmouth, Nova Scotia.

GETTING AROUND

Simply put, the best way to get around New England is by car. The region is relatively small, the highways are good and public transportation is not as frequent or as widespread as it could be.

Air

Regional and commuter airlines connect New England's cities and resorts with Boston and New York City.

There are several regional airlines, especially serving Cape Cod and the islands:

Cape Air (☑800-227-3247; www.flycapeair.com) Flights to several New England destinations, including Cape Cod, Martha's Vineyard and Nantucket.

Nantucket Air (☑800-227-3247; www.nantucketairlines.com) Flights to Nantucket from Boston, New York and Providence.

New England Airlines (☑800-243-2460; www.blockisland.com) Flights to Block Island from Westerly, RI.

Bicycle

Cycling is a popular New England sport and means of transport on both city streets and country roads. Several of the larger cities have systems of bike paths that make bike travel easier and more pleasant. Disused railroad rights-of-way have also been

---

CLIMATE CHANGE & TRAVEL

Every form of transport that relies on carbon-based fuel generates CO_2, the main cause of human-induced climate change. Modern travel is dependent on airplanes, which might use less fuel per mile per person than most cars but travel much greater distances. The altitude at which aircraft emit gases (including CO_2) and particles also contributes to their climate change impact. Many websites offer 'carbon calculators' that allow people to estimate the carbon emissions generated by their journey and, for those who wish to do so, to offset the impact of the greenhouse gases emitted with contributions to portfolios of climate-friendly initiatives throughout the world. Lonely Planet offsets the carbon footprint of all staff and author travel.

turned into bike trails; the Cape Cod Rail Trail between Dennis and Wellfleet is a prominent example.

Bicycle rentals are available in most New England cities, towns and resorts at reasonable prices (often $20 to $35 per day).

Boat

Regular ferry services ply the coast, servicing Cape Cod, Martha's Vineyard, Nantucket and Block Island, as well as some coastal destinations on the mainland.

Bay State Cruise Company (www.boston-ptown.com; round trip adult/child $85/62; SL1 or SL2, South Station) Boston to Provincetown.

Block Island Express (860-444-4624; www. goblockisland.com; adult/child/ bike $25/12.50/10) From New London.

Block Island Ferry (www. blockislandferry.com) From Newport and Point Judith.

Boston Harbor Cruises (Map p40; www.boston harborcruises.com; round trip adult/child/senior $85/62/ 73; Aquarium) Servicing Provincetown and Salem from Boston.

Hy-Line Cruises (508-778-2600; www.hylinecruises. com; Ocean St Dock, Hyannis;) From Hyannis to Nantucket and Martha's Vineyard.

RIPTA (www.ripta.com) Operating between Providence and Newport.

Steamship Authority (508-477-8600; www. steamshipauthority.com; South St Dock, Hyannis;) Hyannis to Nantucket; Woods Hole to Martha's Vineyard.

Bus

Buses go to more places than airplanes or trains, but the routes still bypass some prime destinations, especially in rural places.

The national bus company, Greyhound, as well as Peter Pan, provides service to and within New England. Regional carriers that ply routes within New England include the following:

Concord Coach Lines (Concord Trailways; www. concordcoachlines.com) Covers routes from Boston to New Hampshire (Concord, Manchester and as far up as Conway and Berlin) and Maine (Portland and Bangor).

C&J Trailways (800-258-7111, 603-430-1100; www.ridecj. com) Provides daily service between Boston and Newburyport (Massachusetts), as well as Portsmouth and Dover (New Hampshire).

Dartmouth Coach (603-448-2800; www.dartmouth-coach.com) Servicing Hanover, Lebanon and New London from Boston.

Plymouth & Brockton Street Railway Co (508-746-0378; www.p-b.com) Provides frequent service to the South Shore and to most towns on Cape Cod, including Hyannis and Provincetown.

Car & Motorcycle

Yes, driving is really the best way to see New England. But heads up: New England drivers are aggressive, speedy and unpredictable, particularly around Boston and other cities. You have been warned. Traffic jams are common in urban areas.

Municipalities control parking by signs on the street, stating explicitly where you may or may not park. A yellow line or yellow-painted curb means that no parking is allowed there.

Automobile Associations

The **American Automobile Association** (AAA; 800-564-6222; www.aaa. com) provides members with maps and other information. Members get discounts on

car rentals, air tickets, hotels and attractions, as well as emergency road service and towing. AAA has reciprocal agreements with automobile associations in other countries. Bring your membership card from your country of origin.

Driver's License

An international driving license, obtained before you leave home, is only necessary if your regular license is not in English.

Fuel

Gas stations are ubiquitous and many are open 24 hours a day. Small-town stations may be open only from 7am to 8pm or 9pm. Plan on spending roughly $3.50 to $4 per US gallon in New England.

At some stations, you must pay before you pump; at others, you may pump before you pay. More modern pumps have credit/ debit card terminals built into them, so you can pay with plastic right at the pump. At 'full service' stations, an attendant will pump your gas for you; no tip is expected.

Hire

Rental cars are readily available. With advance reservations for a small car, the daily rate with unlimited mileage is about $50, while typical weekly rates are $300 to $500. Rates for midsize cars are often only a tad higher. Dropping off the car at a different location from where you picked it up usually incurs an additional fee. It always pays to shop around between rental companies.

Having a major credit card greatly simplifies the rental process. Without one, some agencies simply will not rent vehicles, while others require prepayment, a deposit slightly higher than the cost of your rental, pay stubs, proof of round-trip airfare and more.

The following companies operate in New England:

Alamo (☑888-233-8749; www.goalamo.com)

Avis (☑800-633-3469; www.avis.com)

Budget (☑800-218-7992; www.budget.com)

Dollar (☑800-800-5252; www.dollarcar.com)

Enterprise (☑800-261-7331; www.enterprise.com)

Hertz (☑800-654-3131; www.hertz.com)

National (☑800-227-7368; www.nationalcar.com)

Thrifty (☑800-847-4389; www.thrifty.com)

Rent-A-Wreck (☑877-877-0700; www.rentawreck.com) Rents out cars that may have more wear and tear than your typical rental vehicle, but are actually far from wrecks.

Insurance

Should you have an accident, liability insurance covers the people and property that you have hit. For damage to the actual rental vehicle, a collision damage waiver (CDW) is available for about $18 a day. If you have collision coverage on your vehicle at home, it might cover damages to car rentals; inquire before departing. Additionally, some credit cards offer reimbursement coverage for collision damages if you rent the car with that credit card; again, check before departing. Most credit card coverage isn't valid for rentals of more than 15 days or for exotic models, jeeps, vans and 4WD vehicles.

Road Conditions & Hazards

New England roads are very good – even the hard-packed dirt roads that crisscross Vermont. Some roads across northern mountain passes in Vermont, New Hampshire and Maine are closed during the winter, but good signage gives you plenty of warning.

Road Rules

Driving laws are different in each of the New England states, but most require the use of safety belts. In every state, children under four years of age must be placed in a child safety seat secured by a seat belt. Most states require motorcycle riders to wear helmets whenever they ride.

The maximum speed limit on most New England interstates is 65mph, but some have a limit of 55mph. On undivided highways, the speed limit will vary from 30mph to 55mph. Police enforce speed limits by patrolling in police cruisers and in unmarked cars. Fines can cost upwards of $350 in Connecticut, and it's similarly expensive in other states.

Local Transportation

City buses and the T (the subway/underground system in Boston) provide useful transportation within the larger cities and to some suburbs. Resort areas also tend to have regional bus lines.

Taxis are common in the largest cities, but in smaller cities and towns you will probably have to telephone a cab to pick you up. Shuttles may take travelers from their hotel to the airport.

Train

In addition to the routes listed on p439, Amtrak operates the *Downeaster* which runs from Boston's North Station to Brunswick, ME; stops along the way include Exeter, NH, as well as Portland and Freeport, ME.

Other regional train services:

Maine Eastern Railroad (☑866-637-2457; www.maineeasternrailroad.com) Now offers a seasonal service between Brunswick and Rockland in Maine.

MBTA Commuter Rail (☑800-392-6100; www.mbta.com) Boston's commuter rail travels west to Concord and Lowell, north to Salem, Rockport, Gloucester and Newburyport, and south to Plymouth and Providence.

Metro-North (☑800-638-7646, 212-532-4900; www.mta.info) Runs between New York City and New Haven.

Shore Line East (☑203-255-7433; www.shorelineeast.com) The Connecticut commuter rail connects New Haven and New London.

Behind the Scenes

SEND US YOUR FEEDBACK

Things change – prices go up, schedules change, good places go bad and bad places go bankrupt. So if you find things better or worse, recently opened or long since closed, or you just want to tell us what you loved or loathed about this book, please get in touch and help make the next edition even more accurate and useful. We love to hear from travelers – your comments keep us on our toes and our well-traveled team reads every word. Although we can't reply individually to postal submissions, we always guarantee that your feedback goes straight to the appropriate authors, in time for the next edition. Each person who sends us information is thanked in the next edition – the most useful submissions are rewarded with a selection of digital PDF chapters.

Visit **lonelyplanet.com/contact** to submit your updates and suggestions or to ask for help. Our award-winning website also features inspirational travel stories, news and discussions.

Note: We may edit, reproduce and incorporate your comments in Lonely Planet products such as guidebooks, websites and digital products, so let us know if you don't want your comments reproduced or your name acknowledged. For a copy of our privacy policy visit lonelyplanet.com/privacy.

OUR READERS

Many thanks to the travelers who used the last edition and wrote to us with helpful hints, useful advice and interesting anecdotes:
Katharine Barnes, Barry Blain, Richard Durden, Nigel Green, Pauline Jarvis, Ian Jones, Andrew Kemp, Claudio Latanza, Giampaolo Marcellini, JJ Marsh, Alan McCutcheon, Mark Meulepas, Alba Mileto, Ian Ross, Thilo Salmon, Roger Sayers, Lina Swarovski, Mary Sykora, Max Wenger, Dae Yang

AUTHOR THANKS

Mara Vorhees
Thanks to Jennye Garibaldi for many years of leadership and cooperation on *New England* titles – you will be missed! My heart goes out to the victims of the Boston Marathon bombings, all of the runners and the city as a whole. Patriots' Day has always been about facing challenges with courage – it's now true more than ever. Bostonians love their city. Love will prevail.

Gregor Clark
I wish to thank all the generous fellow Vermonters who helped with this project, especially John McCright, Sarah Pope, Namik Sevlic, Saba Rizvi, Sarah Shepherd, Sue Heim and David Alles. Love and thanks as well to Gaen, for sharing my excitement about exploring that next side road, to Meigan for giving me hugs at deadline time and to Chloe, whose infectious love of climbing Mt Mansfield barefoot always makes me smile.

Ned Friary
Thanks to all the people I met along the way who shared their tips, including the helpful folks staffing the counters at the local tourist offices. A special thanks to the rangers at the Cape Cod National Seashore and to Bob Prescott of the Massachusetts Audubon Society for sharing their one-of-a-kind insights.

Paula Hardy
I'd like to thank the following for sharing the best of Connecticut and Rhode Island: Anne McAndrews, Dave Fairty, Pat and Wayne Brubaker, Rick Walker, Sanjeev Seereeram, Cinta Burgos, David King, Dave Helgerson, Harry Schwartz, Elizabeth MacAlister and the Preservation Society of Newport; and in-house, thanks to super commissioning editor Jennye Garibaldi and coordinator Mara Vorhees.

Finally, thanks to Rob Smith for the laughs and letting me bring home Baggo.

Caroline Sieg

Thanks to everyone who took the time to share their tips with me and for the countless friendly conversations at lobster shacks, ski resorts and brewpubs. And a very special thank you to the Schmidt family who keep me coming back to New England year after year.

ACKNOWLEDGMENTS

Climate map data adapted from Peel MC, Finlayson BL & McMahon TA (2007) 'Updated World Map of the Köppen-Geiger Climate Classification', Hydrology and Earth System Sciences, 11, 163344.

Cover photograph: Lobster buoys in Bernard, on Mt Desert Island, Maine, Pietro Canali/4Corners

THIS BOOK

This 7th edition of Lonely Planet's *New England* guidebook was researched and written by Mara Vorhees, Gregor Clark, Ned Friary, Paula Hardy and Caroline Sieg. The previous edition was also researched and written by Mara, Ned and Caroline, alongside Glenda Bendure, Emily Matchar and Freda Moon.

This guidebook was commissioned in Lonely Planet's Oakland office, and produced by the following:

Commissioning Editors
Jennye Garibaldi, Katie O'Connell, Emily K Wolman

Coordinating Editors
Nigel Chin, Kate James, Elizabeth Jones

Senior Cartographer
Alison Lyall

Coordinating Layout Designer Carlos Solarte

Managing Editors
Sasha Baskett, Bruce Evans, Catherine Naghten

Managing Layout Designer
Chris Girdler

Assisting Editors
Susie Ashworth, Alison Barber, Amy Karafin, Erin Richards, Helen Yeates

Assisting Cartographers
Jeff Cameron, Julie Dodkins, Rachel Imeson, Gabriel Lindquist

Cover Research Naomi Parker

Thanks to Anita Banh, Ryan Evans, Larissa Frost, Jane Hart, Genesys India, Jouve India, Trent Paton, Martine Power

Index

Map Legend

Sights
- Beach
- Buddhist
- Castle
- Christian
- Hindu
- Islamic
- Jewish
- Monument
- Museum/Gallery
- Ruin
- Winery/Vineyard
- Zoo
- Other Sight

Activities, Courses & Tours
- Diving/Snorkelling
- Canoeing/Kayaking
- Skiing
- Surfing
- Swimming/Pool
- Walking
- Windsurfing
- Other Activity/Course/Tour

Sleeping
- Sleeping
- Camping

Eating
- Eating

Drinking
- Drinking
- Cafe

Entertainment
- Entertainment

Shopping
- Shopping

Information
- Post Office
- Tourist Information

Transport
- Airport
- Border Crossing
- Bus
- Cable Car/Funicular
- Cycling
- Ferry
- Monorail
- Parking
- S-Bahn
- Taxi
- Train/Railway
- Tram
- Tube Station
- U-Bahn
- Underground Train Station
- Other Transport

Routes
- Tollway
- Freeway
- Primary
- Secondary
- Tertiary
- Lane
- Unsealed Road
- Plaza/Mall
- Steps
- Tunnel
- Pedestrian Overpass
- Walking Tour
- Walking Tour Detour
- Path

Boundaries
- International
- State/Province
- Disputed
- Regional/Suburb
- Marine Park
- Cliff
- Wall

Population
- Capital (National)
- Capital (State/Province)
- City/Large Town
- Town/Village

Geographic
- Hut/Shelter
- Lighthouse
- Lookout
- Mountain/Volcano
- Oasis
- Park
- Pass
- Picnic Area
- Waterfall

Hydrography
- River/Creek
- Intermittent River
- Swamp/Mangrove
- Reef
- Canal
- Water
- Dry/Salt/Intermittent Lake
- Glacier

Areas
- Beach/Desert
- Cemetery (Christian)
- Cemetery (Other)
- Park/Forest
- Sportsground
- Sight (Building)
- Top Sight (Building)

Caroline Sieg
New Hampshire, Maine Caroline Sieg is a half-Swiss, half-American writer. Her relationship with New England began when she first lived in Boston and her best friend moved to New Hampshire and she began heading up to Maine for foodie treats and windswept coastal walks. She was delighted to return to the land of lobster and blueberry pies for Lonely Planet.

OUR STORY

A beat-up old car, a few dollars in the pocket and a sense of adventure. In 1972 that's all Tony and Maureen Wheeler needed for the trip of a lifetime – across Europe and Asia overland to Australia. It took several months, and at the end – broke but inspired – they sat at their kitchen table writing and stapling together their first travel guide, *Across Asia on the Cheap*. Within a week they'd sold 1500 copies. Lonely Planet was born.

Today, Lonely Planet has offices in Melbourne, London and Oakland, with more than 600 staff and writers. We share Tony's belief that 'a great guidebook should do three things: inform, educate and amuse'.

OUR WRITERS

Mara Vorhees

Coordinating Author, Boston, Around Boston Born and raised in St Clair Shores, Michigan, Mara traveled the world (if not the universe) before finally settling in the Hub. She spent several years pushing papers and tapping keys at Harvard University, but she has since embraced the life of a full-time travel writer, covering destinations as diverse as Russia and Belize. She lives in a pink house in Somerville, Massachusetts, with her husband, two kiddies and two kitties. She is often seen eating doughnuts in Union Sq and pedaling her bike along the Charles River. The pen-wielding traveler is the author of Lonely Planet's *Boston* guide, among other titles. Follow her adventures online at www.havetwinswilltravel.com.

Gregor Clark

Vermont Gregor Clark fell in love with Vermont at age 16, while working as a summer conservation volunteer in the state's southwestern corner. His long-held dreams of moving to the Green Mountain State came to fruition in 1997, and he's been here ever since. A lifelong polyglot with a degree in Romance languages, Gregor has written regularly for Lonely Planet since 2000, with a focus on Europe and Latin America. He lives with his wife and two daughters in Middlebury, Vermont.

Ned Friary

Cape Cod, Nantucket & Martha's Vineyard, Central Massachusetts & the Berkshires Ned's college days were spent in Amherst, and traveling around his old stomping grounds always feels like a homecoming of sorts. He now lives on Cape Cod and has explored the region from one end to the other, searching out the best lobster roll, canoeing the marshes, and hiking and cycling the trails. His favorite moment while researching this book: catching the sunset over the Connecticut River Valley from the summit at Skinner State Park.

Paula Hardy

Rhode Island, Connecticut The British half of an American-British couple, Paula spends a lot of time hopping across the pond, torn between the bright lights of London town and Boston, where weekending in the New England countryside is a near-weekly activity. Research for this book though took her way off the beaten path into Connecticut's dairy barns, lobster shacks (yum!) and wine-tasting rooms, and Rhode Island's tiny East Bay villages and breezy Block Island cycling trails – the lasting memories of Baggo defeats and Mudslide sundowners won't be easily forgotten.

OVER PAGE MORE WRITERS

Published by Lonely Planet Publications Pty Ltd
ABN 36 005 607 983
7th edition – Mar 2014
ISBN 978 1 74220 300 3
© Lonely Planet 2014   Photographs © as indicated 2014
10 9 8 7 6 5 4 3 2 1
Printed in China